SOUTH WALES

NORM LONGLEY

www.bradtguides.com

Bradt Guides Ltd, UK
The Globe Pequot Press Inc, USA

Bradt GUIDES

TRAVEL TAKEN SERIOUSLY

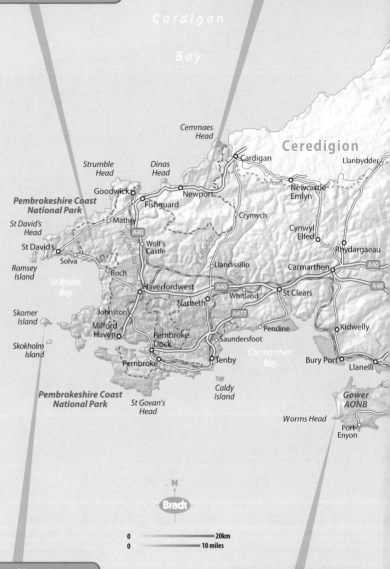

Pembrokeshire Coast Path: At 186 miles long, this is arguably the finest stretch of the Wales Coast Path: wave-bashed coves and monumental beaches, magnificent coastal fauna and a rich tapestry of wildflowers all beckon
page 317

Mynydd Preseli: Little known, the magical Preseli hills combine off-the-beaten-track walking with ancient monuments galore, not to mention the occasional great pub
page 318

Cardigan Bay

Cemmaes Head

Ceredigion

Cardigan

Llanbydder

Strumble Head

Dinas Head

Newport

Newcastle Emlyn

Pembrokeshire Coast National Park

Goodwick

Fishguard

Crymych

Cynwyl Elfed

St David's Head

Mathry

Wolf's Castle

Rhydargaeau

A40

St David's

Solva

Roch

Llandissilio

Carmarthen

A40

Ramsey Island

St Brides Bay

Haverfordwest

A40

Whitland

St Clears

A48

Skomer Island

Johnston

Narberth

A477

Kidwelly

Milford Haven

Pembroke Dock

Pendine

Skokholm Island

Saundersfoot

Carmarthen Bay

Bury Port

Llanelli

Pembroke

Tenby

Caldy Island

Gower AONB

Pembrokeshire Coast National Park

St Govan's Head

Worms Head

Port-Enyon

N

Bradt

0   20km
0   10 miles

Skomer: One of Europe's great migratory seabird destinations, there's not much you won't see on this magical island: puffins, Manx shearwater, razorbills, guillemots, and even short-eared owls
page 300

Lundy

Gower: Whether you're looking for sunbathing or surfing, cave exploration or clifftop walks, the magical Gower Peninsula has it all going on
page 163

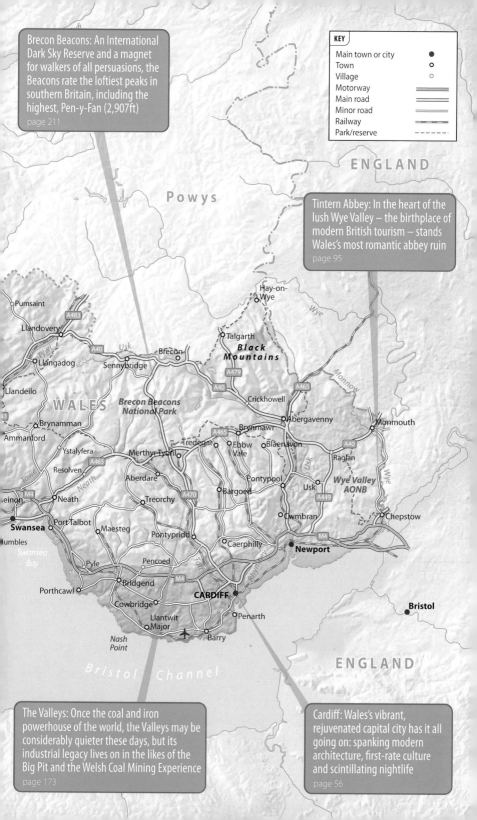

Brecon Beacons: An International Dark Sky Reserve and a magnet for walkers of all persuasions, the Beacons rate the loftiest peaks in southern Britain, including the highest, Pen-y-Fan (2,907ft)
page 211

KEY

Main town or city	●
Town	⊙
Village	○
Motorway	
Main road	
Minor road	
Railway	
Park/reserve	

ENGLAND

Powys

Tintern Abbey: In the heart of the lush Wye Valley – the birthplace of modern British tourism – stands Wales's most romantic abbey ruin
page 95

Pumsaint

Llandovery

Llangadog

Llandeilo

Brynamman

Ammanford

Ystalyfera

Resolven

einon

Neath

Swansea

Mumbles

Swansea
Bay

Pyle

Porthcawl

Hay-on-
Wye

Talgarth

Brecon

*Black
Mountains*

Sennybridge

WALES

Brecon Beacons
National Park

Crickhowell

Merthyr Tydfil

Tredegar

Brynmawr

Abergavenny

Monmouth

Ebbw
Vale

Blaenavon

Aberdare

Raglan

Treorchy

Pontypool

*Wye Valley
AONB*

Port Talbot

Bargoed

Usk

Maesteg

Pontypridd

Caerphilly

Cwmbran

Chepstow

Pencoed

Newport

Bridgend

CARDIFF

Cowbridge

Llantwit
Major

Penarth

Bristol

Barry

*Nash
Point*

Bristol Channel

ENGLAND

The Valleys: Once the coal and iron powerhouse of the world, the Valleys may be considerably quieter these days, but its industrial legacy lives on in the likes of the Big Pit and the Welsh Coal Mining Experience
page 173

Cardiff: Wales's vibrant, rejuvenated capital city has it all going on: spanking modern architecture, first-rate culture and scintillating nightlife
page 56

SOUTH WALES
DON'T MISS...

ISLAND SEABIRDS
Storm petrels on Skokholm, gannets on Grassholm, puffins on Skomer (pictured); a visit to these islands off the Pembrokeshire coast is an unforgettable experience PAGE 5
(CC/VW)

WALKING AND CLIMBING
The Wales Coast Path is the big one, but there are glorious hikes and climbs across the whole of South Wales, including the Beacons Way, which includes an ascent of Pen-y-Fan (pictured) – southern Britain's highest summit PAGE 218
(CC/VW)

BEACHES
From Three Cliffs on Gower to Barafundle (pictured) in Pembrokeshire, the South Wales coastline is peppered with smashing beaches, coves and bays PAGE 287
(BS/S)

THE VALLEYS
Discover why the Valleys were once the beating heart of the Industrial Revolution with a visit to Big Pit PAGE 177
(CC/VW)

CASTLES
Caerphilly is just one of South Wales's blockbuster fortresses, but there are dozens more
PAGE 197
(CC/VW)

SOUTH WALES
IN COLOUR

above
(m/S)
No other building in Cardiff Bay embodies better the wealth of the once-all-powerful coal industry than the Pierhead PAGE 77

below left
(AP/VB)
Cardiff's arcades are a joy to explore PAGE 69

below right
(BS/S)
The colonnaded Welsh National Memorial commemorates those who lost their lives in the Falklands War PAGE 72

bottom right
(CC/VW)
No trip to Wales would be complete without trying a Welsh cake, pictured here on sale at Cardiff Market PAGE 46

Tenby is undoubtedly one of the prettiest coastal resorts in South Wales, if not the UK PAGE 280

above
(BS/S)

The Hay Festival is one of the biggest events in the UK literary calendar PAGE 244

right
(RD/
HOWTIB)

A prosperous little market town, handsome Crickhowell is a great place to base yourself in the Brecon Beacons PAGE 229

below
(BS/S)

above
(CC/VW)

Exploring the length of the country's entire coastline, the Wales Coast Path really comes into its own in South Wales PAGE 50

below left
(CC/VW)

Wales is home to some of the UK's finest surfing spots, such as at Whitesands Bay PAGE 52

below right
(CC/VW)

The River Wye is best explored by canoe PAGE 100

bottom right
(CC/VW)

The steeply wooded slopes of Afan Forest Park make for some of the best mountain biking in Wales PAGE 151

AUTHOR

Norm Longley (w normlongley.com) has travelled around, and written extensively about, South Wales for many years. As well as writing about the country, Norm and his family frequently holiday in Wales, where they are particularly partial to a few days either tucked away behind the mighty sand dunes of Merthyr Mawr in the Vale of Glamorgan or, when feeling more active, taking to the mountains of the Brecon Beacons. Norm grew up in Somerset and spent several years living in Serbia and travelling around the Balkans before returning to the UK. Now an experienced guidebook writer for over more than 20 years, he is the author of two other Bradt guides (*Montenegro* and *Slow Somerset*), and he has written on travel for publications including *The Guardian* and *The Independent*.

AUTHOR'S STORY

I've lived in Somerset on and off for most of my life, so South Wales has always been within touching distance. Moreover, as a child, the South Wales coast usually featured heavily on family outings, with both the Vale of Glamorgan and Pembrokeshire coast firm favourites. Walks weren't particularly high on the agenda then, but growing up the Brecon Beacons became the real draw. For this first edition of South Wales, there were few long-distance trails that I didn't attempt – either wholly or partially – including the Wye Valley Walk, the Offa's Dyke Path and sections of the Wales Coast Path, but again it was the Brecon Beacons, and in particular walking the Beacons Way, that really stood out on this occasion. Trekking aside, South Wales has provided me with some memorable experiences: observing puffins on Skomer, coasteering in Abereiddi, exploring a deep mine, zooming down a zip-line from an old colliery tower, walking with a vulture… and tonnes more beside. Researching and writing this book during the Covid-19 pandemic has not been without its challenges – and inevitably has taken longer than anticipated – but this has made the end result all the more satisfying. South Wales is an absolute blast in every sense. I hope you enjoy it as much as I do.

First edition published February 2023
Bradt Guides Ltd
31a High Street, Chesham, Buckinghamshire, HP5 1BW, England
www.bradtguides.com
Print edition published in the USA by The Globe Pequot Press Inc,
PO Box 480, Guilford, Connecticut 06437-0480

Text copyright © 2023 Norm Longley
Maps copyright © 2023 Bradt Guides Ltd; includes map data © OpenStreetMap contributors; contains Ordnance Survey Data © Crown copyright and database right 2023
Photographs copyright © 2023 Individual photographers (see below)
Project Manager: Laura Osborne
Cover research: Ian Spick, Bradt Guides
Proofreader: Faye Winsor

ISBN: 9781784778378

British Library Cataloguing in Publication Data
A catalogue record for this book is available from the British Library

Photographs Alamy.com: gbimages (gbi/A), Chris Howes/Wild Places Photography (CH/WPP/A), Heidi Stewart (HS/A); AWL Images: Adam Burton (AB/AWL); Hay-on-Wye Tourist Information Bureau: Richard Downs (RD/HOWTIB); National Botanic Garden of Wales: Jac Towler (JT/NBGOW) Shutterstock: abriendomundo (a/S), Wendy Claire Cordes (WCC/S), Dajahof (D/S), Martin Fowler (MF/S), Richard Hayman (RH/S), Helen Hotson (HH/S), muratart (m/S), Keith Pritchard (KP/S), Billy Stock (BS/S), travellight (t/S); SuperStock (SS); Visit Britain: Andrew Pickett (AP/VB); Visit Wales: Crown Copyright (CC/VW)
Front cover Brecon Beacons (AB/AWL)
Back cover Llansteffan Castle (CC/VW); Puffin (CC/VW); Blaenavon (CC/VW)
Title page Llandeilo (CC/VW); Dylan Thomas statue, Swansea (t/S); Llanthony Priory (D/S)

Maps David McCutcheon FBCart.S

Typeset by Ian Spick, Bradt Guides
Production managed by Jellyfish Print Solutions; printed in India
Digital conversion by www.dataworks.co.in

ACKNOWLEDGEMENTS

Big thanks are due to Kim Colebrook, Sian Davies, Julia Blazer, Lizzie Cooper, Nikki Alderslade, Emma and Peter Harrison, Alyson Tippings, Edmund Inkin, Tom Watts, Tezni Bancroft-Plummer, Sophie Harris, Alex Reynolds, Julia Farish, Alix White, Freddie Hitchcock, Paul Williams, Jane Harris, Lewis Phillips (and Harry the vulture), Jessica and Rebecca Griffiths and John Mansfield and Julia Horton Mansfield. Thank you to Laura Osborne for doing such a sterling job of editing, and I also reserve enormous gratitude to the team at Bradt, especially Anna and Claire, who have helped see this project through – their patience has been extraordinary, and very welcome too! Above all, however, love and thanks go to Christian and Anna who accompanied me on too many trips to mention during the course of researching this guide, and who also have also endured endless days and nights of me not being there. Love, too, to Luka, Paddy, Kayleigh and Isla.

FEEDBACK REQUEST

At Bradt Guides we're aware that guidebooks start to go out of date on the day they're published – and that you, our readers, are out there in the field doing research of your own. You'll find out before us when a fine new family-run hotel opens or a favourite restaurant changes hands and goes downhill. So why not tell us about your experiences? Contact us on ✆01753 893444 or e info@bradtguides.com. We will forward emails to the author who may post updates on the Bradt website at w bradtguides.com/updates. Alternatively, you can add a review of the book to Amazon, or share your adventures with us on social:

f BradtGuides
🖷 BradtGuides
🐦 BradtGuides & normlongley

Contents

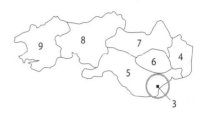

Introduction

In many ways, South Wales is a microcosm of the country as a whole, embracing imperious red sandstone mountains, deeply incised valleys and a long, craggy coastline punctuated with enchanting coastal resorts and some of Europe's finest beaches. Throw in a slew of theatrically sited castles and comely wayside villages – many with an ancient church – and it's clear to see why this region packs a mighty punch.

Working your way east to west – arriving from England as it were – first stop is Monmouthshire, a verdant landscape of rolling countryside peppered with many an old Marcher fortress. A major stop on anyone's list should be Cardiff, the nation's vibrant, youthful capital, a city that's almost unrecognisable from even just a couple of decades ago. Extending like thick veins up towards the Brecon Beacons are the Valleys, once the powerhouse of the Industrial Revolution and perhaps the most instantly recognisable landscape in all of Wales. Factor in some wonderful industrial heritage, outstanding hillwalking and mountain biking, and the Valleys deserve to be far more visited than they are. South of here, the Vale of Glamorgan is also all too often bypassed, but that would be to miss out on a lovely stretch of coastline richly textured by history and nature.

Carmarthenshire, too, remains something of an unknown quantity for many, but as home to some of Britain's finest gardens and castles, it's worthy of extended exploration. The highest-profile region in Wales is Pembrokeshire, in part because it possesses the most popular section of the entire Wales Coast Path but primarily because of its outstanding synthesis of stunning beaches and coves, and a multiplicity of endearing coastal resorts. The Brecon Beacons is not far behind in the popularity stakes, its tangle of well-worn paths furrowed across four geographically distinct mountain ranges variously endowed with chiselled peaks, glacial lakes and waterfalls.

All of these areas offer limitless opportunities for outdoor pursuits, be it trekking the mountains and tramping the coast path, mountain biking in the Valleys, riding cross country in the Black Mountains, or coasteering and kayaking the coastline. Wildlife, too, is as exhilarating here in South Wales as anywhere else in the British Isles, or northern Europe for that matter, especially if birding is your thing: a visit to Skomer or Skokholm – where you will be engulfed by thousands of puffins, guillemots and Manx shearwater – will linger long in the memory.

A land once flush with tin, copper, lead and coal made South Wales one of the richest, most powerful regions in the world, but deindustrialisation left many communities struggling, particularly those in the Valleys where hardship and poverty continue to be a grim day-to-day reality. But the old slagheaps have gone and regeneration continues apace with tourism now the anchor upon which local economies are largely reliant on. The potential is unquestionably huge and this has already been underscored by the development of numerous attractions and facilities.

After its conquest by Edward I in 1278, and its incorporation into England three centuries later by the Tudors, Wales had no governmental existence. All that changed with devolution in 1998, and in the short time since, Wales has attained a greater degree of political autonomy. In tandem with this, the cultural narrative has begun to change too. The Welsh have become more comfortable with seeing themselves as Welsh, which is manifest most spectacularly in the renaissance of the native tongue.

During centuries of British occupation in Wales, the use of Welsh was quelled, but these days a new generation of children can read, speak and write in Welsh, and are obtaining a higher level of fluency than their parents. This linguistic resurgence now pervades every sphere of cultural life, though nowhere more so than in the music industry, which has witnessed a slew of emerging Welsh-language artists and bands. Sport is another great cultural barometer, and the recent success of the national football team in qualifying for its first World Cup since 1958 was driven on by a fanatical set of supporters – known as the Red Wall – who are now more likely to sing in Welsh than they are in English. Although it has been the Scots fervently championing independence in recent times, the Welsh drum may also be beating just a little bit louder in that direction too. The dragon is certainly stirring.

One thing is for sure and that is you'll be warmly received wherever you go in South Wales, but if you can manage to eke out the occasional word of one of Europe's oldest living languages, then you'll win lots more friends.

HOW TO USE THIS GUIDE

AUTHOR'S FAVOURITES Finding genuinely characterful accommodation or that unmissable off-the-beaten-track café can be difficult, so the author has chosen a few of his favourite places throughout the country to point you in the right direction. These 'author's favourites' are marked with a ✳.

PRICE CODES Throughout this guide we have used price codes to indicate the cost of those places to stay and eat listed in the guide. For a key to these price codes, see page 43 for accommodation and page 46 for restaurants.

MAPS
Keys and symbols Maps include alphabetical keys covering the locations of those places to stay, eat or drink that are featured in the book. Note that regional maps may not show all hotels and restaurants in the area: other establishments may be located in towns shown on the map.

Grids and grid references Several maps use gridlines to allow easy location of sites. Map grid references are listed in square brackets after the name of the place or site of interest in the text, with page number followed by grid number, eg: [59 C3].

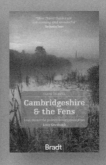

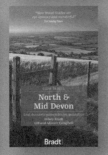

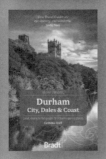

Part One

GENERAL INFORMATION

Location Wales shares a 160-mile-long border with England to the east; Ireland is 45 miles to the west across the Irish Sea

Status Part of the United Kingdom with its own devolved government

National parks Brecon Beacons (520mi^2); Pembrokeshire Coast (243mi^2)

Climate Temperate/maritime; average temperature: January 6.5°C; July 18°C

Capital Cardiff (population 362,000)

Other major cities Swansea, Newport

Language English, Welsh

Religion Church in Wales

Currency Pound sterling

Time GMT (winter), GMT+1 (summer)

International telephone code +44

Electricity 230V

Flag A red dragon on a half-white, half-green background

Anthem Hen Wlad Fy Nhadau ('Land of my Fathers') by Evan James and James James

National holidays 1 January; Good Friday; Easter Monday; early May bank holiday; spring bank holiday (late May/early June); summer bank holiday (late August); Christmas Day; Boxing Day

1

Background Information

GEOGRAPHY

The South Wales landscape is one of sharp contrasts, with flat coastal plains in the south giving way to a largely upland interior, initially characterised by a series of valleys and then a more mountainous range heading into the Brecon Beacons. Formed by four distinct blocks of hills cut through by river valleys – the Black Mountains, the Central Beacons, Fforest Fawr (a designated geopark) and the Black Mountain – the Brecon Beacons is for the greater part characterised by old red sandstone dating back to the Devonian period some 350–500 million years ago, and manifest in variegated colours from light grey-green to dark burgundy. The southern rim of the Brecon Beacons, at the head of the South Wales coalfield, is predominantly carboniferous limestone, an area pockmarked by hollows known as sinkholes, or shakeholes, which has chiselled out a realm of steeply wooded gorges riddled with spectacular cave systems and crashing waterfalls. The Beacons are home to South Wales's highest mountain, Pen-y-Fan, whose height of 2,907ft (886m) just sneaks it into Wales's top-ten peaks, and also makes it the highest mountain in southern Britain. The Brecon Beacons also harbour Wales's second-largest natural body of water, courtesy of Llangorse Lake.

The immense South Wales coalfield, which covers much of the old counties of Monmouth, Glamorgan and Carmarthenshire (with a small incursion into southern Pembrokeshire), is incised with deep, narrow valleys broadly running north–south. Separated by upland moors and hills, this has traditionally made access between the valleys a tricky proposition. The coal measures – from which the mines once extracted their wealth – within the coalfield itself are separated into three distinct areas: anthracite, the deepest, in the far west; steam coal in the central belt; and bituminous in the east. East of the coalfield, heading into Monmouthshire and the Welsh border region with England, the landscape is largely agricultural, shaped by lush, rolling countryside and occasional wooded hills.

The heavily corrugated coastline manifests any number of fabulous geographical features: high limestone cliffs and headlands, coves and bays are the dominant features, but elsewhere you'll come across dune systems like those at Merthyr Mawr and Kenfig, islets, like Gateholm on the Marloes Peninsula, sea caves created by erosion of the underlying rocks, stacks (isolated pillars of rock) – which occasionally go on to form sea arches – and rias (submerged coastal valleys), the best example of which is probably Solva. Then there are the islands themselves: Skomer, Skokholm, Grassholm, Caldey and Ramsey. South Wales also embraces, either wholly or partly, four of the five longest rivers in the country, namely the Severn (which is actually the longest in the UK), the Wye, the Usk and the Tywi.

CLIMATE

The weather in Wales can be gloriously unpredictable, possibly more so than in any other part of Britain, but the one thing that can be said with some certainty is that it rains, a lot. South Wales enjoys a temperate/oceanic climate, meaning that it's largely cool, humid and cloudy for much of the year – and often wet. Wales doesn't generally experience significant seasonal variation in terms of rainfall, hence you should be prepared at all times. Of greater concern is the frequency, and severity, of flooding in recent years, as well as the increasing number of areas that have become susceptible, especially in the Valleys. In 2020, many communities, in particular those in Rhondda Cynon Taf, were hit hard when the River Taff reached its highest level on record. As the impact of climate change continues to be felt, it seems that this is becoming the rule rather than the exception.

Wales is not exactly renowned for its heat, though that's not to say there isn't the occasional spell of scorching weather in the summer months, when the country can be as warm as anywhere in Britain. It's not uncommon for temperatures to hit the 30°C mark, particularly in the capital and coastal areas, though sustained periods of sun-soaked days are rare. Cardiff, too, typically rates a few degrees above anywhere else in the country. As at any time of the year, however, be prepared for the spectre of rain. Spring and autumn are generally pleasant enough, notwithstanding frequent periods of rain, with temperatures generally hovering between 10°C and 15°C. In winter, temperatures throughout South Wales average around 4°C to 6°C, though they do dip below freezing on occasion, especially inland. On higher ground throughout the Brecon Beacons and across to Hay Bluff, there is usually a healthy covering of snow, which can last well into March.

NATURAL HISTORY

MAMMALS Wales's largest native land mammal, **red deer** are almost exclusively confined to the Brecon Beacons, though there have also been occasional sightings in the Lower Wye Valley. Much more widely dispersed throughout South Wales are **muntjac, roe** and **fallow** deer, especially the last, of which there are large numbers in the Wye Valley, though Margam Country Park in Neath is also a good place to see them. Semi-feral **Welsh mountain ponies** roam parts of the eastern Brecon Beacons and, despite their name, inhabit isolated spots of the Pembrokeshire coast such as Stackpole. These small but robust animals are fabulous conservation grazers, helping to keep bracken and gorse under control and grasslands free from invasive scrub.

Around a dozen species of **bat** have been recorded in Wales, though many are in serious decline owing variously to roost disturbance, loss of pasture, disease and climate change. Some of these include Britain's rarest bats, like the **greater** and **lesser horseshoe**, which are mostly confined to parts of Pembrokeshire and Gwent, including Stackpole, which has one of the UK's largest colonies of the greater horseshoe, and the Wye Valley which has a similarly significant population of the lesser horseshoe – Penallt Old Church near Monmouth has an internationally important roosting site. Rarest of them all is the **barbastelle**, believed to inhabit just a handful of isolated breeding sites in South Wales.

A recent success story is the Eurasian **otter**, despite still being categorised as a near-threatened species according to the IUCN Red List. Almost completely wiped out in the 1980s, this secretive, solitary animal frequents many of the waterways within the Brecon Beacons National Park, as well as fast-flowing rivers like the Teifi and Wye, and wetlands such as Magor Marsh on the Gwent Levels. Although they generally keep a very low profile, your best chance of seeing one is early morning or late evening; you are more likely to see their distinctive five-toed footprint or droppings, which are quite fragrant apparently. Magor Marsh on the Gwent Levels and Cosmeston Lakes in the Vale of Glamorgan are also home to **water voles**, another critically endangered animal due to increased predation by American mink, although they are also perfect prey for buzzards, kestrels and the like – a tell-tale sign of a water vole's presence is a deep burrow in the riverbank. A sub-species of the mainland bank vole, the **Skomer vole** is endemic to the island.

Cataloguing **dormice** is notoriously tricky, partly because they are nocturnal, but what is known is that there are scattered populations of this endearing little creature among the woodlands of the Wye Valley and the easternmost flank of the Brecon Beacons, as well as smaller habitats in the Vale of Glamorgan. Dormice typically forage away in dense undergrowth, though are usually only active between May and October before snoozing their way through winter and most of spring.

REPTILES Most of the UK's native reptilian species are present in South Wales, including a healthy population of **adders**, who prefer open heath or moorland. They are Britain's only venomous snake, but will generally steer clear of humans and the only real risk of being bitten is if you step on one. As its name suggests, the **common lizard** can be found in all kinds of habitats throughout South Wales, which sadly isn't the case for the **sand lizard**. Britain's rarest native reptile is a protected species but its numbers remain low – although mostly confined to areas of North Wales, they are present in very small numbers in parts of Pembrokeshire. Other protected species include the **slow worm**, which is not actually a worm or a snake but a legless lizard, and the **great crested newt**, a warty-looking specimen with a bright orange belly whose distribution is fairly widespread. Two important newt sites in South Wales are Cosmeston Lakes and Dyffryn Gardens, both in the Vale of Glamorgan.

BIRDS Thanks largely to their location on the north–south migratory route, the islands of Skomer, Skokholm and Grassholm, just off the Pembrokeshire coast, together make up one of Britain's most important seabird sites. The star attraction is the **Manx shearwater**, more than 200,000 pairs of which settle on these islands following their long flight from South America each March. This staggering number makes it one of the largest concentrations of the bird anywhere in the world, but Manx shearwater are easy prey for gulls so only emerge from, and return to, their shoreline burrows under the cover of darkness, meaning that you'll only see them if you overnight on the islands. Between them, the two islands also hold some 40,000 breeding pairs of **Atlantic puffins** (April to August) and up to 5,000 **storm petrels**, the latter mostly confined to Skokholm. The world's smallest seabird, petrels, like the Manx shearwater, only venture out under the cover of darkness to reduce the risk of predation. Completing this fantastic complement of island seabirds are **guillemots, fulmars, razorbills** and **kittiwakes**, who nest upon the steep cliff ledges. Further offshore, tiny Grassholm Island supports one of the world's largest gannetries, with some 40,000 of these voracious birds taking up residence between late February and September. Elsewhere, the Gower is home to fulmars, cormorants and shags in breeding season, while Carmarthen Bay is of international importance for its 20,000 or so **common scoters** – these small, diving sea ducks were the biggest casualties of the *Sea Empress* oil disaster in 1996 (page 293).

Wales supports many of the UK's most common raptors. Easy to spot thanks to their distinctive forked-tails, **red kites** have made a spectacular comeback to the Welsh countryside in recent years, and while the majority are to be found in North and Mid Powys, the bird is now present across much of the country, even as far south as the Pembrokeshire coastline. Well worth visiting is the feeding station at Llanddeusant in the western Brecon Beacons (page 213). Other common raptors include buzzards, kestrels, sparrowhawks and **peregrine falcons**, which in recent years have become increasingly drawn to urban environments, typically nesting on high ledges that mimic precipitous cliff edges; a family of falcons that nested in Cardiff City Hall's clock tower a few years ago have become a celebrated local attraction, with city pigeons providing these fast, powerful predators with the ideal, ready-made feast. Much less common, and sadly still much persecuted, is the **hen harrier**, which you may catch a glimpse of in upland areas of the Brecon Beacons; the **marsh harrier**, too, is a scarce visitor to the Beacons. All five of the UK's resident **owl** species are represented to some degree throughout South Wales, though again the overall picture is one of steady decline. Most imperilled are the **little owl** and **long-eared owl** – the latter rarely seen – while slightly more populous is the **short-eared owl**, which keeps itself busy along the coastline and in wetland areas and is more commonly seen in winter; Skomer currently has around three pairs. More numerous and widespread are **tawny** and **barn owls**, the latter the most recognisable of the owl family thanks to its heart-shaped head and pure white chest.

Of the woodland bird species, there are currently decent numbers of **redstart**, though both the **wood warbler** and **pied flycatcher** have been in decline and are currently on the Red List. Wales is very much a stronghold for an otherwise relatively small UK population of **choughs** – the rarest member of the crow family – with good numbers along the coastal cliffs of Pembrokeshire and Glamorgan. If you're very lucky, you may get to see the hedgerow-loving **yellowhammer** in parts of Pembrokeshire and the Gower or the brilliantly disguised **nightjar**, a nocturnal heathland bird that makes an unmistakeable churring sound; a dusk-time walk in the Brecons or Afan Forest Park is your best bet of seeing, or at least hearing, one. The upland areas of the Brecon Beacons are also good for spotting **ring ouzels** (a migrant blackbird), **red grouse**, and the stunning **golden plover**, though numbers of all three species are in decline. The Wye Valley, meanwhile, is one of just a handful of UK strongholds for the beautiful but elusive **hawfinch**, the largest member of the finch family.

South Wales's estuaries, coastal marshes and lagoons – such as the Burry Inlet, the Gwent Levels and Oxwich Marshes – host an exciting array of wintering waders, including **avocet, black-tailed godwit, lapwing, dunlin, sanderling, ringed plover** and **redshank**, all of which are listed as either amber or red on the UK conservation list, as well as resident birds like the oystercatcher, Cetti's warbler, little egret and little grebe.

The Gwent Levels has been the site of two notable events recently. In 2016, a pair of **common cranes** nested here, having originated from a successful reintroduction programme on the Somerset Levels. This was the first time since the 17th century that the crane had been seen in Wales – similar to a heron but larger, to see this majestic bird skulking about the marshes foraging for food, or better still, in flight, is quite something. And in 2020, two **bitterns** nested here, the first to do so for more than 200 years. Known for their distinctive foghorn-like call (or 'boom'), these reclusive birds are notoriously difficult to spot owing to their mottled-brown plumage which is tremendously well camouflaged among the dense reedbeds.

INSECTS Although there has been a startling decline in **butterfly** numbers in recent years (though many species do experience fluctuations year on year), the Welsh countryside still harbours some wonderful species. Among the most consistently seen butterflies are the great and small white, the common and holly blue, meadow brown, ringlet, small tortoiseshell and the migrant **painted lady**. Among the rarer species are the once-widespread **marsh fritillary**, a flagship butterfly of the Welsh grasslands that is mostly present in Carmarthenshire; and the **high brown fritillary** – Britain's most endangered species – now confined to just one colony in the Alun Valley in the Vale of Glamorgan. Wales is home to several species of **moth** not found anywhere else in Britain, one of which, the **Silurian**, has been sighted in the Black Mountains. Two extremely rare UK species recently detected in Wales for the first time ever are the **barred-tooth striped moth**, spotted at a woodland site in Monmouthshire, and the **narrow-bordered bee hawk-moth** (a bumblebee mimic), which has been recorded at several sites, among them the Brecon Beacons and Lavernock Point in the Vale of Glamorgan. Another fascinating species is the **Welsh clearwing**, a stunning wasp-like moth that in recent years has been identified in the Black Mountains, which is thought to be its southernmost location; otherwise, it is largely found in the Elan Valley further north. The caterpillar feeds on the bark of mature birch trees before emerging two or three years later, hence the many characteristic exit holes that can be seen in these trees.

Wales counts around 180 different bee fauna, but in line with the rest of the UK, many species are in long-term decline or have become extinct, owing to factors such as habitat loss and degradation, environmental pollution and climate change. It's not all doom and gloom, though. Pembrokeshire and the Gwent Levels are two of just a handful of places in Britain where it's still possible to find the **shrill carder bee**, a species that has been in rapid decline owing to the gradual loss of the flower-rich habitats on which it relies; a late emerging species, it usually goes about its business between May and September. Just as encouragingly, the fields and meadows of the former colliery tips in the South Wales coalfield have become important sanctuaries for a number of bee assemblages, among them the **bilberry bumblebee** and the appropriately named **mini mining bee**, so called because it excavates burrows in the earth to nest. Another scarce species to have recently surfaced in Wales for the first time is the delightfully named **carrot mining bee**, which has been identified at Lavernock Point Nature Reserve in Glamorgan.

MARINE LIFE Although Cardigan Bay is by far the best place in Wales – and one of the best places in the UK – to see **common, bottlenose** and **Risso's dolphins**, as well as **harbour porpoises**, there is often significant activity in the waters off the Pembrokeshire coast, in particular around Strumble Head, Dinas Head, Ramsey Sound and St Bride's Bay. Although dolphins can be seen year-round, the best months are typically July through to September. Of the other cetaceans, there are occasional sightings of **minke whale** and basking sharks, though they inhabit more distant waters. You will, though, see plenty of **Atlantic grey seals** (larger than the common seal) slouching on the rocks of Ramsey and Skomer islands. Although present year-round, September and October are particularly good months to see them as this is pupping season.

With its clean, fast-flowing rivers, remote mountain lakes and vast reservoirs, Wales offers superb angling. First and foremost it's one of the best places in the UK to fish for **wild brown trout**, the country's most widespread species; in South Wales, the Usk is the go-to river for this beautiful specimen. Both the Usk and the strong-flowing Wye are home to another prized game fish, the **Atlantic salmon**, which swim across the ocean to spawn here each spring, though stocks are nowhere near the levels they once were, partly due to rising river temperatures. One of the oldest salmon-fishing techniques is by lave net (a large Y-shaped net), which is practised by just a handful of hardy fishermen on the Severn Estuary (page 105), though they are strictly limited as to how much they can catch. Like the salmon, **sea trout**, which primarily inhabit the Wye, Teifi, Taff and Ogmore rivers, are also in decline.

The Wye is also a prime angling destination for numerous species of coarse fish, including carp, chub, pike, roach and the powerful **barbel**, though the much smaller Taff and Rhymney rivers are also barbel hotspots. Llangorse Lake in the Brecon Beacons is the country's premier pike-fishing spot, while Caerphilly Castle's moat is a spectacular, if unusual, spot to fish for carp. Although closely related to salmon and trout, **grayling** (the 'lady of the stream') is considered a coarse fish and is most commonly found in the Severn and its catchments, as well as the Wye and several of the Valley's rivers such as the Taff, Rhymney and Ogmore. The Wye is also home to several rare and protected fish, among them **twaite shad**, a member of the herring family (and which is only present in three other UK rivers), and the eel-like **lamprey**, both of which are migratory, typically spawning in April or May.

South Wales's coastal waters offer superb year-round boat and shore angling, with bass, pollack, conger eel, flounder, mullet and smooth-hound (a member of the shark family) among the most common species. Indeed, Pembrokeshire is renowned for being one of Europe's premier shark-fishing destinations.

FLORA The South Wales coast is a fantastically plant-rich landscape, with wildflowers in abundance: marsh orchids, knapweed, sea campion, spring squill, English stonecrop, kidney vetch and gorse are among those contributing to a glorious pageant of bright colours; the best time to witness this display is between April and July. The Pembrokeshire coastline, in particular, is a fabulous spot for spring and summer coastal wildflowers, with thrift (colloquially known as sea pink or Mary's pillow) and petalwort especially prolific here – indeed, the coastline boasts one of the UK's largest populations of petalwort.

The coastal dunes and wetlands also present a profusion of exciting plant life. Merthyr Mawr National Nature Reserve counts dune pansies and marram grass among its number, though problems persist with sea buckthorn, a highly invasive shrub that was originally introduced in the mid-19th century to help stabilise the dunes, and work continues in order to reduce its presence. Close by, and one of the UK's most important wildlife conservation sites, Kenfig National Nature Reserve is home to the internationally protected **Fen orchid**. Having been saved from near extinction, this small, rather inconspicuous plant, bearing glossy yellow-green leaves, can only be seen here and on the Norfolk Broads in Britain, and even then only for a very short period between early June and mid-July. Other, more common wild orchids here include bee, marsh, purple and pyramidal, while **sea holly** is another vulnerable species. Another rare native of the dunes is the pale lilac-coloured **sea stock**, which roots down into the shifting sands along more exposed parts of the coast, flowering between June and August.

The high limestone sea cliffs further west on the Gower are home to more rare wildflowers, most importantly **yellow whitlow grass**, a delicate upland Mediterranean species that, between March and May, grows here and nowhere else in Britain. Juniper bushes, basil thyme, goldilocks aster and the delightfully named scrambled egg lichen also put in an appearance at various times of the year. The saltmarsh habitats of North Gower support glasswort, sea aster and samphire, and at Port Eynon Point on South Gower there are often spectacular displays of sea campion, spring squill and wild clary.

There are botanical wonders galore in the Brecon Beacons, whose mountainous outcrops and open moorlands support some fantastically diverse plant life (over 500 species), despite the area's higher altitude and milder temperatures. The Brecons are the southernmost limit in Britain for a number of arctic–alpine species such as **purple saxifrage** and **rosefoot**, while endemic plants found only here include **ley's whitebeam**, a small shrub or tree that's reputedly Britain's rarest species (it's thought that there are no more than 16 remaining) as well as numerous varieties of hawkweed, which are not dissimilar to dandelions in appearance. One of these was discovered as recently as 2004, and subsequently named **Attenborough's hawkweed** (*Hieracium attenboroughianum*) after the celebrated naturalist Sir David Attenborough, the first British species to be named after him.

It's perhaps surprising to learn that Wales is one of Europe's least wooded countries: just 15% of its land area is woodland, less than half of which is native. However, there does now appear to be a sustained commitment to woodland expansion, with the Welsh government's stated ambition being to establish 100,000 new hectares by 2030, partly in response to the climate emergency. In 2020, the government, in conjunction with Natural Resources Wales, launched the National Forest Project, a connected network of 14 woodland sites across the country, five of them in South Wales. The Woodland Trust, meanwhile, has announced plans for the creation of its largest ever woodland, with 150,000 native trees to be planted at Gnoll Country Park near Neath by 2025.

The most heavily wooded areas of South Wales are the Wye Valley, Brecon Beacons and the Valleys, each holding roughly an equal mix of both broadleaf (mostly oak and ash, plus beech, hawthorn and hazel) and conifer (predominantly sitka spruce). These areas include important pockets of ancient **semi-natural woodland** (classified as land that has been wooded for more than 400 years) like Pengelli Forest in Pembrokeshire and Wentwood Forest near Newport, the latter the largest area of ancient woodland remaining in Wales. Dominant tree species include sessile oak, birch, ash and alder. Below the canopy, woodland floors are populated with bluebells, wood anemone, wood sorrel, wild daffodils and ramson (wild garlic), as well as supporting lichen species and their rich moss and liverwort communities. In fact, lichen in Wales represents nearly two-thirds of the total British lichen flora.

HISTORY

PREHISTORIC WALES Early archaeological evidence is scant, but what is known is that stone tools and human teeth, thought to date from around 225,000BC, were unearthed from a cave in Denbighshire, North Wales. More spectacular was the discovery, by geologist William Buckland in 1823, of some red ochre-stained bones in a sea-cave on the Gower. Believing that these bones belonged to a Roman prostitute, the skeleton was subsequently dubbed the '**Red Lady of Paviland**' (page 169) because of the beads and ornaments buried alongside it, but upon further investigation, it was revealed to be that of a male; the name, however, stuck. It was dated to around 24,000BC, leading experts to declare it the oldest anatomically modern human skeleton in Britain and most probably the earliest example of a ritual burial anywhere in western Europe. The skeleton currently resides at Oxford University Museum of Natural History, with a replica at Swansea Museum.

The end of the **Ice Age**, around 9000BC, corresponded with the first period of continuous human settlement on present-day Welsh territory – hunter-gatherers who had migrated here from the European mainland. These **Neolithic** tribes survived by clearing hitherto impenetrable forests to cultivate crops and raise livestock, as well as mining for flint, an easy-to-work material used to produce various tools and implements such as arrowheads, saws and blades. The most compelling evidence of the existence of a Neolithic culture are the many stone-chambered tombs, or cromlechs, distributed around the country, perhaps the finest example being Pentre Ifan in the Preseli Hills in Pembrokeshire. In a similar vein, long cairns – classically a series of chambers set within a long trapezoidal or oval-shaped cairn – were also built to house the remains of the deceased. South Wales has a high prevalence of these, notably in Glamorgan and on the Gower; the most outstanding specimens are Parc le Breos and Tinkinswood, whose capstone is reckoned to be the largest in Britain. Between 2018 and 2020, excavations at Waun Mawn, just south of Pentre Ifan in the Preseli Hills, revealed the remains of four monoliths, which confirmed the existence of what would have once been the third largest bluestone circle in Britain. The dig also confirmed the oft-posited theory that Waun Mawn was almost certainly one of the sites in the Preseli Hills from where many of the bluestones (possibly as many as 80) later erected at Stonehenge were quarried, though why and how these huge slabs were hauled all the way from West Wales to Salisbury Plain remains one of the great mysteries from prehistory. It was also established that the Waun Mawn circle is the only other Neolithic monument in Britain to share the same diameter as the perimeter ditch at Stonehenge.

BRONZE- AND IRON-AGE WALES As the Neolithic era transitioned into the **Bronze Age** around 2000BC, social structures became more organised. This has largely been attributed to the arrival from continental Europe of the Beaker culture, a semi-nomadic race named after the distinctive clay vessels that were buried alongside the dead. While the Beaker phenomenon was not nearly as prominent in Wales as it was in other parts of Britain, a handful of exceptional finds do testify to some sort of presence in the region, notably in Blaenau Gwent. The most significant of these is the Naboth Vineyard Beaker, a beautifully patterned pot found next to the skeleton of a man in a grave near Llanharry in the Rhondda in 1929 while more recently, in 2015, some platforms from a group of ancient huts thought to be of Beaker origin were discovered on a site near the Cwmcelyn Valley. The Bronze Age also saw the introduction of superior methods of metalworking, initially through the use of copper (the mine under the Great Orme in North Wales produced copper on a scale unmatched anywhere else in Europe), resulting in the production of more elaborate jewellery and weaponry. Treasures such as the Llantrisant Fawr Hoard (page 142) and the Llanddewi Skirrid Hoard – both relatively recent finds – demonstrate technically outstanding craftsmanship.

As iron began to replace bronze as the metal of choice, the prevailing systems of wealth and trade collapsed and so the **Iron Age** was ushered in – a period roughly spanning 800BC to AD75. The adoption of this new metal contributed to a period of significant social and cultural advancement: a more sophisticated farming economy emerged – the increasingly widespread availability of iron which, unlike bronze wasn't the preserve of the elite, created a revolution in farming and food production alongside greater mercantile opportunities with mainland Europe and the Mediterranean coast. The most visible legacy from the Iron Age are the 600 or so hillforts stretching across the entire country. Many of these were simple defensive strongholds, while others – particularly those constructed during the latter part of the Iron Age – were larger, more sophisticated enclosures, some even doubling as settlements; among the most impressive in South Wales are Crug Hywel near Crickhowell and the magnificent Foel Drygarn hillfort on Mynydd Preseli in Pembrokeshire. Compared with the many extraordinary treasures unearthed from the Bronze-Age period, meaningful Iron-Age finds from South Wales are in relatively short supply. One exception is the Llyn Fawr Hoard, a repository of items retrieved from a lake in the upper Cynon Valley in the Rhondda in 1913: comprising a cauldron, sword, spearhead and sickle, alongside other pieces, these are among the earliest known Iron-Age objects discovered anywhere in Britain.

THE ROMANS At the onset of **Roman** occupation, which began in Britain around AD43, there were five main tribal groups, or kingdoms, present on Welsh soil: in the north the Ordovices and Deceangli, in mid-Wales the Cornovii, and in the south, the Silures and Demetae. The Demetae were a peaceable, largely agrarian tribe who occupied the territory of modern-day Carmarthenshire and Pembrokeshire, while the Silures – described by Tacitus as 'swarthy of face with curling hair and exceptionally stubborn' – were a hostile mountain people who commanded an area encompassing Monmouthshire, Glamorgan and the Brecon Beacons. One by one, each tribe succumbed to the rule of Rome, though that's not to say the Romans had an easy time of it, owing to the difficult upland terrain they hadn't been forced to encounter in England. First to buckle, around AD48, were the Deceangli, but it took another 30 years before the Ordovician and Silurian tribes – by far the toughest nuts to crack – caved in and by AD75 Wales was finally subjugated.

The Romans established an extensive network of roads that linked a chain of 30 or so auxiliary forts extending as far north as Caernarfon and Anglesey, with as many as 70,000 troops stationed on the territory of Wales. Caerleon, known as Isca during Roman rule and home to the Second Augustan Legion, was established alongside Chester and York as one of three main Roman bases on British shores – and it is here that some of Britain's best-preserved Roman remains are to be found, including a magnificent bathhouse complex and one of Europe's most complete amphitheatres that would have once held 6,000 baying spectators. Nearby Caerwent (Venta Silurum), meanwhile, was designated the administrative centre (*civitas*) for Siluria (the equivalent *civitas* in the Demetae lands was Carmarthen, or Moridunum as it was called then), complete with forum, basilica, baths and so on. Elsewhere, smaller civilian settlements (*vici*) sprang up, and villas, the country mansions of the Roman upper classes, were built. Trade, administration and culture grew up around these garrison towns while at the same time the Welsh lands provided a rich source of mineral wealth: copper, lead, zinc and silver were all extensively mined, as was gold from Dolaucothi in Carmarthenshire, which is the only known Roman gold mine in Britain. The assimilation of the native population into Roman civil society ultimately met with little resistance, although this probably had something to do with the fact that Rome's sphere of influence in Wales was not as complete as it was throughout much of the rest of Britain – for example, the native Brythonic tongue was allowed to co-exist alongside Latin, while certain elements of the ruling classes were permitted to keep their land. The waning influence of the Roman Empire not only coincided with the onset of Christianity but also corresponded with a series of incursions into the region by Germanic Saxons. By around AD390, Welsh lands had escaped the clutches of Roman rule, but new opponents lay in wait.

THE AGE OF THE SAINTS One of Rome's great legacies was Christianity, but now it was the turn of the great Celtic saints to forge their own religious paths. Against a background of increasing religious energy, and despite being surrounded by Saxon enemies who did not share their faith, many Celtic saints came forward to promote

1

a life devoted to prayer and study, taking as their example the Christian hermits from the Middle East. It's generally acknowledged that the first of these saints was Dyfrig (whose monastery, or clas, was at Henllan, in Herefordshire), though the most important was the warrior-cum-monk **St Illtud** who built what is believed to be Britain's first ever centre of learning at Llanilltud Fawr (Llantwit Major); many of Illtud's disciples went on to establish their own class monasteries across Wales, among them St Teilo, who built Llandeilo in the Tywi Valley. This also goes some way to explaining the prevalence of the word Llan, which roughly translates as a 'religious enclosure', as a prefix in so many Welsh place names. The best-known figure of the age, however, and the only native-born patron saint of the countries of Britain and Ireland, was **St David** (Dewi Sant), born around AD500 at St Non's Chapel just south of the city of St David's, which is where he later established an important religious community on or near today's cathedral. Canonised in 1120, he subsequently became the patron saint of Wales. Although St David was not especially well known beyond his native southwest Wales during his lifetime, his influence and legend continued to grow in the centuries following his death around 590, and it was through him that a distinctive form of Welsh Christianity emerged.

THE ANGLO-SAXONS AND THE WELSH KINGDOMS The post-Roman age – often termed the Dark Ages or the Early Christian Age – was also the age of the **Anglo-Saxons**, relentless invaders from southern Denmark and northern Germany who brought with them their own religion and language. At the same time on the territory of modern-day Wales, a multiplicity of **Welsh kingdoms** emerged, among them Ceredigion (the historic county of Cardiganshire); Gwent (southeast Wales); Brycheiniog, roughly the southern half of modern-day Powys incorporating the Brecon Beacons; and Dyfed, which covered most of modern-day Pembrokeshire and the western part of Carmarthenshire, and, like much of western Britain, had largely been settled by the Irish.

In the 8th century, Offa – Anglo-Saxon king of Mercia – built his eponymous dyke, a stupendous piece of engineering that entailed the construction of a linear earthwork demarcating the boundary between Wales (although it did not exist as such then) and Mercia – in today's money from Sedbury near the Severn Estuary to Prestatyn on the North Wales coast – ostensibly to repel raiding warriors from the 'west', or from 'behind the dyke', whom the Anglo-Saxons termed Wēalas (Welsh), meaning to imply 'strangers' or Romanised people. For their part, the Britons increasingly referred to themselves as **Cymry**, 'compatriots' or 'fellow countrymen', from the Celtic word *cambrogi*. In the event, the Britons managed to hold firm in the face of repeated Saxon incursions, though these were mainly confined to the area of modern-day Powys.

Well-honed marauders, the **Vikings** presented a simultaneously awkward threat, and although they primarily had their sights trained on England, Scotland and Ireland, they weren't averse to (the occasional rapacious) sorties on Wales. In South Wales, St David's often bore the brunt, but they also harried other stretches of the coast, establishing minor settlements at Milford Haven, Swansea and the Gower (it's believed that Worm, as in Worm's Head, comes from the Norse word meaning 'Dragon', hence 'Dragon's Back'). Ultimately, they never colonised Wales to anything like the degree they did elsewhere in the British Isles or Ireland. One unifying figure emerged during this period: **Rhodri Mawr**, or **Rhodri the Great**, a leader not only capable of simultaneously repelling both the Vikings and the Anglo-Saxons, but also someone who managed to successfully bring the hitherto fragmented kingdoms together. Upon Rhodri's death, the various kingdoms were dispersed among his sons, leading to inevitable internecine warfare, unlike across the 'border' where the Anglo-Saxons were finally starting to resemble some kind of coherent entity.

Not unlike his grandfather, Rhodri the Great, **Hywel Da** (Hywel the Good) was quite the schemer, and in order to retain a measure of control of his land (by this stage roughly three-quarters of Wales), he forged strong alliances with Wessex, one of his enemies, and orchestrated a strategically arranged marriage to Elen, daughter of Llywarch ap Hyfaidd of Dyfed, thereby putting himself in a position to gain control of much of southwest Wales upon his wife's father's death. Hywel's greatest achievement, however, was the codification and promulgation of Welsh Law, ostensibly to assist in the unification of the Welsh kingdoms; taking place in Whitland, Carmarthenshire, some time around AD930, this body of law was nothing if not meticulous. Regarding divorce, for example, the law stated: 'If anyone send away his wife without lawful cause, and take another in her place, by judgement the woman who has been put out is entitled to come to her home and be in her home until the ninth day...'. Moreover, 'The husband shall have all the pigs, the wife the sheep.' The Law of Wales would remain in place for another five centuries, until it was usurped by the Act of Union in 1536. Upon Hywel's death, further fragmentation ensued, before his great-great-grandson, **Gruffydd ap Llywelyn**, achieved what even Hywel couldn't, and united all the kingdoms.

THE NORMANS AND OWAIN GLYNDWR The next great struggle for the Britons was with the Normans, who arrived on British shores some three years after Gruffydd ap Llywelyn's death. But for the Normans, Wales was a much tougher nut to crack than for their Anglo-Saxon counterparts. Wild and mountainous, especially in the north, and with a multiplicity of leaders to deal with, the Normans were presented with a different set of problems. In the event, they established a collective territory known as Marchia Wallie, or the Marches, across southern Wales – and as was their modus operandi, castles were erected with ruthless efficiency, from Chepstow in the east to Pembroke in the west. Run by Norman, or Marcher, Lords, these strongholds were bastions for raiding land and supressing the locals, who would have suffered the loss of rights and privileges, and sometimes land.

One ruler who refused to be cowed by the Normans was **Rhys ap Gruffydd** (The Lord Rhys) ruler of the Kingdom of Deheubarth, the pre-eminent Welsh kingdom at that time. From his seat of power at Dinefwr Castle in the Tywi Valley, Rhys proved to be quite the persistent thorn (in the Norman side), not only clawing back some of the land previously lost to the Normans, but also skilled enough to negotiate should it benefit him – so much so that he was eventually able to make peace with Henry II; in fact so cordial were relations that Henry made Rhys Justice of South Wales. Rhys was also credited with kickstarting a Welsh cultural revival, and to this end he presided over Wales's first ever eisteddfod at Cardigan Castle in 1176, albeit the next one wouldn't take place until 1451. Moreover, Rhys was instrumental in facilitating the introduction of several Cistercian monastic houses to the region, notably at Strata Florida in Ceredigion and Whitland in Carmarthenshire, in addition to supporting many other religious institutions, including the Order of St Benedict. However, Rhys's unique relationship with the English Crown would break down upon Henry's death in 1189.

In 1267, Henry III formally acknowledged **Llywelyn ap Gruffydd** (Llywelyn the Last) as the Prince of Wales (the first Welsh ruler to receive such recognition by a king of England) in return for homage, and by dint of this, Gruffydd established himself as the most powerful ruler in Wales, although this didn't include Pembrokeshire.

1

However, Henry III's death changed everything, for Gruffydd was unwilling to pay homage to Henry III's successor, Edward I (and nor did he attend his coronation), which prompted Edward to declare war. A year-long campaign ended with a victorious Edward redistributing Welsh lands. Unbowed, five years later Gruffydd joined forces with his brother, Dafydd, although this time the outcome was terminal: death for Gruffydd (in somewhat mysterious circumstances) and the colonisation of Welsh lands by the English. Wales was left powerless, its people bereft, and now with no hope of achieving independence. Edward's I's defining legacy, meanwhile, is an Iron Ring of Castles in North Wales, which just so happened to be inscribed as the country's first ever UNESCO World Heritage Site, in 1986. Worse was to follow in 1349 when the Black Death descended upon Welsh lands, resulting in a quarter of its population being wiped out within just two years. In South Wales, among the worst-hit towns were Abergavenny, Haverfordwest and Pembroke.

A century of English rule was more than enough for one man, however. In 1400, at the ripe old age of 40, **Owain Glyndwr** declared himself Prince of Wales. What started out as a local revolt in Harlech, North Wales, rapidly escalated into a national one, with supporters rising up throughout the country. Deploying guerrilla-like tactics, within just three years, and having seen off the English in the north of the country, Glyndwr – along with his growing army of supporters, set his sights south: Carreg Cennen, Carmarthen and Llansteffan in Carmarthenshire were all captured, as were castles at Usk, Caerleon, Newport and Cardiff among others. There was even an international dimension to the revolt, when in 1405 a 2,500-strong French armada arrived off Milford Haven to proffer its support. However, this rebel with a cause was soon to become a fugitive on the run, as castles that he had once seized, including Harlech, were recaptured – though when and where Glyndwr was killed remains a mystery. While Glyndwr's insurrection undoubtedly inspired a renewed sense of Welsh nationalism throughout all social classes, it came at a high price: huge loss of life, lands wasted and a deleterious effect on the economy. Moreover, it irrevocably damaged what had been a relatively peaceful coexistence – both economically and politically – between the Welsh and English. To this day, though, Glyndwr remains the most enduring figure from Welsh history, manifest in statues and monuments as well as pubs and streets named after him.

THE TUDORS AND CIVIL WAR In the summer of 1485, after 14 years in exile in France, Pembroke-born Henry Tudor landed at Mill Bay near Milford Haven in Pembrokeshire, with one aim in mind: to dethrone Richard. With victory duly gained at Bosworth Field, the newly crowned Henry VII became the first King of England of Welsh descent. Following the death of Henry's son, Arthur, in 1501, the crown – along with Arthur's wife, Catherine of Aragon, and the title of Prince of Wales – passed on to his younger brother, Henry, and it was under his rule, as Henry VIII, that the future of Wales would be dramatically altered.

As its title implies, the **Act of Union** (1536) assimilated the English and Welsh governmental and legal systems, in addition to which it was decreed that English should be the language of the courts, thereby voiding the preceding laws passed under Hywel Da. But far from equalising the two nations, the Act only served to discriminate against monoglot Welsh speakers. Another consequence of the Act was the conversion of the Marcher lordships into shires, with the creation of seven new counties, among them Brecknock, Pembroke, Glamorgan and Monmouth. At around the same time, Henry broke all ties with Rome and placed himself as head of the Church of England. Monasteries throughout Wales were razed, and in South Wales this meant the likes of Ewenny, Margam, Neath and Tintern, once-glorious buildings now subject to what amounted to little more than state-sponsored vandalism. The only group to benefit from this was the Anglo-Welsh gentry, while the landless peasants continued to live in abject poverty. The reign of Elizabeth I coincided with a period of cultural advancement: in 1588 the Bible was translated into Welsh – a singularly towering achievement and just the 13th country in the world to receive its own translation – while Jesus College in Oxford was founded for Welsh scholars. The end of Elizabeth's reign signalled what more or less amounted to the beginning of the commercial age in Wales, which was particularly well established in areas of South Wales. Merchants in Tenby, for example, forged strong links with ports in Portugal, Spain and Morocco, trading in high-end goods like wool cloth, spices and vinegar.

As an essentially royalist-supporting population, the majority of Welsh people sided with Charles I and with tensions growing between king and country (the Parliamentarians), civil war was inevitable. And despite its somewhat misleading name – the English Civil War – many of the most hard-fought battles took place on Welsh soil, including parts of Pembrokeshire, Carmarthen, Swansea and Neath, though none more so than at St Fagans near Cardiff. Cromwell, too, had a personal hand in overseeing some of the sieges, including at Chepstow and Pembroke.

ENLIGHTENMENT AND METHODISM The beginning of the 18th century was a period of cultural and religious efflorescence for South Wales, which in time would play a crucial role in shaping the country's identity. This was in no small part down to the **Methodist Revival**, and in particular three hugely powerful and eloquent figures: a zealous preacher by the name of Howell Harris, the hymn writer William Williams Pantycelyn, and Daniel Rowland, who converted thousands with his powerful sermons (both Harris and Rowland, incidentally, converted to Methodism in 1735). For his part, Williams penned more than 800 hymns, many run through with powerful biblical imagery. A much-improved school system brought about a literary revolution that spread among all sectors of society, while the chapel became the focus of social life. Slowly but surely, the more evangelistic tenet of Calvinistic Methodism took root in Wales, and by 1811 the Calvinistic Methodists had broken away from its rigid Anglican framework.

As they had so often been, religion and education were inextricably entwined. In 1731, Griffith Jones, a rector from Llanddownror in Carmarthenshire, started a system of what were known as circulating, or travelling, schools, some 4,000 of which were established, while also helping organise reading classes for farmers and their families in farm and church buildings. It was a phenomenal success and within 30 years over half of the population was literate, a remarkable achievement by any measure.

THE INDUSTRIAL REVOLUTION From the mid 18th century, South Wales would be changed forever, and on a speed and scale that was hitherto unimaginable. While copper, coal and iron had been mined to some degree or other over the centuries, new technologies and the country's inexhaustible wealth of natural resources would combine to make Wales an industrial powerhouse of global significance, and in the process create extraordinary wealth for the few and abject poverty for the majority.

Just as Swansea would be transformed by the **copper industry** – at its apogee, this area of South Wales accounted for some 90% of copper production in the UK – so great swathes of South Wales would be transformed, not just physically, but economically and socially by the iron and coal industries. As well as being the most technologically advanced copper works anywhere in the world, Copperopolis, as Swansea was known, was the first truly global industry in the sense that it was the first to export its product internationally. Similarly, the perfect combination of natural resources near Merthyr enabled the likes of the Crawshays of Cyfarthfa and the Guests of Dowlais to become two of the wealthiest ironworks in the world: by the mid 19th century, there were more than 25 ironworks in South Wales smelting over a third of Britain's pig iron; the railways of the world were made here in South Wales.

As the demand for iron grew, so too did the demand for more workers. Instant communities sprang up and migrants came from all over, but with too many workers and not enough housing to go around, workers and their families were often forced to live in thoroughly squalid conditions where they would be susceptible to a plethora of diseases, including typhoid and cholera. Given such appalling living and working conditions, along with pitiful pay, it was only a matter of time before the ironmasters had a revolt on their hands. In 1831, up to 10,000 people took to the streets of Merthyr in what would be the first mass uprising on Welsh soil (page 190), but this newly found spirit of rebellion wasn't just confined to the iron towns. **Chartist riots**, fuelled by the government's refusal to accede to a series of demands such as the right for all to vote, broke out in towns across Britain, but nowhere was the struggle more pronounced than in South Wales, and specifically Newport, site in 1839 of the bloodiest confrontation yet seen in industrial-era Wales (page 112). In West Wales meanwhile, an underground protest movement, more commonly known as the **Rebecca Riots**, saw tenant farmers rise up against the payment of tolls in order to use the roads.

But more than iron, it was **coal** that put Wales, and South Wales in particular, on the global map. Although coal had been mined in small quantities since Roman times, and the first deep pits had been sunk as long ago as the 17th century, it wasn't until the late 18th century that coal began to be extracted on a large scale, its demand fuelled, quite literally, by the iron smelters in places like Merthyr and Blaenavon. In 1828, 3 million tonnes of coal were being produced annually, a figure that rose to 4.5 million within 12 years. But nothing before, or indeed since, would compare to the transformation brought about by the growth of the industry from the mid 19th century onwards.

The new coal rush was led by John Patrick Crichton-Stuart, the Second Marquess of Bute, who was not only one of Britain's richest landowners, but also happened to own much of the South Wales coalfield. Keen to exploit the coal measures, Bute's trustees (Bute died in 1848) opened the first pit – the Bute Merthyr Colliery – in the Rhondda Fawr in 1855. Coal was sent down to Cardiff along Bute's newly laid Taff (Vale) Railway, which in turn fuelled Cardiff's fortune, as it was from here that coal would be shipped to all four corners of the earth. Other entrepreneurs followed, with pits opening up on what seemed like a daily basis. The extraction of more coal – which was in particularly huge demand from the Admiralty in London – meant more workers, which necessitated more housing, and so hitherto uninhabited valleys were suddenly run through with serried ranks of terraced houses packed together cheek by jowl, alongside Noncomformist chapels built to support these new populations.

The immiseration facing the miners was all too real, however. These were brutal working environments: accidents were a daily occurrence and major disasters were commonplace too. Many were beyond comprehension, such as those at Cymer in the Rhondda in 1856 when 114 miners died, Ferndale in the Rhondda in 1867 (178 dead) and Senghenydd in 1913 when 439 men were killed. These incidents, alongside the issue of poor pay, were partially responsible for the rise of trade unions, and in 1898, the South Wales Miners' Federation was formed. From early in the 19th century, the coalfield of southern Wales grew to be the richest in the UK. At its peak, in 1913, it provided employment for a quarter of a million miners capable of extracting 57 million tons of the mineral annually – a fifth of Britain's total. In that same year, the Port of Cardiff alone exported 11 million tons of top-quality coal. Llanelli, Barry, Swansea and Newport were also home to huge coal-handling docks and marshalling yards.

THE 20TH AND 21ST CENTURIES At the turn of the century, coal was as popular as ever, yet dreadful working conditions and atrocious pay gave rise to widespread civil unrest and a series of bitter and often violent industrial disputes, nowhere more so than in Tonypandy in 1910 and Llanelli in 1911. Unrest among much of the labourforce was still prevalent at the onset of World War I – incidentally, the prime minister from 1916 onwards was lawyer and Liberal party politician **David Lloyd George**, the first, and still only, Welshman to have held the highest office in government. In the event, more than 40,000 Welshmen lost their lives during the Great War. The worldwide post-war drop in the price of coal led to widespread pit closures and, consequently, high levels of unemployment in the hard-pressed South Wales coalfield – levels that were much higher in Wales than in either England or Scotland.

By this time, the Labour Party – founded by Scots-born trade unionist **Keir Hardie** in 1900, the same year he was elected to parliament for Merthyr Tydfil as Britain's first Labour MP – had usurped the Liberals as the popular party of choice in Wales. Meanwhile, the rise in Welsh consciousness and a growing appetite for social improvement among many sectors of society – a process that had already manifest itself in the foundation of a number of institutions, among them the Welsh Language Society, and the University College Wales and the National Library, both in Aberystwyth – led to the creation of **Plaid (Genedlaethol) Cymru** (the National Party of Wales) in 1925, whose principal aims were the promotion of the Welsh language and political independence.

As elsewhere throughout Britain, Wales suffered great losses during World War II, while many towns and cities were on the receiving end of devastating Luftwaffe raids, none more so than Cardiff – then still one of the world's busiest coal ports – Pembroke and Swansea, the latter almost completely razed over three appalling nights in February 1941. Labour continued to enjoy strong post-war support among South Walians, support that had been strengthened following the newly installed government's commitment to the creation of a welfare state, central to which was the implementation of the National Health Service in 1948. Its architect was Tredegar-born, Ebbw Vale MP **Aneurin Bevan** (page 184), Minister for Health and Housing in Clement Attlee's cabinet, and to this day the scheme remains arguably the single greatest achievement by any 20th-century politician. Another significant post-war landmark was Cardiff's designation as Wales's capital city in 1955; remarkably, the country had been without a capital until that point.

The newly nationalised industries – including iron, steel and coal – powered on in the 1950s and 60s, but with a post-war population hungry for more modern conveniences, light manufacturing businesses – such as the massive Hoover plant in Merthyr – were beginning to supplant heavy industry; for the first time, too, this presented women with the opportunity to join the labour force in large numbers. Despite nationalisation, the number of mines continued to decline and the pits remained perilous places to work. Tragedies were still commonplace and one incident in particular remains seared into the national consciousness nearly 60 years on: the 1966 **Aberfan disaster** (page 193), in which 116 primary children and 28 adults were killed after a massive heap of spoil collapsed on top of their school.

In the 1950s and 60s, the noise around national identity – central to which was the status of the Welsh language – continued to rumble on, yet it wasn't until 1965, under Wilson's Labour government, that the **Welsh Office** was created, tasked with executing government policy in Wales and headed up by the first ever Secretary of State for Wales (Jim Griffiths from Llanelli). Of greater significance though – indeed, a seismic moment in Welsh political life – was the election of the first ever Plaid Cymru politician, Gwynfor Evans in Carmarthen, to Westminster in 1966.

Alongside the Welsh language movement, the other big engine of change in Welsh life in the latter half of the 20th century was **devolution**. In Wales's first ever referendum, in 1979, the electorate emphatically voted 4 to 1 against home rule, a result that could in large part be explained by the much greater concerns people had with regard to jobs and livelihoods rather than nationhood. With industry struggling to compete with the price of oil, between 1976 and 1979 more than 60,000 jobs – mostly in the steel industry, manufacturing and construction – were lost in Wales, while interest rates reached an all-time high of 28%. A second referendum, some 20 years later, would yield a very different result. That said, enthusiasm for the Welsh language was on the rise, for example with the opening of Welsh-speaking schools, albeit in the more traditional Welsh-speaking areas like North and West Wales; another breakthrough came in 1982 when the first Welsh-language television channel, S4C, began broadcasting.

Support for Margaret Thatcher's conservative government remained fairly solid in South Wales in the early 1980s, but the year-long **Miners' Strike** in 1984–85 changed all that. Eventual defeat for the National Union of Mineworkers effectively signalled the end of deep mining, and indeed heavy industry, in South Wales forever. It also ushered in a period of deep economic turmoil, with high unemployment and grinding poverty affecting large swathes of the region, particularly those Valleys' communities that had been sustained by coal, iron and steel for more than a century.

New Labour's commitment to holding a referendum on the creation of a Welsh Assembly – the second following the 1979 vote – resulted in an endorsement for self-governance, albeit by just 6,000 votes. Still, this was a historic moment, the first body of its kind in Wales for more than 600 years. Devolution was also the spur for the transformation of Cardiff Bay, the biggest waterfront regeneration project in Europe, which, among other things, would be home to the Welsh Assembly's magnificent new Senedd building.

In the 2016 **Brexit** referendum, Wales voted to leave the EU by 52.5% to 47.5%, a result that was as surprising as it was depressing given that the country – and particularly South Wales – had long been one of the biggest beneficiaries of EU financial aid. The full effects of Brexit continue to be played out, as do the consequences of the **Covid-19 pandemic**, which, by common consensus, Welsh government members were deemed to have handled well, certainly in comparison with their English counterparts.

GOVERNMENT AND POLITICS

Labour's return to power in 1997 set in train their manifesto promise to hold a referendum on the creation of a Welsh Assembly. In the event, the referendum – held on 18 September 1997 – was a mighty close-run thing with a tiny majority of 50.3% in favour of home rule, though turnout was extremely low, at just over 50%. The Government of Wales Act 1998 duly paved the way for the creation of an

Assembly, which was inaugurated in 1999, though there was widespread discontent that Wales hadn't been given the same primary law-making powers enjoyed by both Scotland and Northern Ireland, the UK's two other devolved nations. Further legislative revisions in 2011 and 2014 extended the Assembly's law-making powers, as did the Wales Act 2017, which more or less aligned Wales to the devolution model originally envisaged, providing for increased executive powers, known as a 'reserved powers' of devolution in a number of policy areas such as law-making and taxation.

In a further nod to its new constitutional status, in 2020 the Welsh Assembly was renamed Senedd Cymru (or the Welsh Parliament, in English) though this still didn't placate many – including numerous prominent celebrities and some ministers, mostly from Plaid Cymru – who were staunchly against the English appendage. The Senedd, incidentally, is in fact the name of the building in Cardiff that houses the parliamentary chamber. Rebranding aside, this was regarded as an historic moment: officially speaking, it had been more than six centuries since the last Welsh parliaments were convened, in Harlech and Machynlleth, and the parliament was the culmination of more than a century of campaigning by devolutionists.

The Welsh Government comprises 60 members – elected every five years and known as Members of the Senedd – 40 of whom are chosen to represent individual constituencies with the remainder representing the five regions of Wales. The government is headed up by the First Minister – the incumbent is Mark Drakeford – and a cabinet comprising 12 ministers plus a counsel general. Since the first elections in 1999, Labour has consistently held the most seats (though always falling just short of the 31 required for a majority), with Plaid Cymru and the Conservatives trailing somewhat in their wake. The current make-up, as of the last elections in May 2021, has Labour with 30 seats, Plaid Cymru 13, Conservatives 16 and the Liberal Democrats 1 – the most notable change being UKIP losing all seven of their seats. These were also the first elections in which 16- and 17-year-olds were allowed to vote. At a local level, Wales is divided into 22 unitary authorities (country or borough councils), each of which is democratically elected every four years and is responsible for delivering local services.

Wales has 40 members represented in the House of Commons (at Westminster). Following the 2019 general election, Labour held 22 of these, losing six seats from the previous election in 2017 to the Conservatives, who currently have 14, followed by Plaid Cymru with four. In terms of South Wales, Labour retained all but one of its 22 previously held seats (losing Bridgend) – a core that spreads west from Newport through the traditional labour heartland of the Valleys to Llanelli and the Gower – despite a disastrous showing in North Wales where they lost several seats and being decimated across large swathes of England. Elsewhere, the Plaid Cymru seat of Carmarthen East is sandwiched in between the Conservative strongholds of Brecon and Pembrokeshire, while Monmouth has long been a solid Conservative seat. The Liberal Democrats, meanwhile, were unceremoniously wiped from the map, losing their one remaining seat. A redrawing of the constitutional boundaries, possibly to 31 seats, has been mooted, though critics argue that would only further diminish Wales's sphere of influence within UK government.

ECONOMY

Long gone are the days when South Wales was a world economic powerhouse. Until the onset of the Industrial Revolution, the Welsh economy was largely rural based: for example, it was the drovers who took livestock on foot to markets in England, as far afield as London. In fact, it was the drovers who established the Black Ox Bank in Llandovery in 1799, which became part of Lloyd's Bank in 1909, at which time the ox was replaced by a horse.

The Industrial Revolution transformed the economic landscape of Wales, albeit bringing vast wealth to the few and abject misery to the majority. Swansea – aka Copperopolis – became the most important port in the world, until it was superseded by Cardiff during the coal boom. Merthyr, meanwhile, was home to four of the world's largest ironworks, among them Cyfarthfa and Dowlais. Such labour-intensive work triggered mass migration from rural Wales, England, Ireland and elsewhere into the new industrial heartlands: at the start of the 19th century, Wales had a population of less than 600,000; by the end of the century, it was 2 million. The steady decline, and eventual collapse, of heavy industry in the 20th century left many communities bereft, with the economic consequences still being felt several decades later.

The question that many commentators are starting to pose is: how long can Wales afford not to be independent if it is to have some say in its own destiny? And while the prospect of a referendum is still some way off (it's certainly much further down the line than Scotland), it's a noise that only looks set to get increasingly louder. Or, to put it another way, *can* Wales afford to be independent? This is especially pertinent given that on key indicators such as productivity, educational attainment, income, material deprivation, health and housing, Wales performs poorly compared with other UK countries and regions.

As in most places, the Covid-19 pandemic wrought tremendous damage on the Welsh economy, while the effects of Brexit continue to be played out. There's no doubt though that the loss of EU funding has impacted in many areas, the sad irony being that South Wales, and the Valleys in particular, were among the areas in the UK with the highest number of Leave votes. Another contentious issue in recent years has been the proliferation of second home-buyers – particularly in popular coastal areas such as Pembrokeshire – which has driven up house prices unsustainably (and it seems that higher taxes on second homes are having little effect), thereby forcing young people to move away, whether they like it or not. In turn, this is exacerbating the problem of Wales's demography: the country is, on average, older than the rest of the UK and ageing at a faster rate; moreover, the elderly population is, in general, poorer and sicker than England's. Rural depopulation is a particularly pressing problem.

One upside of the pandemic, however, has been the number of British people seeking to holiday on home turf – with Wales a particularly popular destination, thanks to its accessibility, spectacular natural beauty, and relative affordability. Although this has re-energised many local economies, these are mostly those areas that rely on tourists anyway, so the spread is very uneven. But overall, tourism in Wales now ranks highly in terms of economic importance. Otherwise, Wales has high proportions of employment in agriculture, forestry and fishing (Milford Haven, with its vast natural harbour, is the region's major fishing port, but overall the fishing fleet is relatively small), manufacturing (especially the automotive and aeronautical sectors) and government, though concomitantly fewer jobs in the financial and business sector. There are still important pockets of heavy industry and manufacturing in South Wales, most obviously the massive Port Talbot steel works – although the threat of closure seems to be ever present – as well as others including the Liberty steel plants in Newport and Tredegar, the Trostre tin-plate manufacturing facility in Llanelli and the Aston Martin car plant in St Athan in the Vale of Glamorgan.

Rome's legacy is still evident in today's Welsh language, with a number of Latinate words such as *pont*, meaning 'bridge', and *eglwys*, meaning 'church', part of the native tongue. But as is often the case, it's difficult to ascertain exactly when the native language might have been first used, whether verbally or as written text. One clue lies in a diminutive 13th-century manuscript called *The Book of Aneirin*, most likely written by a couple of monks. In his poem, *Y Gododdin*, the eponymous poet references, in Welsh, a battle between the Britons and the Angles that took place in the north of England some time around AD600 which makes this the oldest surviving piece of literature in the Welsh language.

Brythonic (which was spoken during Roman rule) was one of the two branches of the Insular Celtic language, which formed the basis for the Welsh language, as well as Cornish (which is currently classified as critically endangered) and Breton which is more widely used. Welsh remained a relatively thriving language in the centuries up to and throughout Norman settlement, a situation that changed following Henry VIII's accession to the throne. As stated in his 1536 Act of Union, 'from henceforth no Person or Persons that use the Welsh speech or Language shall have or enjoy any Manner, Office or Fees within this realm of England, Wales or other of the King's Dominion, upon pain of forfeiting the same Office or Fees, unless he or they use and exercise the English speech or language' – a law that effectively denied Welsh official status and banned the language from the spheres of law and administration, thereby overturning in one stroke the Law of Wales established under Hywel Da some five centuries previously. And in doing so it discriminated heavily against monoglot Welsh speakers. This was followed by the 1549 Act of Uniformity, which decreed that all acts of public worship would be conducted in English. However, this ran somewhat contradictory to legislation introduced by Elizabeth I less than 40 years later, who tasked William Morgan, vicar of Llanrhaeadr-ym-Mochnant, with the not inconsiderable feat of translating the Bible into Welsh. Had Morgan not worked his magic, it's extremely doubtful whether the Welsh language would have survived at all. The fate of the language became inextricably linked to its use within religious circles, in large part due to the rapid spread of Nonconformist religious movements during the 17th century, and as the one Welsh text that most ordinary folk had access to, the Bible did more to reinforce the language's status than anything else. Within a century of the Bible's publication, Wales had one of the highest levels of popular literacy in Europe, and by the beginning of the 19th century it was estimated that some 90% of the population spoke Welsh, the one glaring exception being the small pocket of land in South Pembrokeshire, otherwise, known as 'Little England beyond Wales' (page 278).

This wasn't to last and the Industrial Revolution accelerated the decline of the language. As well as rapid urbanisation, it was the attitudes of the English Establishment, among them mine-owners and capitalists, that did for the language. Many of them believed that Welsh people were uneducated and that this was the root cause of the unrest and instability, so in 1847, a report (the *Brad y Llyfrau Gleision* (*The Treachery of the Blue Books*) was commissioned to judge the state of Welsh education. It was damning in its judgement of both the Welsh language and the morals of those who spoke it, the result being that not only did it illustrate how English people viewed the Welsh and their language, but it also had a serious impact on how Welsh people felt about their own tongue. Moreover, mass immigration brought about by the increase in working opportunities fed other languages into the mix, further diluting the influence of Welsh. Welsh was also forcibly discouraged in schools to the extent that a barbaric practice, known as 'Welsh Not', was employed. Any child caught speaking Welsh would have a piece of wood tied to a leather strap (a *cribban*) hung around their neck, and whoever happened to be in possession of the *cribban* at the end of the day would be soundly beaten.

Following World War I, the number of Welsh-speaking people hit a new low to the extent that it became a minority language. Among the reasons for this was the massive loss of life (young men in particular) suffered during the war, coupled with diminishing chapel attendances, one of the traditional cornerstones of the Welsh-language culture. But hopeful signs were on the way. The year 1925 saw the inauguration of **Plaid Cymru**, the Welsh National Party, whose explicit aim was not only to keep the language alive, but also to make it the official language of Wales. Plaid Cymru were joined in their crusade to revive the Welsh language by the Welsh Language Society (formed in 1962) who embarked on a number of campaigns, among other things including calls for Welsh-language road tax forms and the development of the language, particularly in the realms of broadcasting and education. Indeed, the Welsh Language Act that followed in 1967 not only made provision for Welsh to be taught in primary schools, but also placed Welsh on an equal footing with English for the first time – even now, it's extraordinary to think that it took so long. Since 1999, it has been compulsory for all pupils aged five to 16 to learn Welsh, at least as a second language. But it was the broadcast media that contributed most readily to this new-found sense of Welsh identity, and with it the development of the Welsh language. In 1978, the BBC Welsh-language Radio Cymru began broadcasting, to be followed, just four years later, by the S4C (Sianel Pedwar Cymru) television station.

It is estimated that some 880,000 people (around a fifth of the population) in Wales are able to speak Welsh. In terms of its distribution, it's far from an even spread, although it is returning in strength to areas from which it had partly or totally disappeared. The real stronghold of the language is and always has been North Wales, particularly around Anglesey, the Llyn and Snowdonia, though it is commonly understood in most of West Wales, from West Glamorgan through to Carmarthenshire, Cardigan Bay and northern Pembrokeshire. The language is rarely spoken in the urban, largely anglicised, southeast, or for that matter in southern Pembrokeshire, although there are historical reasons for this (page 278). Moreover, it seems that for the first time, there appears to be greater interest from non-native speakers – whether living in Wales or outside the country – to learn Welsh, certainly if apps like Duolingo are anything to go by.

That the language is experiencing such a renaissance would appear to be fuelled by multiple factors, among them easier access to the language due to the internet, the rise in English nationalism as a result of Brexit (alongside a growing frustration with a post-Brexit Westminster), but perhaps above all, it's just simply that the Welsh are finally proud to proclaim their Welshness. The Welsh government has even released a strategy, Cymraeg 2050, which aims to get a million people speaking and using Welsh daily by the middle of this century – and judging by the way things are going, this seems like one of the government's more meaningful (and realistic) targets.

This new-found willingness to engage in the native tongue is manifest in many areas of Welsh popular culture, though nowhere is it currently stronger than in the sphere of music, which has seen a number of Welsh-language artists come to the fore, and there's even an annual Welsh-language Music Day (Dydd Miwsig Cymru) in celebration of the country's musical heritage. Just as significantly, it's now not uncommon to hear Welsh-language music on mainstream UK stations, particularly the likes of BBC Radio 6 Music. In television, two recent S4C-produced dramas, *Hidden* (*Craith*) and *Hinterland* (*Y Gwyll*), have transferred to the BBC and Netflix to great enthusiasm, with subtitles in English for those Welsh-speaking parts of the programme.

RELIGION

As in much of the rest of Britain, **Christianity** was introduced to South Wales by Roman soldiers, traders and administrators, primarily from Caerwent, although it was largely an urban faith; the earliest Christian discovery on Welsh territory, a Chi-Rho from Caerwent, was dated AD375. In the wake of Rome's departure around AD400, it was left to itinerant missionaries – men and women who had travelled by sea around the westernmost parts of Britain and Brittany – to actively continue the faith, a period more generally known as the Age of Saints (page 11). One of these itinerants was St Illtud, who founded a monastic school at Llantwit Fawr (Llantwit Major). The site is readily acknowledged to be Britain's first seat of learning and continues to be Wales's main place of pilgrimage. Many of St Illtud's students would go on from Llantwit Fawr to establish their own missionaries – one of these was David, who would later become Wales's patron saint and figurehead.

Protestantism was already well established in Wales by the time William Morgan translated the Bible in 1588, but it wasn't long before the rise of **Nonconformism** slowly took hold. The Welsh **Methodist** Revival was a movement unique to Wales among those countries of Britain and Ireland, and was largely driven by a desire to educate what had until that point been a largely illiterate populace. With pre-eminent Methodists like Howell Harris, Daniel Rowland and William Williams Pantycelyn leading the way, there was an explosion of interest among the working and middle classes, a growth that was to continue throughout the 19th century, and which also paved the way for an intense period of chapel building across the country, and especially across South Wales. Although the influence of the chapels was beginning to wane at the beginning of the 20th century, Nonconformists petitioned for disestablishment of the Church in Wales, which duly occurred in 1920, when the Church of England was formally disestablished within Wales by virtue of the Welsh Church Act 1914.

Wales remains a majority self-identifying Christian nation, although declining numbers point to an increasingly secular nation. In the most recent census (2011), 57% of the Welsh population identified as Christian, a steep drop of 13% from the previous (2001) census. Moreover, organised religion forms an increasingly small percentage of this figure and has been on the wane for some time. Of these, 9.5% adhere to the **Catholic** faith. **Islam** in Wales dates back to the early 12th century, though the first mosque in Wales didn't appear until 1947 – there are now around 40 nationwide. Cardiff is home to some of the oldest Muslim communities in the UK, notably Somali and Yemeni, whose merchant seamen were among the first to settle here in the mid 19th century. In Wales today, 1.5% of the population identifies as Muslim, roughly double the number from the previous census, which also makes Islam the country's largest non-Christian faith.

While a **Jewish** community has existed in Wales since at least the 13th century, the first community in South Wales, in Swansea, wasn't established until the 18th century. Wales's position as an industrial powerhouse in the 19th century led to an influx of immigrant workers from Russia and eastern Europe, ensuring a strong Jewish presence in Valleys towns like Aberdare, Pontypridd and Merthyr Tydfil –

a population further bolstered by large numbers of Jews fleeing Nazi persecution in the 1930s. Indeed, Merthyr – which alongside Cardiff was one of the two main centres of the Jewish community in Wales – is home to the country's oldest standing purpose-built synagogue, albeit one that has been defunct since 2006. Plans are currently afoot to convert the building into a heritage centre. Other than that, there are just three working synagogues in the whole of Wales. Unsurprisingly, today's Welsh Jewish population is small, believed to be no more than a couple of thousand, most of whom live in Cardiff. Although this number holds up well against the previous census, it's an ageing population.

CULTURE

FILM For a country that boasts two of the greatest screen actors of all time in Richard Burton and Anthony Hopkins, it's a little surprising that Welsh film hasn't garnered more attention over the years – yet the big screen has played a major part in Welsh cultural life since the late 19th century. One of the earliest pioneers of Welsh film was a little-known chap called **William Haggar**, who toured his travelling theatre throughout Wales to great acclaim in the late 19th century (though it was particularly successful in the industrial heartlands of South Wales) before producing his own films, films that could rightly be considered the first serious contributions to Welsh cinema. One, *A Desperate Poaching Affray* (1903), was even distributed throughout Europe and the States; remarkably, you can view this on YouTube.

Prior to World War I there were in excess of 160 venues screening films, many in Working Men's Halls, a number that, despite the war, had grown to 250 by 1920. Not only that, but during roughly the same period more than 25 films on Welsh subjects had been made. Despite high levels of unemployment, the 1930s was something of a golden time for Welsh cinema: there were more cinemas per capita in South Wales than anywhere else in Britain – if nothing else, it was welcome respite from the daily drudgery of the pits. The first Welsh-language film, *Y Chwarelwr* (*The Quarrymen*), was made in 1935, while the pre-eminent British actor of that time was Ivor Davies, better known as Ivor Novello (page 78). The first truly important film to come out of Wales was *The Proud Valley* in 1940, an affecting film about a Welsh mining community that takes in a black seaman, the seaman in question played by the American singer and activist Paul Robeson, who simultaneously developed a deep and long-lasting bond with the labour movement in South Wales. Released as *The Tunnel* in the States, the film was shot by Pen Tennyson, grandson of the great poet at a cost of £40,000, a pretty sum at the time. The following year, *How Green Was My Valley* – an American drama set in Wales chronicling the life of one mining family – won five Oscars, from a total of ten nominations. Adapted from Richard Llewellyn's much-loved 1939 novel, the film came to define the world image of Wales for generations to come, for better or for worse.

Few actors, Welsh or otherwise, have left such a mark on the big screen as **Richard Burton**, who at one time had few peers in Hollywood (page 149). A much-documented personal life often overshadowed his work, which was hugely impressive. Although he was probably more revered for his theatre work, among his most popular films are *The Spy Who Came in from the Cold* and *Who's Afraid of Virginia Woolf?* Yet despite no fewer than seven Oscar nominations over a long and distinguished career, Burton never walked off with the big prize. Unlike **Sir Anthony Hopkins**, who has a two-out-of-six record thanks to winning Best Actor for his role as the unforgettable Hannibal Lecter in *Silence of the Lambs* in 1991, and as the titular patriarch in *The Father* as recently as 2021. Now well into his eighties, Hopkins's recent career resurgence, culminating in the aforementioned Oscar, also saw him nominated for Best Supporting Actor in 2019's *The Two Popes* alongside Jonathan Pryce (nominated for Best Actor in the film), another fine, though less-heralded, Welsh actor. Of Hopkins's earlier films, *The Remains of the Day*, *Shadowlands* and *Nixon* are among his finest.

The first ever Welsh-language film to be nominated for an Oscar – quite the deal as you might imagine – was the S4C-commissioned *Hedd Wyn* (*Blessed Peace*) in 1992, a stirring account of the North Walian poet Ellis Humphrey Evans who went off to fight in World War I but never returned. Despite not winning, it still retains the honour of being the only Welsh-language film to date to be nominated. A worthy contemporary to Hopkins is **Michael Sheen** who, alongside Burton and Hopkins, completes a remarkable holy trinity of actors hailing from Port Talbot. For all his prolific output (in film, television and theatre), Sheen is probably best known for his character portrayals, most memorably Tony Blair in *The Queen*, Brian Clough in *The Damned United*, and David Frost in *Frost/Nixon* – all terrific films.

Other, purely Welsh films of the last two decades or so worth seeking out include *Submarine*, a delightful coming-of-age drama set in 1980s Swansea; *Pride*, a fabulously entertaining romp based on the true story of how a group of lesbian and gay group came to the aid of the miners during the 1984 strike; and *American Interior*, a typically left-field offering from the Welsh cult musician Gruff Rhys, in which he retraces the steps of a long-distant, 18th-century relative called John Evans.

MUSIC For such a small country, Wales boasts a glorious musical heritage and punches far above its weight. From folk music to great indie-rock bands and a recent resurgence in the popularity of Welsh-language rock music, there's no end to the creative talent emerging from the country. Wales's greatest musical export remains Thomas Jones Woodward, better known as Tom Jones. Born in Pontypridd in 1941, Jones originally made his mark in the theatre hall before establishing himself as one of the industry's great singer/entertainers, a role he played with singular aplomb throughout the 1960s and 70s and beyond – in fact he's still firing on all his octogenarian cylinders today. In a similar vein, Cardiff-born singer Dame Shirley Bassey, also now in her eighties, forged a massively successful solo career, with her two most famous songs soundtracking the James Bond films *Goldfinger* and *Diamonds are Forever*.

Unless you count the likes of rubber-legged Shakin' Stevens and balladeer-cum-foghorn-voiced Bonnie Tyler, plus one or two slightly more rock-oriented artists like The Alarm and John Cale (who formed the Velvet Underground), it wasn't until the mid 1990s that Welsh music could officially rate itself as cool, but even then that was largely on the coat-tails of the wider Britpop movement. Despite being slightly hackneyed, the 'Cool Cymru' label that was pinned to Welsh bands (and Welsh art in general) had substance, and there was certainly an exciting, and definitively Welsh, cultural movement at that time. The most idiosyncratic of all the bands – Welsh or otherwise – to emerge during this period were the **Super Furry Animals**, whose lush, psychedelic sound and wilfully esoteric lyrics singled them out as a group apart. To be honest you could pick any of their dozen or so records and not be hugely entertained, but for starters you could do worse than *Radiator*, *Rings Around the World* and *Phantom Power*. Other prominent bands then included **Catatonia**, whose lead singer Cerys Matthews has since become extremely successful in her own right, not to mention a great champion of all things Welsh, and Carmarthen's

Gorky's Zygotic Mynci, whose whimsical piano-led ponderings are a delight – try *Spanish Dance Troupe* or *The Blue Trees* for size.

The most important band to emerge this side of the Severn Bridge during the 1990s were the **Manic Street Preachers**. All Blackwood born, the four band members – cousins James Dean Bradfield and Sean Moore, plus Nicky Wire and Richey Edwards – met at primary school, becoming friends and going on to form the band whose soundtrack was borne out of an acute sense of alienation derived from their experiences of growing up in the Valleys at the time of the miners' strike. With Edwards as the band's political think tank and a nihilistic post-punk sound with a dash of glam rock thrown in, the band deliberately put themselves out of step with the prevailing laddish party sound, instead focusing on their trademark slogans of boredom and despair. It all added up to quite the formidable package, as demonstrated on their 1992 debut album *Generation Terrorists*, an 18-song *tour de force*, although this was just a primer for the incendiary follow-up, *The Holy Bible*. Edwards went missing in 1995 (and has never been found), a time that coincided with their most commercially successful period to date, thanks to the anthemically driven, hence more accessible, *Everything Must Go*. The band may have toned things down in recent years – for example, the acoustically tinged *Rewind the Film* and their most recent outing, *The Ultra Vivid Lament* – but they remain capable of producing coruscating records such as *Journal for Plague Lovers*, *Resistance Is Futile* and *Futurology*. Among the newer wave of Welsh bands to emerge, and well worth a listen, are The Joy Formidable, an anthemic guitar-driven trio, and Catfish and the Bottlemen, both bands hailing from North Wales.

The Super Furries were also at the vanguard of the Welsh-language rock renaissance, releasing albums in both English and Welsh, as has the band's lead singer Gruff Rhys; their 2000 album, *Mwng* (which is pronounced 'moong' and translates as 'mane'), was the first Welsh-language album to go mainstream. A lo-fi psychedelic masterpiece, it's a hugely enjoyable listen regardless of whether you understand Welsh or not, thanks to Rhys's inimitable vocals. Going back to the 1980s, bands such as the Bangor punk outfit Anhrefn, and misanthropic experimentalists Datblygu from Cardigan Bay, were the first to propagate some form of Welsh identity, but it's only relatively recently that Welsh-language music has entered the mainstream, although it's still relatively niche. But it is certainly the case that the scene is thriving as never before, and as much as it is indebted to Gruff Rhys – and to a lesser degree Catatonia and Gorky's, both of whom use Welsh in their songs – there are now dozens of artists and bands emerging, some of whom have entered the mainstream and are achieving some level of commercial success. Artists such as Gwenno (*Tresor*, *Le Kov*, and *Y Dydd Olaf*) Cate le Bon (*Reward* and *Pompeii*) and Kelly Lee Owens are leading the way, with bands like sonic groovers Roughion from Aberystwyth, indie rockers Candelas from Bala, Ani Glass from Cardiff, and Adwaith, an all-female three-piece from Carmarthen following in their slipstream. This resurgence is celebrated with an annual Welsh-language Music Day (Dydd Miwsig Cymru), with gigs and events taking place throughout the country. Unlike the somewhat manufactured mid-90s 'Cool Cymru' label, this is the real deal, the real Cool Cymru if you like.

One instrument that has long been associated with Wales is the **harp**, which has been played here since at least the 11th century. Wales even has a royal harpist, a tradition that was revived by the Prince of Wales in 2000 after almost a century. The incumbent harpist is Alis Huws, although the instrument's greatest exponent – indeed one of the world's finest – is **Catrin Finch**, a former royal harpist herself. Solo albums aside (*Lullabies* and *Tides*), Finch is a regular collaborator with Seckou Keita, the wonderful *kora* player from Senegal, and to date they have released three sublime albums (*Clychau Dibon*, *SOAR* and *ECHO*) that mix influences from Western classical or folk with African styles to stunning effect; they are also a wonderful live proposition. Another fine harpist is the singer-songwriter **Georgia Ruth** from Aberystwyth; so far, she has made three albums, *Week of Pines*, *Fossil Scale* and *Mai*, and a thoroughly gorgeous five-song EP called *Kingfisher*, as well as collaborating with the Manic Street Preachers on their album *Futurology*.

LITERATURE The literature of Wales is one of the oldest continuous literary traditions in Europe. The earliest Welsh poetry was forged in the battlefields of post-Roman Wales and the old north of Britain, some of which, by the likes of the poets Aneirin and Taliesin, survive in *Historia Brittonum* (AD830) – in the case of Aneirin, his poem, *Y Gododdin*, is preserved in a manuscript known as *The Book of Aneirin* dating from around 1265. The oldest surviving manuscript written entirely in Welsh is believed to be the Black Book of Carmarthen, dating from around 1250, which contains a selection of poetry that was first written down between the 9th and 12th centuries; among the themes are elegies to the princes of Wales, religious and proverbial items, as well as poems related to the early Welsh traditions of Arthur and Myrddin (Merlin).

Wales's most famous text is *The Mabinogion*, a set of Welsh medieval prose narrative tales that many experts rate among the finest within the canon of European folk literature. *The Mabinogion* survives as a series of 13th- and 14th-century manuscripts: the White Book of Rhydderch (c1300–25) and the Red Book of Hergest (c1375–1425), the former copied at the Cistercian Abbey of Strata Florida in mid-Wales. Scholars believe that these tales were passed down by word of mouth to convey information about lineage and landscape by relating myth, magic and monsters to real people and places. The four branches (comprising a total of 11 tales) of *The Mabinogion* – namely Pwyll (Prince of Dyfed), Branwen, Manawydan and Math – weave Celtic mythology with Arthurian romance to dazzling effect, and still today resonate strongly among the Welsh. However, *The Mabinogion* didn't come to general literary prominence until the mid 19th century (1840), which is when the English aristocrat Lady Charlotte Guest edited and published the 11 medieval folk tales under the title *The Mabinogion*.

The first Welsh printed book, in 1547, was *Yn y lhyvyr hwnn* (*In this Book*), which comprised extracts from the Scriptures and the prayer book, and it was from around this time that modern Welsh prose began to assume some kind of definite form. This set the tone for a series of key Reformation-era texts, including the Welsh Prayer Book and William Morgan's translation of the Bible into Welsh in 1588, which to this day remains the single most important text ever translated into the native tongue. The next most fruitful period for Welsh literature occurred during the mid 18th century as a new religious zeal, fostered by the rise in Methodism, led to major growth in the book-reading public. In the 1760s there were some 230 books entirely in Welsh, a number that had doubled by the end of the century. Newspapers, too, were fast becoming important vehicles for political discussion and education. Prolific too was Glamorgan son Iolo Morganwg (born Edward Williams), who was among the great tradition of Welsh Romantic writers, though it was only after his death that many of the ancient works that he claimed to have discovered were actually found to be fake – something which may or may not have been linked to his dependence upon opiates. As voluminous as it was, much of Welsh 19th-century prose was of poor quality, but this changed following the establishment of the University of Wales (1893), which broadened the literary horizons of many a would-be writer.

The list of fine 20th-century Welsh authors is long and illustrious. One such author is Richard Llewellyn, whose 1939 novel *How Green Was My Valley* is an abiding early classic: it's an evocative tale of a Welsh mining family as seen through the eyes of one of the children, although it's the later film adaptation that is often more fondly remembered. No author before, or since, has come close to Dylan Thomas (page 256), who – much like Richard Burton with whom he was friends – was as renowned for his love of booze as he was for the quality of his work. Other celebrated 20th-century Welsh writers include the poet and priest R S Thomas, roughly contemporaneous with Dylan but who never achieved the same levels of acclaim; Alexander Cordell, most of whose novels – including *Rape of the Fair Country* – were set in the Industrial Revolution; Kate Roberts, who was much lauded for her work chronicling the lives of the men, women and children in the northern slate quarries; and Roald Dahl, beloved for his fantastical storytelling. To this list you could also add Jan Morris. Although not Welsh-born, Morris (formerly James Morris) spent most of her life in Wales, and wrote extensively on the country among her many other travel books; *Wales: Epic Views from a Small Country* is as good a place as any to start. Some of the many outstanding contemporary Welsh writers include Cynan Jones, Rachel Trezise and the poet/novelist Owen Sheers, whose writing, much of which is centred on the Black Mountains, is wonderfully evocative. For details of the books by these authors and others, see page 326.

SPORT Welsh identity has long been bound up in one activity: **rugby union**. The sport first developed among the coalfields in the mid 19th century, an environment that was conducive to producing tough and skilful players. This led to the formation of the first clubs in the 1870s, the likes of Neath, Llanelli, Cardiff and Newport, but as in England these were established by a handful of privileged, privately educated men. The game, though, was quickly embraced by the working classes, and the Welsh Rugby Union was inaugurated in 1881, the same year that Wales played their first international, against England. Wales first won the Triple Crown (beating England, Ireland and Scotland) in 1893, and this was followed by six more victories within the first 11 years of the 20th century. For all those earlier successes, it was the 3–0 defeat of the formidable All Blacks in 1905 that really made the rugby world sit up and take notice; in fact, they would defeat the All Blacks in three of their first four encounters, the last of which came in 1953 – they haven't beaten them in 32 matches since.

A period of doldrums followed as many international players were lured to the monied world of English rugby league football, but post-war rugby in Wales saw an upturn in fortunes. The golden era for the sport in the Principality was unquestionably the 1970s, and with a team harnessing the likes of Gareth Edwards, Barry John, Phil Bennett and J P R Williams, Wales swept all before them, on the home front at least, winning three Grand Slams and six Triple Crowns between 1969 and 1979. A rather fallow 20 years followed, but the building of the marvellous new Millennium Stadium (now the Principality Stadium) in 1999 was something of a catalyst as the national team won the Six Nations title six times between 2005 and 2021 (including Grand Slams on four of those occasions) under the helm of New Zealander Warren Gatland, a record unmatched during that period. World Cup success, however, still eludes them, with semi-final appearances in 2011 and 2019 their best achievements to date.

The heartland of Welsh rugby has always been in South Wales, particularly in the Valleys or thereabouts, which is why all four of Wales's regional professional teams are based here: Cardiff Blues, Swansea Ospreys, Newport Gwent Dragons and

Llanelli Scarlets, all of whom play in the United Rugby Championship competing against teams from Ireland, Scotland, Italy and, somewhat bizarrely, South Africa. However, there has long been debate over the viability of Wales being able to support four professional clubs – none of them do particularly well in the Championship – so this structure may well change at some point in the not-too-distant future.

For all the successes of the national rugby team, and as much as the sport remains tied up with the national consciousness, the biggest revolution in Welsh sport in the last few years has come on the **football** field, thanks in no small part to the success of the Welsh national football team. After several near misses in terms of qualification for World Cups and European Championships, the national team not only qualified for the Euros in 2016 but went on to reach the semi-finals in scintillating fashion. They then qualified for the Euro 2020 championships (played in 2021 owing to the pandemic), on this occasion reaching the second round. These achievements were matched in 2022 when they qualified for the World Cup in Qatar, their first since 1958. Much of the team's recent success has hinged on their one truly world-class player, indeed their greatest ever player: Gareth Bale, who is Wales's all-time leading scorer. But perhaps what is even more extraordinary is the notion that football has become as potent a symbol of Welshness as rugby has been for the last century or so, and that's something no-one could have reckoned on a few years ago. It's not unusual now to hear Welsh fans (aka The Red Wall) offer rousing renditions of Welsh songs and hymns, whether that's home or away, and they travel in vast numbers these days. In fact, it's not too far-fetched to suggest that Welsh football fans have become the flag bearers of a modern, bilingual Welsh identity on the international stage.

At club level, both Cardiff and Swansea have spent brief periods of time recently in the Premier League, which has undoubtedly contributed to the overall uplift in the sport in Wales, though both are currently languishing in the Championship, one level below the Premier League. Prior to both clubs' entry into the Premier League, the most successful period for Welsh clubs was the interwar years, when Swansea, Cardiff, Newport, Merthyr, Wrexham and Aberdare were all football league clubs at one stage or another. The high point came in 1927 with Cardiff's FA Cup victory against Arsenal, the first time that a non-English team had won a major trophy, which remained the case until 2013 when Swansea lifted the League Cup.

Boxing is another sport in which Wales has historically excelled, with many of its finest exponents coming from South Wales. In fact, the rules of boxing as they are today were actually devised in South Wales, in Llanelli no less. It was John Graham Chambers, resident of Llanelly House (page 249), who wrote what would be known as the Queensbury Rules, though they were actually named after the Ninth Marquess of Queensbury as it was he who endorsed them. Unsurprisingly perhaps, it's from the Valleys that the greatest Welsh boxers have emerged, the first of whom had been toughened up by pit-fighting and included the likes of Jimmy Wilde ('The Tylerstown Terror') and Freddie 'The Welsh Wizard' Welsh from Pontypridd – both of whom fought an astonishing 150 bouts plus during their careers. Then there was the heavyweight boxer Tommy 'The Tonypandy Terror' Farr who took the great Joe Louis to 15 rounds in New York in 1937. Later heroes from Merthyr included Howard Winstone and Johnny Owen, both of whom are honoured by statues in the town centre; Owen's story was particularly tragic as he died after lapsing into a coma following a knock-out by Lupe Pintor during a world title fight in Los Angeles in 1980. More recently, there has been the super middleweight Joe Calzaghe – rated by many as *the* greatest Welsh pugilist of all time and who remained undefeated during a stellar ten-year career.

Of somewhat more sedate persuasion, **snooker** has also left its mark on the South Walian sporting landscape. Hailing from Tredegar in the Valleys, the best-known Welsh snooker player is Ray Reardon (aka 'Dracula', on account of his swept-back hair and sharp-toothed grin), a six-time World Champion and the first player to be ranked number 1 in the world when the rankings system was introduced in 1976. Following close behind was Llanelli-born Terry Griffiths who won the world title in 1979. Of somewhat more dynamic vintage is another Valleys boy, Mark Williams from Cwm, whose 2018 world title win at the age of 43 came 15 years after his last one in 2003; this also made him the oldest winner since Reardon himself, who was 45 in 1978.

2

Practical Information

WHEN TO VISIT

If you're here to walk, then where in South Wales you want to walk is likely to influence when you come. If you're walking the coast path, then summer is clearly the best time in terms of weather, but you will be reckoning on loads of other people doing the same, and it can get murderously busy, particularly on the more popular sections of the path like Pembrokeshire – notwithstanding the fact that it'll be much harder to find accommodation during this period. That said, it can also depend upon which part of the coast path you're walking. While the Pembrokeshire stretch is the most heavily tramped section, if, say, you wanted to walk the stretch along the Gwent Levels in summer, then you'll find it reasonably quiet by comparison.

For this reason the best time to tackle the coast path is late spring (April/May), not only because of the thinner crowds but also because of the profusion of flora, with wildflowers coming into bloom across the clifftops, as well as the incredible birdlife – auks, razorbills and guillemots – that is just starting to settle. You may also see dolphins and other cetaceans gambolling off the Pembrokeshire coast. September, too, can be a lovely time; the crowds have largely dispersed and the weather is probably at its most reliable, though most of the birds have gone by this stage. The great thing about the coast path of course is that in theory you can walk it any time of the year, so if you're feeling particularly hardy – and don't mind the biting winds – then winter is always an option. It goes without saying that days are shorter so you'll have to plan accordingly. Also bear in mind that some sections of the path are prone to storm damage, and therefore can be cut off or closed at short notice.

The Brecon Beacons is a slightly different proposition: winter and early spring are almost certainly out of the equation, with snow often remaining on higher ground until well into March. Therefore, late spring and early summer is the optimum time to walk, though the weather can change drastically at any time so thorough preparation is paramount; the Brecon Beacons are very exposed, so heat can be just as much of a factor.

As for inland South Wales, again late spring and early summer (before the school holidays) is a good time, as the weather is at its most reliable and everything is open. The Valleys are not exactly a tourist hotspot, so go any time of year and you'll pretty much have the run of the place. Despite being more popular, the same can be said for many parts of Monmouthshire, the Vale of Glamorgan and Carmarthenshire, although areas like the Wye Valley, resorts like Barry and Porthcawl, and Dylan Thomas's hometown Laugharne do tend to draw greater numbers.

If you're here specifically to see wildlife, late spring and early summer is the best time. Puffins, for example, start to arrive on Skomer in late March/early April, along with most of the migrant fauna (guillemots, razorbills, Manx shearwater). September/October is prime pupping time for the colonies of Atlantic grey seals.

As with most cities, Cardiff is a year-round destination, and as long as you're not here on a Six Nations rugby weekend (January to March) – though that can be an absolute blast – then you'll have little problem finding accommodation. Many attractions in Wales, including quite a few of the stately homes and gardens, do close for the winter, so bear this in mind when planning a trip out of season. A final word must go to the rain: Wales is one of the wettest parts of the United Kingdom, and that's because the country lies right underneath the jet stream where hot and cold air collides – so expect a good soaking whenever you go.

HIGHLIGHTS

Monmouthshire's historic towns, **Chepstow** and **Monmouth**, are generally modest and slow paced but merit a day each, especially the former with its immense fortress. Monmouthshire's other great castle is **Raglan**, but the county's siren draw is the quaintly Ruritanian **Wye Valley**, which has within its ranks **Tintern Abbey**, the most atmospheric ecclesiastical ruin in all of Wales. The Romans tramped all over this southern region, leaving the most conspicuous signs of their occupation in the baths and amphitheatre in **Caerleon** and the superb walled town at **Caerwent**. Once the wealthiest docks in the world having made its fortune off the back of the coal industry, the nation's capital, **Cardiff**, is a city transformed and an essential stop on anyone's itinerary.

The **Valleys** are a place apart. The steel and coalmining industries that were once at the heart of the industrial revolution have long been consigned to history, but here, in these somnolent, hard-bitten villages, a doughty spirit remains and you'll be warmly welcomed wherever you go. The Valleys' long and proud industrial legacy is preserved in some fine museums, such as the **Rhondda Heritage Park** and in Big Pit in **Blaenavon**, South Wales's only UNESCO site, as well as moving memorials in **Senghenydd** and **Six Bells**, among other places. The Valleys are reinventing themselves in other ways too, as thrilling new bike parks to rival those in North Wales illustrate. North of the Valleys, the **Brecon Beacons National Park** is a formidable landscape of chiselled sandstone peaks, glacial lakes and wide-open moorland, a magnet for walkers and climbers: the big one, and the highest in southern Britain, is **Pen-y-Fan**. Towns like **Abergavenny** and **Crickhowell** offer respite after a hard day in the hills.

The fast-eroding, fossil-bearing cliffs along the **Glamorgan Heritage Coast** rank alongside their counterparts in Devon and Dorset, yet remain little known. Here too are the twin nature reserves of **Merthyr Mawr** – Wales's most important sand dune system – and **Kenfig**, home to some of Britain's rarest orchids. Most of the Vale of Glamorgan's coastal resorts are of the bucket and spade variety, but both **Penarth** and **Llantwit Major** – the latter a major ecclesiastical centre – are deserving destinations. Further west, **Swansea**, Wales's second city and birthplace of Dylan Thomas, has come of age and is worth a couple of days' investigation before you head out to **Gower**, whose wild, wave-strewn beaches offer great surf and, for the most part, solitude – if you only do one walk out here, make it Worm's Head.

West into Carmarthenshire, the region's mild climate has enabled a slew of fine gardens to flourish: **Aberglasney** and the **National Botanic Garden**, among the very best in Britain, are standout attractions in the county. As is **Laugharne**, hometown and resting place of Thomas, hence *the* place of pilgrimage for the poet's legion of admirers. As elsewhere, the Normans left their mark on the region, as thunderous castles at **Kidwelly**, **Llansteffan** and **Carreg Cennen** testify.

Pembrokeshire's rich complement of world-class beaches, ancient sites, outdoor pursuits and rural peace have made the region perennially popular, and while its authentic character may be partially compromised during the summer season, it's impossible not to fall prey to its considerable charms. Even if you're not here to hike the **Pembrokeshire Coast Path** – and there are worse ways to spend a couple of weeks – there are countless other reasons why you might be. For many it's the world-class birdlife – phenomenal numbers of Manx shearwater, puffins, fulmars, razorbills, guillemots and gannets make the islands of **Skomer**, **Skokholm** and **Grassholm** their home for a few months from spring onwards. Pembrokeshire's beaches too – Barafundle Bay, Whitesands Bay and Marloes Sands among them – more than justify the hype, as do the multiplicity of charming resorts. The coast's star turn, however, is **Tenby**, and while it can get mobbed at the height of summer, it's a magical place any time of year.

The westernmost point is **St David's Peninsula**, at the heart of which is the city of the same name, and itself another centre of pilgrimage as the birthplace of the eponymous saint and its startling cathedral. North Pembrokeshire, meanwhile, is the coast at its wild, wind-battered best, its old centres of industry, primarily quarrying, now comely little fishing villages frequented by hardy folk coasteering and kayaking. While the landscape of the Pembrokeshire hinterland is neither especially wild nor grand, it is consistently seductive, especially up around the **Preseli Hills**, a landscape thick with antiquity: its assemblage of cromlechs and standing stones rival the best that either Scotland or Ireland has to offer.

SUGGESTED ITINERARIES

A WEEK It's all about the coast this week. Begin with a flying visit to Cardiff and some watery action down at the bay before pushing on to Gower and a walk out to Worm's Head – mind the tide! If you've still got the energy, perhaps some surfing? Into Carmarthenshire and Laugharne, hometown and resting place of the nation's greatest poet, Dylan Thomas – the boathouse is a must. Tenby calling, and time for a walk around its creaky old streets and superbly positioned harbour before an afternoon sail to Caldey Island and its ecclesiastical treasures. And if you only do one thing this week, make it a visit to Skomer and its cacophony of birdlife: puffins, razorbills, guillemots and more, the sight and sound of which will remain with you long after you've departed. The wild west beckons next, which can only mean St David's Peninsula: the twin glories of the city's cathedral and bishop's palace await, as does a walk out to St David's Head and some of the finest vistas anywhere along the coast. Back inland to Carmarthenshire via the stunning gardens at Aberglasney, just a little bit more manageable than the equally hypnotic National Botanic Garden up the road, but you choose. It'd be remiss not to squeeze a castle in, so Caerphilly it is before the return home, but not without some cheese.

A FORTNIGHT With another week on your side, it's time to head for the hills. But first a wander around and lunch in Abergavenny, the nation's gastronomic capital. With an extra day to spare, and weather permitting, have a crack at South Wales's highest peak, Pen-y-Fan, doubling up with an assault on nearby Corn Du. A day exploring the Tywi Valley is always time well spent, as is a visit to Wales's most dramatically sited castle, Carreg Cennen, in the foothills of the Brecon Beacons. With this extra time you can expand your exploration of the coast and St Bride's Bay and then head onwards to the North Pembrokeshire coast and gorgeous little Newport.

THREE WEEKS The luxury of an extra week enables you to factor in a visit to the Wye Valley and the gloriously romantic ruins at Tintern, as well as some industrial action at Big Pit in Blaenavon. En route to book-barmy Hay, take a ride over the awesome Gospel Pass via the evocative ruins of Llanthony Abbey. Don't miss the Glamorgan Heritage Coast either, with a walk along its wonderful cliffy seaboard to the marvellous Merthyr Mawr sand dunes – some of the highest in Europe. Resurgent Swansea merits a day of your time. Inland Pembrokeshire is also deserving of further investigation, including its loveliest town, Narberth, and the magical Preseli Hills with their ancient stones.

TOURIST INFORMATION

The main website is w visitwales.com, which provides a comprehensive list of things to see and do, activities and accommodation, with lots of downloadable resources too. Wales's tourist information centres have been pared back heavily in recent years, to the extent that they are the exception rather than the rule, and even in places where you'd expect to find a centre, there isn't one. For example, and inexplicably, there is no tourist information centre in Cardiff, instead just an unmanned hut inside the castle grounds where you can pick up a few leaflets. Many places therefore now rely on the local museum or the local library to stock literature, and staff are unfailingly helpful wherever you try and source your information. Most places have a stash of leaflets on both the immediate and wider area. Opening times can be convoluted so it's best to check in advance, either online or, more reliably, by calling. There are two National Park Information Centres in South Wales, one in Libanus, just outside Brecon, and another in St David's city, while the National Trust also has a presence in some places, like Rhossili on Gower.

MAPS A great companion for any trip is a map, which any good bookshop will stock: Waterstones is always a good bet. More specialised and regional maps can be obtained from travel book shops such as Stanfords (w stanfords.co.uk). Despite the rise of digital mapping, you can't beat the Ordnance Survey maps for walks, though they are equally as useful for cyclists and motorists. The Explorer range maps that cover South Wales are: 12 (Brecon Beacons National Park West); 13 (Brecon Beacons National Park East); 14 (Wye Valley & Forest of Dean); 35 (North Pembrokeshire); 36 (South Pembrokeshire); 151 (Cardiff & Bridgend); 152 (Newport & Pontypool); 165 (Swansea, Neath & Port Talbot); 166 (Rhondda & Merthyr); 177 (Carmarthen & Kidwelly); 178 (Llanelli & Ammanford); 186 (Llandeilo & Brechfa); and 187 (Llandovery). If you haven't managed to buy your maps in advance, most tourist offices (where they exist) sell them.

TOUR OPERATORS AND GUIDES

Many people come to South Wales to walk the coast path or the hills and mountains of the Brecon Beacons, and while these areas don't necessarily present any major difficulties, a knowledgeable guide can really enhance the experience. Moreover, if you don't feel confident tackling some of the more challenging walks by yourself, and/or wish to share the experience with other walkers, a local guide can be a great way to do this; expect to pay around £60 for a half-day trek. The Pembrokeshire coastline and the Brecons have become hugely popular as places to go foraging, and there are several outfits offering expeditions, which typically cost around £35–40 for half a day. Other guides specialise in areas such as archaeology and wildlife.

Brecon Beacons Foraging
w breconbeaconsforaging.com. Experienced Brecon forager Adele Nozedar runs a half-day foraging expedition from Abergavenny on the last Sun of each month, as well as botanical gin-foraging sessions & other bespoke foraging trips.

Beacons Trike Tours m 07484 290039; w beaconstriketours.com. Here's something a little different, a tour through the Brecon Beacons on a trike; while you take one of 2 seats in the back (hence this is ideal for couples) & soak up the scenery, Andy does all the leg work in the front seat.

Muddy Boots m 07577 979062; w muddybootshiking.com. Full-day guided walks (from £80) throughout South Wales, including gentle outings to the Gower & South Pembrokeshire, as well as more moderate & challenging treks in the Brecon Beacons.

Preseli Venture 01348 837709; w preseliventure.co.uk. Among the many activities offered by this established outfit are 5-day guided & self-guided walking holidays along the Pembrokeshire Coast Path including a stay in a 5-star eco-lodge.

Really Wild Emporium 01437 721755; w reallywildemporium.co.uk. John & Julia's great passion is foraging, the results of which sustain many of the recipes in their restaurant & products in their shop (page 307); they offer enlightening trips both inland & along the seashore.

Walk Hay m 07570 946074; w walkhay.co.uk. Guided lowland walks in & around the Black Mountains, so just the bill if you're not looking to exert too much energy. Run by experienced leader Sarah Price, walks range from 4 to 10 miles; she also offers private guided walks.

Wild Trails Wales m 07415 953311; w wildtrailswales.com. Based in the Vale of Glamorgan but offering a variety of full-day guided walks across South Wales, including the Brecon Beacons, the Pembrokeshire coast & the Wye Valley.

RED TAPE

Citizens of all European countries – other than Albania, Bosnia and Herzegovina, Montenegro, North Macedonia, Serbia and most republics from the former Soviet Union – can enter the UK with just a passport for up to three months. US, Canadian, Australian and New Zealand citizens can travel in the UK for up to six months with a passport. All other nations require a visa, available from the British consular office in the country of application.

Now that the UK has left the EU, visa regulations are subject to change, so contact the nearest British embassy or high commission before travelling. Once in Wales you are free to travel into England or Scotland. Check w gov.uk/browse/visas-immigration.

CONSULATES AND EMBASSIES The majority of nations, including the US, Canada, Australia, New Zealand and countries from Europe are fully represented by embassies or high commissions (for Commonwealth members) in London. There are no embassies in Cardiff, but around 20 countries are represented by consulates, including Canada and Ireland; the US has a representative office. A full list of these can be found at w embassypages.com/city/Cardiff. A full list of contact details can be found at w gov.uk/government/publications/foreign-embassies-in-the-uk.

GETTING THERE AND AWAY

South Wales is one of the most accessible parts of Britain to travel to, with excellent road, rail and bus links, though the further west you go, the slightly trickier it gets. The fast mainline train from London serves Cardiff and Swansea, from where you can reach the Valleys and Carmarthenshire/Pembrokeshire respectively. Coaches from quite a few cities in England, including London and Bristol, serve Cardiff and Swansea, and a few places in between.

BY ROAD

By car The main road link into South Wales is the M4 motorway. Originating in London, it crosses into Wales at the Prince of Wales Bridge (until 2018 it was called the Second Severn Crossing, suffice to say that the change of name was not universally popular) before coursing along the foot of the Valleys towards Swansea and then into Carmarthenshire where it becomes the A48 just before Carmarthen. A few miles north of the M4, the M48 (which veers off the M4 a few miles back, in England) crosses the smaller, but original Severn Bridge and emerges a couple of miles south of Chepstow. There are a couple more entry points into Chepstow itself. If travelling from North Wales (or the north of England), the main road south is the A483 towards Brecon.

By coach Coaches also ply the M4 corridor, with both **National Express** (w nationalexpress.com) and **Megabus** (w uk.megabus.com) operating services from London to Cardiff (and which usually call in at either Chepstow or Newport). Buses are roughly every 90 minutes with a journey time of around 3 hours 45 minutes. Fares can vary massively (with both companies), but book far enough in advance and you could secure a ticket for as little as £5 one-way. National Express also operate a handful of buses each day from London to Swansea, via Cardiff and Bridgend, with a journey time of around 5 hours; and from London to Pembroke Dock, calling at Swansea, Carmarthen and Tenby among other places (journey time 6 hours 30 minutes). Hourly coaches from Bristol to Cardiff (journey time 1 hour 15 minutes) also call in at Newport, with buses every 2 hours from Bristol serving Swansea (journey time 2 hours 40 minutes). Similarly, Megabus has a few services a day to Swansea, with tickets from around £10.

BY AIR The likelihood of you arriving in South Wales by air are slim, given that there is only one airport, Cardiff (in Rhoose, to the west of the city), and even they it is serviced by very few flights. It may well be that both **Ryanair** (w ryanair.co.uk) and **Wizz Air** (w wizzair.com), both of whom currently fly to a limited number of destinations from Cardiff, increase the number of flights they offer. In 2021, Ryanair started flying from Cardiff to Dublin, and in 2022 Wizz Air announced that they were to make Cardiff their fourth UK base. Many people intending to visit Wales from abroad do so via Bristol airport just across the border, from where there is a regular bus service direct to Cardiff. Alternatively, you can take a bus into Bristol and then a train from Bristol Temple Meads to Cardiff.

BY SEA There are two entry points into South Wales by sea, both of which originate in Rosslare, southwest Ireland. From Fishguard, in western Pembrokeshire, **Stena** (w stena.co.uk) operate two daily ferries to Rosslare, with a crossing time of 3 hours and 30 minutes or 4 hours (return fare from around £64 adult, from around £260 car). Ferries from Rosslare currently depart at 07.30 and 18.15, while ferries from Fishguard depart at 13.00 and 23.45; these are of course subject to change. **Irish Ferries** (w irishferries.com) also operate two ferries a day to Rosslare, but from Pembroke Dock on the southern Pembrokeshire coast. This crossing takes marginally longer at 4 hours (return fare from around £78 adult, £270 car). From Rosslare, ferries depart at 02.45 and 14.45, and from Pembroke Dock at 08.45 and 20.45.

BY RAIL The most straightforward entry into South Wales by train is the London Paddington line to Cardiff (journey time 2 hours 15 minutes), which also stops at Newport. Trains from Paddington also service Swansea (2 hours 45 minutes), stopping at Bridgend, Port Talbot and Neath en route. Trains run every 30 minutes to Cardiff and hourly to Swansea. The ticketing system is absurdly complex, but generally speaking what you end up paying is dependent upon a number of factors, the most important being when you travel and how far in advance you book; roughly speaking, you can get a single ticket from London to Cardiff for as little as £34, with a third off this if you have a railcard.

A far more agreeable way of reaching South Wales by train is via the **Heart of Wales line** (w heart-of-wales.co.uk), which is operated by **Transport for Wales** (w tfw.wales). The line starts in Shrewsbury, northeast of Birmingham, and enters Wales at Knighton before wending its way down through mid-Wales to Llandovery, Llandeilo, Ammanford, Llanelli and finally Swansea (with a zillion stops in between). There are currently three or four trains Monday to Saturday (two on Sunday) though there are plans to up this to five; the total journey time is around 3 hours 30 minutes to 4 hours, a necessarily slow trip because of all the stops, but you can forgive that because it's gorgeous; this really is slow train travel at its best. On the back of this, there is now also a Heart of Wales trail.

HEALTH

Overall, there's nothing to be overly concerned about in terms of health when travelling in South Wales. The biggest health risks are likely to be when enjoying the great outdoors, but by taking sensible (often obvious) precautions, for example applying suncream if you're out walking and it's hot, you can mitigate against most potential problems. If you are planning on doing any walking – particularly in wooded areas or long grass during spring and summer – one potential hazard to look for is ticks, parasitic arachnids that embed their heads in the skin and suck on your blood (it's not quite as vampirish as it sounds). You can reduce the risk of a bite by wearing lightly shaded, tightly woven clothing, in addition to applying a permethrin-based repellent. Ticks tend to gravitate towards darker recesses of the body, such as the scalp, armpits and genital areas, so do check these areas carefully after an outing. If you do discover one, using tweezers (tick tweezers are worth buying) grasp the tick's head and pull slowly and firmly, but do not twist, ensuring that you remove head and all; after removal, apply antiseptic to the site. Although the potential to contract tick-borne encephalitis from a bite is low, if you experience flu-like symptoms (headaches, fever, aches and pains) as well as/or itching and reddened areas of the skin, seek medical assistance.

The major A&E hospitals in South Wales are Glangwili in Carmarthen, Morriston in Swansea, the Prince Charles hospital in Merthyr, the Princess of Wales hospital in Bridgend, the Royal Glamorgan in Llantrisant, the Grange University Hospital in Cwmbran, Withybush General in Haverfordwest, and the University Hospital in Cardiff. These are complemented by Minor Injuries Units all across the region.

SAFETY

Wales is an extremely safe place to travel, though the usual precautions apply when in some of the bigger cities, especially at night. The biggest risk to one's safety, ironically, is the great outdoors. If, as is likely, you'll be doing some walking here in South Wales, then be wary of cattle. Don't come between a calf and its mother, be a little more circumspect in May when the beasts have just been released from being cooped up indoors for months and always keep your dog on a lead when there are cows about. If you find yourself unsure as to what to do, discretion may be the better part of valour. Walking the coast path, stay away from cliff edges, however tempting it may be to peer over – that said, where there has been rockfall or slips, places are usually fenced off pretty quickly.

Beaches of course present their own dangers. Many beaches in South Wales have lifeguards in the peak summer months, but as many of them are so vast, they are often only able to patrol one section, or zone, which is usually denoted by flags. Be aware of potential rip tides and currents too. As discussed elsewhere, Wales can be very wet, at any time of the year, and anywhere, so do keep a close eye on the forecast. Moreover, it can be very changeable, something to bear in mind especially when in the Brecon Beacons, which are otherwise very exposed. But whatever the weather when you set out, ensure you pack sensible clothing (waterproofs if wet, suncream and hat if hot), suitable equipment (maps, compass), food and plenty of water, and a fully charged mobile phone. The number of people who get caught out, especially in the Brecon Beacons, is quite staggering.

TRAVELLERS WITH A DISABILITY

Much work has been, and continues to be, done in Wales in terms of providing facilities for travellers with disabilities. While older hotels have limited facilities and access, the majority of accommodation providers (even hostels) have at least one accessible room available, with ramps and fully accessible wet rooms.

As transport facilities get upgraded, such as new electric buses, access is becoming increasingly standardised. If travelling with a wheelchair by train, advanced warning will enable station staff to prepare ramps at the appropriate station. Traveline Cymru has comprehensive details on access and facilities on its website w traveline.cymru/accessible-travel, while another useful website is w nationalrail.co.uk/stations_destinations/passenger-assist.aspx.

Many visitor attractions are now fully wheelchair-accessible (certainly most museums), although inevitably there are some buildings whose configurations simply don't lend themselves to decent access, most obviously some (but by no means all) of the region's castles. Visit Wales (w visitwales.com) has a list of some of the accessible accommodation and attractions in South Wales, though this is by no means comprehensive. Another useful website is the RNIB (w rnib.org.uk/wales-cymru).

LGBTQIA+ TRAVELLERS

During the 1984 miners' strike, miners received support from an unlikely source, namely the lesbian and gay community, although they weren't from Wales but from London – manifestations of gay life in Wales were virtually non-existent at that time. Establishing themselves as the Lesbians and Gays Support the Miners (LGSM) group, by the end of the strike nearly a year later, 11 different lesbian and gay alliances from across the UK had emerged in support of the miners, and together had donated more money to their cause than any other fundraiser. These events, and the subsequent relationships that developed between the miners and the gay community were the subject of the fabulously entertaining film, *Pride*, in 2014.

Things have moved on a bit since those dark days, although manifestations of gay life beyond Cardiff and Swansea are still conspicuous by their absence. Cardiff's

Pride event takes place at the end of August, but otherwise there are a few bars and clubs in the city, as well as an excellent shop, Queer Emporium, in the Royal Arcade (page 67).

TRAVELLING WITH CHILDREN

There are endless permutations for kiddie-friendly fun in South Wales. The most obvious target is the coastline and its superb beaches, and whether it's just some good old-fashioned bucket and spade action or dipping in and out of rock pools, you could spend weeks hopping from beach to beach. Pembrokeshire invariably gets most of the attention, but both Carmarthenshire – which has two of the longest beaches in Wales – and the Vale of Glamorgan, with its epic sand dunes, are equally as rewarding.

And what child doesn't like a good castle to root around in? This being Wales, you can take your pick, but if you want to make a good day of it, consider Raglan, the first in Wales to offer an AR (augmented reality) experience, or Caerphilly (for its size if nothing else), though others, like Picton Castle, incorporate added attractions which really lend themselves to making a full day of it, rain or shine: the falconry centre here is excellent, as is the British Bird of Prey Centre at the National Botanic Garden, which has the best flying displays anywhere in Wales.

South Wales is packed with illuminating museums, many of which are geared towards kids (or at least have kiddie-friendly sections) and are both engaging and educational, such as Techniquest in Cardiff, while the enduring St Fagans Museum offers hours of exploratory fun. Several of the old pits have been repurposed into ace museums so your little ones (and you) get to experience what life was like as a miner – the Rhondda Heritage Park and Big Pit in Blaenavon are the two to target here.

South Wales is one of the most exhilarating parts of Britain in which to engage your kids in some outdoor pursuits, and while the prospect of a long hike might not get them scurrying out of the door, there are loads of other thrill-a-minute possibilities. For more adrenaline-driven youngsters, how about coasteering (which was conceived in Wales), snorkelling or kayaking around St David's Peninsula, or in the Valleys, a ride on the world's fastest seated zipline at the old Tower Colliery? The Valleys' bike parks, too, are now a match for those in North Wales, and while one or two of these have been designed with more experienced riders in mind, those at Bike Park Wales in Merthyr and a new one in Dare Valley Country Park offer a potential day's worth of thrills and spills.

If the coast's world-class wildlife doesn't pique their interest in fauna (seabirds, dolphins, seals), then nothing will. Skomer and Skokholm are the big draws, and a few hours spent among the puffins will last long in the memory. If nothing else, the boat ride should be entertainment enough; the RIB trip out to Ramsey Island is rip-roaringly good fun.

Wherever you go, try and take a picnic, at least wherever places allow, and most do. Entrance fees, while generally a bit lower than in England – and there are good discounts for kids and families – can still make a small dent in the wallet, so save some pennies by bringing your own snacks.

WHAT TO TAKE

First and foremost, bring wet-weather gear. It's no secret that it rains in Wales (a lot) so no matter the season, be prepared for a downpour at some point. If you're walking the coast path, a good pair of boots is essential, as is a hat for those windier days, which there will be. In summer, a sunhat and suncream are the essential supplies (it does get hot occasionally in Wales), but even out of season, don't underestimate the sun, especially if you're on the coast path when the wind can reduce your awareness of burning. Mosquito repellent can be useful too, as can a torch, if nothing else but for exploring those burial cairns and sea caves. And if you've any intention of seeking out wildlife don't forget your binoculars, although these can be hired at some nature reserves and, for example, on Skomer. Binoculars aside, you can buy all these things in shops – including many specialist outdoors shops in places like Crickhowell, Brecon and St David's – and supermarkets all across the region.

MONEY AND BUDGETING

The currency in Wales, as in all of the UK, is the pound sterling (£). Just about all accommodation providers, eating and drinking establishments, public transport, shops and visitor attractions accept credit and/or debit cards, and even more so since the pandemic. It's always useful, though, to have some cash on you, as some car parks still take this as a method of payment. You'll find ATMs in most small towns.

Wales can be an expensive destination, but generally speaking is slightly cheaper than England. There are of course ways to keep costs down: staying in a hostel or on a campsite (of which there are plenty), self-catering or getting take-aways, and travelling by public transport will incur a daily spend of around £25–30. Couples staying at a B&B, eating at a middling restaurant and visiting an attraction each day should expect to pay around £70 each – more if renting a car. Staying in the finest hotels and eating at the best restaurants (which are often within the best hotels), you'll likely end up paying stratospheric prices, but then clearly money is less of an issue when you're paying through the roof. Restaurant mains vary wildly, but generally speaking, expect to pay £10–20 for a main course, £8–15 for a bottle of wine, and £3.50–4 for a pint of beer. Prices for some staple products include £1.80 a litre for petrol (although prices were fluctuating wildly at the time of writing) and £1 for a bottle of water.

GETTING AROUND

South Wales is the most densely populated part of the country, and to this end transport links are excellent. The only areas covered in this guide where public transport starts to thin out a little is once you get beyond the Valleys and into the Brecon Beacons, where there are few train lines – though the bus network is still fairly comprehensive – and in West Pembrokeshire, but even there, trains run all the way out to the ferry terminal at Fishguard. All things considered, driving in Wales is a joy, at least once you're done with the M4 and the more congested areas around the bigger cities. Overseeing all public transport is Transport for Wales (w tfw.wales), set up by the Welsh government in 2016.

DRIVING Welsh roads are, for the most part, excellent. With regard to South Wales, the principal entry points from England are the M4 and M48 motorways, the former originating in London and ending in eastern Carmarthenshire, the latter a short 13-mile stretch of road which veers off the M4 in England before crossing the Severn Bridge near Chepstow and rejoining the M4 near Newport. The A40 (which also starts in London) is the main link road between Abergavenny and Fishguard on the coast, skirting the northern rim of the Brecon Beacons National Park en route before going through Carmarthen and Haverfordwest. The recently

For all the main arteries and the necessity of having to get from A to B, there are some genuinely thrilling drives to consider in this part of the world, often blissfully traffic-tree with many an endless distraction.

Not everyone wants to walk in the Brecon Beacons and to this end there are some epic drives. While the A470 (scenic but busy) ploughs straight down the middle of the park from Brecon to Merthyr, some of the roads either side are fabulous. In the eastern Black Mountain range, the A4069 dips and twists between Llangadog and Brynamman with spellbinding views across to Carreg Cennen to the west. East of here, from the A40 just outside Sennybridge, the A4215 heads south before breaking off as an unnamed road before Heol Senni; the road continues over a dramatic switchback (the Devil's Elbow) before emerging near the Maen Llia standing stone and then continuing down to the waterfalls near Ystradfellte. To the east of the A470, and on the other side of Pen-y-Fan, there's a fantastic drive from Talybont-on-Usk around three reservoirs – Talybont, Pentwyn and Pontsticill – before you emerge in Merthyr. In the Black Mountains to the east, the Gospel Pass is one of the most scintillating drives in Wales.

One gorgeous river valley drive not to be missed is up through the wooded gorges of the Wye Valley, perhaps stopping for a waterside picnic along the way. As for Pembrokeshire, any number of coastal drives are likely to end up with an unscheduled diversion or two.

upgraded A465 Heads of the Valleys Road fringes the park's southern range; from here, mostly single-carriageway roads thread their way south towards the opposite end of the Valleys.

Driving in southeastern Wales can be frustrating, particularly around Newport and Cardiff, but apart from that, congestion is not a huge issue. Your biggest frustration in the Brecon Beacons is likely to be sheep rather than other vehicles. though even they somehow manage to take the stress out of driving. The only time when seasonal weather might come into play is winter through to early spring when some of the roads in the Brecon Beacons are quite likely to be cut off.

Petrol stations are ubiquitous, but if you are travelling to some of South Wales's slightly more remote areas, such as the Brecon Beacons, then you'd do well to top up before setting out. Parking will present few problems with plenty of car parks in all towns and cities, for which you'll pay around £1 for 1 hour, £2 for 2 hours and £4 for 4 hours; though the city NCP car parks are much more expensive. There are quite a few National Trust car parks, particularly along the Pembrokeshire coast; £6 a day seems to be the going rate here. Most car parks take cards, or you can use an app, though quite a few still accept cash. Note that quite a few beaches are not accessible by car, particularly the more cove-like bays and beaches along the south coast of Gower and parts of Pembrokeshire; there is, though, usually a car park within a maximum 15–20-minute walk, though that should still be enough to elicit a groan from the kids.

Drink-driving laws are the same as in England. This is 80mg per 100ml of blood (in Scotland it's 50mg), which roughly equates to a pint of beer, but of course the best thing to do if driving is just not drink at all.

BUSES The bus network is generally excellent, with local services run by a bewildering array of companies, though nearly all operate a much-reduced service on Sundays, if they run at all. Moreover, such are the relatively short distances between places in South Wales that no one journey is ever particularly arduous. **Traws Cymru** (w trawscymru.info) operate half a dozen or so medium-to-long-distance services throughout Wales. Of relevance to South Wales are T1 (Carmarthen to Aberystwyth), T4 (Cardiff to Newtown in Powys, via Merthyr and Brecon), T5 (Haverfordwest to Fishguard), T6 (Brecon to Swansea), T11 (Haverfordwest to Fishguard via St Davids) and T14 (Cardiff to Hay-on-Wye via Brecon). These buses are clean, comfortable and have Wi-Fi – and do have Sunday services.

In Pembrokeshire, there are several useful coastal services worth bearing in mind if this area is your intended target. The **Strumble Shuttle** plies the North Pembrokeshire coast between St David's and Fishguard, stopping at all villages in between; the **Puffin Shuttle** works the south coast between St David's and Marloes Sands via St Bride's Bay; and the **Poppit Rocket** runs between Fishguard and Newport to Cardigan further north. There's also the **Coastal Cruiser**, a circular service starting (and ending) in Pembroke Dock, which serves Angle, Bosherston and Stackpole; all these buses do usually run in winter too (October and May) but to a reduced timetable.

Wherever you're looking to go, you'll find all the info you need at w tfw.wales or w traveline.cymru. It's unlikely that even in Cardiff (enormous bus station waiting to open for years) and Swansea (enormous bus station) you'll need to use the local bus service, so compact are both cities.

TRAINS Like buses, the train network in South Wales is generally excellent, if not quite as far-reaching, which is not surprising given the terrain. The main inter-city line is the one from London Paddington whose first stop in Wales is Newport, then Cardiff, Bridgend, Port Talbot, Neath and Swansea. From these stations, suburban and rural services fan out into Monmouthshire, across the Valleys and the Vale of Glamorgan, and, from Swansea and Carmarthen, into Pembrokeshire.

The most glaring gap, unsurprisingly, is the Brecon Beacons, with lines running both east and west of the park. To the west is the wonderful Heart of Wales line (w heart-of-wales.co.uk), which ploughs a very slow furrow from Swansea to Llanelli, Ammanford, Llandeilo and Llandovery before continuing through mid-Wales and on to Shrewsbury in England where it terminates. It does stop at every conceivable halt in between, though that is part of the joy. For all train services in Wales, your best resources are w trainline.com and w traveline.cymru.

If you're considering travelling extensively by train in South Wales (or indeed Wales as a whole), it might be worth considering a pass of some description, most of which are integrated with local bus services. The Explore Wales Pass (£99) offers four days' travel within an eight-day (consecutive) period; in the same vein, but only valid for the South Wales region, is the Explore South Wales Pass (£69). There's also an Explore Cardiff and Valleys day ticket (£13.50) and an Explore West Wales day ticket (£13.50), covering the area between Carmarthen, Milford Haven and Fishguard. You will sometimes also find that some of the heritage and narrow-gauge railways offer deals to holders of the pass. These can only be bought at staffed train stations (including the larger ones in England) and not online.

ACCOMMODATION

Whatever the season, you shouldn't struggle too much to secure the accommodation of your choice, although with the rise in domestic holidays, you may just have to be a little more circumspect in your planning. The choice of accommodation in South

These price codes give an indication of the cost of a double room per night.

£££ £100+
££   £50–100
£   <£50

Wales is extremely varied, with more and more interesting (for interesting read innovative) places coming on stream all the time. Accommodation could therefore range from a secluded farmhouse B&B to a decadent country house, or a clifftop campsite to a mountain hostel. Accommodation is not especially cheap in Wales, or at least it's not appreciably cheaper than in England or Scotland for example. That said, with the exception of most hotels, a lot of places will offer a discount for longer stays, typically anything more than three nights. Conversely, a few places have a two- (or sometimes three-) night minimum stay policy, and this could apply to most types of accommodation, except for hotels usually.

Other than the Valleys, where decent accommodation can be hard to come by, there's a good spread throughout the rest of South Wales. The coast, especially parts of Pembrokeshire, does get chocker in high season, so if you can time a visit for late spring or September when both availability and rates are more favourable, that might be worth considering – and you should still get some of the best of the weather then. The Visit Wales website w visitwales.com has a list of accommodation providers, which are graded using the old-fashioned star system. However, this should be taken with a light pinch of salt, as there is often no hard and fast correlation between rank and price, or standard, but rather it's often more to do with the facilities an establishment has. It is also important to note that not every establishment participates in the scheme (in fact quite a few don't), so the fact that they may not feature on the website is irrelevant.

HOTELS, GUESTHOUSES AND PUBS Welsh hotels run the full gamut, from the ubiquitous chain hotels (though thankfully these are largely confined to Cardiff) which can be cheap as chips if you book far enough in advance, to smaller boutique-type hotels, which, although more expensive, usually come with a dollop of personality. There are some smaller independent chains currently doing good things like Town & Country Collective and the Celtic Collection, both of which have a handful of hotels in different locations across South Wales.

Guesthouses and B&Bs (there's often little distinction between the two) are an excellent alternative to hotels, being less uniform in style and providing a far more personal touch. At the most basic level, this might just be a private house with a couple of rooms, but more usually this is an establishment with multiple rooms and a guest lounge in which you can avail yourself of the facilities.

More and more popular are restaurants with rooms, which typically combine classy accommodation with epicurean levels of cooking, and while these can be expensive, they offer a level of service above and beyond what you'd normally receive – and of course you don't have to leave the premises at any stage. Two of the finest exponents in South Wales are the Felin Fach near Brecon (page 219) and Llys Meddyg in Newport (page 319). Wherever you stay, expect to tuck into a gut-busting breakfast, which will invariably include a cooked option (a cooked-to-order breakfast is always a good sign, though generally only better places offer this).

HOSTELS AND BUNKHOUSES The cities (Cardiff and Swansea) are, surprisingly, poorly served in terms of hostels, Cardiff having lost a few in recent years, including its YHA. Otherwise, the YHA currently has around ten hostels in South Wales: two in the Brecon Beacons and the rest dotted along the coastline, mostly in Pembrokeshire. Some of these are fantastically located, for example those in Talybont-on-Usk, Port Eynon, Manorbier and Goodwick near Strumble Head. Note that some hostels only take group bookings in the winter months, while some may not be open at all during this period. Most hostels now have all the requisite facilities, include kitchen, lounge (occasionally a licensed bar), laundry and bike storage, while some also offer evening meals and packed lunches.

The YHA hostels are complemented by an increasing number of private hostels, which tend to have a bit more personality than the YHA-run ones but with similar facilities. A couple of exceptional ones are the Old School Hostel in Trefin, near St David's (page 313) and the Star Bunkhouse in Bwlch, in the Brecon Beacons (page 226). A more primitive alternative to hostels are bunkhouses, which have traditionally been used by walkers and climbers; expect to pay around £13 for a bed; w bunkhousesinwales.co.uk has a list.

CAMPING AND GLAMPING The Welsh countryside, if not the weather, is made for camping. Given the rural isolation and endless vistas, a week or two under the stars is the perfect antidote to life's modern stresses, so long as the weather's playing ball. Sites range from a simple field with no more than a compost loo to those with modern shower blocks and a fully stocked shop. For pure spectacle, a couple of unbeatable sites are Three Cliffs Bay on Gower (page 167) and West Hook Farm on the Marloes Peninsula (page 300), while for solitude there's the wonderful Ynysfaen in the heart of the Brecon Beacons (page 219).

While many campsites prefer to remain true to their roots and stick to offering a purely canvas-based experience, many more have evolved and now include an element of glamping in their offer, which could mean an unfurnished pod, a more extravagantly furnished shepherd's hut, bell tent, gypsy caravan, or tipi, or any permutation of these. In fact, quite a few hostels are now getting in on the act, and it's not unusual to find a hut or pod of some description available in addition to the hostel accommodation itself.

The number of glamping-only sites has exploded in the last few years, and only seems to be on the increase. There's a reasonably even spread across South Wales, with just as many great sites in Monmouthshire as there are in, say, Pembrokeshire. It's a bit of a loose term, but these too can range from being fairly basic affairs, such as a yurt with just a bed, to an uber-luxurious bell tent with shower, kitchen and woodburner, and perhaps a welcome hamper thrown in for good measure. Some, but by no means all, are open year-round. A couple of cracking glamping sites are Penhein near Chepstow (page 89) and The Roost in Merthyr (page 189).

SELF-CATERING Self-catering was already becoming an increasingly popular choice for accommodation before the pandemic, but since then there appears to be even more demand. Options can range from a clifftop static caravan to the cosy cottage down on the coast experience, for which you will pay a premium, at least during the summer months. Out of season, there are some very good deals to be had. There are dozens of companies advertising properties all over the region.

One of the legacies of the time when holidaymakers from the North of England, and especially the Midlands, hightailed it to the Welsh coast for a couple of weeks during the summer months (and still do) is the endless procession of caravan parks lining some sections of the clifftops. These aren't confined to the coast, though; for example, there's a great caravan park at Llangorse Lake (page 226). Compared with a cottage, farm or apartment, this can be a more affordable way of self-catering, but whatever your choice of self-catering accommodation, you do at least save on eating out, in theory that is.

FAMILIES Families should have little trouble getting something sorted. Of course, the simplest way is to go self-catering, but failing that, nearly all hostels now have a family room of some description, while most hotels are more than happy to accommodate children, whether that's linking through two rooms or using a pull-out sofa bed. In a few instances, some hotels and guesthouses do not accept children under a certain age, and where this is the case, this is indicated where appropriate. If we include dogs as part of the family – as we should – then you'll find Wales incredibly accommodating, to the extent that it's now almost the rule rather than the exception for most places to have dog-friendly rooms – many even go as far as supplying doggie treats.

EATING AND DRINKING

EATING The Welsh culinary scene is almost unrecognisable from even just a decade ago, and it's no longer the UK's poor relation. Both the quality of the produce, much of which is now grown organically, and the types of places where you can sit down and tuck into great gastronomic fare have improved considerably. Moreover, many establishments are seeking to use locally sourced produce wherever possible, and/or are looking to grow their own produce and forage themselves.

With its rich valley pastures providing fine grazing, Welsh **dairy products** are superb. Welsh **cheese** is a serous rival to anything the French can muster, and while Caerphilly's crumbly white cheese is the most well known (so much so that the town has its own cheese festival), there are others, like Perl Wen (White Pearl) from Caws Cenarth, a soft creamy cheese not dissimilar to Brie (they also produce Perl Las, a blue cheese), and Y Fenni, a spiky mustard-and-ale-infused cheddar from Abergavenny. Similarly, this fertile land facilitates the cultivation of abundant **fruit and vegetables**. With its mild climate, Pembrokeshire's early potatoes are rated the best in the land, closely followed by those from Gower – and where would we be without the venerable leek?

The Welsh love their meat as much as any other nation, which is not surprising given the quality and quantity of the produce here. In a land packed with sheep, it's little wonder that lamb is king, in particular **saltmarsh lamb** from Gower, which gains its unique flavour from the animal's diet of sorrel, sea lavender and samphire. You're unlikely to resist if you find this on a menu. In a similar vein, **Welsh Black beef** also has superior flavour, as a result of the cattle – Wales's only native breed – grazing at higher altitude. With so much coastline, **seafood** – including bass, crab, mussels, lobster, sole and mackerel, among other wet treats – comes as standard on menus throughout the region, but of course particularly in Pembrokeshire. The Wye may not be the great salmon river of yore, but it's still fished, as are the Tywi and Usk, both for salmon and sewin (trout), while cockles trawled from Penclawdd on North Gower also make their way on to many a menu.

There are a handful of wonderful Welsh delicacies which it'd be remiss not to try, among them **cawl**, which usually refers to any soup or broth but typically includes a meat of some kind, perhaps lamb or mutton. Described by the actor Richard Burton as 'Welshman's caviar', **laverbread**, which is essentially seaweed, is something of an acquired taste; it's a regular staple on most breakfast menus and must be tried at least once – who knows, you might even like it. In fact **seaweed** is increasingly being used in many recipes, from butter to brownies, not only because of its taste but also because of its extraordinary health-giving properties. A great brunch option is **Welsh rarebit**, a bit like cheese on toast but here the cheese is mixed with beer, mustard and Worcester Sauce, while the legendary **Glamorgan sausage**, made from local cheese and spices, is so good that it is likely to appeal to carnivores too.

The biggest sea change in recent times is the choice available, not just to vegetarians, but also to vegans, and it wouldn't be disingenuous to suggest that Wales currently does vegan better than any other British nation. Most towns, including some smaller ones, can call on at least one dedicated vegan restaurant (or at least a restaurant with a dedicated vegan menu), and some of the cooking is so inventive that it does make you wonder why we ever bother with meat. Anna Loka in Cardiff is the current standout (page 63).

The sweet-toothed are amply catered for. The most traditional Welsh cake (or is it a bread?) is **Bara Brith** ('bara' meaning bread, 'brith' meaning speckled), a traditional tea-loaf. Made from mixed fruit and soaked overnight in tea, it's then combined with dry ingredients and baked the following day. It's best eaten warm with a generous smear of salted butter on top, and with a cuppa. In a similar vein, **Welsh cakes** are cookie-sized morsels packed with currants with a hint of mace and a dusting of sugar to finish. Fantastically moreish, you can buy them in packets from any supermarket but they're best sampled fresh off the griddle. And if all else fails, there's always **ice cream**. Welsh ice cream is probably the finest in Britain (calm down now everyone), a legacy of a wave of Italian migrants arriving here in the early 20th century: Sidoli's, Cadwaladers and Joe's are the names to look out for.

In terms of places to eat, these run the full gamut from pubs and street food markets to smart bistros and Michelin-starred **restaurants**, of which there are currently four in South Wales, all with one star: Home in Penarth, The Beach House in Oxwich (page 168), The Walnut Tree in Abergavenny (page 234), and The Whitebrook just outside Tintern (page 94). Just as good, if not better, are the growing number of restaurant-with-room establishments, where you'll eat and sleep like a king, or a queen. Again, thanks to the widespread Italian influence, there are some terrific pizzerias in South Wales – a shout-out here to the likes of Café Citta in Cardiff and Stone Rock Pizza in Chepstow.

Wherever you dine, service is invariably first rate, rarely too mannered, and typically comes with a warm smile as behoves the natives' welcoming nature. A good place to stock up, be it for an evening in or a simple picnic, are the covered **markets**, such as those in Abergavenny, Carmarthen, Cardiff and Swansea, the country's largest. The biggest and best of South Wales's food festivals (page 48) are those in Narberth and Abergavenny, both in September.

RESTAURANT PRICE CODES

The following codes are used to indicate the average price for a main course.

£££ £25+
££ £15–25
£ <£15

DRINKING In recent years, the big breweries like Cardiff-based Brains (w sabrain. com) have been usurped somewhat by the entrance of dozens of craft **beer** breweries into the market, which has certainly livened things up. From hoppy ales to fruity IPAs, imperial stouts to dark sours, it seems like there's no end to the creativity. Leading the way is the cool Tiny Rebel brewery (w tinyrebel.co.uk) based in Newport, who have also got three bars (two in Newport, one in Cardiff), but others to seek out include Llanelli-based Felinfoel (w felinfoel.com) – Wales's oldest brewery (1878) and the first craft brewery in the world to supply beer in a can (1935), though that's no surprise since Llanelli is home to a tinplate works – Tomos Watkin (w tomoswatkin.com) in Swansea, Evan Evans (w evanevansbrewery.com) in Llandeilo, Pipes (w pipesbeer.co.uk) in Pontcanna, Cardiff, and Tenby Brewing (w tenbybrewingco.com). The pub of course remains an enduring institution, and while there are, sadly, far fewer traditional boozers than there once were, it's still possible to find the occasional hostelry where the locals will stop and have a natter at the bar, even if many of those places now seem to cater more to those in search of food.

Although there is evidence of there being **whisky** stills in Wales as far back as the 4th century, when the Penderyn distillery (w penderyn.wales) started doing so in 2000, it was the first to do so in Wales for more than 100 years. The only other whisky producer in South Wales is the Coles distillery (w coles.wales) in Llanddarog, Carmarthenshire. Penderyn also distils vodka and **gin**, and as seems to be the vogue, specialised gin distillers are springing up all over the place. A couple of interesting ones are the Silver Circle distillery (w silvercircledistillery.com) in Catbrook, the Wye Valley, and Hensol Castle distillery (w hensolcastledistillery. com) just outside Cardiff. To many people's surprise, South Wales is a fertile wine producing area, with both the soil and climate here offering ideal growing conditions. Two excellent outfits are Llanerch (w llanerch.co.uk) in the Vale of Glamorgan and White Castle (w whitecastlevineyard.com) in Monmouthshire.

The artisan **coffee** boom has well and truly hit South Wales and shows no sign of abating. Inevitably Cardiff has the most interesting scene and coffee is brewed with obsessive care, but even in the smaller towns, there should be at least one independent coffee shop doing something interesting. The dominant roaster on the market right now is Coaltown Coffee Roasters in Ammanford. As well as supplying dozens of outlets across South Wales and beyond, you can visit their ace production site-cum-coffee shop and see what all the fuss is about. Unless you're staying in a classier establishment, coffee at breakfast is invariably from a machine, which can be a bit rubbish.

FESTIVALS AND EVENTS

Beyond the most high-profile events – the Hay Literary Festival, the Abergavenny Food Festival and Green Man – the festival scene in South Wales tends to go under the radar, but there are some terrific events worth attending, many of which are even worth planning trips around. As the above selection suggests, books, food and music all play a major part in the Welsh festival scene, but there are other events too – some very offbeat – which revolve around themes such as history, industry, the Welsh language and the great outdoors.

In early March, you can start shedding a few of those winter calories attending the superb **Crickhowell Walking Festival** (w crickhowellfestival.com), nine days of exhilarating treks around the Brecon Beacons, alongside talks and other events (page 229). At the end of the month, the focus switches to Laugharne and all things

Dylan Thomas courtesy of the **Laugharne Weekend** (w thelaugharneweekend.com), three days of readings (some big names come to town), film and music; it's a good one this (page 255). Towards the end of May, the behemoth that is the **Hay Literary Festival** (w hayfestival.com) rolls into this small town, or more accurately an enormous field just outside town. Attended by the most celebrated names in the industry (including big-name politicians and journalists promoting their books) as well as actors, comedians and musicians, this ten-day gathering seems to get bigger every year (page 244). The Valleys has little in the way of festivals, but at the end of June, Blaenavon celebrates its illustrious industrial past in its annual **Heritage Day** (w visitblaenavon.co.uk), with a day of jollity culminating in a colourful town parade.

In July, Caerphilly's famous cheese is celebrated in all its crumbly glory in the rollicking **Big Cheese Festival** (w bigcheesecaerphilly.co.uk) up at the castle, featuring historical re-enactments, a monster tug-of-war, and more cheese than you can shake a cocktail stick at (page 196). August and it's time for **Green Man** (w greenman.net), whose setting in the heart of the Black Mountains, combined with a consistently first-class line up (indie, Americana, alt-rock), as well as a strong focus on art and science, ranks it among the favourites on the British festival circuit. Tickets are invariably snapped up within days of going on sale (page 229). Around the same time, but taking place over two weeks, is the long-standing **Brecon Jazz Festival** (w breconjazz.org), which has been the country's foremost jazz and blues gathering since 1984 (page 220).

The big one in September (though Elvis fans might disagree) is the **Abergavenny Food Festival** (w abergavennyfoodfestival.com), usually around the third weekend in September. One of Europe's premier gastronomic events, it's attended by a who's who of culinary greats, with talks, tastings, masterclasses and much more in venues including the Victorian market hall and castle grounds (page 237). Just a week later, Narberth in Pembrokeshire stages its own **Food Festival** (w narberthfoodfestival.com), and although far more low-key, in its own way it's just as enjoyable (page 276). Nothing, though, in South Wales – or anywhere in Wales come to think of it – compares to Porthcawl's **Elvis Fest** (w elvies.co.uk), the largest festival in the world (how many are there?) dedicated to 'The King'. Some 30,000 'Elvies' descend on this small seaside resort for a riotous weekend of singing and strutting, with official shows staged at the town's Grand Pavilion. It really is a sight to behold (page 137).

As we enter the autumn period, it's time to slow things down a bit with October's **Crickhowell Literary Festival** (w cricklitfest.co.uk), a gentle riposte to Hay's mega event earlier in the year (page 229). Also in October is the **Brecon Baroque Festival** (w breconbaroquefestival.com), four days of premier class concerts in venues such as the cathedral (page 221). Founded by prominent Welsh DJ Huw Stephens, the **Swn Festival** (w swnfest.com) is Cardiff's big annual music hoedown; there's no specific date but it usually takes place in early/mid autumn, its *raison d'être* to showcase emerging acts across multiple city-centre venues, but mostly those in and around Womanby Street like Clwb Ifor Bach (page 66).

One or two events that tend to fly under the radar but are well worth seeking out include **Tafwyl** (w tafwyl.org), a dedicated Welsh-language festival taking place (surprisingly) in Cardiff, at the castle, in mid-June; above all this is a great way to acquaint yourself with Welsh-language music (page 22). Tucked away behind the dunes at Merthyr Mawr, the Woods and Dunes glamping site hosts the thoroughly enjoyable **Between the Trees Festival** (w betweenthetrees.co.uk) at the end of August, with a low-key folk-oriented line up as well as events connected to art, nature and the spoken word (page 137).

SHOPPING

Generally, shops' opening hours are 09.00–17.30/18.00 Monday–Saturday, and 10.00–16.00 Sunday, although these can, and do, vary. The larger malls stay open until 19.00 or 20.00 Monday to Saturday, and 11.00–17.00 Sunday. If you need to stock up on last-minute provisions, there are Co-op and Tesco Express stores all over the place.

In terms of what to buy as a gift (either for yourself or for someone else), you can't go wrong with perishables, and you really could spoil yourself here. Local cheeses, chocolate, a loaf of Bara Brith or a box of Welsh cakes are all mouthwatering possibilities. In terms of alcohol, whisky from Penderyn, wine from Llanerch or White Castle, or gin from Hensol is likely to go down well, literally.

Otherwise, arts and crafty things are usually a good bet. The quintessential Welsh gift is a lovespoon, an intricately carved spoon that was traditionally given as a gift of romantic intent. Most gift shops will have a selection, but there are also dedicated shops. In this land of sheep, the availability of wool is never a problem, so if you're willing to spend a little more then woollen products such as socks, hats, jumpers and blankets make fabulous luxury gifts. Although mostly from North Wales, slate is another popular material used to make various items, such as wine holders and coasters.

ARTS AND ENTERTAINMENT

The Welsh are great connoisseurs of the arts, whether that's **theatre**, **dance**, **ballet** or any kind of **music**: rock, opera, classical, or Welsh-language indie – there is a reason why Wales is known as the Land of Song. Unsurprisingly, Cardiff and Swansea boast the lion's share of venues, from the magnificent Wales Millennium Centre (home to the Welsh National Opera) and the Sherman Theatre in Cardiff to the swanky new Swansea Arena and the venerable Dylan Thomas Theatre in Swansea. But such venues aren't exclusively the preserve of the urban centres. The Savoy Theatre in Monmouth, Theatre Gwaun in Fishguard, and the Torch Theatre in Milford Haven are just some of those that have bucked the trend (and survived the pandemic), and continue to thrive. One thing you should do, given the chance, is attend a **Welsh Male Voice Choir** concert, or at the very least go and watch a rehearsal, where you'll be made to feel very welcome – many of the Valleys' towns have an ensemble, so just ask around (page 207).

You'll find the best of the independent **cinemas** in Cardiff (Chapter) and Swansea (Cinema Co), but that said, they also pop up in some of the most unusual places. A few such places are the fabulous Art Deco Market Hall cinema in Brynmawr (Wales's oldest screen), the Parc and Dare Theatre in Treorchy, and the Phoenix in Ton Pentre, Rhondda. Many of the Valleys' old **mining institutes**, such as Blackwood's superb building, have been repurposed as performance arts spaces and invariably put a good mix of stuff on.

In terms of **nightlife**, few cities in Britain can match the madness of Cardiff of a Saturday evening; Swansea, too, is similarly boisterous. But beyond here, things are pretty sedate. There are fewer places of character to drink in now, though most Welsh villages have as their focal point the **pub**, invariably now serving food too. If you're staying out in the sticks, the chances are that you'll be drinking in the hotel bar, which can be a pleasant, and easy, alternative.

OUTDOOR ACTIVITIES

If you can't enjoy the great outdoors in South Wales, you can't enjoy it anywhere. The walking here is sensational, from the celebrated Wales Coast Path, and its antecedent, the Pembrokeshire Coast Path, to the rugged moorland and high peaks of the Brecon Beacons. Its coastal waters, especially those around Pembrokeshire, attract those seeking more invigorating fare: surfing, coasteering, snorkelling and kayaking, which you can enjoy just as much in the region's lakes and waterways. Back on terra firma, mountain biking has come of age in South Wales, and speed demons will love thrashing about the near-handful of modern bike parks, while those with a preference for two-legged transport can content themselves with a trek along the coastal sands or in the mountains.

WALKING AND HIKING Upon the launch in 2012 of the **Wales Coast Path** (870 miles), Wales became the only country in the world to have a continuous, unbroken path along the length of its entire coastline. The England Coast Path will pass that landmark at some point, but who cares: Wales did it first. More than ten years on, it's as phenomenally popular as ever, and whether you're doing the whole thing in its entirety (technically it goes north to south but it really doesn't matter) or just snippets here and there, it's a thrilling outing. The path really comes into its own in South Wales, in particular the stretch along the Pembrokeshire coastline. Forming part of the Wales Coast Path is the 186-mile-long **Pembrokeshire Coast Path** (page 317), which starts (or ends) in Amroth and continues to St Dogmaels near Cardigan. The PCP is the most popular long-distance trail in the whole of Wales, so if you are wont to tackle it, you'd do well to avoid high season: late spring is the optimum time – you also get the spectacular migrant birdlife coming in to settle then too.

All the high-altitude treks in South Wales are the preserve of the **Brecon Beacons**, and with more than 160 peaks to summit, you could walk for weeks on end and not get bored. The busiest is the central Beacons – thanks in the main to the (literally) crowd-pulling **Pen-y-Fan** (2,907ft) – South Wales's, and southern Britain's, highest mountain. The **Black Mountains** in the eastern Brecon Beacons, and the **Black Mountain** in the western Brecon Beacons, retain their own special character and are far quieter. The Brecons' major trail is the awesome 100-mile-long **Brecon Beacons Way**, an outing of between eight and ten days. For some truly off-the-radar yomping, the **Preseli Hills** take some beating, while the Valleys are growing in stature as a bona fide walking destination.

Two paths covered in this guide, but which spill over into mid-Wales and beyond, are the **Wye Valley Path** and the **Offa's Dyke Path**, both of which begin in Chepstow. Starting at the castle, the first two sections of the Wye Valley trail are delightful. The trail then departs for England briefly before coming back into Wales and continuing inland to its source at Plynlimon, mid-Wales. The Offa's Dyke trail, meanwhile, weaves along the England/Wales border all the way up to the north coast. For all the above, as long as you are armed with a good map (page 34), you can just go and walk, anywhere and as aimlessly as you like.

Wherever you go, and to state the obvious, be prepared. The Welsh weather is notoriously changeable, especially up in the mountains, so check local forecasts assiduously, unless it's obviously going to be a blindingly hot day. You will also need a good map – the excellent and reliable Ordnance Survey Explorer series is far and away the best (page 34), and if you didn't bring one in advance, they are usually available from those tourist offices that do exist or bookshops – if nothing else, they're great for pinpointing local landmarks. Check supplies, too, ensuring that you've got enough food and water for a day out in the hills, and make sure your phone is charged to the max before heading out. The excellent Cicerone guides have guidebooks for all of the above walks and areas, including: *Walking the Wales*

Coast Path, Walking the Pembrokeshire Coast Path, Walking in the Brecon Beacons, Walking the Wye Valley Walk, and *Walking Offa's Dyke Path.*

CYCLING AND MOUNTAIN BIKING Wales is now regarded as one of the world's premier **mountain-biking** centres. It wasn't so long ago that you had to go to North Wales to get your biking kicks, but not anymore. In the last decade or so there has been an explosion of interest in the activity, mostly centred on the Valleys, and in several cases these new centres have transformed many a once-grim mining landscape. At present, there are four mountain-biking centres in South Wales, the biggest and most spectacular of which is Bike Park Wales (**w** bikeparkwales.com) just outside Merthyr. Putting every other bike park in the shade, this enormous facility has a staggering 40 trails (probably more by the time you read this), some of which have been designed with beginners and families in mind, and an excellent uplift service too. Two more are at Cwmbran and Afan Valley (which has two separate centres close to each other) but both of these are for more experienced riders. The newest entrant is at Dare Valley Country Park (**w** darevalleygravity. co.uk), where a couple of blue flow runs should suit beginners and intermediate riders; this too has an uplift service. All these centres have bike-hire facilities, as well as repairs and servicing if you have a problem with your own bike. Most of them also have accommodation close at hand, if not on site itself then certainly within striking distance.

Beyond these dedicated biking centres, there are dozens of good cycling trails, among them the 55-mile-long **Taff Trail** (page 80) from Cardiff Bay to Talybont-on-Usk, which is particularly scenic (and a little bit hilly) as you enter the Brecon Beacons; there are excellent bike-hire outlets in both Talybont and Cardiff Bay. The biggie, however, is the **Celtic Trail**, a 357-mile path that partially takes in Sustrans National Route 4. It starts across the border in England but comes into Wales at Chepstow before weaving its way across the Valleys, Carmarthenshire and then along the Pembrokeshire coastline ending in Fishguard. A shorter ride is the scenic, 6.2-mile Cardiff Bay trail.

HORSERIDING The Welsh have a deep-rooted affinity with all things equine, and this is manifest in the many riding stables across the country. Here in South Wales you're spoilt for choice when it comes to the types of terrain to ride in, with both mountains and coast easily accessible, and plenty of places in between of course; most offer hacks as well as lessons and can usually accommodate novice riders to some degree. Few things are as exhilarating as a ride along the beach, and from their stables on the banks of the River Ogmore in the Vale of Glamorgan, the Ogmore Farm Riding School (**w** rideonthebeach.co.uk) offer 2-hour rides (£60) along Merthyr Mawr and up into the amazing dunes adjacent to the beach as well as 1-hour treks (£40) out on to the local common. In Pendine, Pembrokeshire, the Marros Riding School (**w** marros-farm.co.uk) organise gallops out along the magnificent seven-mile stretch of Pendine Sands, though these are for confident riders and those aged 16 and over. Alternatives include 1- and 2-hour inland treks.

If you like your riding a bit more rugged, the Brecon Beacons is a wonderful place to hack. Here Grange Trekking (**w** grangetrekking-wales.co.uk), based in the tiny hamlet of Capel-y-Ffin, organises half- and full-day rides (£44/75) into the beautiful Black Mountains; the full-day trek along the ridge heading towards Hay Bluff is an unforgettable experience. Others worth looking out for in the Brecon Beacons are Cantref Farm (**w** cantref.com) near Brecon and Ellesmere Riding Centre (**w** ellesmereridingcentre.co.uk) near Llangorse Lake.

WATERSPORTS The main water-bound activity here, and one that continues to grow in terms of participator numbers, is **surfing**, with parts of the Welsh coast acknowledged to be some of the finest areas in the UK for the sport. South Pembrokeshire and Gower, plus one or two isolated spots in the Vale of Glamorgan, are the prime destinations, and although the water is not that warm, the sweeping, wave-lashed beaches offer fantastic conditions pretty much year-round. A top five of surfing beaches would have to include Rest Bay in Porthcawl, Langland Bay on South Gower, Llangennith (Hillend) on West Gower, Freshwater West near Pembroke, and Whitesands Bay on the St David's Peninsula. All of these have consistently good breaks – which makes them great for bodyboarders too – and are also patrolled by lifeguards in high season. Whether you just want to rent a board and/or equipment, or have a lesson (which usually costs around £30 for 2/3 hours), all these beaches have provision; most offer lessons for those aged six or seven and above. Two particularly good surf schools are Porthcawl Surf in Rest Bay (w porthcawlsurf.co.uk) and Llangennith Surf School in Llangennith (w llangennithsurfschool.com).

Stand-up paddleboarding is now well established, and it's often the case that anywhere hiring out surf boards will likely hire out paddleboards too. The spots where you can do this are more varied, and as well as the coastline, the region's lakes and rivers are seeing more and more people take to the water with SUPs. One such place is Llandegfedd Lake near Pontypool (page 180), a huge watersports centre which also offers **pedal boarding**, a bit like cycling on water, as well as all kinds of other activities, including canoeing, kayaking, windsurfing and sailing. Cardiff Bay, incidentally, is also a great place to try out paddleboarding. **Llangorse Lake** in the Brecon Beacons – the largest natural body of water in South Wales – is another terrific spot, though most people here just prefer to pootle around in a little rowboat.

Possibly the most fun you can have getting wet is **coasteering**, which, at its most basic level, entails scrambling along the base of sea cliffs, boulder beaches and sandy coves, while more advanced coasteering will involve scaling sheer rock walls. Although it was 'invented' in some form or other by climbers back in the 1800s as a way of training for technical mountain ascents, the activity as we know it today was initiated in Pembrokeshire in the 1970s, but only emerged as a popular activity in the 1990s. Although most water-based outdoor companies offer coasteering as part of their programme (and all are very good), you'll be in particularly good hands with the likes of Celtic Quest Coasteering in Abereiddi (w celticquestcoasteering.com) and TYF in St David's (w tyf.com), both of whom have years of experience leading trips out. Armed with a wetsuit, buoyancy aid and helmet, and unencumbered by equipment, it's thrill-a-minute stuff and perfectly safe, so much so that weaker swimmers can participate too. The minimum age, however, is usually eight.

Kitesurfing is another very popular activity, and with its Atlantic swells and exposure to the elements, the Pembrokeshire coast, particularly around Freshwater West, is a terrific spot – although these swells and the tides here make this more suited to experienced kite surfers. The Big Blue Experience (w thebigblueexperience. com) in Newgale is a good place to start if you've never done it before but would like to try. A more sedate way to experience the Pembrokeshire coast from the water is in a **sea kayak**, dipping in and out of the bays and coves. Preseli Venture are a good company to try here (w preseliventure.co.uk). The region's rivers can also be just as much fun, with possibilities to kayak along the Wye and the Tywi among others, while those brave enough may be tempted by a **wild swim**.

MEDIA AND COMMUNICATIONS

British daily **newspapers** are all available in Wales, and seem to struggle on in the face of a dwindling readership – not that you'll find much coverage of Wales anyway, unless it's a major news story. For local news, your best bet is go online and check out the likes of w walesonline.co.uk, which offers a broad mix of government news, local stories, sport, travel and a bit of celebrity tat. If you really want to get into the nitty gritty, then most towns or regions have their local rag, but again, this is probably all online.

Wi-Fi coverage is universally excellent, and it's very rare now to go to any accommodation and struggle to get a decent connection. Out and about, mobile reception is usually unproblematic, though in more remote parts of the Brecon Beacons, you may well struggle to receive a signal, if you can get one at all that is. Where you do find a **post office** (and in some of the larger towns and cities this will probably be in WHSmith), opening times are generally 09.30 to 17.30 Monday to Friday and 09.30 to noon or 13.00 Saturday.

Welsh **television** is currently flourishing. BBC Cymru (Wales), whose headquarters recently moved to swanky premises in Cardiff's Central Square, operates two channels: BBC One Wales and BBC Two Wales. The main Welsh television channel is S4C (Sianel Pedwar Cymru, sister channel to the English-language Channel 4), which first aired in 1982 and has since become a major player on the Welsh media scene. Some of its best recent productions, like *Hidden*, have aired on S4C first before transferring to a BBC channel. You can watch many of its programmes with English subtitles.

CULTURAL ETIQUETTE

The Welsh are renowned for their hospitality, and perhaps more than any other area of the British Isles, you'll be welcomed with great enthusiasm, wherever you're from. The supposed animosity towards England and the English is slightly overplayed and really only tends to manifest itself in the sporting arena, especially rugby. That said, the Welsh are more likely to tell it how it is and are often not afraid to proffer their opinion, so don't take it personally!

The Welsh are incredibly proud of their cultural heritage. There has been a renaissance in the number of people speaking the native tongue, and if you can utter a word or two, they will be delighted, in the Welsh-speaking areas at least (page 22). Most signs are now in English and Welsh (since 2016, it has been mandatory to put any new signs in Welsh first), so you'll quite likely pick up the occasional word that way.

General etiquette is in step with the other nations of the UK: it's polite to shake hands with someone when meeting, whether that's a man or a woman; being on time is important (and if you are going to be late, try and inform the person; and if someone buys you a drink in a pub, then an even-handed gesture is to buy the next round. In general, women travellers are unlikely to encounter any specific problems, but as anywhere, if you are travelling alone, or somewhere unfamiliar, exercise caution.

TRAVELLING POSITIVELY

The public transport system in South Wales – which is more comprehensive than in any other part of the country – lends itself to travelling around by bus or train, and you can certainly reduce your carbon footprint substantially should you choose to travel this way. Even along the more remote coastal areas, there are a handful of bus routes serving the numerous scattered villages. Better still, and wherever possible, work your way around by foot – which is what many visitors to South Wales do anyway, at least those with designs on walking the Wales Coast Path.

You can also do much to reduce your carbon footprint by staying in one or two concentrated areas as opposed to travelling widely throughout the region. This way too, you can really get into the nuts and bolts of a place as opposed to covering areas superficially – and of course you can (and indeed should) come back to visit another area another time. The majority of travellers to South Wales tend to home in on the coast – particularly the Pembrokeshire coast – and the Brecon Beacons, both areas that can get swamped at the height of summer. As a responsible traveller, therefore, one of the best actions you can take is to spend more of your time, and money, in some of the lesser-visited parts of the region, where small businesses still struggle to bring in enough customers to make their endeavours sustainable – for example in the Valleys, whose industrial heritage is as rewarding as anywhere else in South Wales.

Part Two

THE GUIDE

3

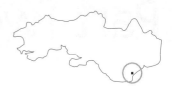

Cardiff

One of Europe's youngest and most dynamic cities, Cardiff is unrecognisable from the city of 20 years ago, having reinvented itself in a way few other capitals have managed, or dared, to do in the intervening period. It was the opening of the Millennium (now Principality) Stadium in time for the 1999 Rugby World Cup that ushered in a monumental rebuilding programme for the city, which centred on **Cardiff Bay**, once a byword for squalor and decay. The stimulus for the bay's metamorphosis into a bona fide visitor attraction was a new barrage, alongside which new and now iconic buildings were raised, such as the Wales Millennium Centre and the Senedd. More recently, the city centre has welcomed the arrival of BBC Cymru (Wales) headquarters to Central Square, with the (nearly but not quite ready) bus station soon to follow.

The arrival of major television production in the city, including the BBC's flagship drama *Doctor Who* and its spin-off *Torchwood*, and a new digital media and drama village at Roath Lock, has done as much, if not more, to boost the city's profile than any tourist board campaign, as did the city's staging of the Champions League final – international club football's most prestigious prize – in 2017. There's a palpable buzz about Cardiff these days, its youthful appeal bolstered by a large student body that lends the city a wonderful dynamic. Cardiff wears its sociability well, manifest in a thriving music scene and some of the most exuberant nightlife anywhere.

For a capital city, Cardiff is not especially well endowed with major attractions, but in **Cardiff Castle**, the **National Museum Cardiff** and the awesome **Principality Stadium**, it does possess three big-hitters. At the heart of the city, the River Taff meanders through the gracious green acres of **Bute Park** – offering a degree of respite from the noise – before continuing its journey north past impressive **Llandaff Cathedral** and beyond towards the Valleys and the Brecon Beacons. North and west of the centre, the village-like areas of **Canton, Roath** and **Pontcanna** – the first one of the city's most multicultural neighbourhoods, the last its most urbane – are worth exploring for their suburban idiosyncrasies.

Cardiff's principal satellite attractions are **St Fagans National Museum of History**, with its marvellous assemblage of vernacular architecture, and the dramatically sited **Castell Coch,** both of which make for easy and satisfying excursions.

HISTORY

Like many cities, Cardiff's earliest history is somewhat foggy, but what is known is that the Romans arrived some time around AD55, forming a settlement (possibly called Tamium) as part of their strategy to fortify the Severn. But it wasn't until the Normans, commanded by Robert FitzHamon, pitched up in 1093 that something approaching an identifiable settlement began to emerge – the most obvious legacy being Cardiff Castle's keep.

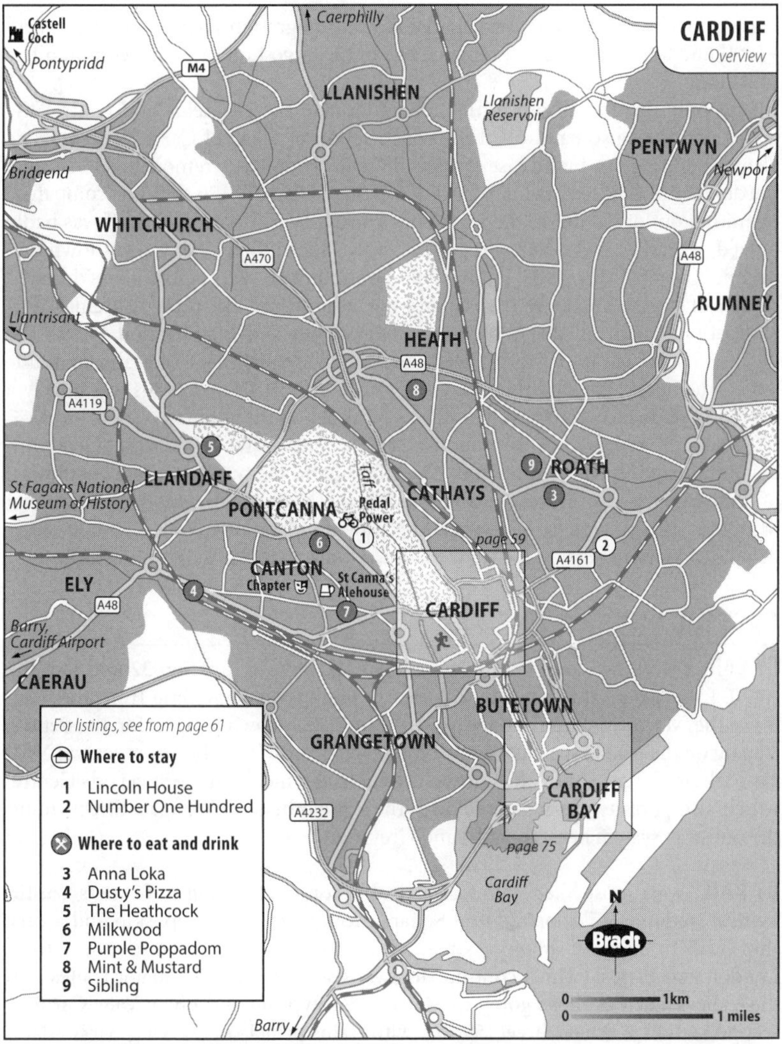
CARDIFF
Overview
Castell Coch
Pontypridd
Caerphilly
M4
LLANISHEN
Llanishen Reservoir
PENTWYN
Newport
Bridgend
WHITCHURCH
A470
A48
RUMNEY
Llantrisant
HEATH
A48
A4119
LLANDAFF
ROATH
St Fagans National Museum of History
CATHAYS
Taff
PONTCANNA
Pedal Power
page 59
A4161
CANTON
Chapter
St Canna's Alehouse
ELY
A48
CARDIFF
Barry, Cardiff Airport
CAERAU
BUTETOWN
GRANGETOWN
CARDIFF BAY
A4232
page 75
Cardiff Bay
N
Bradt
0 1km
0 1 miles
Barry
For listings, see from page 61
Where to stay
1 Lincoln House
2 Number One Hundred
Where to eat and drink
3 Anna Loka
4 Dusty's Pizza
5 The Heathcock
6 Milkwood
7 Purple Poppadom
8 Mint & Mustard
9 Sibling

Boom-time Cardiff coincided with the Industrial Revolution. The opening of the Glamorgan Canal, between Merthyr Tydfil (then Wales's largest town) and Cardiff, in 1794 opened the floodgates, quite literally, initially for shipments of iron and steel, then coal, the latter on an epic scale. This was facilitated by John Crichton-Stuart, the Second Marquess of Bute – one of Britain's richest landowners – who built the first dock (Bute West) here in 1839, and following completion of the Taff Vale Railway in 1841, Cardiff was well on the way to becoming the world's largest coal-exporting dock, which in turn fuelled the growth of the city as a whole. By 1850, Cardiff's population had risen six-fold to more than 26,000, and by the beginning of the 20th century that figure had reached 170,000, a figure bolstered by a massive influx of immigrants, mainly from the Arabian Peninsula, West Africa and the Caribbean, but also from Europe (particularly Ireland and Italy) and the Indian subcontinent, most of whom settled in Cardiff Bay – or Tiger Bay as it was known locally – and Butetown. Large-scale immigration continued after World War II and to this day Cardiff remains one of the largest multi-ethnic communities in Britain.

Not only did the all-powerful Butes dominate the coalfields and control the docks, but they also bankrolled the construction of many of Cardiff's great Civic Centre buildings, or in the case of Cardiff Castle, completely remodelled it. Despite the devastation caused during World War I, there were still 120 shipping companies operating out of Cardiff at the war's end. During World War II, Cardiff was badly blitzed, its docks and other parts of the city reduced to rubble. Cardiff town had become Cardiff city in 1905, but it would be another 50 years before it was declared capital of Wales, and only then after what now seems like pretty unremarkable competition, with all due respect to Aberystwyth and Llandrindod Wells. The decline of the coal trade in the 1960s and the subsequent lack of seaborne traffic sealed the docks' fate and they were left to rot. The 1970s and 1980s was largely a period of stagnation for Cardiff, as it was for much of the country.

The city's renaissance in the late 1990s and early 2000s coincided with devolution and the development of Cardiff Bay, and today, any national institution of consequence in Wales is here in Cardiff: the National Assembly, the National Museum, the Principality Stadium and National Opera, BBC Wales, with its shiny new headquarters outside the train station, as well as all the major film studios.

GETTING THERE AND AWAY

BY CAR Travelling along the M4 from the east, leave at junction 32 and join the A470, from where the city centre is clearly signposted. Travelling from the west, leave the M4 at junction 33 and join the A4232 following signs for the centre; staying on the A4232 will take you all the way to Cardiff Bay. There are several NCP car parks in the city centre, the most convenient of which is in the St David's Centre, which also permits overnight parking. There are others on Westgate Street (mind the one-way system here, though) and Greyfriars.

BY RAIL Your most likely point of arrival if coming by train is Brunel's **Cardiff Central station** [59 E4] on Central Square, from where it's a hop, skip and a very short walk to the main shopping streets. The station is served by hourly trains from London and Bristol (which continue to Swansea), as well as the major routes into the Valleys, such as those going to Merthyr, Pontypridd and Ebbw Vale. Cardiff's second station is **Queen Street** [59 F2], with trains principally serving Barry Island and some of the Valleys as well as Cardiff Bay.

BY BUS Since the main bus station was bulldozed in 2015 to make way for the regeneration of Central Square, including the new headquarters of BBC Wales, Cardiff has been without a dedicated bus station. However, a new station is finally being constructed on Westgate Street [59 E4], slated to open in summer 2023. Until then – unhelpfully and confusingly – buses leave from different parts of the city for different places, so your best bet is to consult w cardiffbus.com. Some of the main destinations include: Abergavenny (roughly hourly Mon–Sat) and Pontypridd (every 20mins), from Greyfriars Road; Barry Island (every 30mins), from Park Street; Caerphilly (every 20mins) and Newport (every 30mins), from Kingsway; and Penarth (hourly), from Canal Street and Park Street. National Express has its own terminus in Sophia Gardens in Bute Park, with long-distance buses operating across Wales and to many destinations in England.

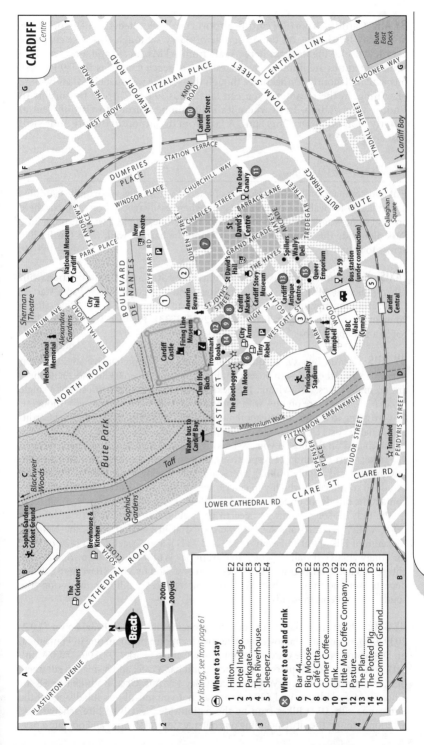

10 Cardiff Queen Street

11 The Dead Canary

7 St David's Centre

2 Aneurin Bevan

1

12 Firing Line Museum

14 The Bootlegger

6 The Moon

8 City Arms

9 Tiny Rebel

13 Cardiff Antique Centre

15 Wally's Deli

Queer Emporium

3

5

BBC Wales (Cymru)

Par 59

Cardiff Central

Bus station (under construction)

National Museum Cardiff

City Hall

Cardiff Castle

Troutmark Books

Clwb Ifor Bach

Water bus to Cardiff Bay

Principality Stadium

The Cricketers

Brewhouse & Kitchen

Sophia Gardens Cricket Ground

Bute East Dock

Tramshed

For listings, see from page 61

Bradt

0   200m
0   200yds

N

3

Cardiff   GETTING THERE AND AWAY

59

BY AIR Cardiff Airport (w cardiff-airport.com) is located 12 miles southwest of the city in Rhoose, on the other side of Barry – though there are currently very few useful flights from here. Apart from ATMs, a café and a few car-hire firms, amenities are limited. The fastest way to reach Cardiff is the T9 Express bus with half-hourly connections, though this service was suspended at the time of writing: in the meantime you can take a bus (905; £2) from the airport to Rhoose train station, from where it's a 40-minute journey to Cardiff Central (hourly Mon–Sat, every 2hrs Sun). A taxi from the airport to the city centre will cost around £30.

GETTING AROUND

Flat and compact, and with most sites of interest within close proximity, Cardiff is a terrific city for walking. Not only is everywhere easily reached on foot, but there are also some wonderful walks in their own right: for example, a walk through Bute Park alongside the River Taff to Llandaff, and the barrage walk from Cardiff Bay across to Penarth.

TAXIS The main taxi rank is to the right as you exit Cardiff Central station, with other ranks on Mill Lane, Greyfriars Road and St Mary's Street. Fares start at £2.50, and a journey across the city should cost no more than £8–10. A few reliable companies include **Dragon Taxis** (☏ 029 2033 3333), **Premier Taxis** (☏ 029 2055 5555) and **Capital Cabs** (☏ 029 2077 7777).

BY BUS Cardiff Bus (w cardiffbus.com) runs a comprehensive and efficient network across the city, with buses running roughly between 05.30 and 23.30; there are no night buses. As a visitor, the tickets you are most likely to use are a single ticket (£2 – exact fare on bus, with both cash and contactless accepted), though if you are going to explore a little more widely, the 'Day to Go' ticket covering Cardiff and Penarth costs £4, and one covering those two plus Barry costs £5.80; these can be purchased on the bus. If you are looking to travel for a few days, then 'Week to Go' tickets cost £15 and £21 respectively, though to get these you will first need to buy an 'iff Card' (apply online); thereafter only weekly (or monthly) tickets can be added to the card, which you can do on the bus. In the event of lost property, contact the bus depot on Sloper Road (◷ 06.00–19.00 Mon–Fri).

The only reason you might need to use public transport within Cardiff is to get to outlying attractions such as the cathedral in Llandaff (#25), the National Museum of History at St Fagans (#320 and #321), and Castell Coch (#26 or #132 for Tongwynlais). If walking down to Cardiff Bay is beyond you, then you have the choice of a half-hourly train from Queen Street station or a bus (Baycar #6), which departs every 30 minutes from Wyndham Street and Cardiff Central station (the south side on Penarth Road).

BY BIKE There are two excellent bike-hire schemes in Cardiff. **Pedal Power** (☏ 029 2039 0713; w cardiffpedalpower.org) has two locations: the main one in Pontcanna, on Dogo Street near the Cardiff Camping and Caravan Park (◷ 10.00–17.00 Mon–Sat), which also does repairs and servicing and has a café; and a smaller, summer-only outlet on Porth Teig Way in Cardiff Bay (◷ Apr–Oct). Both charge £8 for 1 hour, £16 for 4 hours and £20 for the day, but you must book in advance at the Pontcanna site. **OVO Bikes** (run by the nationwide Next Bike hire scheme) has locations around the city (including one outside Central station) and operate a pay-as-you-ride scheme (£1 for the first 30mins, then another £1 for every subsequent 30mins, up to a max of £10 for 24hrs); they've also got e-bikes costing £2 for every 30 minutes up to £30 for 24 hours.

TOURIST INFORMATION

Inexplicably – especially for a capital city – there's no tourist information centre in Cardiff, just an unmanned hut inside the castle grounds where you can pick up a few leaflets (w visitcardiff.com; ⊕ same opening times as castle).

 ## WHERE TO STAY

Cardiff's best accommodation revolves around a select bunch of high-end hotels, but otherwise there's not much available in the mid-range sector, and even less in the budget sector, unless you fancy one of the ubiquitous chain hotels. Alternatively, there is a smattering of guesthouses along Cathedral Road, which is an easy walk from the centre. Hostels are in surprisingly short supply (the main YHA has closed), but there is a decent caravan park and campsite in Pontcanna Park.

Hotel Indigo [59 E2] (122 rooms) Dominions Arcade, Queen St; ☎0871 942 9104; w ihg.com. Despite being part of an international brand, this sparkling city-centre hotel feels very much part of the neighbourhood. Themed rooms can sometimes feel a little earnest, but those here – 'Made in Wales', 'Welsh Industry' & 'Music' – have been brilliantly executed; the 'Music' rooms in particular are fiendishly cool with spotlights, drumstick lamps & pictures of musical icons, while the 'Industry' rooms feature coal scuttle bins. Throughout, bathrooms are tiled in varying shades of green in homage to the Welsh countryside. Public spaces include the Cwtch lounge & Marco Pierre White's Steakhouse Bar & Grill. **£££**

Lincoln House [map, page 57] (6 rooms) 118–120 Cathedral Rd; ☎029 2039 5558; w lincolnhotel.co.uk. The pick of the guesthouses (it's a small hotel really) along this wide, tree-lined avenue linking the city centre with Pontcanna. Its immaculately serviced en-suite rooms include a twin, a 4-poster & a penthouse sleeping 4. Secure parking available. **£££**

✳ **Parkgate** [59 E3] (169 rooms) Westgate St; ☎029 2274 5595; w theparkgatehotel.wales. Cardiff's newest kid on the block, the Parkgate occupies the combined buildings of the former head post office & county court, which date from 1897. Later acquired by the Welsh Rugby Union (it's a conversion kick away from the stadium),

these buildings lay empty for the best part of 20 years until the hotel's opening in 2021. From the moment you step inside reception, it's clear that this is a cut above anything else in town. The rooms certainly don't disappoint: understatedly cool & mercifully uncluttered, they are run through with classy touches like anglepoise lamps & pull-out lights on each side of the bed; the suites have a separate bunk room. A formal but far from snooty restaurant, lounge bar & a gorgeous top-floor spa (costing extra) rounds things off in exemplary fashion. **£££**

Hilton [59 E2] (197 rooms) Kingsway, Greyfriars Rd; ☎029 2064 6300; w hilton.com. A city-centre favourite on the busy Kingsway that's still setting the standards. Rooms on 7 floors are arranged around each side of a soaring triangular atrium, with those on the castle side affording a panorama into the castle grounds, & the higher up you go (floors 6 & 7 have the executive rooms), the better the view; other rooms overlook the Civic Centre buildings & the City Hall's immense clock tower. The rooms themselves are smart & spacious but without any of the fancy-pants stuff you find in so many modern hotels (& that's a good thing). For families, there are dbl rooms & plenty of suites. **££**

Number One Hundred [map, page 57] (7 rooms) 100 Newport Rd; ☎029 2010 5590; w icardiff.co.uk. Not the most flattering of locations, on one of the busiest roads into the city, but if you can get past that, then this attractive Edwardian terraced house is well worth considering. Many of the period features have been retained in the warmly decorated rooms, such as the original fireplaces, which are otherwise furnished with wood-framed mirrors, elegant side lamps & bespoke beds dressed with snazzy cushions & throws. Guests can also avail themselves of the lounge & dining room, which has a microwave. **££**

🏠 **Sleeperz** [59 E4] (74 rooms) Station Approach, Saunders Rd; 📞029 2047 8747; w sleeperz.com. Surely the first rule of travel is don't stay in a hotel anywhere in the vicinity of a train station, right? Wrong, at least where Sleeperz is concerned. Turn immediately right out of the station & you'll find this blocky building harbouring minimalist but surprisingly high-spec rooms decorated in bold reds, oranges & greys; floor-to-ceiling windows allow light to flood in

while the wet-room bathrooms are big enough to squeeze a small army into. Given that some rooms back on to the tracks, the absence of noise is quite an achievement, thanks to superior double-glazed windows. The location couldn't be any more convenient, either for the station or the city centre. Buffet b/fast extra. A selection of accessible & family rooms is available too. **££**

🏠 **The Riverhouse** [59 C3] (12 rooms) 59 Fitzhamon Embankment; 📞029 2010 5590; w icardiff.co.uk. Just a 5min walk from the centre & with head-on views of the Principality Stadium, this is about as restful a stay as you could wish for. Owned by the same folk who run Number One Hundred (page 61), the spotlessly clean rooms, some with bunks but all with shared bathrooms, sleep between 1 & 4 people, & there's also a communal kitchen & dining room. Continental b/fast costs £4. **£**

✖ WHERE TO EAT AND DRINK

While it's not unkind to suggest that Cardiff doesn't rank that highly in the pecking order of Britain's fine-dining destinations (interestingly it's the only capital city in the UK and Ireland without a Michelin-starred restaurant, for what it's worth), there's no question that the scene is changing for the better. With a few exceptions, the city centre itself is a little bereft when it comes to worthwhile restaurants, hence you'll need to root around some of the outlying areas in order to find Cardiff's best dining establishments.

You don't have to travel quite so far for good coffee, with a dense concentration of independent coffee shops in the city centre (the arcades are always worth staking out), but again, some of the more innovative places are emerging in some of the further-flung corners.

RESTAURANTS

✳✖ **Clink** [59 G2] HMP Cardiff, Knox Rd; 📞029 2092 3130; w theclinkcharity.org; ⏱ noon–15.30 Thu–Sat, noon–15.30 Sun, plus 18.00–21.30 Fri & Sat. The concept at Clink is as bold as it is brilliant. As part of their training for a City & Guilds qualification in food & beverage services, inmates are trained up in bartending & waiting among other things. But make no mistake, this is professional-quality food; the restaurant uses only British produce that's in season & from local suppliers, including the gardens at HMP Prescoed in Pontypool & HMP Send in Woking; the one caveat is that there is no alcohol. Moreover, the restaurant does actually look like a restaurant; in fact it looks & feels very classy, with some of the furniture made by prisoners from HMP

Frankland in County Durham. A memorable dining experience is assured, but it won't just be the food you're raving about when you leave. Perhaps most importantly, though, not only have statistics shown that the rate of reoffending at the 4 prisons in the UK currently running the scheme has dropped dramatically, but many former prisoners have also gone on to work in restaurants up & down the country. **£££**

✖ **The Heathcock** [map, page 57] 58–60 Bridge St; 📞029 2115 2290; w heathcockcardiff. com; ⏱ 17.00–23.00 Mon & Tue, noon–23.30 Wed & Thu, noon–00.30 Fri & Sat, noon–16.00 Sun. Located amid the leafy lanes of Llandaff, this is another promising addition to the city's burgeoning roster of exciting restaurants. It's a pleasantly utilitarian space of pub dining room

& bar, with a menu of small plates & sharing dishes alongside a healthy selection of mains; with its farm-to-fork (or sea-to-fork) ethos, dishes comprise the likes of slow-roasted Vale of Glamorgan lamb & Welsh-landed fish (pan-fried pollock with red-wine-braised cuttlefish); it offers lush puds too such as damson soufflé, & buttermilk pudding & honeycomb. They also make all their own sourdough bread on site. If you don't fancy going large, you can munch on flaky sausage rolls from the bar menu, perfect with a pint of Bragdy Twt Lol Twti Ffrwti from the Trefforest Brewery in Pontypridd. Note that food is not served on Mon & Tue. £££

✕ **Pasture** [59 D3] 8–10 High St; m 07511 217422; w pasturerestaurant.com; ⊕ 11.45–23.00 Mon–Thu, 11.45–midnight Fri & Sat, 11.45–18.00 Sun. Along with the Potted Pig across the road, Pasture is one of the few city-centre restaurants worth considering, & it has garnered no end of plaudits since opening in 2020. Moreover, it was about time the city had a decent steakhouse, & it's clear from the meat cleavers & saws hanging ominously on the walls & the beautiful cuts of meat – all the beef is taken from cattle reared on Welsh farms & raised on pasture (wouldn't you know) before it's aged for a minimum 35 days – that this place means business. A quality selection of wines & cocktails too. £££

✕ **The Potted Pig** [59 D3] 27 High St; ✆ 029 2022 4817; w thepottedpig.com; ⊕ 18.00–21.00 Tue, noon–14.30 & 18.00–21.00 Wed & Thu, noon–14.30 & 17.00–21.30 Fri, noon–15.30 & 17.00–21.30 Sat, noon–15.30 Sun. Sequestered in the reconditioned vaults of an old bank & one of the few restaurants in town that has stayed the course, the Potted Pig continues to offer food & service unmatched by most other places in the city. The menu, as the name suggests, is largely piggy-oriented (crispy pig's ear with black pudding, three pork cassoulet, or a whole suckling pig if you can manage it), but there's much more besides, like lamb sweetbread & peas, & rabbit pappardelle with wild mushrooms. It's at the slightly pricier end of things but good value nonetheless. £££

✕ **Purple Poppadom** [map, page 57] 185a Cowbridge Rd; ✆ 029 2022 0026; w purplepoppadom.com; ⊕ 17.00–23.00 Tue–Sat, 13.00–21.00 Sun. It's not the most promising location in the world, but the Purple

Poppadom has consistently been one of the city's finest restaurants – Indian or otherwise – for some 15 years now. Overseen by Kerala-born chef Anand George, many of the dishes reflect his love of the sea, with mouthwatering concoctions like crispy crab croquettes & tiffin seabass with curry leaf-infused mash & raw mango. Indian food doesn't get any better than this, not here in Cardiff anyway. £££

✳ ✕ **Anna Loka** [map, page 57] 114 Albany Rd; ✆ 029 2048 9773; w anna-loka. com; ⊕ 10.00–14.00 & 17.00–21.00 Tue–Sat, 10.00–16.00 Sun. In a city that is becoming increasingly vegan-oriented, Anna Loka is leading the way. It was opened by Adam, a Hare Krishna monk, back in 2015 when veganism was still quite niche, & if Adam can't preach the goodness of a plant-based diet then frankly no-one can. The menu is just as likely to appeal to carnivores as it is to vegans, with all kinds of clever variations on wraps, burgers & other mains (from fish & chips to chana masala), many with nods to Indian & Asian flavours. Out in Roath, a 20min walk from the centre. ££

✕ **Bar 44** [59 D3] 15–23 Westgate St; ✆ 0333 344 4049; w bar44.co.uk; ⊕ 16.30–23.00 Wed, noon–23.00 Thu, Fri & Sat, noon–18.00 Sun. A small slice of Iberia comes to Cardiff courtesy of this convivial tapas bar, 1 branch of a small local chain, with others in Cowbridge & Penarth. There's a busy but easy-going vibe about the place, with waiting staff scuttling around with vibrant plates of food like sherry-soaked Payoyo cheese with rosemary sea salt, & cider-poached Leon chorizo; most dishes go for between £5 & £10 a pop. The all-Spanish wine list includes a terrific selection of vegan wines. ££

✳ ✕ **Café Citta** [59 E3] 4 Church St; ✆ 029 2022 4040; w cafecitta.has.restaurant; ⊕ noon–23.00 Tue–Sat. Discreetly tucked away on a busy pedestrianised street, this fabulous, family-run pizzeria has comfortably seen off most of its city-centre competitors over the years & there's little sign that standards are slipping. No airs or graces here, just good old-fashioned wood-fired pizzas made using doughs & sauces prepared on site & locally sourced ingredients. If pizza doesn't take your fancy, there's plenty more like *salsicce* & *spinaci* (sautéed Italian sausage with spinach & chillis) & *linguine citta* (sun-blushed tomatoes with ricotta cheese & roasted pine nuts). ££

✖ Dusty's Pizza [map, page 57] The Boneyard, Papermill Rd; **m** 07566 798627; **w** dustyspizza. co.uk; ⏰ 17.00–23.00 Wed–Fri, 10.00–23.00 Sat, 10.00–15.00 Sun. If you're committed to tracking down the best pizza in town, then head west to this atmospheric (covered & heated) outdoor seating venue situated amid a funky little artistic hub near Victoria Park. These are not your run-of-the-mill pizzas, but instead expect creative morsels like the seafood one with Penclawdd cockles & laverbread. Take-aways too. **££**

✖ Milkwood [map, page 57] 83 Pontcanna St; **** 029 2023 2226; **w** milkwoodcardiff.com; ⏰ 08.00–16.00 Mon–Fri, 09.00–16.00 Sat & Sun. During the pandemic, the folk here at Milkwood changed their modus operandi from high-end bistro to something approaching a café/diner, & it's still brilliant. All-day brunches (hands down the best in town) are its forte, but there's plenty more besides including *huevos rancheros* (a Mexican-style b/fast), *cubano* sandwiches & salads. **££**

✖ Mint & Mustard [map, page 57] 134 Whitchurch Rd; **** 029 2062 0333; **w** mintandmustard.net; ⏰ 17.00–22.00 Mon–Fri, noon–22.00 Sat & Sun. Although not as refined as the Purple Popaddom (page 63), Mint was the city's original pioneer of Indian fine dining, & its staying power is testament to its sustained quality. You'd do well to begin with their signature starter, the melt-in-the-mouth *bombay chaat* (dough balls with sweet yoghurt, tamarind & chickpea) but choices get tricky thereafter: the curries, including salmon chatti & paneer masala, are sensational, as are the tandoori grills & thalis (veggie/vegan, meat or fish). The restaurant itself looks great & the service is attentive without being overbearing. There's now also a branch in Penarth. **££**

BAKERIES AND COFFEE SHOPS

☕ Big Moose [59 E2] 4–5 Frederick St; **m** 07542 850251; **w** bigmoosecoffeecompany.co; ⏰ 10.00–15.30 Mon–Fri & Sun, 09.30–16.00 Sat. The idea for Big Moose came about when the café's owners were running a soup kitchen for the city's homeless, which morphed into this quiet little retreat just off busy Queen St & has proved to be quite a hit. All the proceeds go back into providing therapy, intervention & other services related to

mental health, homelessness & suicide prevention. The coffee's not bad either. **£**

☕ Corner Coffee [59 D3] 13 High St; **** 029 2132 0400; **w** cornercoffee.uk; ⏰ 09.00–17.00 daily. Easy-going city-centre joint run by a team of coffee obsessives who know their beans; be it a cappuccino, ristretto or lungo, the quality is consistently high & the service impeccable. There's just about enough seating inside, but in warmer weather the tables out in the arcade are very pleasant indeed. **£**

✷ ☕ The Little Man Coffee Company [59 F3] Ivor Hse, Bridge St; **m** 07933 844234; ⏰ 08.00–17.00 Mon–Sat, 10.00–16.00 Sun. If you prefer your coffee in the comfort of quieter surrounds, then come to the Little Man, occupying a corner building that was once home to a bank & post office. The space is light & airy (making it a good place to work), it's restful, & the coffee is first rate (there are usually a couple of blends on the go at any one time), as is the selection of sticky cakes. As an inducement to take up residence for the day, they offer unlimited coffee, a cake & lunch for £16. **£**

☕ The Plan [59 E3] 28–29 Morgan Arcade; **** 029 2039 8764; ⏰ 08.45–17.00 Mon–Sat, 10.00–16.00 Sun. A bright & buzzy 2-storeyed coffee bar in one of the city's more elegant arcades, The Plan was one of Cardiff's original coffee pioneers & remains one of the best destinations in town. Lots of tempting coffee options, from a heart-stopping espresso to a *piccolo*, a single espresso shot with a creamy layer of milk. The food's pretty good too, with b/fast, brunches & light lunches all served. **£**

✷ ☕ Sibling [map, page 57] 39 Lochaber St; **w** siblingcardiff.co.uk; ⏰ 08.00–16.30 Tue–Thu, 08.00–21.00 Fri, 09.00–21.00 Sat. Unless you're in Roath visiting its great park, you're unlikely to venture out this way, which is a shame as you'd be missing out on one of the city's best neighbourhood coffee shops. Formerly a brothel, brother-&-sister team Will and Georgie have done a terrific job renovating the small space, which is little more than the counter & a trio of thin communal tables plus an itsy bit of outdoor space. All the magic comes from a single grinder, your coffee & is best enjoyed with some sourdough toast & Welsh honey, or a pastry from the Ty Melin bakery. On Fri & Sat evenings the venue morphs into a brilliant little wine bar with small plates, though wine is also available to try throughout the day. £

⊑⚹ Uncommon Ground [59 E3] 10–12 Royal Arcade; **w** uncommon-ground.co.uk; ⏰ 07.30–18.30 Mon–Sat, 10.00–17.30 Sun. Frankly, you could take your pick from any number of coffee shops sheltered within the city's arcades, but this place is definitely up there, both for its delicious array of caffeine fixes brewed various ways (aeropress, V60, espresso) & its thoughtfully designed interior – squishy leather sofas, communal tables & hollowed-out copper kettles for lights; the best seats are those underneath the big bay windows (great for gawping) or the pew-style benches outside in the arcade itself. A word of warning, though – they don't take too kindly to laptop squatters; you have an hour, give or take, unless you keep topping up that is. £

ENTERTAINMENT AND NIGHTLIFE

Cardiff is renowned for its boisterous nightlife, and that's putting it mildly: a youthful population combined with a huge student contingent ensures that on any given night of the week the city's pubs and bars are rammed. Many of Cardiff's pubs have histories that stretch back centuries, while others are unaltered Victorian or Edwardian period pieces. Factor in a plentiful supply of trendy, modern bars, and there's enough to cater for all preferences. For years, the only brewery in town was Brains, established in the late 19th century, but an emerging craft brewery market has shaken things up a bit; ones to look out for include Crafty Devil in Canton and Pipes Up in Pontcanna.

Although there's a dearth of decent small-to-medium-sized live music venues, you can normally hear live jazz, folk and rock in one or other of the city's pubs, and for really big events, the Principality Stadium or the grounds of Cardiff Castle are pressed into service.

PUBS AND BARS

⊑⚹ Brewhouse and Kitchen [59 B1] Sophia Cl; ☎ 029 2037 1599; **w** brewhouseandkitchen.com; ⏰ 11.00–23.00 Tue–Thu, 11.00–midnight Fri & Sat, noon–23.00 Sun & Mon. In the shadow of the cricket ground at the entrance to Sophia Gardens, the old gatekeeper's lodge has recently been taken over by an ambitious brewpub group, though it does appear to have retained the cool disposition of its legendary forerunner, Mochyn Du. Interior furnishings are sympathetic to the character of the building itself (large barrel tables, bottle lights) while the beer, brewed on site, is excellent, with at least half a dozen core (cask & keg) beers on the go plus seasonal specials & a brewer's tap choice. This has always been the most 'Welsh' of the city's pubs & to this end all signs & menus are in the native tongue.

⊑⚹ City Arms [59 D3] 10–12 Quay St; ☎ 029 2064 1913; **w** sabrainpubs.com; ⏰ noon–23.00 daily. Just a conversion kick away from the Principality Stadium, you can't beat this good old-fashioned boozer for its rollicking atmosphere, especially on match days when half of Cardiff seems to decamp here. Although a Brains pub, the beers here aren't limited to the brewery, with a decent selection of guest ales & bottled beers also available. If you haven't got a ticket for the game, there are plenty of big screens – standing room only mind.

⊑⚹ The Cricketers [59 B1] 66 Cathedral Rd; ☎ 029 2034 5102; **w** cricketerscardiff.co.uk; ⏰ noon–23.00 daily. So-named because it's just a short hit away from the Sophia Gardens cricket ground, this handsome Victorian townhouse is one of Cardiff's more refined hostelries. The pretty, sun-kissed courtyard is perfect in warmer weather, where you might even hear the sound of leather on willow across the way. They do a mean Sun lunch too.

⊑⚹ St Canna's Alehouse [map, page 57] 42 Llandaff Rd; **m** 07890 106449; **w** stcannas. com; ⏰ 16.30–23.30 Mon–Fri, noon–23.00 Sat, noon–22.00 Sun. There's a fabulous community feel about this tiny micropub, in a red-brick corner building just across the road from Chapter (page 66). In fact you might just as well be in someone's living room such is this happily cluttered space where locals huddle around small tables supping

3

lovely beer & idly chatting. Live music/gigs, open mic on Wed & plenty of other fun happenings.

Tiny Rebel [59 D3] 25 Westgate St; m 07377 414204; w tinyrebel.co.uk; ⏰ noon–02.00 daily. 1 of the 3 brew bars belonging to the ace Newport-based venture (the other 2 are in Newport), this big, bare-bricked venue gives you the opportunity to sample any number of their bewildering long list of beers, like the award-winning Cwtch red ale, a refreshingly crisp 313 pale ale, or the fun & fruity Seacider, a blood orange-infused cider; there's good food too to soak it all up. Entertainment comes in the form of live music, comedy, a cracking quiz every 3rd Wed of the month, & yoga & beer evenings, though to be honest we're not quite sure how that one works.

Par 59 [59 E4] Basement Unit at Imperial Gate, St Mary St; ☎ 029 2252 0059; w par59. com ; ⏰ 17.00–midnight Mon–Wed & Sun, 15.00–midnight Thu, noon–01.00 Fri–Sat. Which is the total par score for the 2 9-hole mini-golf courses that have been creatively integrated into this cool underground bar, the brainchild of Welsh superstar footballer Gareth Bale, who was frequently accused by Real Madrid fans of putting golf before footie – a sly retort perhaps? Of course you don't *have* to play golf to enjoy this place, but it'd certainly be far more entertaining if you did.

The Dead Canary [59 F3] Barrack Lane; ☎ 029 2023 1263; w thedeadcanary.co.uk; ⏰ 17.00–late Tue–Sun. Brilliant name aside, The Dead Canary is something just a little bit different. Firstly you need to book online, then upon arrival – it's the graffitied, black-painted building with a 'Fire Exit/Keep Clear' door with a birdcage above it – ring the bell (as instructed) & you'll be escorted down a corridor & into a gorgeous, grown-up cavern. The playful menu offers a wide & unusual range of cocktails bearing wondrous names like Vortigern's Dragon (turmeric-infused gin, marmalade syrup & lemon), Quetzalcoatl (tequila, blood orange, agave & lime) & Birds of Rhiannon (Arette Blanco tequila, cucumber, strega egg white & matcha tea), & for those of a non-alcoholic persuasion there's a thoughtfully curated selection of mocktails. Each drink will set you back around £9–12.

LIVE MUSIC

The Bootlegger [59 D3] 5A Womanby St; ☎ 029 2037 3482; w bootleggerbars.com. Directly opposite Clwb Ifor Bach, Bootlegger has tapped into the jazz market, but there's also soul, hip hop, funk & 50s/60s rock'n'roll; upstairs is a classy cocktail bar.

Clwb Ifor Bach [59 D3] 11 Womanby St; ☎ 029 2023 2199; w clwb.net. 40 years old in 2023, Cardiff's, & Wales's, musical roots are still firmly anchored within this stalwart club, which is renowned for both the quantity & quality of the bands it fosters, many of whom are of Welsh origin. In 2022, the Manic Street Preachers played the club 32 years after their one & only previous appearance here at an anti-poll tax gig. They also have some belting club nights.

The Moon [59 D3] 3 Womanby St; w themooncardiff.com. Completing the remarkable trio of live music venues on this one (very short) street, the Moon is an intimate 140-capacity non-profit live music venue staging gigs as well as stand-up, poetry, spoken word & raucous club nights.

Tramshed [59 C4] Clare Rd; ☎ 029 2023 5555; w tramshedcardiff.com. The city's best small-to-medium-sized venue (though still with only a capacity of only 1,000), Grangetown's popular Tramshed attracts established indie bands (Metronomy, Maximo Park) as well as hosting regular club nights, occasionally with a big name to the fore like Paul Oakenfold.

THEATRES, CINEMAS AND ART CENTRES

Chapter [map, page 57] Market Rd; ☎ 029 2031 1050; w chapter.org; ⏰ 09.00–22.00 Sun–Wed, 09.00–23.00 Thu–Sat. Occupying the old Canton High School premises since opening in 1971 (following a benefit gig in Sophia Gardens featuring Pink Floyd & Black Sabbath), the wonderful, multi-artform Chapter was Wales's first arts centre, & remains one of its most outward-looking. Under the one roof are 2 cinemas showing independent, world & mainstream movies, 2 theatres hosting contemporary visual art & performance works, a gallery, artists' studios & a buzzing café-cum-bar, worth a visit even if you're not here for a performance.

New Theatre [59 E2] Park Pl; ☎ 0343 310 0041; w newtheatrecardiff.co.uk. Popular city-centre venue that delivers a packed programme of crowd-pleasing fare, from music & comedy to musicals & panto, much of it oriented towards a younger audience.

Sherman Theatre [59 E1] Senghennydd Rd; ☏029 2064 6900; w shermantheatre.co.uk. Since its inception in 1973, this well-respected theatre has consistently produced compelling, often provocative, theatre, including many radical reworkings of classic texts. Moreover, the theatre's strong Welsh orientation (many performances are in Welsh & English) makes it very popular with native speakers. Things lighten up around Christmas when the theatre stages some of the city's best pantos.

St David's Hall [59 E3] The Hayes; ☏029 2087 8444; w stdavidshallcardiff.co.uk; ⏰ 09.30–17.00 Mon–Fri on non-performance days. Opened in 1979 & located within the shopping centre of the same name, this big old auditorium (capacity 2,000) is showing its age a little these days, but remains a popular venue for touring bands &

musicians – of a certain age shall we say, although they do host some contemporary folk & world musicians too. There's a mixed bag of other stuff too, including comedy, dance & ballet, plus regular performances by the BBC National Orchestra of Wales (although their 'home' is the Millennium Centre) & other classical ensembles.

Wales Millennium Centre Bute Pl; ☏029 2063 6464; w wmc.org.uk; ⏰ 10.00–18.00 daily on non-performance days. Home to no fewer than 9 cultural organisations, including the Welsh National Opera, the BBC National Orchestra & Chorus of Wales, & National Dance Company Wales, this marvellous building, housing the acoustically superb 1,900-seat Donald Gordon Theatre, in addition to several other performance spaces, stages everything from opera & dance to ballet & comedy, & touring West End musicals. Don't pass up the opportunity to catch a performance here if you possibly can.

SHOPPING

Despite the relentless march of the big chains – most of which are corralled into the St David's Centre (including the only branch of John Lewis in Wales), and to a lesser extent along Queen Street – it's still possible to track down some excellent independent traders. The best places to start investigating are the wonderful Victorian arcades, where you'll find all manner of singularly unique outlets selling anything from secondhand books and antiques to bespoke clothing and skateboard gear. There's also the indoor market, whose wraparound balcony is home to vendors whose wares range from vintage threads to vinyl. Cardiff's markets are well worth making time for too.

Cardiff Antique Centre [59 E3] 21 Royal Arcade; ☏029 2039 8891; ⏰ 10.00–16.30 Mon–Sat. Small shop with shelves groaning under the weight of just about anything you can think of: Corgi toys, Hornby trains, scale models & Groggs (page 200).

Queer Emporium [59 E3] 2 Royal Arcade; w thequeeremporium.co.uk; ⏰ 11.00–18.00 daily. The name's a bit of a giveaway. This cool, colourful store brings together some 20 LGBTQIA+ business ventures under 1 roof, selling anything & everything, from clothes, hats & bags to art & books; there's a great little outdoor café for once you're done browsing. A great roster of events too, from stand-up to literary evenings.

Spillers [59 E3] 27 Morgan Arcade; ☏029 2022 4905; w spillersrecords.uk; ⏰ 11.00–17.00 Tue–Sat. The world's oldest record store, established

in 1894. Don't be fooled by the relatively small interior as there isn't much you won't be able to source here (CDs & vinyl), whether it's punk & hardcore or Welsh dub-reggae, & the informed staff really do know their stuff. Loads of great T-shirts too. Keep an eye out for both local & big-name in-store signings and gigs; past visitors have included James Dean Bradfield from the Manics & The Pixies. The website has a comprehensive new release list each week.

Troutmark Books [59 D3] 39–43 Castle Arcade; ☏029 2038 2814; w troutmarkbooks. com; ⏰ 10.00–17.15 Mon–Sat, 11.15–16.00 Sun. Shuffling through this narrow shop with its teetering bookcases unnervingly stuffed to the ceiling with titles of every possible genre, you'll think you've seen it all, only to find a further warren of rooms downstairs in the basement.

Cardiff boasts several terrific weekly farmer's markets (w riversidemarket. org.uk), ideal for stocking up on picnic supplies or for a few treats for home. The original (and biggest) one is the **Riverside Market** on the Fitzhamon Embankment (opposite the Principality Stadium) every Sunday (⏲ 10.00–14.00), where you can pick up anything from homemade jams, honeys and breads to cheese and fresh fruit and veg – there are also plenty of street-food vendors doling out steaming curries, oak-fired pizzas and the like. As well as this, there's a **Riverside night market** (⏲ 17.00–20.00) on the last Wednesday of each month. On Saturday mornings (⏲ 09.30–13.00), **Roath Market** on Keppoch Street features some of the traders from the Riverside Market, and on Fridays (⏲ 10.00–13.00) it's the turn of the cool little **Rhiwbina Market**, 5 miles north of the centre at Ye Old Butcher's Arms on Heol-y-Felin; if you don't fancy the walk from the centre, it's a 10-minute stroll from Rhiwbina train station. There's often live music at these markets too.

Wally's Deli [59 E3] 38–42 Royal Arcade; ☏ 029 2022 9265; w wallysdeli.co.uk; ⏲ 08.30–17.30 Mon–Sat. A Cardiff institution, the shelves here heave with colourful, mouthwatering produce, expertly conditioned Welsh farmhouse & artisan cheeses, charcuterie, as well as organic wines & beers, chocolates & confectionery, & loads more.

WHAT TO SEE AND DO

Compared with most cities, Cardiff's commercial centre – bounded by Central station to the south, Queen Street station to the east, the castle to the north, and the Principality Stadium to the west – is surprisingly compact. Packed with the familiar high-street retailers, **Queen Street** is the main shopping thoroughfare and the location for a quartet of heavy-cast bronze sculptures by Robert Thomas, one of the founder members of a Rhondda-based group of artists in the 1950s. Walking east to west, there's *The Miner*, which speaks for itself, as do *The Family* and *Mother and Son* just beyond. Bookending the street, atop a large pedestal, is an oversized sculpture of a neatly coiffured **Aneurin Bevan** [59 E2], former Labour Minister for Health and founder of the NHS (page 184) – occasionally he'll have a traffic cone on his head.

St Mary's Street is the place for restaurants and bars – certainly not an area for the faint-hearted of a Saturday evening, with stag and hen parties carousing between pubs. It is worth glancing up at the appealing mélange of Victorian and Edwardian architecture, as well as having a nose around **Cardiff Market** [59 E3], which has stood on this spot – originally site of the old town gaol – since 1891. Look out for the plaque at the High Street entrance to the market denoting the spot where Dic Penderyn, one of the principal antagonists in the Merthyr Rising (page 190), was hanged in 1831. There's not much you won't be able to find here on the market's two floors (the upper floor is balconied), with shops and stalls selling fruit and veg, cheese, confectionery, books, records and vintage clothing among other things.

Running parallel to St Mary's, the **Hayes** is a far more appealing thoroughfare, albeit flanked on one side by the **St David's Centre**, a gargantuan two-tiered mega mall that was massively extended in 2009 to elevate Cardiff into the premier league of British shopping destinations, and also incorporates the St David's Concert Hall (page 67). At the point where the Hayes forks between Trinity Street and Working Street is the **Old Library** (1882), which, aside from the modern glass entrance porch, retains much of its Victorian grandeur. This was home to the city library until 1988 (now located at the southern end of the Hayes) and today houses the **Cardiff Story Museum** [59 E3], which offers a short but enjoyable romp through the city's history courtesy of locally donated objects. While here, don't pass up the opportunity to view the floor-to-ceiling tiled corridor, which was the library's original entrance; the tiles were designed by Maw & Co and depict images of the four seasons. The corridor can be accessed even when the museum is closed. Two floors of the building have recently become the home of the Royal Welsh College of Music, thereby ensuring the Old Library's status as one of the city centre's most vital cultural hubs.

Infinitely more pleasant places to shop are Cardiff's 19th-century **arcades**. Of the seven, the two most appealing are the **Royal Arcade** – the first to open in 1858 – and **Morgan Arcade**, both of which run between the Hayes and St Mary's Street, with the others clustered together up towards the castle. Within each one, you'll find all kinds of emporia selling everything from vintage clothing and graphic art to musical instruments, board games and Cuban cigars; here too are some of the city's best delis and independent coffee houses.

Central Square has also seen quite some changes recently; exit the station and you're now confronted by the glassy headquarters of BBC Cymru (Wales), to the right of which the long-awaited bus station is finally beginning to take shape, though they've been at it for years. Across the road from the BBC building, on Wood Street, is a statue of Wales's first black headteacher and campaigner, **Betty Campbell** (1934–2017) [59 E4]. It's chiefly remarkable in that it was the first statue of a named non-fictionalised woman to be erected (in 2021) in a public space anywhere in Wales; but just like buses, they all seem to come along at once and there is now a second statue dedicated to the writer Elaine Morgan in Mountain Ash in the Valleys.

CARDIFF CASTLE [59 D2] (Castle St; ✆ 029 2087 8100; w cardiffcastle.com; ⊕ Mar–Oct 10.00–18.00 Mon–Fri, 09.00–18.00 Sat & Sun, Nov–Feb 10.00–17.00 Mon–Fri, 09.00–17.00 Sat & Sun; £14.50) Tucked into the southeastern corner of Bute Park and hemmed in by two of the city's busiest roads, the spacious grounds of Cardiff Castle make for some welcome relief from all the outside noise. A Gothic Victorian fantasy of the most ostentatious kind, the main castle building as you see it today was the work of the coal-rich Third Marquess of Bute (John Crichton-Stuart) and maverick architect William Burges. Unimpressed with the way the castle had previously been restored, Bute employed Burges – a man with a similarly obsessive take on medieval kitsch – to fulfil his wildest Gothic fantasies. Following the marquess's premature death in 1900 at the age of 53 (Burges died in 1881), the estate passed over to the Fourth Marquess, also John Crichton-Stuart, who continued work on the castle until he died in 1947, whereupon the Bute family bequeathed both the castle and Bute Park to the city; there's some footage of the handover on YouTube.

The castle's history goes much farther back than Lord Bute, however, as determined by sections of the outer wall where red, Tetris-like patches of Roman stonework can clearly be seen on the south-facing side, to the right of the entrance. Bute was so keen to preserve what was left of the castle's Roman identity that he decided to reconstruct on top of the old fort, which makes this singularly unique anywhere in Europe. More obvious is the lofty, 12-sided Norman motte-

and-bailey **keep**, the finest of its kind in the country – it was certainly the most well-protected part of the complex. From the top there are sublime views of the castle grounds spread out below and the spidery white steel girders of the Principality Stadium.

Within the **castle** itself it's possible to view a selection of rooms on a self-guided tour but you'll get to see more areas if you take a guided tour, for which there is a small additional fee. The most impressive rooms are the church-like Banqueting Hall, featuring a gloriously kitsch chimneypiece, the well-stocked library, complete with Burges's original bookcases and tables, and another superb fireplace, above which are carvings signifying the five ancient languages: Greek, Hebrew, Assyrian, Hieroglyphics and Runic. Burges was also an innovator, and when he had central heating installed, radiators here in the library were concealed within the bases of the tables. A guided tour gets you access to all the above rooms plus the Winter Smoking Room, Roof Garden, Nursery and Lord Bute's Bedroom, notable for its bevelled ceiling mirrors and walnut enclosed bathtub, which was about as extravagant as it got in those days.

If you've still got the energy, in the basement of reception the **Firing Line Museum** (included as part of the castle entry) documents the history of The Queen's Dragoon Guards and The Royal Welsh Regiment. All the major conflicts are covered, including the Battle of Waterloo, Rorke's Drift (part of the Anglo-Zulu wars), both World Wars as well as more recent deployments in Iraq and Afghanistan. A bigger crowd favourite is the animal wall, a series of cheeky, stone-carved creatures perched atop the wall to the left of the castle entrance all the way to the bridge. Curiously, none of the animals – the drawings for which were conceived by Burges, though he died before the wall was complete – are native to the United Kingdom; among them, there's a leopard, a vulture, a bear and an anteater, whose nose was replaced after being chopped off.

NATIONAL MUSEUM CARDIFF [59 E1] (Cathays Park; ☎ 0300 111 2333; w museum. wales/cardiff; ⏲ 10.00–17.00 Tue–Sun; free) More compact and restrained than neighbouring City Hall, the National Museum was inaugurated in 1927 by King George V, a statue of whom stands opposite. The museum is a two-parter: the **Evolution of Wales Gallery** on the ground floor is a whistle-stop tour through the geology of the nation, though, oddly, much of what is on show comes from other continents, even the moon; a chunk of basaltic rock from the 1969 Apollo moon landing has somehow found its way to Cardiff. Elsewhere, there are gold nuggets from Dolgellau and a coarse-grained gabbro rock from Old Radnor in Powys, which, at 702 million years, makes it the oldest known specimen in Wales. All kinds of weird and wonderful fossils are on display, but the star of the show is a more recent discovery. In 2014, two brothers out at Lavernock Point stumbled across some dinosaur remains (skull, claws, teeth and a foot bone), which were subsequently determined to be those of a Jurassic-era dinosaur, the first found on Welsh soil. It was given the title *Dracoraptor hanigani* ('Dragon Robber'), the second part named in honour of the brothers. Also on the ground floor is the eminently missable Natural History section, full of the usual stuffed suspects.

The museum's strongest suit is its art collection. Though by no means as vast as national collections found elsewhere in Britain, its coverage of Welsh art is unrivalled, while it also includes a clutch of exquisite Old Masters and some superb Impressionist works. The gallery also benefits greatly from being a manageable size, its series of airy rooms enlivened by imaginative displays and a pleasantly unrushed atmosphere.

The Welsh landscape – its mountains, valleys, lakes, coast, castles and coalfields – have provided inspiration to legions of painters for centuries, and it comes together spectacularly in the **Welsh Landscapes Gallery** (no 7). The most celebrated of a formidable trio of artists, which included William Parry and Thomas Jones, was Richard Wilson (1713–82), who not only revolutionised Welsh landscape art but is considered by many to be Wales's finest ever painter and a worthy contemporary to the likes of Hogarth and Reynolds, both of whom are represented in gallery 4 (Art in 18th-century Britain). Having spent his formative painting years in Italy, Wilson returned to Wales, painting among others *Caernarfon Castle* and *Pembroke Town and Castle* – both to lustrous effect – and, although not in Wales, *Lydford Waterfalls*, where you can just about make out the figure at the top of the hill. One of Jones's contributions is *A View from Radnorshire*. But the Welsh landscape wasn't solely the preserve of its native painters: L S Lowry's large-scale *Six Bells, Abertillery* evokes beautifully the industrial grimescape of the valleys.

Turning towards some of the great European painters, the museum is heavily indebted to two local sisters, Margaret and Gwendoline Davies, who bequeathed an outstanding number of paintings, including pieces by Cezanne, Degas, Pissarro and Sisley, whose *Cliff at Penarth* resonates more than any other picture here as he was the only major French Impressionist to come to Wales to paint. The sisters also left more than half a dozen paintings by Monet, though it is Van Gogh's superlative *Rain, Auvers*, painted shortly before he took his own life, that most visitors gravitate to first. Other crowd-pleasing names include Matisse, Picasso and Renoir, whose *La Parisienne*, a near-life-size woman sporting a luscious blue bustle dress, is one of the museum's most enduring paintings – the sitter is the French actress Henriette Henriot who modelled for Renoir on several occasions.

Important later Welsh artists include Pembrokeshire siblings Augustus and Gwen John, both featured here in gallery 15, entitled British Art around 1900. Gwen, who spent most of her life in France where she had a ten-year affair with Rodin, never received the same level of recognition as her more flamboyant younger brother. She was also more conservative, for example her fresco-like *Girl in a Blue Dress* (most of her sitters were anonymous females), which contrasts with Augustus's effervescent family portraits *Dorelia McNeill in the Garden at Alderney Manor* and *Pyramus John* (Dorelia, his wife and Pyramus, his son who died aged just eight). Wales's most important mid 20th-century artist was Ceri Richards (1903–71), whose largely Surrealist work was inspired by music and poetry, and specifically Dylan Thomas – for example, the wildly colourful *Cycle of Nature* was based on Thomas's 1933 poem *The force that through the green fuse drives the flower*. Muscling in on this predominantly Welsh collection are some of England's most celebrated names, including Freud, Bacon, Hockney and Whiteread, all of whom are represented by a piece or two at least.

Sir William Goscombe John, a key figure in the Welsh cultural revival of the late 19th century and one of the foremost British sculptors of the time, is represented by a generous number of works in the rotunda. Basing much of his work on Rodin, whom he studied in Paris for a year, Goscombe John is known above all for his public memorials, which you'll come across all over South Wales and beyond (there's even one in Baghdad in Iraq), but he was no less adept at smaller, more intimate pieces, many of which verge on the homoerotic, like the lithe *Morpheus* and the bronze relief *Glamour of the Rose*. Interestingly, one of several pieces here by Rodin is the bronze *Head of Whistler's Muse (Head of Gwen John)* in gallery 16 – a nod (excuse the pun) to his relationship with the Welsh artist.

CATHAYS PARK AND THE CIVIC CENTRE Beyond the grand ceremonial avenue that is Boulevard de Nantes (named after the city twinned with Cardiff), Cathays Park is an area of neatly proportioned Edwardian buildings. Together these comprise the Civic Centre, front and centre of which is **City Hall** [59 E1] (🕘 08.30–17.00 Mon–Fri; w cardiffcityhall.com), an Edwardian-Baroque extravagance dating from 1906 graced by a bulbous, dragon-topped dome and a 194ft-high clock tower which tapers steadily upwards – the architect deliberately ensured that this was higher than the castle clock tower, while the clock face itself is hewn from a single piece of cast iron. In recent years, the tower has become an attraction for a very different reason, since a pair of peregrines decided to nest here. Train your eyes long enough and you may catch sight of them, though a pair of binoculars would come in handy.

The hall itself is actually the fifth building in Cardiff to have served as the seat of local government, though none of the previous four town halls survive. The building is usually open to the general public during office hours, so if you've got a few minutes to spare, it's worth having a nose around those areas that are accessible, including the resplendent Marble Hall with its columns of Siena marble and statues of Welsh heroes (all men incidentally) chiselled from Seravezza marble: among them are Owain Glyndwr by Alfred Turner, Henry Tudor by Ernest Gillick, and Sant Dewi (St David) by the ubiquitous Goscombe John. Here too is a smattering of artwork, and while there's nothing to rival anything in the adjacent National Museum, there are one or two impressive pieces on display. Assuming access isn't restricted owing to council business, take a peek inside the Council Chamber, unusual for being entirely circular as opposed to semicircular, and richly furnished in oak panelling and Breccia marble.

Tucked away behind City Hall, the neatly symmetrical **Alexandra Gardens** [59 D1] rarely get a look in, most folk either blissfully unaware of their presence or content to head back into the city centre after visiting the National Museum. But this is a lovely spot to sit in quiet contemplation. Centre stage is Sir Ninian Comper's **Welsh National Memorial** [59 D1], a bombastic colonnaded structure cast from Portland Stone. Close by is a somewhat more restrained memorial honouring those who lost their lives in the 1982 Falklands War; the big lump of rock from the Mount Harriet battlefield in the Falklands atop the plinth was gifted to the city by the islanders, while the plinth itself bears the names of all 255 servicemen who fell, 32 of whom were Welsh Guards, along with three of the island's civilian residents – it's a beautifully worked and gently affecting memorial. Spreading north beyond the Civic Centre, the neighbourhood of Cathays itself is the city's main student enclave.

PRINCIPALITY STADIUM [59 D3] (Westgate St; ☎ 0844 249 1999; w principalitystadium.wales; 🕘 tours at 10.00, noon, 14.00 & 16.00 daily, except on matchdays; £16.50) When it opened in 1999 just in time for the Rugby World Cup, the Millennium Stadium, as it was then known, was widely acknowledged as one of the most state-of-the-art stadiums in the world, and while it may have been superseded by other stadiums in the intervening 20 or so years, it remains a brilliant architectural achievement. It's still one of the most atmospheric stadiums in world sport, and aside from the rugby, it occasionally hosts the Welsh national football team as well as mega bands.

To make way for the new structure, the National Stadium, which had sat on an east–west axis, was mostly demolished, but in order to accommodate not only an increased capacity (74,500) but also the mechanisms required to support a fully retractable roof (the first in the UK and the third largest in the world), the new stadium had to be rotated 90 degrees; given the tight physical constraints – hemmed in by buildings on three sides and the Taff on the other – this was no mean feat. The result is a cavernous bowl with steeply banked rows of seats, each and every one affording a fantastic unencumbered view.

Tacked on to the north side of the Principality Stadium is the much-loved, if now slightly dilapidated, Cardiff Arms Park, which is home to the Cardiff Blues, one of Wales's four professional regional rugby union clubs. The site's early history is often overlooked, but in the late 19th century this was the location for the Cardiff Arms Hotel, hence the name of the ground. After that was torn down, this large swathe of reclaimed land – like much of Cardiff it was owned by Lord Bute – was used to stage cricket matches (notwithstanding the fact that the ball would quite often end up in the Taff, flooding was a regular hazard) and then football.

If you can't get tickets for a match at the Principality (and you probably won't), then the next best thing is a stadium tour, which takes in the changing rooms, pressroom, hospitality boxes and then a walk down the players' tunnel to pitchside. Either way, there's not much that beats Cardiff on match day, especially when hordes of beer-guzzling Scots or Irish roll into town swelling the already packed pubs and bars to bursting point.

BUTE PARK [59 C1] Extending north from Castle Street up to Blackweir Woods, with the River Taff bordering one side and the A470 the other, Bute Park is one of Cardiff's greatest assets. You could quite easily spend a day exploring its outstanding collection of trees, ancient ruins and modern sculptures, or simply ambling alongside the riverbank.

As its name suggests, the park's history is inextricably linked to that of the Bute family, and in particular the Third Marquess (Lord Bute) who, with his head gardener Andrew Pettigrew, pursued its creation in the late 19th century – essentially to complement the work Bute and Burges had started on the castle, whose private gardens consisted of what is now the southern portion of the park. Its Victorian layout remains much as it did then, though were Lord Bute to visit today, he certainly wouldn't have recognised the magnificent arboretum, which was established after the park (along with the castle) had been gifted to the city by the Fifth Marquess of Bute in 1947.

Bute Park is home to more than 3,000 catalogued trees, among them 41 **Champion Trees** (those deemed to be the tallest or broadest examples of their kind within Britain), a number unrivalled among municipal parks in Britain and Ireland. Among the most important species here are Siberian Elm and Chinese Ginkgo Biloba, and if you want to seek them out, there are two Champion Tree trails (north and south), in addition to another trail mapping out a dozen or so of the park's signature species; these can be obtained from the visitor centre (page 74).

Skirting the easternmost boundary, the Dock Feeder Canal is the park's secondary water corridor, originally built to supply the West Bute docks down in the bay with fresh water that had been flushed away each time the lock was emptied, a function it still fulfils to this day. The canal follows the course of an old leat, which once fed the mills and tanneries here. There are even specially designed dog steps so your pooch can have a paddle. During the summer, *Gunnera* plants, or 'giant rhubarb', hang lazily over the water's edge, while demoiselle damselflies and the occasional kingfisher make their presence known. The northernmost sector of the park is given over to **Blackweir Woods**, an ancient broadleaved woodland home to lots of birdlife, including greater spotted woodpecker, blackcap and goldcrest, as well as an abundance of bats, with half of the UK's 18 species found here. It's worth popping into the park's visitor centre, hidden behind the Secret Garden's high red-brick wall, to pick up trail leaflets and also inspect a small exhibition on the park's history; note that the park is also the departure point for water taxis down to the bay (see below).

SOPHIA GARDENS AND THE MUSEUM OF WELSH CRICKET [59 B1] On the other side of the Taff lie Sophia Gardens, which take their name from the Second Marquess of Bute's wife, who established the gardens in 1857. These days, they are dominated by the cricket ground of the same name, which has been home to **Glamorgan County Cricket Club** (Wales's only first-class county cricket club) since 1967. Following redevelopment in 2008 the ground staged its first ever international test match in 2009, and it couldn't have been bigger: the opening match of the Ashes series between England and Australia (it was a draw). You could do a lot worse than spend a long leisurely afternoon watching a session or two of cricket in this lovely setting (tickets are somewhat easier to get than for the rugby), but if you haven't the time or inclination for that, it's worth considering a stadium tour, where you get to see the pavilion, dressing rooms and media centre; your ticket also includes entry to the **Museum of Welsh Cricket** (⚲ 029 2041 9383; w www.cricketmuseum.wales; ⊕ Apr–Sep 10.00–16.00; £5). Gleaming glass cabinets packed with memorabilia recall the history of the sport in Wales – it's believed that the first match in South Wales took place in 1783 – and that of the club itself, which was formed in 1888. The club greats are celebrated too, among them Viv Richards, the legendary West Indian batsman who spent three seasons here in the early 1990s. Sophia Gardens extend north towards **Pontcanna Fields**, an even larger green space.

CARDIFF BAY

Heading down the ceremonial-like Lloyd George Avenue, with its faceless apartment blocks and offices, it feels as if you could be anywhere. But as you get closer to the bay, the great, hump-backed beast that is the Wales Millennium Centre hoves into view alongside Roald Dahl Plass (meaning 'plaza' or 'space' in Norwegian), a vast oval basin that has an almost continental airiness about it. Beyond here an assortment of buildings vie for attention, from the sublime (the Pierhead and Senedd) to the plain ugly (Mermaid Quay), the latter a modern excrescence packed with restaurants and bars that doesn't do justice to its fabulous waterside setting. Despite its critics, and there have been quite a few, the overall project has had a transformative effect on both the bay and the city in a way few could have envisaged a couple of decades ago.

Wind back 20 years and the bay area looked very different, a squalid wasteland whose once world-renowned docks had long since been consigned to history. Prior to their decline, these were the busiest docks in the world, with consignments of coal from the Valleys distributed all around the globe, as far as Australia and Brazil. But just as the bay's fortunes were dependent upon coal, so too was it the cause of its demise, and when coal no longer became a viable export in the 1960s, the port slid into inexorable decline. Colloquially, it's known as **Tiger Bay**, a title that was first coined in the late 20th century when the docks gained a reputation as a notorious locality – the presence of sailors and merchants certainly gave the place a cosmopolitan, if rough and slightly seedy, edge – although its provenance remains disputed. Regardless, its name is more likely to resonate with some thanks to *The Girl from Tiger Bay*, a gorgeous anthem penned by the Manic Street Preachers for Dame Shirley Bassey, the bay's most famous export.

It was the US city of Baltimore – whose horseshoe-shaped Inner Harbour mirrored that of Cardiff's and which, like Cardiff, had been a major exporter of coal

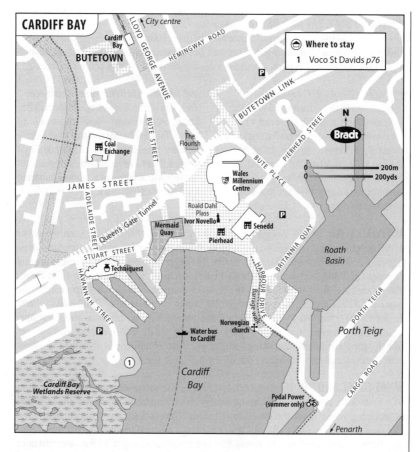

Where to stay

1 Voco St Davids *p76*

but then experienced a sustained period of post-industrial decline – that served as the model for the regeneration and long-term economic development of the bay. Key to the entire redevelopment was the construction of a barrage, which would do away with the mudflats and stabilise the water level, as the tidal waters here are among the highest in the world. The Port of Cardiff has three remaining operational docks – Roath Basin, Roath Dock and Queen Alexandra Dock – the main activity being timber and steel, and while you may catch sight of the occasional supersized tanker edging its way out into the Bristol Channel, there appears to be little activity (though there's not even much of that these days). But with berths having been approved for cruise liners, perhaps this is the future?

GETTING THERE AND AWAY If you don't fancy the walk down to the bay from the city centre – and to be honest, it's a pretty dull trudge – there are several alternatives. The Baycar **bus** (#6) departs every 30 minutes from outside Cardiff Central station (on St Mary Street), or there's the **train** from Queen Street station every 15 minutes. More fun is the **waterbus** (w aquabus.co.uk; £6), which departs from Bute Park on the hour from 10.00 to 17.00 (10.30–16.30 from the bay), passing the Principality Stadium, and stopping on request at Taff's Mead Embankment (for the train station) en route. Buggies, bikes and wheelchairs can all be accommodated.

🏠 WHERE TO STAY, EAT AND DRINK *Map, page 75*

The bay's one outstanding hotel occupies a superb location, but otherwise it's surprising and disappointing that no-one has yet had the presence of mind to open a halfway-decent restaurant down here. Instead, it's dominated by the usual chain suspects.

🏠 **Voco St David's** (142 rooms) Havannah St; ☎ 029 2045 4045; w stdavids.vocohotels.com. Easily identifiable by its seagull-like roof, it's not just the unbeatable waterside location that's great about this refurbished 5-star hotel. Although now part of the newly launched Voco brand, St David's still retains heaps of personality, from its soaring curved atrium to the rooms themselves, which are categorised in 4 tiers. All are amply sized & decorated in sunny yellow & petrol blue tones, with wide-screen watery vistas from their floor-to-ceiling windows – some also have a balcony. The adjoining spa is a small affair (kids can attend between 08.00 & 09.00, & 17.00 & 18.00), & there's a very commendable restaurant that's emphatically superior to anything on offer at nearby Mermaid Quay. **£££**

ACTIVITIES **Bay Island Voyages** (Lower Board Walk, Mermaid Quay; m 07393 470476; w bayislandvoyages.co.uk) is an excellent outfit offering various waterborne trips around the bay and along the coast. These include 60- and 90-minute coastal voyages (£30/40), which take in both Flat Holm and Steep Holm, but if it's thrills you're seeking, do the Bay Blast (£12), a 15-minute high-octane rip around the bay in a RIB. **Cardiff International White Water** (Watkiss Way; ☎ 029 2082 9970; w ciww.com), located in the International Sports Village, offers a host of water-bound activities on manmade rapids, including white-water rafting and tubing, hot dogging (inflatable kayaking), stand-up paddleboarding and kayaking. Most activities typically cost around £60–65 for a 2-hour session.

WHAT TO SEE AND DO The main catalyst for the bay's regeneration was the creation of a 1km-long **barrage**, which many experts had long been advocating as a means of trapping water from the exceptionally tidal Severn Estuary, without which the bay would have been left without water for large parts of the day. To do this, water was impounded from nearby rivers and the area transmogrified into a freshwater lagoon. It was a phenomenal bit of engineering, though one not without controversy given the concerns over rising groundwater as well as potential habitat loss. In the event, fears over the former have gone unfounded, and although some of the existing wetlands were sacrificed, there was recompense with the creation of the Newport Wetlands National Nature Reserve further along the Gwent Levels (page 106). Other critics of the scheme argued that more of the money should have been spent on public housing for the impoverished Butetown community.

One of the most enjoyable ways to experience the bay is the **barrage walk** across to Penarth, which should take no more than an hour and a half at a very leisurely pace; this is also part of the Wales Coast Path, so you can tick this section off. Starting at the Senedd, walk past the Norwegian church, just behind which is *Antarctic 100*, a memorial to the Antarctic mission which set sail from this spot in 1910: the white-tiled ceramic sculpture has Scott and his crew caught in a snowdrift. The walk continues past Porth Teigr (location for the BBC studios) and the Pedal Power bike-hire station (you can cycle the barrage too), beyond which there are several diversions: an outdoor exhibition on the coalmining industry, a skate plaza and a children's play area. The barrage then narrows before you reach Penarth's three huge locks, which effectively marks your entry into the Vale of Glamorgan; there's a seasonal café here for refuelling. Once beyond the locks, you have several options: continue into Penarth, take a waterbus back to the bay, or return from whence you came. Having got this far, though, it makes sense to carry on into Penarth via the well-signposted Coast Path which winds through a series of imposingly hilly streets to a viewing point that delivers a sublime vista of the pier below and the islands of Flat Holm and Steep Holm in the distance.

Wales Millennium Centre (Bute Pl; ☏029 2063 6464; w wmc.org.uk; ⏱ 10.00–17.00 daily; free) An architectural triumph of the first order, the monumental Wales Millennium Centre is a suitably fitting home for the Welsh National Opera. Constructed solely from native Welsh materials – stratified layers of multi-coloured slate from North Wales, hardwood timbers from mid-Wales and stainless steel from Pontypool – its most impressive aspect is the sweeping copper portico emblazoned with words composed by Wales's first national poet Gwyneth Lewis: 'In these stones horizons sing', and 'Creu gwir fel gwydr o ffwrnais awen', the Welsh translating as 'Creating truth, like glass, from the furnace of inspiration', a firm nod to Wales's industrial might of yesteryear. These three rows of prose that stand taller than a double-decker bus.

Yet the building might not have happened at all. It was originally envisaged that the site would be home to an opera house, cue what appeared to be a winning bid from the late Zaha Hadid; in the event, her design was controversially rejected by the Millennium Commission – ostensibly because of concerns pertaining to finance and construction, but many observers, including Hadid herself, were of the opinion that prejudicial forces were at play. It would be another five years or so before the Commission coughed up the cash to support the Millennium Centre project. Hadid had the last word, though, with the very same revolutionary design finally coming to fruition in the Chinese city of Guangzhou in 2010.

The interior is just as dramatic: steel-clad walls, timber-lined stairs and polished wooden balconies. The main auditorium, the Donald Gordon Theatre, is a stunning space boasting sensuous curves, superb acoustics and perfect sightlines. Even if you aren't here for a performance, do have a nose around – the centre did run tours at one stage, but these are currently suspended and may or may not be on the agenda again at some point in the future. In any case, there are several cafés and bars on the ground floor from which to take in this wonderful building.

Pierhead (Maritime Rd; ☏ 0300 200 6565; w senedd.wales; ⏱ 09.30–16.30 Mon–Fri, 10.30–16.30 Sat & Sun; free) No other building in the bay embodies better the wealth of the once all-powerful coal industry than the splendid neo-Gothic terracotta red-brick Pierhead. The one constant amid the flush of modern architecture, the Pierhead (1897) was commissioned by the Third Marquess of Bute and designed by William Frame to replace the Bute Dock Company offices that had burnt down five years earlier. The Bute Dock Company was subsequently renamed the Cardiff Railway Company to reflect the increasing reliance on the railways and, conversely, the decline in seaborne traffic.

The interior is a riot of ornate plasterwork, walnut panelling and glazed tiles decorated with images of birds and fish, a theme its architect, Lord Bute, returned to time and again – as you'll have seen if you've visited Cardiff Castle. Three rooms have been given over to an exhibition on the history of the building, the docks, and the neighbouring Senedd which owns the Pierhead. The single most important exhibit is the binnacle (a stand housing the ship's compass) from the SS *Terra Nova*, which set sail from Cardiff Bay bound for the South Pole on 15 June 1910 with Captain Scott and 65 crew aboard – the men perished, but incredibly the ship made it back from the Antarctic in 1913, whereupon the binnacle was presented to the city. The *Terra Nova* continued work as a seal-fishing vessel before being redeployed to the Arctic for wartime activity assisting allied bases in Greenland, where she did finally sink in 1943. At the entrance to the Hotel Royal on St Mary's Street in the city centre, a blue plaque identifies the building as where the ill-fated expedition team held their farewell supper.

Behind the Pierhead is a statue of **Ivor Novello** (1893–1951), one of Wales's most celebrated actors, dramatists and composers. Chair-bound with a book and a pen at the ready, Novello cuts a svelte figure as he turns inwards to the Millennium Centre. Not hugely well known outside Wales, most people will have probably heard of Novello in relation to a prestigious annual award named after him which acknowledges outstanding songwriters: previous recent winners include Elbow and Jamie Cullum. If you're heading towards Canton, a blue plaque on the house at 95 Cowbridge Road marks this out as his birthplace.

Senedd
(✆0300 200 6565; w senedd.wales; ⊕ 09.00–16.30 Mon–Fri; 10.30–16.30 Sat & bank hols; free) The main anchor among all this waterside development is the stunning Senedd, designed by Sir Richard Rogers as a permanent home for the Welsh Assembly, now called the Welsh Parliament. Looking as fresh and modern as it did when it was inaugurated in 2006, it's an adventurous, beautifully executed building that, like the Millennium Centre, makes astute use of native materials: slate from Blaenau Ffestiniog, and cedar and oak wood from mid-Wales.

The Senedd is also one of the most environmentally conscious parliament buildings in the world, benefiting from a ground source pump that services the building with heated water, a biomass boiler that burns recycled pellets, and, inside, an enormous, mushroom-like funnel which serves as a lightwell. On the outside of the funnel, a wind cowl supplies the entire building with natural ventilation, while the roof itself functions as a rainwater harvesting system.

Two of the building's three levels are open to the public who are welcome to watch over a plenary session in the circular debating chamber, which was deliberately designed that way to advocate a more consensual style of politics – it's worth noting then that Wales is one of the few countries in the world where women are in the majority in the cabinet. You can also partake in some refreshments in the café, at the same time as savouring fabulous bay views. Note that if you are planning to visit, expect a thorough security check upon entry.

Norwegian church
(✆ 029 2087 7959; w norwegianchurchcardiff.com & welshnorwegian.org; ⊕ 10.30–16.00 daily) Alongside the Pierhead, the bay's only other formative building is the much-loved Norwegian church, a white, stumpy-spired structure fixed on its own little grassy terrace on the east side of the harbour. The oldest Norwegian church outside Norway, it was founded in 1868 by Herman Lunde from Oslo at what was then Bute West Dock – where the Wales Millennium Centre now stands – to provide sanctuary for the thousands of Norwegian sailors who travelled to the docks each year on ships laden with timber for use as pit props in the coalmines. One of their number was Roald Dahl's father, Harald, who ended up settling in Cardiff, and in 1916 Roald was christened at the church.

Having fallen into a state of disrepair, the church was deconsecrated in 1974, before being dismantled and re-erected on its present site in 1992, since when it has functioned as an arts centre and café. More recently, threats by the council to pass the church over to a commercial venture never materialised, though only after a petition, and in 2021 it was agreed that the current lease would be transferred to a charitable body led by the Welsh Norwegian Society. Norwegian Day is celebrated on 17 May, so if you happen to be in Cardiff at that time, do come down and see the parade and flag-raising ceremony. Inside, on the wall of the main hall you'll see two crossed oars (symbolising good luck), discovered under the floorboards when the church was moved from Bute West, alongside a picture of Roald Dahl.

Techniquest (Stuart St; ☏ 029 2047 5475; w techniquest.org; ⊕ check website for opening times; £10.90) Occupying a sleek, glass-fronted building to the west of Mermaid Quay, the revamped Techniquest deals with all things science and technology: in fact the revamp is so up to date that there's even a section on Covid-19. While chiefly aimed at children, there's more than enough interactive wizardry here to entertain and inform everyone, with opportunities to create your own animation or tuck yourself into a space shuttle seat among some of the possibilities across its two fun-filled floors.

The museum is grouped into five different gadget-packed zones, themed on chemistry, space, biomedical science, the environment and world issues. You'll have your own favourite area, but one of the most popular zones is biomedical science, especially if you don't mind exerting a little energy (how long can *you* hang from a bar or go full pelt on a bike machine?), though there are more thought-provoking activities like working a virtual operating table. Best of all are the imaginatively recreated natural disasters whereby you can get blasted by hurricane-strength winds or experience what it's like to be in an earthquake. The older retro section, despite now looking a little tired, is also a great deal of fun and will probably resonate more with those of a certain age. The Science Theatre has several daily shows (£2 extra), which could be about anything from how energy works to how dinosaurs fly, while the Planetarium (also £2) is a 360-degree cinema that gives a wonderfully immersive film experience. Inevitably, it's busiest during school holidays and at weekends, so if you can visit outside these times, you'll get more out of your time there.

Butetown 'The only place in Britain where you can see the world in one square mile' was how local historian Neil Sinclair once described Butetown. Hemmed in by the city centre to the north, the bay to the south, and housing developments east and west, Butetown is still home to one of the most diverse and oldest multi-ethnic communities in Britain, with many of its members originally drawn here in the early 20th century by the promise of work in the docks: Greeks, Portuguese, Jews and Somalis are just some of the dozens of nationalities that made the bay their home. A few decades ago, it wouldn't have been unusual to find, for example, Cypriot barbers or Jewish pawnbrokers among the businesses touting for custom along Bute Street, Butetown's main artery. For years, Butetown has been one of the most deprived areas in Wales, with high levels of unemployment and poverty, crime and anti-social behaviour all contributing to a legacy of stigma – and despite its proximity to both the city centre and the bay, it remains a community on the margins, yet the folk here are defined by their warmth and generosity.

Among the depressed housing estates and dull new-build developments – many of which were substituted for neighbourly terraced houses in the 1970s – one or two buildings of distinction have held firm, or have been scrubbed up, like the **Coal Exchange** on Mount Stuart Square, an area of otherwise well-appointed residences. Built in 1886 as a trading centre for the wheelers and dealers of the coal industry, it was here in 1901 that the first million-pound deal in the UK was struck, or so the story goes; as business declined, so did the importance of the Exchange and the floor closed in 1957. The Exchange has since endured a

A 55-mile-long mostly traffic-free route between the mouth of the Taff in Cardiff to its source in the Brecon Beacons, the Taff Trail traverses some of the most beguiling landscapes in southern Wales, utilising old railways, tramways and towpaths, as well as forest trails, country lanes and other public rights of way. Equally suitable for walkers and cyclists – it doubles up as the final section of the National Cycle Network Route 8 from Holyhead to Cardiff – the trail was opened in 1988. Parts of the trail are also used by horse riders.

Starting in Cardiff, the first seven miles or so of this lovely riparian trail are a great way to get acquainted with the city's parks and green spaces, leading you through its centre on an easy traffic-free path along the west bank of the river and onwards to the village of Tongwynlais, overlooked by the eminence that is Castell Coch. Beyond here the trail winds its way up the Taff Valley to Pontypridd and Abercynon before reaching Merthyr. After Merthyr, the landscape abruptly changes, from urban and industrial to open countryside and wild uplands. The ascents are necessarily steeper too, though nothing beyond anyone with average fitness. The trail snakes along the western side of the Pontsticill Reservoir, then sweeps east and up along the eastern side of the Talybont Reservoir – the highest point of the trail – before ending at the Canal Basin in Brecon, where you can refuel at the theatre's excellent café.

It doesn't really matter which way round you do it, but for the sake of speed you're best off starting in Brecon and heading south as it's a slightly more downhill trajectory. However, travelling south to north, you save the most dramatic scenery until last – either way, if you've time to spare, the trail is best approached over a leisurely two or three days. Bikes can be rented in both Cardiff and Talybont (pages 60 and 227).

troubled history, primarily functioning as a concert venue but with intermittent periods of closure, although its latest incarnation as a plush four-star hotel has finally given the building purpose. Even if you're not staying here (and it ain't cheap), take a peek at the interior with its rich wood panelling, oak balcony and stained-glass windows.

Cardiff Bay Wetlands Reserve Occupying a small parcel of land between Voco St David's and the mouth of the Taff, the Cardiff Bay Wetlands Reserve is a minor conservation area carved out of a former saltmarsh when the barrage was built in 2002, effectively to offset the loss of wading-bird habitats. It's largely been a success, the dense reedbeds supporting healthy numbers of great crested grebes, reed warblers and reed bunting, any of which can be seen flittering around the vegetation. A further wander around the site may also turn up sightings of herons and kingfishers. It won't take long to walk around, but it does offer some peaceful respite away from the bustle of the harbour itself.

AROUND CARDIFF

LLANDAFF CATHEDRAL (Cathedral Close, Llandaff; ☏ 029 2058 4554; w llandaffcathedral.org.uk; ⏰ see website; free) Nine hundred years old in 2020, Llandaff Cathedral is Cardiff's most important place of pilgrimage, yet it doesn't receive nearly as many visitors as it should, partly, one suspects, because of its relatively remote location two miles northwest of the city. Evidence suggests that Llandaff's Christian roots can be traced back to the 6th century, given its proven associations with three prominent Welsh saints, namely Dyfrig, Teilo and Euddogwy – indeed the church's full title is the Cathedral Church of Saints Peter and Paul, with Saints Dyfrig, Teilo and Euddogwy. The first reliable reference to Llandaff as a diocese dates from 1119, which was most likely the work of the Normans.

Ironically, the cathedral's position, largely sheltered from view in a steep hollow, was designed to protect it from potential marauders, though it didn't count on the Luftwaffe, who, during the night of 2 January 1941, dropped a parachute mine on the graveyard which ripped the roof off, blew out the windows and blackened much of the interior – only Coventry fared worse among Britain's cathedrals during World War II.

As a result of multiple restorations, the most significant of which took place in the mid 19th century and the last of which was in the 1950s under the charge of George Pace, the current building is an architecturally inconsistent beast, though this doesn't detract from its appeal. The church's most contradictory aspect is most obvious in the western façade: the square, left-sided Jasper Tower pre-dates the right-sided Prichard Tower – distinguished by its needle spire and some exceptional statuary – by some 400 years, the former having been constructed in 1485.

Entering the building, the nave's perfectly proportioned parade of columns and arches stretches out before you, although the view down through the main aisle is marred by an unsightly concrete parabola whose cylindrical organ case is surmounted by Jacob Epstein's cumbersome *Christ in Majesty* statue. Beyond the nave and choir, the sanctuary supports a superb Norman arch embellished with fancy zig-zag mouldings and roundels. At the far end of the cathedral, the Lady Chapel manifests a beautifully painted vaulted ceiling, which looks down upon a 15th-century reredos inlaid with garish bronze panels representing different types of native flora. This whole ensemble is overseen by the *Tree of Jesse* window, a replacement for the original one destroyed in 1941. By way of contrast the St David (or Welsh Regiment Memorial) Chapel is a bland 1956 appendage, but do stop to admire the fine Norman doorway, which is not dissimilar to the one in the sanctuary, as you head back into the cathedral.

Elsewhere, the church is packed full of minor treasures: in the north aisle, there are stained-glass windows by William Morris and an effigy of Charles Vaughan (founder of the Cathedral School) by Goscombe John (a former choir member), and, in the St Dyfrig Chapel, an unusual reredos comprising a set of ceramic tiles, collectively titled *Six Days of Creation*, made to designs by Edward Burne-Jones – though this is usually sealed off so you'll have to crane your neck in order to see it. For all the above, the cathedral's single most important work of art is the John Marshall Panel: taken from the 15th-century throne of the eponymous bishop – and a very large chair it must have been for it's a substantial piece of oak – the painting depicts the Virgin Mary, cloaked in a gold-coloured mandorla and escorted by instrument-playing angels as she ascends towards heaven. That it survived the Reformation at all is remarkable, but here you'll find it, gloriously restored in the south aisle.

It's worth taking time to explore the grounds too. Dating from 1860, the restored **Prichard's Bridge** – built wide enough to allow access for carriages – straddles a now non-existent stream that once fed a local mill. On the other side lies a properly overgrown Victorian cemetery with its assortment of crumbling and tumbling gravestones, and beyond here, the Taff River and trail, from where you can walk back into the city centre. On the small hill near Cathedral Green lie the crumbly remains of the old bell tower – all but decimated by Glyndwr's men in the 15th century – and Goscombe John's World War I memorial bearing three bronze figures: that of a female, either side of which are two men, one representing all those from the Cathedral School who died, the other representing the men from the local parish who fell.

A short walk from the cathedral, the High Street is worth perusing for its coffee shops and delis. Fans of **Roald Dahl**, meanwhile, will delight in seeing a plaque on the wall of No 11 marking this out as the site of Mrs Pratchett's sweet shop – which the author frequented as a young boy and which also served as the inspiration for one of his most beloved characters, the shop proprietor whom he described as 'a small, skinny old hag'; her real name was believed to be Katy Morgan. Dahl lived in Llandaff until the age of nine. The cathedral actually lies right on the Taff Trail (page 80), but if you don't fancy the walk, take bus #25 from Greyfriars Road in the city centre to the village (get off at the Black Lion pub), from where it's a 5-minute walk.

CASTELL COCH (Tongwynlais; ✆ 03000 252239; w cadw.gov.wales; ⊕ Mar–Jun 09.30–17.00 daily, Jul & Aug 09.30–18.00 daily, Sep & Oct 09.30–17.00 daily, Nov–Feb 10.00–16.00 daily; £8.30) With its sharp conical towers rising like witches' hats from a thickly wooded limestone crag overlooking the Taff Valley, Castell Coch looks every inch the fairytale castle. Yet despite its medieval good looks, the 'Red Castle' (so-named after the colour of the castle's stone) is actually a fairly modern creation, having been rebuilt in the late 19th century under the patronage of the Third Marquess of Bute, who, together with William Burges, had overseen Cardiff Castle's extravagant revamp. Bute once again turned to Burges to help him reconstruct Castell Coch, which, although much smaller, was almost ruinous. There had in fact been a stronghold of some description here since the end of the 11th century, albeit one of no significance, and by the time the Butes got their hands on it in the mid 18th century, there was little here but a pile of rubble.

For the exterior, Burges rebuilt the gatehouse, reinstated the *chemin-de-ronde* (wall-walk) and heightened the existing towers, simultaneously equipping them with their distinctive roofs. With the same team of craftsmen that worked on Cardiff Castle, Burges employed similar themes inside too, the result being another hallucinogenic triumph. The octagonal drawing room is perhaps Burges's finest work anywhere; here, gilded stone ribs arch upwards towards a steeply vaulted ceiling painted with butterflies, parrots and other birdlife. The chimneypiece bears a sculpture entitled *The Three Fates*, which dwells on themes of mortality, and the walls bear murals depicting Aesop's Fables. Lady Bute's circular bedroom is no less dramatic, a red and gold painted double dome above the bed inlaid with 28 panels depicting monkeys in various states of cheeky pose – and the less said about the crystal globes on the bedposts the better.

Following Burges's untimely death in 1881, the remaining craftsmen were tasked with completing the job, although the Marquess disliked the reworked designs – he described certain aspects as 'lascivious' – to the extent that he never again returned to the property. The castle was requisitioned by British and American troops during World War II before the Butes handed it over to the municipal authorities following the death of the Fourth Marquess. An excellent audio guide is included in the admission price. To get here, take bus #26 (which continues to Caerphilly Castle) or #132 from Cardiff to Tongwynlais, from where it's a 10-minute walk to the castle.

ST FAGANS NATIONAL MUSEUM OF HISTORY (St Fagans; ☏ 029 2057 3500; w museum.wales; ⊕ 10.00–17.00 daily; parking £6.50) For many visitors to Cardiff, the city's most enjoyable attraction is the marvellous St Fagans National Museum of History, four miles west of the city in the village of the same name. A branch of the National Museum of Wales, the museum is located within the grounds of St Fagans Castle, which is not really a true castle, but a grand Elizabethan manor house and one-time home of the Earl of Plymouth. Although it's possible to enter the building, the interior has been heavily remodelled and is decidedly dour in tone, but in any case there's more fun to be had elsewhere.

The museum comprises two elements: the indoor galleries and an outdoor display of vernacular architecture, which was the first museum of its kind in Britain, conceived in 1946 as the Welsh Folk Museum by the poet Iorwerth Peate who had been inspired by the *skansen* in Stockholm. Wherever you start, you should allow plenty of time for a visit, so pick your day wisely (preferably a sunny one), and pack a picnic.

It's a marvellous ensemble of more than 50 dwellings, farmhouses, workshops, churches, shops and other structures from all over Wales, spanning the late 12th to early 20th centuries. A good cross-section of these can be entered, while suitably attired guides are on hand to lend a touch of living history to proceedings. One of the first buildings to be donated to the site, in 1955, was the 17th-century Kennixton Farmhouse from the Gower, unmistakeable by its red-painted exterior and whose bulk indicates that it belonged to a family of some wealth – there's even a sleeping platform over the fireplace.

Few buildings here are as redolent of the Victorian era as that of the squat **St Mary's (Maestir) Board School** from Lampeter, which is no more than an entrance porch, side room and classroom. Built in 1880, the school closed less than 30 years later owing to dwindling pupil numbers, though it may also have had something to do with the fact it was a 'sink' school – or 'inadequate' in Ofsted speak. Another favourite is the late 18th-century **Rhyd-y-car terrace**, built by the iron baron Richard Crawshay (page 192) and consisting of half a dozen ironworkers' cottages from Merthyr Tydfil that have been fitted out to represent different eras, from 1805 through to 1985; the adjoining garden plots are delightful. A few paces away, the Gwalia Stores is a gloriously old-fashioned grocery and ironmonger's shop from Ogmore Vale where you can indulge in all your sweet-toothed fantasies, and next to this is an elegant Victorian urinal transplanted here from Llandrindod railway station. If savoury is your thing, the waft of freshly baked bread will have you scurrying over to the early 19th-century Derwen Bakehouse, originally from Aberystwyth, and opposite here is the diminutive Blaen-waun post office from Whitland in Carmarthenshire.

The museum's ecclesiastical buildings are worth hunting down: the Pen-rhiw Chapel from Dre-fach Felindre in Carmarthenshire has been a Unitarian meeting place since 1777, and still hosts the occasional service, but it's clear from its simple, rectangular shape that this was originally conceived as a barn of sorts. Nor is this the only building on site believed to be haunted, for it is said that phantom funerals, accompanied by *canwyll corff* (corpse candles), take place here after dark – far-fetched, possibly, but a good story nonetheless. The solitary headstone in the chapel grounds, meanwhile, is that of Iorwerth Peate, the museum's founder. Much older is St Teilo's Church from Llandeilo Tal-y-bont in Glamorgan, which has a more conventional nave-and-side-aisles floorplan; the wall paintings were only discovered during the rebuild.

The museum's most recent acquisition is sure to be one of its most popular when complete. Between 1853 and its closure in 2012, **The Vulcan Hotel** in Adamstown served as one of the city's most famous hostelries, frequented by a loyal band of drinkers as well as some of the good and great of the music industry. The hotel had already survived one threat of closure before it was eventually deemed to be an unviable proposition, and it was only saved from disappearing altogether thanks to museum staff who dismantled it, brick by brick, before bringing it here to St Fagans. Its reconstruction – which will feature the original sign and exterior green and brown tiles, the ornate urinals, and best of all, working pumps – is slated for completion some time in 2023, although whether any of the old-timers can be persuaded to head all the way out here for one last nostalgic pint, only time will tell.

Reopened in 2018 after a six-year revamp, the **galleries** display objects from the National Museum of Wales's history and archaeology collections, many of which had never been on show before. The Wales Is gallery is a series of themed areas pertaining to the people and events that have shaped the country's fortunes. It's well laid out, with some stellar exhibits and refreshingly concise explanations. Archaeology, costume, education and industry are all covered, and there's particular emphasis on the 1984 Miners' Strike, with a police riot shield and various pins and badges, including some from the LGBTQIA+ community (page 205).

Wales's marvellous musical heritage is duly celebrated courtesy of the harp made by Evan James, who composed the Welsh national anthem, alongside Joseph Parry's baton (page 191). More sobering is the section devoted to Wales's drowned villages: in 1965, Capel Celyn, a hamlet near Bala in North Wales, was flooded in order to create a reservoir for Liverpool: 12 houses, alongside farms, a post office, school and a church were submerged and 48 people were forcibly evicted – on display here is the village road sign. More poignantly still, at the far end of the room in a cabinet all of its own, is the small, battered clock from Pantglas Junior School in Aberfan (page 193), its hands frozen at the time (09.13) the landslide hit in October 1966. Recovered from the debris by volunteer rescuer Mike Flynn, the clock was presented to the museum in 2022. Coming right up to speed, there's coverage of the Black Lives Matter movement, with placards retrieved from protests that took place in Cardiff in the wake of George Floyd's death in 2020.

The Life Is gallery is distinctly underwhelming by comparison, though there are one or two items that might arouse your curiosity, such as the bedstead belonging to Sir Rhys ap Thomas (who would appear to have been a pretty small chap judging by the size of the bed), carved all the way round in shallow relief with self-aggrandising images of him in battle at Bosworth alongside spear-wielding horsemen. There's also the rugby blazer belonging to the Wales captain Claude Davey on the occasion of their test match against the New Zealand All Blacks in Cardiff in December 1935, a match the Welsh famously won 13–12. To put this into context, they've only beaten New Zealand once in the intervening 85 years; there's some remarkable footage of the game on YouTube.

Buses #320 and #321 both stop in the village, from where it's a 5-minute walk to the site.

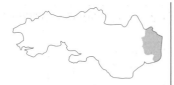

4

Monmouthshire and Newport

Whichever bridge you choose to enter South Wales by, Monmouthshire will be your first port of call. Crossing the original Severn Bridge, you're within striking distance of **Chepstow**, a personable town with a mighty castle and which is the starting point for forays up the **Wye Valley**, whose eponymous river marks the border with England. A long, narrow gorge deeply incised into the limestone plateau, the valley still trades on its reputation as the birthplace of British tourism, as well it might given the glut of natural and historic attractions here. The Wye Valley's most memorable stop is **Tintern**, courtesy of its glorious abbey, but away from the river, there are some lesser-known spots worth seeking out, **Trellech** and **Catbrook** among them. With plenty of time and a reasonable level of fitness, the most rewarding way to explore the Wye Valley is on foot – with both the Offa's Dyke and Wye Valley trails, two of the country's most popular long-distance hikes, running its length and beyond, albeit with the occasional cross-border detour into England. Both trails pass through **Monmouth**, a spruce, slightly old-fashioned town but with more than enough to rate a leisurely day's exploration.

The region's only city is **Newport**, a lively, gutsy place, albeit one that few visitors bother with, especially with its more famous and glamorous big-city rival just down the road. But with its historic Chartist links and a maritime legacy to rival that of cities twice its size, it shouldn't be dismissed.

Extending from the Severn Bridge all the way down to Cardiff, the Monmouthshire coastline is entirely given over to the **Gwent Levels**, a big-skied expanse of pristine chequerboard fields, mudflats, saltmarshes and manmade ditches carved out to alleviate flooding. Once submerged beneath the Bristol Channel, this precarious, sparsely populated landscape presents a melancholy aspect, but its unique ecology attracts an abundance of fabulous winged fauna: nesting waders, grebes, warblers, bitterns and kingfishers are among the regular visitors – even the once-extinct Common Crane has been spotted here in recent times. The **Newport Wetlands National Nature Reserve** is the gold-star destination here, but there are other important habitats, like Magor Marsh, which can be explored from the never-ending Wales Coast Path. Indeed, the Levels offer ample yet undemanding walking and cycling, perfect for those with an aversion to hills.

Anyone even remotely interested in the Roman Empire could happily spend an unhurried day or two exploring **Caerleon** and **Caerwent**, the former home to Britain's finest Roman amphitheatre and the only extant legionnaires' barracks in Europe, the latter making a good case for being the most complete example of a civilian Roman town in Britain. As the one-time realm of border battles and powerful Marcher lords, it's little surprise that so many castles litter the Monmouthshire landscape, the Normans having left many impressive statements of intent. **Raglan** is the finest specimen, though a cluster of craggy ruins a little further north –

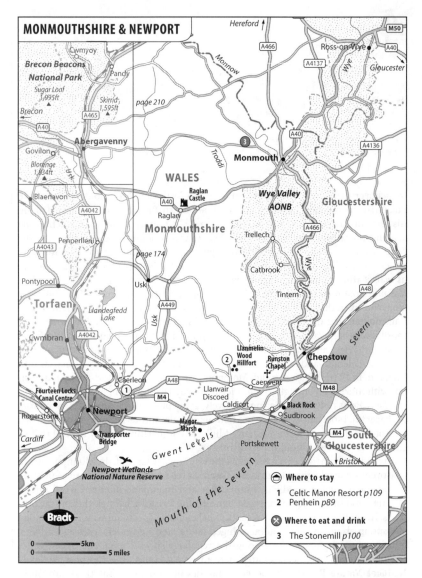

MONMOUTHSHIRE & NEWPORT

Hereford ↑

M50

Cwmyoy

Ross-on-Wye ● A40

A40

Brecon Beacons
National Park

Pandy

A466

A4137

Wye

Gloucester

Sugar Loaf
1,995ft

Skirrid
1,595ft

page 210

Monnow

A40

A4136

Brecon

A465

Monmouth ●

3

Abergavenny

Govilon

Troddi

WALES

Blorenge
1,834ft ▲

Raglan
Castle

Wye Valley
AONB

Gloucestershire

Blaenavon

A40

A4042

Raglan

Monmouthshire

Trellech

A466

Penperlleni

A4043

page 174

Catbrook

A48

Pontypool

Usk

Tintern

Torfaen

Llandegfedd
Lake

A449

Usk

Wye

Cwmbran

A4042

Llanmelin
Wood
Hillfort

2

Severn

Runston
Chapel

Chepstow

Caerleon

1

A48

Llanvair
Discoed

Caerwent

M48

Fourteen Locks
Canal Centre

M4

Caldicot

Black Rock

Rogerstone

● Newport

Magor
Marsh

Sudbrook

M4

South
Gloucestershire

Cardiff

Transporter
Bridge

Gwent Levels

Portskewett

↓ Bristol

Newport Wetlands
National Nature Reserve

Mouth of the Severn

N

Bradt

0 ——— 5km
0 ————— 5 miles

⌂ Where to stay
1 Celtic Manor Resort *p109*
2 Penhein *p89*

✕ Where to eat and drink
3 The Stonemill *p100*

Skenfrith, Grosmont and White castles – are all enticing prospects, particularly as these can be visited on a very satisfying two-day circular walk, or in one day if you are very quick, and reasonably fit. A lesser fortress at **Usk**, a comely little market town on the river of the same name, retains its own idiosyncratic charm.

CHEPSTOW

The first major settlement this side of the border, hence one of the most anglicised of all Welsh towns, Chepstow (Cas-Gwent in Welsh, meaning 'Castle of Gwent') sits in a hairpin bend of the River Wye – in fact, its Norman name was Striguil, likely taken from the Welsh word 'ystraigyl' meaning 'bend in the river', before it appropriated the English version from the words 'ceap', meaning market and 'stowe' meaning place.

Although Chepstow's history is, inevitably, bound up with that of its castle, it was the arrival of a market in the late 13th century, alongside the construction of a port wall and town gate, that helped transform it into Wales's most important medieval port, which it remained until it was superseded by Cardiff and Swansea during the Industrial Revolution. The town later became an obligatory stop on the Wye Tour as popularised by the likes of John Egerton and William Gilpin, and to this day it remains a convenient base for forays up the Wye Valley and elsewhere within the Monmouthshire countryside.

Notwithstanding some clumsy modern development, Chepstow is a place of not inconsiderable charm, thanks to its neat medieval layout and a colourful medley of whitewashed cottages and Georgian townhouses spilling down the hill towards the castle. The castle is without doubt the town's big draw, and alone makes Chepstow worth a diversion, though there's plenty more to stick around for – and if you're tackling one of the three long-distance trails that start (or finish) here, you could do worse than stay overnight and have a gander before setting off.

GETTING THERE AND AWAY Chepstow is one of the most easily accessible places in South Wales, thanks to its proximity to both the M4 and M48, the latter crossing the Severn Bridge just a few miles south of town. Chepstow is also reachable from England via the A48, from the direction of Gloucester, and the Old Wye Bridge a little further up the river. There are plenty of pay-and-display car parks in the town

A TALE OF TWO BRIDGES AND A TUNNEL

Until 1886, the only way to cross the tidal Severn Estuary was by boat between New Passage in South Gloucestershire on the English side and Portskewett near Sudbrook on the Welsh side, a treacherous journey at the best of times; alternatively, it entailed a lengthy detour via Gloucester. That year, after taking 13 years to complete, the **Severn Tunnel** opened, and was the longest underwater tunnel in the world at the time, which it remained until 1987. Just over four miles long (2¼ miles of which is under the estuary itself), it was also the longest railway tunnel in the UK until 2007 when HS1, part of the Channel Tunnel Rail Link, opened. It even has its own pumping station which pumps out 14 million gallons of water a day so as to prevent flooding from an underwater spring (page 105); without this it's estimated that the tunnel would completely fill in under half an hour, which is a fairly sobering thought. It was undoubtedly one of the great feats of 19th-century engineering, and the crowning glory for Great Western Railway's chief engineer Sir John Hawkshaw.

The original **Severn Bridge**, which links England and Wales via the M48 just south of Chepstow, was opened in 1966, with tolls imposed at the same time. It wasn't until 30 years later that the much longer and grander **Second Severn Crossing**, which carries the M4, was opened, with the same tolls applied. The controversial, and expensive, toll scheme was finally scrapped on both bridges in 2018, though no less controversial was the decision to rename the Second Severn Crossing the **Prince of Wales Bridge** in 2018 (ostensibly to mark 50 years since Prince (now King) Charles was given the title), which, if nothing else, had the Welsh nationalists up in arms. In fact, only 17% of people surveyed approved of the name change.

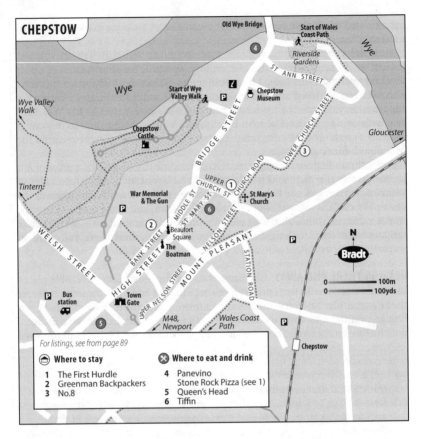

CHEPSTOW

Old Wye Bridge

Start of Wales Coast Path

Riverside Gardens

ST ANN STREET

Wye

Wye Valley Walk

Start of Wye Valley Walk

Chepstow Museum

BRIDGE STREET

LOWER CHURCH STREET

Gloucester

Chepstow Castle

UPPER CHURCH ST

Tintern

War Memorial & The Gun

MIDDLE ST

ST MARY ST

CHURCH ROAD

St Mary's Church

WELSH STREET

BANK STREET

Beaufort Square

NELSON STREET

The Boatman

HIGH STREET

UPPER NELSON STREET

MOUNT PLEASANT

STATION ROAD

N

Bradt

0 — 100m
0 — 100yds

Bus station

Town Gate

M48, Newport

Wales Coast Path

Chepstow

Chepstow

For listings, see from page 89

🛏 **Where to stay**

1 The First Hurdle
2 Greenman Backpackers
3 No.8

✕ **Where to eat and drink**

4 Panevino
  Stone Rock Pizza (see 1)
5 Queen's Head
6 Tiffin

centre, but you'd do well to seek out one of the free car parks down near the train station; there's also some street parking in the vicinity of the train station.

Chepstow's Grade II-listed **railway station** – designed by Isambard Kingdom Brunel – is a 5-minute walk from the town centre on Station Road. Its position on the Cheltenham to Maesteg line makes travelling here by train an attractive proposition; trains to Maesteg (via Caldicot, Newport and Cardiff) run more or less hourly, with services in the other direction to Gloucester and Cheltenham Spa also running hourly – though not all services go to Cheltenham, in which case you have to change in Gloucester. Note that there are no bike-storage facilities at Chepstow station.

The **bus station** is at the top end of town on Thomas Street, just beyond the West Gate, so an even closer walk to the centre. Bus links are excellent, with services to Caldicot (6 daily), Monmouth (10 daily), Newport (10 daily), Tintern (8 daily Mon–Fri, 5 Sat), Trellech (4 daily Mon–Sat), Usk (5 daily Mon–Sat) and Bristol (hourly Mon–Sat, 4 Sun). If travelling to Cardiff, you'll need to change in Newport.

TOURIST INFORMATION In the car park across from the castle, the small tourist information office (✆01291 623772; w visitmonmouthshire.com; ⊕ 10.00–15.00 daily) is actually more of a coffee shop, with a limited selection of leaflets on the town and Wye Valley plus a few walking guides to buy. Still, the staff are helpful and knowledgeable and, should you require it, can book accommodation for a £2 fee.

🏠 WHERE TO STAY *Map, opposite, unless otherwise stated*

Chepstow is well served with places to bed down for the night, useful if you're heading out on one of the long-distance trails.

🏠 **The First Hurdle** (12 rooms) 9–10 Upper Church St; ☎ 01291 622189; w thefirsthurdle. co.uk. In an ideal location between the castle & the town centre, this family-run guesthouse offers a dozen well-appointed rooms across 2 conjoined townhouses, with a mix of sgls, twins & dbls plus an attic room sleeping 4. An attractive b/fast room & a warming snug round things off rather nicely. They also just happen to have one of the best pizzerias in South Wales (see below). **££**

🏠 **No.8** (3 rooms) 8 Lower Church St; ☎ 07799 888335; w no8chepstow.co.uk. This sensitively restored 18th-century townhouse (a former public house) retains 3 drink-themed rooms (gin, whisky & rum), all of which are finished to an extremely high standard; note, however, that the stairs are steep & narrow. Guests can also avail themselves of the kitchen lounge & courtyard garden; there is a car park close at hand if you can't park on the street next to the property. **££**

🏠 **Greenman Backpackers** (10 rooms) 13 Beaufort Sq; m 07773 553397; w greenmanbackpackers.co.uk. Owners Mick & Ness have got every angle covered here, from the clean, well-designed rooms – which include single-sex dorms, en-suite twins & dbls & private family rooms – & the farmyard-like kitchen (a self-service continental b/fast is included) to the lounge & bar areas, where you can have a tipple while observing the comings & goings on the main square below. There's parking & bike storage, & if you've had a particularly soggy outing on one of the long-distance trails, they've got a drying room & laundry facilities. They can also organise canoe hire for use on the Wye. **£**

✴ ⛺ **Penhein** [map, page 86] (8 tents) Discoed; ☎ 01633 400581, w penhein.co.uk. 8 miles west of Chepstow, just outside the village of Discoed, the sprawling Penhein Estate is home to a wonderful back-to-nature glamping site which has 6 Iranian *alachigh* tents, all sleeping 5 & fitted out with kitchen, woodburner & firepit. You even get a gorgeous little welcome hamper. Each tent has its own loo attached, though showers are taken in a communal block, which is next to a small kitchen & pantry, where you can buy food for the fire as well as beer & a few other treats. There's so much to do on site that you'll not want to leave, including a wildlife challenge in the wildflower meadow, an adventure playground & fantastic tree swings, plus some brilliant walks. At certain times of the year different pursuits are available including foraging & bushcraft. **£££**

✕ WHERE TO EAT AND DRINK *Map, opposite*

✕ **Panevino** 28 Bridge St; ☎ 01291 409568; w panevino-restaurantchepstow.com; ⏰ 11.00–23.00 Mon–Sat, 11.00–21.00 Sun. After several incarnations, this Grade II-listed building on the banks of the Wye (it's still known locally as Afon Gwy) has happily settled into life as an outstanding Italian restaurant. It combines tried & tested classics (pizza & oven-baked pasta) alongside fish (pan-fried monkfish with mussels & leeks) & chicken dishes (breast with mushrooms in marsala wine cream sauce). Consummate service rounds things off in style. **££**

✴ ✕ **Stone Rock Pizza** 9 Upper Church St; ☎ 01291 621616; w stonerockpizza.co.uk; ⏰ 16.00–21.00 Mon–Fri, noon–21.30 Sat & Sun. Run by the owners of the First Hurdle guesthouse (see above), pizzas in Wales do not get much better than this (& in a land full of great pizza-makers, that's saying something). Pasquale, the restaurant's resident *pizzaiolo*, knocks up some mouthwatering recipes from his clay oven, such as The Forest of Dean, an action-packed pizza of Somerset mozzarella, wild boar, red-wine salami & venison carpaccio – there's no shortage of vegetarian & vegan options either. Try & bag a table out on the stone-walled patio, a lovely spot to eat whatever the time of year, with overhead heaters & blankets available to warm the bones in colder weather. **££**

🍺 **Queen's Head** 12 Moor St; m 07793 889613; w queensheadchepstow.co.uk; ⏰ 15.00–22.00 Tue–Thu, 14.00–22.00 Fri & Sat, 15.00–20.00 Sun. There's a paucity of decent hostelries in town, but when you've got one as good as this 1-room micropub, then it really doesn't matter. The owner, Glen, usually has half a dozen or so real ales on tap at any one time (& these will often change daily),

so if deciding is too onerous, try a flight of thirds. Refreshingly, there is no music, TV or Wi-Fi, which is just the way the locals like it. ££
💷 **Tiffin** 8 St Mary St; ⊕ 10.00–15.00 Mon–Sat. There are many good reasons to like this colourful teahouse, with its floral formica tablecloths, pastel-painted wooden chairs & lines

of bunting. As well as serving the best coffee & cake in town, there are dedicated teacake & crumpet menus, alongside more substantial lunch options (like Spanish omelette with chorizo). In warmer weather take a seat out in the gravel courtyard &, if it's free, bag a seat in the green-painted shed. ££

WHAT TO SEE AND DO

Chepstow Castle (Bridge St; ✆ 03000 252239; w cadw.gov.wales; ⊕ Mar–Jun 09.30–17.00 daily, Jul & Aug 09.30–18.00 daily, Sep & Oct 09.30–17.00 daily, Nov–Feb 10.00–16.00 daily; £8.30) Perched high above the cliffs, its sides dropping almost sheer into the muddy waters of the River Wye, Chepstow Castle was described by the late, great Jan Morris as 'like a huge fist of rock at the very gate of Wales' – and there's no question it's a mightily impressive sight. It also stakes claim to being the oldest surviving stone-built castle in Wales – not a bad boast considering that there are over 100 castles still standing in the country. The Domesday Book records that the first stones were laid here in 1067 by William Fitz Osbern, close companion of William the Conqueror; its position on this spur of rocky land (part of the last cliff on the River Wye before it reaches the Severn Estuary) affording Fitz Osbern the opportunity to secure the westernmost fringes of the Marches – as a statement of Norman power, it certainly took some beating. Indeed, such is the regard in which Fitz Osbern is held that Chepstow was twinned with Cormeilles, his Normandy home, in 1976.

After Fitz Osbern, construction of the castle continued in piecemeal fashion over the next two centuries under different rulers. First up was William Marshal (he also helped draft the *Magna Carta*) who constructed the eponymous tower, gatehouse and prison, before each of his five sons, at some point or other, oversaw development of the Upper Barbican as well as transforming the Great Tower. The last major phase of construction was undertaken by Roger Bigod III, Fifth Earl of Norfolk, who was responsible for most of what you see in the lower bailey, though there were some 17th- and 18th-century additions, notably the curtain wall, raised to replace earlier war damage. The castle actually remained unbreached until 1648 when Parliamentarians seized control of the town. It was then converted into barracks and a prison before falling into neglect; the garrison was disbanded in 1685.

From the imposing main gatehouse, the complex is more or less linear and neatly sectioned into lower, middle and upper baileys. It makes sense, chronologically at least, to start in the **Great Tower**, the oldest, and only Norman-built, part of the castle, although much of its base is formed of large yellow sandstone blocks believed to be of Roman origin. A vast rectangular hall-like space measuring over 130ft long, it would have originally had an upper and lower floor, as the pair of sawn-off arches – hewn from Purbeck marble and still bearing some beautifully crafted mouldings – would indicate. There's plenty of subtle ornamentation elsewhere too: train your eye carefully on a spot just to the right of the first open window on the south wall and you can detect the shallow remains of a Roman relief, which is thought to depict Venus and her nymphs, and in the left-hand recess at the west end are some fragmentary remains of a wall painting.

The Great Tower aside, the most rewarding part of the castle is the suite of buildings dispersed around the **Lower Bailey**. Prominent here is the domestic range, comprising the roofless great hall, the heavily restored and minimally refurnished Earl's Chamber, the kitchen and service passage, and, beyond here, a dank cellar possessed of a finely vaulted ceiling and a window through which wine and barrels of ale would be winched up from the river directly below. Standing in the great hall porch, you can't fail to miss the pair of gatehouse doors: in situ until 1962, these magnificently preserved specimens – bearing iron-clad planks constructed from green oak – date from the late 12th century, hence are reckoned to be the oldest surviving castle doors anywhere in Europe. Opposite the range stands Bigod's other main contribution, the well-proportioned **Marten's Tower**: this massive defensive unit was originally equipped with private lodgings and a chapel before being converted into Tudor apartments. Incidentally, the best views of the castle are to be had from the opposite side of the river in England; walk across the old bridge and turn left.

Chepstow Museum (Bridge St; ✆01291 625891; w monlife.co.uk; ⏲ 11.00–16.00 Thu–Tue; free) Directly opposite the castle car park, in a handsome cream-coloured Georgian mansion, the Chepstow Museum is a minor delight. Through a series of packed rooms, it recalls the history of the town, with emphasis on the trades that sustained it, including shipbuilding along the Wye. There's also reference to the time when the building, unlikely as it seems, functioned as a Red Cross Hospital during World War I and then as a district hospital. Upstairs is a particularly fine series of topographical prints of Chepstow Castle.

A walk around town It's surprising how few people make it to Chepstow's town centre, most content to push on elsewhere after visiting the castle. This is a shame because there's enough to warrant a couple of hours' exploration, starting with the **Old Wye Bridge**, an elegant, cast-iron specimen built in 1816 by the splendidly named John Urpeth Rastrick, a renowned railway engineer. Costing around £17,850 (about £1.2 million in today's money), the five-arch bridge actually replaced a 500-year-old wooden structure. A cluster of plaques on the wall by the bridge relay all manner of fascinating facts and figures about both the bridge and the river: one contends that of all the iron arch road bridges built before 1830, this is the only one remaining, while another states that the tidal rise here is the fastest in the world, typically surging to 42ft (13m) in just 4 hours. The neighbouring **Riverside Gardens** hold some further points of interest: a large floor mosaic denotes the start (or finish) of the Wales Coast Path (page 50), while a blue plaque on the wall of La Ribera restaurant marks the spot from where John Frost and other convicted Chartists (page 112) left aboard a ship bound for Tasmania in 1840, a journey that would take four months.

Heading back up Bridge Street, you'll come to **St Mary's Church** at the end of Upper Church Street. As with the castle, the church was founded by William Fitz Osbern in 1072, just a few years after the former, as a Benedictine priory. Beyond the superb Norman doorway, with its zig-zag and lozenge-style stonework, the church interior is a relative mish-mash of styles. Now very much ageing, and in parts crumbling, a number of structural issues currently plague the building and there have even been threats of closure, so its future remains uncertain.

Taking pedestrianised St Mary Street, you'll come to **Beaufort Square**, at the heart of which, next to the War Memorial, stands **The Gun**, a grey-painted deck gun seized from a German UB-91 submarine during World War I and presented to the town by King George V in honour of a fallen Chepstow soldier. A few paces further along the High Street is the *Boatman*, an oversized bronze sculpture of a naked fisherman sat atop a boat-shaped granite plinth. Designed by London-based sculptor André Wallace, the *Boatman* is certainly a well-endowed chap, which caused a few mutterings of

Running for 136 miles from Chepstow to the source of the Wye in Plynlimon high up in the Cambrian Mountains, the Wye Valley Walk may be less well known than the neighbouring Offa's Dyke Path, but that doesn't make it any less an attractive proposition. Outlined here is a brief description of the walk's first two stages (the stretch between Chepstow and Monmouth), beyond which the walk – which crosses into England before looping back round to Hay-on-Wye on the Welsh side and then continuing northwest to Plynlimon – falls outside the area covered in this book.

One way of sampling both trails in the same day (especially if you need to be back in Chepstow) is to walk from Chepstow to Tintern along the Wye Valley Path, cross the old wireworks bridge into England, and then head south along the right bank of the Wye on the Offa's Dyke Path, a round trip of around 12 miles – a pamphlet (£1) from the visitor centre illustrates this route. Otherwise, jump on one of the hourly buses back to Chepstow. Either way, Cicerone's *The Wye Valley Walk* guide (£12.95) is an excellent companion.

CHEPSTOW TO TINTERN (6 miles; 3hrs 45mins) The trail starts at the car park by the castle. The first stage is, on the whole, fairly steep: in fact, the elevation gain of 1,578ft is the third highest of the route's 17 stages. Denoted by a leaping salmon, beyond The Dell running alongside the castle, it's a bit of a drudge, along a main road and then through a school car park, but once you reach the woodland path, it's fabulous. The first of several designated viewpoints – all of which were laid out in the mid 18th century by Valentine Morris, erstwhile politician, slave owner and proprietor of the Piercefield Estate (through which the trail passes) – is the Alcove, a stone seat long since shorn of its arched roof. Beyond The Grotto – a cave-like stone shelter – you come to the Giant's Cave, a slight misnomer given that this 40ft passage was hewn out of a huge chunk of rock. Taking its name from a stone giant that once supposedly guarded the entrance, the wide view from its platform is tremendous. Your next staging post is the Lower Wyndcliff car park and the A466. Cross the road and you have two options in order to reach the Eagle's Nest: tougher, but much more fun, is the path to the right, which is actually 365 knee-jarring steps, though once at the top you are rewarded with stupendous views of the almost entirely circular bend of the river (you are now just over 700ft above the Wye), as well as Chepstow Castle, which looks a surprisingly long way

discontent among some of the more conservative members of the community when it was unveiled in 2005. Either way, it's guaranteed to raise a wry smile.

Continuing uphill, the road narrows as it approaches the 13th-century **Town Gate**: firmly wedged between two buildings, this was once the principal route in and out of Wales, its original purpose as a collection point for tolls. Facing the gate, to the left is tiny Place de Cormeilles (it's not as grand as it sounds) where a substantial section of the **Old Port Wall** – built at the same time as the town gate – extends down to the main road before continuing on the other side and cutting awkwardly through a housing estate and beyond to the railway line.

TINTERN AND THE WYE VALLEY

'If you have never navigated the Wye, you have seen nothing,' remarked the author and cleric William Gilpin in his 1782 guide *Observations on the River Wye*, a book away now, and the Severn Bridge in the distance. Thereafter, the walk levels out through thick woodland before a gentle descent through fields and more woods and then into Tintern.

TINTERN TO MONMOUTH (9 miles; 4hrs 30mins) Compared with the first stage, the second leg is, on the whole, flatter and follows the course of the Wye for much of the way. From the abbey (though you could start anywhere in the village), walk through the village along the roadside path (unfortunately there is no riverside path) and just before the Wye Valley Hotel on the bend in the road, take the path that goes right to **St Michael's Church** (page 96). Go through the church grounds and enter the big open field, taking the riverside path. This sweeps round to a gate and some steps, which lead up to the **Old Station** (page 96). Continue north along the old Wye Valley track bed to Brockweir Bridge (the village of Brockweir is on the opposite side of the river) and take the steps up to the main A666 road. Cross the road (with care!), and take the path that continues into the woods, which is pretty much opposite a bus shelter. The initial bit is fairly steep before becoming more gradual. When you reach the Trellech road, with Hazelgrove House on your right, walk along here for 100 yards or so before the path heads off right, passing the Botany Bay Activity Centre. Follow the path, over a stream (which may be dry), before you come to another road. Turn left here, walking along the road for another 100 yards or so, before heading back into woodland on your right. Carry on through Bargain Wood, pausing at a couple of viewing points, before reaching **Cleddon Falls**, allegedly the spot from where Wordsworth wrote *Lines Composed a Few Miles above Tintern Abbey*.

From the falls, continue straight ahead, passing between a couple of properties along the track before entering more woodland. Carry on until you reach the hamlet of **Pen-y-Fan**, walking along the surfaced lane with views over the Wye and Bigsweir Bridge to your right. At the gateway to 'The Folly', the path turns right and goes down to the Whitebrook road. Continue down here, and with Tump Farm on your left, turn left at the bend in the road and continue for two miles alongside the river. At the Boat Inn (time for some refreshments?), cross Redbrook Bridge and into England, with the village of **Redbrook** on your right. From here, the path continues in gentle fashion alongside the river for another 2½ miles to Monmouth.

that effectively marked the beginning of tourism in Britain as we know it today. Gilpin had in fact sailed the Wye some years earlier (1770), though not before John Egerton, a rector from Ross-on-Wye and later the Bishop of Durham, had already designed a boat to transport passengers along the Wye. Following the publication of *Observations*, boat tours along the Wye became increasingly popular, early precursors to the modern-day package tour if you like. Gilpin's writing developed the idea of 'picturesque tourism', which marked a shift away from traditional sightseeing (typically history and architecture) towards scenery and landscapes, which the Wye Valley possessed in abundance – and still does of course, albeit rarely viewed from a boat these days.

Between Chepstow and Tintern, the Wye assumes the character of a tide river, hence the murky waters and thick, muddy banks, and while the river may have lost some of its sheen since Gilpin's day, there is more than ample compensation in the surrounding scenery – and this is what really makes walking the valley (whether that's along the Wye Valley Path or the Offa's Dyke Path) such a joy. From Tintern the Wye wriggles and worms its way up through heavily wooded slopes to Monmouth, which tops out the Lower Wye Valley.

TINTERN A long, linear village situated on a tidal stretch of the Wye, Tintern has been a magnet for visitors ever since Gilpin, Wordsworth and chums pitched up here in the 18th century seeking out the abbey ruins. And while this magnificent time capsule is undoubtedly the most compelling reason to visit, there's much else to enjoy here – in any case, there's a good chance you'll be passing through if you're hiking the Wye Valley or Offa's Dyke trails.

Getting there and away Bus #69 does the run between Chepstow and Monmouth, stopping at Tintern en route; the main stop is outside the Wild Hare, though the bus does stop elsewhere within the village, so if you're bound for the Old Station, for example, you can get off there. There are usually eight or nine buses per day in either direction on weekdays, four on Saturdays and none on Sundays.

🏠 Where to stay, eat and drink

🏠 **The Whitebrook** (8 rooms) Whitebrook; 📞 01600 860254; **w** thewhitebrook.co.uk; ⏱ 19.00–21.00 Thu, noon–13.30 & 19.00–21.00 Fri–Sun. Some 6½ miles north of Tintern, this beautifully located restaurant-with-rooms has a Michelin star courtesy of chef Chris Harrod, who worked with Raymond Blanc at Le Manoir. As much as possible is foraged from the neighbouring woods, so you may be tucking into the likes of truffle-baked parsnip with Hen of the Woods mushroom & salted plum, or suckling pig with garden chard & garlic purée. The cheapest way to eat is the 3-course set menu (£49), but if you really want to go for it there's an 8-course tasting menu for £110. Once you've eaten, you can sleep it all off in one of their immaculate rooms, 4 on the 1st floor & 4 on the 2nd floor, which are smaller & have a combined bath & shower (but are cheaper). Note that rooms are also only available Thu–Sun. **£££**

✱ 🏠 **Hop Garden** (5 units) Monmouth Rd; 📞 01291 680111; **w** thehopgarden.co.uk. The good folk of the Kingstone Brewery (page 97) at the northern end of the village also have 5 terrific on-site retreats (all sleeping 2 & with their own shower facilities), 4 of which are Scandi-style cabin-like structures mostly fashioned from wood – the pick of these is Brambling Cross, situated within a fenced-off garden, with an enclosed cabin

bed inside & firepit & hot tub outside. The 5th unit is a cleverly converted horsebox with a bed above the cab & a woodburning stove in the corner. **££**

🏠 **Wild Hare** (14 rooms) Monmouth Rd; 📞 01291 689205; **w** thewildharetintern.co.uk. This graceful little hotel has a suite of 5 differently graded rooms (lovely, fabulous, wonderful, luxury & suites) variously split between the main building & an exterior annex fronting a willow-fringed garden. Dogs are welcome in some rooms, for which there's a £10 charge. The restaurant, while not meriting a special diversion, is of a good standard, with a few eye-catching dishes like harissa-spiced lamb bon bons & roast cod loin with Welsh rarebit & creamed mash; service is cheerful enough if slightly ponderous. **££**

🍴 **Filling Station Café** Monmouth Rd; **m** 07770 544592; ⏱ 09.30–16.30 Mon & Fri, 08.45–17.00 Sat & Sun. As the crowd of bikes parked up outside this roadside café testify, this place is a popular refuelling spot for the hundreds of cyclists (that's no exaggeration) who pass through each weekend – & with good reason too. Vin, the owner & a keen cyclist himself, offers a cracking little menu of hot sandwiches, oggies (pasties), cakes & coffee, which he will happily prepare to your desired strength; they also run a tidy little ice cream parlour across the road. **£**

What to see and do Surveying Tintern's arcadian surrounds, it's hard to imagine that the village was once something of an industrial powerhouse, with Britain's first water-powered wire-drawing works established here in 1566 and, a little later, a major ironworks. By the mid 18th century, wire had become a much-sought-after commodity, variously used in the production of nails and fishing hooks as well as carding combs for the country's burgeoning wool industry. There's scant evidence to show for this today, save for a few ponds along the Angidy Valley, whose eponymous river (a tributary of the Wye) powered the furnaces and forges, and the **old wireworks bridge**, which was constructed to provided a rail link (the Tintern Wireworks line, a branch of the Wye Valley Railway) to the wireworks site on the other side of the river. In the event, the Abbey Wireworks Company had already closed at the time of the bridge's opening in 1876, and although a tinplate manufacturing company subsequently acquired the site, they ceased trading in 1901, leaving the railway line redundant and bringing to an end nearly 350 years of metalworking in Tintern. Closed just before World War II, the track was sold off and the bridge converted into a footpath, which it remains to this day. The only surviving waterwheel (there were 22) is in the grounds of the **Abbey Mill** (⊕ 10.30–16.30 Wed–Fri, 10.30–17.00 Sat & Sun), formerly the tidal dock. The restored wheel still turns occasionally, but the mill is otherwise now a busy craft-cum-shopping complex and tearoom.

Tintern Abbey (✆03000 252239; w cadw.gov.wales; ⊕ Mar–Jun 09.30–17.00 daily, Jul & Aug 09.30–18.00 daily, Sep & Oct 09.30–17.00 daily, Nov–Feb 10.00–16.00 daily; £6.60) No matter how many times you see it, Tintern Abbey is always a majestic sight, and it's little wonder that this place has inspired writers, painters and poets over the centuries, from the likes of Snyed Davies who extolled the glory of the abbey ruins in his 1745 poem, *Describing a Voyage to Tintern Abbey, in Monmouthshire, from Whitminster in Gloucestershire*, to Turner and Wordsworth, both of whom were frequent visitors. Others have been similarly enraptured, such as the priest and historian William Coxe who, on a tour through Monmouthshire in 1798, recorded that: 'the picturesque appearance of the ruins is considerably heightened by their position in a valley watered by the meandering Wye and backed by wooden eminences which rise abruptly from the river, unite a pleasing intermixture of wildness and culture, and temper the gloom of monastic solitude with the beauties of nature.'

Founded by Walter FitzRichard of Clare in 1131, Tintern was only the second Cistercian house in Britain after Waverley in Surrey (1128), and initially home to 13 choir monks from l'Aumône in Normandy, in addition to the abbot. The abbey's subsequent patronage included the Earl of Pembroke, William Marshal I and the Bigod Earls of Norfolk, one of whose clan, Roger (who had already overseen the development of Chepstow Castle) had a new abbey church built to replace the previous timber one. Consecrated in 1301, this ushered in a period of great prosperity for the abbey, which lasted until 3 September 1536 when it was surrendered to Henry VIII's officials following the dissolution of the monasteries. Appropriated by Henry Somerset, Earl of Worcester, many of the monastic buildings were subsequently employed as cottages and workshops for labourers from the nearby wire- and ironworks, but even by that stage the abbey was already in an advanced state of neglect.

The abbey's fortunes were partially reversed in the mid 18th century under the stewardship of Henry James, Fifth Duke of Beaufort, who had rubble and fallen masonry removed and the ground levelled and turfed. By this time, the abbey – and the Wye Valley as a whole – was emerging as a bona fide tourist destination, thanks to the recognition it had started to gain from some of the foremost writers, poets and painters of the time.

Beyond the reception, the path leads straight ahead to the **Warming House**, which, kitchen aside, was the only part of the abbey permitted a fire. After hours

Monmouthshire and Newport **TINTERN AND THE WYE VALLEY**

4

spent between the icy chill of the church, cloisters and dorms, this would have offered welcome respite for the monks. The Warming House is flanked on one side by the **Day Room** (aka Novices' Hall) – where monks would engage in various tasks such as writing manuscripts – and on the other by the **refectory**, a deceptively large space whose ornate stone doorway and slender window columns hint at its former splendour; you can still see the serving hatch adjoining the kitchen and the chute for dispensing waste. The monks' one daily meal, taken in silence, typically consisted of bread, veg and a few beans, with eggs, cheese and fish served on feast days – more generous was the daily beer allowance of one gallon per person. Collectively these quarters were among the first buildings constructed here at Tintern, around the mid 13th century. A later, 14th-century addition to the complex was the **abbot's residence**, which ranged across an extensive area northeast of the church and comprised a house (note the fireplace), hall and chamber, the latter with its own private chapel, in keeping with the abbot's high status. The rest of the site is consumed by the knee-high remains of the **infirmary buildings**, comprising hall, kitchens and cloister. Almost a mini monastery in itself, this is where the needs of the sick and elderly monks would have been attended to. Seek out, too, the extant drain, an ingenious example of medieval water management.

Constructed in the shape of a cathedral, the **church** is the abbey's great glory and one of the finest specimens of Gothic architecture in Britain, if not Europe. Upon entering the church through the mighty west front, whose skeletal seven-light window retains its exquisite stone tracery, Coxe commented that 'the eye passes rapidly along a range of elegant gothic pillars…from the length of the nave, the height of the walls, and the aspiring form of the pointed arches, first impressions are those of grandeur and sublimity.' And it's been the same for most visitors ever since. Bar the roof, an almost entire shell remains, and yet despite being stripped of almost all its ornamentation, it exudes a befitting sense of authority. Beyond the six bays that comprise the high and wide three-aisled nave, four massive cross-arms mark the divide between the nave and presbytery, and the north and south transepts; the space in between is the choir, so-named as this is where the choir-monks sang and prayed. In the presbytery, the great east window, unlike the west window largely devoid of all tracery, frames the distant hills perfectly.

Before exploring the complex, it really does pay to buy a guidebook (£4.95) here, as there is much to take in but information around the site is minimal.

Elsewhere in Tintern Most visitors to Tintern are content to view the abbey and move on, which is a shame because the village itself is deserving of further exploration. Heading north from the mill along Main Road (there's no riverside path to walk along at this point), you'll come to Tintern Parva (originally a separate parish but which was amalgamated with Chapel Hill to form Tintern as it is today), location for the squat **St Michael's Church**. Heavily rebuilt in 1846, St Michael's is originally of medieval descent, and while there are some vestigial remains, notably the inner wall of the south porch, a window in the chancel south wall and the font bowl, the church is predominantly Victorian in outlook. In theory it's open 10.00–16.00 each day but if it is closed ask around for the key.

From the church, continue into the field along the footpath that tracks the bend in the river (you are still on the Wye Valley Path) until you see signs for the **Old Station** (⊕ Apr–Oct 10.00–16.00 daily). One of just four stations that served the Wye Valley Railway, the line closed to passengers in 1959, and to freight around 25 years later, but the site has been well restored. Three carriages are here in situ, one with an exhibition on the Wye Valley, another packed with railway memorabilia, and the third nominally functioning as an information point/souvenir shop. You can also visit the old signal box and on Sundays the miniature railway gets an outing. Otherwise, partake in some refreshments in the restored Victorian waiting room – or you can camp on site too.

The brewing of ale in this part of the world has come on a bit since the days of the monks down at the abbey, and one local place to sample a few of the latest offerings is the **Kingstone Brewery** (✆ 01291 680111; w kingstonebrewery.co.uk; ◷ 11.30–16.00 Mon–Wed & Sat, though these times do change so ring ahead) just across the road from the Old Station. An independent, four-barrel micro-brewery, it is run by owner Ed Biggs and his small team, who hand brew and hand bottle eight different unfiltered and unpasteurised beers, ranging from a fine golden ale to a stronger premium stout, which you can enjoy in the courtyard garden or purchase from their Real Ale Shop. On the first Saturday of each month they have a pizza evening, but again do check in advance. They've also got some cool on-site accommodation (page 94).

AROUND TINTERN
Silver Circle Distillery
(✆ 01600 860702; w silvercircledistillery.com; ◷ 10.00–18.00 Thu–Sat) Operating out of a green corrugated-iron barn at the aptly named Pleasant View Barn in the village of Catbrook, just 3 miles northwest of Tintern, this small craft spirit producer was founded by Nina and Joe Howden in 2019. Gin is the name of the game here, with ingredients – which could be anything from mugwort and black garlic to blackberry leaves – foraged from the surrounding hills, fields and hedgerows. The result is more than half a dozen varieties of gins and cocktails, all of which are handcrafted and hand bottled on site. All the magic happens courtesy of a single still, named Rhiannon, a column hybrid that dispenses around 200 bottles every two weeks. Chief distiller Patrick talks visitors through the process in a 45-minute presentation (£15), before you get to sample their signature product, Wye Valley Gin, and a few others – perhaps a honey gin or a fruity damson negroni. Driving? Don't worry, as you'll receive a miniature to take away. If you fancy indulging in a little gin sorcery of your own, sign up for the 2½-hour gin school (£110). Otherwise, the small bar is open to the public on Friday and Saturday evenings, and street-food events are held on various dates throughout the summer.

Trellech If it's antiquity you seek, then Trellech (meaning 'Three Stones'), two miles north of Catbrook, is a must, as the village holds a remarkably disproportionate number of ancient monuments for such a modest settlement.

If driving, park in the small village car park, from where each of the four sites is no more than a 5-minute walk away. Start opposite the car park and walk along the path which passes through Court Farm towards **The Tump**, a curious, bramble-covered mound which, legend has it, should not be disturbed lest there be deadly reprisal. Thankfully no such fate is likely to pass once you've climbed it, but what you will get are some wonderful views, even from its very modest height of just 40ft. It's believed that a rudimentary wooden castle surmounted the mound some time in the 13th century, and the fact it's encircled by a shallow ditch would appear to support this assumption.

The most noteworthy monument in the village is the **Lost City of Trellech** (✆ 01291 625831; w lostcityoftrellech.org), some 400 yards due south of the car park along the Catbrook road. Following initial excavations in the early 2000s, Stuart Wilson – the site's current director and an archaeology graduate – bought the field at auction,

4

having been alerted to the possibilities here when he found some 13th-century pottery fragments dug up by moles. It's fair to say that many at the time thought he was bonkers, but having devoted much of his time (and money) to attempting to unearth its secrets, Stuart has been handsomely rewarded. Further excavations have uncovered the remains of five medieval stone structures, including a manor house and a courtyard well, as well as a few other bits and bobs: coins, cooking vessels and part of a leather shoe, for example. Although hard to reconcile looking at today's site, it has been reliably determined that this was an iron-working centre of some importance, whose eventual decline, and subsequently that of the village, coincided with the demise of the ruling de Clares, a powerful marcher lordship family who had also built Caerphilly Castle. It's an open access site, and in truth there's not an awful lot to see, but for the really keen, Stuart runs dig days on weekends between April and October, as well as guided group talks for a fee.

Returning to the main village junction, turn left on to the B4293 Llanishen road and about 150 yards up on your left-hand side are three prehistoric standing stones, these being the stones from which the name of the village derives. Also known as **Harold's Stones** (on account of the eponymous king, though any association is tenuous at best), these three thick fingers of puddingstone rock – each bearing a discernible drunken lean – are thought to date from around 3500BC, and while it has been proposed that their presence has some ritual or astronomical meaning, they were just as likely marker posts.

Finally, around 400 yards along the road to Tintern (in a field through a gate partially obscured by bushes), the **Virtuous Well**, or more properly St Anne's Well, has long been a place of spiritual significance, thanks to its iron-rich waters, which are alleged to contain medicinal properties. Set within a horseshoe-shaped wall, the well itself is likely to be of medieval origin. Candles and offerings placed inside the apsed niche, together with an untidy tangle of coloured ribbons tied to the tree, testify to the popularity of this slightly odd place.

Also of note in Trellech is **St Nicholas's Church**, whose mostly 13th-century nave is bookended by a 15th-century tower and a 19th-century chancel: it's worth a peek but no more.

MONMOUTH

Enclosed on three sides by the rivers Wye and Monnow, the former county town of Monmouth merits a decent day's exploration, though if you happen to be walking either of the Offa's Dyke or Wye Valley trails, it makes for a convenient stopover after completing the first (or second if you are at it) leg. While it's not exactly at the vanguard of culture, and certainly can't boast anything quite as grand as Chepstow Castle, the town prides itself on its historical associations: Henry V is said to have been born here, both Horatio Nelson and Charles Rolls have strong links to the town, and it was the site of the last mass treason trial in Britain.

As a border town, defence has always had an important role to play in Monmouth, ever since the Romans built a fort called Bestium. Following the Norman Conquest, the prolific Fitz Osbern designed a typically muscular fortification – initially timber but then augmented with stone defences – to which town walls and a fortified bridge were later added. It was as a market town and agricultural centre, as opposed to any particular industrial might, that the town really prospered, although the availability of excellent stocks of local wool did sustain a profitable knitting industry – the Monmouth cap was a much sought-after item, popular among soldiers and sailors, and even exported to the continent. Monmouth was really put on the map in 1839,

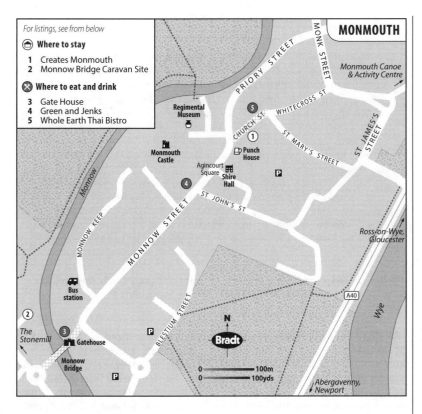

when the trial of John Frost and other Chartists was held here (page 112), an event
that the town has made great play of ever since.

GETTING THERE AND AWAY Monmouth is not on a railway line (the closest
stations are Chepstow and Hay-on-Wye), but bus links are good, with connections
to Abergavenny (4 daily Mon–Sat), Chepstow (10 daily Mon–Sat), Tintern (8 daily
Mon–Fri, 5 Sat), Trellech (4 daily Mon–Sat) and Usk (6 daily Mon–Sat). The bus
station is at the bottom of Monnow Street.

TOURIST INFORMATION A small information desk (⏰ 11.00–16.00 Mon, Tue & Sat)
just inside the Shire Hall dispenses leaflets and the staff can assist with any queries.

 WHERE TO STAY *Map, above*
Accommodation options in Monmouth are surprisingly limited given the town's
prominent position on both the Offa's Dyke and the Wye Valley trails.

🏠 **Creates Monmouth** (8 rooms) 7 Church
St; ☎ 01600 460492; w createsmonmouth.com.
Run by Ben Price & his husband Kenny John, this
divine little guesthouse is comfortably the most
appealing overnight option in town. Ben is the
creative force behind the interior design, with
all rooms conceived on the theme of woodland
animals, hence names like Hare's Warren &
Squirrel's Drey, & lots of playful design touches
including acorn-shaped lamps & a wall-bound
suitcase masquerading as a shelf. Continental b/
fast is taken in the restaurant, which otherwise
serves as a very impressive in-house art
gallery. **££**

If you were wondering what all the buzz was about in Monmouth, well, in 2020, Monmouth was designated Britain's first Bee Town. On the back of the county council's pilot project 'Nature Isn't Neat', the town council and Bees for Development – a Monmouth-based charity that uses beekeeping as a way to help alleviate poverty around the world – joined forces to promote a bee-friendly environment in the town through, for example, selective mowing of council green spaces and by encouraging locals to create pollinator-friendly gardens. The town also happens to be home to a high density of beekeepers anyway.

Naturally, there is an annual **Bee Festival** (w monmouthbeefestival.co.uk), which usually takes place on the first weekend of July each year across two town-centre sites, Chippenham Fields and the Nelson Garden. There are talks and demonstrations, bee-related products to sample, a bee walk, activities for kids, a tea party and loads more. If the sun is shining, it's a fabulous day out.

🏠 **Monnow Bridge Caravan Site** Drybridge St; ☎01600 714004. This tidy little site, just a few minutes' walk from the town centre, has space for both tents & campervans; facilities consist of a shower block & toilets. **£**

✗ **WHERE TO EAT AND DRINK** *Map, page 99, unless otherwise stated*

✗ **The Stonemill** [map, page 86] Rockfield; ☎01600 716273; ⏰ 10.00–15.00 & 18.00–21.00 Wed–Sat, noon–14.30 Sun. 2 miles west of town, the classy Stonemill offers top-drawer country dining in a superbly converted 16th-century barn. There's very little on the menu that's not sourced locally, with the likes of Pant-ys-gawn goats' cheese mousse (with beetroot remoulade & dukkah) & Raglan lamb (served with mint gnocchi & rosemary jus) the sort of scrummy morsels you can expect to dine on; otherwise, all bread, pasta & ice cream is made on site, with fruit, vegetables & herbs sourced from the kitchen garden. **£££**

✗ **Whole Earth Thai Bistro** 10 White Swan Court; ☎01600 715555; ⏰ 09.00–16.00 Mon–Thu, 09.00–22.30 Fri & Sat. Located at the top of Monmouth High St, this super little bistro has been dishing up some of the best Thai food in South Wales for many a year now. Curry aficionados will be very satisfied, as will those hankering after a good pad stir-fry. BYO too (£2 corkage). **££**

🍺 **Gate House** 125 Monnow St; ☎01600 713890; w the-gate-house.com; ⏰ 11.00–23.00 Mon–Thu, 11.00–late Fri & Sat, noon–23.00 Sun. In a town rather well endowed with pubs, this fine Georgian building just about shades it as the pick of 'em, largely by virtue of its position next to the Monnow Bridge & with outdoor seating overlooking the water, but also because it has the best selection of ales – the food's not half bad either. **££**

☕ **Green and Jenks** 11 Agincourt Sq; ☎01600 711657; w greenandjenks.com; ⏰ 09.00–17.00 Mon–Sat, 10.00–17.00 Sun. The lengthy queues outside this inviting deli-cum-café testify to its popularity, & with good reason. Most folk come here for the excellent coffee or ice cream (or both) but there's loads more besides including a delicious selection of *merendas* – flat, sausage-roll-like snacks stuffed, for example, with cheese, vegetables & walnuts. The upstairs floor is essentially an art gallery, but if you'd rather be outside, to the rear of the shop a raised seating area overlooks a smartly designed sunken terrace. **£**

ACTIVITIES Monmouth is the ideal spot from which to explore the River Wye, and to this end, the excellent **Monmouth Canoe and Activity Centre** (Castle Yard, Old Dixon Rd; ☎01600 716083; w monmouthcanoe.co.uk) offers both canoe (£60/70 half/full day) and kayak hire (from £40/50 half/full day) as well as guided trips along the river.

WHAT TO SEE AND DO Most things of interest in Monmouth are on, or just off, Monnow Street, itself bookended by the River Monnow at one end and the Shire Hall at the other. Spanning the Monnow is a handsome, 17th-century three-span pedestrianised stone bridge, itself crowned by a chunky **gatehouse** dating from 1262 – thus rendering it the last remaining fortified river bridge in Britain. Tours of the gatehouse – which has variously functioned as a tollhouse and lock-up – are sometimes possible, so it's worth checking with the tourist information office if you're keen.

From the bridge, Monnow Street gently inclines, and despite the usual proliferation of chain stores, it's not an unattractive thoroughfare, flanked on either side with pleasing two- and three-storeyed coloured buildings. The top end of Monnow Street opens up on to **Agincourt Square**, so named after Monmouth-born Henry V's victory at the eponymous battle in 1415. And it's a statue of Henry V, one arm aloft, that adorns the central first-floor niche of the grand Shire Hall (see below), the town's most arresting building. Not to be overshadowed is William Goscombe John's flamboyant **statue** of Charles Stewart Rolls holding a biplane aloft (in front of the Shire Hall). Although well known for his motoring exploits – the name will be familiar as one half of the Rolls Royce empire – Rolls, whose parents were from nearby Llangattock, was also a pioneering aviator. In 1910 he became the first man to pilot a double-flight over the English Channel, so it was somewhat ironic (though no less tragic) that just a month later he was the first Briton to die in an air crash, at the Bournemouth air show.

Shire Hall (Agincourt Sq; ☎01600 775257; w monlife.co.uk; ⏰ 11.00–16.00 Mon, Tue & Sat; free) A splendid Baroque edifice built in 1724 to house the County Court of Assizes, the six-arched Shire Hall wouldn't look out of place in Bath, thanks to its smooth limestone façade. Until 1974, the hall functioned as Monmouthshire county's administrative centre, but following the creation of Gwent Council and the transfer of the county court to Abergavenny in 2002, the building was stripped of any real purpose. But its history does loom large.

In 1839, the Shire Hall was the scene of one of the most noteworthy trials in British history, when John Frost, alongside fellow ringleaders William Jones and Zephaniah Williams, stood trial for their roles in the Chartists' riots in Newport earlier that year (page 112); their resultant death sentences were subsequently commuted to deportation. The courtroom in which the trial took place – and which functioned as a court of law until 2002 – offers little real insight into the events surrounding the trial, though it is possible to view the claustrophobic holding cells in which the protagonists (and other miscreants over the years) were held. More illuminating is an exhibition entitled Dig Monmouth, a small but exceptional hoard retrieved from a handful of excavation sites around town. Among the many exquisite items on show are a Roman disc brooch, some rare Venetian glass fragments, pieces of rouletted pottery, clay pipes, marbles and, most eye-catching of all, a handful of items hewn from bone, namely a comb, flute and die.

Monmouth Castle and Regimental Museum (Castle Hill; ☎01600 772175; w monmouthcastlemuseum.org.uk; ⏰ Apr–Oct 14.00–17.00 daily; free) On the opposite side of Agincourt Square to the Shire Hall, a path leads up to the largely ignored ruins of **Monmouth Castle**, which was (mostly) obliterated during the Civil War, though three sides do remain more or less intact. The ruins carry some historical clout, for it was here in 1386 (or thereabouts) that Henry V was born, as a plaque on one wall recalls. King of England between 1413 and 1422, Henry V's greatest military success by far was a routing of the French at Agincourt in 1415, a cracking away victory if ever there was one.

Just across the way, the Great Castle House (itself constructed from some of the castle's remaining bricks) is the headquarters of the Royal Monmouthshire Royal Engineers, the second-oldest regiment in the British army, and unique for having the word 'Royal' twice in its title. The Engineers' illustrious history – it has provided unbroken service since 1539 – is relayed in the **Regimental Museum**, and although for much of the piece it's a fairly dry affair, with cabinets stuffed with the usual medals, documents, weaponry, battleground mementoes and suchlike, the sections on the regiment's engagements in more recent conflicts like the Falklands, Bosnia and Iraq are worth lingering over.

GWENT LEVELS

A low-lying, estuarine landscape of alluvial wetland, salty lagoons and marshes, and intertidal mudflats, the magical Gwent Levels are a place apart. Indeed, this gorgeous slice of pancake-flat lushness comes as one of the most unexpected landscapes in all South Wales, home to no fewer than eight Sites of Special Scientific Interest (SSSIs), among them Black Rock, Magor Marsh and the Newport Wetlands National Nature Reserve. Yet they are all too easily bypassed by visitors in a dash to reach Cardiff or the more obvious destinations further west; the fact that the M4 runs more or less parallel to the Levels just to the north offers little incentive to slow down (and explore more locally), but it's also certainly the case that they just aren't that well known – certainly not as well known as their more celebrated counterparts across the bridge in Somerset.

Attempts to tame, or, more accurately, reclaim the Levels from the sea have been ongoing ever since the Romans set foot here over two millennia ago. Evidence points to the construction of a seawall and the cutting of drainage channels (reens) even back then, a process continued in earnest fashion by Benedictine monks from the long-since-gone Goldcliff Priory. Following the dissolution of the monasteries, control and management of the land passed to a few select, and very wealthy, landowners, among them the Duke of Beaufort and the Morgans of Tredegar, who continued the process of digging drains and rebuilding or relocating sections of the seawall. Increased industrialisation in the 19th century had a transformative effect on the Levels, what with the construction of the Chepstow to Swansea railway line and the Severn Tunnel, although there was also a degree of depopulation as people moved away from the area to take up employment in the increasingly urbanised towns and cities.

A more recent, and existential, threat to this precarious landscape was the proposed construction of an M4 relief road, which, had it gone ahead would (according to many experts) have resulted in the destruction of many precious habitats. But after years of political wrangling and tireless opposition from locals and environmentalists, the project was canned in 2019, the primary reason given being the environmental impact – although there's no doubt that cost was an equally determining factor. This, though, hasn't stopped the UK government from suggesting that they might overrule the devolved administration at some point in the future.

The most obvious appeal of the Levels is its fantastic birdlife, though it offers sanctuary for all kinds of other wildlife too: bees, butterflies and beetles, plus mammals like otters and water voles. There's also terrific cycling and walking to be had here with little, if any, real exertion required, including a substantial section of the Wales Coast Path, while the many villages strung out along the Levels – such as Goldcliff, Portskewett, Redcliff and Nash – offer a flavour of the area's heritage, most boasting an ancient church at the very least.

RUNSTON CHAPEL AND LLANMELIN WOOD HILLFORT Hidden away in perfect rural isolation about a mile north of the village of Crick, the 12th-century **Runston Chapel** (m 07847 658653; w cadw.gov.wales; ⊕ open access) is all that remains of a medieval village, abandoned some time in the 18th century. It's been reliably determined that the village (which historians believe pre-dated the chapel by at least a century) consisted of around 20 dwellings, in addition to a manor house – and while there's now nothing tangible to see, it is possible to detect a few turf-covered banks here and there, which most likely correspond to the layout of the houses. Most probably built by the Normans following their conquest of the region, the chapel itself – roofless and half surrounded by a shallow stone wall – remains an evocative sight, and also retains some impressive architectural features, notably an almost completely intact chancel arch and a couple of well-preserved lancet windows in the nave.

The chapel is tricky to find, though that does increase the sense of satisfaction once you've actually made it. To reach it, head up Crick Road from the village and after about a mile on your right you'll come to a small gap in the trees, which is the entrance to Wye Valley Archery (it's not signposted so is easy to miss), whereupon you should be able to open the gate and park up. Either way, and if you are determined to visit the site, your safest bet is to contact Lee, owner of the archery club and self-styled 'Guardian of the Chapel', though the site is under CADW's stewardship. If he is there, he'll happily walk you up to the chapel and give some spiel on the place too.

If you're with wheels, then 3 miles northwest of Runston Chapel, near Llanvair Discoed, is **Llanmelin Wood Hillfort** (w cadw.gov.wales; ⊕ 10.00–16.00 daily), which is marginally easier to find as it is at least signposted. Heading through the twisting lanes you'll arrive at Coombe Farm on your right, opposite which is a small patch of grass, just big enough for a couple of cars. From here a path runs alongside a cornfield and then dips and bends through woods before emerging at the hillfort. It's immediately recognisable thanks to its steep banks and deep ditches, though these are now so heavily overgrown that a bit of wading is required. Moreover, the site is surrounded by a thick ring of trees, thus obscuring any potential views. But it's a colourful sight, having been heavily colonised by the likes of St John's wort and rosebay willowherb, the latter's tall pink spires blanketing much of the site in summer – you may even spot the occasional alpine strawberry. Initial excavations of Llanmelin, led by Victor Nash-Williams in the 1930s, established that the fort was most likely begun around 2500BC, with further phases of development in later years, possibly as late as 50BC. Recent digs have unearthed items of pottery and metalwork alongside animal and human remains. The fort was probably abandoned around AD75, just as the Romans began settling in Caerwent and Caerleon.

CAERWENT Situated in the centre of the broad Nedern Valley, Caerwent (meaning 'stronghold of Gwent') wouldn't normally merit a diversion, but the fact that it retains the best-preserved defences of any Roman town in Britain renders it a real highlight on any tour of the region. Strategically located on a major Roman highway between Glevum (Gloucester) and Isca (Caerleon), Venta Silurum, or 'market town of the Silures', was established around AD75 just as Romanisation of the region was gathering pace. For the next 300 years or so, Venta functioned as one of the smallest tribal capitals in Britain, as well as the main administrative centre of the Silures, who had been granted a degree of self-governance. But like so many outposts in Britain, the town's fortunes waned when the Romans upped sticks, and by the end of the 5th century its decline was complete.

Enclosing much of the modern village, the **old town wall** is a mile-long girdle of Roman handiwork reckoned to be the finest in Britain: an easy-paced circuit should take no more than 45 minutes. Although you can pick up the wall pretty much anywhere, your best bet is to park in the main car park near the West Gate. From here, turn right and cross the road before hopping up on to the grassy ramparts of the West Wall, though it's just as much fun walking along the base, because from here you can fully appreciate their scale. Up to 16ft high in places and peppered with crumbling bastions, the largely intact South Wall exerts a formidable presence; factor in some lovely views across the valley and this is easily the most rewarding section of the walk. In the southeastern corner, an 11th-century Norman motte marks the start of the East Wall, which gradually tapers down to the East Gate, of which very little remains. Just above here, the Coach and Horses pub suffices for a brief thirst-quencher on a hot day. Much of the North Wall has been lost under grass or obscured by gardens, so could easily be skipped if you're pushed for time.

Within this immense fortified perimeter wall (itself bisected by a main road running between the East and West gates) lie the vestigial remains of several **Roman buildings**, which were excavated periodically between 1899 and 1984. The area contained within the walls would have comprised a planned system of streets, variously parcelled up into different-sized plots, or *insulae* – I, II, III and so on up to 20 here at Venta. Roughly opposite the church is the old Roman-Celtic temple, which bears a near-complete and very well-defined floor plan, though the focal point of the town would have been the forum and basilica, abutting each other just behind the temple: the forum was essentially an open market sheltering offices, shops, stalls and the like, while the basilica (whose remains are more visible) comprised three aisles, as its substantial foundations demonstrate. A cluster of buildings over in Pound Lane, near the car park, include what would have been a very comfortable 15-room courtyard house, another 4th-century house with 13 rooms and the extensive remains of a hypocaust (an elaborate heating system), and some neighbouring shops. Interpretation panels do a good job of explaining each site's function, alongside images depicting how each one might have looked.

While here, pop over to the **village church** to view the so-called Paulinus Inscription, a magnificently chunky stone block discovered in 1903 bearing a dedication to Tiberius Claudius Paulinus, a commander of the Second Augustan Legion at Caerleon in the early 3rd century. The inscription not only documents the legate's military achievements but it also sheds light on the structure of the civil administration.

DEWSTOW GARDENS (Dewstow Rd, Caldicot; ✆01291 431020; w dewstowgardens. co.uk; ⊕ May–Sep 10.00–15.30 daily; £8) It's a little surprising that Dewstow Gardens aren't more well known, but that's no bad thing as this means that you're more likely to have them all to yourself, at least outside the school holidays. These enchanting gardens appeared to be lost to eternity until 2000, when current owners John and Lisa Harris, whose family acquired the estate in 1980, began the process of rediscovering, and simultaneously renovating, the site – and the job they've done is fantastic. The garden's history is first worth recalling: confiscated by Parliamentarians in 1657 during the Civil War, and then owned by the vicar of Magor, the estate was subsequently purchased in 1893 by Great Western Railway director Henry Oakley, who commissioned eminent landscaper James Pulham – responsible for the likes of Sandringham and Buckingham Palace – to rework the grounds. Although Pulhamite designs (distinguished by their fantastical rockwork creations) were not particularly unusual within the UK during the Victorian era, both the nature and scale of the gardens here at Dewstow render these the most unique – and certainly justifies their Grade I-listed status. Oakley managed the gardens up until his death in 1940, after which time they fell into disrepair, to the extent that they were almost completely buried in the 1960s when spoil excavated to build the nearby M4 motorway was dumped here.

The Harris's excavations, made all the more difficult by having no plans or records of what had gone before, led to some unexpected discoveries, the most surprising of which was a sequence of subterranean **grottoes** concealing dry pools, streams and hidden caverns. Subsequently named Fern, Tufa and Lion, these jungle-like spaces now support many kinds of sub-tropical flora as well as plenty of fish. A tunnel from one of the grottoes leads to the timeworn Tropical House, whose rusting cast-iron columns stand much as they've always done.

Back above ground, the fragrant **rock garden** is planted with African daisies, wood cranesbill, cinquefoil and Himalayan honeysuckle. Close by, a neatly tended herbaceous border bristling with colour (red bistort, blue globe thistle, acanthus) frames an inviting croquet lawn, beyond which further paths slope down to a succession of ponds and gardens connected by a series of narrow paths and low stone bridges. The place teems with colourful plant life: lilies, sunflowers, dahlias, gooseneck and much more. You'd do well to bring a picnic too, the rolling, baize-like lawns fronting the family house inviting a lengthy pause as well as the promise of Severn Estuary views. Gardens can often come across as being rather stuffy places, but Dewstow is not one of those and caters brilliantly to families and younger visitors.

BLACK ROCK Just outside the village of Portskewett, and within touching distance of the Prince of Wales Bridge, Black Rock is home to Wales's only existing lave net fishery, an ancient method of fishing that has been present here since the 1600s, though it's a way of life now sadly under threat. With their wide, willow-framed Y-shaped lave nets, the fishermen (there are currently eight) wade out waist-high into the Severn Estuary and wait to snaffle any passing salmon. The season is short, running from the beginning of June until the end of August, and the fishing itself is tide-dependent, so catch is rare. Despite this, in 2021 Natural Resources Wales imposed a mandatory catch-and-release rule, owing to what they claim are reduced stocks, but these restrictions, say the fishermen, now make it virtually unsustainable for them to carry on. But carry on they do, for the time being at least, and while all is not quite lost, the future for the lave fishermen remains uncertain. Adjacent to the car park, the net house has a small display and occasionally opens up on fishing days, though these are random (and not at weekends) so your best bet is to check the website (w blackrocklavenets.co.uk).

Whatever the future holds, this unique piece of fishing heritage is celebrated in the form of a gigantic wooden sculpture of a lave fisherman attempting to catch a salmon. From the picnic site, where there's a fabulous view of the entire span of the bridge, there's an easy 3-mile **circular walk**, and while not the most scenic stroll, it does takes in a few interesting aspects of the local heritage. Starting at the sculpture, follow the Wales Coast Path for about half a mile before entering the village of **Sudbrook**, built to house some 3,000 workers during construction of the Severn Tunnel in the late 19th century (page 87); indeed, many houses were built using excavated material from the tunnel. This outstanding feat of engineering is recalled in the **Sudbrook Tunnel Centre** (☏ 01291 420530; w visitmonmouthshire. com; ⏱ 10.30–17.00 daily), which occupies one room of the Sports and Social Club on Camp Road, formerly the pay office. The adjacent water-pumping station is still in working order, which is just as well because up to 20 million gallons of water flow into the tunnel each day. The village has grown since those days, with the old workers' cottages joined by ranks of faceless housing estates.

Beyond the Tunnel Centre, follow the path round to some rather sorry-looking 12th-century **chapel ruins**, all that remains of a long-lost medieval village, and an **Iron-Age camp**, though you wouldn't much know it standing here. At this point you can either carry along the coast path or continue the circular walk, in which case cut through the gap in the rampart (on the other side of the football field just beyond the goalposts) and back into the village. Once out of the village (the road bends around to the right), go through a gate and a series of fields running parallel to the main railway line. Cross the tracks via the footbridge and take a right into **Sunnycroft** – continue along here and at the end turn right again down Black Rock Road all the way back to the picnic site.

MAGOR MARSH (w gwentwildlife.org) Seven miles west of Black Rock, and just a couple of miles south of junction 23A of the M4, Magor Marsh is a tranquil area of relict fenland covering a varied terrain of reedbeds, meadows, woodland, grazing pasture and ditches (or reens), which are narrow, manmade channels designed to alleviate flooding in marshy coastal areas such as this. Not only do these function as an important flood-protection measure, but they support a healthy population of water voles, which were reintroduced at Magor less than ten years ago. The fact that these semi-aquatic rodents (Britain's largest) do thrive here is mainly due to the absence of American mink in the area, which have decimated the animal in many other parts of the country. Their deep burrows can be detected along the grassy banks, and although you're unlikely to see a vole itself, you might hear a faint 'splosh' as it dives into the water. Similarly elusive are otters and stoats, but they are here, as is the king diving beetle, the largest and rarest of the water beetles – so rare, in fact, that this is one of the very few habitats anywhere in Wales.

From the car park a raised, buggy-friendly **boardwalk** wends its way around the marsh, with one path breaking off towards a hide overlooking the pond, where you'll likely spot reed and sedge warblers, herons and egrets; you may even catch the blue flash of a kingfisher skimming the water. Wildflowers flourish here too: bittersweet (woody nightshade), meadowsweet and ragged robin, while, in July and August, frogbit – a small, lily-like plant bearing three white-petalled flowers – masses across the water's surface. A leisurely stroll around the site should take no more than 45 minutes to an hour.

Architectural oddities pop up in all sorts of unexpected places across South Wales and Magor is no exception. Less than half a mile from the marsh (back in the direction of the village) stand the skeletal 16th-century remains of a **Procurator's House**, which is believed to be the last building of its kind still standing in Wales, and probably just one of two or three in the whole of Britain. Incongruously located beside the village church and opposite a modern housing estate, the house – which also goes by the names of Magor Mansion and Church House, as it was unclear as to whether it was indeed used for ecclesiastical purposes – still bears two reasonably intact sides.

NEWPORT WETLANDS NATIONAL NATURE RESERVE (West Nash Rd; ☏ 01633 636363; w rspb.org.uk; ⏱ 09.00–17.00 daily; £4 parking for non-RSPB members)

Sited next to the gaping mouth of the River Usk, the Newport Wetlands National Nature Reserve was only designated as such in 2008, having been conceived a few years earlier in response to the loss of numerous habitats in the area caused by the creation of the Cardiff Bay Barrage (page 76). Indeed, the site's transformation from an ash-covered wasteland – waste that was mostly dumped here years ago from the neighbouring, though now-redundant, Uskmouth power station – is as remarkable as it is exciting. Four easily walkable (and buggy-/wheelchair-accessible) paths, varying in length from a mile-long trail to a three-mile loop that combines elements of the three other paths, cut through a large area of mostly reedbeds and water channels, as well as smaller tracts of woodland, scrub and wet grassland. Beyond the high seawall that marks the southern boundary of the reserve – you are now on the Wales Coast Path – lie the wide, open mudflats.

The wildlife here is premier-league class, and although you'll get most out of a visit during late spring and summer, there's activity all year round: resident birds include little egret, Cetti's warbler and bearded tit, the latter identifiable (contrary to its name) by its distinctive black 'moustache' and which can usually be seen flittering among the reeds. Winter has its own special appeal, with plenty of waders: dunlin, lapwing, oystercatcher and the charismatic curlew probe the mudflats in search of a good meal. But there are few more memorable spectacles than the murmurations. Each day at dusk, tens of thousands of starlings fly in cleverly co-ordinated formations as they bed down among the reedbeds for the night – the most common explanation for this strange avian dynamic is that by grouping together in such large numbers, this affords the birds a greater degree of protection from potential predators such as sparrowhawks and peregrines. December and January are the best months to see this. If your luck is in, you may spot a marsh harrier or bittern, though the latter is notoriously shy and difficult to spot, such is its brilliant disguise.

It's not just about the birds, though: these wetlands are home to one of Britain's rarest and most endangered bees, namely the shrill carder, which makes merry among the abundant wildflowers – late spring sees a wave of colour wash across the reserve, with several varieties of orchid (including marsh and bee), as well as buttercups, yellow iris and grass vetchling, or grass pea. Otters and grass snakes do their best to be avoided, but there are good numbers of these here too.

Halfway along the seawall stands the **East Usk Lighthouse**, dating from 1893 and one of two lighthouses that guarded the entrance to the Usk Estuary. While the West Usk Lighthouse is now a wedding venue, this one is still operational, despite its legs being buried in fly ash dumped here from the power station. The visitor centre at the reserve entrance has a small exhibition, café and RSPB shop, a good place to stock up on bird feed for your own garden. Don't worry if you forget your binoculars; they can be hired here for a fiver. Wheelchairs and mobility scooters can also be hired here.

NEWPORT

Most people simply bypass Newport en route to Cardiff, and it's fair to say that Wales's third-largest city doesn't rank highly on the list of most visitors' planned destinations. It's true that years of industrial decline, which culminated in the closure of the city's last steelworks in 2020, has taken its toll, yet the common perception of an industrially depressed and culturally bereft city is a little off the mark. Among the pockets of deprivation, you'll find vestiges of antiquity, sterling Victorian architecture and world-class engineering (here's looking at you, Transporter

4

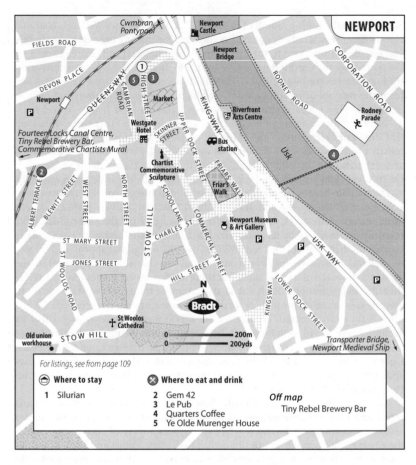

Cwmbran,
Pontypool

Newport
Castle

Newport
Bridge

FIELDS ROAD

CORPORATION ROAD

DEVON PLACE

QUEENSWAY

CAMBRIAN ROAD

HIGH STREET

Newport

P

Market

Riverfront
Arts Centre

RODNEY ROAD

Rodney
Parade

Westgate
Hotel

SKINNER STREET

UPPER DOCK STREET

KINGSWAY

Bus
station

Usk

Fourteen Locks Canal Centre,
Tiny Rebel Brewery Bar,
Commemorative Chartists Mural

Chartist
Commemorative
Sculpture

FRIARS WALK

Friar's
Walk

ALBERT TERRACE

BLEWITT STREET

WEST STREET

NORTH STREET

STOW HILL

SCHOOL LANE

CHARLES ST

COMMERCIAL STREET

Newport Museum
& Art Gallery

P

USK WAY

ST MARY STREET

ST WOOLOS ROAD

JONES STREET

HILL STREET

COMMERCIAL STREET

P

KINGSWAY

LOWER DOCK STREET

P

N

Bradt

St Woolos
Cathedral

Old union
workhouse

STOW HILL

0 — 200m
0 — 200yds

Transporter Bridge,
Newport Medieval Ship

For listings, see from page 109

🛏 **Where to stay**
1 Silurian

❌ **Where to eat and drink**
2 Gem 42
3 Le Pub
4 Quarters Coffee
5 Ye Olde Murenger House

Off map
Tiny Rebel Brewery Bar

Bridge). Factor in a growing portfolio of independents – shops, breweries and coffee shops – and Newport's trajectory, it seems, is slowly being reversed.

The first known recorded name of present-day Newport was Novus Bergus, which was bestowed by the Normans in the 11th century, who subsequently built a castle up on Stow Hill. As the iron and coal industries boomed in the early 19th century, so did the city's docks, which grew to become Wales's largest coal port and one of Europe's major trading hubs, handling not only coal, steel and iron but other cargo such as vehicles, food and tobacco. But the combined impact of two World Wars (though it was largely spared from the Luftwaffe's bombs), together with post-war recession, contributed to its inevitable demise.

Newport is a city steeped in history, with a formidable track record of liberal radicalism – it was here that the infamous Chartist Rising of 1839 occurred, the last major armed insurrection in mainland Britain. Politics aside, Newport has often possessed an edgy energy: it was at the forefront of the alternative Welsh music scene in the 1990s – though it was quite different (and indifferent) to the Britpop movement that was to follow and which had more in common with Cardiff just up the road – and it remains a fertile breeding ground for new artists. Sport also plays an important role in community life, with the Newport Gwent Dragons – one of Wales's four professional rugby union regional teams – providing the weekend blood and thunder; match days in the streets around the antiquated but much-loved Rodney Parade ground are usually charged with good-natured beery fervour. The city has had its moments in the international spotlight too: in 2010, nearby Celtic Manor hosted the Ryder Cup golf tournament between Europe and the United States, then in 2014 the same venue hosted the NATO summit, welcoming more than 60 world leaders to town, including Barack Obama, remarkably the first serving US president to visit Wales.

GETTING THERE AND AWAY As Wales's gateway city, Newport has excellent road, rail and bus links. It's on the main London to Cardiff railway line with hourly services to the capital, half-hourly services to Bristol and trains to Cardiff at least every 20 minutes. There are also regular services to Abergavenny (every 30mins), Caldicot (hourly), Chepstow (hourly) and Pontypool (every 45mins). The city's station (which is as close as many people get to actually visiting the city) is on Queensway, just a 2-minute walk from the centre. Buses, which depart from the huge main bus station below Friar's Walk, fan out to all areas, including Abertillery (hourly), Cardiff (every 15mins), Caerleon (every 20mins), Chepstow (hourly), Raglan (7 daily Mon–Sat) and Usk (7 daily Mon–Sat).

TOURIST INFORMATION The Newport Museum and Art Gallery (page 111) has a limited rack of leaflets, though the staff can help out with any general queries.

WHERE TO STAY It's unlikely that you'll need (or indeed want) to stop the night – particularly with Cardiff just down the road – which is just as well because options are limited. There are, however, one or two appealing possibilities, including the Celtic Manor Resort, just outside town, which rates as one of the country's most exclusive (and expensive) venues.

Celtic Manor Resort [map, page 86] (548 rooms) Coldra Woods, Usk Valley; ☎01633 410262; w celtic-manor.com. It's a beast of a building when viewed from the M4, but unabashed glamour pervades this vast resort spread among lovely parkland 3½ miles east of Newport, & which hosted both the 2010 Ryder Cup & 2014 NATO summit. The main Resort Hotel is the showstopper – effortlessly classy rooms with marble bathrooms & state-of-the-art audio-visuals – while the 19th-century Manor House is 1 level of luxury below; then, thirdly, there's the more affordable Coldra Court Hotel. Factor in a couple of glitzy spas, half a dozen restaurants & its own mini shopping mall & there's really no reason to want, or need, to leave at all. Golf aside (it's got the small matter of 3 championship courses), there are activities galore, from archery & tennis to high ropes & laser combat. Good luck fitting it all in. **£££**

Silurian Hotel [map, opposite] (61 rooms) 55 High St; ☎01633 533050; w silurianhotel.com. There are no airs or graces about this appealing mid-range hotel, which occupies a convenient location across the road from the train station & is close to the city's most enjoyable pubs & restaurants. The rooms are crisp, clean & well insulated from the neighbouring streets, ensuring a decent night's sleep. Excellent cooked b/fasts to order too. **££**

WHERE TO EAT AND DRINK *Map, opposite*

Gem 42 42 Bridge St; ☎01633 287591; w gem42.co.uk; ⏰ 17.30–23.00 daily. The location, on the busiest of main roads near the top of the railway bridge, couldn't be any less appealing, but that's immediately forgotten once inside this sublime restaurant run by the Cinotti brothers. Between them (Sergio does mains & Pasquale desserts), they conjure up a thrilling quartet of 4-course tasting menus (including separate vegetarian & vegan ones), each costing £45; sample plates might include scallop with egg yolk & wasabi vinaigrette, or smoked chocolate-

4

rum crémeux, with wine pairings an optional extra. This really is food as art. ££

Le Pub 14 High St; 01633 256326 **w** lepublicspace.co.uk; 16.00–midnight Tue & Sun, Wed & Thu, 16.00–02.00, 16.00–03.00 Fri, noon–03.00 Sat. The city's live music scene is in good hands at this ace community-run pub-cum-arts space at the top of the High St. With just a 100-person capacity, it's small & sweaty, but the quality of the bands, which are mostly from Cardiff & Newport, is top drawer; there are typically 2 or 3 gigs a week with tickets costing in the region of £6–8. They also serve food, with a creditable vegan-only menu. ££

Ye Olde Murenger House 52 High St; 01633 263977; noon–23.00 daily. With its half-timbered black-&-white frontage & dimly lit orange lights flickering beyond frosted windows, it doesn't take much persuading to be enticed into this Dickensian-like lair. Dating from 1533, & erstwhile home of both the High Sheriff of Monmouthshire & Chartist hero John Frost, the pub takes its name from 'murage', a medieval-era tax levied for the upkeep of the town walls. Although very much a local's boozer, all-comers are warmly welcomed. ££

Tiny Rebel Brewery Bar Wern Industrial Estate, Chartist Dr; 01633 547378; **w** tinyrebel. co.uk; 11.00–23.00 daily. A barn of a building, the headquarters of this ace independent brewery, 3 miles west of the city centre, also comprises an adjoining bar-cum-restaurant; a long bar fronts a vast seating area where you can sample until your heart's content (or your head's all fuzzy) & tuck into burgers and chips. Without wheels, it is a fiddle to get to – indeed, you may well ask what the point is in heading all the way out here when there's a city-centre bar – but it's great fun. Moreover, they do brewery tours (though these were suspended at the time of writing), which include a beer at the end. £

Quarters Coffee Millennium Walk; **m** 07920 037837; **w** quarterscoffee.com; 10.00–15.00 Wed–Sun. Located on the east bank of the Usk at the end of the Millennium footbridge, this smart little coffee house has a lovely aspect over the river through its floor to-ceiling windows. With its cheery crew & a fabulous repertoire of coffees & homemade cakes, Quarters has it nailed. It's just a shame about the short opening hours. £

WHAT TO SEE AND DO Newport's one landmark building, the **Westgate Hotel**, at the top of Commercial Street, is also its most infamous, as it was here on 4 November 1839 that 22 Chartist sympathisers were gunned down by waiting troops during the Newport Rising (page 112). A dignified four-storey building, the hotel has had several incarnations since opening in 1709 – the present, Renaissance exterior dates from 1887 – though it's a rather forlorn sight these days, having been boarded up for more than 20 years. As it awaits its fate, plans have been mooted to convert its public spaces (including the once-magnificent ballroom) into exhibition and event rooms, a café, restaurant and so on, though this is unlikely to happen any time soon. For now, you can just admire the Regency-style porch with its fluted iron pillars and beautifully sculpted capitals. Outside the hotel, the **Chartist Commemorative Sculpture** is a collective of three sculptures representing Union, Prudence and Energy, titles taken from the motto of the Chartists' convention.

Instead of continuing along Commercial Street, the embattled main shopping thoroughfare, head up Stow Hill, the road down which the Chartists marched on that fateful day. A calf-stretching 10-minute walk later and you reach the red-brown-brick **St Woolos Cathedral** (01633 267464; **w** newportcathedral.org.uk), named after the 5th-century saint Gwynllyw (loosely meaning 'Woolos'), who, it is said, founded a church here around AD500. That has long since gone of course (if it ever existed at all), but scant foundations from the subsequent Saxon church do remain. Most of what you see today is of Norman origin, and quite superb it is too, not least the entrance arch, which also blends Roman stonework recycled from Caerleon. The nave, meanwhile, manifests chunky pillars and elegant rounded arches with clerestory windows and a fine, recently restored medieval timber ceiling

– the modern chancel extension, however, is rather jarring in comparison with the rest of the church. Somewhere in the cemetery are the unmarked graves of ten Chartists, and while you won't find them, there is a dedication stone embedded in the wall just beyond the entrance gate. Continuing along Stow Hill (where it flattens out) for another 200 yards or so, look out for a plaque on a red-brick building by the entrance to the hospital, identifying this as the **old union workhouse** where, on the evening of 3 November 1839, soldiers from the 45th Regiment were garrisoned ahead of the following day's clashes with the Chartists – some of whom were then detained here.

Back down in the city centre, attempts to revitalise the **waterfront area** have led to a spate of rather disjointed developments, most conspicuously the Friar's Walk shopping complex, and there have been as many casualties here as in Commercial Street. Across the busy main road, the shallow dock next to the Riverfront Arts Centre was the site of the discovery of the *Newport Medieval Ship* in 2002 (page 113); the nearby 100ft-long Steel Wave sculpture, created by Peter Fink in 1990 and supposed to reflect the area's history of steel manufacturing, is an oversized eyesore and does nothing to enhance this stretch of the riverbank. Regeneration of the area is scheduled to continue with the demolition of the ageing Newport Centre, which will be replaced with a state-of-the-art leisure facility, though this is a couple of years off yet.

A once-proud waterfront fortress overlooking the muddy waters of the Usk, **Newport Castle** makes for a more ghostly presence these days. Having replaced an earlier Norman motte-and-bailey up on Stow Hill in the 14th century, the castle's chequered history entailed being sacked by Glyndwr in 1402 and then being taken by Cromwell during the Civil War, before finding favour as a tannery and brewery. The castle's ignominy was complete in the 1970s when a road was built through the western end of the site, and although it was open to the public, it has now been closed for the best part of a decade with no plans, it seems, to reinstate access. Despite its fairly anonymous status, the castle has provided sufficient inspiration to a number of artists over the years, among them J M W Turner, whose 1796 painting, *Newport Castle*, currently resides in the British Museum. The best view of the castle's largely intact three towers – two polygonal end towers and a central rectangular tower, each separated by a chunky stone wall – is from the far end of the road bridge.

Newport Museum and Art Gallery (John Frost Sq; ☎ 0163 656656; w newport. gov.uk; ⊕ 09.30–17.00 Tue–Sat; free)

For a comprehensive overview of both the city and the wider area, make a beeline for the exhaustive Newport Museum and Art Gallery, up on the first floor of the library building. The museum crams in an awful lot, though themed sections do make it easier for visitors to decide which subjects they'd most like to see; there's also a leaflet that identifies the museum's ten most prized exhibits. The **prehistory** section mostly dotes on finds from the Gwent Levels, with the oldest bits dating back to 7500BC, among them some beautifully sculpted and polished axeheads, although the most arresting thing here is the skeleton of an auroch (a large wild cattle) dating from 2700BC, found buried in the mudflats – the beast having got stuck there and collapsed.

The **Roman** era is represented by a similarly eye-catching array of treasures, many of which were retrieved from Caerwent, including column and capital fragments, a near-complete mosaic from the old basilica, and the so-called Chi-Rho hoard – significant here is the pewter dish engraved with a 'chi-rho', a chi-rho being the first two letters of Christ's name in Greek, hence this is generally acknowledged to be the earliest evidence for Christianity found in Wales. Keep an eye out too for

4

THE CHARTISTS

Townsmen, much of the evils of life proceeds from the ignorant, corrupt, and oppressive men in authority. The object of the Chartists is to place in the House of Commons, able, honest and industrious men.

John Frost

The first mass political movement in the United Kingdom, Chartism was borne out of the People's Charter, a document drafted by Cornish-born radical William Lovett in 1838. Set within the overall context of parliamentary reform, the charter sought six key changes: a vote for every man over the age of 21, a secret ballot, equal voting constituencies, annual parliamentary elections, no property qualification for members of parliament, and payment for MPs. By the summer of 1839, amid growing discontent among the working-class population, more than 25,000 had joined democratic associations, and while Chartism was keenly supported in many of Britain's newly industrialised towns and cities, such as Birmingham, Glasgow and Manchester, it was the radical heartlands of South Wales – especially among the coalmining and ironworking communities – where support was strongest.

As unrest grew, so hitherto peaceful protests turned increasingly violent, culminating in the most infamous incident of the movement's history. On the morning of 4 November 1839, around 5,000 sympathisers (mostly coal- and ironworkers) from across South Wales, under the leadership of John Frost (a former Newport mayor), converged on the city's Westgate Hotel. However, they didn't reckon on waiting troops from the 45th Regiment, and in the ensuing battle 22 protesters were killed. At the subsequent trial at the Shire Hall in Monmouth, Frost, along with arch conspirators Zephaniah Williams and William Jones, were charged with high treason and sentenced to death, though this was later commuted to transportation; on 3 February 1840, the three convicted men boarded a ship from Chepstow bound for Van Diemen's Land (present-day Tasmania). While Williams and Jones remained in Tasmania, Frost returned to Bristol, living to the ripe old age of 94.

Chartism continued in a weakened form for another 20 years or so, and by the time the movement disbanded in 1858 not one of its proponents' demands had taken effect. However, their endeavours hadn't entirely been in vain, as subsequent groups continued the struggle. By 1944, all but one of their demands (that of annual parliamentary elections, which has never been implemented) had been enshrined in law.

Both Newport and Monmouth have well-laid-out Chartist trails documenting the key sites; you can pick up leaflets in the town's respective museums, while the Newport Museum and Art Gallery (page 111) has a dedicated exhibition.

some of the more obscure objects: enamelled brooches, coloured gaming counters, white clay statuettes and bronze figurines, though the semi-erect phallus will no doubt raise the wryest of smiles. The medieval section is mostly concerned with the story of the *Newport Medieval Ship* (see opposite), with cabinets containing items recovered from its hull: a leather poulaine shoe, gaming pieces and pottery, and the star object, a petit blanc – a small silver coin which had been purposely concealed within the keel.

The exhibition on the **Chartists** is the museum's most rewarding, and the one to single out if time is tight. A compelling overview of what remains one of the most important political reform movements in British history, it documents the rise of the movement and its key players, though inevitably the focus is on the Newport Rising itself (page 112); to this end, the most pertinent exhibits are the three pistols belonging to the leader, John Frost. Upstairs, the exhibition on the **Transporter Bridge** is similarly captivating: alongside panels exploring the history of this type of bridge (between 1893 and 1916, 18 were built worldwide), there are some fabulous photos as well as a few associated items including the ceremonial trowel, one of the bridge's two dedication plaques (the other one was stolen), and a huge wicker basket used for hoisting workmen up and down. More remarkable still is the footage of the bridge's opening in 1906, one of the earliest known recordings in Wales: in a fascinating 4 minutes of soundless film, all three of the bridge's leading players – the donor Lord Tredegar, and the engineers Ferdinand Arnodin and Robert Haynes – make an appearance (this can also be viewed on YouTube). Another floor up, there are some intermittently interesting bits of art, and although there's nothing particularly exciting worth hanging around for, if you like teapots, then you'll enjoy the Wait Collection of Edwardian kitsch. Otherwise, you'll probably have had enough by then anyway.

Transporter Bridge (Brunel St; w newport.gov.uk) With its vast spidery frame visible for miles around, Newport's Transporter Bridge remains one of South Wales's most iconic sights. One of just six such operational bridges in the world (and one of just two in Britain: the other is in Middlesbrough), this magnificent Grade I-listed structure was built in 1906 by French engineer Ferdinand Arnodin, 13 years after he designed the world's first transporter bridge (the Vizcaya Bridge) in Bilbao, Spain. The bridge was built to facilitate the movement of workers from the city to the Lysaght steelworks across the river without disturbing the shipping: the alternative was a laborious ten-mile round trip by road (though there were allegedly 28 pubs en route!), while a ferry was deemed too unsafe in these extreme tidal waters. As simple as it is ingenious, the bridge carries cars across the river on a cable-suspended gondola, itself powered by the bridge's original twin electric motors. For a more exhilarating experience, albeit strictly one for those with a head for heights, you can walk up 278 steps and then along the gantry, a mere 74m (242ft) high. For the foreseeable future, though (until 2023 at least), the bridge remains closed pending its biggest ever overhaul, which, in addition to repairs and maintenance, will also incorporate a visitor centre complete with a virtual view from the top for those whose can't make, or face, the climb. In the meantime, it's still worth inspecting close up, especially at night when it's lit up.

AROUND NEWPORT
Newport Medieval Ship (Queensway Meadows Industrial Estate, Estuary Rd, Spytty; ☏01633 274167; w newportship.org; ⊕ 10.30–16.00 Fri, Sat & bank hols; free) In the summer of 2002, building work for the city's new arts centre on the muddy banks of the River Usk revealed the partial remains of a 15th-century ship, rendering this one of the most exciting maritime archaeological finds on British shores in recent history. Using dendrochronology (the study of data from tree-ring growth), experts have established that the *Newport Medieval Ship*, as it has since been named, was a three-masted, clinker-built merchant vessel constructed in the Basque region some time around 1450, and which appeared to have foundered here while undergoing repairs following the collapse of its support structures. Evidence

suggests that the ship most likely carried wine, iron ore and other goods from southern Iberia to northern European ports such as Bristol.

The ship's component parts are currently held within a large warehouse on an industrial estate in Spytty, three miles southeast of Newport, pending a lengthy restoration programme – and by lengthy, this means the best part of 25 years from the time of its excavation to its reconstruction, making this by far the world's largest ancient ship rebuild project. Run by a team of cheerful volunteers, the centre welcomes visitors through its doors to observe the ongoing restoration programme, alongside photographs illustrating how the ship was excavated, panels depicting what the vessel might have looked like, and a cleverly conceived digital reconstruction of the ship – this can also be viewed online at w livinglevels.org.uk.

Following excavation, the process of cleaning and recording each and every one of the ship's 2,500 or so Spanish oak timbers (the keel is made of beech wood) took around three years before attention turned to their conservation. Now nearing completion, this painstaking task entails soaking the planks in ammonium nitrate and polyethylene glycol before they are freeze-dried in a designated facility in York and returned to the centre's climate-controlled storerooms. The wreck also gave up hundreds of artefacts, many of which now reside in the Newport Museum and Art Gallery (page 111). These included leather shoes, gaming pieces, bits of pottery and an archer's brace, as well as animal bones, which suggest that the ship would have carried livestock. The most exciting find, however, was a petit blanc, a silver coin that had been hidden away in an aperture between the keel and the stern.

It's anyone's guess as to when the ship's reconstruction might be complete, but a conservative estimate is around 2030. It'll be some event when it does happen, and great reward for the patience of all those involved, not to mention the vast sums of money invested in the project – the hope is that the *Newport Medieval Ship* does for Newport what the *Mary Rose* did for Portsmouth following that famous ship's recovery in 1982. Before that, though, the challenge is to find a building large enough to accommodate its reassembly; the question then becomes where to display it.

To get here from the centre, take bus 43 to Nash College or bus 74C to Tesco at Spytty Park, from where it's a 10-minute walk.

Fourteen Locks Canal Centre (Cwm Lane, Rogerstone; ℘ 01633 892167; w mbact.org.uk; ⊕ 10.00–17.00 daily; free) It may be unnavigable these days, but the Fourteen Locks, or Cefn Flight, just 2 miles west of Newport city centre, remains one of South Wales's great engineering marvels. Located on the Crumlin Arm of the Monmouthshire and Brecon Canal – which once connected Crumlin and its tramways to the docks at Newport and comprised 32 locks over 11 miles – the Fourteen Locks collectively comprises one single lock (21), five pairs of locks and a group of three locks, which you can inspect on an easily walkable (and wheelchair-accessible) heritage trail taking around 45 minutes there and back. Opened in 1799 to carry mostly coal and iron, the last tolls were collected here in 1935, though boats probably still used this stretch until the end of World War II. The greater vision is not only for all 14 locks to be restored, but also for the canal to return to full navigation, though this is years, if not decades, away from being a reality.

The trail begins at lock 21, which, like all the locks down to and including 17, has been restored in the past ten to 15 years, though they are already starting to look a little worse for wear. Beyond here, the remaining locks have slipped into quiet decay, dry and weed-strewn. Note that in parts, there is quite a deep drop from the embankment into the canal, so watch your footing! As the towpath descends gently, you'll pass Pensarn Cottage, the old lock keeper's cottage next to lock 13 before crossing an old stone bridge. Take a quick look at the remains of an old limekiln and continue past lock 11 (now on your right), which is curious for the two 'shelves' located one on either side, a feature that has long vexed experts. As you approach lock 8, the M4 roars into earshot, a sobering reminder of how much has changed since this once-bustling waterway was operating at full tilt. At this point you can either return to the centre or extend your walk into a 3-mile circular route, though this entails muddy fields, uneven paths and some steep steps; some sturdier footwear might be in order too.

The centre itself is little more than a café (serving full meals) and craft-cum-souvenir shop, though there are some good canal-related books and maps for sale. If travelling by car, the centre is well signposted from the centre; from the M4, leave at Junction 27, from where it's a 2-minute drive.

Commemorative Chartists Mural If you have the time and inclination, it's worth making the effort to view the Commemorative Chartists Mural, a couple of miles west of the centre in the suburb of Rogerstone. Completed in 2019 by Oliver Budd, this four-panel mosaic mural is a one-tenth replica of the original Chartist mural designed by Oliver's late father, Kenneth, in 1978, and which adorned an underpass in John Frost Square until it was bulldozed in 2013 to make way for the new Friar's Walk shopping complex. It was an extraordinary act of vandalism by the council, which, unsurprisingly, resulted in widespread condemnation, both locally and nationally. But just like its predecessor, this new commission is a fabulous piece of work, depicting colourful banner-waving Chartists marching through Newport en route to the Westgate. Unlike his father's mural, however, this also features an accompanying timeline. Easily missed, the mural is just before the roundabout at the junction of Cefn Road and Chartist Drive – if you're coming by car, it's on the right-hand side just before the roundabout, and conveniently there's a lay-by to pull into.

CAERLEON

In 1865, Tennyson wrote that: 'The Usk murmurs by the windows and I sit like King Arthur at Caerleon. This is a most quiet village of about 1,500 inhabitants with a little museum of Roman tombstones and other things.' Little has changed, it seems, in the intervening years. Less than four miles north of Newport, on the other side of the M4, Caerleon's history belies its modest size – and for that it can thank the Romans. From around AD75, Caerleon – whose meaning is a corruption of the Latin words *castrum* (fortress) and *legio* (legion) – was one of just three permanent legionary fortresses in Britain (the others being York and Chester), which, together, provided a formidable linked chain of command for the Romans. Known as Isca, the Romans chose this site by the River Usk (from which the name Isca is derived) as the base for the 6,000-strong Second Augustan Legion owing to its accessibility to the Severn. But this part of Wales was by no means an easy nut to crack for the Romans, because not only was the terrain harsher than anything they'd encountered previously, but they also had to contend with the resilience of the ruling Silures – once subjugated, however, the Silures were forced to adopt Romanised ways. With more pressing commitments elsewhere, the Romans upped sticks around AD300, leaving Caerleon's fortress redundant – unlike those at Chester and York, which developed into fully fledged cities – though it may have been occupied by a smaller civilian population for a short while thereafter. The town's fortunes ebbed and flowed, and despite enjoying brisk maritime trade on occasion, Caerleon largely missed out on the Industrial Revolution, eventually being surpassed in importance by Newport, which it became a suburb of, and effectively remains so to this day.

In the 12th century, the celebrated historian Geoffrey of Monmouth ventured that:

> the city was of undoubted antiquity, and handsomely built of masonry, with courses of bricks, by the Romans. Many vestiges of its former splendour may be seen: immense palaces, formerly ornamented with gilded roofs, in imitation of Roman magnificence; a tower of prodigious size; remarkable hot baths; relics of temples, and theatres, all enclosed with fine walls.

Fast forward to today and Caerleon still provides a wonderful evocation of Roman Britain, its legacy secure courtesy of Europe's only extant legionary barracks, the most complete Roman amphitheatre in Britain, and the extensive remains of fortress baths.

GETTING THERE AND AWAY Buses (27 or 28) depart from Newport's bus station on Friar's Walk every 30 minutes for the 15-minute journey to Caerleon, where they set down outside the post office on the High Street.

✗ WHERE TO EAT AND DRINK

Coffiology 29 High St; m 07771 222888; w coffiology.com; ⏲ 08.00–16.00 Mon–Sat, 10.00–16.00 Sun. Not before time, Caerleon finally has a decent place to grab a coffee, & it's really good stuff too, from the Coaltown Roastery in Ammanford (page 271). With bread & croissants from the Angel Bakery in Abergavenny, a selection of heavenly cakes from other local suppliers, & scrumptious sourdough sandwiches (salt beef, Welsh brie & bacon), you'll probably just want the lot. On Fri & Sat evenings, the venue morphs into a lively wine bar with charcuterie plates (meat, cheese or mixed) – booking is advised. The place looks cool too, the light industrial/rustic aesthetic manifest in aluminium ceiling pipes, LED pendant lighting, & communal wooden tables & bench seating; no frowning at laptop users here either, with lots of power points for charging. £

WHAT TO SEE AND DO

Legionary Barracks and Amphitheatre (Broadway; ✆03000 252239; w cadw. gov.wales; ⏲ Mar–Oct 10.00–16.00 daily, Nov–Feb 10.00–16.00 Mon–Sat, 11.00–16.00 Sun; open access; free) As with most legionary standings, the standard layout of the fortress here at Caerleon incorporated an earthen rampart surrounding a grid of streets dividing the complex into roughly four sections, with the incipia, or headquarters, located at the very heart of the complex. Neatly laid out across well-manicured fields a 5-minute walk from the High Street, the foundations of four legionary **barracks** occupy what would have been the northwesternmost corner of the fortress. It remains an impressive site, despite the fact that most of the original stonework was plundered long ago for modern building material. There were originally 60 barracks here, first built in timber but later reconstructed in stone, each one housing between 80 and 100 men – and with around eight men to a room, meagre furnishings were the order of the day. The barracks aside, it's also possible to make out the remains of a latrine, complete with an outside drain, and a kitchen block with the bases of at least ten large circular ovens – it was a big legion that needed feeding.

Around 200 yards southwest of the barracks, just beyond what would have been the old fortress walls, Caerleon's commanding **amphitheatre** – the finest in Britain – was the last of the main structures to be built here, around AD90. Initial excavations in 1909 brought to light the amphitheatre's basic structure, although its full extent wasn't determined until further digs in 1926, which established that the arena was in fact oval and its walls stood some 13ft high. Eight massive vaulted entrances are separated by steep, thickly turfed banks, which, back in the day, would have accommodated ranks of bloodthirsty spectators among its tiers of half-timbered seats – more or less enough seats for the full complement of the legion. Two processional entrances, one for gladiators and one for animals, were located at either end, with the other six entrances reserved for spectators who gained access by presenting their 'ticket' in the form of a lead token. Out on the arena floor, gladiators – who were typically picked from slaves, criminals or prisoners – were pitted not just against each other, but wild animals too, typically bears, boars and wolves from the nearby forests, though the amphitheatre was also used for drills and parades.

Fortress Baths (High St; ☎ 03000 252239; w cadw.gov.wales; ⏰ 10.00–17.00 daily; £4.80) Public bathing was at the very heart of Roman social life, and it was no different here in Caerleon, whose fortress baths afforded legionnaires some relief from the day-to-day drudgery of soldiering. The complex here at Caerleon incorporated both indoor and outdoor pools, as well as exercise yards – an antique leisure centre if you will. The bathhouse stood derelict for more than 1,000 years following the Romans' departure, before it was mostly demolished. But in the 1960s, the discovery of a mosaic during excavations on neighbouring Backhall Street also exposed the foundations of what was left of the baths, which have since been preserved in situ.

The original building would have comprised a suite of three bath halls: frigidarium (cold plunge pool), tepidarium (warm bath), and caldarium (hot bath) – which bathers would have used in that sequence. Only the first of these has survived (and is still visible), along with the now-covered outdoor pool (*natatio*), which is the first one you see as you enter – since shortened, this pool was originally longer than the Great Bath at Aquae Sulis (in Bath). The only other extant aspect is the changing room (apodyterium), whose sawn-off brick pillars were part of a sophisticated underground heating system (hypocaust), itself a remarkable feat of engineering for the time.

Excavation of the bath's main drain system in the late 1970s uncovered an exceptional miscellany of small items, including gaming pieces, animal bones and jewellery, notably 88 differently coloured gemstones which now reside in the Roman Legion Museum. Here too were hairpins and milk teeth, which came as quite a surprise to archaeologists who had previously assumed that the baths were off-limits to women and children; whether mixed bathing ever occurred, however, is unlikely given that all patrons were obliged to bathe naked. What could potentially be a rather dry (excuse the pun) experience is anything but, thanks to cleverly conceived sound and light effects which give the illusory appearance of water being present in the pool.

National Roman Legion Museum (High St; ☎ 0300 111 2333; w museum. wales/roman; ⏰ 10.00–17.00 daily; free) Having left such a massive imprint on the town, it's little surprise that so many extraordinary artefacts have been recovered, most of which have found their way to the National Roman Legion Museum. The museum itself is housed within a much worked-over building whose only original feature is the portico, dating from 1850. Death and burial feature heavily, with a superb collection of weather-beaten funerary and dedication stones, though the

The Arthurian legend is ubiquitous, in history, folklore and place names all over Britain. Yet despite competing claims from the likes of Winchester, Tintagel in Cornwall, Glastonbury and Cadbury Castle (both in Somerset), numerous locations throughout Wales itself, and even Brittany in France, the most compelling evidence suggests that Arthur's Camelot, his chief court and fortress, was here in Caerleon. But did King Arthur exist at all? The evidence (or rather lack of) suggests that the Arthurian legend is more fancy than fact, but whatever his origins, the narrative has taken on a life of its own.

It was the Welsh monk Nennius who first made mention of Arthur in his work *Historia Britonum* (*History of the British*) around AD800, before stories of his epic deeds – including how this great Celtic hero-warrior repelled waves of invading Anglo-Saxons – were recounted and inflated by various medieval chroniclers. Among these was Geoffrey of Monmouth who, in his monumental 12-volume *Regum Britannicae* (*History of the Kings of Britain*), asserts that Caerleon was the home of Camelot, at the same time as introducing various other characters into Arthurian mythology, not least the wizard Merlin, who is based on the Welsh legend Myrddin Wyllt (Merlin the Wild); Thomas Malory, meanwhile, writes in his classic 15th-century tome, *Le Morte d'Arthur* (*The Death of Arthur*), that Arthur's coronation took place here in Caerleon, though he maintains that Winchester was the site of Camelot. Arthur's legend was further romanticised by Alfred, Lord Tennyson, who wrote part of his fabled Arthurian cycle, *Idylls of the Kings*, during a visit to Caerleon in 1856, when he stayed at the Hanbury Arms.

most attention-grabbing exhibit is that of a skeleton reposed within an open stone coffin. Discovered in 1995, the remains are those of a 40-year-old local man, and the fact that he was buried and not cremated suggests that he came from a family of some wealth.

Cabinets hold a miscellany of coinage, tools, pottery and glassware, but it's the smaller, less conspicuous items that captivate, including bronze belt buckles, leaden bread stamps, and several objects hewn from bone, such as a bottle stopper, tweezers and a die. There are also stacks of jewellery, notably a cache of 88 brightly coloured gemstones retrieved from the fortress baths, exquisite specimens rich with imagery: one, for example, depicts a palm tree with dates, another an Indian green parrot engraved with symbols signifying justice, fortune and prosperity. Once done, take a look at the recreated Roman gardens out back.

USK

Straddling the wide, languid river from which it takes its name, the orderly little market town of Usk was the location of Wales's first Roman fort (Burrium), which was constructed here in AD55, although this was superseded by the much larger legionary fortress in Caerleon. Under the governance of the superbly named Richard 'Strongbow' de Clare, both the town and castle grew up alongside each other in the 12th century. Industrialisation largely passed the town by, though it was home to an important Japanware company for a period in the late 18th century, and it has remained a predominantly agricultural settlement. Usk has few sights as such (some romantic castle ruins and a pleasingly old-fashioned museum), but in any case it's really a place to amble, enjoy the river – one of the country's best for salmon fishing – and dip in and out of its many cafés and restaurants.

GETTING THERE AND AWAY The nearest train station to Usk is Pontypool, 7 miles away, but buses connect the town with Newport (7 daily Mon–Sat), as well as Chepstow (5 daily Mon–Sat), Monmouth (6 daily Mon–Fri, 3 Sat) and Pontypool (4 daily Mon–Sat). The main drop-off point is Twyn Square.

WHERE TO STAY, EAT AND DRINK

Three Salmons Hotel (24 rooms) Bridge St; 01291 672133; w threesalmons.co.uk. Dating back 300 years & one of the town's landmark buildings, these luxe, tasteful rooms (some with 4-poster beds) offer splashes of country art & the occasional artefact to keep things fresh. The well-kept public areas include a very creditable restaurant, a cosy, fire-warmed lounge & garden terrace. Dinner & B&B rates also offered. **£££**

The Nags Head Inn Twyn Sq; 01291 672820; w nagsheadusk.co.uk; 09.30–14.30 & 17.00–22.30 daily. A proper pub this is, where little has changed in the past half a century. It has been passed down through 3 generations of the Keys family, meaning that you're in welcoming hands. The interior is all heavy wood & thick stone walls bearing horse brasses, lanterns, farming implements & other curios, & although first &

foremost a drinker's refuge, the food is excellent too, the menu featuring traditional pub mains like Gloucester Old Spot sausages with mash & onion gravy as well as some mouthwatering in-season game dishes (guinea fowl in a wine & fig sauce, rabbit pie). **££**

Café Sprokwobbles 22 Bridge St; 01291 672048; 09.30–16.30 Mon–Sat. Ace name aside, there are other very good reasons to make a beeline for this gorgeous little café/deli, which has a vaguely vintage/Art Deco thing going on. Food runs the gamut from soups & pasties to baguettes & salads, plus cakes galore, including plenty of options for vegans. Cyclists, meanwhile, receive a small discount. The sunny courtyard often plays host to evenings of entertainment, which could be live music, comedy, wine tasting, or some such jollity. **£**

WHAT TO SEE AND DO The town's focal point is **Twyn Square**, a wide elongated space centred on a red-brick Victorian clock tower and fringed by a neat kernel of Georgian tenement buildings – for good measure, there's a decent pub here too, the Nags Head Inn (see above). One name mentioned more than any other in association with Usk is the naturalist **Alfred Russel Wallace** (1823–1913), a bust of whom was unveiled in the square by comedian (and Wallace fan) Bill Bailey in 2021. An indomitable explorer and voracious collector – in 1848 he spent eight years in the Malay Archipelago gathering some 120,000 specimens – Wallace was one of the two co-originators of the theory of natural selection, yet while Darwin is most often credited with the idea, Wallace, who worked independently of Darwin but whose contributions were no less significant, became the forgotten man. Wallace is also remembered with a memorial outside St Madoc's Church at Llanbadoc.

Usk Castle (Monmouth Rd; 01291 672563; w uskcastle.com; 10.30–16.30 Mon, Thu & Sun; £4) Secluded within an enclave of pretty gardens, this eccentric little castle has been owned by the Humphreys family since 1908, prior to which its schizophrenic history included life as a farmhouse, dame school and fern garden. Unmanicured and idiosyncratic, this is exactly what a castle ruin is meant to look like, yet its tranquil setting betrays a stormy past. The two most significant figures in the castle's history are Richard 'Strongbow' de Clare, who laid its stone foundations some time around 1174, and William Marshall (Earl of Pembroke), who further strengthened its defences with a long curtain wall and a few towers for good measure (and to keep it in the family, he married Strongbow's daughter, Isabella). Pulverised by Glyndwr's forces in 1402, the castle was then one of the main battlegrounds during the Battle of Usk just three years later, but on this occasion Glyndwr fared less well and was routed. The Welsh endured catastrophic losses and 300 prisoners were massacred in front of the castle. The castle never recovered, falling into neglect with much of the stonework pilfered for use in local building projects. It's therefore surprising that quite so much remains intact, notably Marshal's French-style Garrison Tower, a superb example of a circular keep, and Strongbow's gatehouse which has also stood the test of time well. You'll likely be joined by geese, ducks and chickens as you potter, so if you are bringing a dog, then do make sure it's on a lead. Although you can drive up here, you're just as well parking in the town car park and walking from there.

Rural Life Museum (New Market St; ☎ 01291 673777; w uskmuseum.org; ⊕ Apr–Oct 11.00–15.00 Thu–Sun; free) Housed inside an old malt barn part way down New Market Street, the Rural Life Museum offers an engaging, if slightly disjointed, trawl through local history, roughly spanning the period between the early 1800s and the end of World War II. Monmouthshire folk are well known for their practical skills in agriculture, such as fencing, hedging and ploughing, and this is reflected in the wealth of agricultural paraphernalia, especially a fine assemblage of horse-drawn ploughs and vintage tractors including John Deere, Allis-Chalmers and Fordson F models. The world's first mass-produced tractor, the Fordson F (manufactured by Henry Ford and Son of Ford Model T car fame) was of a smaller and lighter design – hence also much more affordable – than existing models, and as such helped to revolutionise the farming landscape at the end of World War I. Some of the adjoining buildings have been mocked up as interiors of tradesmen's workshops (blacksmiths, cobblers, wheelwrights), which helps bring the experience to life a little.

AROUND USK
Raglan Castle (Castle Rd, Raglan; ☎ 03000 252239; w cadw.gov.wales; ⊕ Mar–Jun, Sep & Oct 09.30–17.00 daily, Jul & Aug 09.30–18.00 daily, Nov–Feb 10.00–16.00 daily; £8.30; bus #383 or #60 from Newport) Visible for miles around, Raglan Castle does more to give the impression of a palace than it does of a 15th-century fortification, which should come as no surprise because it was in fact originally built almost entirely as a statement of wealth and influence, more concerned with securing fabulous views – which it has in abundance – than defending the local territory. Whatever its *raison d'être*, kids will love having the run of the place, with its big towers and never-ending spiral staircases, gunloops and slits, and damp, dingy caverns, all in the name of endless exploration.

As far as Welsh castles go, Raglan was a relatively late entrant on to the scene, of mid 15th-century origin courtesy of Sir William ap Thomas, though he never saw the fruits of his early labours – most likely just the Great Tower and the South Gate – and instead it was left to his son, also called William but who took the surname Herbert, to continue his father's work. This he did but on an even grander scale, and notwithstanding some later Tudor and Jacobean rebuilding, more or less what you see today is his handiwork. Following Herbert's death, the castle was passed into the hands of the Somersets (Earls of Worcester) whose greatest contribution to Raglan was the landscaped gardens, none of which now remain.

Having held out against Cromwell's forces for the best part of two months, the castle finally succumbed in August 1646, and that was more or less it for Raglan. In common with other castles, it was plundered for building material but otherwise condemned to decay, although, much like nearby Tintern, its ivy-covered ruins were a source of much curiosity among the new breed of so-called Romantic tourists at the beginning of the 19th century. In his journal of 1802, Sir Richard Colt Hoare remarked, 'I cannot but regret when I see this grand relic of baronial magnificence that it has been so long neglected and uninhabited'.

The main approach into the castle is via the well-protected gatehouse range, framed by two superb hexagonal towers, which each contain four levels of rooms. The most striking aspects of the gatehouse range are its machiolations (arched openings at battlement level), which suggest a heavy French influence. Beyond here lies the **Pitched Court**, a sloping cobbled courtyard that was principally the reserve of the household staff: service rooms, accommodation and so on. The impressive hexagonal **Kitchen Tower** retains its two impressive fireplaces, oven and drains, while the basement – known as the **Wet Larder** – would have kept all the meat, cheeses and other perishables. To the left of the Pitched Court, and very much at the heart of the complex, is the mid 16th-century **Hall Range**, by far the most complete of the castle's remaining chambers; the great Tudor oriel window at the dias end of the hall is especially superb. Adjacent is the grass-covered **Fountain Court**, named after the white marble foundation that once stood here – only the base now remains. Integral to the Fountain Court was the chapel, whose one remaining wall is shared with the Great Hall, the other three sides now reduced to no more than shin-high remains. Otherwise, the Fountain Court would have once held a suite of well-appointed apartments, reached via a double flight of steps opposite the chapel.

The *pièce de résistance* is the hexagonal **Great Tower**, a five-storeyed behemoth encircled by a pondweed-covered moat and an apron wall punctuated by half a dozen partially severed turrets. Otherwise known as the 'Yellow Tower of Gwent' on account of its ashlar stone, the tower is completely open on two sides, having been blasted to bits by Cromwell's henchmen following the desperate three-month-long siege in 1646. Spiral up to the top for superior views across the complex and the Black Mountains in the distance. There's also a pleasing walk around the moat, whose sidewall is studded with empty niches that would have once contained statues of Roman emperors.

There's no café here (they appear to have missed a trick there), but in any case this is perfect picnicking territory – the raised terrace opposite the Great Tower (reached via the South Gate) was the castle's old bowling green, as played on by King Charles I on a visit here in 1645. As neat as an Oxbridge lawn, the green would have fronted a series of stepped terraces, which, together with a magnificently landscaped parkland, including the 'great poole', at one time comprised one of the finest Renaissance gardens in the country, as laid out by the fourth and fifth earls of Worcester from the mid 16th century onwards.

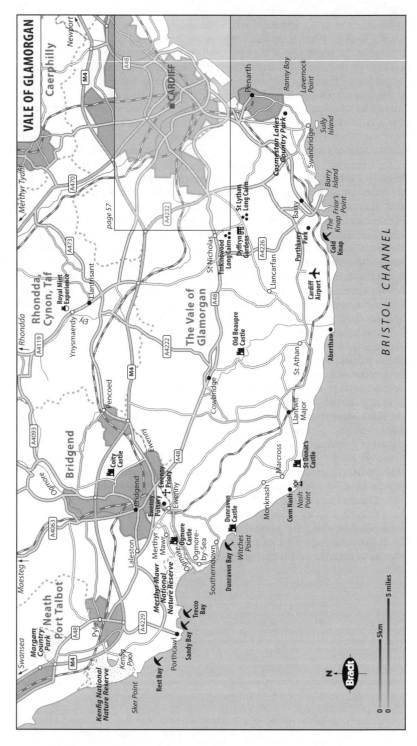

5

Vale of Glamorgan, Swansea and Gower

The Vale of Glamorgan is not somewhere that resonates as much as, say, the Valleys or Pembrokeshire – or Carmarthenshire for that matter – which is perhaps one reason why it attracts relatively few visitors. But it's got charm by the bucket load and a few days spent exploring its coast and interior will yield a few surprises.

The Vale's unsung coastline is, in parts, comparable to anything Pembrokeshire has to offer. Solidly old-fashioned resorts like **Barry** and **Porthcawl** – now a key surfing destination – cheerfully serve the bucket-and-spade brigade, but it's the **Glamorgan Heritage Coast**, a geological marvel to rival Dorset's Jurassic Coast, that you'll recall long after visiting: spectacular stratified cliffs eaten away to form fantastic shapes, huge wave-cut platforms caused by thousands of years of erosion, and immense dune systems like that at **Merthyr Mawr**, which boasts some of the wildest, highest dunes in Europe. Another is **Kenfig**, which offers endless scope for fun and exploration with its rich tangle of colonising grasses, as well as slacks, orchids and birdlife. Here too, of course, the coast path weaves its magic, in parts as impressive, but much less tramped, than those sections further west.

Although not as emphatically scenic as the coast, the Vale's hinterland, a flattish green patchwork of countryside, is speckled with small towns and villages, castles and churches, all stitched together by narrow, high-hedged lanes. Well-heeled **Cowbridge** is where folk go to eat and shop and hilltop **Llantrisant**, on the cusp of the Valleys, is home to the compelling Royal Mint. The Vale's most startling church is **St Cadoc's** in Llancarfan, by virtue of some recently discovered wall paintings, while gracious ruins at Ogmore, Ewenny, Newcastle and Coity serve to emphasise the region's one-time status as a Norman frontier land.

This chapter also includes the Vale of Neath, another once-great centre of industry, and the Afan Valley, reinvented as an activity centre. Neither of these are in the Vale of Glamorgan, nor are they part of Swansea, but they both look more towards Cymric Swansea than they do anglicised Cardiff. Like **Bridgend** further east, the area's towns, **Neath** and **Port Talbot**, are usually ignored, a glimpse of their harsh industrial surrounds – in the case of Port Talbot, Wales's largest steelworks – usually enough for most people to keep on going to the more obvious attractions further west. But to ignore these places completely would be to miss out on some unanticipated delights: magnificent abbey ruins in Neath and a Banksy-inspired art trail in Port Talbot for example.

Out on the yawning curl of Swansea Bay, Wales's second city, **Swansea**, is resurgent. Once the country's greatest industrial metropolis and long in the shadow of Cardiff, its setting, along with a clutch of fine museums – including one of South

Wales's best galleries – and Dylan Thomas connections (he was born, and drank quite a lot, here), demand a day or two of your time, before saving the best till last. Edging out into the Bristol Channel, **Gower**'s reputation as one of Wales's great beauty spots is fully merited. It's a place to spend some unhurried days – to drop off the radar for a bit. Not that you'll have much choice, especially if travelling by public transport – this is Slow Travel as it should be.

Getting around is relatively straightforward: the M4 effectively separates the Vale of Glamorgan from the Valleys, with any number of junctions giving access to the coast. Fast trains from Cardiff call at Bridgend, Port Talbot and Neath before terminating in Swansea. Otherwise, trains also depart Cardiff for Penarth, Barry and Llantwit Major before cutting inland and terminating in Bridgend. For the remainder of the coast you'll be reliant on local bus services, which are more than adequate, as they are throughout the rest of the Vale.

PENARTH AND AROUND

Part suburb, part Victorian seaside resort, well-heeled Penarth hasn't quite been absorbed into Cardiff's orbit, for which it can thank the River Ely that separates the two. This small and deceptively hilly little town therefore offers a gentle reprieve from the hurly-burly of its big-city neighbour, thanks to its elegant confection of Victorian and Edwardian buildings, green parks and a clutter-free esplanade with a long pebble beach (dogs permitted October to April).

GETTING THERE AND AWAY The most satisfying way to arrive here is on foot via the Cardiff Bay Barrage (page 76), but otherwise, you have the choice of buses #7, #92, #93 and #94, which run every 15–30 minutes (Mon–Sat) from Canal Street or Park Street in Cardiff to Windsor Terrace in Penarth, or the train from Cardiff Central (every 15mins; Sun hourly) to the station on Station Approach. From here it's a 5-minute walk into the town centre or a 10-minute walk down through Alexandra Park to the seafront.

🏠 **WHERE TO STAY, EAT AND DRINK**

🏠 **Sain Y Mor** (9 rooms) 3 Penarth Pier; ☎ 029 2071 0779. There's no real reason to need to stay in Penarth, lovely as it is, but if you do, then this is a good best bet, primarily for its location on the seafront. Occupying the brightly painted buildings on the opposite side of the pier (you can't miss 'em), this gorgeous little hotel has perky rooms, some of which have unencumbered sea-facing views. The others look out on to the back terrace, & as such are around £10 cheaper. **££**

🍴 **Brød** 6 Glebe St; ☎ 029 2070 0835; w thedanishbakery.co.uk; ⏰ 09.00–16.00 Tue– Sat, 10.00–15.00 Sun. What an absolute charmer this branch of the original Danish bakery in Cardiff is, where all the breads & pastries are lovingly crafted in-store each morning, for example *københaver* (vanilla puff pastry sprinkled with poppy seeds), *kanel snegl* (cinnamon-filled pastry

topped with icing), & *pølsehorn*, a Danish-style sausage roll-cum-hot dog. The décor is naturally very Scandi: pine-clad walls & hardwood flooring complement the rough-edged stonework, & there's also the odd curiosity like a wall-mounted bike & a display cabinet of old cameras; the owner, Betina, was a photographer prior to entering the world of baking. It all adds up one lovely big dose of *hygge*. **£**

🍴 **Coffi Co** The Esplanade; w coffico.uk; ⏰ 08.00–20.00 daily. The interior is a little charmless but the wrought-iron balcony terrace fronting this ornate Victorian building is rather lovely, as is the rooftop terrace – if nothing else it's worth stopping by for the outstanding views. The coffee is excellent (nicely roasted, strong & hot) & they do a good selection of hot meals if you're feeling peckish. **£**

plates like lamb shank with minted gravy & mash – & that's before you've even got to the cornucopia of delicious deli goodies. Located directly opposite the train station. £

WHAT TO SEE AND DO Penarth is home to one of just one of two surviving pleasure **piers** along the South Wales coast, the other one being in Mumbles on Gower (page 165). Opened in 1895, thus pre-dating Mumbles by three years, the 658ft-long pier was quick to receive pleasure steamers that paddled their way up and down the Bristol Channel, though its glory days didn't last long as it was requisitioned by the military for use during both World Wars before falling into disrepair. Beset by further calamities (including a fire and several boat-on-pier collisions), it wasn't until 2013 that the pier was faithfully restored, as was its pavilion, an elegant late 1930s Art Deco building refurbished to incorporate a cinema, events space and café. Between September and May, fishing is permitted on the pier, and the good news is that neither a licence nor a fee is required.

If you can tear yourself away from the seafront, the red-brick **Turner House Gallery** (📞 029 2070 0721; **w** turnerhouse.wales; 10.00–16.30 Thu–Sun; free), opposite the train station on Plymouth Road, is well worth an hour of your time. An offshoot of the National Museum Cardiff, the gallery was conceived by Somerset-born James Pyke Thompson who had the building constructed by Edward Seward (architect of the Old Library and Coal Exchange in Cardiff) in a corner of his garden in 1888. Its programme, which exhibits anything from photography to contemporary crafts and applied art, is invariably first class: recent exhibitions have included works by Eduardo Paolozzi, Matisse and Quentin Blake. Penarth's coastal light has long drawn artists to the area, including the French Impressionist **Alfred Sisley**, one of the very few international painters who actually visited Wales. Sisley completed at least six oils during his time in Penarth, two of which are on display in the National Museum Cardiff, and in fact he even got married in Cardiff, in 1897 when both he and his partner were dying of cancer.

Behind the Turner House, sloping up steeply between the seafront and the centre of town, is **Alexandra Park**. Laid out in 1901, the park delights with its luxuriant lawns and immaculately trimmed topiary, and what Victorian park in South Wales wouldn't be complete without an old-fashioned bandstand or indeed the obligatory offering by Goscombe John, here a towering white granite obelisk commemorating the fallen from World War I.

Cosmeston Lakes Country Park Less than a mile inland from the Wales Coast Path, just before Lavernock Point, is Cosmeston Lakes Country Park, whose former life as a limestone quarry and then a landfill site makes what you see before you today all the more surprising, but at the same time very welcome. These days, it's flora and fauna that thrive here, including the recently reintroduced water vole: along with Magor on the Gwent Levels, Cosmeston is home to one of the largest populations of this critically endangered rodent in Wales. Ponds too have been created here at Cosmeston, ostensibly to support a small population of great crested newts, yet another threatened species. Spring and summer bring the possibility of observing lots of fantastic winged fauna: blackcaps, chiffchaffs, and several species of warbler, and in winter you might get lucky sighting a bittern. Butterflies, damselflies and dragonflies are as prevalent here as they are just down the road at Lavernock. Cosmeston is the only site in Wales – and only one of two in Britain (the

5

other is the Norfolk Broads) – where the critically endangered Starry stonewort, a translucent freshwater algae, grows. The park is easy enough to navigate, being cut straight through by Mile Road (it's actually a footpath), either side of which are two large lakes (formerly the quarries), fringed by high reedbeds.

An area in the south of the park has been given over to the recreation of a **medieval village** (⊕ Apr–Sep 10.00–17.00 daily, Oct–Mar 10.00–16.00 daily; free), in lieu of one that stood here back in the 14th century. During work on the park in the late 1970s, digs uncovered the foundations of an ancient settlement, which upon further investigation was revealed to have been a village called Costentinstune, after the local de Costentin (or Constantine) family. It is likely to have consisted of a handful of dwellings clustered around a more substantial manor house, although when or why the village vanished remains something of a mystery.

Constructed upon the original foundations, the recreated buildings comprise thatched-roof crofts, including one of the earliest examples of a semi-detached cottage anywhere in Britain, barns, an inn, a bakery, and some neatly laid out medieval gardens, although in total this represents just a fraction of what was probably here. While it can in no way compare with St Fagans in Cardiff, it's a fascinating portal to an ancient way of life, which is further enhanced with a small museum packed with information and artefacts pertaining to life in a crofting village. Digs, both at the time of the original excavation and in later years, unearthed some genuinely exciting items, including some highly decorative pottery fragments, one a rare ram's head from an aquamanile (a jug or vessel in the shape of an animal).

Entry is free but it's worth paying the small fee for a self-guided audio tour; costumed guides may or may not have resumed tours by the time you read this. Cosmeston Lakes is served by an hourly bus (#94) from Cardiff, which also passes through Penarth.

Lavernock Point From Penarth it's an invigorating clifftop walk along the Wales Coast Path high above Ranny Bay to Lavernock Point, 2 miles distant. It was here, on 13 May 1897, that Guglielmo Marconi delivered the words 'Are you Ready, Can you hear me?', to which his colleague, George Kemp, stationed on Flat Holm Island some three miles distant, replied, 'Yes, loud and clear' – a brief exchange that was the world's first radio transmission across open water. A plaque on the side of the wind-battered **St Lawrence Church** commemorates this milestone in telecommunications history, while on the cliff edge stands the ramshackle hut in which Marconi stored his equipment. Following the successful transmission here at Lavernock, Marconi further advanced his reputation, establishing successful transmissions across both the English Channel in 1899 and the Atlantic Ocean in 1901.

Most visitors to the headland inevitably prioritise the Marconi connection but what often gets overlooked is the fact that Lavernock Point is a Site of Special Scientific Interest (SSSI), rich in both flora and fauna and one of the best birdwatching spots along this stretch of coast. Green woodpeckers, long-tailed tits and sparrowhawks can all be seen at one time or another, as can a variety of birds nibbling among the berry-rich hedgerows. Moreover, it is especially rich in wildflowers (early purple orchid, bee orchid, devil's bit scabious and the rarely seen adder's tongue fern), all of which attract large numbers of butterflies, among them red admiral, painted lady and small tortoiseshell. In among the scrub stands the **Lavernock battery and fort**, built in the 1860s during the short-lived war between Britain and France, and one of the few remaining gun emplacements along this stretch of coast.

There is limited parking in the car park at the end of Fort Road, and if you don't fancy the full walk here, bus #94 from Cardiff runs to Ford Road, about half a mile from the reserve.

Sully Island If you've still got the energy, it's worth continuing the walk to Sully Island, around two miles on from Lavernock Point. Tethered to the village of Swanbridge by a low, rocky causeway, the small, elongated island trades on its reputation as a one-time smugglers' haunt – one such sea robber was Alfredo de Marisco (aka The Nighthawk) who established a base here in the 13th century, earning notoriety for his daring raids on merchant ships trading in the Bristol Channel. For such a small area – it's just a quarter of a mile long – the island has had an eventful past: in 1916, the Antarctic survey vessel SY *Scotia* caught fire just offshore and was wrecked here, and although you won't see that, you will find the slime-covered ribs of another unidentified wreck alongside the remains of a Danish fort. A circular walk around the foreshore should take no more than an hour. The island can be accessed at low tide and although there is a traffic-light system in place indicating when it's safe to cross (which takes around 20 minutes), it's surprising just how many people get marooned. If you do get stranded, under no circumstances should you try and swim back.

BARRY

Said to be named after Baruc, a 6th-century saint who had the misfortune to drown in Whitmore Bay after journeying back from Flat Holm, Barry is an entirely different proposition after Penarth's sedate charms. For most people, Barry means Barry Island, one of South Wales's most popular seaside resorts, yet it's one that still gets a bad rap from time to time. Tourism is nothing new here, however: on a visit to Barry in 1803, the travel writer Reverend John Evans remarked 'to a party, who have all their amusements among themselves, it may be tolerable for a time', going on to suggest 'for those desirous of sea-bathing in retirement…the water and sands are reasonable inducement.'

Much has changed since then of course, and it's quite likely that the Reverend wouldn't be too enamoured with the place today, with its bleeping arcades and rickety fairground rides, ice cream parlours and candy stalls – but plenty of people are. Moreover, and despite appearances to the contrary (donkey rides, saucy postcards), there are a few concessions to culture: a brace of ancient ruins and parks, a heritage railway and a quirky little museum, as well as some very agreeable local walks.

Barry's popularity as a seaside resort in the late 18th century coincided with the town's growth as a major port, and before long it was rivalling Cardiff as one of the most prolific coal ports in Europe: at its peak it was shipping in excess of 4 million tonnes of coal per year (11 million tonnes in 1913). In 1881 just 85 people lived in the parish of Barry, a figure that had risen to 27,000 by 1901 – the speed at which it was urbanised was quite staggering. The industry's decline, however, was as swift as its rise, and with the closure of the docks the town became more reliant than ever on seaside custom to sustain the local economy.

Barry owes much of its recent popularity to the hit television programme *Gavin and Stacey*, which was mostly filmed here. Fans of the show – with its cast of wonderfully idiosyncratic characters – will be familiar with the steep rows of red-brick terraces climbing down the hill from the top of town and the amusement arcade and kiosk on the prom – rarely has the phrase 'TV tourist' been so apt as it is here in Barry. Barry has also become a desirable proposition for potential house buyers who have been priced out of Cardiff and other towns and villages in the Vale, thanks to its affordability and excellent transport links. There's not much in the way of accommodation in Barry, but it's easily day-trippable from Cardiff.

GETTING THERE AND AWAY Trains depart every 15 minutes from Cardiff Queen Street station, stopping at Barry Docks and Barry before terminating at Barry Island. Bus #95 runs roughly every 30 minutes (Sun hourly) from Park Street in Cardiff to Barry Island.

✗ WHERE TO EAT AND DRINK

☐ Academy Espresso Bar The Pumphouse, Unit 1, Hood Rd; **w** www.academycoffee.co.uk; ⊕ 09.00–18.00 Sun–Tue, 09.00–23.00 Wed–Sat. Having comfortably settled into life within the immaculately restored Grade II-listed pumphouse, the Academy Bar is about more than just great coffee. Come sundown the place morphs into a funky cocktail bar while on Thu–Sat evenings at 17.00 there's a different street vendor on site; chuck into the mix a regular roster of events (open mic, quizzes, etc) & a good time is guaranteed. They've also got a drive-through at the Goodsheds just across the road. **£**

☐ The Goodsheds Hood Rd; **w** goodshedsbarry.co.uk; ⊕ noon–21.00 Wed–Sat, noon–19.00 Sun. Occupying a mix of repurposed shipping containers & railway carriages in the former docklands area, this has been touted as Wales's first sustainable urban high street. You certainly won't want for choice on the grub front, with cheerful traders rustling up everything from Greek to Mexican & Japanese to Indian, & for vegans there's the very dependable Mother Nature. Seating is outside, indoors (well, under a canopy) or you can take away. You're unlikely to spend more than a tenner wherever you decide to eat, but if you don't mind parting with a bit more cash, then make for The Shed in the old railway sidings building: run by Michelin-starred chef James Sommerin, this is exceptional food served at affordable prices, for example chicken kiev with caramelised cauliflower & chicken butter sauce (£19). A craft beer bar & a drive-through espresso bar round things off. Tidy, as they say in this part of Wales. **£**

WHAT TO SEE AND DO Described once in the *New York Times* as a 'stubby peninsular' – which while not entirely flattering is fairly accurate – Barry Island was only joined to the mainland in the late 19th century, until which point it stood aloof from the town, at that time believed to have been a retreat for hermits and holy men. Most of the island's action centres on the gently curving, white-sand beach of **Whitmore Bay**, fronting a long promenade packed with all the usual resort paraphernalia. Beach pursuits and other sundry tack aside (the less said about the Pleasure Park the better), there are a few pleasant surprises in store.

Opened in 1888, the main purpose of the **Barry Railway** was to create an integrated rail and dock system to rival that of Cardiff's, and while it couldn't count on the kinds of riches that Cardiff had courtesy of the Butes, it did have the backing of David Davies Llandinam, owner of some of the most important collieries in the Rhondda Valley. Trains laden with coal trundled down from Bridgend to Barry before looping up to Trehafod. On Saturdays and Sundays between 09.00 and noon there are heritage rides on a stretch of track (same details as for the war museum).

The last thing one would expect to see in Barry is a **war museum** (**m** 07443 870136; **w** barrywarmuseum.co.uk; ⊕ 11.00–14.00 Wed & 11.00–16.00 on 2nd Sun of month; free) but here it is, tucked away within the confines of Barry Island railway station. This small private collection is stuffed with all kinds of military paraphernalia, and while they've tried hard to make costumes, some weaponry and a bunch of medals look interesting, this is probably one for fans only. In any case, it's only open for three hours a week(!) so you'd do very well to get your timings right. However, the station building has just been put on the market by the council so the museum may move at some point.

From Whitmore Bay, there's an easy walk west out along an extended finger of land to **Friar's Point** or, better still, head across to the **Knap**, which comes from the Old English *cnæpp* ('hilltop'), which gives us the Welsh word *cnap* (a lump or knob in the landscape). The Knap was once the site of Wales's largest lido, but like so many others it was filled in years ago and is now somewhat more prosaically a landscaped park. You can still make out its rectangular imprint, as well as that of its curving chalets and changing rooms. Beyond the Knap lies **Cold Knap beach**, a forever expanse of pebble, which in stark contrast to Barry's main beach, receives

BARRY TO PORTHKERRY WALK

For an alternative perspective of Barry, there's an easy 3½-mile circular walk from the car park above Cold Knap beach to Porthkerry Country Park. Heading west from the car park, some 3rd century AD **Roman ruins**, incongruously located among some modern housing just behind the public loos, come as the first surprise. Uncovered in the 1960s during construction work, these low walls once belonged to a mansio (guesthouse or inn), and are all that is left from the time when the Romans constructed a harbour at Cold Knap – it's quite conceivable that there are more treasures lurking hereabouts.

Continue towards The Knap, passing the harp-shaped lake and park and rounding the headland by a watchtower before turning north along Lakeside Road towards **Romilly Park**, a mix of freshly cropped lawns and woodland that was laid out by (and named after) one of Barry's most prominent families in 1898. Continue up to Park Road junction and turn left, whereupon **Barry Castle** beckons you across for a quick nose around. Formerly the seat of the Du Barris, what remains of this mostly 13th-century building is more akin to medieval manor house than castle, but whatever its status at the time, the extant structure – essentially the gatehouse and south range – is in pretty good nick.

The Romilly family were also responsible for landscaping **Porthkerry Country Park**, a mile or so further west of the castle. Predominantly (a mixture of) meadows and woodland, it's a delightful spot for a ramble, but has had other uses over the years, such as when it was used to station troops and machinery ahead of the D-Day landings during World War II. The park's defining feature is its viaduct, a 16-span beauty designed by the wonderfully named Szlumper brothers in 1897 to service the newly inaugurated Vale of Glamorgan railway line between Barry and Bridgend.

The southernmost section of Porthkerry rubs up against the coastline and the now-defunct golf course, where an exciting project to rewild part of the course (which had became unplayable owing to persistent flooding) is well underway. This includes plans to return the area to wildflower meadows, ponds and saltmarshes in the hope of attracting new species. The early signs are certainly encouraging: in 2021, the rare carrot mining bee was spotted here for the first time. From the golf course, return to Cold Knap beach along the coast path. Of course, you don't have to undertake this walk in order to enjoy the park: it's a worthwhile visit in its own right and there's plenty of parking next to the visitor centre available if coming by car.

far fewer visitors – it's an excellent place to fly a kite too. A little tip here: the free car park above the beach is a good place to park, so long as you don't mind a longish stroll into town and back.

AROUND BARRY

Dyffryn Gardens (St Nicholas, CF5 6FZ; ☏029 2059 3328; w nationaltrust.org. uk/dyffryn-gardens; ⊕ 10.00–18.00 daily; £11) Another stuffy old National Trust property? Nope, far from it. Dispensing with the airs and graces typically found in so many of their estates, Dyffryn Gardens is quite different – it's a more hands-on experience (you can even play snooker) – and is also one of the reasons why it also makes for such a popular outing for families. The fact that both the house and gardens remain a work in progress only adds to its charm.

Prior to its acquisition by the National Trust in 2013, Dyffryn House was used as a police training centre and a conference venue. Its early history, however, is somewhat more conventional. Although the estate dates back as far as AD640, the first manor wasn't raised until the 16th century, but what you see today was built off the vast riches created by the coal industry and one man in particular, John Cory, who procured Dyffryn in 1891 and set about remodelling the house. Cory's daughter Florence was the last person to live here, in 1936, before it was leased out to the local council. Restoration has been a necessarily slow process, such was the building's parlous state, but during this time there have been some revealing finds. In 2018, there was a recovery of a stash of paintings by the portraitist Margaret Williams, who, during a long and distinguished career, painted some of the most illustrious names in the world of royalty and politics, among them The Queen and Winston Churchill. Of the 11 or so rooms available to view, many are still in a pleasing state of dilapidation. The most interesting are the Great Hall, bearing some gorgeous stained-glass windows, and the oak-panelled Billiards Room, which still retains a useable snooker table. Upstairs, the Red Library has a secondhand bookshop and comfy sofas.

Once considered among the finest Edwardian gardens in Britain, Dyffryn owes everything to the vision of Thomas Mawson, who was tasked with designing the grounds following Cory's acquisition of the estate. Yet despite his prolific output, Mawson, a self-taught horticulturalist, never received the same level of acclaim as Jekyll and Lutyens, those other titans of Victorian gardening. Today, this 50 acres of landscaped loveliness – walled and courtyard gardens, lawns, meadows, a fernery and arboretum – is utterly enchanting, though there's an awful lot to pack in so it might pay to be selective if time is short. Not to be missed is the walled garden, abundant with fruit and vegetables, which nestles up against the glasshouse, a steamy paradise of cacti, orchids and vines from the world over. Of the garden rooms, seek out the Pompeian and Mediterranean gardens before a ramble around the arboretum, many of whose trees were collected by John Cory's third son Reginald, a world-renowned plant gatherer.

St Lythan and Tinkinswood long cairns If you're a fan of such things, there are couple of intriguing megalithic tombs worth tracking down in the vicinity of the gardens, close to the village of St Nicholas. South of the gardens, by the lane junction of Dyffryn Lane and St Lythan's Road, is the 4,000-year-old **St Lythan Long Cairn** (open access). Looking something like a prehistoric bus shelter, the chamber comprises three upright mudstone slabs supporting a 13ft-long, slightly sloping capstone ceiling. Among the many legends attributed to the cairn, one is that on Midsummer's Eve, the capstone spins around three times before all the stones pop down to the river for a quick bath.

More impressive, and probably even older, is the **Tinkinswood Long Cairn** (open access), north of the gardens towards the village. A phenomenally heavy 40-tonne capstone monolith – which rates it one of the largest, if not *the* largest, in Britain – the chamber is fronted by a small 'forecourt', from where a narrow passage leads to a solitary chamber. During excavations in 1914, the bones of around 40 to 50 people were dug up along with broken bits of pottery.

THE GLAMORGAN HERITAGE COAST

Wending its way for 14 miles between Aberthaw and Porthcawl, the Glamorgan Heritage Coast is one of the most unheralded seascapes anywhere in Britain. The name was conceived as such in 1973 as a means of preserving this part of the South Wales coastline's unique geology: ancient lias limestone, shale and (Jurassic and Triassic) mudstone cliffs, interspersed with shingle or rock pavement beaches and occasional sandy bays. With the second highest tidal range in the world after Fundy Bay in Canada, and Atlantic storm swells frequently battering the coastline, these near-vertical cliffs are subject to a faster rate of erosion than many other parts of the coast.

Beyond Aberthaw's enormous power station, the first town is Llantwit Major, one of the key centres of early Celtic Christianity. Beyond here, the coast threads west towards Dunraven, Southerndown and Ogmore, where its eponymous river spills into the sea. On the other side of this small estuary lies Merthyr Mawr Nature Reserve, an expansive, internationally important sand dune system, before this designated stretch ends at the cheerfully appealing resort of Porthcawl.

LLANTWIT MAJOR History resonates powerfully in Llantwit Major, a snoozy little town 10 miles along the coast from Barry. It was here, some time in the early 6th century, that a chap called Illtud pitched up and established Britain's formative seat of learning, one that attracted students from all over, many of whom would go on to become religious leaders and missionaries themselves. Llantwit is very much a town of two halves: its eastern part comprises grey modern housing estates and a few tired-looking shops, while the older, far more agreeable western core manifests a neat kernel of 16th-century buildings and grey stone cottages, as well as Llantwit's great glory, St Illtud's Church. And with one or two very good places to eat and drink, there are good reasons to stick around a while.

Getting there and away The train station, which is on the Vale line serving Cardiff (via Barry) and Bridgend, with hourly trains to both, is a 5-minute walk from the modern part of town. Buses from Cardiff, Barry and Bridgend (all hourly) arrive on Le Pouliguen Way near the train station.

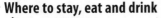
Where to stay, eat and drink

🏠 **The West House** (6 suites, 6 rooms) West St; ☎01446 792046; w townandcountrycollective. co.uk. A 5-minute stroll from the town square, the West House is your best bet if you're looking to bed down in Llantwit for the night. It offers 2 room types: standard rooms in the original part of the hotel & superior rooms in the newer part of the building, which are larger & benefit from garden views. Dogs are more than adequately catered for,

with canine-friendly amenities including beds & bowls plus a few doggie treats. A warming lounge bar rounds things off nicely. **££–£££**

✕ **The Cwtch** East St; ☎01446 792048; w the-cwtch.co.uk; ⏱ noon–14.00 & 18.00–21.00 Thu–Sat, noon–14.00 Sun. Inviting town-centre restaurant with big bay windows, smartly laid tables & colourfully upholstered chairs. The menu is accented towards Mediterranean dishes,

One of the most significant figures in the religious history of Wales, St Illtud (c465–c525) ranks alongside St Dyfrig and St David (St Teilo) as being among the most venerated of all Welsh saints. Little is known about Illtud's early life, only that he was possibly the son of a Breton king and a Welsh princess, and that he was at some stage a soldier under the employ of his (alleged) cousin, King Arthur. What is more certain is that Illtud was a disciple of – and may have been ordained by – St Germanus of Auxerre, in southwest France, though some scholars dispute this owing to some chronological discrepancies. Whatever the facts, there's no doubt that Germanus was a major influence on Illtud's future teachings.

Following his studies at Llancarfan, Illtud established a monastic school, called Cor Tedws, here in Llantwit Major (or Llanilltud Fawr as it was then), in or around 495. Among Illtud's students, said to number a thousand or more, were Samson, Aurelian and Gildas (supposedly the author of the first history of Britain), though claims that St David and St Patrick were also among his number are fairly wide of the mark, certainly where Patrick is concerned. Although David is referred to in a number of documents, his presence at Llanilltud Fawr has never been definitively proven. Not only was Illtud a man of superior intellect, which would appear to correspond with Samson's description of him as being 'a most wise magician, having knowledge of the future', but he also managed the not inconsiderable feat of bringing Christianity to the countryside, whereas under Roman rule it had largely been confined to urban areas.

The monastic community itself probably dispersed some time just before the Norman invasion at the end of the 11th century, leaving behind little more than an enclosure ('Llan') around, or near, the present-day church. But Illtud's influence was such that there are said to be 16 churches in South Wales dedicated to him, and a further seven in Brittany, one of which, somewhat fancifully, claims to hold his bones. However, the likelihood is that if he's buried anywhere, it's at the church of Llanilltud on Mynydd Illtud in the Brecon Beacons.

for example, tagine & chicken, or for veggies a Mediterranean tart, while the service is attentive but not overbearing. ££
Old Swan Inn Church St; 01446 792230; w knifeandforkfood.co.uk; noon–23.00 daily. Llantwit's oldest public inn has been courting visitors since some time in the 16th century, Neville Chamberlain & William Randolph Hearst, one-time owner of nearby St Donat's Castle, among its more distinguished guests. Split into 2 sections, the front bar is popular with hardcore ale drinkers, while the restaurant to the rear serves

pub classics, including a pie of the day, alongside more sophisticated plates like pork tenderloin with dauphinoise & apple purée. ££
Café Velo 3 Church St; 01446 792564; 09.00–15.00 daily. Everything in this brilliant, bike-friendly café is geared (excuse the pun) towards welcoming the saddle-sore, or anyone else for that matter, from the posters & jerseys on the walls to a television in the corner relaying live coverage of a race going on somewhere in the world. Both the coffee & cakes (banana choc chip, toffee loaf) are delicious. £

What to see and do Located on, or near, the site of Britain's oldest seat of learning, **St Illtud's Church** (w llanilltud.org.uk; 10.00–16.00 daily) was, according to John Wesley who preached here in 1777, 'abundantly the most beautiful church in

Wales', and it'd be hard not to disagree. Although there's nothing left of those 6th-century buildings today, the incumbent church is not a bad sub. The church actually constitutes three distinct parts, or more accurately, two churches and a chapel: the Norman-built West Church, erected around 1100; the 13th-century East Church; and tacked on to the end of the West Church, the newly rebuilt Galilee Chapel.

It's believed that the West Church replaced an earlier Celtic timber construction, though most of what you see today is mostly 15th century, with the arch above the main door leading to the entrance and the font all that remain from the Norman edition. Otherwise, interest centres on the fabulous oak roof adorned with wooden bosses depicting eminent families from the Vale of Glamorgan, and carvings of human heads. While the West Church was effectively the parish church, the East Church – the two are connected by the tower – was primarily a place of worship for the monks. The East Church is of less interest, architecturally at least, but it does bear a fine, and still fairly well-coloured, fresco of St Christopher on the north wall, possibly dating from around 1400, and a reredos, or stone screen, whose 22 niches would have at one time been in possession of a statuette. Only one survived (Madonna and Child) and this now resides in one of the south windows.

Until 2013, the 13th-century **Galilee Chapel** – a galilee being a vestry where priests prepared for service – had stood as a roofless ruin for more than 250 years. As much as was possible, the chapel was rebuilt using the same materials that were used in its original construction – local lias limestone, timber and slate – and although the result is pleasing enough, the modern glass windows and tiled flooring do mar the overall effect a little. Still, it's a beautifully reworked space, one that's been given over to the church's outstanding collection of 9th-century Celtic stones, among the most valuable and oldest-known inscribed Christian stones in Britain. Variously recovered from the church grounds and some local gardens, three of the stones illustrate some form of inscription, the most prized of which is the **Illtud Cross**, a chunky 8th-century boulder bearing the faintest outline of the letters, ILT (and half of a U), as in ILTU, the Latin for ILLTUD. The most impressive stone here, though, is the partially fractured **Houelt Cross**, one of the finest examples of a wheel cross anywhere. It's precisely decorated on both faces using a combination of plait work, interlace and fret (straight line), and with a Latin inscription on the base indicating that Houelt had the cross prepared upon the death of his father, Res (or Hywel app Rhys), erstwhile King of Glamorgan.

From the church, Colhugh Street wriggles its way down towards the town **beach**. Part sand, part pebble, it's a small affair but great for surfing, fossil hunting or just idling.

SOUTHERNDOWN AND DUNRAVEN BAY

A surf-washed pebble beach hemmed in by high, bowl-like cliffs, Dunraven Bay sees fewer visitors than most other beaches along this stretch of coast, which in itself makes it an enticing proposition for an outing. The beach is also lifeguarded between July and September. There is a car park here, but it's more fun to park at Southerndown and walk back along the short section of coast path to the bay, which takes around 15 minutes.

Arcing around the left-hand side of the beach (looking seawards) is the prominent headland known as **Witches Point**. A satisfying climb to the top affords superlative views of the beach below and the striated cliffs running away to the east – from here it feels that if you stepped off the edge you'd plummet into the sea, but in actual fact layers of rock steadily bump their way down, almost but not quite, to the water's edge. You'll probably find a lone fisherman enjoying some peace and quiet, though fishing is not recommended if you haven't done so here before.

This 4½-mile walk starts from Nash Point car park (£3), 4 miles west of Llantwit Major, where's there's a café open in summer. Head back inland along the road towards the village of **Marcross,** where the early 12th-century Holy Trinity Church is worth a peek for some lovely aspects of Norman architecture, notably the semicircular chancel arch with its exquisite roll moulding and an oversized font. A few paces further on, turn right before the Swn-y-Mor bungalow, following the track around to the left and on towards a stile. Through here, walk straight ahead with the hedge immediately on your left. Within this field are two sharp left turns: at the second of these turns, ignore the footpath that leads off to the left and instead continue towards a stone stile. Stay left, following the hedge towards the road. Turn right here, and with Elms Cottage on your left and Marcross Farm on your right, walk down the tarmac path for just over 150 yards. Go through the (partially concealed) stile to your left and walk towards another stile directly opposite, then diagonally across the well-worn path to another stile. Go left along the path to a wall stile at the end of the field. Follow the path round to the left of the building to another stile that gives way to a lane, to walk between the garage and Park Farmhouse.

Go through the gate and head down through the woodland (ignoring the slightly uphill path to the right), where you'll eventually reach a road with the impressive bulk of St Donat's Castle rising sheer above. Down to the right, at the foot of a crag upon which the castle stands, **St Donat's Church** is most likely a 12th-century construction, with piecemeal add-ons over the centuries. The Lady Chapel is notable for its marble tombs of various members from the Stradling family, owners of the castle between roughly 1300 and 1740. The font is another supreme example of Norman craftsmanship, but note too the Calvary cross in the cemetery, to the left as you enter through the gate.

An immense mock-Gothic fortification, **St Donat's Castle** originally dates from the 12th century, but most of its present (interior) appearance dates from the 1920s following extensive renovation work by the American media magnate William Randolph Hearst, who purchased it for £27,000, then lavished another £280,000 on it. Not one to do things by halves, one of Hearst's more ambitious projects was to completely deconstruct Bradenstoke Hall, from Bradenstoke

En route to the top you'll notice the scant ruins (a few bits of masonry and a near-intact arch) of **Dunraven Castle**. As hard as it is to imagine today, a manor was recorded here in the 16th century – although evidence points to continuous occupation since the Celts, which comes as little surprise given its formidable location. Illustrated information boards give you some idea of what it might have looked like. The castle's demolition, however, is relatively recent, for it was used as a convalescence hospital during both World Wars, then as a tourist authority guesthouse until 1963.

Back down at the bottom of the hill, a vaulted stone arch with a heavy wooden door beckons you into Dunraven's old **walled gardens** (open access), the only surviving part of the castle. Following substantial funding a few years ago, the gardens were restored and reopened by Lady Dunraven, who owns this land. Enclosed by a high, mostly crenellated wall, the gardens – which are once again looking neat and sprightly – are portioned up into four plots, which slope ever so gently down to the far western wall and a corner tower, or folly, which probably accommodated an icehouse.

Priory in Wiltshire, and have it rebuilt here. By all accounts his gatherings were quite something: among his many distinguished guests Clark Gable, Errol Flynn, David Lloyd George and Churchill. The castle was subsequently passed over to Atlantic College, who continue to run it as a residential sixth-form college for international students.

From the church, walk back up the road (with the car park on your left) to the main road. Taking a sharp right here, pass the college entrance on your right and follow the road round as it bears left. Just over 200 yards further on, just beyond the lay-by, go through the kissing gate and walk through the field towards the coast. Having now joined the Wales Coast Path, turn right and follow the path through the woods until you emerge at St Donat's Bay and the college's castellated perimeter wall and flanking towers. Walk along the gently sloping sea wall and up the steps into more woods before you reach a field. Slightly confusingly, two paths fork here, but you can take either of these.

Continue along the path until you reach **Nash Lighthouse**, erected in 1832 in response to the loss of the Frolic on the notorious Nash Point sandbanks the previous year when 78 men perished. A graceful 121ft-high cylindrical tower constructed from the local blue lias stone, the lighthouse is currently presided over by Deryn Gully, the country's first (and presently only) lady lighthouse attendant. From the lighthouse continue across the meadow to the car park.

If you want, you can extend the walk to include another loop, which is of a similar length to the one outlined above. From the car park dip down into the valley and up the other side to **Nash Point**, before continuing along a long and easy stretch of coast path towards (the Sphinx-like head of) **Cwm Nash**. In 2019, concerned members of the public alerted police to the possibility of human remains embedded within these cliffs. Following excavation and forensic analysis, it was determined that these were the remains of six, possibly more, males (including a child) who probably ended up here as a result of a shipwreck, and as the cliffs eroded, the bones had become increasingly exposed. From Cwm Nash, walk inland along the steep-sided valley towards the village of **Monknash** where the Plough and Harrow (w ploughandharrowmonknash.co.uk) awaits to rid any hunger pangs.

✖ Where to eat and drink

✖ **Frolics** Beach Rd, Southerndown; ☎ 01656 880127; w frolicsrestaurant.co.uk; ⏰ noon–15.00 & 18.00–22.00 Tue–Sat, noon–16.00 Sun. While the location is rather odd & the building bland, this cheerful Portuguese/Brazilian-owned restaurant is fabulous. A good starter would be the crisp beetroot & walnut salad, before tucking into a plate of wild mushroom linguini with red onion & garlic, then finishing with the house tiramisu. If you want to save some cash, there are great-value discounted 2- & 3-course lunch & dinner menus Tue–Thu. ££

OGMORE-BY-SEA AND EWENNY From Southerndown it's a short hop along the coast to Ogmore-by-Sea, a village of straggling houses along the road high above the shoreline. A turning in the tight bend just before the estuary leads down to a couple of busy car parks and a big area of sand and shingle beach below some low rocky cliffs. Here, the River Ogmore spills into the sea, meaning that you can't access Merthyr Mawr beach on the opposite side – instead, you'll have to walk up to Ogmore Castle and cross there.

Nudged up against the Ewenny River about a mile or so inland on the road towards Ewenny village stand the small but surprisingly atmospheric ruins of **Ogmore Castle**, which roughly dates from the time of the Norman Conquest in 1100. Centred on a solid stone keep built by Maurice de Londres, son of William de Londres, one of the Twelve Knights of Glamorgan, the Normans had it positioned it here so as to guard the mouth of the river, which also explains the deep ditch. By around 1400, the castle's purpose had been served and so began its slow decline. As enjoyable as the castle is, more fun are the dozen or so stepping stones across the Ewenny River, the only access point to the fields on the other side, and from where you can walk to Merthyr Mawr village around 15 minutes away. This shallow riverbank is a lovely spot for a picnic. Alternatively, from the other side of the road opposite the castle, you can walk up on to Ogmore Down, a large tract of limestone heathland – just watch out for stray golf balls.

Continuing inland for a couple of miles or so, a leafy lane just northeast of Ewenny village leads to **Ewenny Priory**, founded in 1141 by Lord Maurice de Londres (author of Ogmore Castle's stone keep) as an adjunct to Gloucester's Benedictine Abbey. It was by no means a large priory, home to just one prior and 12 monks, and by the time of its dissolution in 1536, it's quite likely that there were only two or three monks remaining. The priory's powerful, thick-set precinct walls are punctuated by three towers including the mighty North Gate(house), with its deeply incised slots denoting where the portcullis would have been positioned, and ominous-looking 'murder holes' in the ceiling.

Within the precincts, the priory house and grounds are now in private hands so, unless you want to get married there, these are off-limits. What you can view, however, is the neighbouring **priory church**, a bold, squat Romanesque structure built by Maurice's father William, and as such pre-dating the priory by some 15 years. It's divided into two sections: you enter via the western section, or nave, its roof supported by chunky Norman columns but which is otherwise bare save for some fine Norman-era stained-glass windows. This part of the church still serves as the parish church. Through the door – beyond the medieval rood screen – the eastern chancel or monastic chapel holds a fine collection of carved stones and tombs, among them the flamboyant tomb slab of Maurice de Londres, and next to that, the broken-up grave slab of his son William. Look out for a small section of medieval floor tiles, which can be discerned by their different colourings. On the east side of the presbytery, you can just about detect the faint outline of some wall paintings, reputedly the oldest in Wales. The priory church also attracted the attention of J M W Turner on his tour of the region in 1795; his subsequent watercolour, the gorgeously light-filled *Transept of Ewenny Priory*, has a sculpted knight reposed atop an altar tomb alongside roaming pigs and chickens. It was displayed at the Royal Academy in London in 1797 and now resides in the National Museum Cardiff, though is not normally on show.

If you've time, it's worth popping into the **Ewenny Pottery** on the main Ewenny Road (✆ 01656 653020; w ewennypottery.com; ⏲ 09.30–13.00 & 14.00–16.30 Mon–Sat), Wales's oldest potters. Here you can view Caitlin Jenkins – the eighth generation of Jenkins potters – at work, as well as peruse (and perhaps buy) a selection of her beautifully crafted items.

MERTHYR MAWR NATURE RESERVE From the village of Merthyr Mawr, itself little more than a handful of thatched and whitewashed cottages, a narrow road bumps along a wooded glen before terminating at Candleston car park and the dishevelled, ivy-draped ruins of a 15th-century fortified manor house, which was abandoned as the sands encroached. This is Merthyr Mawr National Nature Reserve, at the heart of which is one of the largest dune complexes in Europe. This was once a prodigious belt of sand stretching all the way to the Gower Peninsula but which has now been reduced to two locations: here at Merthyr Mawr and the other at Kenfig (page 140) on the other side of Porthcawl. Such is their scale that they have occasionally doubled for Middle Eastern desertscapes, most memorably for a handful of scenes in David Lean's 1962 Oscar-winning film *Lawrence of Arabia*.

Presently, there is relatively little bare sand across the reserve, and with that comes the threat of it being overrun with vegetation, typically grass and scrub, none of which are conducive to supporting the variety of insects, fungi and other pioneer plant species here. To this end, there have been concerted efforts to rejuvenate the dunes, one of the projects being to cut large troughs in the frontal dunes so that sand can be funnelled inland, but it's a long process.

As it is, the dunes are abundant with flora. There are healthy colonies of purple-coloured wild pansy, and for a short period in June, marsh orchids make their appearance. Prevalent too is marram grass, whose long roots help stabilise the dunes. Rarer species include sea holly and rock sea lavender, though less welcome is sea buckthorn, a thorny, non-native shrub that smothers existing vegetation and therefore has a detrimental effect on sand growth. You may also see the occasional slow worm (technically a legless lizard) cross your path. Having picked your way through the dunes, you'll eventually emerge on to pristine, flat white sands. And because it requires some effort to get here, Merthyr Mawr beach sees relatively few visitors, certainly compared with Ogmore on the other side of the estuary. Enjoy the solitude.

Back at the car park, signs point to the **Big Dipper**, which at 200ft is the second-highest single dune in Europe after the Dune du Pilat in western France which rates a whopping 377ft – it's an awesome sight and an even more awesome climb, if you're feeling up to the challenge.

Where to stay

⋀ Woods and Dunes Candlestones Campsite; m 07754 734556; ◪ woodsdunes. Among thick woodland & just a stone's throw from the dunes, this wonderful site is about as blissed out as it gets. There are 10 yurts scattered around the site each sleeping 4, with loos & showers in the main barn building, which also doubles as the site's social hub; b/fast is taken here & there's also a licensed bar. The huge firepit is the focal point for nightly acoustic sessions, which anyone can partake in. The owners, Dawn & Andrew also organise the wonderful Between the Trees Festival each Aug, which is largely soundtracked by contemporary folk acts, but music aside, it strives to reconnect younger generations with the natural world through talks, debates & films. **££**

PORTHCAWL AND AROUND A former iron and coal terminus turned popular seaside resort, Porthcawl somehow feels harder to categorise than either Barry or Penarth, lacking the buzz (though thankfully the tack) of the former, and the demonstrable charm of the latter. That said, the town scrubs up pretty well and suffices for all things of a practical nature, though there's very little to see or do in the centre itself. But when you've got so many beaches on your doorstep, that's no big deal, and in recent years Porthcawl has made a name for itself as a popular surfing destination, to add to its status as one of Wales's premier golf resorts. One time you may not want to be here (or maybe you do) is at the end of September when thousands of Elvis clones (over 20,000!) hit town for the annual Porthcawl Elvis Festival (w elvies.co.uk). Shows take place inside the Grand Pavilion, but really it's just one big silly carnival.

Getting there and away Porthcawl is a 10-minute easy diversion off the M4. It's best to avoid trying to park in the centre and along the seafront and instead head to one of the large car parks east of the centre out towards Trecco Bay. Buses from Bridgend (every 20–30mins) and Cowbridge (every 20–30mins) set passengers down on St John Street, right in the centre.

Where to stay, eat and drink

Olivia House (6 rooms) 44 Esplanade Av; ☎ 07968 841992; w oliviahouse.com. Discreet Edwardian townhouse just up from the seafront concealing half a dozen theatrically designed rooms, each of which plays on a different theme (for example, the French Room & the Angel Room). Guests are also encouraged to enjoy the lounge, where you can read, play chess or just sip a glass of wine. Breakfast, meanwhile, is a delicious affair with the likes of kippers & smoked salmon to tempt you out of bed. £££

39 John Street (3 rooms) 39 John St; ☎ 01656 771991; w 39johnstreet.com. Porthcawl's most exciting accommodation option offers 3 fun & funkily designed studio rooms (all sleeping 4), each one named after a line from a song from a famous band, namely 'Here comes the sun', 'Sweet dreams are made of this', & 'Scaramouche, scaramouche, will you do the fandango?' – we'll leave you to work it out. Each room has a kitchenette with microwave & Nespresso machine, a dining area & lounge, & Netflix-enabled TV. ££

Double Zero Pizza Unit 2, Jennings Bldg; ☎ 01656 507608; w doublezeropizza.co.uk; ⏰ 10.00–22.00 Tue–Fri, 09.00–23.00 Sat, 10.00–20.00 Sun. It's not quite the 'Slice of Italy' it purports to be, but there's no doubt that the pizzas here are very good indeed; all the usual suspects plus a few pasta dishes, salads & the like. Located east of the centre by the harbour. ££

Rest Bay Café Bar Rest Bay Watersports Centre; ☎ 01656 771877; w restbaycafebar.co.uk; ⏰ 09.00–21.00 daily. Glass-fronted 1st-floor café inside the watersports centre affording glorious views out across the bay. B/fast (served until 11.30) comes in all guises, with a particularly appetising line in egg-based dishes plus veggie/ vegan options, while lunches run the full gamut from sandwiches & paninis to fish & chips & steak burgers. Come sundown it makes a terrific spot for a beer or a glass of wine. Dogs are not permitted in the café but are allowed in the sheltered downstairs kiosk. No bookings – it's first come first served. £

Sports and activities

Cycling
Rest Bay Bike Hire Rest Bay Watersports Centre; m 07376 303917; w restbaybikehire.co.uk. There are bikes of all denominations available for hire here, including mountain bikes (£10/15 2/4hrs) & fat bikes (£15/25 2/4hrs).

Golf
Royal Porthcawl Rest Bay; ☎ 01656 782251; w royalporthcawl.com. Endorsed by some of the world's greatest golfers (including Tom Watson no less) & frequently rated one of Britain's finest courses, Royal Porthcawl is a magnificent seaside links, but it's by no means easy, or cheap: a round of 18 holes in summer will cost £175 (£250/ day), though the price is much reduced in winter (£100/18 holes).

Surfing and paddleboarding
Porthcawl Surf Rest Bay Watersports Centre; m 07583 348013; w porthcawlsurf.co.uk. One of Wales's best surf centres offering year-round tuition (£35/2hrs) & rental (£10/day for a board, £5 for a wetsuit). Also for hire are stand-up paddleboards (£10/90mins) & kayaks (£10/1hr).

What to see and do Occupying the Grade II-listed former premises of the old police station halfway down the main pedestrianised high street, Porthcawl's **town museum** (☎ 01656 773861; w porthcawlmuseum.com; ⏰ 11.00–15.00 Wed, Fri & Sat; £2.50) is a minor delight. The core of the museum's displays usually revolve around a series of rotating exhibitions, which more often than not tend to coincide with a significant anniversary: in 2022, there was an exhibition commemorating the 40th anniversary of the Falklands War. Outside, there's an old Anderson bomb shelter and the Porthcawl cannon, discovered on a local beach and now resubmerged to preserve it. Beyond the old prisoners' yard, the three holding cells – still with their original graffitied metal doors – house temporary exhibitions. Otherwise, there are plenty of artefacts and memorabilia pertaining to local history and events, and any of the friendly volunteers here will be happy to show you around. Afterwards, it's worth a stroll along the Esplanade for a quick gawp at the impressively domed and colonnaded **Grand Pavilion** and then for a coffee in one of the many seafront cafés while taking in the wide watery views.

If it's beaches you're after, there are seven to choose from. Closest to the town centre is **Sandy Bay**, a flat, sandy expanse overshadowed by the all-singing, all-dancing Coney Beach Amusement Park. Next along is **Trecco Bay**, a blue flag beach overlooked by an unsightly sprawl of mobile homes. In part this is a legacy of the institution known as the Miners' Eisteddfod, when, during the last week in July and the first week in August, miners and their families would pile down to Porthcawl for respite from the daily drudgery of the pits. A far more appealing blue flag beach is **Rest Bay**, a 20-minute walk northwest of town and renowned for having some of the finest surf in Wales; here too is where you'll find all the requisite amenities, courtesy of a shiny new watersports centre. The most westerly pair of Porthcawl's beaches, and the best of the lot – partly because they can only be reached on foot from either Rest Bay or the Kenfig Nature Reserve and are therefore quieter – are **Pink Bay** and **Sker Beach**, which respectively lie south and north of Sker Point, site of one of Wales's worst ever shipwrecks (see below).

The beaches have become a popular spot for **fat biking**, which involves cycling around on large-rimmed bikes whose grip and traction is designed to traverse

SHIPWRECK!

A notorious stretch of water, the Bristol Channel has a long history as a shipping hazard, with many wrecks smashed against its shores, in the process claiming the lives of hundreds of seafarers.

In 1947, the rocky bluff of Sker Point was the scene of Wales's worst peacetime maritime disaster when, on the afternoon of 23 April, the US-built steamship SS *Samtampa*, en route from Middlesbrough to Newport, was driven on to the rocks during a great storm. Worse was to follow when the Mumbles-based lifeboat, *Edward Prince of Wales*, capsized in the act of trying to rescue the crew of the Samtampa, with all eight of its men drowning. In total 48 men were lost from the two vessels, 12 of whom were laid to rest in Porthcawl cemetery. Parts of the *Samtampa's* wreck are visible at very low tide including, remarkably, a section of its engine; close by, just off the coastal path and in among the rocks, is a commemorative plaque at the site where the lifeboat perished, and where it was subsequently burnt, as is RNLI tradition.

In 1906, the *Sage* was carrying a cargo of slate tiles from North Wales when it was blown ashore near the harbour. Here, just below Porthcawl lifeboat station, it's possible to make out some of the barnacle-encrusted tiles melded into the rocks. One of the more mysterious wrecks in these waters was that of the steamship Kendy, which sank half a mile or so out from Rest Bay on 27 August 1928, although the exact whereabouts of the wreckage has still to be determined.

pretty much any terrain, including mud, sand and rocks. One of the best stretches is between Coney Beach all the way to, and in among, the dunes at Merthyr Mawr. Give it a go, it's an absolute blast. They are available to rent from Rest Bay Bike Hire (page 138).

KENFIG NATIONAL NATURE RESERVE (✆ 01656 743386; w kenfignnr.blogspot. com; ⏁ open access) Covering 1,300 acres of land between Porthcawl to the south and the belching stacks of the Tata steelworks to the north, Kenfig National Nature Reserve was once the site of a medieval village named Cefn-y-ffignon (a corruption of 'A Ridge on a Marsh') but it has long since been lost to time, and sand, and the only vestige is the rather sad stump of the castle.

Currently only 8% of the site comprises bare sand, hence there continues to be a concerted effort to repopulate slacks in order to smother existing, invasive vegetation and encourage the colonisation of pioneer species such as petalwort, as well as other habitats. This is where the reserve's livestock comes in. As well as sheep, between May and October Kenfig is home to around 75 Highland cattle, brought here to assist in controlled conservation grazing.

As an open habitat, it's comparable to Merthyr Mawr (page 136), but what sets it apart from those dunes, or any other dune system in Wales, is the breadth of its flora and fauna, in particular orchids and birdlife. In spring and summer, the reserve is a wonderful floral cornucopia. Among the 15 or so species of orchid recorded so far at Kenfig are bee, pyramidal, twayblade and the red-listed Dutch helleborine, a rare beauty that you won't find anywhere else in Wales. Kenfig also has one superstar species: along with the Norfolk Broads, it is the last bastion in the UK of the **Fen orchid** (though numbers are far greater here than they are in Norfolk), and it's no exaggeration to say this small, pale yellow and fairly inconspicuous flower attracts botanists from all over the world, such is its status. If you're keen to see it, there's a short window of opportunity between early June and mid-to-late July. Other orchids flower at various times between April and September.

There's fantastic birdlife here too: redshank, ringed plover, little ringed plover, Cetti's warbler, the hard-to-detect bittern, as well as raptors including sparrowhawks, peregrines and goshawks. One of the best places to see some of these are the two hides next to freshwater **Kenfig Pool**, which you can walk around between July and October although swimming is strictly forbidden at all times. Important here is the presence of stonewort, a rich source of food for fish and other aquatic organisms, while the cleanliness of Kenfig Pool is also attractive to medicinal leech (*Hirudo medicinalis*), a species that is rarely found in the wild – did you know that a (painless) 20-minute bite from one of these little blood-suckers is enough to supply them with nine months' worth of nutrients? Therefore consider your deed done if you do succumb. During medieval times, leeches were used to remove blood from patients (a process known as 'bloodletting') and today they are still used in microsurgery as a means of preventing blood from coagulating. Otherwise, the grassy banks by the pool are popular with picnic-toting folk.

Look out too for basking lizards, and the occasional otter by the bridge on the reserve's marshier, quieter, north side. Kenfig specialises in many other rare and unusual species, be it flora or fauna, including the shrill carder bee, a species in serious decline, and the great crested newt, one of just four protected amphibians in the UK. If there's something you'd specifically like to see here, seek out Chris Jones, Kenfig's highly knowledgeable warden. As the old adage goes, what Chris doesn't know about birds, bees and orchids – but especially fungi – isn't worth knowing about. There aren't as yet any official trails through the site but it's easy to pick your way through the dunes on clearly defined paths. The visitor centre building no longer functions as such, but Chris does host free guided walks on the last Saturday of each month; a good source of up-to-date information is his Twitter feed (🐦 @kenfigwarden).

MARGAM COUNTRY PARK

MARGAM COUNTRY PARK (📞 01639 881635; **w** www.margamcountrypark.co.uk; ⏰ summer 10.00–18.00, winter 10.00–16.30; parking £6.80) Within roaring earshot of the M4 lie the thousand acres of Margam Country Park. If you've come expecting to see inside its showpiece castle, you'll be disappointed. Save for the grand entrance with its splendid octagonal lantern tower and staircase (and a few mildly diverting photos of past visiting dignitaries), it's not possible to venture any further inside the building. But there's certainly no shortage of other ways to spend your time in the park, especially if you've got kids in tow, to whom most things seem to be geared towards anyway.

A Tudor-Gothic behemoth, the heavily turreted castle was raised in the 1830s by Christopher Rice Mansel Talbot, who installed no fewer than 29 bedrooms but just one bathroom, which gives a whole new meaning to shared shower facilities. It was sold to a local colliery owner in 1942, but he considered the place too large (which somewhat begs the question: why on earth did he buy it in the first place?), and it was largely ruinous by the time it was acquired by the council in 1974. Gutted by fire three years later, its fortunes have fluctuated ever since and most of its rooms are now given over to events. The castle's list of previous visitors is as illustrious as it is long, among them Lord Admiral Nelson and his mistress Lady Hamilton, Isambard Kingdom Brunel, and General Eisenhower, who called in on troops stationed here during World War II.

A few paces down from the castle are the atmospheric remains of the Cistercian Abbey, a mid 12th-century outpost to France's Clairvaux Abbey that was mostly demolished by Sir Rice Mansel when he bought the estate from King Henry VIII. There's little of substance to see, but the 12-sided chapter house retains most of its vaulted ceiling. Far more impressive is the neighbouring orangery, a gorgeous Georgian masterpiece, which, at 327ft, is the longest in Britain. The surrounding gardens are rather lovely too. It was around the same time that the monastery was built that deer were introduced to the park, and they have remained an enduring presence ever since. Mostly red and fallow deer, there's also a small population of endangered Père David deer.

Kids can burn off some energy (and parents can have some respite) in the castle-themed adventure playground, or Fairytale Land, with its child-size storybook cottages, although it is looking slightly tired these days. Elsewhere there are a couple of marked trails, one of which takes in an iron-age hillfort, a miniature railway (though its operating times are erratic), and Go Ape, which is independently run.

LLANTRISANT

Casting an impressive shadow high above the Ely River Valley, the market town of Llantrisant feels somewhat out of place here on the dividing line between the Vale of Glamorgan and the Valleys, as if reminiscent of a small French hilltop town. Everything in the village revolves around the **Bull Ring**, so named after the bull baiting that used to take place here. In the centre stands an oversized statue of William Price (1800–93), Llantrisant's most famous son and one of Wales's most colourful and controversial 19th-century figures. A fervent nationalist, as well as doctor, chartist, heretic and archdruid, Price clearly had many strings to his bow, but it was one incident in particular that he is chiefly remembered for: in 1884, following the death of his infant son, Iesu Grist (Welsh for 'Jesus Christ'), he attempted to cremate the boy on a pyre up on Llantrisant Common, an act that, while considered blasphemous (and illegal), did pave the way for cremation to become legalised, culminating in the Cremation Act 1902. Price's notoriety was such that when he himself was cremated, some 20,000 people gathered to observe proceedings. As an interesting aside, Robert Downey Jr based his character Dr Dolittle (the titular protagonist of the 2020 film of the same last name) on Price.

Across from the statue, where the two roads fork, is the sweet little **Llantrisant Gallery Model House** (📞 01443 238884; w llantrisantgallery.com; ⏰ 10.00–17.00 Tue–Sat, 11.00–16.00 Sun), a contemporary craft centre, exhibition space and shop selling hand-crafted Welsh products. There are some lovely pieces here if you're on the hunt for a gift.

A 2-minute walk from the Bull Ring, on a grassy terrace with commanding views over the Vale of Glamorgan, the 13th-century **Parish Church** is chiefly notable for a stained-glass window (the east window behind the altar) by Edward Burne-Jones depicting a beardless Christ, thought to be one of only three such windows to exist. A few paces away are the stumpy remains of the old town castle's Raven Tower. There are half-hourly buses from Cardiff (departing from Castle Street) to Llantrisant.

ROYAL MINT EXPERIENCE (Heol-y-San, Ynysmaerdy; 📞 0333 241 2223; w royalmint. com; ⏰ 09.15–16.15 daily; £13.25) Ask people where British coins are minted and the likelihood is that the majority wouldn't have the foggiest. Pushed further they'd probably venture London, and until 1967 that was the case. It therefore comes as quite a surprise to many to learn that the Mint is actually based here in South Wales, on an ordinary industrial estate just outside Llantrisant.

Remarkably, the Mint was founded way back in AD886, since which time (at least until its move here) it operated out of London, initially the Tower of London then Tower Hill. The move was prompted by the need to work from larger premises as the United Kingdom prepared to go decimal in 1971, and Llantrisant won the bid, which may or may not have had something to do with the fact that the Chancellor of the Exchequer at the time, James Callaghan, also happened to be MP for Cardiff. Fittingly, it was Her Majesty the Queen who struck the first coin in December 1968. Today, some 5 million coins per week (or 850 coins per minute) are minted here.

Following a brief introduction, where you can view three of the original 19th-century presses from Tower Hill and a few other bits and bobs, the **tour** continues over at the plant itself, though for obvious reasons, it's not possible to enter the production room so instead you view proceedings through a glass screen, which includes the coins being struck at machine-gun speed. At the end you'll be given the opportunity to strike your own coin, which will cost you £5 – save your money.

Better is the **museum** that follows the tour, which you are free to peruse at leisure. Showcasing Britain's illustrious history of coinage, there are some wonderful artefacts on display, going all the way back to the 9th century and the Alfred the Great Penny, inscribed with the word LVNDONIA (the Latin word for London), to the 1489 Gold Sovereign of Henry VII, the largest, most valuable coin of its day. What is less well known is that the Royal Mint has been producing coins for circulation overseas since 1325, and today supplies currency to more than 60 countries, many of which are on display here. But the Mint's remit goes far beyond coins. Medals – lots of them – have been minted here, ever since 40,000 individually named Waterloo campaign medals were issued to every participating soldier in 1816. And for the London 2012 Olympic and Paralympic Games, all 4,700 medals were struck here.

The Mint has contributed in other ways too: during World War II it assisted in the manufacture of munitions, and more recently during the Covid pandemic it was pressed into service as a production line for medical visors: around 2 million were made. In 2021, the Mint unveiled a monster 10kg gold coin, part of the Queen's Beasts commemorative coin collection. Purchased for a cool £10,000, it's little surprise that the identity of the buyer has remained a secret. As for the rarest United Kingdom coin currently in circulation? That'll be the 50p coin with an image of Kew Gardens on the back, so keep an eye out – it could be worth a few bob.

COWBRIDGE AND AROUND

One of Wales's most affluent small towns, Cowbridge retains an air of genteel respectability, its well-groomed main street liberally sprinkled with enticing cafés, restaurants, wine bars and boutique shops. Although you wouldn't think so, Cowbridge is the only town in the old county of Glamorgan to have retained its medieval walls, and on Church Street (just off the High Street) you can walk through the last remaining, albeit much-remodelled, gatehouse – one of what were originally four that punctuated these walls.

GETTING THERE AND AWAY There is no rail line here but half-hourly buses from Cardiff and Porthcawl, as well as buses from Llantwit Major (#8, Mon–Sat), stop near the Town Hall on the High Street.

WHERE TO STAY, EAT AND DRINK

The Bear (33 rooms) 63 High St; 📞01446 774814; w townandcountrycollective.co.uk. It's the sort of place you expect to see out in the sticks, but even in the middle of the high street The Bear retains genuine warmth & cosiness; rooms are split between those in the main building & those in the courtyard annex, though to all intents & purposes the furnishings & décor are the same. Both the grown-up, glamorous-looking stone vaulted restaurant & lounge bar & grill offer enticing menus with treats like braised fennel, asparagus, orange & burrata lasagne; b/fast is taken across the road in the Penny Farthing restaurant. **££**

Arboreal 68 Eastgate St; 📞01446 775093; w arboreal.uk.com; ⏰ 18.00–22.00 Thu, 15.00–22.00 Fri, noon–22.00 Sat, noon–16.00 Sun. Everything at Arboreal – presently the town's standout restaurant – is wood-fired, from the starters (sticky pork ribs) & flatbreads (Peking duck) to all the mains (spring lamb rack) & pizzas (spicy Mexican). The restaurant itself looks brilliant & the service is consummate. **££**

Pear Kitchen 15 High St; 📞01446 772001; ⏰ 11.00–15.00 Tue–Sat. Ignore the slightly clinical feel of the place & just enjoy the exceptional food in this well-priced vegan diner.

Korean cauliflower fritters with Asian slaw, & katsu burger in a crispy *seitan* (bun) with curry sauce & pickled onions are two of the staples, though the daily specials chalked up on the board are often a good bet. It keeps short hours so this is essentially a lunchtime option. £

📖 **Penny Farthing** 54 High St; ✆01446 774999; w townandcountrycollective.co.uk; ⏰ 08.00–16.00 Wed–Sun. Directly opposite The Bear (it's under the same management),

this 17th-century coaching house retains many of the building's original features, such as the curved bay windows & the arched stone alcoves down one side, perfect for a romantic tryst; even the 50ft-deep well remains in situ. Food-wise, nothing in particular stands out, rather it's all done exceptionally well, from the gut-busting all-day b/fasts & brunches to light bites & mains like Welsh beef pie; look out for the one-off Gourmet Nights too. ££

WHAT TO SEE AND DO It's one section of Cowbridge's walls that frames one side of the **Physic Garden** (⏰ summer 10.00–18.00 daily, winter 10.00–16.00 daily; w cowbridgephysicgarden.org). Just half an acre all in, this small but neatly tended garden is located within the grounds of what was once part of Old Hall, former home of the wealthy Edmondes family, who acquired it in the mid 18th century and left in the 1930s. The garden as you see it today has only been like this since 2006, its revival possible thanks only to the dedicated work of local volunteers, before which time it was a kitchen garden and tree nursery for the local grammar school and council respectively.

The garden is arranged into 12 triangular beds, each named after, and containing, plants that have had medicinal properties attributed to a part of the body or a particular illness, for example bones, muscles and glands, or digestive organs. This fragrant site extends to the perimeter, which is planted up with a selection of fruit trees: apple, pear, walnut and quince among others. If you want to learn more, volunteers are usually on hand most Thursday mornings. The site is wheelchair accessible but there are no other facilities here.

The only other site of note in Cowbridge is **Old Beaupre Castle** (⏰ open access), 2 miles south of town in the direction of St Athan. It's a bit of a misnomer really, for Beaupre (which translates as 'the fair meadow') is essentially a fortified manor house, one that was built in two stages, the first part raised in the 14th century and the second stage by the resident Bassett family who conducted an almost complete revamp in the 16th century. The architectural highlight is the three-storey gatehouse – The Tower of the Orders – centred on a magnificent stone-carved Renaissance porch which bears the date 1586 and the letters R B (Richard Bassett) and C B (Catherine Bassett). Built in three sections, the gatehouse manifests a pair of pillars surmounted by exquisitely crafted Doric, Ionic and Corinthinan capitals in ascending order. There's rarely anyone here so you'll probably have the run of the place.

St Cadoc's Church (Llancarfan; ✆ 01446 781453; w stcadocsllancarfan.co.uk; ⏰ 09.00–18.00 daily, except 09.30–11.00 Tue & 10.30–12.30 Sun when services held; free) Eight miles southeast of Cowbridge in the hamlet of Llancarfan, St Cadoc's Church – named after the venerated saint credited with founding the monastery here – merits a special diversion. Chasing away some damp from the south wall in 2007, architects stumbled upon some faint, ochre-coloured lines, and sure enough, concealed under at least 20 layers of limewash, a series of murals gradually revealed themselves, leading church historians to declare these the most complete wall paintings to be revealed anywhere in Britain for some time, certainly this millennium.

Following a long and complex operation (which partly entailed injecting slaked lime putty behind the paintings), it was established that the paintings were completed around 1485, some 70 years before being whitewashed during the Reformation, although ironically, rather than erasing them, what this actually did was protect the paintings from the elements – their discovery in 2007 was the first time they had seen the light of day for more than 500 years. Their discovery was all the more important for the fact that so few church paintings are known to exist in Wales.

Not only are they remarkable because of the quality of the work and the brilliance of the colours, but also because of the completeness of the stories recalled within. The dominant image is of George lancing a fiery-mouthed dragon, a spectacular tableau quite possibly unmatched anywhere else in Britain, and while it's thought that there are only two other murals of St George in Welsh churches (in Llangattock and Llangoed), neither compares with the one here at St Cadoc's. To the left of St George, a princess and a lamb await sacrifice (unless George completes the job first) as her anxious-looking parents (a very handsomely bearded king) peer over the battlements; to the right of St George stands the Virgin Mary, appearing to bless the warrior.

Lower down, wrapped around the window embrasure, is a rare painting (certainly the only one of its kind in Wales) entitled *Death and the Gallant*, which is a variant on the famous *Danse Macabre* (or *Dance of Death*), a mural more usually found in churches across France, where it originated, and northern European countries. Symbolising the equalising power of death, in the gruesomely powerful image here, a fashionably dressed young man wearing a traditional Monmouth cap is led to purgatory by a worm-infested skeleton. The mural above the door illustrates the seven deadly sins, where spitting, swirly tailed devils goad a couple into lustful activity while another pours beer into a red-coated glutton.

The structure of the building is also unusual, in that it deviates from the traditional cruciform plan and instead consists of two, almost ruler-straight aisles – south and north – separated by a centre parting perforated with rounded arches. Given the majesty of the paintings, it's easy to bypass the rest of the church. In the north aisle chancel, for example, is a resplendent 16th-century polychromed reredos.

BRIDGEND

A once ancient settlement that guarded the entrance to the Ogrw, Garw and Llynfi valleys, as evidenced by the remains of two hulking Norman castles, Bridgend generally gets a pretty bad rap. And on the surface it's not difficult to see why. Its doleful-looking streets are blighted by the usual rag tag assortment of discount stores, barber's shops and bookies, cheap eateries, and just as many vacant premises. There is, though, some salvation in the aforementioned castles, and one or two other ancient structures.

Bridgend has always looked to manufacturing for its economic prosperity. During World War II the town was home to the largest of eight Royal Ordnance factories in Wales, at one stage employing an incredible 40,000 people, mostly women – which made it the largest single-site employer in Britain at the time. Under its operational title of Filling Factory no 2, the work here – the filling and storing of ammunition – was both arduous and dangerous. Fast forward some 40 years and Bridgend was chosen as one of Ford's largest car manufacturing plants, making it the town's single biggest employer by far. However, its closure in 2020 with the loss of nearly 1,700 jobs was a particularly savage blow to an already beleaguered community, whose workers and their families were just as reliant on the car manufacturing industry as those workers in Port Talbot are on the steelworks.

GETTING THERE AND AWAY Bridgend is a useful transport interchange, its proximity to the M4 making for convenient access. It is also on the main Cardiff to Swansea line, with trains going in both directions at least every 30 minutes; the station is a 2-minute walk from town on Station Hill. The large and efficient bus station is even closer on Querella Street, with half-hourly services (hourly on Sun) to Swansea, Cardiff, Porthcawl and Port Talbot among other destinations.

🏠 WHERE TO STAY, EAT AND DRINK

🏠 **Coed-y-Mwstwr** (35 rooms) Coychurch; 📞01656 860621; w townandcountrycollective. co.uk. In vast acres of parkland 3 miles east of Bridgend, this 3-storeyed red-brick Victorian mansion was the erstwhile home of Arthur Williams & his wife Rose Crawshay, daughter of Merthyr ironmaster Richard Crawshay. Lloyd George & Ivor Novello were among the distinguished house guests before its conversion to a girls' school & then a hotel in the 1970s. It remains a very civilised country residence, its rooms – including 7 in the renovated Coach House on the opposite side of the car park – are easy on the eye & well endowed with furnishings. The smartly decorated public areas, including the lounge with its sweeping parkland views, are good spots to eat, especially in the absence of anywhere decent to go in Bridgend itself. **££**

✖ **The Black Rabbit** Wind St, Laleston; 📞01656 652946; w theblackrabbitlaleston. co.uk; ⏲ noon–15.00 & 18.30–22.00 Tue–Sat, noon–15.00 Sun. 2 miles west of Bridgend in the village of Laleston, the well-regarded Black Rabbit has been welcoming drinkers to its homely environs since the 14th century. Owner & head chef Jonathan Lewis conjures up some hugely enticing plates, like chorizo croquettes, garlic & smoked paprika aioli, & cod loin, chive mashed potato & chive beurre blanc sauce. It's just as much fun to come here for a pint. **££**

WHAT TO SEE AND DO The centre of town might not have much going for it, but there are one or two points of interest. A short way down **Elder Street**, the town's oldest, you'll find a tidy little sculpture ensemble depicting six animals – duck, fish, rabbit, ram, cow and pig – representing the seasonal produce that was once sold along here. In order to reach the first of Bridgend's two castles, you'll need to cross the town's single-span **stone bridge**, dating from 1425 and built to link what were the villages of Newcastle and Oldcastle, although that it has survived at all is pretty remarkable given the entirely modern surrounds. Once on the other side of the dual carriageway, head up Newcastle Hill to the pretty village-like square next to the church. You can't fail to miss the Coleman's Mustard and Starch signs plastered all over the walls of the terraced corner house, which presumably suggests that this was once a shop.

On the far side of the square, and raised slightly higher than the church which it may have once ringed, is the entrance to **Newcastle** (⏲ 10.00–16.00 daily; free), whose name belies the fact that it was originally built in 1106. A clearly defined D-shaped defensive structure with heavy-set walls nearly 20ft high in places, the castle was founded by William de Londres, one of the semi-mythical Twelve Knights of Glamorgan, a supposed group of mercenaries loyal to the Norman conqueror Robert Fitzhamon. Beyond the late Norman-decorated doorway, there's nothing to see as such, but the views, high above a bend in the Ogmore River, are worth the calf-straining walk to get here.

More substantial, and of roughly similar age, is **Coity Castle** (⏲ 10.00–16.00 daily; free), located just over a mile northeast of town in the suburb of the same name. Constructed by another of the Twelve Knights, the splendidly named Sir Payn 'the Demon' de Turberville, the castle is more or less buttressed up against residential streets on two sides with sheep-filled fields on the other. A large outer ward encloses the original keep and a bunch of disparate domestic buildings in various states of disrepair, including the remnants of the central octagonal pier for the castle's vaults, though the whole is impressive. The site is currently fenced off pending restoration work, but you can still obtain respectable views standing on top of the earthen rampart which is accessible via the footpath running alongside the church.

VALE OF NEATH AND AFAN VALLEY

Another part of South Wales that flies very low under the radar is the **Vale of Neath** (or Neath Valley), which runs between the town of **Neath** and the villages of Glynneath and Pontneddfechan at the foothills of the Brecon Beacons. This northern extremity of the valley also encompasses a memorable group of waterfalls, but for convenience sake these are covered in the *Brecon Beacons* chapter. The Vale has much in common with the mining valleys to the east, in so far as it too once marched to the beat of heavy industry – here it was the tinworks at **Aberdulais** and the **Cefn Coed** deep anthracite mine.

East of here, the heavily wooded **Afan Valley** has emerged as another exciting mountain-biking destination, though this is one for more serious riders. The one village not to miss, whether you're in need of another industrial fix or happen to be a fan of Richard Burton, is **Pontrhydyfen**. At the tail end of the valley lies **Port Talbot**, one of Britain's great steel towns.

NEATH Despite its proximity to the M4, few people visit Neath, and seen from the motorway there would appear to be little incentive to. Yet that might be remiss, because root around a bit and you'll find antiquities from the Roman, Norman and medieval periods. Moreover, despite usually being lumped in with Bridgend and Port Talbot as a place that's not worth bothering about, Neath's town centre is far livelier than either (not difficult, admittedly).

✖ Where to eat and drink

✖ **The Mine Bistro** 24 High St, Cwmgwrach, 10 miles northeast of Neath; 📞 01639 720968; w theminebistro.co.uk; ⏰ 17.00–21.30 Wed & Thur, 16.30–22.00 Fri, noon–22.00 Sat, 12.30–18.00 Sun. That it took so long for anyone in the Valleys to come up with the idea of a colliery-themed restaurant is surprising, but here it is & it's great, despite its odd location tacked on to the back of a Premier Shop. The mine-themed décor is manifest in thick cable reels repurposed as tables, sheet metal for wall decoration & a memory wall plastered with photos of miners. The food, served on shovels, is nothing fancy (homemade lasagne, bad boy burgers, upside-down curry), but is done with aplomb. The nearest town is Neath, 10 miles away, so it does take a bit of effort to get to but is well worth it. Book ahead, though. **££**

What to see and do Ingloriously sited above Morrisons car park are the slight remains of **Neath Castle**, whose gatehouse is flanked by a pair of dignified round towers, but you can't enter the site so there's not much more to see. Originally a Norman construction, these masonry remains date from the 12th to 14th centuries, and although there was some phased renovation in the early 1990s, everyone seems to have given up since then. With entrances on The Parade and Green Street, the old **covered market** (founded 1837) might yield the odd exciting find, with florists, leatherworkers and antiques dealers among the many battle-hardened traders.

Given the paucity of visitors to Neath, it's little surprise that **Neath Abbey** (w cadw. gov.wales; ⏰ 10.00–16.00 daily; free) – once the largest monastery in Wales – doesn't get the numbers it should do and that's a shame because its extant ruins are among the most memorable in South Wales. The abbey was founded around 1130 by Richard de Glanville – pre-dating Tintern by one year (though it's some 30ft shorter than Tintern), thus earning the right to call itself Wales's oldest abbey – for

5

a group of Savignac monks, after which time it royally prospered like many other monasteries in these lands. Having stood firm in the face of 13th-century Welsh uprisings (under the patronage of Robert de Clare), the abbey suffered the same fate as many other monasteries and was dissolved in 1539. It was then converted into a Renaissance-style residence, before being swallowed up by the local iron- and copper-smelting works, and following the demise of those industries, the abbey and its grounds were left to picturesque decay, which is how they remain today – although CADW has done a good job of cleaning up the site (over 7,000 tonnes of spoil was removed in the 1920s) and installing information boards and listening posts.

The abbey's brooding ruins retain a palpable sense of grandeur, from the almost complete western range, formerly the lay brothers' dormitories, to the great abbey church itself, whose footprint remains clear to see. In one of the partially intact walls of the south transept, you can quite clearly make out the night stair with its smoothly rounded handrail – see if you can spot the carved face. Elsewhere, fragments of stonework on the chapel walls offer a tantalising glimpse into the workmanship that went into this place. Anomalous to the rest of the site is the late 16th-century Tudor mansion over in the southeastern corner, which was largely built from the remains of the dissolved abbey: it carries a fine vaulted ceiling but otherwise most of its windows are blocked out.

Lying alongside, and easily visible from, the A465, the abbey is well signposted from both that road and the town centre, although its location at the back end of an industrial estate does come as a slight surprise. A 5-minute walk north along the River Clydach brings you to the old **Neath Abbey ironworks**, founded in 1792 by two Quaker families, one of whom, Joseph Tregelles Price, was the founder of the first world peace movement. Pressed into the cliff face, the two jaw-droppingly large blast furnaces, one of which is over 60ft high and with a heaving crack down the centre, are among the best preserved in the world.

Aberdulais and Cefn Coed Colliery
Just 3 miles up the road from Neath, Aberdulais (✆ 01639 636674; w nationaltrust.org.uk/aberdulais; £6) was the Welsh equivalent of the great Cornish tin-mining enterprises. In seeking out a site to begin copper smelting, the Mines Royal Society settled upon Aberdulais, given that all the constituent elements required for mass production were present in abundance: seclusion, dense woodland, and most importantly a powerful, fast-flowing river, the Dulais. And so, in 1584, the first copper-smelting works in Wales were established here, setting in train more than 300 years of industrial endeavour. After the copper works came corn milling, then iron forging and finally, tinning, an industry that made it through to 1939, just as war beckoned.

With such resources on its doorstep, Aberdulais was able to realise 520 tonnes of ore a week. Copper was becoming a much-sought-after product, used to sheath the hulls of warships (hence the term 'copper-bottomed'), in the minting of coins, then later in the manufacture of domestic products like saucepans. After viewing the site's impressive extant remains, including segments of wall from the tinning house and furnaces, the lithe chimney stack and the largest electricity-generating waterwheel in Europe – which currently generates enough energy to power the site – walk up to the head of the falls for a close-up view of the foam-flecked water. A second underground turbine generates surplus energy, which is sold back to the National Grid, underscoring the site's commitment to self-sustainable practices. There's a fascinating historical overview of the site courtesy of an exhibition in the old stable block, with lots of exquisite tin-plated items including toys and beer cans.

Aberdulais was another stop on J M W Turner's tour of the region in 1795, and he was as captivated by this place as he was with any other in South Wales, completing a number of sketches and paintings, most of which are held in Tate Britain. The old school house is now a tearoom.

RICHARD BURTON: THE GREATEST SHOWMAN

'It has been said, and we all agree, his was the greatest voice of the English language', proclaimed Dr Hywel Francis, MP for Aberavon. Widely regarded as the finest stage and film actor of his generation, Richard Burton was born Richard Walter Jenkins, the 12th of 13(!) children born to Richard 'Dic' Walter and Edith Jenkins. While Dic lived until the age of 81, which was no mean feat for a hard-drinking miner in those days, his mother died when Burton was just two, whereupon he moved in with his eldest sister, Cecilia (Cissy) and her family, at that time living in the Taibach area of Port Talbot. He stayed in Port Talbot until the age of 21.

Although both Cissy and his older brother Ifor, whom he idolised, were his formative influences, it was Philip Burton, the head of drama at Port Talbot secondary school (as well as Burton's commanding officer at the local Air Training Corps), who cultivated Burton's obvious love of, and natural gift for, poetry and words. Such was their bond that not only did Burton become Philip's ward, but he also took his surname. Burton did actually serve three years in the RAF but left because of poor eyesight.

Initially, Burton successfully managed to dovetail stage and screen work, and made his debut in front of the cameras in the critically lauded but commercially unsuccessful *Last Days of Dolwyn*, in 1948. But it was his appearance alongside Sir John Gielgud (who also cast Burton) in *The Lady's Not for Burning* at London's Globe Theatre – a show that was subsequently transferred stateside, thereby exposing the rising star to an American audience for the first time – that Burton's first Hollywood film was *My Cousin Rachel*, a film for which he received the first of seven Oscar nominations, though he lost out that time, as he would do on every other occasion. But triumphant roles back on the stage in London, firstly as Hamlet, and then Henry V at the Old Vic cemented his status as one of theatre's finest Shakespearean actors alongside the likes of Gielgud and Olivier. Back on screen, Burton was commanding the kind of money commensurate with his status as a bona fide Hollywood superstar; notable films included *The Spy Who Came in From the Cold* and *Who's Afraid of Virginia Woolf?*, the latter one of several films he co-starred in with Elizabeth Taylor.

Not only was his love life one of great tumult – notwithstanding his legendary womanising, Burton married five times, including, famously, twice to Elizabeth Taylor (the first time in 1964 and then again in 1975, though the second marriage lasted less than a year) – but his predilection for alcohol, an affliction he shared with his father, was just as destructive. As Burton himself once said, 'I have to think hard to name an interesting man who does not drink.' Burton was certainly never not interesting, and he certainly liked a drink.

Burton spent nearly half his life in Switzerland, moving there (with his then wife Sybil) when he was 27, ostensibly to avoid the burdensome tax bills he was subject to in the UK, and this is where he died on 5 August 1984 – he is buried at the Vieux cemetery in Céligny.

This 5-mile walk is an easy circular outing, beginning and ending in the village of Pontrhydyfen, taking in open countryside, woods and rivers, and many facets of the area's industrial past. For the most part, the walk is along well-maintained paths, with the occasional mud track or gravel path, plus a few bits of road here and there. Part of National Route 887, the trail can also be cycled.

From the **Rhyslyn** car park (which is well signposted from the main road), walk around 200 yards back down the road to where it forks and take the right (higher) path passing a row of neat cottages and some garages on your right. Turn left on to the 75ft-high **aqueduct**, built in 1825 to convey water to the water wheels for the blast furnace at the local Oakwood ironworks; to your right, in the distance, there's a good view of the viaduct, which you will traverse towards the end of the walk. Once across the aqueduct, keep going and bear right past the **Bethel Baptist Chapel**, first built in 1850 but now sadly defunct – the chapel was used for Burton's memorial service in August 1984, attended by the great and good of the movie world.

Approaching the crossroads, with the mint-green-coloured church straight ahead (now deconsecrated and smartly converted into a house), take a left down Penhydd Street, and stay left as you walk down the lane to the junction of Oakwood Avenue. Take another left here and walk towards the rugby pitch, taking the path that runs around to the right until you get to the waymarked junction. Continue left (direction Cwmafan/Cwmavon) with the River Afan below on your right and the wooded slopes of the **Mynydd** up to your left.

After a gently undulating mile or so through mostly open countryside, you'll come to the **Portrait Bench**, three steel cutouts, one of Burton, another of Swansea-born funny man Rob Brydon, and a third of former Afan Valley Park head ranger Dick Wagstaff – and in case you were wondering why Dick is in such

A further 3 miles up the A4019 (which breaks off the A4565 shortly after Aberdulais), the **Cefn Coed Colliery Museum** (w npt.gov.uk) offers another small window into a lost way of life, or at least it would do if it were open. As things stand, a lack of funding alongside some serious structural issues has undermined attempts to reopen the site, which has endured a troubled recent history. The Grade II-listed winding head frames were dismantled a few years ago with a view to restoring them, while plans were drawn up for the construction of a new visitor centre, but none of this has happened and whether it ever will, only time will tell. The best thing to do is keep an eye out for updates on the website.

Sunk in the 1920s, Cefn Coed was formerly the deepest anthracite mine in the world, with miners (and ponies) working at depths in excess of 2,250ft, which earned it the sobering moniker 'The Slaughterhouse'. For this reason, conditions were manifestly much harder here than in many other mines, but another factor that made Cefn Coed such a difficult environment to work in was the lack of community: with no village here, miners had to travel what would have then been considered a long distance to get to work. The pit closed in 1968, so workers were transferred to the nearby Blaennant drift mine, before that shut its doors in 1990.

PONTRHYDYFEN Almost as hard to say as it is to find, Pontrhydyfen (meaning Bridge over the Vale, or Valley) is singularly famous for being the birthplace of Richard Burton (page 149), Wales's greatest stage and screen actor. But it's not only Burton's illustrious company, he was nominated by members of the local community. Turn the dial and you can listen to Burton's mellifluous tones reciting passages from *Under Milk Wood* and other plays.

After a well-earned pause, press on towards **Cwmafan** about three-quarters-of-a-mile distant. Cross the bridge and turn immediately right on to the path, which is initially tarmac then a mud track. At the point where it looks as if you can go no further (you can, a little bit, but don't or you'll end up in the river), head up the scruffy bank and on to the main road. After less than 200 yards, there's a gap on your right; go through this and across the bridge so that you are now back on the east bank of the river. On the other side, take the left-hand path (and not the one straight ahead) and you'll be back on the path you were on earlier. At the intersection with the same three waymarkers you were at before, carry straight on towards a green metal gate, beyond which is the **viaduct** that once linked the nearby Tonmawr collieries, via the Pelenna River, with the docks at Port Talbot (and from where you can now see the aqueduct in all its glory away to your right). After around 800 yards, you'll reach a gravel track; take an immediate right down the hill and to the foot of the viaduct for superior, close-up views of its nine beautifully proportioned arches.

Now on the road, and just before the aqueduct, is **Burton's birthplace**, the house (2 Dan-y-Bont) with the gable end facing you and a conservatory tacked on to the front. As unassuming as any other house in the village, this semi-detached terrace was where Burton was born on 10 November 1925 and where he lived for just the first two years of his life, before moving to Port Talbot. Otherwise unidentified, take a peek through the conservatory window (you won't be the first or the last) and you can clearly make out a plaque on the right-hand side of the door and a photo of Burton on the left-hand side.

associations with the village that that make it worth seeking out. Picturesquely sited at the confluence of the Afan and Pelenna rivers, and enclosed on all sides by precipitous hills, the village retains some authoritative reminders of its industrial past in the form of an immense four-arch aqueduct and a nine-arched, red-brick viaduct, both of which you'll cross on the walk outlined in the box above, although the best views of both are from the valley floor. This is also wonderful walking country.

Incidentally, the sign on the opposite side of the road to Burton's birthplace (page 149) house identifies the singer and actor Ivor Emmanuel, whose most famous role was as Private Owen in the 1964 film *Zulu*, and soprano Rebecca Evans, as having been born here too, just so as they don't feel left out presumably.

AFAN FOREST PARK Just two miles east of Pontrhydyfen, the steeply wooded slopes of Afan Forest Park make for some of the best mountain biking in Wales, and it's fairly low-key compared with many other bike parks in Wales. The six **trails** here (ranging from 6km to 40km) take in a mix of forest road and tracks and open hillsides – the latter offering consistently superb views – though with the exception of one (the Rookie Trail), the other five are really only for competent riders, as names such as Y Wâl (The Wall) might well suggest.

The same can be said for the trails at Glyncorrwg Mountain Bike Centre (page 152), 5 miles up from the visitor centre at the head of the Afan Valley. The big one here is the **Skyline Loop**, a 28½-mile-long monster whose potential rewards are amazing, with views of the Brecon Beacons, the Preselis and the coast, on a clear day at least. But the park is not solely the preserve of mountain bikers: a series of well-laid-out walking trails have been devised and lack the crowds you get in the Brecons.

Within the Afan Forest Park Visitor Centre (see below) there is a small **mining museum** (w swminers.co.uk; ⊕ summer 10.00–16.00 Tue–Sun, winter 10.30–15.30 Tue, Wed & Fri; £3), which comprises an outdoor section with a few monumental pieces of equipment (lamp room, winding engine) as well as a working miniature steam train, and an indoor part which entails a mock-up tunnel and a display of gorgeously crafted miners' lamps alongside photos and documents.

Tourist information and bike hire

🛈 Afan Forest Park Visitor Centre Cynonville; ☎01639 850564; w dramaticheart.wales; ⊕ Apr–Sep 09.30–17.00 Mon–Fri, 09.30–18.00 Sat & Sun, Oct–Mar 09.30–16.00 Mon–Fri, 09.30–17.00 Sat & Sun. Lots of good information here, & also houses the mining museum (see above) & the Afan Valley Bike Shed (m 01639 851406; w afanvalleybikeshed.co.uk; ⊕ 10.00–17.00 Mon & Wed–Fri, 09.00–17.00 Sat & Sun), an excellent outfit with different bikes to hire including standard hardtail (£20/30 half/full day) & e-bikes (£95/day). They also offer comprehensive bike servicing & repairs, & can advise on any aspect of the trails here.

🛈 Glyncorrwg Mountain Bike Centre Glyncorrwg Ponds, SA13 3EA; ☎01639 699802; w dramaticheart.wales; ⊕ 10.00–17.00 Mon, Wed & Fri, 10.00–18.00 Thu, 09.00–17.00 Sat & Sun. Not so much an information point, but instead home to Afan-a-Blast (m 01639 699802; w afan-a-blast.business.site; ⊕ 09.30–17.00 Mon & Wed–Fri, 09.00–17.00 Sat, 09.00–16.00 Sun), offering bike rentals & repairs alongside showers & bike-wash facilities. The on-site Corrwg Cwtch café serves light refreshments, tea, coffee & so on.

Where to stay, eat and drink

🏠 **Afan Lodge** [map, page 155] (16 rooms) Afan Rd; ☎01639 852500; w afanlodge.wales. With a name like this, & the accompanying views, you could almost be forgiven for thinking that you were in the Swiss Alps, but the Welsh rain is a bit of a giveaway. Still, this is a very comfortable & very well-run hotel with modestly proportioned, minimally furnished rooms (try & bag a valley-view room if you can) in addition to a creditable restaurant. Located roughly midway between the 2

mountain-bike centres, it was formally the Duffryn & Cynon Welfare Hall & Institute, which makes its transformation all the more impressive. **£££**
🏕 **Glyncorrwg Camping** Mountain Bike Centre, Glyncorrwg Ponds; ☎01639 699802; w dramaticheart.wales. Basic site with pitches for tents as well as spaces for motorhomes & caravans, with hook-ups too. Wash & shower facilities available at the centre. **£**

PORT TALBOT

No other town in Wales has been as reliant upon one industry as Port Talbot, which takes its name from the dock, opened in 1837, and named after Christopher Rice Mansel Talbot of Margam, its principal sponsor. With its landscape of silos, blast furnaces, cranes and chimneys, the **steelworks** (owned by Tata, the Indian-based conglomerate that acquired UK-based Corus Steel in 2007) has shaped life for the majority of the town's residents for the past 120 years or so and continues to be its single biggest employer by far, although the 4,000 or so current employees is a substantial drop from the 20,000 who worked here in the 1960s. Despite the perennial threat of further job losses, or worse still, closure (which almost became reality in 2016), the steelworks – which produces strip steel, the kind used in cars, building materials and domestic appliances – remains Britain's largest, accounting for more than a third of all its production.

In the town centre, Station Road is symptomatic of the malaise that has afflicted the town, as is the deserted Aberafan shopping centre at its far end. There is hope, though. The once-magnificent Art Deco Plaza Cinema on Talbot Road is currently undergoing major restoration and will be repurposed as a community hub complete with theatre, studios, café, and business and retail units. And for a town that counts Richard Burton, Anthony Hopkins and Michael Sheen – three of the greatest actors in the history of film, Welsh or otherwise – among its number, it's not before time.

Ty'r Orsaf, the former police station building opposite the train station, was the temporary home of Banksy's *Season's Greetings* until its removal in February

WHEN BANKSY CAME TO PORT TALBOT

In December 2018, Port Talbot found itself in the international spotlight. On the side of a garage in the Taibach area of town, close to the Tata steelworks, a mural was discovered: from one angle it shows a child standing under a snow shower trying to catch what appear to be snowflakes on their tongue, but from the adjacent wall, it's clear that what is actually falling on the child is ash from a skip fire – the not so subtle statement being the impact of pollution and its effects on the most vulnerable in society, an issue that has particular resonance here in the industrial heartland of South Wales. Banksy, the highly secretive street artist, later confirmed via a video message to his followers that the piece – entitled *Season's Greetings* – was his.

The mural attracted thousands of visitors, not just from Port Talbot, but from all over the country and beyond, thus necessitating round-the-clock security – fundamentally to prevent it from being vandalised, even though it had been fenced off and a screen erected – while it also spawned a cottage industry in souvenirs. But as many had predicted, this was always quite likely to end in tears, and so it proved, at least for the residents of Port Talbot: in May 2019, an Essex art dealer, John Brandler, bought the piece from the garage owner for an unspecified six-figure sum and it was moved to the town's former police station on the square in front of the train station where it could be viewed without the prospect of being damaged.

When the owner of that building decided that he wanted its space back, Brandler suggested that the artwork remain in Port Talbot (he even proposed a street art museum for the town), but the council contended that they were in no position to pay for its removal, reinstallation and subsequent upkeep. The strong suspicion among many, however, was that the council actually had no intention of retaining it, given that the message of *Season's Greetings* reflected poorly on the town. Moreover, they were evidently nervous about upsetting the steelworks, who to all intents and purposes were the target.

Despite the circus that grew up around *Season's Greetings*, that the mural was eventually removed from the town in 2022 remains a source of much regret and anger in Port Talbot, with many adamant that more could, and should, have been done to keep it. There's no doubt that this was a huge missed opportunity to make something for the town. The piece is now somewhere in England, though there are plans to either tour it or find it a home of some description. However, as well as putting Port Talbot on the map, the Banksy artwork appears to have given a boost to the cultural life of the town, not least the creation of ARTwalk Port Talbot (see opposite).

2021 (page 153). During its residency, the plaza was a whirr of activity with hundreds turning up every day, but now it's mostly empty. However, on the back of the Banksy affair, an urban art trail entitled **ARTwalk Port Talbot** has grown up around town, the first and only graffiti art trail of its kind in Wales, featuring pieces by both international and local artists (among them Ame72, Hazard One and Mike22inks from the vibrant Bristol scene, as well as local talents Rarebit, Bims and SoK). To see where these works are (there are presently around 20), download the app theatr3.com.

A couple of miles west of the centre, **Aberavon beach** is a 3-mile stretch of golden sand spearing north all the way up to the Neath Estuary. Running for most of its length is a tidy promenade, behind which a landscaped park offers various activities (adventure playground, aqua-splash, mini golf and so on), but is otherwise pleasantly devoid of all the usual seaside clutter.

SWANSEA

'An ugly lovely town' was Dylan Thomas's oddly contradictory assessment of Swansea (Abertawe), Wales's second-largest city, with a population of around 310,000. Like Cardiff, Swansea was once a great centre of industry. But more than that, it could lay rightful claim to being Wales's first industrial town, and by extension the birthplace of modern Wales. Its copper and pottery works were among the largest in the world – within Swansea and its environs, there were no fewer than 20 copperworks at one point, smelting two-thirds of the copper ore imported into Britain and responsible for as much as 90% of all copper production in Britain – earning it the moniker 'Copperopolis'. The Swansea Blitz was appalling: over the course of three nights, between 19 and 21 February 1941, 30,000 incendiaries rained down on the city, almost wiping out the centre in its entirety, hence much of its blandness today.

One enthusiastic observer in the late 18th century suggested that, 'Swansea, in point of spirit, fashion and politeness, has become the Brighton of Wales'. A little misplaced, maybe, and while it certainly has spirit, few would contend that Swansea has ever been fashionable. But there has been much progress and no little ambition in recent years, which was kickstarted by the redevelopment of the old docks, now a glitzy waterfront zone of swanky apartments and office blocks with the odd restaurant and coffee shop thrown in to keep the neighbours happy. A more recent upgrade on the Maritime Quarter is the spanking new Copr Bay development, centred on the magnificent Swansea Arena – a gentle poke in the eye for Cardiff, which in recent times has owned the rights to all the big flag-waving projects.

Swansea has its heroes too, none greater than hometown boy Dylan Thomas, whose imprint is all over the city, from the superb Dylan Thomas Centre down by the Tawe and the theatre bearing his name, to his birthplace a few miles away in the well-heeled Uplands suburb. But Swansea's cultural treasures don't just start and end with Thomas: both the National Waterfront Museum and the Swansea Museum merit extended visits, while the wonderful Glynn Vivian Gallery will satisfy those thirsting for some art. It may not be instantly loveable, but Swansea is a grower so don't be too surprised if you find yourself staying here a little longer than you anticipated.

As an aside, one wouldn't normally recommend visiting the depressed suburb of Townhill to the north of town, but from its summit on Pantycelyn Road there really is the most extraordinary panorama of Swansea Bay, curling all the way around to Mumbles Head one way and the smoking steelworks at Port Talbot the other. There are few more expansive views anywhere else in Wales, or indeed Britain.

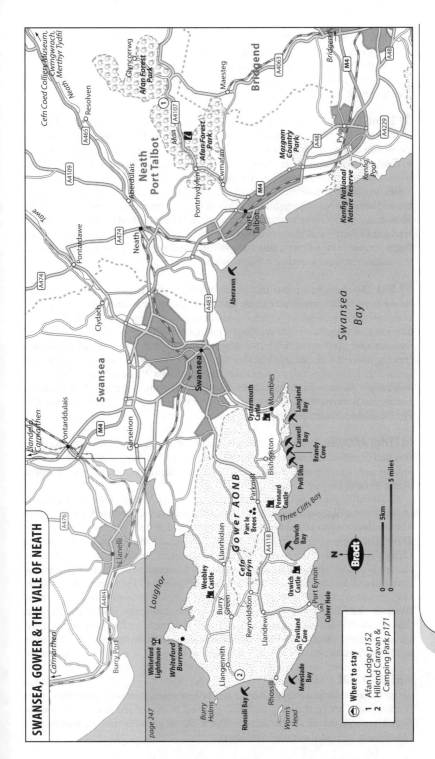

Vale of Glamorgan, Swansea and Gower   SWANSEA

5

SWANSEA, GOWER & THE VALE OF NEATH

Where to stay
1 Afan Lodge *p152*
2 Hillend Caravan &
   Camping Park *p171*

page 247

Neath
Port Talbot

Bridgend

Swansea

Gower AONB

Swansea
Bay

155

GETTING THERE AND AWAY

By car Coming from the M4 along the A483, it's a fast and direct drive into the heart of the city. Driving into and through the city can be confusing and frustrating owing to the convoluted one-way system. There is no end of car parks, including plenty of multi-storeys.

By train Located a 10-minute walk north of the city centre at the top end of the High Street, the train station is the terminus for trains from London Paddington via Bristol and Cardiff; trains runs hourly to Bristol and London, and half-hourly to Cardiff, stopping at Neath, Port Talbot Parkway and Bridgend en route. Swansea is also the terminus for the lovely Heart of Wales line which runs through mid-Wales stopping at Llanelli, Ammanford, Llandeilo, Builth Wells, Knighton and finally Shrewsbury in Shropshire, plus lots of other smaller stops in between (4 daily Mon–Sat, 2 Sun). Going west, there are services to Carmarthen (hourly), Fishguard Harbour (2 daily), and Haverfordwest and Milford Haven (8 daily Mon–Sat, 3 Sun). There are one or two direct trains a day to Tenby and Pembroke Dock, but otherwise this usually requires a change at Carmarthen.

By bus Swansea's enormous bus station (probably the largest in the country) is smack bang in the centre next to the Quadrant shopping centre and is served by a comprehensive network of both local and long-distance buses (including National Express and Megabus). The excellent TrawsCymru T6 service operates between Swansea and Brecon via Neath, the Aberdulais Falls and Dan-yr-Ogof Showcaves (hourly Mon–Sat, 5 Sun), while the T1S service has three buses (Mon–Sat) to Carmarthen, one of which stops at the Botanic Gardens Wales. Otherwise, there are half-hourly buses to Bridgend, Carmarthen and Llanelli, and every 20 minutes to Neath. The information desk here is open from 08.30 to 17.30 Monday to Saturday. For local bus services, see below.

GETTING AROUND Swansea is a manageably small and eminently walkable city, and you'll really only need to use public transport if visiting some of the lesser-known sights in the outlying suburbs, such as Uplands and Sketty – or if you're heading out to Gower.

As a visitor, your most likely local destinations are Mumbles and Gower, both of which are well served by buses, though some services don't run on Sundays. Bus #2 trundles along to Mumbles every 15 minutes and 2C to Caswell Bay. Adventure Travel currently operate buses #14 from Swansea to Bishopston and Pennard Cliffs, via the university (every 90mins Mon–Sat, 5 Sun); #116 to Llanrhidian (hourly), two or three of which carry on to Llangennith; #118 to Rhossili via Parkmill and Reynoldston (7–8 daily Mon–Sat); while #115 is a circular between Llangennith and Port Eynon. An adult single ticket to anywhere in the Swansea Bay area costs £4.70, but if you plan to explore a little more widely, the Explore Gower day ticket, which allows unlimited, all-day travel within Swansea and the Gower, is good value at £7.50. A Swansea Day Inner Zone ticket costs £4.50 and an Outer Zone £7.50.

▲ WHERE TO STAY *Map, opposite*

Given the city's size and with all the recent redevelopment, Swansea's accommodation stock is poor, hence you may well find yourself in one of the many chain hotels dotted around the city. Alternatively there are some agreeable guesthouses in Mumbles as you head out towards Gower.

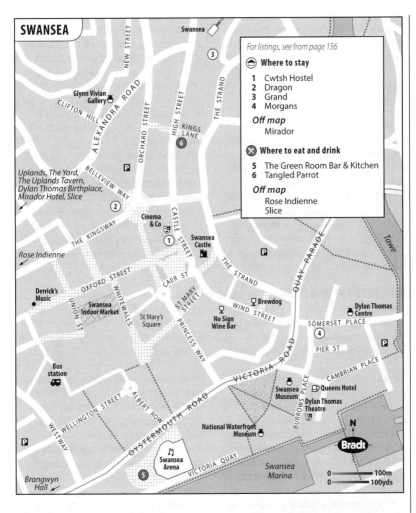

SWANSEA

For listings, see from page 156

Where to stay

1 Cwtsh Hostel
2 Dragon
3 Grand
4 Morgans

Off map
Mirador

Where to eat and drink

5 The Green Room Bar & Kitchen
6 Tangled Parrot

Off map
Rose Indienne
Slice

Morgans Hotel (42 rooms) Somerset Pl; 01792 484848; w morganshotel.co.uk. Formerly home to the city port authorities, Swansea's finest hotel is as grand as the Edwardian building it occupies. Due deference is paid to its maritime heritage, such as in the ship-bound stained glass, wave-form lamps & the big anchor on the stairs. Rooms are good-sized with sturdy polished hardwood floors, high ceilings & large wooden box beds with thick mattresses & Egyptian cotton bedsheets; heavy suede curtains offer the promise of a solid night's sleep while Nespresso machines ensure that there's decent coffee on tap. The suites are almost twice the size, with double vanities & mood lighting (pointless but fun) among the extras. B/fast is served in the glass-roofed atrium on the top floor, while the glamorous bar is the spot for a nightcap. Rooms are also available in a refurbished Regency townhouse opposite. **£££**

Dragon Hotel (106 rooms) 39 The Kingsway; 01792 657100; w dragon-hotel. co.uk. Neither the location – lots of main roads blather noisily past – nor the exterior is likely to get the juices pumping, but beyond the bland façade is a well-run hotel with well-appointed, if slightly dated, rooms in 4 or 5 different categories. Additional facilities include spa & gym. **££**

Grand Hotel (53 rooms) Ivey Pl; 01792 645898; w thegrandhotelswansea.co.uk. If it's convenience & not a pretty location you're after, the Grand is just the ticket as it's the 1st building you see upon exiting the train station. An appealing, sandy-coloured building dating from the 1930s, the Grand's rolling refurbishment plan is almost complete & the sleek rooms (classic, deluxe & suites) are nothing if not bold: floral print armchairs in some, zig-zag floor patterns in others plus further chintzy flourishes here & there; the 3 top-floor rooms open up on to private balconies with hot tubs. The sporty vibe bistro/bar is a convivial spot for a bite to eat or a beer while watching big-screen rugby or footie. **££**

🏠 **Mirador Hotel** (7 rooms) 14 Mirador Cres; 📞01792 466976; w themirador.co.uk. It might be a little too kitsch for some, but the Mirador's rooms, each named & decorated in the style of a particular country or region, are enormous fun. Take the Roman room, for example, featuring

playful cherubs on the mantelpiece & grape vines (not real) wrapped around the bathrooms, or the Africa room with its leopard-print wallpaper & elephant-stand table. You could come here on 7 occasions & have a different experience each time. Although on a quiet residential street, its location in the very pleasant Uplands district makes it a good base from which to explore some of the city's best bars & pubs. **££**

🏠 **Cwtsh Hostel** (9 rooms) 10–14 Castle St; 📞01792 986556; w cwtsh-hostel.co.uk. In a great city centre location, this new hostel has 5 dorms, variously sleeping 4, 10 & 12 (1 dorm is female only) each with cool pod-like beds & their own shower facilities, in addition to some private dbls. Other facilities include a kitchen, coffee shop/crêperie & bike storage. *Dorms* **£**, *dbls* **££**

✖ WHERE TO EAT AND DRINK *Map, page 157*

Swansea is by no mean a gastronomic paradise, but there are one or two standout restaurants, and if you're up for a good curry make a beeline for St Helen's Road. The coffee scene has improved no end, to the extent that you no longer have to rely on the ubiquitous chain coffee shops to get a decent caffeine fix here.

✖ **Slice** 73–75 Eversley Rd; 📞01792 290929; w sliceswansea.co.uk; 🕐 18.15– 21.15 Thu, 12.30–14.00 & 18.15–21.15 Fri–Sun. A cut above anything else Swansea has to offer, this small 16-seater restaurant occupies an unusual wedge-shaped corner building (hence the name) in the western suburb of Sketty. Owners Adam & Chris have been cooking together since their college days & they've curated some superb 2- & 3-course lunch & dinner menus in addition to a 6-course tasting menu – expect dishes like Jerusalem artichoke with confit egg yolk & fresh truffle, & Galician beef fillet with oxtail cottage pie & onion puree. **£££**

✖ **Rose Indienne** 73–74 St Helen's Rd; 📞01792 467000; w rose-indienne.co.uk; 🕐 17.30– midnight Mon–Thu, noon–14.00 & 17.30–01.00 Fri & Sat, noon–midnight Sun. This just about shades it as the pick of the city's many excellent Indian restaurants, & the fact that it's been around for eons speaks volumes. As well as there being plenty to please seasoned curry connoisseurs, with classics like dal makhani & chicken tikka on offer, the mind-bendingly long menu features other tasty treats like cauliflower masala, Ajwaini fish tikka & *laiz pasliya* (charcoal grilled lamb).

The all-you-can-eat Sun buffet (noon–17.00) is a steal. **££**

✖ **The Green Room Bar & Kitchen** Coastal Park, Oystermouth Rd; 📞01792 123456; w thegreenroomswansea.co.uk; 🕐 10.00–17.00 Tue–Sun. Located in the newly landscaped park next to the Swansea Arena, the Green Room (in a nod to its neighbour) is serious about its coffee, which is supplied by Coaltown Coffee in Ammanford (page 271). They also serve draught beer from the excellent Tiny Rebel brewery in Newport as well as b/fast, brunch & lunch. It's worth noting that the café is at its busiest early to mid-morning, in which case you may have to settle for a seat outside – lovely on a warm day, not quite so on a wet one. **£**

☕ **Tangled Parrot** 222 High St; 🕐 10.00– 17.30 Mon–Sat. Run by music-fan Matt & coffee-man Tony, the Parrot is a terrific combo of the 2, with wall-bound vinyl on one side (which makes this only the 2nd shop in Swansea to sell vinyl, alongside Derrick's) & a neat little drinking area to the rear where you can hunker down with your laptop & soak up the latest tunes. Unlikely as it may seem, they squeeze in the occasional gig here too. **£**

ENTERTAINMENT AND NIGHTLIFE While not as numerous as in Cardiff, Swansea's pubs and bars can be just as lively as those in the capital. Wind Street is the city's noisy drinking hub but if you want a calmer time of it, make for the Uplands area. As you'd expect, there's hardly a pub in town (the more traditional ones at least) that doesn't have some association with Dylan Thomas.

Pubs and bars

Brewdog 19 Wind St; ☎01792 721321; w brewdog.com; ⏰ 11.00–23.00 daily. Brewdog may have evolved into one of the biggest pub chains in Britain but their bars do at least retain a sense of their own identity. Their beer, with at least a dozen on tap, is fantastic, as is the food; Wed is unlimited wings night. If you do dare venture on to Wind St of an evening, then trust that Brewdog remains a haven of sanctuary while chaos reigns elsewhere.

No Sign Wine Bar 56 Wind St; ☎01792 465300; w nosignwinebar.com; ⏰ noon–23.00 Mon–Thu, noon–01.00 Fri & Sat, noon–20.00 Sun. Established in 1680, which makes it Swansea's oldest hostelry (according to its owners at least), this is, alongside Brewdog, the one place worth seeking out on Wind St. Popular with the 1930s bohemian set – Thomas drank here – it still attracts a slightly raffish crowd.

The Yard 38 Uplands Cres; ☎01792 447360; ⏰ 14.00–midnight daily. Borne out of Noah's Yard (Noah left a few years ago), which was credited with kickstarting the transformation of the Uplands drinking scene, The Yard is carrying on the good work. An easy-going wine-cum-cocktail bar, it plays host to various events (chess club anyone?), but Mon nights are where it's at with live jazz.

Queens Hotel Gloucester Pl; ☎01792 521531; ⏰ 11.00–23.00 daily. Tucked away among the quiet streets down by the waterfront, a few paces along from the Dylan Thomas Theatre, this good old-fashioned boozer has changed little since the time when Thomas drank here while working as cub reporter for the *Evening Post*. It's actually one of the city's few remaining traditional pubs, popular with locals but you'll be made to feel just as welcome: lively chat, a convivial atmosphere & good beer come as standard. The food also gets good reviews with many swearing by the Sun roast.

The Uplands Tavern 42 Uplands Cres; ☎01792 458242; w greeneking-pubs.co.uk; ⏰ noon–23.00 Mon–Thu & Sun, noon–midnight Fri & Sat. You can't visit Uplands & not have a pint in the Tavern, Thomas's favourite Swansea boozer (though it was then known as the Uplands Hotel), although less well documented is that Kingsley Amis was also a regular client. Thomas's memory is preserved in a corner snug, with the obligatory photos & so on, while the large central bar lends the place an air of genial conviviality.

Music, theatre and cinema

Brangwyn Hall Swansea Guildhall, Guildhall Rd; ☎01792 475715; w brangwyn.co.uk. Named after the eponymous artist, this magnificent hall – much enlivened by the artist's 16 large-scale decorative panels – hosts classical music concerts as well as other musical genres; free lunchtime organ recitals too.

Cinema & Co 17 Castle St; ☎07305 908260; w cinemaco.co.uk; ⏰ 10.00–16.00 Tue–Sun plus evening film screenings. Brilliantly innovative social & cultural hub incorporating the city's only independent cinema, with heavy emphasis on young local film makers. Seats are in the form of wheel-mounted upcycled pallets, which can be removed so as to turn the same room into a gallery as well as space for other live events, including outreach programmes & Q&A sessions. During the day, the cool, chipboard-designed bar operates as a conventional café.

Dylan Thomas Theatre Gloucester Pl; ☎01792 473238; w dylanthomastheatre.org.uk. The forerunner to this wonderful community theatre near the Waterfront Centre was the Swansea Little Theatre in Mumbles, where Thomas himself is said to have rehearsed on occasion. Wall panels around the foyer illustrate that old venue's history – there's also a framed letter from Dylan & a lithograph by Ceri Richards depicting the characters from *Under Milk Wood* – which you can view any time during box office opening hours (10.00–14.00 Mon–Fri). This venue is still run by the Swansea Little Theatre, who put on around half a dozen of their own productions in the 150-seat-capacity auditorium, as well as hosting a fantastic repertoire of outside productions including drama, dance, music, comedy & cabaret.

Swansea Arena Oystermouth Rd; 📞 0333 009 6690; w swansea-arena.co.uk. The new Copr Bay development's (see opposite) flagship building has given the city a much-needed boost, both in terms of adding a bit of pizazz to the area and the genuine need for a good-sized venue. The 3,500-capacity arena hosts big name bands, artists & comedians.

SHOPPING

Derrick's Music 221 Oxford St; 📞 01792 654226; w derricksmusic.co.uk; ⏰ 09.00–17.30 Mon–Sat, 11.00–16.00 Sun & bank hols. Venerable record shop that originally operated out of a small unit in Port Talbot before moving to this site in 1968, since which time it has just about managed to withstand the vagaries of the record-buying public. Both vinyl & CDs sold here, as well as tickets for concerts, both in Swansea & further afield. It's also the best place to get info on upcoming gigs in the city.

Swansea Indoor Market Oxford St; 📞 01792 654296; w swanseaindoormarket.co.uk; ⏰ 08.00–17.00 Mon–Sat. Swansea may be starved of genuinely exciting shopping opportunities, but its indoor market is one of the best in Wales. Fishmongers, florists & fruiterers, bakers & butchers, seamsters & sweetie shops, you'll find them all here – and what's more, most are run by local families. Whatever you're on the hunt for, you'll most likely source it here. Goods acquired, head to the Market Garden for some refreshments.

WHAT TO SEE AND DO

The city centre As much as anywhere, the centre of the city is **Castle Square**, an unadventurous concrete plaza flanked on three sides by depressingly ill-conceived modern buildings. On the other side stand the pigeon-pooped remains of **Swansea Castle**, now much diminished and of little interest to anyone it seems beyond the massed ranks of birds ranged along its high walls ready to pounce on any scraps of food left in the square below. A substantial pile, the castle was originally raised in the early 11th century but what you see now – chiefly the semicircular arcades – dates from around 1330.

South of Castle Square, freshly tarted-up **Wind Street** (pronounced as 'whined') is Swansea's notorious nocturnal thoroughfare, packed cheek-by-jowl with chain bars, pubs and restaurants, though there are one or two places with genuine personality here too – that said, Wind Street is not for the faint-hearted at weekends. Heading west from Castle Square brings you to the main shopping precincts, bounded by The Kingsway to the north, Oystermouth Road (A4067) to the south, and the Westway. The one thing likely to detain you here is the excellent, glass-domed **indoor market** (see above), which opened on this site in 1830 – this one dates from 1961 after the original one was destroyed during the Blitz – and is still the largest in Wales. Arrowing north from Castle Square in the direction of the train station is the somewhat frayed **High Street**, though it is slowly being re-energised, with galleries moving into redundant shops and some excellent coffee shops taking up residence.

A better reason to venture out this way, though, is the wonderful **Glynn Vivian Gallery** (Alexandra Rd; 📞 01792 516900; w glynnvivian.co.uk; ⏰ 10.00–17.00 Tue–Sun; free). A Grade II-listed building dating from 1911, the gallery has ten ground- and first-floor rooms set around a glorious, light-filled atrium, although some of these are set aside as working studios. Born into wealth as the son of copper magnate John Henry Vivian, Richard Glynn Vivian (1835–1910) had no time for his father's business and instead dedicated his life to travel, which in turn fed his insatiable desire to accumulate. Journeying across the world, initially to Ireland but then as far afield as North America, China, Japan and the West Indies, Vivian amassed an astonishing number of artefacts from all ages and cultures, though he held a particular regard for ceramics. He bequeathed his entire collection to the museum (which opened after he died), some of which is on display here (principally in rooms 4 and 5) – for example, Meissen vases, Cloisonné enamels, fans and miniature watercolours. Best of all are three gorgeous leather-bound travel albums, one of which is open so as you can view Vivian's sketches. In addition to the atrium, other rooms display paintings from Vivian's bequest, and it's high-calibre stuff too: Kyfin Williams, Augustus John, Cedric Morris and the like.

The Maritime Quarter Swansea's three key attractions (Dylan Thomas Centre, National Waterfront Museum and Swansea Museum) are concentrated to the south in and around the regenerated dockland area, aspiringly called the Maritime Quarter. The city's urban transformation has continued apace with the arrival of **Copr Bay** in 2022 – a major new cultural and leisure hub costing a cool £135 million and centred on the spectacular **Swansea Arena**, itself clad in gold-coloured perforated metal panels. The adjoining bridge – freckled with laser-cut origami shapes – has inevitably already acquired various sobriquets, among them 'the Crunchie' and 'the Taco'. The Copr Bay development also incorporates a newly landscaped coastal park and a cool café/bar (page 158).

Dylan Thomas Centre (6 Somerset Pl; ℡01792 463980; w dylanthomas.com; ☉ 10.00–16.30 Wed–Sun; free) Considered disposable by Swansea Council, the Dylan Thomas Centre was only saved from closure in 2011 when the University of Wales agreed to lease the venue from the council, and it's a very good job they did too because this is a brilliant tribute to Wales's most revered poet. The centre occupies the dignified Old Guildhall building, dating from 1829, and was originally opened by the former US president, and lifelong Dylan fan, Jimmy Carter in 1995.

Entitled 'Love the Words', the exhibition (encompassing the largest collection of Thomas-related material in the world) is thoroughly absorbing and by the end of your visit there's not much you won't know about the man and his life. Arranged chronologically, it therefore begins with his childhood in the Uplands area of the city, where he schooled in Mirador Crescent before going to Swansea Grammar, although he cared little for academia, instead preferring to spend his time reading, writing and debating, or playing cricket. His time at the *Swansea Evening Post* – which is where he really started to forge his poetic identity – is also recalled with samples of his writing.

Rarely acknowledged are Thomas's political leanings, and to this end the centre holds his only known painting, a watercolour titled *A Petition to the Government*. There's intensely personal stuff here too, such as a hastily scribbled note on the back of a bank paying-in stub where Thomas writes 'my darling own dear Cat, I love you for ever and ever…I had no time, from the BBC, to get to bank between 10 & 3.' There's plenty of other thrilling memorabilia too, like the tablecloth purloined from a New York restaurant on which Dylan and Caitlin have doodled various messages. More poignant are some of the last photos taken of Thomas, including one of him in the bar of Swansea's (now-demolished) Bush Hotel, and another of him propping up the bar in New York's White Horse Tavern a few days before he died. There's also a telegram sent to his friend (and composer of the score to *Under Milk Wood*) Daniel Jones, informing him of the poet's grave condition, as well as the Harris Tweed jacket he wore on that last trip.

Thomas's influence on other artists is apparent here too: among others, Peter Blake, Bob Dylan and John Lennon all cited him in some form or other – did you know, for example, that Thomas appears on the cover of the Beatles' *Sergeant*

Pepper's Lonely Hearts Club Band, a copy of which is on display here? There are also some sketches of Thomas by his good friend, the Scottish poet Ruthven Todd. For all the above, the most instantly recognisable (and certainly the largest) exhibit here is the sky-blue door from his writing shed in Laugharne, which fronts a mocked-up version, complete with original manuscripts and workings, notes and books.

National Waterfront Museum (Oystermouth Rd; ☏0300 111 2333; w museum. wales/swansea; ☉ 10.00–17.00 daily; free) An old warehouse zhuzhed up with ultra-modern glass, steel and slate, the National Waterfront Museum emerged from the ashes of the old Welsh Maritime and Industrial Museum formerly based in Cardiff – the one thing Cardiff didn't hang on to during the dock's rebirth. Nearly 20 years after it opened, some of the exhibits could do with freshening up, but it's still an excellent introduction to Wales's industrial might, pulling together the many strands of the country's disparate industries – transport, coal, iron and steel, shipping and the sea – under one gigantic roof, with colour-themed sections to help as you go around. The hi-tech interactive nature of many of the exhibits also makes this a favourite with adults and kids alike.

There are some big bits of machinery of course, including a magnificent 1907 Robin Goch (redbreast) monoplane, a working replica of Trevithick's engine (the original did grace the old Cardiff Museum, alas not so here), and a lovely old Mumbles tram – what the locals wouldn't give to have that reinstated. But where the museum really excels is its focus on social history, for example the trade unions and the old colliery brass bands in the Organisations gallery, or the lives of your everyday 19th-century Swansea worker in the People section.

Swansea Museum (Victoria Rd; ☏01792 653763; w swanseamuseum.co.uk; ☉ 10.00–16.30 Tue–Sun; free) An appealingly old-fashioned collection in a grandiloquent Greek-revival building, Swansea Museum was established in 1841 by the Royal Institution of South Wales, making it Wales's oldest museum. There is likely to be something for everyone to enjoy here, whether that's the vast collection of ceramics, including some fine samples from the local Cambrian Pottery (1764–1870), or its extensive archaeological treasures – cabinets packed with cave finds, many of which were excavated from Minchin Hole in Pennard on Gower, including an exquisite Roman bone comb with, remarkably, almost all its teeth intact. The only surprise is that so little is made of the city's once all-conquering copper-smelting industry.

In 1823, the remains of a skeleton dubbed the Red Lady of Paviland, but who was actually a man (page 169), were discovered in a cave on Gower's southern peninsula, and subsequently identified as being the oldest ever found – but before you get too excited, what you see here are replica bones, as the original ones are currently reposed at the Oxford University Museum of Natural History, much to the vexation of locals. Were the original skeleton on display here, it would unquestionably be the museum's prize exhibit, but in its absence that honour goes to the **Mummy of Hor**, which has been a fixture here (along with the beautifully painted wooden coffin) since Field Marshal Lord Francis Grenfell – a keen Egyptologist – brought it over from the country in 1888. Kept within a small, dimly lit room in between the two first-floor galleries at the top of the grand double staircase, X-rays determined that Hor (the only mummy in Wales) was a priest from Akhmim north of the Nile, and probably lived between 250 and 200BC; alongside this, there's a fascinating short film illustrating the work of the mummy's conservationist. One of the two busts either side of the room containing Hor is that of Gower's favourite son,

Edgar Evans, who perished alongside Scott during the ill-fated Antarctic mission of 1912 (page 169). The temporary exhibitions here are always worth investigating, and might cover anything from Welsh costume to natural history.

Dylan Thomas Birthplace (5 Cwmdonkin Drive; ✆ 01792 472555; w dylanthomasbirthplace.com; ⊕ tours 10.00–15.00 Wed & Sun, book in advance; £8) Halfway up steep Cwmdonkin Drive, in the urbane, middle-class enclave of Uplands, a 30-minute walk west of the centre, a blue plaque marks out an ordinary suburban semi as the birthplace of Dylan Thomas. There's nothing original here from Dylan's time but the house has been faithfully recreated to evoke the atmosphere of early 20th-century Swansea, with tiled hearths in the front room, a deep cast-iron claw tub in the bathroom and original books from 1914 in his father's old study – in fact such is the owner's commitment to authenticity that this is the one room visitors are allowed to smoke in, just as D J Thomas did. Dylan's tiny box bedroom, meanwhile, has the only working gas lamp in the house. It's best to pre-book a visit as there isn't always someone here, but more fun is the possibility of sleeping at the house, which is let out as a whole for anyone wishing to stay.

'Pretty park nearby. Sea a half mile off…Lunatic asylum a mile off', Thomas once observed. One can't vouch for the asylum these days (though presumably it's long gone), but the park in question is **Cwmdonkin** directly opposite the house, where he would frequently go for walks. A memorial stone here affectionately recalls a line from *Fern Hill*, one of his most beloved poems: 'Oh as I was young and easy in the mercy of his means time/held me green and dying/though I sang in my chains like the sea.' The park itself is most pleasant, with a play area, an old-fashioned bandstand, walking trails and a tearoom, as well as splendid views of Swansea Bay, as referenced by Thomas in that earlier quote.

GOWER

The first area in Britain to be designated an Area of Outstanding Natural Beauty (AONB) in 1956, Gower is deserving of all the superlatives that frequently come its way. In fact, to quote a few visitors to South Wales it eclipses many of Pembrokeshire's finest spots. Gower has been inhabited since Paleolithic times, as the much-vaunted discovery of a skeleton at Goat's Hole Cave in 1823 indicated (page 169), but evidence points to many other periods of human habitation here: a chambered tomb at Parc le Breos, an Iron-Age hillfort at Rhossili, and a Roman villa at Oystermouth.

On the edge of Gower, and effectively a suburb of Swansea, Mumbles is charm personified and a good place to stock up on provisions, especially if you're planning to hunker down for a few days out west. Originally settled by the Normans, wind-bitten south Gower is the most built-up part of the peninsula – and notwithstanding the odd bit of bungalow blight – is possessed of a string of fabulous blue flag beaches backdropped by sometimes sheer cliffs. Many of the smaller coves and beaches here can't be reached by car, so if it's a bit of solitude you're after, these are the ones to target. Three Cliffs Bay is the main one, but the likes of Oxwich Bay (home to one of Wales's few Michelin-starred restaurants) and Port Eynon are just as rewarding.

West Gower brings with it world-class coastal scenery courtesy of Worm's Head out beyond the village of Rhossili, from where it's an exhilarating walk along Rhossili Bay up to Llangennith and its campsite, popular with surfers. Compared with south and west Gower, mid- and north Gower receive far fewer visitors, which is not that surprising given how relatively remote these areas are and the difficulties of reaching them by public transport. Beyond the sheep-filled fields of the central tract – a long, red sandstone ridge – the north coast is Gower at its most elemental: spectral castle ruins, vast acres of marshes and mudflats, cockle beds, and the odd, time-warped village. It's also where Wales's finest meat, Gower saltmarsh lamb, hails from. Indeed, with its fertile farmland, endless coastline and mild winters, Gower is blessed with an exceptional natural larder: shellfish, Penclawdd cockles, asparagus and seaweed – tons of the stuff – all of which finds its way on to menus both here in Gower and beyond.

With its white-tipped waves lashing the shoreline, Gower has some of the best surfing in the country: Langland Bay, Oxwich and Llangennith all have something for everyone, from beginners to pros. There's fantastic walking too of course, with the Wales Coast Path hugging the wildly exposed Gower coastline, plus less obvious tramps, for example along the top of Rhossili Downs. There's not much by way of accommodation on Gower, so staying in Mumbles is likely to be the most viable proposition.

GETTING THERE AND AROUND

By car The narrow, often single-lane roads make for wonderful driving, with endless opportunities (for diversions) to stop and admire the next fabulous view – though patience will be required, if not with other motorists, then certainly sheep.

By bus Gower is pretty well served by buses, though it's important to note that many services don't run on Sundays. The main buses of concern are #14 from Swansea to Bishopston and Pennard Cliffs, via the university (every 90mins Mon–Sat, 5 Sun); #116 to Llanrhidian (hourly), two or three of which carry on to Llangennith; #118 to Rhossili via Parkmill and Reynoldston (7–8 daily Mon–Sat); while #115 is a circular between Llangennith and Port Eynon.

MUMBLES The well-heeled seaside town of Mumbles – whose name is a corruption of the Norman French word 'mammelles', or 'breasts', a term first thought to have been coined by French sailors when they encountered the two bulbous lumps of rock near Mumbles Head – has been a popular destination since Victorian times.

Mumbles' original denizens were mostly fishermen, but when heavy industry began to encroach on the village in the early 18th century following the advent of coalmining in the nearby Clyne Valley, the character of the town was substantially altered. Mumbles became linked to the port of Swansea via iron rails which ran the length of the bay, and by 1807 it was already accepting fare-paying passengers, and could therefore lay claim to being the world's first passenger-carrying horsecar railway. Later upgraded to steam and then electric, the tramcar was prematurely closed in 1960, replaced by motor buses; you can see one of its old carriages in the National Waterfront Museum in Swansea (page 162).

Despite elements of gentrification, Mumbles has retained its Edwardian earthiness and is devoid of any of the tackier elements of your average seaside resort. In fact Mumbles is one of those places where really you don't need to do very much at all, except promenade, eat and drink. In recent years Mumbles has forged quite a reputation as bit of a foodie destination, and while places do come and go, you can expect to gorge well here. There are plenty of pubs too – it isn't dubbed the 'Mumbles Mile' for nothing – though presumably there are not quite as many here now as there were when Dylan Thomas staked out the *locales*.

Getting there and away Buses (#2 and #2A) from Swansea make the 35-minute trip out here every 20–30 minutes, alighting at Newton Road opposite the police station, from where everything is within easy walking distance. If travelling by car, there are plenty of pay and displays along the seafront, as well as a small parking area just below the castle off Castle Street.

Where to stay, eat and drink

Langland Cove (4 rooms) 4 Rotherslade Rd; 07411 545685; w langlandcove.co.uk. Sparkling little guesthouse with bright & sunny rooms, each of which has been individually fashioned; 1 has a snug seat that converts into a dbl bed, hence is suitable for families. Rooms come with a few little extra treats too, including ground coffee, fresh milk (there's a fridge so you're welcome to bring your own drinks) & homemade cakes or biscuits. **££**

Langland Road B&B (5 rooms) 17 Langland Rd; 01792 361170; e langlandroad@ hotmail.co.uk. Quiet, comfortable guesthouse a short walk up from the seafront with impeccably kept rooms – 2 of which are twins – spread across 3 floors. Expect terrific hospitality too. **££**

Tides Reach Guesthouse (5 rooms) 388 Mumbles Rd; 01792 404877; w tidesreachguesthouse.com. A tidy, well-presented guesthouse on the road into Mumbles with 5 individually decorated rooms, one of which is a cosy loft room with widescreen views of Swansea Bay. The tremendously helpful hosts rustle up a superb brekkie to see you on your way to Gower. **££**

The Front Room 618 Mumbles Rd; 01792 362140; w thefrontroomcafe.co.uk; 09.30–16.00 Wed–Fri, 09.00–16.00 & 18.00–20.30 Sat, 09.00–16.00 Sun. Homely & welcoming seafront tea room/bistro combo run by a couple of amiable chaps offering b/fast (until noon), brunches & lunches (Welsh rarebit, *croque madame*, beetroot, red onion & tomato tart), as well as evening meals on Fri & Sat. Best of all is a delicious, calorie-packed high tea featuring finger sandwiches, buttermilk scones with clotted cream & jam, pastries, & tea or coffee. **££**

Gin & Tapas 61 Newton Rd; 01792 361764; w gintapas.com; 16.00–late Tue–Thu, noon–late Fri & Sat, noon–18.00 Sun. Cosy, family-run restaurant dishing up homemade tapas (3 for £15), with standards including creamy garlic mushrooms, Spanish meatballs & *patatas bravas*, in addition to monthly specials like herb-encrusted cod with seafood sauce. On Sun you can go the whole (hog) roast. Gins & cocktails galore with a happy hour 21.00–22.00 Fri & Sat. **££**

Gower Seafood Hut Promenade Tce; w gowerseafoodhut.co.uk; Mar–Sep 13.00–18.00 Tue–Sun. Tuck in to scrumptious morsels of fishy things in this repurposed horsebox located roughly halfway along the promenade near Southend Gardens; crispy chilli prawns, plaice goujons, whitebait, calamari & dressed crab are all up for grabs. If it's fish & chips you want, you'll have to go elsewhere. **£**

Verdi's Knab Rock; 01792 369135; w verdis-cafe.co.uk; Apr, May & Sep 10.00–21.00 daily, Jun–Aug 10.00–21.30 daily (until 22.00 during summer holidays). A local institution, you can't come to Mumbles and not visit Verdi's. Located down towards the pier this venerable gaff has been doling out the town's finest gelato (including some eye-popping sundaes) since time immemorial, though just as many folk pile in here for their scrumptious pizzas. Good coffee too. **£**

What to see and do The joy of Mumbles is simply strolling – preferably with ice cream in hand – along the mile-long promenade. At its southern end stands the resolutely old-fashioned **Mumbles Pier**, one of Wales's six remaining iron piers. Opened in 1898 and formerly the terminus for the Swansea & Mumbles Railway, the pier has led a charmed, if occasionally troubled, existence including periodic episodes of restoration in the past decade or so, though it's fair to say that it's seen better days.

The end of the pier is home to the **RNLI boathouse**, which replaced the original boathouse on the north side of the pier in 2014. It was from the latter that, on 23 April 1947, *Edward Prince of Wales* set out to assist the *Samtampa*, which had been driven on to rocks at Sker Point near Porthcawl, but in the rescue attempt all eight crew members perished along with 39 men from the ship; a plaque at the spot where the lifeboat was washed up recalls the tragedy (page 139). All those who died are also commemorated with a stained-glass window inside **All Saints' Church** on Church Park Lane, which is set back from the main road just along from the Methodist Church.

Just offshore, on the outermost of the two small islets, is **Mumbles Lighthouse**, built in 1793 by the prolific Swansea architect William Jernegan and unusual for its two-tiered and octagonal, as opposed to circular, configuration. There had been a lighthouse keeper present here since its inception, but automation in the 1930s deemed it no longer necessary; it's now electrified using solar panels. It is possible to reach the island for a short period at low tide across the slippery, seaweed-strewn rocks, but beware the incoming tide, and if you do happen to get stranded, do not try and swim back!

If you are thirsting for a drop of culture, then **Oystermouth Castle** (m 07557 481467 (Mon–Fri), 07917 200064 (Sat & Sun); w swansea.gov.uk; ⊕ Apr–Sep 11.00–17.00 daily, Oct same times Sat & Sun; £5) will provide it. Perched atop a modest hill overlooking the bay, Oystermouth possesses neither the raw power of, say, Caerphilly, nor the wealth of Raglan, but it trumps both of those with its superior views of the wide curve of Swansea Bay. Neat and compact, the first castle was raised here in 1106 following the capture of Gower by the Normans, but what you see today is mostly the result of work by the ruling de Breos family (1203–1322), though their stay was fairly short-lived and by the mid 15th century the castle was already just a footnote. An extensive revamp ten years ago included, among other things, the installation of a 30ft-high glass bridge leading into Alina's Chapel, a 14th-century appendage named after the daughter of William de Breos III, Lord of Gower. At the time of writing, however, work was about to commence on restoring some of the chapel's masonry which had been invested with vegetation that damaged the wall paintings, so this may be off-limits for a short while.

SOUTH GOWER
Langland Bay to Three Cliffs Bay
The first beach outside of Mumbles and in Gower proper is **Langland Bay**, which, of all Gower's beaches, comes closest to imitating the classic Victorian seaside resort with its curving strip of green and white beach huts along the promenade. Council-owned, they are allocated by public ballot each year. Langland Bay is popular with both surfers and families, thanks to its facilities (good parking, a café, outdoor showers) and the presence of lifeguards between May and September, but regardless, it's a fantastic sweep of sand and the sunsets are terrific.

Just around the headland, the next beach is **Caswell Bay**, another family-friendly beach and even more picturesque than Langland Bay. The next few beaches along are not so car-friendly, so a bit of legwork, quite literally, is required here. Beyond Caswell Bay, the landscape takes a decidedly more rugged turn, and the only way to reach **Brandy Cove** – a one-time haunt for smugglers – is by foot, either along the beach from Caswell at low tide or via one of the lanes from the village of Bishopston at any other time. Also accessible from Bishopston is pebbly **Pwll Dhu** (meaning 'Black Pool'), a pearl of a beach whose clear, chilly waters are perfect for a dip. As at Brandy Cove, there are no facilities here.

Continuing westwards over the Pennard Cliffs you'll come to the gaunt ruins of the early 12th-century **Pennard Castle**, and while structurally not especially impressive (a couple of rooms and the front of the gatehouse), its setting overlooking **Three Cliffs Bay** is what sets it apart. If you're with wheels, the easiest way to access the bay is to park (£4) at the **Gower Heritage Centre** (☎ 01792 371206; w gowerheritagecentre.co.uk; ☉ 10.00–17.00 daily; £5, £2.50 for anyone arriving by bike or on foot) in the village of Parkmill, and walk from there. A working 12th-century water-powered mill – the last remaining one on Gower, where there were once 50 – the centre is effectively a rural life museum-cum-crafts centre. The museum element comprises a woodturner's room, woollen mill, blacksmiths and a replica cottage from the 18th century, plus a few other bits and bobs. Resident craft workers and other businesses occupy the remaining space: a jeweller, bakery, cider-maker, cheese-maker and so on. A couple of further curiosities here include a puppet theatre and La Charette, a 23-seat railway carriage with velvet seats, flock wallpaper and hand-cranked curtains thought to be one of the world's smallest cinemas – it's certainly the smallest in Wales. Built at home by electrician and movie buff Gwyn Phillips, it had been operational in his back garden for 55 years before its relocation here in 2009 – the guest of honour at its reopening was none other than Kenneth Branagh.

A mile or so from the heritage centre, reached via a narrow lane, is a Neolithic trapezoidal-shaped chambered tomb, which was subsequently named **Parc le Breos** in honour of the 13th-century lords of Oystermouth on whose land it was discovered. The tomb likely dates from around 3800BC and most probably remained in use for somewhere between 300 and 500 years; although partially restored and now roofless, it's still an arresting site. In 1869, workmen digging for stone chanced upon the cromlech which had enshrined the remains of more than 40 people (men, women and children), as well as animal remains and shards of pottery, in a quartet of chambers linked to a central passage. The tomb was later identified as belonging to the so-called Cotswold–Severn group of long barrows, whose number probably exceeded 200 across western Britain.

Where to stay, eat and drink

⌂ Parc le Breos Hotel (16 rooms) Parkmill; ☎ 01792 371636; w parc-le-breos.co.uk. Imposing country house set amid lush parkland with swanky, if somewhat ostentatiously decorated, rooms, many of which, surprisingly perhaps, cater well to families. The high-brow restaurant (☉ closed Mon & Tue) serves lunches, dinners & afternoon teas. There are some lovely local walks from the hotel too, either heading down to & along the coast or further inland. **£££**

Å Three Cliffs Bay Parkmill; ☎ 01792 371218; w threecliffsbay.com. Run by the same family that opened the original site on nearby North Hill Farm in 1948, Three Cliffs regularly appears in Top 10 lists for the UK's best this or that campsite & it's easy to see why. Right on the coast path & with direct access to the beach, the site has both sea- & country-view pitches, the latter less exciting though slightly cheaper. No fires permitted but charcoal BBQs are. Glamping comes in the form of 5-man, dog-friendly yurts & bell tents (again with sea or country view), each with its own BBQ & gas stove. The shop is abundantly stocked with food & provisions as well as loads of beach gear. **£–££**

Oxwich Bay Somehow the beaches seem to get better the further west you go, and so it is with Oxwich Bay just around the headland from Three Cliffs Bay, which is accessible by foot at low tide. A three-mile sweep of soft pale sand, with safe, shallow sea, good surf and acres of space, this pretty much has everything you could wish for in a beach. It's also ecologically sound thanks to its status as a national nature reserve, **Oxwich Burrows**, which embraces dune slacks, lakes, saltmarsh and woodland – quite an unusual combination in a relatively confined area. There are plenty of botanical superstars to go hunting for, among them bee, common twayblade and pyramidal orchids, yellow flag irises, round-leaved wintergreen and the bright purple dune gentian. Birds often seen here include little grebes and water rails as well as lots of wildfowl.

Oxwich has its own **castle** too (w cadw.gov.wales; ⊕ May–Oct 10.00–17.00 on specific days – see website; £4.80), looming large atop a headland at the southern end of the bay. But it's not really a castle in the true sense of the word. It was Sir Rice Mansel, owner of Margam Abbey (page 141), who kicked things off by remodelling the original 14th-century structure into a Tudor-style mansion, but his son, Edward, managed to trump his father's efforts with an extravagantly designed south range incorporating a long gallery. Ironically it's the latter that now stands in ruins. Before leaving do take a look at the immense dovecote, drilled through with some 300 nesting holes which would have once been used to store eggs, meat and other provisions. Remarkably the castle is still owned by descendants of the Mansels.

🏠 *Where to stay, eat and drink*

🏠 **Oxwich Bay Hotel** (42 rooms) Oxwich beach; ☎01792 390329; w oxwichbayhotel.co.uk. Classy hotel in a plum seafront location at the far southern end of the beach with mostly sea-facing rooms of some description, but if you're looking to penny-pinch, the 4 standard rooms at the rear of the hotel (which have no sea view) are around £20 cheaper. Better still are the half a dozen wood-clad garden pods, all sleeping 2 with bathroom, pull-down beds & tea- & coffee-making facilities, though these don't have views either; those staying here take b/fast in the hotel. The bistro welcomes all-comers, though nothing beats a beer out on the grassy terrace when the sun is doing its thing. **£££**

✖ **Beach House Restaurant** Oxwich beach; ☎01792 278277; w beachhouseoxwich.co.uk; ⊕ noon–14.00 & 18.30–20.45 Wed–Sat. One of just 5 Michelin-starred restaurants in Wales – but you can bet that none of the others have an outlook quite like this. Formerly sous chef at Ynyshir Hall in Machynlleth (which now has 2 stars), owner & head chef Hywel Griffiths has created something special of his own here; 3-, 6- and 8-course tasting menus (plus vegetarian menus) are simply listed as, for example, Llandeilo fallow deer, Jerusalem artichoke, cod & Bara Brith soufflé; the delight is in what comes with them. Reservations required. **£££**

Port Eynon

The next bay along from Oxwich and the most southerly point on Gower, **Port Eynon** is quite possibly named after the eponymous 11th-century prince. Back in the day, the bay had high levels of salinity, hence the ruinous presence of an old salt house (possibly 16th century) at Port Eynon Point at the far western corner of the bay – today a scheduled ancient monument, some of its structures now lay buried in the sand. At high tide the seawater would enter the building's chambers and be stored in a reservoir. The water would then be pumped into large iron pans and slowly heated and evaporated. As the salt formed, it would be scooped off and stored in another chamber to dry. Close by, the former lifeboat station, which closed in 1919, is now a superb hostel (see below); a new lifeboat station opened at Horton on the eastern side of the bay in 1968.

Beyond the headland to the west of Port Eynon is **Culver Hole**, a manmade cave that may have originally been built as a dovecote, though later was quite likely used as a smuggler's retreat. Some 2½ miles further along the coast is **Paviland Cave**, the site of one of the most remarkable finds in human history (see opposite), though it is accessible for only a couple of hours each day. The last beach of note before reaching Rhossili is **Mewslade Bay**, accessible via a path from Pitton.

🏠 *Where to stay, eat and drink*

🏠 **Port Eynon Youth Hostel** (8 rooms) Old Lifeboat House; ☎0345 371 9135; w yha.org.uk.

Occupying the old lifeboat station, this terrifically sited hostel right on the water's edge offers

On 18 January 1823, William Buckland, a professor of geology at Oxford University and a prolific digger, was exploring deep within Paviland Cave (aka Goat's Hole Cave by the locals) on the south side of the Gower Peninsula when he chanced upon some human bones stained red ochre (naturally occurring red oxide). Upon retrieval and analysis, Buckland concluded that these were the remains of a woman, hence he dubbed her the Red Lady of Paviland. Later research, however, identified this as being the skeleton of a man (though the female part of the title stuck), dating from around 34,000 years ago, which makes this the oldest anatomically modern human skeleton found in Britain – and by implication Paviland Cave the site of the oldest ceremonial burial in western Europe. Analysis also suggested that the man was probably in his late twenties, around 5ft 8ins tall and weighing around 11 stone, while ivory rods found close by indicate that this chap was of some standing, possibly a religious leader. Unfortunately, the 'Red Lady' now resides across the border in the Oxford University Museum of Natural History, and the likelihood that she'll ever see her way back across the Severn Bridge is pretty slim.

dorm rooms with multiple beds & shared shower facilities, as well as private rooms, some with bathrooms. Cosy lounge & self-catering kitchen plus a bike-storage facility. **£**

RHOSSILI AND AROUND 'Bleak and barren' was Dylan Thomas's rather curt observation of **Rhossili Bay**, which bears the full brunt of the mighty Atlantic swell at the far western tip of the peninsula. It's fair to say that most visitors would be inclined to disagree with Thomas's assessment, for this is one of Wales's great beauty spots, a 3-mile stretch of smooth sand, 2 miles of which is owned by the National Trust. Moreover, dogs are permitted on the beach all year round. So named because the Vikings thought it resembled a sleeping dragon, **Worm's Head** (page 170) is the most sought-out landmark on Gower, and one of the most memorable geographical landmarks anywhere along the British coastline, up there with the likes of Durdle Door and the Old Man of Hoy.

From Worm's Head, soft, straw-coloured sand arcs north as far as the eye can see, bounded by the towering ridge of **Rhossili Down** – where the 193m-high Beacon marks the highest point on Gower – on one side, and crashing rollers on the other. You can walk all the way to Llangennith from here, and beyond to Llangennith Burrows and **Burry Holms**, which, like Worm's Head, is another tidal island so only accessible at low water. Back towards the southern end of the beach, the spiky remains of the *Helvetia*, a Norwegian barque that foundered here in 1887, are visible through the sand at low tide.

There's very little to Rhossili village itself but it's worth having a peek inside the (diminutive) wind-lashed **church of St Mary** for its memorial to local boy Edgar Evans, the first of the four men to die during Scott's 1912 Antarctic mission; the remaining members perished later, before reaching the *Terra Nova*. The white marble tablet, which was erected by his widow Lois in 1914, reads: 'To seek, to strive, to find and not to yield.'

Getting there and away If coming by car it does feel like a minor achievement to have made it to the end of Gower. The National Trust car park (£3/2hrs,

A WALK ALONG WORM'S HEAD

A long, rocky promontory at the southern end of Rhossili Bay, the island is divided into three parts (Inner, Middle and Outer Head), the last of which can be reached via a tidal causeway within a roughly 5-hour window each day – note, though, that Outer Head is off-limits between March and August to protect nesting birds. Tidal times can be obtained from the visitor centre in the village, or you can check online. The 4½-mile return walk entails a mix of rocky foreshore, a few easy paths and some scrambling: from the village, walk along the coast path above Rhossili Bay and then down on to the island itself, initially along the fairly steep-sided Inner Head. Beyond Low Neck, you reach Middle Head and a spectacular natural arch, aka the 'Devil's Bridge', before the final leg, a short rock scramble to Outer Head and with that, glorious views across the Bristol Channel to Lundy Island. If for some reason you do get cut off, stay there and wait for the next low tide.

£6/day) is directly opposite the Worm's Head Hotel. Note that overnight parking is not permitted. Bus #118 from Swansea/Mumbles stops by the hotel.

Tourist information

National Trust Visitor Centre ☎01792 390707; ⏱ 10.00–16.00 daily. As much shop as information centre, but you can pick up a few leaflets as well as information on local walks & maps. The centre also has tide times if you're planning to walk Worm's Head.

Where to stay, eat and drink

Worm's Head Hotel (17 rooms) ☎01792 390512; w thewormshead.co.uk. In truth, some of the rooms here (standard & superior categories) are in need of a revamp, so before you wonder why they are so expensive, you only need to look out of one of the windows: the views are glorious – some with dual aspect, though not all rooms are sea-facing. Food is average, nothing more. **££**

Pitton Cross Caravan and Camping Park ☎01792 390593; w pittoncross.co.uk. Tidy, well-run site a mile back out along the road from Rhossili with tremendous views from some of its pitches. Comprehensive facilities include men's and women's shower blocks, laundry, & a brilliant shop well stocked with produce, maps, board games, fishing gear & kites, so you may be tempted into a purchase before heading down to the sands. The bus to Rhossili stops right outside the entrance. **£**

Bay Bistro ☎01792 390519; w thebaybistro. co.uk; ⏱ 10.00–16.00 Mon–Fri, 09.00–17.00 Sat & Sun. Surfer-friendly café just behind the Worm's Head Hotel with a laid-back beachy vibe – stripped-back wood, lots of bright colours & wall-bound coastal pictures – & simple but good food to boot such as club sandwiches, burgers & BBQ pulled pork. From the terrace there are fantastic wide-screen views of Rhossili Bay & at low tide you should be able to pick out the gaunt ribs of the *Helvetia*. **££**

LLANGENNITH The big deal in Llangennith is its **beach**, a mile or so from the village down Moor Lane. A yawning expanse of dune-backed golden sand, it's one of the best surfing beaches in Wales, popular with everyone from hot locals to complete novices. There's an excellent surf school based at the Hillend campsite (see opposite), which is where most people end up staying anyway. Pleasant as it is, there's very little to Llangennith itself, save for the **church of St Cennydd** on the grassy village green, and the popular King's Head Pub opposite. Raised in the 12th century on the site of a previous llan (churchyard) founded by the eponymous saint, this sizeable church with its overbearing central tower is one of the best-preserved buildings on Gower.

There are a few interesting bits of detail, such as a 14th-century tombstone of a knight from the de la Mare family and a fragment of a 9th-century cross on the western wall.

Getting there and away To reach Llangennith by foot from Rhossili, it's a fabulous 3-mile walk along the beach, and then a few windy lanes up into the village, but travelling by car entails a somewhat more circuitous route via Llanddewi and Burry Green.

Where to stay, eat and drink

Kings Head (27 rooms) Llangennith; 01792 386212; w kingsheadgower.co.uk. Comfortable accommodation is provided at this nicely aged 17th-century inn run by the same family since the 1980s, so consistency is the watchword here; rooms are divided between the adjoining house & 2 stone barn conversions to the rear, though all are similarly furnished. There's no other option to eat close by but that's no bad thing as the pub does more than passable food. **££**

Hillend Caravan and Camping Park [map, page 155] Llangennith beach; 01792 386204; w hillendcamping.com. Fabulous location behind the dunes, & perfect for the hoards of surfers that pile down here & don't want to go anywhere else, this large site is well equipped with 3 types of pitches (standard, large & electric hook-up), modern shower blocks for males & females (plus a few outdoor showers), launderette, shop & play area, as well as an ace on-site café, Eddy's (Apr–Oct). **£**

Activities

Llangennith Surf School Llangennith beach; m 07855 420062; w llangennithsurfschool.com. Long-established outfit on the beach offering surf lessons to anyone from the age of 7 up, from novices to more competent boarders looking to up their game. Lessons are 3hrs long (10.00–13.00 & 14.00–17.00, depending upon tide) & cost £35, which includes all equipment hire; showers available too.

PJ's Surf Shop Llangennith; 01792 386669; 09.30–17.30 daily (to 16.30 in winter). Open since 1979, this legendary shop has been run by former European British & Welsh surf champion Pete Jones. All kinds of surfing equipment to hire including hard boards (£15/day), soft boards (£12), bodyboards (£8) & wetsuits (£12); they've also got SUPs for hire (£30/day).

MID AND NORTH GOWER Mid Gower is defined by the brackeny backbone of **Cefn Bryn**, a 500ft-high sandstone ridge that stretches all the way across the peninsula to Rhossili Downs. Inland Gower's main settlement is **Reynoldston** and it'll come as little surprise to learn that its focal pint, sorry, point, is the pub, and a fine one it is too. From Reynoldston, the road heads northwest to Fairyhill, beyond which one road heads west to Llangennith and the other east to the village of **Llanrhidian**, whose historic and much-loved pub, the Dolphin Inn, closed in 2020. However, there have been rumblings that this may reopen in some form or other under new owners, so watch this space.

A short way west of Llanrhidian, **Weobley Castle** (w cadw.gov.wales; Apr–Oct 09.30–18.00 daily, Nov–Mar 09.30–17.30 daily; £4.60) was originally raised by the de la Bere family in the late 13th century, though it was more fortified manor than fortress, as its present outline would suggest. Later lived in by an assortment of people, including Rhys Thomas and the Mansels of Oxwich Castle, it first took a battering during Glyndwr's uprising in the early 15th century. There's enough left to make it interesting (kitchen, great hall and part of the accommodation), but it's the view that makes the entrance fee worth paying.

The area around Weobley is the home of Gower's famous saltmarsh lamb, while beyond is the marsh-ringed **Loughor Estuary**, where waders, ducks and geese –

curlew, oystercatchers and brent geese among them – gather in good numbers in search of a good meal. Here too cockles are picked and seaweed collected before being made into laverbread. The area's one beach is the 2-mile-long **Whiteford Burrows**, a short way north of Llangennith in the northwest corner; just offshore stands the only cast-iron lighthouse to be built in Britain, in 1865.

Where to stay, eat and drink

King Arthur Hotel (18 rooms) Higher Green, Reynoldston; 01792 390775; w kingarthurhotel. co.uk. As popular with locals as it is with folk tramping the nearby hills, the best thing about the King Arthur is grabbing a pint at the bar (⏰ 10.00–23.00 daily) & heading outside on to the green along with the sheep. There's good food too & if you want to stay, you can do that too, with rooms in both the main pub & in the well-designed annex to the rear. That said, it has become quite a popular wedding venue so check ahead. **££**

Britannia Inn Llanmadoc; 01792 386624; w britanniagower.com; ⏰ noon–23.00 daily. The late 17th-century Britannia Inn is the sole survivor of the 4 pubs that once served Llanmadoc, & it really is the quintessential community pub. The lounge has beams allegedly repurposed from shipwrecks, & elsewhere there is the original fireplace, gas lamps & bread oven. Food is ambitious, featuring starters such as oak-smoked mackerel with cucumber salsa, &, as you'd expect in this neck of the woods, lamb is a mainstay: sous-vide Welsh lamb shoulder with butternut puree, & Moroccan-style braised lamb are just 2 ways they do it. Decent ales from the Gower too. **££**

6

The Valleys

The 'Valleys': a name that resonates, a name that is instantly familiar to just about anyone – even those not from Wales. For more than a century the Valleys of South Wales were the heartbeat of the Industrial Revolution, names like Blaenavon, Ebbw Vale, Merthyr Tydfil and the Rhondda synonymous with the once-mighty coal, steel and iron industries. There were few communities that weren't part of the industrial machine, but while rapid industrialisation brought immense wealth for a few, it brought a life of misery for the majority. As industry expanded, populations grew exponentially – Merthyr Tydfil grew from a population of 7,700 in 1801 to more than 50,000 within six decades, while Pontypridd grew from a humble settlement of 1,000 to 150,000 in the 60 years prior to the outbreak of World War I. With so many people crammed into such narrow valleys, a unique urban architecture evolved: towns and villages defined by ribbon-like rows of densely packed ranks of steep terraces tucked neatly into the folds of the hills – it's a sight you'll see everywhere, and remains one of the most evocative in Wales.

The decline of the coal industry hasn't been kind to the Valleys' towns and villages and post-industrial hardship remains a fact of life here. Some 40 years after the last closures, the Valleys' belt of former mining communities have been left floundering to regain a foothold, and many still mourn the loss of a common identity. Yet while poverty and economic stagnation remain prevalent, many places have embraced tourism in a way that has enhanced rather than degraded their assets, and has also helped keep some miners (don't call them ex-miners!) in work. In both the **Rhondda Valley** and **Blaenavon** – South Wales's only UNESCO World Heritage Site – visitors can head underground and get as close as they ever will to experiencing life as a miner. Others have been even more innovative, like the old Tower Colliery in Rhigos which has been repurposed into one of Wales's four Zip World centres. Elsewhere the Valleys are littered with moving memorials honouring those that served, and often died, in the mines, such as at **Senghenydd** and **Six Bells**, while spirited little community museums, like those at **Brynmawr** and **Pontypool**, offer fascinating insight.

Another beneficial consequence of the collapse of industry is that scenery once disfigured by slag, spoil and smog has been relandscaped in dramatic fashion: the old heaps have turned green and rivers that once ran black with dust now run clear. This has facilitated the presence of new and fresh flora and fauna, with herons, kingfishers and peregrine falcons all common sights here now. Nature has certainly been doing its bit to heal some of the Valleys' physical scars. This resculpting of the landscape has also generated an exciting new drive towards adventure tourism, so much so that in recent years the Valleys have stolen some of North Wales's thunder when it comes to outdoor pursuits. Bike parks are popping up all over the place – Bike Park Wales near Merthyr is the big one but there are other action-packed possibilities in **Dare Valley**, with more likely to follow. The lakes, too, are packed with potential: at **Llandegfedd** near Pontypool, you can canoe, kayak, paddle and

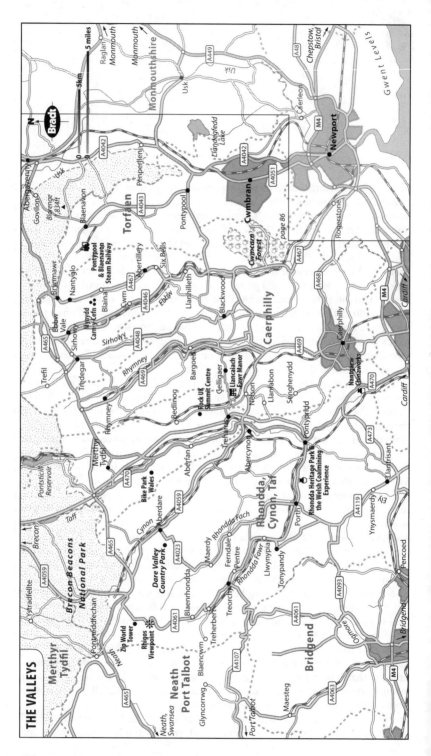

paddleboard, or wild swim. The Valleys are also reinventing themselves as a walking destination, the main difference here being that you won't find the crowds you do in the Brecon Beacons or Pembrokeshire. Away from industry and adventure, there are one or two fascinating historic sights, none grander than **Caerphilly Castle**, the greatest bastion of Norman impregnability, and **Llancaiach Manor**, home to all sorts of spooky carry-ons.

Given the densely populated nature of the Valleys, **getting around** is easy. Most, but not all, the different valleys are served by trains, usually originating in Cardiff or Newport, though there are one or two obvious exceptions, like Blaenavon. Otherwise, the bus network is very comprehensive and fills in any gaps. Cycling, too, is now a great way to explore the Valleys, not just on the waymarked routes but also on the much larger network of lanes, tracks, byways and old tramways.

BLAENAVON

Huddled under rolling moorland, Blaenavon is the archetypal Welsh mining streetscape of ruler-straight stone or rendered terraces of two-up, two-down houses. True, it can be bleak here when the wind and rain come off the Brecon Beacons, and walking around, there's an oddly melancholic air about the place, something that's apparent in its tatty shop frontages and boarded-up pubs. But Blaenavon's doughty community spirit remains intact and you'll be greeted warmly.

During the 19th century, Blaenavon was pre-eminent among the world's coal and iron-ore producers, and for this, the town and surrounding landscape was inscribed on UNESCO's World Heritage List in 2000, the second in Wales and currently one of just four in total in the country. Today this legacy is brilliantly brought to bear in a brace of heavyweight attractions: the enduringly popular Big Pit, and the awesome Blaenavon ironworks – add the Pontypool and Blaenavon steam railway into the mix and there's more than enough here to warrant a full day's exploration. The only disappointment is the obvious paucity of facilities – just one hotel and a couple of average places to eat, which is hardly an inducement to linger once you've seen the sights.

GETTING THERE AND AWAY Blaenavon lies a few miles south of the A465 and is linked to Pontypool by the A4043 and Brynmawr by the B4248. There are plenty of free car parks in town, including the Prince Street car park next to the Queen Victoria pub below the heritage centre, although you can just as well park at the ironworks and reach everywhere from there; you can also park on most streets without any trouble.

Blaenavon has no train station, so you'll be reliant on buses if travelling by public transport. From Pontypool in the south, bus #X24 makes the trip every 15 minutes (hourly on Sun), continuing down to Newport, while bus #31 makes the short journey across to Brynmawr every hour (Mon–Sat). Buses stop on the High Street, near the junction with Burford Street.

TOURIST INFORMATION
Blaenavon Heritage Centre Church Rd; ☎ 01495 742333; w visitblaenavon.co.uk; ☉ 10.00–17.00 Tue–Sun. Provides stacks of info, both local & regional; there's also a worthwhile little exhibition & a decent café (page 176).

WHERE TO STAY, EAT AND DRINK
⌂ **Lion Hotel** (12 rooms) 41 Broad St; ☎ 01495 792516; w thelionhotelblaenavon. co.uk. Given the absence of anywhere else to stay in Blaenavon, it's just as well that its 1 hotel is

halfway decent. Perkily decorated rooms have modern furnishings, plump mattresses & cool, creamy marble bathrooms with big walk-in showers, though some also have clawfoot tubs. Somewhat unexpectedly there's also a small health suite with sauna & steam room. The Lion also doubles up as the best (if not the only) place to eat in town, with a menu featuring pubby standards alongside occasionally more adventurous fare like pork belly bao buns or venison pie with bone marrow sauce. Sun lunch is a good bet but book ahead. **££**

🖥**Heritage Tea Rooms** Church St; 📞01495 742339; 📱 07709 501295; ⏰ 09.15–16.30 Tue–Sun. With such meagre pickings in town, there's a good chance you'll find yourself at this little tearoom inside the Blaenavon Heritage Centre at some point. Tea, coffee & cakes are served alongside light lunches, but the best thing is the view as you tuck in. **£**

WHAT TO SEE AND DO Growing up around the pit and ironworks was the town itself, its buildings and institutions typical of a Valleys town: shops and public houses, churches and chapels, a works' school and a working men's institute. By the late 19th century, the town supported a diverse array of shops, businesses and co-operatives – possibly as many as 150 – and had a population approaching 12,000, a number that had halved by 2000.

The logical place to start is the **Blaenavon Heritage Centre** (page 175), which rates its own little nugget of history, for this is the oldest surviving works' school building in Wales, built in three phases between 1816 and 1860. Interestingly, when it opened there were 120 children on the roll, a much lower number than those actually working the pits and ironworks. In the adjacent grounds, the **parish church of St Peter** is worth a peek for its collection of cast-iron tomb covers and pillars – even the font is made from iron. It was built by the town's ironmasters Hill and Hopkins, both of whom are buried here in iron-topped tombs, and consecrated in 1805 – if it's not open, you can get the key from the heritage centre.

Across the road stands Blaenavon's most recognisable building, the **Blaenavon Working Men's Hall**, an immense grey-stoned edifice which, depending upon your perspective, is either the best or worst of Victorian excesses. Bearing a close resemblance to the Miners' Institute building in Blackwood (page 187) – though this is considerably larger – the hall was used by local miners and their families for educational and recreational purposes, upon payment of a halfpenny a week. It still occupies a role within the local community, hosting the occasional concert, but otherwise, it's now mostly taken up by an engaging **community museum** (📞01495 790991; ⏰ 10.00–15.00 Mon, Tue & Fri, 10.00–13.00 Sat; £2), which dotes upon the town's history and its major personalities. One of these was Alexander Cordell, the pen name for one George Alexander Graber (1914–97), whose most well-known work was the provocatively titled *Rape of the Fair Country*, actually the first in a trilogy about life in early industrial Wales. Some of Cordells's personal effects are on display, like his jacket, typewriter and tippex-splashed table. Elsewhere, the town's choir, churches and chapels, trades and trade unions, sporting clubs and societies are all given due prominence.

From the institute, walk past the Horeb Baptist Chapel (1862) on the opposite side of the road – one of 18 places of worship here in Blaenavon at the turn of the 20th century – and turn left on to Ivor Street. A little way up, in the triangle at the junction of Ivor Street and Broad Street, is a statue of hometown hero **Ken Jones** (1921–2006), arguably Wales's greatest ever all-round sportsman. Crafted from iron, naturally, the spindly figure, clutching a rugby ball, was one of Wales's most celebrated players, receiving 44 caps for his country, but is most often remembered for scoring the winning try against the New Zealand All Blacks in 1953. Such was his speed that he represented the Great Britain team at the 1948

London Olympics, reaching the semi-finals of the 100m and winning silver in the 4x100m relay.

Broad Street itself is the town's main thoroughfare, though any semblance of life seems to have been sucked right out of it. Records state that there were once more than 40 licensed premises in Blaenavon, many here on Broad Street, but these days you'll be lucky to find more than one or two, and that's if they're not boarded up.

Big Pit

Big Pit (✆029 2057 3650; w museum.wales/bigpit; ⊕ Mar–Jun 10.00–17.00 daily, Jul & Aug 10.00–18.00 daily, Sep & Oct 09.30–17.00 daily, Nov–Feb 10.00–16.00 daily; free) With its towering steel headframe standing sentinel, Big Pit is not only one of South Wales's most popular visitor attractions, but it's also the Valleys' most authentic mining experience. Moreover, tours are led by ex-colliery personnel who entertainingly convey the hardships of life underground.

Although parts of Big Pit technically date to the early 19th century, it was opened officially in 1860, before being sunk to its present depth of 300ft in 1880. So-called because it was the only pit in Wales large enough to service two tramways, Big Pit served as the area's principal colliery for the next 100 or so years, at its peak producing 100,000 tonnes of coal per annum. As well as being one of the most productive mines in the coalfield, it was also one of the most technologically advanced, with its pithead baths and winding-engine house – a direct result of nationalisation of the coal industry in 1947. Coal extraction ended in 1980 and the museum opened just three years later.

Kitted out with helmet, lamp and battery pack, visitors are lowered to a depth of 300ft in the original cages (if you're of a claustrophobic disposition this may not be for you), before the walk along a labyrinthine web of tunnels to the old coal face, sections of which were sunk in the original, abortive development 50 years before the pit opened properly. Off the main tunnel are a series of narrow pillar-and-stall alcoves that one man would work, and gloomy underground stables that were home to the pit ponies who hauled the trucks of newly cut coal; the ponies' names are still painted above each cubicle. Children as young as six or seven would also endure long days down here, for which they were paid a paltry twopence for a gruelling six-day week; more children worked the mines than went to school.

Back above ground, you can make a bit more sense of what you've just experienced in a couple of exhibitions, one an audio-visual presentation entitled *King Coal: The Mining Experience*, and another in the old pithead baths. Constructed in 1939 and one of around 400 built throughout Britain during the inter-war period, the baths (which were actually showers) had heated lockers, and also incorporated a canteen, medical rooms and laundry – thus sparing miners' wives the grinding daily chore of washing their blackened clothes. Writing of his own experiences down a mine in *The Road to Wigan Pier*, the author George Orwell commented: 'I needed two complete baths after going down a coalmine. Getting the dirt out of one's eyelids is a ten minutes' job in itself.'

Blaenavon Ironworks

Blaenavon Ironworks (North St; ✆03000 252239; w cadw.gov.wales; ⊕ Apr–24 Oct 10.00–17.00 daily, Jul & Aug 10.00–18.00 daily, Sep–Oct 09.30–17.00 daily, 25 Oct–Mar 10.00–16.00 daily; £6.60) Blaenavon's magnificent ironworks is one of the most complete sites of its kind anywhere in the world, yet it wasn't so long ago (the 1970s) that they were slated for demolition, before being taken into the care of the state. Established in 1788 under the partnership of Thomas Hopkins, Benjamin Pratt and Thomas Hill, the enterprise was set up with astonishing rapidity, with Furnaces 1, 2 and 3 already in situ by 1792 – a rare example at this time of a multi-furnace site. The partners also set about an ambitious programme of house-building to cater for an ever-expanding workforce, which included the dwellings still standing on Stack Square. The ironworks here were well disposed to take advantage of the area's rich natural resources, which, for the purposes of smelting, were limestone, coke and iron ore.

The site's dominant structure, and its finest architectural specimen, is the hulking **balance tower** – a relatively late addition in 1839 – where water diverted from a stream was used to lift raw materials from the yard below on to tramlines and thence the Brecknock and Abergavenny canal. You can walk to the top of the tower via a looped path, from where there's a superb bird's-eye view of the site, not to mention a vertigo-inducing peek straight down its throat to the bottom. Adjacent are the almost complete remains of three Georgian **blast furnaces** (two more were pulled down long ago), the foundry and a cavernous cast house – here, the furnace clanks and roars, steam hisses, and bright orange veins representing liquid molten iron course along the floor.

Opposite the cast house is **Stack Square**, another of the site's original 1788 buildings and comprising Middle Row and Engine Row. A rare example of early iron company housing, these tiny limewashed cottages would have originally been home to specialist workers brought here to set up the ironworks, before being converted into more humble, and very cramped, dwellings for lower-paid labourers. Two of these cottages were fitted out for the 2007 BBC television series *Coal House* and have been left that way since; in the real world, these were inhabited as recently as 1971.

The adjacent Engine Row harbours two more fully furnished cottages, with a couple more given over to an exhibition and a fine model of the site as it would have once looked. Next door, occupying the last building on Engine Row, is a mocked-up 'truck' shop (truck meaning exchange), where workers could purchase basic goods, but given that it was owned by the ironworks company, and in the absence of anywhere else to shop in town, prices were hugely inflated. Moreover, with wages usually paid late, the common practice was to buy on the 'slate' or 'tab', whereby purchases were credited against future earnings, thus ensuring that families were trapped in a cycle of debt. The truck system was eventually abolished.

As at Big Pit, working here was a brutal existence, especially for children, some of whom were as young as five, unfathomable as that seems. A government-led commission in 1842 identified 185 children under the age of 13 working at the ironworks, some of whom even worked the furnaces. Regardless of whether you were an adult or child, you'd be expected to work a 12-hour shift, six, sometimes seven, days a week, and that's without factoring in the many hazards – burns, broken or crushed limbs, and carbon monoxide poisoning were among the most common injuries and ailments. The working life of the average ironworker was typically over by the age of 40, assuming they made it to that age at all.

Pontypool and Blaenavon Steam Railway (Furnace Sidings, Garn Yr Erw; ☏ 01495 792263; w bhrailway.co.uk; ⊕ Apr–Sep Sat & Sun, plus bank hols & Wed in summer hols – see website for timetable; £11)

Just under 2 miles northwest of the town centre on the A4248 road between Blaenavon and Brynmawr, a signpost invites railway enthusiasts to the Pontypool and Blaenavon Steam Railway, and while there may be more scenic heritage rides in Wales, this is still an enjoyable little outing. Built by the Brynmawr and Blaenavon Railway in 1866 before it was leased to the London and North Western Railway in 1869, the line operated as the main line for Big Pit until 1980, before its reincarnation just three years later as a heritage railway.

It's an odd little run, though. From the Furnace Sidings (where there's a car park and the ticket office), the train trundles the short distance past the Garn Fawr lakes to the Whistle Inn halt, site of a small pub and campsite. It then returns back past the sidings and continues down to the Big Pit halt (where you can alight if visiting the museum; page 177) and then on to Blaenavon High Level station – before returning to Furnace Sidings. For the best views, sit on the right-hand side heading out to the Whistle Inn halt, and on the left-hand side going in the other direction. Reckon on about an hour for the entire trip. There are tentative plans to extend the line beyond the Whistle Inn, though this is unlikely to happen any time within the next few years.

For the hardcore train enthusiasts among you, pop along to the Railway Shop at 33 Broad Street in Blaenavon town centre which has a wide selection of model railway equipment, books, toys and memorabilia – you can also buy tickets for the railway here.

PONTYPOOL AND AROUND

Another Valleys town that has hit upon hard times, Pontypool is unlikely to register on most people's radar, and while there's no reason to visit the town centre itself – its largely deserted main street the usual parade of betting dens, vaping parlours and charity shops – it does have a quirky museum and a fine park with a couple of whimsical Victorian curiosities to keep you occupied for a couple of hours.

A sprawling, hilly town on the Llwyd River, Pontypool was never a coalmining centre, but it was home to numerous other industrial enterprises, including an important nylon factory as well as a tinplate-making works, a japanning works and ironworks. Many of these businesses were established by local landowners and industrial pioneers, the Hanburys, and although Richard Hanbury was the founding father, it was John Hanbury (1664–1734) who pursued these various business interests and oversaw the development of the town as a whole – at one stage Pontypool was richer than Cardiff.

GETTING THERE AND AWAY Pontypool is just west of the A4042, roughly midway between Newport and Abergavenny. Bus #X24, from Blaenavon to Newport, stops on Park Road, a 5-minute walk from the museum and park.

WHAT TO SEE AND DO Housed in a slightly run-down Georgian stable block that was attached to the estate of a mansion belonging to the Hanburys, just across the river from the town centre is the **Torfaen Museum** (℡01495 752036; w torfaenmuseum. org.uk; ⊕ 10.00–16.00 Tue–Thu, 13.00–16.00 Sat & Sun; £5), which just about manages to make some sense of the town's history. Its most worthwhile section is on japanning, the process of finishing and ornamenting a metal (for example iron or tin), wood or papier-mâché with a hard lacquered finish. Britain's first japanning industry was developed here in Pontypool by John Hanbury around the turn of the 18th century, though the Chinese had been practising the art as long ago as AD6. There's a lovely display of japanned domestic products here, like trays, baskets, canisters and bookends.

The art gallery has a series of rotating exhibitions, but the one constant is Thomas Barker's endearing *The Woodsman and His Dog*, a large-scale oil canvas depicting the grizzled, pipe-smoking huntsman George Kelson outside his cottage together with his faithful hound. A contemporary of Gainsborough, hence his slightly strange moniker 'Barker of Bath', the Pontypool-born painter completed this in 1790, before it was presented to the people of Pontypool in 1858.

There are traces of Pontypool's former wealth in the trim swathes of the town **park**, laid out by John Hanbury in 1704. Entering the park near the museum, you'll pass a small Italian garden, a bandstand and the **rugby ground**, a vast oval basin whose main stand is named after the late, great Ray Prosser, former Wales and British Lions player. Before the era of professional rugby, Pontypool was one of the great names in the British game, but today they play in the second tier of Welsh club rugby.

From the leisure centre just beyond the rugby ground, a sign points to the **Shell Grotto**. It is, though, a fairly stiff 20-minute climb up the side of the valley, initially along an uneven rocky path, before you reach the summit and the grotto – and it'll probably be raining, so come prepared. The rewards are worth it, however, not so much for the grotto itself, surrounded by an ugly barbed wire-topped fence, but for the marvellous view across the Usk Valley towards the Severn Estuary. A circular structure with a conical roof, the Shell Grotto was conceived around 1794, ostensibly as a summerhouse for the Hanburys. It's not possible to view the interior (except on special days), which is a huge pity because it's a startling sight, its fan-vaulted ceiling and walls plastered with molluscs, minerals and stalactites, and animal bones and teeth set within the floor.

Continue along the ridge of the hill and follow signs to the more conventional **folly tower** – the original was demolished by the RAF during World War II because it was located near a munitions site, hence too obvious a target, with this one erected in 1994.

Llandegfedd Lake (Coed Y Paen; ☎01633 373408; w llandegfedd.co.uk; ⏰ Mar–Oct 09.00–17.00 daily, Nov–Feb 09.00–16.00 daily) A 434-acre supply reservoir constructed in the 1960s 6 miles east of Pontypool, and now owned by Welsh Water, Llandegfedd Lake has recently been transformed into a major activity and watersports centre. Not only that, but the lake has been designated a Site of Special Scientific Interest, such are the numbers of wintering wildfowl, which is why it's only possible to use the lake between March and October.

There's no shortage of water-bound activities here: windsurfing, canoeing, kayaking, sailing, paddleboarding and pedal boarding, which is a bit like cycling on water but not quite as fast, are all available. Located in the southeastern corner of the shore, the watersports centre has all the equipment and wet gear available for hire, but you can bring your own equipment; you can also get tuition in most activities – a full list of activities and prices are on the website. The lake is a fabulous spot for a dip on a hot day, and it is now possible to open-water swim, with trained lifeguards in attendance, but with the caveat that you need to join as a member and complete an induction session first. Swimmers are also required to wear wetsuits, which can be hired from the centre if you don't have your own.

If, however, you prefer to keep your feet on terra firma, there are four easily navigable walking trails, ranging from an simple mile-long stroll to a moderately strenuous 6-mile lakeside walk, which is well worth the effort if you've time; the latter veers some way from the lake itself at one point and is only open between April and September. After all that exertion, catch up with a bite to eat in the Lakeside Café, whose floor-to-ceiling windows (and balcony) offer an almost bird's-eye view of the lake.

FROM BRYNMAWR TO CWMCARN

Many of the communities along the A467 – from Brynmawr near the A465 down to Abertillery and Six Bells around 6 miles to the south – were among the hardest hit following the closure of the mines. But while there are still plenty of physical scars, there have been some wonderful efforts to preserve the area's mining heritage, as well as coax back nature to parts of the landscape. One way to explore most of those places covered in this section is to walk or cycle the **Ebbw Fach Trail** (w ebbwfachtrail.org.uk), a short 9-mile trail between Brynmawr in the north and Llanhilleth in the south. They are actually two separate trails: the walking trail lies to the east of the A467, and the cycling route to the west – en route you'll encounter Mynydd Carn-y-Cefn, a Bronze-Age burial cairn halfway between Nantyglo and Blaina, as well as chapels and churches, mining memorials, woodland and wetland habitats. There are regular buses between Brynmawr and Cwmcarn.

BRYNMAWR The small town of Brynmawr merits a visit for its town **museum** (☏ 01495 313900; w brynmawrmuseum.org.uk; ⊕ 08.30–noon & 14.00–16.00 Thu, 10.00–noon & 14.00–16.00 Fri, 10.00–noon Sat; free), which like so many community-run museums in the Valleys is a minor joy. Housed inside the old Carnegie Library, and run by a handful of cheerful elderly ladies (if they like you enough they'll probably invite you into their office for a cup of tea), there's very little that this terrific little place doesn't pack into its handful of rooms, most of which are items donated by locals.

First and foremost the museum makes great play of its furniture collection, which, on the surface, does sound a trifle dull, but Brynmawr furniture became a much sought-after commodity during the inter-war years. This was as a result of the so-called Brynmawr experiment (it's not as sinister as it sounds), which was an attempt by local Quakers to reduce mass unemployment in the town and surrounding area by creating a local furniture-making industry utilising mainly unskilled workers. Although the company was fairly short-lived (1929–40), not only was it incredibly prolific, but it also supplied some of the biggest names in the world of British retail, among them Browns of Chester and Harrods in London. The furniture itself was mostly made from imported European oak and had a minimalist aesthetic not all that dissimilar to the Biedermeier style of early- to mid 19th-century central Europe – on display here are some sample pieces including tables, armchairs, chests and bedsteads and the like.

Pottery was another well-respected local craft and here you can view some smartly engraved flagons, a stoneware hot water bottle, and even a gentleman's urinal! Other areas of local life are covered: the police and military, hospitals, the Church, transport, sports clubs and associations, and trades such as pharmacy, optometry and dentistry (the Victorian tooth extractor doesn't bear thinking about, frankly). Among some of the more esoteric stuff on display is an Etch-a-Sketch (one for 1970s and 80s kids, that) and a booklet entitled *Fifty Facts about Hitler*. Remembered here too is Tom Cable, one of the 23 victims of the 1958 Munich air crash involving the Manchester United football team. Cable, the chief flight steward aboard the flight on 6 February, was born in Brynmawr and schooled his whole life here before going on to have successful careers with both the RAF and British Airways. He is buried in the town's St Mary's Church.

Once done in the museum take a look – or better still, go and see a film – at the beautifully renovated Art Deco **Market Hall Cinema** (☏ 01495 310576; w markethallcinema.co.uk) next door. Thought to be Wales's oldest cinema (1894), it's got just one screen and all tickets are under a fiver.

NANTYGLO A couple of miles south of Brynmawr in the sprawling upland settlement of Nantyglo, brown signposts point you in the direction of one of the area's more curious monuments. Standing at the entrance to Roundhouse Farm is a remarkable **fortified roundhouse** possessed of 4ft-thick walls and an iron-plated door with musket loop-holes. It was built in the 19th century by local ironmaster Joseph Bailey, an English Anglican renowned for his callous treatment of workers – lest his workers attempt to exact revenge, Bailey had this mini castle constructed. It's in a parlous state, nettles and weeds sprouting from every orifice and the crumbling interior enveloped in scaffolding, hence it can only be viewed from the outside. That said, the owner of the small row of white cottages adjacent to the tower (see below) does have the key to the tower, so if you can track him down he'd be happy to show you inside and take you up on to the roof. There is a second, much better-preserved roundhouse on the other side of the long barn in the yard, but you're unlikely to be able to access this one.

🏠 Where to stay, eat and drink

🏠 **Roundhouse Farm** Waen Ebbw; w holidaycottages.co.uk. Located on the former ironworks site – right next to the fortified roundhouse – this trio of Grade II-listed cottages (Henrietta, William & Mary) have been sensitively restored to accommodate between 2 & 4 people (& dogs in Henrietta). All are clean, bright, modern & extremely comfortable. There's a communal terrace with a firepit for guests, plus an electric vehicle charging point. A fabulous stay in the heart of the Valleys. **£££**

EBBW VALE AND CWM Three miles southwest of Brynmawr, **Ebbw Vale** is the largest town and administrative centre in Blaenau Gwent Borough, and although not worth a diversion, it's worth recalling that this was once one of Europe's largest steel towns. Originally the Ebbw Vale Ironworks, as the Ebbw Vale Steelworks it produced the steel that helped drive the Industrial Revolution, manufacturing steel for some of the world's most prestigious projects, from the Stockton and Darlington Railway to the Sydney Harbour Bridge. As the demand for steel declined, the works bowed to the inevitable and closed in 2002, leaving the town with one of the highest rates of unemployment in the UK. Tellingly, 62% of the population voted Leave during the Brexit vote, the highest proportion of anywhere in the country. Despite pockets of investment, and the arrival of a new railway from Cardiff a decade or so ago, Ebbw Vale remains a depressed place.

Travelling south beyond Ebbw Vale, the village of **Cwm** was an insignificant little spot until the Marine Shaft was sunk here in 1889. Closed exactly 100 years later, the old pit site has since been reclaimed by nature and now goes by the name of the **Silent Valley National Nature Reserve**. In early spring the precipitous upper slopes are awash with bluebells, but otherwise they are covered by huge canopies of ancient semi-natural beech woods. The reserve is organised to the extent that there is a car park here and two easy walking trails – wellies advised, as it gets very muddy.

ABERTILLERY AND SIX BELLS A typically workaday Valleys town, **Abertillery** (Market St; ☎ 01495 211140; w abertilleryanddistrictmuseum.org.uk; ⏱ 10.00–13.00 Thu–Sat, but do call ahead; free) merits a visit for its engaging museum, which had various homes until it moved into the Old Market Hall in 2021. There's very little that's not covered here, from lots of early archaeological artefacts (Bronze Age axes, Roman pottery) to agricultural implements and domestic machines, though the most rewarding displays pertain to the early and mid 20th century, including an original World War II Anderson shelter and, inevitably, stacks of stuff on the local mining industry. There's even a tŷ bach (outside loo) complete with sound effects.

Within easy walking distance of Abertillery, **Six Bells** was the scene of one of the worst post-war pit disasters, when 45 miners were killed in an explosion at the Six

Bells Colliery on 28 June 1960. The miners are duly commemorated thanks to what is the undoubtedly the most striking (and certainly the biggest) of all the Valleys' mining memorials. Unveiled on the 50th anniversary of the disaster, on the site of the old colliery that's now a freshly landscaped park, the *Guardian* **monument** is the towering creation of Welsh sculptor Sebastian Boyesen. Perched atop a 23ft-high circular sandstone plinth inscribed with the names of all those who died is a 40ft-high bare-chested miner with arms outstretched, the whole ensemble comprising more than 20,000 fabricated strips of steel. When viewed from afar, the miner appears as an almost transparent figure, but up close, it's clearly one solid block.

You can learn more about the construction and installation of the *Guardian* monument at the **Ty Ebbw Fach** (✆ 01495 211732; w sixbellsconferencecentre. co.uk; ⏰ 09.00–16.00 Mon–Fri) building on Chapel Road, a 5-minute walk away from the memorial. Also documented is the history of the mine, which opened in 1892, peaked around World War II employing more than 2,450 men, and then closed in 1988, by which time it had merged with the nearby Marine Colliery in Cwm. Boots, lamps, mandrels and the like have been donated by miners, while you can listen to moving tales of mining life in the Story Chair. There's a pleasant café next door too.

CWMCARN FOREST (✆ 01495 272001; w cwmcarnforest.co.uk; ⏰ 09.00–17.00 daily; parking £1/3 2hrs/day) One of the most enjoyable outings anywhere in the Valleys is Cwmcarn Forest, another previously mined area but which in recent years has become a favourite destination for hardcore mountain bikers and walkers. For the more sedentary-minded, a unique forest drive – the only one of its kind in Wales – offers all the views but without having to leave the comfort of your vehicle.

There are three **mountain-biking** trails in the forest (all free), though with two designated red and one black, these are really for experienced downhillers only, but if you do fancy tackling one of these and don't have your own wheels, PS Cycles (w pscycles.co.uk; ⏰ 10.00–16.30 Wed–Fri, 09.30–17.30 Sat & Sun) hire out bikes (£32.50/day) from their shop in the car park. Walkers are also well catered for, courtesy of five **walking trails**, ranging in distance from 1 to 9 miles; the last of these a pretty strenuous workout.

Reopened in 2021 following a six-year closure in order to fell some 150,000 trees blighted by *Phytophthora ramorum* (larch disease), the **Cwmcarn Forest Drive** (⏰ Mar–Oct 10.00–18.00 daily, Nov–Feb 10.00–16.00 Sat & Sun; £8/4 car/ motorbike) is a 7-mile figure-of-eight loop through lush mountain scenery and with cracking views to boot. Well tarmacked, the drive starts at a barrier (which is also where you pay) about half a mile beyond the visitor centre. En route there are seven stopping points (denoted P1, P2, etc, all with loos and tables and benches), where you can stretch your legs and go for a walk (if so desired), have a picnic, or simply admire the view. Kids will love it too, not only because this is one trail they don't have to walk, but because there are also three brilliant adventure play areas along the way, particularly the one at P4 (Carn Valley). If you're gunning for a walk, the 5-mile return P7 (Head of the Pass) is the one to aim for, as from here there's a terrific ramble up to **Twmbarlwm**, an Iron-Age hillfort. Just make sure you pick a clear day for the drive to make the most of the outstanding views. Allow at least 2 hours, more if you plan to do any walking.

Where to stay, eat and drink The **Cwmcarn Forest Information Centre** (⏰ 09.30–16.00 Sat–Thu, 09.30–15.30 Fri) has an adjoining café that is good for a coffee or a spot of lunch.

⋀ Forest Drive Campsite (10 pods) ☏ 01495 272001; w cwmcarnforest.co.uk. Take your pick between a pitch or a pod, the latter coming furnished or unfurnished & sleeping between 4 & 6 – shower & cooking facilities are available to be shared by all; or one of the 6 new fully furnished, en-suite lodges, which sleep up to 6. The campsite itself is neat & level, & if you can't be bothered to cook, you can eat at the on-site café. *Pods* **££**, *camping* **£**

THE SIRHOWY VALLEY

TREDEGAR AND AROUND

Tredegar A close-knit little town at the head of the Sirhowy Valley, Tredegar is the birthplace of Aneurin Bevan, founder of the NHS (see below). The town's other

ANEURIN BEVAN

Born in Tredegar in 1897, Aneurin Bevan was introduced to life down the pits at the youthful age of 13, but it wasn't long before he was already concerning himself with issues of health and welfare. By the age of 21, he was already running a club that provided medical assistance to the local community, and at 26 he became leader of Tredegar Urban District Council. Greater things beckoned: as a prominent trade unionist in the South Wales coalfields, Bevan led miners in the 1926 General Strike, and just three years later secured the seat of Ebbw Vale, serving as the Labour MP here for the next 31 years.

An avowed Marxist, Bevan was considered a radical within his own party, frequently clashing with leading members, including the Prime Minister Lloyd George, and at one point was expelled for his support of the Spanish Popular Front, though that didn't stop him from being appointed Minister of Health in the wake of Labour's 1945 election victory. One of the key reasons behind Labour's landslide win was the party's commitment to greater social reform and the creation of a welfare state: better council housing, support for the unemployed, a drive towards state-owned industries, and a national health service that would provide free health care for all. Presiding over the last of these policies – and one that would ultimately be his lasting legacy – was Bevan himself, who had already pioneered a similar scheme in his hometown some years earlier under the slogan 'Free Health Care for All'. Indeed it was his avowed mission to 'Tredegarise the whole country', and this was his template for establishing the NHS, although his skills as a canny negotiator and powerful orator – he would often practise speeches up on the Brecon Beacons – were a major factor too.

Bevan resigned his cabinet post in 1950, railing at the imposition of prescription charges, but he remained a hugely divisive figure, establishing a left-wing faction known as the Bevanites. One of Bevan's closest allies was the former Labour leader Michael Foot, whose two-volume biography, *Aneurin Bevan: A Biography*, is a good starting point for anyone keen to know more about one of Britain's greatest rhetoricians; better still is a more recent study of Bevan by Nicklaus Thomas-Symonds called *Nye: The Political Life of Aneurin Bevan* (page 327). Diagnosed with terminal cancer in 1959, Bevan encouraged Foot to stand in his Ebbw Vale seat, which Foot duly won following Bevan's death in July 1960. Despite the many well-documented problems with the NHS, it remains the greatest legislative achievement of any British government to date.

The *Guardian* monument at Abertillery commemorates those who lost their lives in one of Wales's worst post-war pit disasters PAGE 183 above left (CH/WPP/A)

Newport's Grade II-listed Transporter Bridge is one of just six such bridges in the world PAGE 113 top right (BS/S)

Blaenavon's ironworks is one of the most complete sites of its kind anywhere in the world PAGE 177 above right (CC/VW)

Explore the industrial history of the Valleys at Rhondda Heritage Park PAGE 203 below (BS/S)

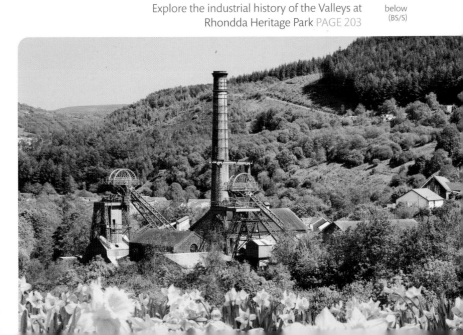

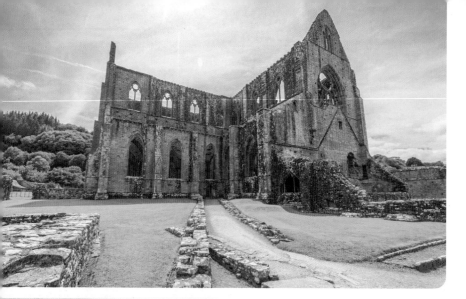

above
(CC/VW)

Tintern Abbey is the most atmospheric ecclesiastical ruin in Wales PAGE 95

left
(CC/VW)

Caerleon's commanding Roman amphitheatre was built around AD90 PAGE 116

below
(CC/VW)

Dylan Thomas's writing shed in his hometown of Laugharne is one of the author's most important legacies PAGE 258

Perched atop a vertiginous limestone outcrop on the Carmarthenshire/Brecon Beacons border, Carreg Cennen is one of the country's finest fortresses PAGE 268
above left
(CC/VW)

With its endless battlements, cannon ports and hidden staircases Kidwelly Castle is still a marvel to explore PAGE 253
above right
(CC/VW)

The largest prehistoric tomb in Wales, Pentre Ifan is some 5,000 years old PAGE 321
below
(RH/S)

above (gbi/A) Merthyr Mawr is home to one of the largest dune complexes in Europe PAGE 137

below left (CC/VW) Strumble Head is the closest Wales gets to the Irish mainland PAGE 314

below right (BS/S) The colourful seaside town of Barry combines good old fashioned beach pleasures with bracing walks PAGE 127

bottom right (CC/VW) Atlantic grey seals are present off the coast at Ramsey and Skomer year-round PAGE 7

Three Cliffs Bay is the poster child of the Gower PAGE 167

above
(BS/S)

Abereiddi's Blue Lagoon is a popular coasteering spot PAGE 312

right
(HH/S)

Llanelli's Millennium Wetland yields a fantastic variety of birdlife PAGE 250

below
(CC/VW)

above
(CC/VW)

In 2012, the Brecon Beacons National Park became the first place in Wales to be designated an International Dark Sky Reserve PAGE 224

left
(SS)

Sgwd yr Eira is the most impressive of the waterfalls on the Four Falls Trail PAGE 214

below
(HS/A)

Overlooking the Valleys and the Brecon Beacons, the Rhigos Viewpoint is a great spot for a picnic PAGE 207

The disconcertingly narrow Gospel Pass is one of the most thrilling roads in Wales PAGE 241

above
(a/S)

Looking like an enormous spaceship, the great glasshouse at the National Botanic Garden of Wales is the largest single-span great glasshouse in the world PAGE 263

below left
(JT/NBGOW)

The Dan-yr-Ogof Showcaves were discovered only in 1912 PAGE 216

bottom left
(CC/VW)

Kenfig National Nature Reserve is one of the UK's last bastions of the internationally protected Fen orchid PAGE 140

below right
(MF/S)

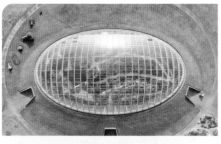

above (WCC/S) Grassholm sees around 40,000 pairs of breeding gannets return each spring PAGE 302

below left (CC/VW) Guillemots are one of the many species of seabird spotted on the islands off South Wales PAGE 5

below right (CC/VW) Get up close with red kite at the feeding centre in Llanddeusant PAGE 213

bottom right (KP/S) Head to Skomer to see some 120,000 pairs of Manx shearwater PAGE 300

political heavyweight was Michael Foot (former leader of the Labour Party), who served as a Member of Parliament for both Ebbw Vale (1960–83, the seat left vacant following Bevan's death) and Blaenau Gwent (1983–92), holding surgeries in a cottage here in Tredegar for more than 30 years.

Tredegar's one noteworthy site is **Bedwellty House and Park** (✆ 01495 353370; w bedwelltyhouseandpark.co.uk; ⊕ house 09.30–16.30 daily, park 08.30–20.30 daily; free), a handsomely proportioned Regency building somewhat at odds with the earnest character of the rest of town. Built in 1822 for the Homfray family, co-founders of the Tredegar Iron Company, Bedwellty remained the main residence for subsequent ironmasters until 1899 when Lord Tredegar acquired the property, before he promptly relinquished it for public use. It remains one of the most complete examples of an ironmaster's residence in South Wales, albeit one that was heavily restored in 2009–11 following major investment.

Ultimately, though, the house is a disappointment, in the sense that there's little of substance to see, and in keeping with today's fashion is mostly used for weddings and other ceremonies. There is, though, compensation in its grounds: fountains, cascades and ponds, a walled kitchen garden and grotto, a rare ice-house, and, its pièce de résistance, a monster block of coal weighing 15 tonnes, heavy enough for it to be considered the largest piece of coal ever cut – it had been intended for display at the 1851 Great Exhibition in London, but without any practical way of transporting it, a smaller piece was sent instead. Most visitors to Bedwellty come for refreshments in the quaint Orchid House Tea Room adjoining the house.

A 5-minute walk up the road from Bedwellty House, Tredegar's **clock tower** is an eloquent reminder of the town's once-proud iron-making industry. Raised in 1858 on the Circle, at 72ft it's reputedly the tallest free-standing clock in Britain, but whether that's true or not, it's a superb specimen. If you happen to coincide a visit with CADW's Open Doors event in September, then you may have the opportunity to climb up the inside the clock.

Sirhowy Another salient reminder of the region's once industrial might is the **Sirhowy Ironworks**, located behind a little housing estate on Grahams Yard, just off Dukestown Road. The site is not very easy to locate, but if you do get stuck, ask around and someone should be able to point you in the right direction.

One of the Valleys' few extant ironworks, Sirhowy roared into life in 1778 with just the one furnace, but by the 1840s there were five in blast, supplying pig iron to the Ebbw Vale works just down the road. By the late 1870s, however, smelting was no longer deemed profitable and the remaining furnaces were decommissioned, though coke continued to be produced here for Ebbw Vale until around 1905. Despite the trees, grass and weeds that have ambushed its three massive barrel-vaulted arches pressed into the bankside (each of which would have been joined to a casting house in front), it remains a poignant site. There's little by way of interpretation, save for an information board by the perimeter fence which in theory you're not meant to climb over.

On a gentle rise about half a mile northeast of Sirhowy on the A4047, you can't fail to miss four enormous, but seemingly random, lumps of rock. Collectively known as the **Aneurin Bevan memorial stones**, they were erected here in 2002 as a tribute to the work of the founder of the NHS (see opposite) – the largest stone bears a plaque with the words 'It was here that Aneurin Bevan spoke to the people of his constituency and the world', and indeed this was the spot where Bevan frequently preached to mass gatherings, the great orator that he was. Looking across to the grey skies and brooding hills in the distance, it's probably worth pausing for a

From Trefil there's a wonderful walk up on to Mynydd Llangyndir, a vast undulating plateau whose southern slopes begin in Blaenau Gwent and extend into the Brecon Beacons down to the village of Llangyndir in the valley of the River Usk, after which the mountain is named. Mynydd Llangyndir is mapped as open country so walkers are free to roam at will, but there are few defined paths (just two that run north–south), so an OS map is pretty much essential.

A designated Site of Special Scientific Interest, Mynydd Llangyndir's most distinctive geographical features are tumps (small lumpy mounds) and depressions (or shake holes) that have formed as a result of the limestone ceiling collapsing. As for archaeological heritage, there are burial cairns dotted all over the landscape. Like many other remote moorland areas in Britain during World War II, decoy fires were employed on Mynydd Llangyndir as a means of diverting enemy bombs away from their intended targets, which, in this part of Wales, would have been the local steelworks. This ingenious method of deception (known as urban decoy) entailed lighting diversionary fires, which were designed to replicate the fire effects the enemy would expect to see when their target has been successfully hit – thus duping the second wave of attackers into bombing the same target. Stark yet exhilarating, it's not difficult to see why this landscape has long appealed to television and film producers; productions have included *His Dark Materials*, *Wrath of the Titans* and *The Hitchhiker's Guide to the Galaxy*.

Many people head up on to Mynydd Llangyndir to seek out the **Chartist's Cave** (Ogof Fawr) where, in 1839, activists stockpiled their weapons ahead of the ill-fated Newport march on 4 November (page 112), as the commemorative plaque by the cave entrance acknowledges; such is the cave's remoteness, it's little wonder they chose this site. Beyond the low, arched mouth of the cave it's possible to venture a short distance inside – there's one passage to the left and another to the right, but mind your head! The panorama standing atop the cave – Hay Bluff and the Black

moment to reflect upon the value of the National Health Service, and of Bevan's work, especially in light of the recent pandemic.

Trefil Three miles north of Tredegar on the other side of the A465, Trefil – officially the highest village in Wales (1,342ft) – was once a hive of activity owing to its location close to the vast limestone quarries, from where the material would be shipped via the Brinore Tramroad to Tredegar in the south and Talybont, in the Brecon Beacons, to the north. The old tramroad ran straight past the Top House (see opposite), as popular a hostelry today as it was back then; it was also a favourite watering hole of Aneurin Bevan, who occasionally stopped for a pint after a day spent walking and rehearsing his speeches in the nearby hills. Aside from the excellent Top House, there's no specific reason to visit the village, other than to use it as a starting point for forays up on to Mynydd Llangyndir (see above). Villagers in Trefil like to tell anyone that's interested that they've got the highest rugby pitch in Wales.

⌂ Where to stay, eat and drink

⌂ **Tredegar Arms Hotel** (10 rooms) Morgan St, Tredegar; ☏ 01495 788463; w tredegararms. co.uk. Recently returned to something like its former glory, the town's singular hotel, close to

Bedwellty Park, offers 10 rooms of no little charm & style, which, among other things, feature exposed brick or stonework, splashes of artwork & clawfoot tubs; extremely good value. The hotel's

Mountains to the east and the high peaks of the Brecons (Pen-y-Fan and Corn Du) to the north – is sublime. You won't see many other people up here: instead, the landscape is largely the preserve of sheep and mountain ponies, none of which will be the slightest bit bothered by your presence.

A 10-minute walk west from the cave is **Garn Fawr**, a Bronze-Age burial cairn that's easily identified as a prominent mound of grey stones – and, at 1,827ft, it's also the highest point on Mynydd Llangyndir. From the cairn, continue west towards **Trefil Quarry**, a scheduled monument that was worked prolifically between the late 18th and early 19th centuries, fluxing stone for a handful of different iron and steelworks. Walk around the edges and you'll see sheep nestled precariously inside small hollows dug into the sides of the quarry.

On the other side of the quarry road is **Duke's Table**, a grassy 'table' partially embedded with stone blocks, which is enclosed within a shallow ditch and an outer ring, or 'bench', also comprised of turf-covered stones. Local legend has it that this little ensemble served as a picnic table for the Duke of Beaufort during his hunting expeditions, which is not the most implausible of theories. Rather conveniently, they would have gathered their water from the nearby spring, which you can do too before the final leg back to Trefil, a 15-minute walk south along the **Brinore Tramroad** or old quarry road. Engineered by George Overton, who had already overseen construction of the Penydarren Tramroad in Merthyr, the 8-mile-long tramroad was operational between 1815 and 1865 and connected the Tredegar Ironworks and the quarries with the Monmouth and Breconshire Canal, variously transporting coal and limestone. Llangyndir is very exposed, so bring a hat and suncream if it's warm, and if there's even the slightest suggestion of rain, a raincoat too. A walk up to the Chartist's Cave and back will take around 1½ hours, but if you want to take in everything here, then allow at least 3 hours.

Coach House restaurant is worth a punt too, particularly if you enjoy a nice hunk of steak. **££**
🍴 **Railway Tavern** Dukestown Rd, Sirhowy; 📞01495 722574; w therailwaytredegar.biz; 🕐 09.00–21.30 Mon–Fri, 09.00–20.00 Sat & Sun. Less than a mile north of Tredegar, in the smaller village of Sirhowy, the Railway Tavern doesn't look like the most inviting of venues from the outside. Fronted by a grubby car park, the inside initially feels a little impersonal but that's probably just the size of the place, with tables & chairs healthily spaced out around a long, deep bar. But the Railway comes recommended, thanks both to the welcome & the good food. Despite the meat & steak-heavy menu, there are several veggie/vegan alternatives such as spring green risotto & a plant-based root burger. **££**

❋ 🍴 **The Top House** Tafarn Ty Uchaf, Trefil; 📞01495 616510; w www.thetophouse-tredegar. foodndrink.uk; 🕐 11.00–midnight Wed–Sun. Occupying a lovely whitewashed cottage at the far end of the village, the Top House is the last public house before the Brecon Beacons, a place where tramroad workers & quarrymen would gather for a pint after a long shift. It's a bit more refined these days, the quarrymen too replaced by villagers, as well as passing walkers & cyclists. A broad range of unfussy but well-cooked dishes include house specials like the Top House burger & the Top House chicken, in addition to a pie or a curry of the day – & if you enjoy a Sun roast (served noon–17.00), you'll not find a better one anywhere in the Valleys, but do make sure to book ahead. **££**

BLACKWOOD In the lower reaches of the Sirhowy Valley, the village of Blackwood is worth a brief diversion for a look at the **Miners' Institute** (📞 01495 227206;

w blackwoodminersinstitute.com; ⊕ 09.00–21.00 Mon–Fri, 09.00–14.30 Sat). Institutions of this kind were the bedrock of many Valleys' communities at the turn of the 20th century, serving as libraries and reading rooms as well as a place of recreation for miners and their families. Most were constructed from contributions of the miners themselves, such as Blackwood's, which was built in 1925, originally as a snooker hall. Its demise coincided with the local pit closures, but following a sensitive restoration, it's now home to a well-restored multi-purpose arts centre. Blackwood's main claim to fame, however, is as the birthplace of the Manic Street Preachers (page 26), whose members spent their formative years here and who still retain a fervent local following; in 2011, they played a memorable hometown gig at the Institute, 25 years after their last.

MERTHYR TYDFIL AND AROUND

On the cusp of the wind-blown Beacons, Merthyr Tydfil was the beating heart of the Industrial Revolution. By the late 18th century, the town had emerged as the greatest iron-making centre in the world, with four major sites: Dowlais (established 1759), Plymouth (1763), Cyfarthfa (1765) and Penydarren (1784); even Lord Nelson popped by on one occasion to purchase a few cannonballs. By the mid 19th century, the ravenous appetite for iron – particularly within the burgeoning railway industry – ensured that the works here in Merthyr continued to boom. And with so much work available, Merthyr inevitably attracted migrants from all over the world, which helped swell its population to more than 60,000 by 1860 (more than Cardiff, Newport and Swansea combined), easily making it the most populous town in Wales.

With World War II on the horizon and the ironworks on the wane, Merthyr was chosen by the giant American firm Hoover to help spearhead the post-war domestic revolution in the manufacture of white goods, principally washing machines. The firm's closure in 2009, therefore, was another hammer blow to Merthyr, and the town has struggled to regain a foothold since. It remains a place of high unemployment and social deprivation, and the town was one of the worst affected in the UK during the Covid-19 pandemic. Yet despite the obvious problems, Merthyr's residents take great pride in their town, certainly more than the recurring negative media representation of the town might suggest. What Merthyr lacks in aesthetic appeal – and its crestfallen main street does present a pretty depressing sight – it makes up for in its surprisingly diverse cultural diversions, which are inevitably bound up in its formidable industrial past. Moreover, the town has repositioned itself as something of an adventure sports hub, home to Wales's best mountain-bike park and of course some superb walking on its doorstep.

GETTING THERE AND AWAY

By car Merthyr is extremely well connected by road with the fast A465 shooting east–west across the top of town and the A470 running north–south from the Brecon Beacons and down towards Pontypridd and the M4 (just 20 minutes away from Merthyr). Given that most things of interest lie on the outskirts of town, you'll probably not need to park centrally, but if you do, your best bet is the Tesco Extra car park south of the High Street, though there may be a limit on how long you can stay.

By train and bus Merthyr's train station is just a couple of minutes' walk southeast of the centre on Tramroad Side with half-hourly services to Cardiff and Pontypridd. For Aberdare, you'll need to change at Abercynon.

The bus station is close to the train station at a new interchange on Swan Street. Bus links are excellent, with services to Abergavenny (hourly Mon–Sat), Cardiff (every 30mins Mon–Sat, hourly Sun), Pontypridd (every 20mins) and Rhymney (every 20mins). If you're looking to travel north from Merthyr, a useful service is the T4 (part of the Traws Cymru medium- to long-distance bus service), a route that starts in Cardiff then stops in Merthyr before continuing through the Brecon Beacons to Brecon town and beyond to Newtown in Powys (7 daily Mon–Sat, 3 Sun).

TOURIST INFORMATION In the absence of a tourist office (though you can pick up leaflets from Cyfarthfa Castle), consult the excellent website w visitmerthyr.co.uk.

WHERE TO STAY, EAT AND DRINK

The Tiger Inn (7 rooms) 75 Pontmorlais W, High St; m 01685 722555; w thetigerinn.wales. One of the few bright spots along the High Street, this sparkling little hotel harbours minimalist, nearly all-white rooms offset with splashes of lime. The on-site Tiger Lounge & Café is 1 of just 2 places in Merthyr worth eating at, & is also the best spot in town to grab a coffee. **££**

The Roost (5 cabins) Ash Rd, Troed-y-rhiw; m 07484 697392; w roostmerthyr.co.uk. A fabulous biker-/hiker-friendly site run by a very welcoming family 3 miles south of the town centre. There's a choice here of heated cabins, each sleeping 2 adults & up to 2 children & all have a bike/equipment-storage area; 1 cabin is en suite, while occupants of the others have allocated showers as well as well-equipped self-catering 'inside-outside' kitchens. Bike wash, drying room & washing line also available. It's small, & very

popular with bikers using the nearby Bike Park Wales, so book ahead. There are also a couple of pitches for campervans. **£**

The Mine at CF47 & Castelanys Fine Dining 24 High St; 01685 385947; themineandcastelanys; ⊕ noon–23.00 Wed–Sun. Sister restaurant to the brilliant Mine Bistro in Cwmgrach, Merthyr finally has a decent restaurant of its own. Well, it's 2 actually, because the bistro shares premises with Castelanys, a split establishment comprising a 1st-floor Italian restaurant & a ground-floor tapas-style bar. Co-owner & head chef Marius Castelany has a solid grounding, having served as an apprentice under Antonio Carluccio & here he prepares dishes with understated flair such as risotto with chicken, Italian sausages & roasted red peppers with pecorino cheese. The Mine menu is of the burgers, fried chicken & BBQ ribs variety, all of it very fine. **££**

WHAT TO SEE AND DO All of Merthyr's key sites, including Cyfarthfa Castle and Park, are located to the north and east of the town centre, in which case there's little reason to venture here, but if you do find yourself in the neighbourhood, there a couple of things to look out for. At one entrance to the moribund shopping centre is a statue of the boxer **Johnny Owen**, which was raised in 2002, 22 years after his death in a fight with Lupe Pinto, who unveiled it himself in a touching ceremony; at the other entrance is a statue of Merthyr's other great fighter, Howard 'The Welsh Wizard' Winstone, perched on his corner stool.

Walking north along the High Street, you can't miss the former town hall, renamed the **Redhouse** following an immaculate £8 million revamp a few years ago. This magnificent red-brick and orange terracotta building was completed in 1896 to house the local seat of government (including law courts and holding cells), although its last incarnation prior to closure was as a nightclub, hence the precarious state it found itself in prior to renovation. Now a cultural centre used primarily by the local college as a performing arts space, the lobby scrubs up beautifully (Doulton tiles, mosaics) with, front and centre, a majestic imperial staircase flanked by the original pillars, above which is a beautifully restored stained-glass window bearing an image of Queen Victoria. Merthyr has its own Goscombe John statue too, that of **Henry Seymour Berry** outside the library next to the Redhouse. Berry's brothers get plaques around the base, including James Gomer Berry, former proprietor of the *Sunday Times* and a director of the Reuters News Agency in the 1950s.

The next building in line to be revived is the former **Jewish Synagogue**, a 5-minute walk east of the Redhouse on Bryntirion Road. A turreted, Gothic Revival edifice, it's the oldest purpose-built Jewish building surviving in Wales and served a community up until 1983. A Jewish presence has been identified in Merthyr as far back as the 1830s, with the first synagogue here around 1848; as the ironworks grew, so too did the number of Jewish merchants, eager to capitalise on a large, relatively well-paid workforce. With a growing congregation, the original synagogue on John Street was deemed too small and replaced by this one on Bryntirion Road. After World War I, there were still around 400 Jews in Merthyr, though that number is now down to single figures. The synagogue was recently acquired by the Foundation for Jewish Heritage (**w** jewishheritage.wales), whose plan is to convert

MERTHYR RADICALS

Social disaffection in Merthyr had been fermenting during the early years of the 19th century, culminating in the 1831 Merthyr Rising, or Merthyr Riots, an armed revolt by industrial workers angered by low pay, abject poverty, and hellish working conditions – ire that was exacerbated in the knowledge that their ironmaster bosses were lording it up in their grand mansions.

On 1 June, somewhere between 5,000 and 10,000 protesters began the march, but after a week of intermittent engagements with the authorities, the revolt had been crushed, at the cost of 24 protesters' lives. The most iconic moment of the protest was the raising of a red flag that had been soaked in calf's blood, which is believed to be the first time that such a symbol had been used as a gesture of worker revolt on British soil – a symbol that, later, would be adopted internationally by Communists and Socialists.

The leading personality of the uprising was Lewsyn yr Heliwr ('Lewis the Huntsman'), a renowned political agitator and the proverbial persistent thorn. Lewis was sentenced to death for his part in an alleged robbery, although this was later commuted to transportation. Lewsyn's cousin, 23-year-old trade unionist Richard Lewis (Dic Penderyn), didn't fare quite so well, carted off to Cardiff and hanged for allegedly stabbing a soldier, though by common consensus his sentence was based on the fact that the authorities required a high-profile scapegoat – even the wounded soldier refused to identify Penderyn as the perpetrator. In the event, Penderyn's last words were 'O Arglwydd, dyma gamwedd!' ('O Lord, what an iniquity!'). Some 40 years later, a Welshman by the name of Ianto Parker confessed that it was he who injured the soldier before fleeing to America to evade capture, an admission that secured Penderyn's status as one of the great Welsh martyrs. There have been attempts since to have Penderyn pardoned.

Despite eventual defeat, the rising only served to galvanise the Valleys' communities, with union lodges emerging across the region and beyond. Compared with the Peterloo massacre in Manchester 12 years earlier, the Merthyr Rising has historically garnered relatively little attention, yet is widely regarded as the birth of Britain's working-class order. The town's political conscience is still alive and kicking thanks to the **Merthyr Uprising Festival** (**w** merthyrrising.uk), a cracking three-day jamboree of music, arts, talks and debate taking place in mid-June; a weekend ticket costs around £110.

it into Wales's national centre for Jewish history – all things being equal, by 2025. As an architectural specimen, it's quite unusual: the entrance is approached via a double flight of steps that draw upwards to the entrance, although the synagogue's most intriguing element is a red sandstone dragon, its claws jammed on to the apex of the entrance bay pediment. What few Hebrew inscriptions that remain have been badly eroded, and are almost indistinguishable.

Anyone familiar with *Myfanwy* (*My Dearest*) – and if you've ever heard a Welsh male voice choir, you will be – will know that it was composed by Joseph Parry, one of Wales's all-time leading musicians and the first to compose an opera in the Welsh language (*Blodwen*). Parry was born in 1841 in a sweet little two-up, two-down ironworker's cottage at 4 Chapel Row, which is now known as **Joseph Parry's Cottage** (✆ 01685 727371; w visitmerthyr.co.uk; ⊕ by appointment only, contact Cyfarthfa Castle Museum). The downstairs rooms have been recreated as per the time, and upstairs there's a small museum in honour of Parry. Parry lived the latter part of his life in Penarth, where he is buried. Parry was also responsible for the much-loved hymn, *Aberystwyth*, which some insist (though just as many refute) formed the basis for *Nkosi Sikelel' iAfrika*, South Africa's co-national anthem.

There are few better examples in South Wales of a blowing engine house than the **Ynysfach Engine House** (w wellbeingmerthyr.co.uk) on the eastern bank of the Taff behind Merthyr College. A sturdy four-storey building dressed in blue pennant sandstone and limestone quoins, Ynysfach is the last of four engine houses that originally stood here, and dates from 1836 when the local ironworks were at the peak of their powers. It's now a heritage centre where you can inspect some of the internal workings downstairs and read about the history of the building. However, the Engine House was closed at the time of writing and it was unclear as to when it might reopen, so it's worth checking the website from time to time.

Cyfarthfa Castle and Park (Cyfarthfa Park, Brecon Rd; ✆ 01685 727371; w wellbeingmerthyr.co.uk; ⊕ 10.00–16.30 Tue–Sun; £2.30) Nowhere in South Wales embodied the wealth and optimism of the iron industry more than the castellated pomposity that is Cyfarthfa Castle, built in 1825 by William Crawshay II, grandson of Richard Crawshay – who, while not the originator of the Cyfarthfa Ironworks, established it as the biggest in the world. It's actually two buildings within one: the castle itself and a school tacked on to the back in the 1920s, though this closed in 2014.

Much of the building is now in an advanced state of decay, yet is still home to the **museum and art gallery**, itself in need of a little love and attention, though there's still much to enjoy. Heading down into the basement beyond the café, the first few rooms document the town's formidable industrial heritage and history of innovation. It was in Merthyr that the world's first steam-powered locomotive, designed by Cornish engineer Richard Trevithick, successfully ran: this was actually the result of a wager in 1804 between Samuel Homfray, proprietor of the Penydarren Ironworks, and Richard Crawshay, owner of the Cyfarthfa works, in which the former bet the latter 1,000 guineas that he could design an engine (subsequently named the *Pen-y-Darren*) that could haul ten tons of iron from Merthyr to Abercynon, 9 miles distant. With Trevithick on board (excuse the pun), Homfray succeeded, albeit only after a slight hiccup when the chimney smashed into a bridge and had to be repaired. Somewhat less successful (and something those of a certain age may well recall) was the infamous, and short-lived, Sinclair C5, a weird-looking electric tricycle manufactured at the local Hoover factory; a model of this is on display here.

Moving away from industry, the upstairs rooms are a miscellany of different themes, but begin with an overview of the Crawshays themselves, with numerous cabinets packed with items illustrating the family's ostentatious wealth: tea sets, glassware and the like, plus some personal effects. Elsewhere, there are dresses by Merthyr-born designers Julien Macdonald and Laura Ashley, ceramics from Nantgarw (page 198) and, more surreally, a stuffed king penguin brought back from Shackleton's 1914 Antarctic trip.

South Wales is renowned for producing world-class boxers, nowhere more so than here in Merthyr. Two of Britain's finest pugilists were Howard 'The Welsh Wizard' Winstone, a former world featherweight champion in the 1960s, and the

ANY OLD IRON

Taking a lead from Abraham Darby's successful attempts to smelt iron using coke at Coalbrookdale in Shropshire, an embryonic coke-iron industry began to supplant charcoal as the main fuel in South Wales, and by 1788 the area was producing over 15% of Britain's total output – a figure that had doubled within 20 years – and its output began to exceed even that of Shropshire and Staffordshire. Demand was principally fuelled by the Royal Navy, which was becoming involved in an ever-greater number of conflicts around its expanding empire, although the coming of the railways would fuel further demand.

Given the abundance of raw resources available locally – coal, limestone, iron ore and fast-flowing streams – Merthyr Tydfil became the epicentre of iron production, with almost half of the ironworks within its legal jurisdiction, most of which were owned by the four biggest estates in the region: Dowlais, Cyfarthfa, Plymouth and Penydarren, who between them employed around 15,000 men by 1830. The owners of these works were typically wealthy businessmen from London or Bristol, like Richard Crawshay, boss of the Cyfarthfa works. The Blaenau Gwent Valleys – Sirhowy, Ebbw Fawr and Ebbw Fach – were also among the largest iron manufacturing concerns in the world. By the late 1830s, South Wales was producing at least 40% of Britain's iron, which itself was the largest iron-producing country in the world, and by the mid 19th century, there were no fewer than 25 ironworks in the region smelting over a third of all Britain's pig iron. One of the corollary effects of such growth was the creation of a network of canals, such as the Glamorganshire and the Monmouthshire and Brecon canals, which were a far more efficient means of transporting iron and steel from the Valleys down to Cardiff and the sea than the wagons and horses previously used.

Such was the reservoir of expertise and talent in South Wales that workers from here helped establish fledgling ironworks as far afield as Pennsylvania and Ohio in the US, and the Donetz Basin (Donbass region) in the Ukraine, where Merthyr-born ironmaster John Hughes helped found the Hughesovska works. Numerous factors contributed to the decline in demand for wrought iron in the 1870s, among them the depletion of resources and the large-scale importation of cheaper Spanish hermatite ore. Meanwhile, technological advancements ensured that less iron was required to manufacture the same number of products as previously, although some iron-working centres, such as those at Ebbw Vale and Tredegar, were in a position to diversify into manufacturing steel.

tragic boxer Johnny Owen – aka the Merthyr Matchstick – who, aged 24, died after fighting the Mexican Lupe Pinto in Los Angeles in September 1980; the gloves he wore that night are displayed here. Statues in the centre of town commemorate both men (page 29). Finally, the old library is now a small, permanent art gallery. Although fairly underwhelming, there are a couple of evocative Valleys' paintings by Cedric Morris (*The Tips, Dowlais*) and Kyffin Williams (*Mountain Landscape*).

After years of consultations, a long-term plan has been engineered to transform Cyfarthfa Castle and its park into a world-class visitor attraction. Under the Cyfarthfa Plan, the park will be extended along the valley to twice its current size, with regreening at its heart; the castle will be renovated with new museum galleries; and the badly degraded furnaces will not only be stabilised and restored but will also be connected to the castle via a high-level walkway. It's a bold statement of intent, and if it does ever bear fruit, the benefits to the town and surrounding area will be immeasurable.

Bike Park Wales (Gething Woods, Abercaid; ✆01685 709450; w bikeparkwales. com; ⏲ summer 10.00–16.00 Mon, Thu & Fri, 09.00–13.30 & 14.30–19.00 Sat & Sun, winter 10.00–16.00 Mon & Thu–Sun; daily in school hols; uplift pass £38–48 depending upon the day; bike rental from £55) The opening in 2013 of Bike Park Wales, 3 miles south of Merthyr in Gethin Woods, not only massively boosted the town's much-maligned profile, but it also did much to correct the imbalance between North and South Wales in terms of not just mountain-biking facilities, but adventure pursuits more widely. Suffice to say it's been a thrill-a-minute success ever since, so much so that many riders now consider this the most rewarding bike park in Wales. That's not to say it was designed with just elite or competent riders in mind; one of the park's four founding members is former Welsh downhill champion Rowan Sorrel, who was keen to create a facility for all-comers.

To this end the park can count on more than 40 gravity-fed trails, many sporting wonderfully nutty names like Melted Welly, Rim Dinger and Dai Hard, with a roughly equal split between blue (intermediate), red (advanced) and black (expert) runs, though beginners need not worry as there are also a couple of green trails (Bushwhacker and Badgers Run). The blue ('flow') runs are probably the most popular, owing to the generally smoother ride they give, and even novices shouldn't have any problems negotiating these. The excellent uplift service transports bikers to the summit which stands at a height of 1,610ft (491m); in fact the view from the top of many of the runs are superb. While this is no Verbiers, the vibe here at Bike Park Wales is not dissimilar to that of a ski resort, from the graded runs to the 'après-bike' café-cum bar. It's an absolute blast.

THE TAFF AND CYNON VALLEYS

ABERFAN Once the archetypal monochrome mining village, Aberfan, 6 miles north of Abercynon, is associated with one of the worst mining disasters in Wales. On the morning of 21 October 1966, an unsecured slag heap high above the village crashed down the hillside, crushing the local Pantglas primary school and many of the surrounding houses; 144 people lost their lives, including 116 children, almost half the number in the village. To this day, it's a figure that remains beyond comprehension.

One of scores of communities in South Wales that huddled at the foot of spoil tips, this was, by common consensus, a tragedy waiting to happen, given the consistently complacent attitudes of the coal bosses towards safety, not just here in Aberfan but throughout the Valleys. Repeated complaints had been made to the coal board about the risks posed by the tips – including a petition from the school itself several years earlier – yet these warnings continued to go unheeded. During the last days of the tribunal, Lord Robens, Chairman of the National Coal Board, finally appeared to admit fault on behalf of the board, and when the tribunal finally retired to consider its verdict in August 1967, two months after the trial started, it was unequivocal in apportioning blame to the coal board. In the aftermath, campaigns throughout South Wales led to the removal of larger tips, in the process reshaping much of the local landscape, but even today there are some isolated tips in parts of the Valleys still at risk of collapsing.

Aberfan's victims are buried in the cemetery on the slopes high above town; you can't miss it, two neat rows of white arched headstones inscribed with all kinds of unbearably sad valedictions from bereaved parents. To get there, head past the site of the old school along Bronheulog Terrace, before veering right and heading uphill along the winding road. The old school site is now an affecting **memorial garden** – opened by the Queen in 1997 – which has been laid out to replicate the footprint of the school. Meanwhile, the clock from the school, which stopped at 09.13, is on display at St Fagans Museum in Cardiff (page 83). More than 50 years on, it's a tragedy that still haunts the village.

Numerous books have been written about Aberfan, but two of the most affecting are *The Green Hollow*, an eloquent portrayal of that dreadful day by the poet and novelist Owen Sheers (which was based on an earlier BBC TV film), and *Aberfan*, a moving testament as recalled by Gaynor Madgwick, one of the survivors and whose brother and sister died.

ROCK UK SUMMIT CENTRE (✆ 01443 710090; w rockuk.org/centres/summit-centre; ◷ 10.00–21.00 Tue–Thu, 10.00–17.00 Fri & Sat; climbing wall £9.50) Nine miles north of Pontypridd, on a minor road in between the villages of Trelewis and Bedlinog in the heart of the Taff Bargoed Valley, the site of the old Trelewis Drift Mine has been put to excellent use as the Rock UK Summit Centre, one of the country's premier indoor climbing centres. The valley's pits – Trelewis plus Deep Navigation and Taff Merthyr – closed in the early 1990s leaving a community bereft, but a site once deemed too polluted and dangerous to enter was cleaned up and in 1997 the Welsh Climbing Centre (as it was then) opened its doors.

The purpose-built hangar harbours all kinds of walls, some 60ft high, with walls tailored for use by both experienced and beginner climbers; these include overhanging and roof walls in addition to bouldering walls. If you fancy trying your hand at something else instead of (or in addition to) climbing, there are some 20 or so different activities to try, high ropes, archery and kayaking among them.

The centre is popular with, and largely geared up for, residential groups, so do check ahead. It is at the heart of the **Taff Bargoed Country Park**, a major land reclamation project that has successfully entailed the reintroduction of previously lost habitats, including ponds, reedbeds and grassland, which in turn has encouraged the return of different kinds of flora and fauna.

LLANCAIACH FAWR MANOR (Nelson, Treharris; ✆ 01443 412248; w llancaiachfawr. co.uk; ◷ 10.00–17.00 Tue–Sun; £8.50) South Wales doesn't lack for properties purporting to possess some degree of paranormal activity, but Llancaiach Fawr Manor, situated on the B4254 between the villages of Nelson and Gelligaer, probably has greater claim than most. To this end, all manner of markings designed to prevent evil spirits from entering the house – including Marian Marks (overlapping Vs, denoting the Virgin Mary, scratched on to stone walls) and witch marks (black stains scorched into the wooden beams) – have been uncovered over the years, and are still being discovered.

A stern, three-storey residence built around 1530 but remodelled in the 17th century, Llancaiach Manor was the seat of the Prichard family whose chief protagonist was Edward, born around 1610. Erstwhile Sheriff of Glamorgan and Justice of the Peace, Prichard was originally on the side of the Royalists during the Civil War, yet despite a visit to the manor by King Charles I persuading him to remain onside, Prichard swapped allegiance and joined forces with the Parliamentarians. The Prichards relinquished the manor at the end of the Civil War and thereafter it settled into a comfortable life as a farmhouse.

Visits to the house are by guided tour only, but what elevates a tour here above your average one is the presence of actors in period costume speaking 17th-century English (ironically, the Master of the House disapproved of the use of Welsh) and generally having a jolly good time. Although it sounds tacky, it's not at all. With flames crackling and candles flickering, it's very atmospheric and very entertaining. There are plenty of amusing anecdotes along the way, though younger visitors may occasionally find the patter beyond the scope of their understanding, and patience.

The house is frozen in time – 1645 to be precise, at the height of the Civil War – as the cast leads you around half a dozen or so rooms, including the kitchen, dining room, great hall, counting house (arms store) and bedrooms; note, under Prichard's bed, the rolling truckle bed in which his servant would be obliged to sleep, lest he be required to attend to his master's needs during the night. Who knows, you might even see Prichard himself, one of the four ghostly beings said to patrol the manor. But if that's not spooky enough for you, there are dedicated ghost tours on Friday and Saturday evenings throughout the winter months.

SENGHENYDD Few villages in South Wales have felt the shattering effects of a mining tragedy as much as Senghenydd, 6 miles east of Pontypridd. While the Valleys are littered with episodes of appalling mining tragedies, two incidents here stand out, if only because of the sheer numbers involved. On 14 October 1913 at the Universal Colliery in Senghenydd, 950 men descended the pit for their morning shift. As they did so, a massive blast ripped through one of the shafts killing 439 men, and in the event one rescuer. The manager, Edward Shaw, was convicted of eight charges (nine were dismissed), though the pit owner, Lord Merthyr (of Lewis Merthyr Consolidated Collieries) had already died by the time the verdict was passed. It remains the single most serious industrial disaster in UK history and among the worst mining disasters to be recorded anywhere in the world.

The even greater tragedy was that this should never have occurred at all, or at least not on the scale that it did. Twelve years earlier, 81 men lost their lives in the same pit, but the Coal Mines Act of 1911 that followed as a result of that incident (and which proposed numerous measures in order to prevent another similar tragedy) had yet to be fully implemented by the time of the 1913 disaster. The mine closed in 1928 and the two shafts at Senghenydd were finally filled in 1979.

Somewhat belatedly, a memorial was unveiled in October 2013 on the 100th anniversary of the second disaster. Located on the site of the old colliery at the northern end of Commercial Street, the **Welsh National Mining Memorial and Universal Colliery Memorial Garden** is a beautifully worked piece, at the centre of which is *The Rescue*, a dramatic bronze sculpture depicting a stricken miner being

6

hauled away by a rescue worker. The names of all those killed in both 1901 and 1913 are remembered on individual plaques, while floor-bound slate plaques recall every other pit disaster in Wales in which five or more miners died – there were more than 150.

The victims of the two pit disasters are further remembered in the wonderful **Aber Valley Heritage Centre** inside the Senghenydd Community Centre on Gwern Avenue (✆ 029 2083 0445; w abervalleyheritage.co.uk; ⏰ 11.00–14.00 Tue–Sat; free). As well as various reports, letters and photos, including one of William Harris, the sole survivor from the 1901 incident, there's stacks of other mining memorabilia – tommy (lunch) boxes, tobacco boxes, lamps, photos and so on – in addition to objects relating to the town and Valleys' wider history.

🏠 **Where to stay, eat and drink**

🏠 **Llechwen Hall** (44 rooms) Llanfabon; m 01443 742050; w llechwen.co.uk. A longhouse, prison & school were just a few of this remarkable building's many previous incarnations, but these days it's a charming country house hotel with 4 categories of room (classic, superior, premium & 4-poster), though all are blissfully comfortable & peaceful. This is also far & away the best place to eat for miles around, its restaurant housed within a gorgeous oak-beamed orangery & serving irresistible dishes like lamb rump pie with spring cabbage & parsley emulsion. **£££**

CAERPHILLY AND AROUND

A reluctant suburb of Cardiff, just 8 miles down the road, the small market town of Caerphilly is likely to resonate with most people for two things: its castle and cheese. One of the most recognisable names on the British cheese market, Caerphilly (Caerffili) was first produced in the town around 1830, then very much a staple of a coal miner's lunch. It's a hard white cheese that manifests a mild, buttery taste, not that dissimilar to cheddar – not that much of the stuff is made here in Wales these days: ironically, most Caerphilly cheese is now produced across the border in the West Country, such as Gorwydd Caerphilly which hails from Weston-Super-Mare in Somerset, though there has been a recent revival locally – one to look out for is Cenarth Caerffili from the Caws Cenarth creamery in Carmarthenshire. The cheese is celebrated in all its crumbly glory at the end of July during the **Big Cheese Festival**, a three-day jamboree taking place in and around the castle grounds and entailing all manner of events from street theatre and medieval re-enactments to a funfair and food stalls, before a big fireworks finale. Naturally there's a cheese race.

Before entering the castle, take a look at the oversized bronze statue of the comedian **Tommy Cooper**, wearing his iconic fez. He was born here in Caerphilly in 1921, though he moved to Exeter at the age of three.

GETTING THERE AND AWAY Caerphilly is just east of the A468/A469, 10 miles from Cardiff's centre. It is easily reached by train from Cardiff Central (every 15mins) and bus #26 (hourly) from The Kingsway in Cardiff, though this takes double the time of the train.

✕ **WHERE TO EAT AND DRINK**

✕ **Volare** 87 Cardiff Rd; ✆ 029 2132 2077; w volarewales.co.uk; ⏰ closed Mon. This Italian restaurant, just a short walk south of the castle, rates highly among the locals. Along with the stock pizza menu, there's an appealing main cast of pasta & risotto dishes as well as some more unexpected plates like pork loin in balsamic honey sauce with sautéed potatoes. Cheaper lunchtime offerings are worth considering if you're just visiting the castle for the day. **££**

WHAT TO SEE AND DO

Caerphilly Castle (☎ 0300 0252239; w cadw.gov.wales/visit/places-to-visit-caerphilly-castle; ⊕ Mar–Jun 10.30–17.00 Mon–Fri, 09.30–17.00 Sat & Sun, Jul & Aug 09.30–18.00 daily, Sep & Oct 09.30–17.00 daily, Nov–Feb 10.00–16.00 daily; £10.10) Britain's second-largest castle after Windsor – and the third largest in Europe – Caerphilly Castle is an astonishing sight, not only because of its bulk, but also because of its concentric design, a design that preceded Edward I's strongholds in North Wales by several years and which was also the first of its kind in Britain. Parts of the castle are due to undergo a much-needed makeover estimated at £5 million, which will eventually include the renovation of the Great Hall, better interpretation around the site and a new visitor centre – improvements that will finally do justice to this world-beating monument, though these are unlikely to be complete until 2024 at the earliest.

Starting in 1268, the 'Red Earl', Gilbert de Clare – second only to the royal family as the wealthiest person in Britain at the time – took just three years to complete Caerphilly Castle, which was remarkable given that during this time it came under sustained (but ultimately futile) attack by Llewelyn ap Grufudd in 1270. De Clare's death in 1295 ushered in a largely uneventful period for the castle, with ownership having passed to the Despensers and not much happening by way of any meaningful action. Pressed into action once more during the Civil War – although its role during this time remains unclear, much of the site was undermined. It then lay derelict until the Butes got their hands on the property, another to add to their portfolio of mighty southern Welsh fortresses, Cardiff Castle and Castell Coch being the others. Restoration of the castle continued under successive marquesses, though it was the Fourth Marquess, John Crichton-Stuart, whose hand was most prominent. His most profound, and controversial, initiative, however, was the clearance of hundreds of houses and businesses so that the original lakes could be reflooded, a process that duly took place in 1958.

The approach to the castle is across the outer moat and through the **outer main gatehouse**, itself flanked by the north and south dam platforms. The wall along the north dam platform to your right betrays a perceptible inward lean as it shadows the grassy bank up to the north gatehouse, from where a road once stretched all the way to Morlais Castle in Merthyr. The south dam platform – which was effectively the outer ward back in the day – offers up a few interesting features, like some rarely seen remains of an old corn mill that likely functioned until the 17th century, and, further along, a display of replica siege engines, which are occasionally pressed into action during festivals.

From the south platform, another bridge traverses the inner moat (itself part of the wider lake) to the central island on to which the main castle buildings are grafted. The middle ward is fronted by the **outer east gatehouse**, an extraordinary proposition even by this castle's impressive standards, but even that pales when compared with the **inner east gatehouse**, which invites access to the **inner ward**. Never breached, the inner ward is defined by its four great **towers**, one of which, the southeast tower, is the castle's most iconic structure on account of its disconcerting lean. Various theories have been posited for its 10-degree slant, but the most probable explanation is that it was a combination of a few cannonballs and a good old bit of subsidence. The best view of the tower's huge rupture (and it does look as if the whole thing could topple over at any moment) is from within the overgrown terrace of the neighbouring kitchen annex.

Ranged along the southern curtain wall is the much-reworked **Great Hall**, initially the work of de Clare but heavily modified by Despenser around 1317. It acquired a new timber roof in 1871 under the Third Marquess of Bute, with some further tinkering as recently as the 1960s. For the most part featureless, there is some extant ornamental detail in the guise of some moulded ball-flowers, a popular form of Gothic decorative art, and the occasional corbel. A door at the end leads through to the former earl's apartment, and while there's little to see here now, the impression remains of a once-grand abode. The rooms in the adjoining **inner west gatehouse** are largely bare, save for an entertaining animated film illustrating the castle's history.

Be sure to take a walk along the northern curtain wall too, with its reconstructed fighting gallery, known as a hourd; there is a fine view of the north lake from here. The last part of this 30-acre site to be investigated is the western island, and although this cannot be accessed from the main castle, it can be reached via a walk along the north bank, an extended grass strip running from the outer gatehouse between the moat and north lake. In fact you can take this in as part of a circular walk around the castle.

Nantgarw Chinaworks (Tyla Gwyn, Nantgarw; ☎ 01443 844131; ᴡ nantgarwchinaworksmuseum.co.uk; ⏱ 10.00–16.00 Wed–Sun; £2.50) In 1813, the painter William Billingsley relocated from Derby to Nantgarw (which translates as 'rough brook' in Welsh – Nant meaning 'brook' and Garw meaning 'rough' – and pronounced 'nant-ga-roo') just to the southwest of Caerphilly to set up a porcelain works, attracted here by the ready-made supply of coal to fire the kilns and the nearby Glamorganshire Canal, which he could utilise both for the transportation of raw materials and to export his goods. Working alone, Billingsley became obsessed with manufacturing the finest porcelain the world had ever seen, a product to rival Sèvres in France, and he largely succeeded, thanks to his unique alchemy and exquisite floral artwork. Billingsley was a perfectionist, however, and rejected more than 90% of everything he made. Combined with his evident lack of business acumen, he was forced to shut up shop in 1820, penniless and hunted down by creditors.

The site was revived a few years later under a different guise. Under the ownership of William Henry Pardoe, whose father Thomas was a noted enameller, Nantgarw reopened in 1833, but now producing earthenware pots and jugs, stoneware bottles and clay pipes. There are some lovely examples on display here. Although a less profitable occupation, it was more reliable, but by the end of World War I, cigarettes had usurped pipes as the preferred choice of smokers, which effectively signalled the end for the factory and it finally closed in 1920.

Nantgarw porcelain is scarce these days, and while there are a few items on display here at the museum, most of what's left is now kept within the National Museum Cardiff (page 70) and the V&A in London; there are also small collections in the Glynn Vivian Gallery in Swansea and Cyfarthfa Castle in Merthyr. In the back garden, one of the original bottle kilns has been restored, with ambitious plans for this to one day be fired up again. Elsewhere, studio space has been created within the museum to allow a new generation of ceramicists to continue the work of their predecessors. After browsing you can enjoy a cuppa and a slice of cake here, all of which is served using original Nantgarw porcelain, naturally.

Travelling by public transport, the bus from Caerphilly (hourly) stops at the Cross Keys Inn in Nantgarw, from where it's less than a 10-minute walk to the chinaworks.

PONTYPRIDD

Affectionately known as Ponty by the locals, the busy market town of Pontypridd sits at the confluence of the Taff and Rhondda, a location that has often left it at the

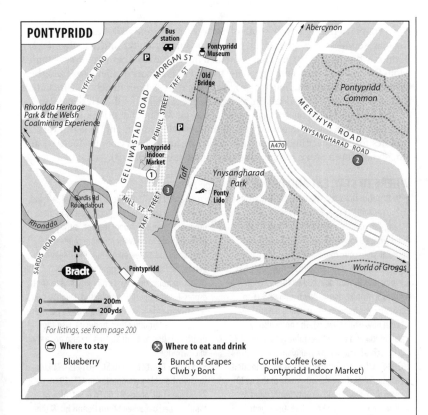

Bus station

Pontypridd Museum

MORGAN ST

TAFF ST

Old Bridge

TYFICA ROAD

Abercynon

Pontypridd Common

Rhondda Heritage Park & the Welsh Coalmining Experience

GELLIWASTAD ROAD

PENUEL STREET

MERTHYR ROAD

YNYSANGHARAD ROAD

A470

Pontypridd Indoor Market

1

3

Taff

Ynysangharad Park

Ponty Lido

2

MILL ST

TAFF STREET

Sardis Rd Roundabout

Rhondda

SARDIS ROAD

N

Bradt

Pontypridd

World of Groggs

0 ———— 200m
0 ———— 200yds

For listings, see from page 200

⌂ **Where to stay**
1   Blueberry

✕ **Where to eat and drink**
2   Bunch of Grapes   Cortile Coffee (see
3   Clwb y Bont   Pontypridd Indoor Market)

mercy of these two powerful rivers. So it sadly proved once again in 2020, just a month before the pandemic, when Storm Dennis caused the Taff to burst its banks and water surged through the town. It was the opening of the Glamorganshire Canal in 1794 that paved the way for the town's future prosperity, with coal mined at the nearby Lewis Merthyr Colliery sent straight to the ironworks in Merthyr further up the canal. Other industry followed, like the Brown Lennox Chainworks who supplied chain cables and anchors for merchant vessels (and closed as recently as 2000), in addition to a rail mill and tinplate works.

The town's compact nature, tucked into a tight wedge between the Taff and the railway line with the park located between the right bank of the Taff and the A470, lends itself to getting around by foot. Pontypridd also makes a good base for exploring the two arms of the Rhondda Valley just a few miles northwest of town.

GETTING THERE AND AWAY

By car Pontypridd is probably the best-connected town in the Valleys, easily accessed by car with the M4 within striking distance and the fast A470 north–south road linking Cardiff and Merthyr (which continues through the Brecon Beacons). There's plentiful parking in the town centre, the most convenient spot being Gas Road car park parallel to the High Street on the west bank of the Taff, or the Goods Yard car park directly above the bus station.

By train and bus Pontypridd's fine Edwardian train station, with its curving platforms (one of which was the longest in the world when it opened in 1970) is just a couple of minutes' walk south of the town centre and park next to the A4058. Regular services to both Cardiff (every 20–30mins daily) and Merthyr (every 30mins Mon–Sat, 7 Sun) are complemented by services to Aberdare (every 30mins Mon–Sat, hourly Sun) and up along the Rhondda Fawr (valley) to Treherbert (every 30mins Mon–Sat, hourly Sun), stopping at all stations in between, including Trehafod for the (Welsh Coalmining Experience at the) Rhondda Heritage Park.

The bus station is on Morgan Street, just above the Old Bridge at the top of the High Street. Buses depart every 30 minutes for Cardiff, and at least every 20 minutes for Merthyr (hourly on Sun), and there are also services to Aberdare and Abercynon (both every 20mins) and Caerphilly (every 30mins).

🏠 WHERE TO STAY, EAT AND DRINK *Map, page 199*

🏠 **Blueberry Hotel** (9 rooms) 6–8 Market St; ✆ 01443 485331; w blueberryhotel.co.uk. Accomplished little hotel right in the heart of the town whose 9 rooms are split into 2 categories: imperial-style Loire rooms, which, as the name suggests, are run through with French flourishes; & White rooms, with polished white-on-white fixtures & fittings, goose-down pillows & crisp Egyptian cotton sheets (& sparkling bathrooms, all with powerful showers). The hotel also accommodates a very respectable restaurant. **££**

🍴 **Bunch of Grapes** Ynysangharad Rd; ✆ 01443 402934; w bunchofgrapes.pub. Curiously located on a residential street the other side of the A470 flyover, the Grapes' food is consistently good & well above your average pub fare. Open your lunch account with pan-fried cockles with leek & pancetta, before a main of hot salt beef with horseradish mash & fried gherkins, then wrap up with caramelised pear & chestnut tart tatin. Or just come for beer, which is damn fine. **££**

✳ 🍴 **Cortile Coffee** Indoor Market, Market St; w cortilecoffee.co.uk; ⏱ 09.00–16.00 Wed, Fri & Sat, 09.00–15.00 Tue & Thu. A mini caffeine empire, this fab little café, tucked away in the otherwise fantastic indoor market, is the place in Pontypridd to get your morning coffee fix. The family roast their own beans in Bridgend before the Fracino coffee grinder works its magic pumping out heart-stopping double-shot espressos among other caffeinated delights; cakes & toasted sandwiches too. If you wish to purchase some beans (among other products), visit their dedicated shop at 4 Taff St. They've also got a shop in Cowbridge. **£**

☆ **Clwb y Bont** 85a Taff St; ✆ 01443 491424; w clwbybontblog.wordpress.com; ⏱ 19.00– 23.00 Tue–Thu, noon–01.00 Fri & Sat. Almost totally wiped out when Storm Dennis hit, & then closed, like many other venues, because of the pandemic, this ace club is now back on its feet & once again championing local musicians & artists, as it has done since 1983. Regular themed nights include sing-a-longs & bilingual quizzes, as well as evenings of jazz, folk & blues on different Weds each month.

SHOPPING

World of Groggs 159–160 Broadway, Treforest; ✆ 01443 405001; w groggs.co.uk; ⏱ 09.00–15.00 Mon–Fri, 10.00–15.00 Sat. Your face is likely to light up upon entering this wonderful shop – you can't miss its brazen red & green-painted frontage – whose owners, the late John Hughes, and now his son Richard, have been handcrafting these clay caricatures ('Groggs') since 1965. What started off as a small hobby creating mythical creatures evolved into modelling Welsh sporting heroes, then actors, musicians & a few other celebrities, as well as sheep & dragons, naturally. Although most Groggs are miniatures, there are quite a few larger pieces; either way, they're not especially cheap (expect to pay around £35 for a miniature), but as a gift, they are certainly unique.

WHAT TO SEE AND DO Ponty's main point of reference is its sturdy **Old Bridge** (1775), which, as hard as it is to believe today, was once the largest single-span stone bridge in Europe, at the time exceeding that of the Rialto in Venice. Mind you, it did take amateur stonemason William Edwards several attempts (four in fact) before he cracked it, his previous three bridges having ended up in the Taff.

Pontypridd Museum (℡01443 490748; w pontypriddmuseum.wales; ⊕ 10.00–16.00 Mon–Fri; free) Abutting the river on the west side of the bridge stands the old Tabernacle Chapel, these days home to the Pontypridd Museum, whose basement was flooded during Storm Dennis in 2020, destroying or damaging more than 1,000 items. Although the building closed as a place of worship in 1983, the chapel has retained its elegant, pea-green cast-iron columns which support the beautiful wood-panelled balustrades reached via steps on the left-hand side. The organ is an impressive specimen too.

All the exhibits are up on the three-sided gallery overlooking the ground floor, and cover a broad range of topics from industry to entertainment, but the most enjoyable sections are those on music and sport, and Pontypridd has a fine pedigree in both. One of Ponty's most famous sons is Sir Geraint Evans (1922–92), one of Britain's finest operatic bass-baritones who reprised more than 70 roles in a dazzling international career, including Mozart's *Figaro* over 500 times: one of these was at La Scala in Milan in 1960, the first performance there by a British singer since the end of the war. Stored here in a darkened cabinet is the costume he wore when playing Falstaff, though the less said about the mannequin the better. Hometown heroes don't get any bigger, though, than Sir Tom Jones. Born Thomas Jones Woodward in Pontypridd in 1940, the indefatigable crooner, now well into his eighties, continues to make new music and tour. Not forgetting either the wonderful Côr Meibion (Pontypridd Male Choir), who use the building for rehearsals (page 207).

Among the pantheon of Welsh boxing greats, Pontypridd rates two of its very own. Wales's first true sporting hero was the American-Welsh boxer Frederick Thomas (better known as Freddie Welsh, aka the 'Welsh Wizard') who, in a remarkable but little-documented career, fought in excess of 150 bouts, losing just five and winning the world lightweight title in 1914; it's also believed that the eponymous character in F Scott Fitzgerald's Great Gatsby (Jay Gatsby) was modelled on Welsh, whom, it is alleged, Fitzgerald may have even sparred with. Like another great Welsh hero, Dylan Thomas, Welsh was found dead in a New York hotel room in 1927. The second great Ponty-born pugilist – but again little known – was Frank Moody, who is believed to have fought over 200 times, including three bouts at New York's Madison Square Garden; on display here are his well-worn leather gloves.

More unusual is a pair of weighty quoits (metal rings) belonging to Welsh international quoit player (yes, it's an international sport!) W J Perkins. While starting out as a pastime, the game – which is thought to have originated from the Greek discipline of discus throwing – quickly evolved into a competitive sport, with dedicated clubs emerging in towns and villages throughout the Valleys in the late 1880s.

Ynysangharad Park and Ponty Lido (Lido: ℡0300 004 0000; w rctcbc.gov.uk; ⊕ Jun–mid-Sep 07.30–19.15 daily; £2.50; visitor centre: Mar, Apr & Oct 09.00–16.00, May, Jun & Sep 09.00–17.00, Jul & Aug 07.00–19.00, Nov–Feb 09.00–15.00) Wedged into a neat triangle between the Taff and the A470, the barely pronounceable **Ynysangharad Park** is the town's popular green lung. Ynysangharad was conceived as a memorial park after World War I, its two original memorials – one dedicated to those killed during both World Wars and the other to those who died during the Falklands War – joined in 2011 by another one remembering those who lost their lives in other conflicts such as those in Palestine, Korea and the Suez.

Elsewhere in the park is Goscombe John's memorial to father and son Evan and James James, represented by allegorical statues symbolising poetry and music. The pair were responsible for the rousing *Hen Wlad fy Nhadau* (*Land of my Fathers*), composed in 1856 (Evan wrote the lyrics, James the melody) and later adopted as the de facto Welsh national anthem.

Dating from 1927 and largely funded by local miners, **Ponty Lido** (also known as the National Lido of Wales) was part of the lido boom that swept across Britain during the 1920s and 30s. It was the second-largest open-air pool in Wales after Cold Knap in Barry, but after that closed (it's since been demolished), Ponty was left as the country's sole survivor, astonishing when you consider that there were once 57 open-air pools in Wales alone, many here in the Valleys. The lido closed in 1991, condemned to ruin before plans were hatched to restore it to its former glory.

Reopened in 2015, some of its original features – the turnstiles and wooden changing cubicles – have been retained, but otherwise it's all sparkling new, with three heated pools: a 25m main pool, an activity pool with loads of inflatables, and a splash pool for tots and younger kids. Done swimming, you can enjoy a bite to eat in the Waterside Café, above which is a visitor centre displaying (sepia-tinted) photos and other memorabilia. And as if that wasn't enough kid-friendly entertainment for one afternoon, there's a spanking new adventure park next door, with several wheelchair-accessible swings and rides.

Pontypridd Common On the other side of Ynysangharad Park across the A470, Pontypridd Common (or, to give it its proper title, Coedpenmaen Common) is a rare quiet spot in town. A walk around the common takes in a few interesting features, including a rocking stone (so-called because it's said to move if enough people jump up and down on it at the same time), the remnant of a retreating ice sheet, which itself is ringed by a circle of smaller stones placed here in 1850. Look out, too, for a burial cairn, prehistoric standing stone and a war memorial as you walk around.

THE RHONDDA

Other parts of the Valleys may call it differently, but the Rhondda was the crucible of the Welsh coal industry. Exploratory pits in the 1850s and 60s revealed abundant seams of high-grade steam coal, leading to ever-deeper shafts being sunk. Alongside the coal boom, towns and villages were grafted on to the precipitous valley cliffs to accommodate the massive surge in the population – in 1801, the population was somewhere in the region of 550, and just over a century later, nearly 153,000.

By World War I, the Rhondda had 53 large mines, each one employing at least 1,000 men. In 1913 the Rhondda eked out 9 million tonnes of coal, around a sixth of the entire South Wales coalfield. As well as more houses – in excess of 15,000 were built in the Rhondda in the 30 years prior to World War I – more people meant more shops, pubs, clubs and theatres, workmen's institutes and chapels, and by the end of the 19th century there were around 150 chapels in the Rhondda.

By the end of 1914 more than 40,000 miners from South Wales, the majority from the Rhondda, had enlisted for the war. The huge losses suffered, along with the Great Depression – which hit mining harder than any other industry – essentially reversed much of the previous 100 years' growth, leading to mine closures throughout the area. The last to close in the Rhondda was Maerdy in 1990.

The Rhondda is actually two river valleys: the **Rhondda Fach** (Little Rhondda) which wriggles northwest for 16 miles to Maerdy, and the **Rhondda Fawr** (Great Rhondda), which runs parallel to the River Fach to Blaenrhondda. Fairly remote reaches by Valleys standards, neither Rhondda Fach nor Rhondda Fawr offer much by way of tangible sights (the Rhondda Heritage Park aside), but set against that, the scenery can be tremendous and the hills offer some fantastic, yet little-known, trails – and if you've an aversion to crowds, this will be very much to your liking.

GETTING THERE AND AWAY It's a pleasant, if slow, journey up through the valleys by car, with the scenery becoming increasingly more attractive the further up you go. Half-hourly trains (hourly on Sun) from Pontypridd travel the length of the Rhondda Fawr Valley all the way up to Treherbert, stopping at all points along the way, including Trehafod (for Rhondda Heritage Park), Tonypandy and Treorchy. The Rhondda Fach is served by buses only (every 30mins), with buses also serving all the villages in the Rhondda Fawr, though these are a little more frequent, roughly every 20 minutes.

 WHERE TO STAY, EAT AND DRINK

🏠 **Heritage Park Hotel** (43 rooms) Coedcae Rd, Trehafod; ☎01443 687057; w heritageparkhotel.co.uk. A complete makeover has improved this hotel just a couple of minutes' walk from the Rhondda Heritage Park no end. Despite its undistinguished exterior, the rooms are spruce & spotless, with nice plump beds & faux-tartan carpets. Both the bar &restaurant impart an open & immediately friendly feel, while the food itself is solid without being spectacular: chicken tandoori, hanging kebabs & pizza from the wood-fired oven – that sort of thing. Trehafod train station is a 10-minute walk away. **££**

✳ ✗ **Colliery 19** Pontrhondda Rd, Llywnypia; ☎01443 663202; w cymoedd.ac.uk; ⏰ 17.00–20.00 Mon, noon–14.00 Thu. One of 4 local training restaurants attached to Coleg y Cymcoedd (Cymcoedd College), this laudable enterprise has students cooking & serving (fine-dining) meals. It's a great opportunity to enjoy high-end food at stupidly low prices, with a constantly changing menu that might include dishes like pot roast duck breast with vegetable royale & duck leg samosa. The £15 3-course lunch is an absolute steal. The smart but unfussy table settings & lack of pretence lend a welcome air of informality to proceedings, while the mining-themed artwork rounds things off in style. Note that the restaurant is only open 2 days a week & with limited opening times; it's also closed during school holidays, so you'll have to be on your game to bag a table. **££**

WHAT TO SEE AND DO
Rhondda Heritage Park and the Welsh Coalmining Experience (Coed

Cae Rd; ☎01443 682036; w rctcbc.gov.uk; ⏰ 10.00–15.00 Tue–Sat; free, tour £7.95) Wedged between the road and railway 3 miles west of Pontypridd in Trehafod, not far from the entrance to the Rhondda Valley, is the site of the old Lewis Merthyr Colliery, now the Rhondda Heritage Park and the Welsh Coalmining Experience. The colliery was established in the mid 1870s by W T Lewis (later Lord Merthyr) after an amalgamation of the Coedcae and Hafod collieries, which had originally been sunk in 1850. With Lewis's money, the colliery grew to become one of the most productive and wealthiest in the area, at its peak producing 20,000 tonnes of coal per week and employing more than 5,000 men. The colliery merged with Tymawr in 1958 before both closed in 1983, a year before the miners' strike. Its headframes, alongside two engine houses (named Bertie and Trefor after Lewis's two sons), the chimney stack, two fan houses and a lamproom make this the most complete group of colliery buildings anywhere in Wales.

Within the absorbing **Black Gold exhibition** is all kinds of fascinating memorabilia, including all the requisite bits of equipment (mandrels, lamps, wedges, curling boxes). Among the more sobering exhibits is a pocket watch belonging to Gildas Jones, one of the nine men killed in the 1956 disaster here, a Dead Man's Bath

BLACK GOLD

Coal beds were laid down as long as 350 million years ago in a geological age known as the Carboniferous period – which simply translates as 'coal-bearing' (from the Latin carbo (coal) and fero (bear or carry) – and South Wales was replete with them. There were essentially three types of coalfield within the Valleys: bituminous or household coal in the south and east, steam coal in the centre, and anthracite in the west. The other two great Welsh coalfields were in the northeast and Anglesey. Although coal was a popular source of fuel during Roman times, when it was burned in heath and fireplaces, it wasn't until the 18th century that it started to be properly exploited when technological advancements saw the replacement of watermills, windmills and horses in favour of steam-powered automation. Then came the Industrial Revolution.

Death was part of the fabric of life in the early days of the pits. The biggest danger – and which made working the coalmines more perilous than any other industry – was the presence of methane, the cause of so many explosions and a never-ending catalogue of death and injury. On top of this, miners had to contend with fatal roof-falls, flash floods, runaway coal wagons and faulty lift mechanisms. The first incident to take more than 100 lives occurred in Cymer in the Rhondda Valley in 1856. Two disasters followed a decade later just up the valley in Ferndale: the first, in 1867, claimed 178 lives, and just two years later another resulted in 53 deaths – and on it went. The greatest loss of life came at the Universal Colliery in Senghenydd in 1913 when 440 men were killed (page 195).

Nationalisation of the coal industry in 1947 (under the National Coal Board) led to an immediate improvement in working conditions, both in terms of advanced mechanisation, such as the introduction of hydraulic chocks (by the end of the 1960s all coal was cut by machine as opposed to by hand), and better pay. The work, however, remained incredibly dangerous, as the disasters at Six Bells in Abertillery in 1960, when 45 men were killed, and the Cambrian Colliery in Clydach in 1965, when 31 men died, served to emphasise.

By the 1950s, Britain had become totally reliant on coal for its energy and heating, a situation that proved unsustainable. In 1956, the same year as the Clean Air Act was introduced in response to London's great smog that killed 4,000 people, coal use peaked at 210 million tonnes. That same year, the world's first

– no prizes for guessing what that was for – and many informative wall panels recalling all the disasters in the Rhondda mines. There are some poignant photos too, including men working the last shifts at the mine in 1983.

To look around the site, and view the Black Gold exhibition, is free, but the **guided tour** is what really makes a visit here worthwhile. These are led by former miners who interweave lots of fascinating factual stuff (and a few mannequin tableaux thrown in for good measure) with tales of what life was like working underground. The tour begins with an overview of the site, including a visit inside the magnificent engine winding houses whose titanic wheels would raise up to 1,000 tonnes of coal a day; still in perfect working order, one of these is usually cranked into action. Suitably helmeted, you then step inside one of the cages (back in the day these would drop at a rate of 30ft a second) and descend to an unknown depth before a walk through a series of manmade tunnels, which had to be constantly reinforced owing to the pressure bearing down on them; you'll then get to experience a boom of a simulated explosion. The tour concludes civil nuclear programme was developed at Windscale, Cumbria, and then came the electrification of the railways in the late 1960s. Strikes in 1972 and 1974 were harbingers of what was to come. In 1984, the proposed closure of Cortonwood Colliery in South Yorkshire prompted a strike that would last two days' shy of one whole year. During that period, there were repeated clashes between the police and miners, while the minority (around 6%) who did go back to work ('scabs' as they were labelled), were ostracised; the social and economic effects on communities were profound. With Margaret Thatcher unrepentant and funds dwindling, the defiantly left-wing and militant National Union of Mineworkers (NUM) was eventually defeated, and with that came widespread colliery closures, not just in South Wales but across Britain (before the industry was privatised in 1994), though the reality is that many mines had already closed by the time of the strike.

During the strike, the miners received support from an unlikely source, in the form of the gay community (LGB as it was known then), with activists from London rallying and forming a dedicated LGSM (Lesbians and Gays Support the Miners) group. Together they worked raising funds and joining marches, events memorably portrayed in the 2014 film *Pride*.

For the first time, the strike also shone a light on the role of miners' wives, who were as prominent on the picket line as they were busy organising soup kitchens. Interestingly, women were forbidden to work underground following the 1842 Mines Act, though that didn't stop some, who managed to circumvent this by dressing up as men. Few, if any, households at that time could afford to have just one member of the family earning. Otherwise, women were heavily involved in clerical, medical and other work within the industry, notwithstanding the fact they were also tasked with doing all the cooking, cleaning and washing at home; in fact, more women died of tuberculosis or overwork than men.

The mining industry left in its wake a catastrophic human toll, not just in the many lives lost, but also in terms of pollution and disease: asthma, cancer, heart and lung ailments were just some of the devastating effects – emphysema and 'Black Spit' (or 'Black Lung') were particularly nasty perils which claimed the lives of many men by their forties.

with a virtual ride in a dram, the name given to the small trucks used to transport coal through the mines.

RHONDDA FACH Nowhere was the closure of the mines felt more keenly than in the Rhondda Fach, whose poor transport links (there's no railway line) have long contributed to a feeling of isolation among the communities here. Amenities and jobs remain scarce, which, to some extent, is reflected in some of the lowest property prices in Britain, while those who do have jobs have to make the daily commute down the valley to Pontypridd or Cardiff, or even further afield to Bristol.

With its long rows of stone cottages, **Ferndale**, whose first pit was sunk in 1857, is one such village, though efforts have been made to knit the community together. One such initiative is the **Arts Factory** (w artsfactory.co.uk), an environmental graphic and design business that also offers well-being groups as well as classes in art, dance and other activities. Naturally it also has its own male voice choir, the **Côr Meibion Morlais**.

A couple of miles up the road, **Maerdy** was the very last working pit in the Rhondda coalfield to close, in 1990. During the inter-war years, the village was renowned, and indeed feared by politicians, for its militant tendencies, earning it the moniker 'Little Moscow' – which also goes a long way to explaining the prominent role Maerdy's miners and their wives played during the 1984 miners' strike. At the foot of the mountain road as you enter the village from the north (and just south of the old colliery) is the **Maerdy Gateway Memorial and Garden**, represented by a dram of coal and a pithead wheel embedded in the bankside surrounded by stones from the now-demolished workmen's hall; the statue of a miner embracing his family is a nice touch. Heading north back out of the village, the A4233 road continues to Aberdare, 5 miles distant.

RHONDDA FAWR Unlike the Rhondda Fach, the Rhondda Fawr can count on a railway line to connect its many villages. After **Porth** (meaning 'Gateway') where the Rhondda splits, the first settlement of any real size is **Tonypandy**, which is associated with one of the Valleys' most infamous episodes. During the strike of 1910, with miners protesting against poor pay and living conditions, riots took place in a number of communities across South Wales, but these were particularly acute in Tonypandy where rioters destroyed shops and attacked properties belonging to the pit owners. In response, the then Home Secretary Winston Churchill sent in troops to restore order, a move many commentators deemed excessive; the popular historical myth that troops subsequently fired on protesters has never been proven.

Travelling through Pentre, 3 miles further along the valley, you can't fail to miss the roadside **St Peter's Church**, optimistically called the Cathedral of the Rhondda. Pentre was also the birthplace of Jimmy Murphy (1910–89), the legendary Manchester United coach who was instrumental in nurturing the feted Busby Babes team of the 1950s, many of whom were subsequently killed in the Munich air crash of 6 February 1958 – a flight that Murphy was also due to have taken. A blue plaque (one of several in the Rhondda commemorating celebrated local figures) at his childhood home, 43 Treharne Street, a 5-minute walk from the church on the other side of the A4058, remembers him.

The next village along is **Treorchy**, whose internationally renowned choir remains by far its biggest draw (see opposite). Like the old miners' institute in Blackwood (page 187), the old and very grand Parc and Dare Hall on Station Road has been converted into an entertainment venue, now called the **Parc and Dare Theatre** (w rct-theatres.co.uk). Dating from 1892 it was originally just a library and bar, before a theatre was appended in 1913 and a cinema a few years after that. It offers a varied diet of film, music, theatre and comedy among other art forms.

From Treorchy the train line continues the short distance to its last stop at **Treherbert**, from where the road straggles onwards and upwards to **Blaencwm**, and beyond to **Blaenrhondda**, where the Rhondda officially ends. Ambitious plans are afoot to reopen the **Rhondda Tunnel**, which originally linked Blaencwm in the Rhondda and Blaengwynfi in the Afan Valley – which is otherwise an 11-mile road journey via Treorchy and Bwlch Mountain, wonderful in summer but often treacherous in winter. Driven in the late 1880s, the tunnel was used continuously until its closure, on safety grounds, in 1968, and then buried a decade later. Currently doing its best to get things moving is the **Rhondda Tunnel Society** (w rhonddatunnelsociety.co.uk), who have committed to turning this into a mini tourist hub, complete with café, visitor centre and bike hire – should they pull it off, the economic boost to the area would be immeasurable. Exploratory investigations

Not for nothing is Wales known as the land of song, and for this it can thank its wonderful male voice choirs. Choirs are present in communities right across the country, but it is here in South Wales where the tradition is strongest, and the voices loudest it seems. This cornerstone of Welsh musical culture has its roots going back to the time of the monastic choirs, but the tradition of Côr Meibion (the male voice choir in Welsh) as we recognise it today emerged in the late 19th century as a result of the Industrial Revolution, which brought miners, steelworkers and quarrymen together in large numbers.

The chapel was typically the focal point for these musical gatherings, ostensibly because they were the only venues capable of accommodating such large numbers, notwithstanding the fact that the prevailing temperance movement precluded meeting in pubs. Touring was popular too, even back then, with the United States a popular destination owing to its large Welsh immigrant communities.

While not as prevalent as they once were – ageing congregations and fewer singers to replace them, plus a scarcity of funding, are all contributory factors – most Valleys' towns are still home to a choral ensemble of some description. Perhaps the most famous, and certainly the oldest, is the **Treorchy Male Voice Choir** (w treorchymalechoir.com), who were formed in 1883 and still tour, both in Britain and occasionally further afield. Like most choirs they have a staple repertoire, which typically includes *Cwm Rhondda*, *Sosban Fach* (*Little Saucepan*) and the rousing *Hen Wlad Fy Nhadau* (*Land of my Fathers*), the de facto national anthem.

Given half a chance, you shouldn't pass up the opportunity to see a choir in action. Your best bet is to check each choir's website, which should have up-to-date listings of performances, but otherwise it is usually possible to catch a rehearsal. The Treorchy choir have rehearsals at Treorchy Primary School at 19.00 on Mondays and Thursdays, while the Côr Meibion Pontypridd (w malechoir.com) meets for rehearsals in the Tabor Hall on Vaughan Street at 19.30 on Sundays; however, do call ahead and check first.

have determined that the existing structure is in pretty good condition, despite inevitable defects and some water ingress after all these years. If it is completed, it will be the longest walking and cycling tunnel in Europe – trumping the mile-long (1,672m) Combe Down Tunnel in Bath, which reopened in 2013 – and the second longest in the world after the 2½-mile-long Snoqualmie Tunnel near Seattle.

NORTH OF THE RHONDDA Beyond Blaenrhondda/Treherbert, the road leaves the Rhondda and snakes up and over a fabulous mountain pass towards the **Rhigos Viewpoint**, 10 miles distant. If the weather's playing ball, it's a great spot to stop for lunch while soaking up the views of the Valleys and Brecon Beacons.

About 3 miles and a couple of hairpin bends further on, you'll arrive at **Zip World Tower** (Rhigos, Hirwaun; ☏01685 706666; w zipworld.co.uk; ⏰ 09.00–16.30 Tue–Sat; Phoenix Zipline £50 for 2 zips; Tower Coaster £25 for 3 rides; Tower Flyer £15 for 3 zips), the fourth of the Zip World sites to open (in 2021) but the only one in South Wales; the rest are all in Snowdonia. Thrill-seekers will love it, with a choice of three activities to get those juices pumping: Phoenix, which purports to be the fastest seated zipline in the world, up to 70mph; Tower Coaster, an industrial-style kart that races along a 0.6-mile length of track; and Tower Flyer, a more sedate zipline for those not tempted by Phoenix.

Zip World Tower is located on the site of the old Tower Colliery, the oldest continuously working deep coalmine in the UK. It was originally closed by British Coal in 1994 but then almost immediately bought out by a co-operative of local miners who resumed operations until a second and final closure in 2008. It's certainly one of the more novel ways a decommissioned colliery has been put to good use.

✕ Where to eat and drink

✕ **Cegin Glo** Zip World Tower; 📞 01865 706666; w zipworld.co.uk/cegin-glo; ⏱ 09.00–17.00 Mon, Tue & Fri–Sun. After all that activity you're going to want to refuel, in which case make a beeline for Zip World's on-site bar & bistro, Cegin Glo, pronounced 'Keg-in Glorr', which translates as 'Coal Kitchen'. The food is simple but beautifully cooked classic Welsh dishes like cawl & Welsh rarebit, plus fish & chips, burgers & the like – for anyone looking to go large try the Phoenix Burger, a substantial lamb patty with minted raita in a charcoal bun. The floor-to-ceiling windows permit unencumbered views across to the Rhigos Mountains & the zip line itself. £

Dare Valley Country Park Lying within the shadow of the cupped peaks of the Brecon Beacons, one of the best-kept secrets in the Valleys is Dare Valley Country Park, the first country park in Wales and the first to be designated as such on reclaimed land. Extending all the way up a glacial valley called the Darren, the 500-acre park – a sylvan mix of open land, meadows, cliffs and pockets of woodland – occupies the site of two collieries, the only reminders of which are a couple of modest spoil heaps. Mining here in the Dare Valley was once a serious proposition, and at its peak there were 19 pits here. Since being cleared, nature has reasserted itself in spectacular fashion: nothing has been planted, but instead has been left completely to its own devices.

During spring and summer, bird activity in the park is fantastic, and to this end there are a couple of viewing platforms, brilliantly positioned so that you can view the treetops at eye level and observe willow warblers, black caps and chiffchaffs, as well as peregrine falcons, who are drawn to the inaccessible ledges and open terrain, ideal for catching prey. Rarer is the ring ouzel (the park emblem), although this migrant bird may occasionally be glimpsed feeding on berries en route back to Africa for the winter. You may also see lizards basking on grassy tumps. A small chain of lakes sees abundant moorhen, coots and grebes, and if you're really lucky, the occasional kingfisher stalking prey in the water.

This is also ideal walking country, with three waymarked trails, ranging from 2 to 4 miles, mapped out for visitors to explore the park. Information can be obtained from the **visitor centre** where the Black Rock Café rustles up good lunches. Alternatively, grab a hot drink and make your way over to the adventure playground where you can let the kids off the leash.

An exciting new addition to Dare Valley is **Gravity Bike Park** (📞01594 729007; w darevalleygravity.co.uk; ⏱ 09.30–12.30 & 13.30–16.30 Mon & Wed–Sun, also 17.00–20.00 late-night Fri; £13 per session, £12 late-night Fri). A short walk from the visitor centre, it may be small in size – there are currently just a couple of blue flow runs – but it's an absolute belter with split-track options and mini pump-track loops for added variety. The runs take in a mixture of forest and open countryside with stunning views of Cwm Dare most of the way.

The uplift service shuttles up and down the mountain at the times shown above. Note that the driver stops for lunch at 12.30 for an hour, and while you can walk to the top, it's a long haul, even without a bike, so you'd do well to take your break at the same time (assuming you are booked in all day). Otherwise, passes are sold for either a morning or an afternoon session, with a maximum of four runs permitted per session. Gravity is more family-oriented (and far less busy) than other bike parks, so will be of little interest to more advanced riders. You're welcome to bring your own bike, but both adult and children's bikes can be hired (£15–20), and there's a workshop should you need any repairs.

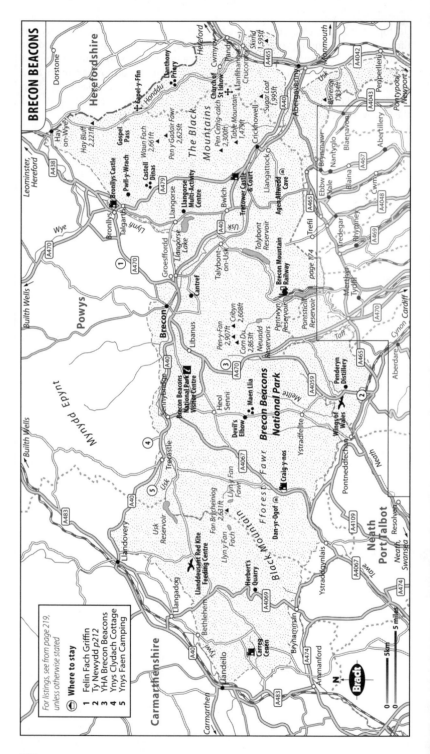

For listings, see from page 219,
unless otherwise stated

Where to stay

1 Felin Fach Griffin
2 Ty Newydd *p212*
3 YHA Brecon Beacons
4 Ynys Clydach Cottage
5 Ynys Faen Camping

Herefordshire

Dorstone

Hay
on-Wye

Hay Bluff
2,221ft

Gospel
Pass

Capel-y-Ffin

Llanthony
Priory

Cwmyoy

Skirrid
1,595ft

Pandy

Pen Cerrig-calch St Ishow
2,300ft

Waun Fach
2,661ft

Pen y Gadair Fawr
2,625ft

Church of
St Ishow

Llanfihangel
Crucorney

The Black

Mountains

Table Mountain
1,479ft

Sugar Loaf
1,995ft

Crickhowell

Abergavenny

Usk

Monmouth

Penperlleni,
Newport

Pontypool

Abertillery

Blaenavon

Brynmawr

Nantyglo

Leominster,
Hereford

Bronllys Castle

Pwll-y-Wrach

Castell
Dinas

Langorse
Multi-Activity
Centre

Bwlch

Tretower Castle
& Court

Llangattock

Agen Allwedd
Cave

Trefil

Ebbw
Vale

Blaina

Cwm

Brynmawr
934ft

Wye

Bronllys

Talgarth

Llyn Syfaddan

Llangorse

Langorse
Lake

Groesffordd

Cantref

Talybont-
on-Usk

Usk

Talybont
Reservoir

Brecon Mountain
Railway

page 174

Pontsticill
Reservoir

Merthyr
Tydfil

Tredegar

Rhymney

Powys

Builth Wells

Brecon

Libanus

Brecon Beacons
National Park
Visitor Centre

Heol
Senni

Penyfan
2,907ft

Cribyn
2,608ft

Corn Du
2,863ft

Neuadd
Reservoirs

Pentwyn
Reservoir

Pontsticill
Reservoir

Taff

Penderyn
Distillery

Aberdare

Cynon Cardiff

Mynydd Epynt

Builth Wells

Sennybridge

Maen Llia

Melte

Brecon Beacons

National Park

Devil's
Elbow

Craig-y-nos

Ystradfellte

Wings of
Wales

Pontneddfechan

Neath

A470

A465

A4059

A467

A469

A4048

A4043

A4042

Felin Fach Griffin

Usk

Trecastle

Fan Brycheiniog
2,631ft

Fforest Fawr

Llyn y Fan
Fawr

Llyn y Fan
Fach

Black Mountain

Dan-yr-Ogof

Herbert's
Quarry

Neath

Port Talbot

Neath,
Swansea

Resolven

Pontneddfechan

Usk
Reservoir

Llandovery

Llanddeusant Red Kite
Feeding Centre

Carreg
Cennen

Ystradgynlais

Tawe

Llangadog

Bethlehem

Carmarthen

Llandeilo

Brynamman

Ammanford

Carmarthenshire

A40

A483

A4069

A474

A4109

A4067

A40

A483

N

Bradt

0   5km
0   5 miles

7

Brecon Beacons

The Brecon Beacons is walking country *par excellence* – there are some 163 peaks here – and although in parts as popular as Snowdonia, it is still large enough that you can find your own little corner. For the more adventurous, or those with some time, the 100-mile Beacons Way (page 219) presents the ultimate challenge.

The park ranks the twin peaks of **Pen-y-Fan** and **Corn Du** as its highest – and by extension the loftiest in southern Britain. Both are eminently doable for anyone with a reasonable level of fitness, but during summer walkers home in on these two summits in big numbers, so you may want to divert elsewhere. The forbidding **Black Mountain** area spanning across the western Beacons holds out the promise of fewer signs of life, and while the old quarry scars still remain, this is a tremendous wilderness. As is the neighbouring **Fforest Fawr**, an internationally significant geopark thanks to its outstanding geological structure. These brooding mountains are veined with watercourses, which hurtle south through a limestone porous landscape culminating in a spectacular series of waterfalls between **Ystradfellte** and **Pontnedfecchan**, and cave systems such as those at **Dan-yr-Ogof**.

On the opposite side, bordering England, the **Black Mountains** (an entirely different part of the Beacons to the Black Mountain area in the west, despite the almost identical name) more or less constitute the easternmost third of the national park. For centuries, these thrillingly remote hills have drawn artists and recluses into their solitudinous embrace. The highlight here is the memorably lush **Vale of Ewyas**, whose remote confines are a wonderful antidote to the stresses and strains of modern life. The valley is home to a trio of unique churches: the resonant priory ruins at Llanthony and the singularly hard-to-reach churches at **Cwmyoy** and **Partrishow**. From here, it's an awesome drive over the **Gospel Pass** towards Hay Bluff, which stands sentinel over the book-besotted town of **Hay**, itself with one foot almost in England.

Here too within the bosom of the Black Mountains are its two most popular, and populous, towns: food-obsessed **Abergavenny**, and just up the road, smaller and fiercely independent **Crickhowell**, whose terrific spread of festivals make it an appealing proposition. Both Abergavenny and Crickhowell are perfect bases from which to head off into the mountains: Crickhowell for walks up to Table Mountain and the immense limestone wall at Llangattock, and Abergavenny for assaults on three of the park's most iconic peaks: Sugar Loaf, Skirrid and Blorenge. Nearby **Talgarth** is similarly well placed for mountain exploration, while **Llangorse Lake** – the largest natural body of water in South Wales – offers some respite from the hills with lots of watery distractions.

GETTING THERE AND AROUND

BY CAR The main road through the national park is the north–south A470, which spears through the heart of the Beacons between Brecon town and Merthyr Tydfil,

Brecon Beacons   GETTING THERE AND AROUND

though this is by no means the most spectacular of the park's roads (page 41). The fast A40 from Abergavenny runs up the park's western flank before curling around to Brecon and then looping back down along the eastern flank en route to Carmarthen.

BY TRAIN Of the places in this chapter, only Abergavenny has a train station, from where you can transfer to a bus to Brecon and Crickhowell. Otherwise, the Heart of Wales line skirts the park's western boundary, with stations at Ammanford, Llandeilo and Landovery, from where you could get a bus to Brecon town.

BY BUS In the absence of trains, you'll be heavily reliant on buses in this region. The main routes are #43 from Abergavenny to Brecon via Crickhowell; #39 from Brecon to Talgarth and Hay-on-Wye; and the #T6 from Brecon to Swansea.

BY BIKE Of course, the most eco-friendly way of travelling is by bike, and the Brecon Beacons are ready-made for cyclists of all persuasions, whether that's easy road cycling or tougher mountain-bike trails. There are some excellent-bike hire companies in the Brecons, including **Bikes & Hikes** in Talybont-on-Usk (page 227) and **Drover Cycles** in Hay (page 243).

THE WESTERN BEACONS

Bleaker and wilder than any other area of the Brecon Beacons, the untamed western Beacons can be classified as having two distinct parts, namely the Black Mountain, not to be confused with the easterly Black Mountains (ie: plural) range, and Fforest Fawr, roughly somewhere between the Black Mountain and the central Beacons. Few visitors take to the higher, more hostile interior of the western Beacons, preferring instead to stick to the beauty spots and attractions clustered in and around the southern fringes, like the Mellte and Pontneddfechan waterfalls and the caves at Dan-yr-Ogof.

 WHERE TO STAY, EAT AND DRINK *Map, page 210*

Ty Newydd (28 rooms) Penderyn Rd, Hirwaun; 01685 813433; w tynewyddhotel. co.uk. Once a farmhouse, this vaguely grand 1930s country house hotel is not far from the southern entrance to Penderyn village. The rooms – a good mix of dbls, twins & sgls – are perfectly fine, & some have lovely garden views, though could use a bit of tidying up around the edges. There's a decent restaurant to boot, which is just as well because there's nothing much else close by. **££**

BLACK MOUNTAIN Contrary to its name, the Black Mountain (Mynydd Du) is not a singular peak but instead the name given to an area of mountains roughly spread between Ammanford in the southwest and Sennybridge in the north. Geologically, the greater part of the range comprises old red sandstone, essentially an extension of the same rock that makes up neighbouring Fforest Fawr, its most striking features being the twin glacial lakes of **Llyn y Fan Fach** ('Lake of the Small Peak') and **Llyn y Fan Fawr** ('Lake of the Big Peak'), not far from which is its highest peak, **Fan Brycheiniog**, topping out at an impressive 2,631ft.

The Black Mountain's inaccessibility means that it receives relatively few visitors, certainly compared with much of the rest of the Brecon Beacons, and therein lies much of its appeal. This elusive, untamed mountainous area also provides some of the most challenging walks in the national park, as well as some exceptional bike rides and drives, but whichever your preferred mode of transport, you'll barely meet another soul here.

The main A4069 road through the Black Mountain is superb. From Llangadog, roughly midway between Llandeilo and Llandovery, the road snakes its way up to a couple of fantastic switchbacks (Tro Tir-y-Gat and Pant-y-drefnewydd), before arriving at **Herbert's Quarry**. This part of the Black Mountain was once an area of heavy quarrying, the limestone here extracted before being burnt in kilns to produce lime (calch) for use as agricultural fertiliser, as well as in the building trade (for plaster and mortar), and as an ingredient in the production of iron in the Valleys. By the 1870s the lime trade was on the wane, owing to a combination of factors: a depressed agricultural industry; the availability of cheaper alternatives to lime, especially from South America; and the rising cost of coal required to fuel the kilns. By the beginning of the 20th century, many of the kilns here were redundant, but the quarry struggled on, finally closing in 1958.

Cut into the hillsides, the kilns here mostly date from the early 19th century, with the oldest (partially collapsed) ones at the bottom and the more 'modern' ones higher up. Towards the top of one of the kilns is the leftover of one of the workers' huts, where they would work during the lime-making season. Helping to make some sense of it all is a dedicated quarry walk, which starts from either of the two car parks, with audios and interpretation panels along the way; it's around 4 miles so can be done in a leisurely couple of hours. The Beacons Way (page 219) passes directly through the quarry.

Dropping down into **Brynamman**, don't be fooled by the presence of the **Black Mountain Centre**. While they do stock some limited material, this is a community centre and not really given to assisting tourists. Heading in the other direction (ie: south–north), there's another sensational drive/bike ride starting in **Ammanford**, 5 miles west of Brynamman. Northeast of town, head up Wern Ddu for a few hundred yards, then turn right along Heol Ddu, which continues into the hills. Away to your left are magnificent views of Carreg Cennen (page 268) atop its limestone crag. Carry on along this road and you'll eventually join the A4069.

Just to the north of the Black Mountain escarpment is the **Usk Reservoir**, one of the least-visited parts of the entire national park, which is a little surprising as it's fairly easily reached and offers a terrific walk around its mostly wooded perimeter. Built in 1955 with materials quarried in the Black Mountain itself, the reservoir, through which the River Usk passes on its journey down through the mountains before emptying in the Severn Estuary, is regarded as one of the best still-water trout fisheries in the country. Day tickets (£22) can be bought from the bank and there's parking a short way along from the dam, while in summer there's usually a little hut here for refreshments.

Llanddeusant Red Kite Feeding Centre (w redkiteswales.co.uk; ⊕ Thu–Sun,
school hols daily (closed Jan); £6) It's not nearly as well known as Wales's larger kite-feeding centres in Rhayader and Bwlch-y-Nant, but this red kite feeding centre is nevertheless a great opportunity to see these charismatic birds up close. Once protected by royal decree, red kites (*Milvus milvus*) were hunted to death in the 19th century. The kite was left on the brink of extinction after being branded as vermin and erroneously charged as livestock killers, alongside incidents of poisoning (from gunshot pellets in the carrion they would scavenge) and the widespread theft of their eggs. A sustained conservation effort, which included more sophisticated nest-protection initiatives, has not only ensured their survival but has also seen numbers increase exponentially, so that there are now thought to be around 600 breeding pairs in Wales alone, which has traditionally been a stronghold for the bird. Each day at 15.00 (14.00 in winter), anywhere between 50 and 100 birds

(buzzards and ravens like to muscle in on the action) converge here in a frenzied scrap for food. With their magnificent 6ft wingspans and mermaid-like splay tails, they are a beautiful sight in flight. If coming by car, you should park at the Cross Inn pub, from where it's a short walk to the feeding station.

FFOREST FAWR (✆ 01874 620415; w fforestfawrgeopark.org.uk) A member of the European Geoparks Network and the UNESCO Global Network since 2005, Fforest Fawr translates as 'Great Forest', which is actually a bit of a misnomer because there's hardly any forest here at all. Instead, this 300-square-mile area of moorland between the Black Mountain and the central Beacons takes its name from when it was used as a royal hunting ground. Broadly speaking, Fforest Fawr is bounded to the east by the A470, which darts north–south between Brecon and Merthyr Tydfil, and to the west by the A4067 Sennybridge to Ystradgynlais road. One of just two geoparks in Wales (the other is GeoMôn in Anglesey), and eight in total in the UK, Fforest Fawr is a landscape some 500 million years in the making, from the Ordovician and Silurian rocks, the oldest, through to the red sandstone of the Devonian (400 million years) and Carboniferous limestone (350 million years) rocks, which are the two main materials that comprise this immediate landscape. The southern edge of the park gives way to the Coal Measures, whose seams were once at the heart of the Industrial Revolution.

In May, the excellent two-week **GeoFest** gives visitors the opportunity to explore the area under the expert guidance of park officers. The festival programme includes a number of circular walks as well as talks that take place throughout the park; most events are free.

Maen Llia and Ystradfellte
While both the A470 and A4067 roads are scenic – and are useful if you need to get a move on – neither can compare to the unclassified road that splits the pair of them. With time on your side, and good weather too, this is as good a drive or cycle as anywhere in South Wales. The best approach is from the National Park Visitor Centre in Libanus (page 218). From here, it's 5 miles southwest to the hamlet of **Heol Senni**, whereupon a narrow mountain road climbs up the **Devil's Elbow**, a thrilling switchback that climbs nearly 600ft in just over a mile. Cyclists love it, and the views back down the valley from whence you've just come are simply glorious.

Continuing south, the landscape begins to plateau, and on your left (don't go too fast or you'll miss it), all by itself, is **Maen Llia**. Of all the Beacons' many standing stones, this diamond-shaped, red sandstone beauty, some 13ft high, is the finest, and the most mysterious. Thought to date from around 4000BC, it was possibly a marker stone (or it could have been – no-one knows for sure); whatever the reason for its existence, there's certainly no denying Maen Llia's powerful primeval presence – and of course where there's a stone, there's a legend. Of Maen Llia, it's said that on Midsummer's Eve, she heads down to the nearby Mellte River to drink. You can park by the side of the road and hop over the stile to view it up close.

Beyond Maen Llia, the road drops down in the valley of the Afon Llia, and the hitherto predominant sandstone rocks begin to yield to huge belts of limestone, resulting in the spectacular grouping of caves and waterfalls around the village of **Ystradfellte**, itself useful as a base and for picking up provisions.

Four Falls Trail and the Pontneddfechan Waterfalls
From Ystradfellte, it's 2 miles south to both the Gwaun Hepste and Cwm Porth car parks and the waymarked 4½-mile-long **Four Falls Trail**, a walk that should take around 3 hours there and back. Note that, for obvious reasons, it does get very wet along the trail,

so do wear sturdy footwear and mind your step. The first of the falls is **Sgwd Clun-Gwyn** (White Meadow Fall), where the Mellte crashes some 50ft over a pair of oblique rocks before hurtling down towards **Sgwd Isaf Clun-Gwyn** (Lower White Meadow Fall) and the more powerful **Sgwd y Pannwr** (Fall of the Fuller). Beyond, at the confluence of the Mellte and Hepste rivers, lies the **Sgwd yr Eira** (Fall of the Snow), the best of the lot owing to the fact that you can walk around, or behind, the waterfall; you can bathe here too.

Another quartet of picturesque waterfalls await near the village of **Pontneddfechan**, 4½ miles south of Ystradfellte. Note that the Waterfall Centre, which still appears in some maps and books, closed some time ago, but the trails are well marked. If you want to see all four falls (officially called the Elidir Trail), it's roughly a 5-mile round trip north from the village up to the Pont Melin-Fach car park. Up first is the **Sgwd Gwladus** (Lady Falls) an easy-ish mile or so along the verdurous River Nedd Valley. The overhang is big enough here to allow you to walk behind the crashing curtain of water, which is great fun. If you're with younger kids, then this might be enough as you've still got to walk back (so count on a round trip of about 45 minutes). Otherwise, retrace your steps to the main path, bear left and carry on a short while to **Sgwd y Bedol** (Horseshoe Falls), alas nothing quite like those in Canada but very pretty all the same. Continuing on you'll come to the twin falls of **Sgwd Ddwili Isaf** (Lower Gushing Falls) and **Sgwd Ddwili Uchaf** (Upper Gushing Falls), which, as their names suggest, generate huge volumes of water, especially after heavy rainfall. In theory, you could carry on walking from here to the Four Falls Trail.

Penderyn Distillery

Penderyn Distillery (☎ 01685 810650; w penderyn.wales; ⏲ 09.30–17.00 daily (summer to 18.00); tours £12.50) Wales not only had a once-thriving distilling industry itself, but played a major part in the fortunes of the whisky business elsewhere. Jack Daniel's was created by an American of Welsh-born parents, while another stateside bourbon, Evan Williams, was launched by a Pembrokeshire family who emigrated there in the 18th century. However, the emergence of Methodist chapels throughout Wales in the 18th century, and the corresponding growth of the temperance movement, effectively signalled the end of the distilling industry in Wales, unlike in Scotland and Ireland where ministers and priests were demonstrably more accommodating when it came to the consumption of alcohol.

So when the first malts in Wales for more than a century rolled off the line at the Penderyn Distillery in 2004, it was quite some cause for celebration. The location itself was chosen for its abundant springs, one of which the distillery sits on and is used to marry the whisky spirit. Uniquely, the distillation process here at Penderyn is done just once – unlike in Scotland where it is twice and in Ireland where it is thrice – thanks to a revolutionary copper pot still invented by a descendant of the celebrated scientist Michael Faraday. The whiskies are then finished off in different cask types, including sherry, port and Madeira, and there's a peaty version, which is cultivated using barrels from Islay. Forty-five-minute tours of the site begin with a short film explaining the history of Penderyn, before you are taken into the distilling area to view the mash tun, washbacks and the beautiful Faraday-designed copper stills. Previously it had been possible to view the bottling plant and warehouse, but both those processes now take place elsewhere. The tour concludes in customary fashion with a couple of tastings, before exiting into the shop, where you will have the opportunity to make a purchase or two.

Wings of Wales

Wings of Wales (☎ 07800 986673; w wingsofwales.com; tours from £120) Originally from London, Lewis Phillips (the self-styled 'Cockney Conservationist') established his own falconry near Penderyn in 2015 and now has around a dozen birds of prey under his charge, among them a white-tailed (sea) eagle, bald eagle, harris hawk and several owls. His real passion, however, is vultures, and to this end Lewis has made it a very personal mission to help save this declining breed. It is estimated that, globally, only around 9,500 vultures remain in the wild, with 14 of the 22 species threatened with extinction..

Lewis offers a range of half- and full-day excursions into the nearby hills (the Neath Disturbance) with one or more of the birds, some of which involve handling and flights to the glove, though the most popular outing is with Harry the vulture. Born in the Netherlands (his parents are in Moscow Zoo), Harry is a Rüppell's vulture, an interior-organ-eating bird found mainly in East Africa but which is currently critically endangered. Factors attributed to its alarming decline include poisoning, human use for medicine or meat, and loss of nesting sites and potential food sources. For most experiences, you'll meet Lewis at the Ty Newydd hotel (page 212) then head up to nearby Pantcefnfforrd Farm where you'll meet the birds and head out into the hills. A reasonable level of fitness is required – especially if you are out for the whole day – as there might be some considerable walking including some steep inclines.

Dan-yr-Ogof Showcaves (Brecon Rd, Pen-y-Cae; ✆01639 730284; w showcaves. co.uk; ⊕ Apr–Oct 10.00–17.00 daily (last entry 15.00); £17.50) By the standard of most cave discoveries, those here at Dan-yr-Ogof were quite late. In August 1912, two local farmers, Jeff and Tommy Morgan, set out to find the source of the River Llynfell but instead they managed to track the water back to a labyrinth of caves. Their curiosity piqued, they returned with boats and managed to push on past four lakes before they could go no further – but that was enough and it wasn't long before they started charging curious tourists to see these mysterious chambers. The caves were officially opened to tourists in 1939, just weeks before the outbreak of World War II, but that didn't stop them from serving a purpose. As was the case with many a cave system during the war, those here at Dan-yr-Ogof were put to good use as a storage facility for priceless works of art from Cardiff and Swansea. There was then a prolonged hiatus before the caves reopened in 1960, which was about the time that a local girl, Eileen Davies, chanced upon several more miles' worth of chambers.

Despite all feeling a little contrived, there's no disguising the natural splendour of the caves themselves, which you visit on a self-guided tour and with audio commentary – courtesy of the Morgan brothers themselves – emanating from wall-bound speakers. Although the total extent of the caves so far explored is around ten miles, you get to see around a mile on a loop. It's all well lit, spacious, fairly flat and dry, and there are three caves in all to explore.

First up is the **Dan-yr-Ogof Cave**, reputedly the longest showcave in Britain, though no doubt others would argue their case. Either way, it's an enjoyable trek through a series of tunnels, chambers and passages framed by weird and wonderfully shaped stalactites (hanging down) and stalagmites (pointing up). Look out, too, for some of the more unusual individual features, like 'curtains' – transparent, gossamer-thin formations perched at precarious angles, a phenomenon caused by water running off the ceiling.

Back outside, beyond the roaring dinosaurs and recreated Iron-Age village, you enter the **Cathedral Cave**, much broader than its predecessor and with a series of chambers culminating in a vast 150ft-long, 70ft-high cavern complete with son et lumière show. Lastly, and slightly more awkward to reach via a steep path up behind

Dino Park, there's the **Bone Cave**, so-called owing to the discovery of the remains of more than 40 Bronze-Age human skeletons, and lots of animals; the mannequins are a bit daft, though. As well as the caves, there is the aforementioned dinosaur park (which is as tacky as it sounds but the kids will love it), the replica Iron-Age farm, a shire horse centre, Victorian farm and play area – in short enough to detain you for the best part of 3 or 4 hours.

Craig-y-nos Castle and Country Park (Brecon Rd, Pen-y-Cae; ☎01639 731167; w craigynoscastle.com; ☉ open access; free, tours £10) Less than a mile south of the caves is the spiky shape of the 19th-century Craig-y-nos Castle (roughly translating as 'Rock of the Night'), originally a small folly built by the High Sheriff of Brecknock, Captain Rice Davies Powell, but which was extended in 1878 for the pre-eminent Italian-American opera singer Adelina Patti. Born in Madrid of Italian parents, Patti's fame was assured when, just aged 19, she sang for Abraham Lincoln in the White House (Verdi was a huge fan too), and it wasn't long before she was a Royal Opera House regular, able to command fees of up to £1,000, an inordinate amount in those days of course. To the house she added central heating, a chapel, a theatre seating 150 – which also incorporated a hydraulic lift so it could be converted into a ballroom (literally at the flick of a switch) – and acres of gardens. Patti retired in 1906, though she did sing again at the Royal Albert Hall in 1914, and died in 1919; she is buried in the Père Lachaise Cemetery in Paris. You can see more of her personal effects in the y Gaer museum in Brecon (page 223).

Following Patti's death, the hotel served as a TB hospital, closing in 1980 before years of careless development and neglect left it in a bit of a state. Bought out in the 1990s, it was originally a hostel but was upgraded to a hotel, which is as it is today, though principally one that serves large wedding parties, and is heavily marketed as such. Anyone is free to have a nose around the ground-floor rooms (though they'd much rather you came and had lunch), including the exuberant Patti Bar, with fireplace tiles depicting the novels of Sir Walter Scott, and the Grade I-listed theatre itself, but if you wish to see more of the building – including Patti's boudoir and dressing room – tours are scheduled at 10.30 Monday to Friday, although do call ahead to make sure these are running.

Patti employed an army of landscape gardeners to cultivate what is now a **country park** that offers a very pleasant stroll around its extensive 40-acre grounds, with meadows and woodlands either side of the River Tawe.

THE CENTRAL BEACONS

Slightly confusingly, the central Brecon Beacons is the area after which the whole national park is named. Although not approaching the heights of much of Snowdonia, the terrain here is still unmistakeably mountainous, comprising great walls of the same red sandstone that characterises much of the national park and sharp peaks that rise abruptly from the glacially carved landscape.

This is prime Beacons walking territory, and of all the areas within the park, the one where you're likely to meet the greatest number of fellow walkers, most of whom are targeting the twin peaks of **Pen-y-Fan** (2,907ft) and **Corn Du** (2,863ft), South Wales's – in fact southern Britain's – two highest mountains. These summits lie almost immediately due south of **Brecon**, a very likeable small town with a coterie of interesting sites, as well as excellent accommodation and dining, hence why many people choose to use this as the place to base themselves if they're intending to spend any length of time in these mountains.

TOURIST INFORMATION AND ACTIVITIES

ⓘ Brecon Beacons National Park Visitor Centre Libanus; 01874 623366; w breconbeacons. org; ⏱ 09.30–16.30 daily). All the info you need on the park plus maps, guides & other bits & bobs. Gift shop, crafts centre, café & children's play area. There's acres of outdoor seating with tables & benches so bring a picnic. Parking £1/2hrs, £2/4hrs, £3/day; electric charging too. The #T4 bus from Brecon to Merthyr stops in Libanus, but it's a fairly gruelling 30min uphill walk from there to the visitor centre. From the visitor centre take a walk out on to Mynydd Illtyd Common, a wide, open space swathed in heather & bracken that offers 360-degree views of the surrounding peaks.

Brecon Beacons Park Society
w breconbeaconsparksociety.org. Working with the park authorities to protect & conserve the Brecon Beacons, this well-run society also organises walks throughout the park on most weekends (and other

selected days) throughout the year. Walks, which take place all over the park, including in Fforest Fawr & the Black Mountains, are graded from blue (easy) to red (strenuous). Free to members, but otherwise there's a small fee to pay. The excellent online calendar details them all.

A Good Day Out Ynysclydach Farm, 2½ miles northwest of Sennybridge; ☎ 01874 749092; w gooddayout.co.uk; ⏱ noon–22.30 Mon–Sat, noon–16.00 Sun. From her farm just outside Sennybridge, Julia runs what must be the only activity of its kind anywhere, namely dinky-donkey & piggy walks. Leading the 2 miniature Mediterranean donkeys, Maverick & Goose (cool or what?), you head up into the hills through farmland & ancient tracks before stopping for a picnic & then returning. The only difference with the little porkers is that it's a 'pig-nic' of course. Whether you love donkeys & piggies or not (& let's

CLIMBING PEN-Y-FAN AND CORN DU

While it may not come close to the mighty peaks of Snowdonia, **Pen-y-Fan** (2,907ft) is the park's highest mountain, which alone makes it an irresistible pull for the majority of walkers and climbers who visit the Beacons. And given that **Corn Du** (2,863ft), the park's second-highest peak, is so close, an assault on both peaks is normally the done thing.

The easiest and most direct ascent of the two peaks starts from the **Pont ar Daf car park**, half a mile south of the Storey Arms on the A470 (roughly midway between Brecon and Merthyr), from where it's a steady, though not hugely arduous, 5-mile round trip up and around the mountains' southern flanks. Longer, but infinitely more rewarding, is the **'Gap' route** (the old Roman road), an 8-mile circuit (4–5hrs) that starts at the old Victorian **Neuadd reservoirs** southeast of Pen-y-Fan and north of the Pontsticill Reservoir (page 227).

From the car park, head north along the road to the Lower Neuadd reservoir and go through a gate with a Welsh Water sign before cutting down to a bridge on the left. Cross this and go up on to the dam, and then through a gate in the fence. From here, continue west alongside the forestry fence (to your left) then head right (north) along a well-defined path onto the ridge above. Here, on **Graig Fan Ddu**, there are magnificent views west towards the Carmarthen Fan and the Rhigos, and down below, Cwm Crew. Follow the path along the sandstone ridge and, where this ends, descend to the col at Bwlch Duwynt, just shy of the first peak, **Corn Du**. From here it's a short and obvious hike down into the saddle and up to **Pen-y-Fan**. From there, the path descends southeast along **Craig Cwm Sere** before splitting: one path breaks off east up to **Cribyn** – at 2,608ft, the third-highest peak in the Beacons – while the main path continues south. Either way, you'll end up at Bwlch ar y Fan, from where the path continues south through the 'Gap' across Tor Glas and back down to the Neuadd reservoirs.

face it, who doesn't?), this is great fun. Julia also organises sheepdog experiences & hedge-laying courses. Walks cost £35, a portion of which goes to the Brecon Mountain Rescue services.

 WHERE TO STAY, EAT AND DRINK *Map, page 210*

✳ 🏠 **Felin Fach Griffin** (8 rooms) Felinfach, A470, 5 miles northeast of Brecon; ☎ 01874 620111; w eatdrinksleep.ltd.uk. Having garnered plaudits galore in the national press in recent years, the Felin Fach has become one of the most well-known & well-respected restaurants-with-rooms in Wales, & deservedly so. Everything about the place oozes class. Its dbl rooms (some dog-friendly) are categorised according to the size of the bed (smaller, better, good, best) & while some can be noisier than others, depending upon which side of the building you are on, they are all fabulous: handcrafted Welsh blankets, books, wall-bound art & photography, & fresh flowers (& milk) – & no TVs either, just Roberts radios. The Griffin's short, concise menu (which changes daily) is strongly underpinned by ingredients from its vegetable garden, so might feature plates like lamb breast, asparagus & confit tomato, or hake with celeriac, fennel & smoked leek. The nicely put-together Vegetable Patch menu costs £35 for 3 courses. If you fancy just popping in for a pint, you can do that too, & there's plenty of choice with half a dozen local breweries represented, including Wye Valley & Brecon Brewing. Its location next to the busy A40 is a little distracting if you're outside, but that's a minor gripe; in every other sense, the Felin Fach is top drawer. **£££**

🏠 **Ynys Clydach Cottage** 2½ miles northwest of Sennybridge; m 07917 695559; w 2bedcottageinwales.co.uk. You won't find a quieter, more restful spot in all the park (though technically it's just outside the park) to bed down

for a few nights. All the amenities you need are here in this warm & intimate 2-bed stone cottage, with a well-equipped kitchen, slate-floored lounge/diner & inglenook fireplace. Dog-friendly too. **£££**

🏠 **YHA Brecon Beacons** 7 miles southwest of Brecon, near Libanus; ☎ 01874 624261; w yha.org.uk. Unsurprisingly, this is massively popular with walkers & climbers (& groups, so check ahead). A converted 19th-century farmhouse, there's lots of choice of different accommodation here, from hostel rooms themselves (dorms, en-suite dbls) to camping & land pods with heating & lighting (all sleeping 4), & wild camping in the woodland, where fires are permitted. Hearty, home-cooked food & good beer at the bar. Usefully, the #T4 bus from Brecon to Merthyr stops on the road at the top. **£**

🛖 **Ynysfaen Camping** Cwmwysg, 11 miles west of Brecon; ☎ 01874 636436; w campingatynysfaen.co.uk. Out towards Usk Reservoir, this gloriously isolated site offers flat tent & campervan pitches as well as a shepherd's hut (2 adults), glamping bell tent (2 adults) & empty bell tents sleeping 4. Facilities include a unisex shower/toilet block, while fire pits, logs & kindling (£5), plus BBQs with charcoal (£5) can be supplied. Make sure you bring all the supplies you need as there's no shop here, though their chickens will oblige. No cars allowed on site but there are barrows to cart your stuff around, & no larger motor homes or caravans here either. **££**

BRECON AND AROUND A brightly coloured foil to the brooding, chiselled peaks of the Beacons to the south, Brecon is the only town of any significant size in the national park. Within its neat and compact historic core are a couple of terrific museums which are complemented by a sprightly assortment of cafés, pubs and restaurants, a handful of galleries, and a superb theatre, so there's more than enough to detain you for a couple of days at a leisurely pace, whether you intend to use it as a base for forays into the mountains or not

Historically, Brecon has long been a place of some importance ever since **Y Gaer**, an early Roman fort, was established around AD75. The Acts of Union in the 16th century recognised Brecon as the county town of the newly formed Brecknockshire, and with that the headquarters of one of the four circuits of the Court of Great Sessions, which by implication made it one of the capitals of the four 'quarters' of Wales. Although not an industrialised town itself, Brecon's location close to those areas where industrialisation was rapidly expanding, in particular the Valleys, made it an attractive proposition to the new middle classes: the lawyers, bankers and businessmen of the steel and ironworks. Brecon's status was further enhanced in 1800 when it became the first town in Wales to obtain a canal link, a vital element in the growth of its economy. Brecon is Wales's major garrison town, home to the Administrative Headquarters for the Army in Wales (160th Brigade), and with the Sennybridge Army Camp and Training Centre on its doorstep, you'll become accustomed to seeing uniformed officers around town. In 2021, news that the barracks, which the UK government had threatened with closure, were to remain in Brecon was a major lift for the town.

Brecon has one of the more exciting festival scenes in South Wales. Starting in 1984, the **Brecon Jazz Festival** (w breconjazz.org) remains one of the country's most

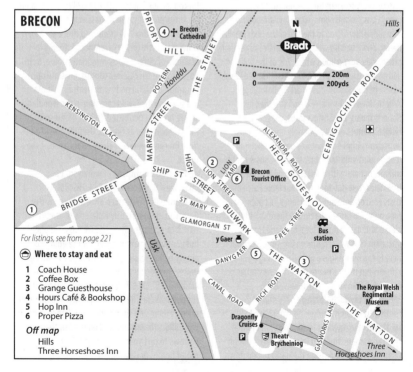

BRECON

For listings, see from page 221

🏠 **Where to stay and eat**

1 Coach House
2 Coffee Box
3 Grange Guesthouse
4 Hours Café & Bookshop
5 Hop Inn
6 Proper Pizza

Off map
Hills
Three Horseshoes Inn

respected music events. Taking place in mid-August, this lively four-day gathering sees some of the biggest names in the business performing venues all over town, including St Mary's Church, the cathedral, and several pubs and bars. Running concurrently is the **Brecon Fringe**, an open-access series of events in pubs, bars, galleries and anywhere else that fancies hosting. There's music of a different genre in October courtesy of the superb **Brecon Baroque Festival** (**w** breconbaroquefestival. com), four days of high-class concerts, featuring international musicians, held in Theatr Brycheiniog and the cathedral.

Getting there and away   Brecon is well connected with several main roads converging on the town: travelling north–south, the A470 cuts through the heart of the Beacons from Brecon down to Merthyr Tydfil, while the A40 from Abergavenny passes directly through town and continues across the northern edge of the Brecon Beacons National Park to Llandovery in the west. Car parking is plentiful, the largest, most convenient spot being Lion Yard car park.

There's no railway here (the nearest station is Abergavenny 22 miles away) so you'll be reliant on buses for public transport, though fortunately connections are good: there are hourly buses to both Crickhowell and Abergavenny as well as half-hourly buses to Cardiff and Hay.

Tourist information

Brecon Tourist Office 11 Lions Yard; 01874 620860; **w** visitbrecon.org; 10.00–16.00 Mon–Sat. Small office but with plentiful supplies of information, both on the town & the national park, including a selection of maps & guidebooks to buy.

Where to stay, eat and drink   *Map, opposite*

Coach House (6 rooms) 12 Orchard St; 01874 620043; **w** coachhousebrecon.com. Classy outfit in the Llanfaes district of town & a 5min walk across the Usk, the 6 sumptuous rooms (1 is a mini suite) here are a cut above anything else in town, packed with subtle touches. The b/fast menu features their signature Welsh rarebit. No children under 16. **££**

Grange Guesthouse (8 rooms) 22 The Watton; 01874 624038 **w** thegrange-brecon. co.uk. Gorgeous stone-built guesthouse along the handsome main thoroughfare leading into Brecon, the warm & welcoming Grange offers pristinely prepared rooms, but better still is the en-suite bothy in the garden. They've also got cycle storage & electric-car charging points. **££**

Hills Bishop's Meadow, Hay Rd; 01874 611714; **w** hillsbrecon.co.uk; 16.00–21.00 Tue–Thu, noon–15.30 & 17.00–21.00 Fri & Sat, noon–16.00 Sun. Providing the perfect sustenance for weary walkers, this is no ordinary burger house: the Juan Hilario (sobrasado, confit onion & pimento ketchup), & a Peking duck cheeseburger give you some mouthwatering idea of what to expect. Vegans will be just as content with the likes of vegan bangers & mash & a vegan pickle & spice burger. A bit of a pain to get to without wheels – it's a mile or so north of town – but worth very bead of sweat. **££**

Proper Pizza 11 Lion Yard; 01874 620036; **w** properpizzas.co.uk; 16.00–21.00 Wed–Sat, 15.00–20.00 Sun. Operating out of a shop next to the tourist information centre in Lion Yard, this small, family-run pizzeria rustles up scrumptious take-away pizzas, which are made using their own (gluten-free) dough recipe; moreover, any one of the pizzas on the list can be made into a vegan version. Book your slot for collection & away you go. In the absence of anywhere remotely appealing to sit down & eat near the shop (the car park doesn't really cut it), head down to the canal basin. **£**

Three Horseshoes Inn 3 miles east of Brecon in Groesffordd; 01874 665672; **w** threehorseshoesgroesffordd.com; noon–15.00 & 17.00–22.00 Mon–Thu, noon–22.00 Fri–Sun. This smart pub's location – at the end of a residential cul-de-sac – is as odd as it is unexpected, but don't let that take away from the fact that this is one of the finest places to dine in the Brecon Beacons. Each dish completely rocks with flavour, for example crab Scotch egg with brown crab mayo, crispy pork belly with glazed pig cheeks & potato terrine, or duck-egg custard tart with rhubarb. Dedicated veggie & vegan menus too. The service is also first class. £££

Hop In 37 The Watton; 01874 622092; w hopinbeerandgin.co.uk; noon–22.30 Mon–Sat, noon–16.00 Sun. Blink & you might just miss it, which would be a shame because this beer & gin house is well worth a visit. There are typically 8 beers on tap at any one time, including a couple of cask ales (all available in thirds' & two-thirds' pints), plus a choice selection of gins, some unusual ones too. There's tasty food as well, of the small plates variety (ham hock terrine with caramelised walnuts, mussels in garlic & white wine), plus a cracking Sun lunch offering. Park up inside or head through the wafer-thin corridor to a suntrap courtyard where there's more seating. If you haven't got time to hang around, you can grab a 4-pack 'growler' of beer to take away. ££

Coffee Box 7 Lion St; 01874 938628; w coffeeboxonline.com; 09.00–17.00 Mon–Sat, 10.00–16.00 Sun. Bright, bustling coffee house that does the best coffee-&-cake combo in town. Take a seat by one of the big bay windows & enjoy the comings & goings as you devour a slice of caramel & pecan cake washed down with a steaming latte or mug of tea. £

Hours Café & Bookshop Cathedral Cl; 07726 375274; w thehoursbrecon.co.uk; 10.00–16.00 Tue–Wed & Fri–Sat, 11.00–16.00 Thu. Perennially popular café/bookshop that's just moved from its much-loved & very wonky Tudor building on Ship St to the heritage centre in the more serene surrounds of the cathedral. It's still as inviting, & indeed there are few better ways to spend an hour or so than poring over a few titles with a mug of tea & a slice of coffee & walnut cake to hand. £

Entertainment

Theatr Brycheiniog Canal Wharf; 01874 611622; w brycheiniog.co.uk; box office 10.00–18.00 Mon–Fri, 10.00–16.00 Sat. One of Wales's more progressive art centres, this terrific theatre puts on a diverse programme of events from music & theatre to comedy & film, plus there's also a strong commitment to Welsh-language performances. The café here is great too: grab a panini or some coffee & cake & head out to the wharf.

Activities

Cantref Upper Cantref Farm, 5 miles south of Brecon; 01874 665223; w cantref.com; Easter–mid-Jul & Sep 10.30–17.00 Sat & Sun; school hols 10.30–17.00 daily. Long-established family-run trekking centre offering treks (£24.75/1hr, £41.25/half day, £68.50/full day) into the Brecons & riding lessons, from £42/hr for an adult (£36.75 for a child). As well as riding, they've also got an adventure farm (animals, outdoor activities & indoor soft play), so you could quite easily make a day of it with the kids here.

Dragonfly Cruises Brecon Basin; m 07831 685222; w dragonfly-cruises.co.uk; cruises Mar–May noon Tue–Sun, Jun noon Mon–Sat, Jul noon Mon & noon–15.00 Tue–Sun, Aug noon & 15.00 daily, Sep noon Tue–Thu & noon–15.00 Sat & Sun, Oct noon Tue, Wed, Sat & Sun; £10. If you're done with walking for a while, consider a jolly out on the water. From its base at the head of the Brecon & Monmouthshire Canal, this excellent outfit offers scheduled narrowboat trips along a 2-mile stretch of the canal up to Brynich, a round trip of 2hrs. Informed on-board commentary gives all you all the lowdown on the canal, & you can even join the 'skip' at the helm. They've also got self-drive boats available for hire, each carrying up to 8 people (£35/1hr, £45/2hrs, £55/3hrs).

What to see and do Brecon is small and easily navigable, and a walk from the **Watton** – a wide, handsome thoroughfare lined with variously coloured Georgian townhouses, which then segues into the Bulwark before continuing up through the High Street and then dipping down to the bridge over the Usk River – should take no more than 15 minutes. The castle, at the confluence of the Usk and Honddu rivers, is now a hotel.

The Royal Welsh Regimental Museum (The Watton; ☎ 01874 613310; w royalwelshmuseum.wales; ⏰ 10.00–17.00 Mon–Fri, Easter–Sep 10.30–16.00 Sat (Aug 10.30–16.00 Sun also); £5) Voluminous hardly begins to describe the amount of stuff on display in The Royal Welsh Regimental Museum. In fact they've got so much stored away that a move to a larger premises has been mooted, but this has yet to materialise and there have even been fears that the museum may have to close if they are unable to vacate the current premises. For the time being, you can immerse yourself in more than 300 years of military history, covering every conceivable war (Boer, Crimea, World War I and II, Bosnia, Iraq and Afghanistan), with uniforms, medals, weapons and suchlike.

The one exhibition that captures most people's imaginations is on the South African Zulu Wars, which was of course immortalised in Stanley Baker's 1964 film, *Zulu*, starring Michael Caine. During the course of the 1879 Battle of Rorke's Drift, 150 soldiers repelled more than 4,000 Zulu warriors – seven men from the 24th Regiment of Foot (one of the preceding regiments) were awarded Victoria Crosses for their role in the stand, although those on display here are replicas, the originals having been placed in vaults. Among the many exceptional items retrieved from the battlefield is the Union flag, discoloured and blotted with white patches where it had been folded, and the only surviving drum from the Battle of Isandlwana, the first major encounter of the Anglo-Zulu wars.

y Gaer (Glamorgan St; ☎ 01874 623346; w ygaerpowys.org.uk; ⏰ 10.00–16.00 Tues & Thu–Sun; free) Reopened in 2019 after a lengthy and costly revamp, y Gaer (meaning Hill Fort or Fortress) brings the Brecknock Museum and Art Gallery, the old Court of Assizes, and the town library all together under the one roof of the Neoclassical Shire Hall, itself raised in 1842. You first pass through the old **Court of Assizes**, preserved in all its pompous splendour, although the furniture, which is original, is not in situ, having been reconfigured during the renovation. Proposed alongside the construction of the Shire Hall itself, the court served as the seat of the county's more serious criminal cases until its closure in 1971. Next door an old Victorian schoolroom amply demonstrates how cramped conditions were for what would have been a few dozen children crammed in here.

In the craft gallery, delicately embroidered samplers, beautifully carved walking sticks and centuries-old love spoons (traditionally given as a gift of romantic intent) are packed cheek-by-jowl into gleaming glass cabinets. The small but action-packed art gallery usually has rotating displays; don't be surprised to see lots of local landscapes – Pen-y-Fan, Fforest Fawr, the Black Mountains and so on – by the likes of Augustus John, Roger Cecil and Thomas Jones.

Up on the first floor, the **Brycheiniog Gallery** offers a thoroughly enjoyable romp through Brecknockshire life, with themed displays covering religion, festivals, trades, the landscape, military affairs and more. There are too many outstanding items to list them all here, but do try and seek out the following: a medieval stone cresset lamp; the *Maiden Stone*, a Roman tombstone carved with images of a Roman citizen and his wife (presumably found at Brecon Gaer Roman fort); and a fantastically well-preserved *crannog* (log boat or dug-out canoe) retrieved from Llangorse Lake in 1925 and dating from around AD800. On a more abstruse note, there's a display on the great Italo-American opera singer Adelina Patti (page 217), who lived at Craig-y-Nos Castle at the turn of the 20th century and some of whose possessions are on display here, including, weirdly, her stuffed dog.

Brecon Cathedral (Priory Hill; 📞 01874 623857; w breconcathedral.org.uk; 🕐 09.00–18.00 daily; free) Surmounting Priory Hill, Brecon Cathedral – or to give it its full and proper title, the Priory Church of St John the Baptist – was elevated to the status of cathedral as recently as 1923, following the Church of Wales's disestablishment from England three years earlier, and the subsequent founding of the Diocese of Swansea & Brecon. There has, though, been a place of worship on this site since 1093 when a priory was founded as a dependent of Battle Abbey in Sussex, before further enlargement in the 13th and 14th centuries. A fair proportion of the church's present appearance owes much to the serial restorationist George Gilbert Scott, whose phased Gothic Revival work between 1860 and 1872 entailed, among other things, the reconstruction of the fine timber roof and the relaying of the floors.

The exterior is not especially prepossessing, but inside there is something of interest in just about every corner. In fact, three of the cathedral's finest ancient monuments are closely grouped together just inside the entrance. First up is an exuberantly carved Norman font bearing shallow reliefs of birds and beasts, and a so-called Green Man: often grotesque mask-like faces with foliage spewing from one or more orifice, these were among the most common decorative motifs of medieval sculpture. It has long been a popular pub name, and is also from where the eponymous music festival, held in Crickhowell in August (page 229), takes its name. Close by is the largest cresset stone (a word of French origin) in Britain, a square stone slab bearing 30 cup-shaped hollows into which candles would have been

DARK SKY AT NIGHT

In 2012 the Brecon Beacons National Park became the first place in Wales, and at the time only the fifth in the world, to be designated an International Dark Sky Reserve. As of 2022, there were 20 International Dark Sky Reserves worldwide, and remarkably, seven of these are in Britain and Ireland; the only other one in Wales is Snowdonia. Certified by the International Dark Sky Association, dark sky areas are classified as public or private land possessing an exceptional or distinguished quality of starry nights and nocturnal environment that is specifically protected for its scientific, natural, educational, cultural, heritage and/or public enjoyment. While there are obvious rewards to designation, such as the potential for increased tourism, there are other, more environmentally friendly benefits, one of which is the requirement for local authorities to adopt planning rules that enforce a high standard of lighting in order to minimise light pollution.

On a clear night in the park, you might see the Milky Way (which appears as a cloud owing to the number of stars in it), major constellations, bright nebulas, shooting stars, and maybe even a comet. Some of the best places in the park to set up a telescope are Llangorse Lake, the National Park Visitor Centre in Libanus (both of these are easily accessible), Usk Reservoir, Hay Bluff, and nearby Llanthony Priory looking across to Hatterall Hill – which *really* is remote, and quite wonderful. It's not unusual for some accommodation providers in the Brecon Beacons, particularly self-catering cottages, to have their own stargazing equipment (there are even 'stay-and-gaze' options), so it's always worth asking. And a few final tips: wrap up warm, even in summer (it can get very chilly up here of an evening) and take a torch with a red light to assist with night vision.

placed; although fairly commonplace in England, this is the only known specimen in Wales. Thirdly, there's the Games Monument, a tomb dedicated to the eponymous family but which was destroyed save for an oak-carved figure of a woman, hands clasped in prayer and minus her nose which has been unceremoniously hacked off. Architecturally, the most arresting aspect is the magnificently proportioned brick-vaulted chancel (the oldest surviving part of the building), though the reredos is of more recent vintage (1936). The neighbouring Harvard Chapel is also known as the Regimental Chapel of the Royal Welsh, hence the presence of various military regalia, including a faded flag from the 1879 Battle of Rorke's Drift.

LLANGORSE LAKE AND AROUND The curious, dog-leg-shaped Llangorse Lake (w llangorselake.co.uk), a mile southwest of the village of Llangorse, is the largest natural lake in South Wales and the second largest in the country after Bala in Snowdonia. You could conceivably spend an entire day here, whether pottering by, or on, the water; walking some of the trails, the best of which is the 4-mile walk down to Llangasty on the southern shore; staking out the hide near Llangasty, where you'll probably see reed warblers, Cetti's warblers, sand martins, chiffchaffs and great-crested grebes; or just relaxing in the water meadows.

The centre of the lake is crowned by Wales's last remaining *crannog* – an artificial island built out on to a lake as a defensive dwelling. These were fairly commonplace throughout Scotland and even more numerous in Ireland. Initial excavations in 1869, followed by more extensive research in the late 1980s, determined that this *crannog* probably dates from the time of the 9th-century court of Brycheiniog. The dwelling has long gone, and instead a simple thatched roundhouse (made from the same thick reeds that grow in the lake) has been erected on stilts at the end of a pontoon, where panels inform on the history of the lake and the lives of its natives; the hut is wheelchair accessible. Note that on OS maps the island is marked as Bwlc.

According to legend, and first chronicled in the 15th century, the lake has its own beast: the Afnac of Llangorse, or as it's known colloquially, Gorsey. Either way, it is said that Gorsey is partial to a nibble, as was reported in *The Guardian* in 1999 when a waterskier was bitten by a mysterious creature from the depths. With no sense of irony, the victim likened it to a scene out of *Jaws*; it was in fact just a very large pike, for which the lake is renowned – it's said that the largest ever pike caught in British inland waters was here at Llangorse in 1846, though one suspects that documentary evidence for this is scant. Monsters aside, you are likely to see horses here, who like to amble down from the nearby riding school for a drink, much to the surprise of onlookers.

From the hut by the lake you can hire rowing boats seating 4 (£19.50/hour), stand-up paddleboards (£17.50/hour), kayaks/canoes (£16.50/hour) and Canadian canoes and double kayaks (£26/hour); you are permitted to bring your own boats too. There is no bank fishing here, but fishing is permitted on the lake, for which a permit is required (£9). These can be purchased online or from the shop next to The Lake Café, and fishing boats can be hired (£30/day) from the hut too.

One mile south of the lake in Gilfach is **Llangorse Multi-Activity Centre** (⏃01874 658272; w activityuk.com; ⏀ 09.30–17.00 Mon & Fri–Sun, 09.30–21.00 Tue–Thu). The two main activities available here are indoor climbing (£9.50/day plus any equipment hire), alongside climbing tasting sessions (£30) and horseriding, from a 1-hour beginner's ride (£30) to half-day hacks (£50) for the more experienced; they also offer activity sessions which entail climbing, bouldering, zip-wire and high ropes.

7

Where to stay, eat and drink

Star Bunkhouse (6 rooms) Brecon Rd, Bwlch; 01874 730080; w starbunkhouse. com. Don't let the noisy roadside location put you off: Pete & Emma's terrific bunkhouse offers 6 small dorms sleeping between 2 & 5 (showers are separate), a well-equipped kitchen & a small warren of cosy, communal areas with woodburners & packed with books, guides, maps & games. Additional facilities include a BBQ which guests are free to avail themselves of, laundry & bike wash. Both Pete & Emma are trained mountain guides & are happy to lead hikes anywhere within the national park. **£**

Lakeside Caravan and Camping Llangorse Lake; 01874 658226; w llangorselake.co.uk; mid-Mar–early Nov. Set back from the lake on the other side of the water meadow, this large site has 4- & 6-berth static caravans for hire alongside pitches for tents & tourers; facilities include modern shower blocks & laundry, while the café & shop are just across the way for all your supplies. Min 2-night stay for camping & caravans (3 nights for caravans in summer). *Camping* **£**, *caravans* **£££**

New Inn Brecon Rd, Bwlch; 01874 730215; w beaconsbackpackers.co.uk; 17.00–22.00 Wed–Fri, 14.00–22.00 Sat, noon–20.00 Sun. Directly across the road from the Star Bunkhouse,

Neil & Sarah's convivial inn serves some of the best nosh for miles around. Although meaty treats abound on the menu – the Welsh black beef pie is a popular staple & they take their venison from the farm shop just up the road (see below), veggies & vegans are well catered for (pea & mint fritters, chargrilled aubergine & butterbean stew). The beers are top notch as well, as are the locally brewed ciders, which is why you'll always find a merry band of locals chuntering away at the bar. **££**

The Lake Café Llangorse Lake; m 07583 988730; Mar–Oct 09.00–17.00 daily. Although you really should bring a picnic if you're intent on spending the day at the lake, this cheerful seasonal café (owned by the caravan site) has lengthy b/ fast & lunch menus, plus coffees, teas & ice creams, which can be enjoyed either inside or outside on the big, gravelly terrace. Take-aways too. **£**

Welsh Venison Centre Middlewood Farm, Bwlch; 01874 730929; w beaconsfarmshop. co.uk; 08.00–16.30 Tue–Sat, 10.00–16.00 bank hols. Just off the A40 about a mile north of Bwlch, this tidy farm shop café is an ideal spot to refuel for lunch after an early-morning assault on the mountains; they do b/fasts too, as well as coffee, cakes & ice creams. Lovely deli too selling baked goods, cheese & meats, which of course includes their own venison. **£**

TALYBONT-ON-USK Six miles southeast of Brecon, and about 8 miles northeast of Crickhowell, Talybont-on-Usk is a busy little activity hub owing to its position on the Monmouthshire & Brecon Canal and the Taff Trail (page 80), which runs alongside it, as well as its proximity to two enormous reservoirs (see opposite) and of course the mountains themselves. To that end, the village is brilliantly geared up, with enough accommodation and dining possibilities to go around, plus excellent bike-hire facilities. The village is more or less centred on a short stretch of the main through road (running parallel to the canal) where you'll find a couple of pubs, the excellent village shop, with a café (shop 07.00–19.00 Mon–Sat, 08.00–17.00 Sun; café 08.00–16.00 daily), and a little further along, the village hall and car park – avoid trying to park along the main road if you can, the locals don't much like it.

One popular walk from Talybont is along the old **Brinore Tramroad** – an early 19th-century horse-drawn railway. This steady 8-mile hike (around 3hrs) starts at the canalside wharf behind the White Hart Inn and takes you south to the village of Trefil (Wales's highest village – page 186) just shy of the A465.

Where to stay, eat and drink

Coity Bach Farm 01874 676675; w coitybach.co.uk. Just over a mile west (& uphill) of the village, this pleasantly chaotic working farm offers a mixed bunch of accommodation,

from 2 self-catering cottages & a wooden cabin to a gypsy caravan & semi-wild camping in the top field – which, incidentally, is a terrific spot for stargazing. There are usually various animals wandering around, including a couple of (very friendly) dogs. £££

🏠 **YHA Danywenallt** 📞01874 676677; w yha.org.uk. A mile south of the village at the northern end of Talybont Reservoir, this converted farmhouse occupies a superb location with mountain view. Dorms & private rooms (some en suite), in addition to a couple of bell tents plus camping in the apple orchard. Facilities include a lounge with warming woodstove & a decently equipped kitchen. Meals available on request. £

🍺 **Star Inn** High St; 📞01874 676635; ⏰ noon–22.30 Tue–Sun. The Star seems to have had innumerable owners over the years but still it ploughs on, welcoming all-comers & serving the best beer in the village; the food's not bad either. It's more atmospheric than the White Hart down the road & is also possessed of a cracking beer garden. Look out too for evenings of live music & the occasional beer festival. £

🍺 **White Hart Inn** High St; 📞01874 676227. It does get mixed reviews but it's a fine old building with a roaring log fire in winter & on a good day the food – pub standards – can be very good. They've also got a bunkhouse attached, with 4- & 6-bed rooms & shared shower facilities; laundry & bike storage available. B/fast costs extra. £

Activities

Bikes & Hikes Next to the Talybont Stores shop; m 07909 968135; w bikesandhikes.co.uk. Excellent little outfit operating out of a small hut by the village shop. As well as offering bike hire (£30/35 3hrs/day), Keith, the owner, can also deliver bikes, as well as do repairs & servicing. Just down the road at the village hall, there's a bike hub, where you can wash down both your bike (£1) & yourself (in a shower that is).

RESERVOIRS AROUND TALYBONT Crowded in by steep, conifer-forested hillsides, **Talybont Reservoir** is the largest reservoir in the Brecon Beacons, and was completed in 1938 to supply water to Newport, though that did necessitate the flooding of 25 farms and nearly 3,000 acres of land. It was (then) created as a local nature reserve (in 1975) in recognition of its ornithological importance, particularly with regard to wintering migrants. The Taff Trail (which you can start in Talybont) runs along a ridge above the eastern side of the water, before sweeping east towards a grouping of waterfalls on the Nant Bwrefwr.

From here you can either continue north towards the **Neuadd Reservoirs**, from where you can make a twin assault on Pen-y-Fan and Corn Du (page 218) or head south towards the **Pentwyn** and **Pontsticill reservoirs**, which is the route the Taff Trail takes. The trail wends its way down along the western side of these two reservoirs, and is likely to be relatively busy, so if you fancy a more solitudinous – and slightly harder – walk, cross the dam at the northern end of the Pontsticill Reservoir, turn right and follow the course of the Brecon Mountain Railway for a bit before taking the path that veers east up rocky slopes to higher ground. The views from here are some of the best in these mountains. Pontsticill (also known as Taff Fechan) is the second-largest reservoir after Talybont, and was created in 1927 to supply the Valleys' towns. Submerged somewhere in its depths are the remains of the Bethlehem Independent Chapel, though it's said that in rare times of drought the chapel does resurface. Beyond the dam at the southern end of the reservoir, the Taff Trail continues down into Merthyr, which feels like stepping into a cold shower after what has just preceded.

BRECON MOUNTAIN RAILWAY (Pant station; 📞 01685 722988; w bmr.wales; ⏰ times vary so check website) Opened in 1980 following the closure of the Brecon and Merthyr Railway in 1964 – originally built to transport coal from Merthyr to Brecon – this 5-mile section of railway is a gentle little ride along the eastern side of Pontsticill Reservoir. It starts in Pant, itself just three miles north of Merthyr, and runs straight through to Torpentau station at the northern end of the reservoir. On the return leg it stops at Pontsticill station for 25 minutes – enough time to look around and have a drink from the snack bar (though you could also just wait for the next train to pass through if you fancy hanging around a bit) – before the last leg back – it's about 90 minutes all in. Facilities at Pant station include a tearoom and gift shop; there are no facilities at all at Torpentau.

TALGARTH A welcoming, community-minded village located at the intersection of roads to Brecon, Crickhowell and Hay, Talgarth has been a milling settlement since the 12th century. The existing **mill** (☏ 01874 711125; w talgarthmill.com; ⊕ 10.00–15.00 Wed–Sat; free) has been here since 1780, but by the end of World War II was a wreck; it was only saved from complete dereliction in 2011 when lottery funds were made available to bring it back to health, and it now looks a million dollars – though only the waterwheel is original. Formal tours of the mill have been suspended for a while now but may be up and running again at some point in the future. Failing that, you are free to look around and watch the resident miller working his magic – better still, try some of the goodies in the on-site café afterwards.

A short but pleasant walk is to **Pwll-y-Wrach**, meaning 'Witches Pool', a local beauty spot about a mile along the road heading south out of the village. From the car park and gate at the entrance to the wooded reserve, a path dips and weaves alongside the River Enning to the pool (so-named as this is where those accused of being witches were taken for a ducking), into which water tumbles from a 33ft (10m)-high waterfall – quite spectacular after heavy rainfall. From here you loop left, taking either the woodland track or the road back to the starting point. Depending on the season, you can expect to see white wood anemones, yellow celandines, bluebells and wild garlic; there is a small colony of dormice, but the chance of happening upon one is slight.

Travelling north out of the village on the road to Hay, on your right-hand side you'll catch a glimpse of **Bronllys Castle** (⊕ open access), actually less a castle than the sizeable remains of a 12th-century cylindrical stone tower, or keep, perched atop the motte mound. A chain at the top of the stairs currently bars entry, hence it's not worth stopping off for, but if you do want a closer look, usefully there's a lay-by on the opposite side of the road.

Tourist information

⧉ Talgarth Tourist Information Office The Square; ☏ 01874 712226; ⊕ 10.00–14.00 daily. This friendly, volunteer-run tourist office inside the Tower Shop has plenty of information on both the town & surrounding areas, including a selection of maps & guidebooks to buy.

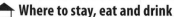 Where to stay, eat and drink

⌂ Tegfan Suite Tegfan, Wernfawr; ☏ 01874 711121; w tegfangardensuite.com. A mile or so southeast of Talgarth, this nicely secluded self-contained property occupies the property's erstwhile Victorian greenhouse. As well as a dbl bed, there's a dbl pull-out, so effectively this place sleeps 4, ideally 2 adults & 2 kids; kids (& maybe adults too) will also love the fact that there is also a PlayStation here. The suite also has a well-equipped kitchen, & upon arrival you'll be received with a little hamper containing a few lovely treats including the owner Helen's own jam. If you ask nicely she may just let you play the crazy golf course hidden away in the garden. **£££**

⌂ Castle Hotel Bronllys; ☏ 01874 712272; w thecastlehoteltalgarth.com. A 5min walk from the centre out on the Bronllys Rd, this steady ship is run by jolly proprietor, Ian. The refurbished rooms provide decent value for money, while the restaurant/bar is a good spot to rest up in after a hard day in the mountains; there's also a cracking little take-away fish & chip shop attached. **££**

Honey Café Bronllys; 01874 711904; w honeycafe.co.uk; 09.00–16.00 daily. Just over a mile north of Talgarth on the road to Hay, the perky Honey Café is a popular refuelling spot for passing motorists. Originally a malt house & brewery, & used as a cellar nightclub for a stint in the 60s, it has remained in the same family's hands since 1933. The bright red- & orange-painted exterior is as likely to draw you in as much as the menu: b/fasts, wraps & sandwiches, homemade pies & burgers, & a long-standing Tex-Mex menu are all fair game. **££**

Gertie's Talgarth Mill, The Square; w gerties.co.uk; 10.00–15.00 Wed–Sat. With fresh flour milled in the room next door, where better to sample a freshly prepared sandwich & other freshly baked goodies than the mill's on-site café, which has just been taken over by new tenants; some lush-looking cakes & good coffee too. **£**

Strand Regent St; 01874 711195; w thestrandtalgarth.com; 10.00–14.00 Mon, 11.00–15.00 Thu, 10.00–17.00 Fri & Sat, noon–16.00 Sun. With a menu as long as your left leg, you'll have no idea what to choose – there really is nothing that this quirky corner café-cum-bookshop doesn't offer (b/fasts, paninis, pies, pizza, curry, custard pudding?), & you're unlikely to spend more than £8–10 on any one dish. **£**

CRICKHOWELL AND AROUND

A prosperous little market town tucked under the folds of the Black Mountains, Crickhowell (Crug Hywel) has made a bit of a name for itself in recent years with its success in managing to repel various attempts by national chain stores to muscle in on its patch. One recent example of this was when a redundant pub that was earmarked for development by one chain was subsequently bought by the local community and is now home to a zero-waste shop, antiques shop and café. The town's wide and handsome High Street therefore remains an unyielding bastion of independence: a butcher, bakery, florist, ironmongers and a wonderful bookshop are all testament to that.

CRICKHOWELL FESTIVALS

Crickhowell boats a triumvirate of festivals that towns ten times the size would be envious of. First up in March is the **Crickhowell Walking Festival** (w crickhowellfestival.com), with dozens of guided walks taking place over nine days, ranging from easy strolls to hard, full-day hikes of up to 20 miles in length. Most require a small fee but it's a great way of exploring these mountains without the stress of trying to navigate everything by yourself, and in the company of like-minded folk too. Mid-August sees the four-day **Green Man Festival** (w greenman.net) come to town, or more specifically, the Glenusk Estate just up the road. It's not just its beautifully positioned location in a verdant Welsh valley that sets it apart from just about any other major festival in Britain, but it's also the consistently high quality of its artists: a blend of indie, alt-folk and Americana. In 2022, the likes of Kraftwerk, Michael Kiwanuka and Kae Tempest performed, while there's invariably a performance by the de facto godfather of Welsh rock Gruff Rhys, frontman of the Super Furry Animals. It's also well known for being one of the more child-friendly festivals on the circuit, and there's stacks more going on including comedy, film, literature and performing arts events. The town's even spread of festival year culminates in October's five-day **Crickhowell Book Festival** (w cricklitfest.co.uk), and who needs Hay when there's this little beauty?

Crickhowell is certainly bucking the trend of your average high street, and although some have suggested that that's because of the town's demographic (and it is fairly wealthy by the standards of most rural Welsh towns), this is perhaps a little disingenuous because like any small rural settlement, Crickhowell has its problems, and in any case many of the shops and businesses have been present here for generations. While there's little of discernible interest in town – certainly nothing to see by way of conventional sights – Crickhowell is a great place to base yourself if you're considering spending any length of time in the neighbouring Black Mountains. There is one site of intrigue, though: from the High Street it's a short walk down to the Usk and Crickhowell's 18th-century **bridge**, not only Wales's longest, but one that offers an element of intrigue on account of the fact that it has 12 arches upstream and 13 downstream!

GETTING THERE AND AWAY Crickhowell is close to three major roads: the A40 which runs right through the heart of town, the A479 to Talgarth, and the A465 a few miles to the south.

The nearest train station is Abergavenny 6 miles away, from where the X43 bus runs hourly (every 2hrs Sun) to Crickhowell, stopping on Beaufort Street at the top of the High Street. There are also hourly services to Brecon (none on Sun).

TOURIST INFORMATION

🛈 Crickhowell Resource and Information Centre 1 Beaufort St; ☏01874 811970; w visitcrickhowell.wales; ⏲ 10.00–17.00 Mon–Sat. The excellent, efficient community-run tourist office has loads of information on both the town & walks in the surrounding area, with plenty of maps & guidebooks to buy. There's also a gift shop, & a café with Wi-Fi here.

WHERE TO STAY, EAT AND DRINK

🏠 Gliffaes Country House (23 rooms) 4 miles west of Crickhowell; ☏01874 730371; w gliffaeshotel.com. Secreted away within 33 lush acres of woodland at the end of a long, tree-lined avenue lies this Italianate Victorian manor built by the Reverend West in 1895. Owing to the building's design, each room is differently configured, &, broadly speaking, differently styled, though throughout there are antique dressers & beautifully reupholstered chairs, tile-rimmed fireplaces, splashes of artwork, retro Roberts radios & shelves loaded with books; some of the deluxe & superior rooms are river-facing. There's no lift. Glamorous, grown-up public areas include the lounge bar, drawing room & restaurant, & while dinner can be pricey, lunch – best enjoyed on the summery terrace overlooking the valley – is much more affordable. James, the owner, is a committed dendrophile & has devised a tree trail within the grounds which anyone is free to enjoy, whether staying here or not. Moreover, each overnighting guest is liable to a £1.50 tree tax, to which James will add £1. Other activities include tennis, fishing (permits issued here), & in warmer weather, wild swimming. **£££**

🏠 The Bear Hotel (35 rooms) Beaufort St; ☏01874 810408; w bearhotel.co.uk. This rambling, resolutely old-school inn has been welcoming guests since 1432 believe it or not. Its ancient creaking floors, wonky doors & low oak beams (mind yer head) are all part of its effortless charm, with rooms split between those in the main building (categorised as cosy, good, better, best, very best) & those in the old courtyard stables, which offer a few more concessions to modernity. The public areas include a couple of warming bars with wood-panelled walls & wooden settles – perfect after a muddy ramble in the mountains – & the restaurant, where you can slide into a *cwtch* (nook) & get your chops round a Melting Bear burger with Monterey Jack cheese. **££**

🏠 Dragon Hotel (15 rooms) 47 High St; ☏01873 810362; w dragoninncrickhowell.com. A low-key alternative to The Bear at the other end of the High St, the salmon-pink-painted Dragon is renowned for its popularity with walkers, be it those stopping the night or just popping in for a pint & a bite to eat. Rooms here are all the same, save for those up in the eaves, which have shower attachments over the baths as opposed to standalone cubicles. Dog-friendly too, with pooches welcome in the bar & in some rooms. **££**

✳ 💻 **Book-ish** 18 High St; 📞 01873 811256; **w** book-ish.com; 🕐 09.00–17.00 Mon–Thu & Sat, 10.00–16.00 Fri & Sun. Grab a book to browse from the shop out front & head into the bookshop's bright & airy split-level café to the rear. Among the b/fast options are dippy eggs with buttered soldiers & for lunch filled sandwiches & paninis, as well as hot dishes like sweet potato falafel with tabbouleh; superb coffee & cakes too. **£**

SHOPPING

Book-ish 18 High St; 📞 01874 811256; **w** book-ish.com; 🕐 09.00–17.00 Mon–Thu & Sat, 10.00–16.00 Fri & Sun. Fantastic little bookshop stocking titles from all genres, including the most up-to-date releases (often author signed), but it's all the other stuff that the shop's relentlessly energetic owner, Emma Corfield-Waters, organises that makes it so much fun. These include high-calibre book signings, a monthly writing group, Mon night book club, Book-ish quiz & games evenings. Also, & just for good measure, Emma curates the Crickhowell Literary Festival in Oct (page 229). The café is rather marvellous too.

Crickhowell Adventure 1 High St; 📞 01874 810020; 🕐 crickhowelladventure.co.uk; 🕐 09.30–17.00 Mon–Sat. A one-stop shop for all your walking gear, plus loads of other paraphernalia for campers, climbers, cavers, canoeists, cyclists & any other Cs you care to think of. Located directly opposite the Market Cross.

Webb's High St; 📞 01874 810331; **w** webbscrickhowell.com; 🕐 08.30–17.30 Mon–Sat. Trading since 1936, there's almost nothing you can't buy in this traditional ironmonger's, a labyrinthine emporium where anything goes; you'll certainly end up spending more time here than you intended – and in all likelihood leaving with more than you intended.

WHAT TO SEE AND DO

Tretower Castle and Court (Tretower; 📞 03000 252239; **w** cadw.gov.uk; 🕐 Apr–Oct 10.00–17.00 daily, Nov–Feb 10.00–16.00 Thu–Sun; £8.30) Under one of the Beacons' windswept ridges a couple of miles north of Crickhowell is Tretower Castle and Court, of which there is far more left of the former than the latter. This late-medieval manor house was originally built to a design by Sir Roger Vaughan, who was gifted the property by his half-brother, Sir William Herbert of Raglan Castle. Vaughan began with the impressive West Range, incorporating the Great Hall – here heavily mocked up with replica furniture but having retained its magnificent timber framework – and then the adjacent galleried North Range, which was probably used as accommodation. From Roger, the house passed to his son Thomas, whom it is believed was responsible for the remaining two sides of the court – the east and south curtain walls; a nice symmetry all told. The court ceased to be the family residence in the early 18th century and was eventually incorporated into the neighbouring farm.

Much of what you see today is actually as a result of a 40-year-long restoration programme, which began in 1930 following the acquisition of the court by the Brecknock Society, who subsequently entrusted the work to HM Office of Works for conservation. Apart from those rooms in the west range, the remaining rooms are stripped bare. The court's completeness also renders it a popular spot for shooting films: in 2004 Johnny Depp pitched up here for filming of *The Libertine*. There's also a gorgeous little walled garden adjacent to the manor house, though this is a 1991 recreation of how it might have looked during Vaughan's day.

Before the mansion, however, came the castle, which stands isolated on the other side of what was known as Castle Green. All that remains these days is a round, four-floored 13th-century tower (Tretower literally translates as 'the place

Crickhowell makes a brilliant base from which to strike out on any number of thrilling walks. One of the most enjoyable is a 4-mile circular route from Llangattock village, 1½ miles south of Crickhowell, up to Craig-y-Cilau, a cliffside nature reserve noted for its outstanding limestone flora and hidden caves. After an initial couple of tough steep ascents, the walk levels off before the descent back down to the village.

The walk starts just beyond the village of **Llangattock** by a sharp bend in a minor road. From here, cross the stile and follow the path on the left through a gate (ignoring a stile on your left) and continue straight ahead. Go through another gate and continue past the Cwm Bach holiday cottages on your left. A little further on you come to a small stream; cross this and ahead of you, ever so slightly to your right, is a very steep, rocky slope – this is the old quarry incline. After a sapping 200m or so you reach a small open area where, just to your right, is a bench – a good time for a breather and to take in the superlative views of the Black Mountains across the valley, including Table Mountain and Pen Cerrig-calch straight ahead.

With your back to the bench, take the uphill path slightly to the left and keep ascending until you finally emerge above the hedgeline at the foot of the scarp. Turning to your right – you are now in the **Craig-y-Cilau nature reserve** – walk along the flat grassy terrace that curls under the sweeping curtain of rock to an information board. Not only is this one of the largest upland limestone cliffs in Wales, but it's also one of the country's outstanding botanical sites. Among the many rare wildflowers here are mossy saxifrage, limestone fern and Llangattock hawkweed, which is found here and nowhere else in Wales. In the 19th century, this entire area was a site of heavy industry, an enormous quarry from where limestone was extracted for the ironworks in Nantyglo in the Valleys. Its gradual reclamation by nature has been spectacular, as are the views from this lofty position.

Beyond the information board, carry on until you get to a junction. Before you take the waymarked path that breaks off down to the right, continue along to the end of the terrace where you'll see the entrance to **Agen Allwedd Cave**, one of several cave systems dotting these mountains; it's also home to a significant colony of lesser-horseshoe and long-eared bats. Returning to the junction, head downhill to another waymarked post and take the path to the right, carrying on downhill. At the bottom turn right and walk along the valley floor beside the stream until you reach the bottom of the quarry incline that you walked up earlier, from where you can retrace your steps back towards Llangattock.

of the tower'), this one having replaced an earlier earth and timber fortification established by Picard around 1100. Take a look at the gigantic hooded fireplaces on both first- and second-floor levels, which suggests a dwelling of some luxury.

Castell Dinas Six miles further up the A479, from the hamlet of Pengenffordd, it's a short walk up to the Iron-Age hillfort of Castell Dinas, whose 2,500-year-old ditches and grass ramparts lie at 1,500ft, sufficiently high enough to afford uplifting views down the valley of the River Rhiangoll.

Although there's nothing wildly exciting to do in Abergavenny itself – though the castle with its museum and the outstanding priory church demand a couple of hours of your time – it's the town's reputation as a gourmet hub, combined with its urban amenities and proximity to some of the most eminently walkable peaks in the Black Mountains, that make Abergavenny such an attractive proposition.

There was almost certainly a Roman outpost here before the Normans pitched up and built the castle. A lethal combination of the Black Death, which was rife here, and a good sacking by Owain Glydnwr then brought the town to its knees. Abergavenny was located just a little too far north of its near neighbours in the Valleys to be invested in the iron and coal industries, but it did sustain important weaving and tanning trades from the 16th century onwards, and together with its market, the town prospered. In many ways the market still remains the beating heart of town, but post-lockdown(s), it's the town's culinary assets that remain its strong suit.

GETTING THERE AND AWAY Abergavenny is well located for drivers, just west of the A465, and is the starting point of both the A40 to Brecon and the western half of the A465 to Neath. The town is served by trains from Cardiff, Newport and Hereford across the border, typically every 30–45 minutes. The train station is a 10-minute walk southeast of town on Station Road. The bus station is 5 minutes closer to town on Monmouth Road. There are at least hourly services to Brecon, Cardiff, Crickhowell, Monmouth and Raglan, the last for its castle.

TOURIST INFORMATION

ℹ️ Abergavenny Tourist Information Centre Town Hall, 61 Cross St; 📞01873 853254; w visitmonmouthshire.com; ⏰ 10.00–16.00 Mon–Sat. Great location inside the town hall, this excellent office has all the information you could possibly need on both the town & walks in the surrounding area, with plenty of maps & guidebooks to buy. They also offer a bed-booking service.

WHERE TO STAY *Map, page 234*

✳ 🏠 **The Angel** (35 rooms) 15 Cross St; 📞01873 859050; w angelabergavenny.com. Enduringly classy hotel that has been providing some of South Wales's finest hospitality since 1832. Behind its stately Georgian façade the Angel's rooms are built for enduring comfort, from the fired-earth bathroom fittings & percale linen to eye-catching wall pieces from their art shop across the road. Dinner & b/fast are served in the Oak Room restaurant or there's more casual dining/drinking in the atmospheric Foxhunter Bar – named after the legendary racehorse (page 239). The hotel is much feted for its afternoon tea, for which it has won legions of awards, though you will need to book ahead & save your pennies – it's £44. **£££**

🏠 **The Kings Arms Hotel** (11 rooms) 29 Nevill St; 📞01873 855074; w kingsarmsabergavenny. co.uk. This warm 16th-century apricot-coloured building – the site of an inn during medieval times – runs the Angel close, both in terms of accommodation & food. The rooms ooze character, as well as plenty of original features, including heavy wooden beams, leaded windows & rippled slate floors – 1 or 2 rooms even come with their own bit of old town wall; the pick of the rooms is the intimate attic room with its slipper bath. **£££**

🏠 **The Abergavenny Hotel** (20 rooms) 21 Monmouth Rd; 📞01873 859050; w abergavennyhotel.com. Opposite the bus station, this good-looking red-brick-&-stone Victorian building is a low-key alternative to its sister hotel, The Angel, further up the road. Rooms, available in different categories, namely Classic for Sole (ie: singles), Premier & Studio rooms, & Studio Terrace rooms, are done out in light palettes with oak furnishings & all the requisite mod-cons. Continental b/fast is served here. **££**

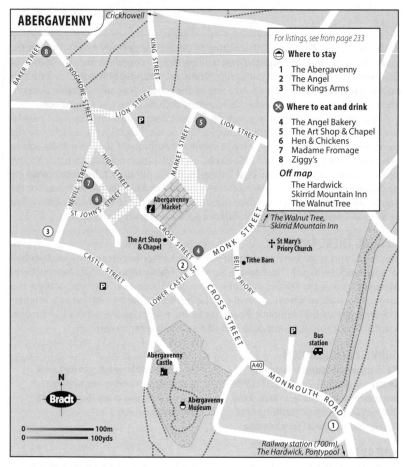

ABERGAVENNY

Crickhowell

For listings, see from page 233

Where to stay
1 The Abergavenny
2 The Angel
3 The Kings Arms

Where to eat and drink
4 The Angel Bakery
5 The Art Shop & Chapel
6 Hen & Chickens
7 Madame Fromage
8 Ziggy's

Off map
The Hardwick
Skirrid Mountain Inn
The Walnut Tree

The Walnut Tree,
Skirrid Mountain Inn

St Mary's
Priory Church

Tithe Barn

The Art Shop
& Chapel

Abergavenny
Market

Bus
station

Abergavenny
Castle

Abergavenny
Museum

N

Bradt

0 ———— 100m
0 ———— 100yds

A40

MONMOUTH ROAD

Railway station (700m),
The Hardwick, Pontypool

✗ WHERE TO EAT AND DRINK *Map, above*

✗ The Walnut Tree 3 miles northeast of Abergavenny on the B4521, Llanddewi Skirrid; ☏ 01873 852797; w thewalnuttreeinn.com; ⊕ noon–14.30 & 18.00–21.00 Wed–Sat. Opened in the 1960s under the helm of legendary chef Franco Taruschio, the Walnut Tree was the original Brecon fine-dining establishment, and the one that many other places have tried, unsuccessfully, to emulate. For a while his head chef was Stephen Terry, who became the proprietor in 2001, earning the restaurant its first Michelin star the following year. A few troubled years later, it was taken over by Shaun Hill, who now holds his own star. The interior is pleasantly understated & unlike many starred establishments the food is unpretentious: you can choose from a set menu or an à la carte menu for lunch, & à la carte for dinner, but

a couple of Shaun's signature dishes are the Lancashire bomb cheese soufflé with Welsh white truffle, & monkfish with crab & green curry. If you're staying at The Angel, then a complimentary taxi is provided. £££

✗ The Art Shop & Chapel 8 Cross St; ☏ 01873 852690; w artshopandchapel.co.uk; ⊕ chapel 09.30–17.00 Tue–Sat. Another fabulous corner of the Angel's mini empire, these are actually 2 different venues a couple of minutes apart from each other, with the chapel (incorporating the kitchen) just around the corner from the shop on Market St. It's a thoughtfully designed space in which to enjoy dishes that are prepared using foraged or home-cultivated ingredients wherever possible, & with bread from its own bakery of course (see opposite). The majority of dishes, be they b/fast (Za'tar eggs with Greek fava & spinach) or lunch (stout rarebit on Angel Bakery sourdough with tomato chutney) are veggie-oriented. Regularly stages art, music & other events. £

The Hardwick 3 miles south of Abergavenny on the B4598 (Old Raglan Rd); 01873 854220; w thehardwick.co.uk; 11.00–23.00 Wed–Sat, noon–15.30 Sun. Run by Stephen Terry, one-time owner of The Walnut Tree, the food at this no-fuss gastropub is as good as anywhere else in South Wales. A 3-course menu might look something like Black Mountain smoked salmon with deep-fried avocado for starters, slow-cooked shoulder of Brecon lamb with Italian broad beans & potato gnocchi for main, & topped off with panna cotta, stem ginger & Wye Valley rhubarb. It's not cheap, hence the 3-course lunch (£35) & Sun lunch (£37.50) menus are well worth considering. Even the children's menu has been well thought out, offering a more exciting take on the usual dreary formula, such as Brecon lamb shepherd's pie with seasonal greens, & all mains are under a tenner. £££

Hen & Chickens 7 Flannel St; 01873 853613; w sabrainpubs.com; noon–23.00 daily. It's been around for eons & remains as popular, & as timeless, as ever. It's a Brains pub so the choice of beer isn't the most varied, but there are usually a couple of guest ales on the go at any one time. Also serves reassuringly solid grub at reassuringly cheap prices. £

Skirrid Mountain Inn 5 miles north of Abergavenny in Llanfihangel Crucorney; 01873 890258; w skirridmountaininn.co.uk; 17.30–23.00 Mon, 11.30–14.30 & 17.30–23.00 Thu & Fri, 11.30–23.00 Sat, noon–22.30 Sun. By some distance Wales's oldest pub – some say as early as 1110 but no-one knows for sure – this storied pub is well worth a diversion. At any time of the

year the Skirrid has its own special atmosphere, but especially so in winter when the enormous log fire crackles & spits away. While here, don't discount the possibility of a strange encounter or 2, for this is reputedly Wales's most haunted hostelry. It's said that the notorious Judge Jefferies ('The Hanging Judge') frequently held court here, with the condemned sentenced to death by hanging from the oak beams over the stairwell – hence the scorch marks from the rope that are still visible. You have been warned… ££

Madame Fromage 16 Neville St; 01873 856118; w madamefromage.co.uk; 10.00–17.00 Mon–Sat. In 2021, the owners of this splendiferous café-cum-deli took the bold decision to relocate here from Cardiff where the shop had been a huge success for 17 years. But they needn't have worried because the punters keep on comin'; with lovely lunch plates like hot homemade sausage roll with coleslaw, grilled goat's cheese salad, & baked camembert with chutney, plus platters too, you'll have a hard time choosing – you'll just have to come back again. ££

The Angel Bakery Lower Castle St; 01873 736950; w theangelbakery.com; 09.00–16.00 Tue–Sat. The Angel's bakery has forged a fantastic reputation for itself, & you'll find very few cafés or delis in the area that don't stock their goodies in some guise or other. Everything is made here on the premises: big slabs of sourdough, toasties, patisseries & supersized croissants, all & any of which is best washed down with a strong cup of coffee; sit in or take away. £

Ziggy's 53 Frogmore St; 01873 855706; 08.30–16.30 Mon–Sat. Cracking coffee house whose bi-fold doors open on to a small, sunny (when the sun's shining) terrace, the perfect spot to indulge in an almond croissant alongside a mug of the town's tastiest, strongest cappuccino. £

SHOPPING

Abergavenny Market Town Hall, 61 Cross St; 01873 853254; w visitmonmouthshire.com; 09.00–17.00/18.00. You'll find something going on under the blue wrought-iron girders of the town's most gilded building most days of the week, including a general market on Tue, Fri & Sat – look out for Y Fenni (a mustard-infused cheddar)

& freshly griddled Welsh cakes; & a flea market (mostly arts & crafts) on Wed. There's a craft fair on the 2nd Sat of each month, an antiques fair on the 3rd Sun of the month, & an artisan (produce & art) market on the 4th Thu of each month. There's occasionally a collectors' fair taking place too.

WHAT TO SEE AND DO Abergavenny is a fairly small town, with most things of interest centred on, or just off the main thoroughfare, Cross Street, including the blue-turreted Victorian Gothic Town Hall, home to all manner of various markets (page 235), and the tourist information office. Cross Street then becomes the quietly bustling High Street, which is doing much better than your average town-centre high street these days, with enough independents to keep things interesting.

Abergavenny Castle and Museum (Castle St; ✆01873 854282; w monlife.co.uk; ⊕ 11.00–16.00 daily except Wed; free) Loftily perched above the Usk, Abergavenny Castle is an extremely modest affair by the standards of most Welsh castles. One of the grimmest episodes in its history took place at Christmas 1175 when William de Braose, then lord of the town, invited the Gwent chieftain Sitsyllt ap Dwfnwal and guests to the castle, only for them all to be unceremoniously put to the sword – a revenge act, one suspects, for Dwfnwal's capture of the castle from de Braose a few years earlier, though it was Dwfnwal himself who then had the fort repaired. It was pretty much downhill all the way after that: sacked by Owain Glyndwr and then laid to waste during the Civil War, all that really remains beyond the roofless gatehouse as you enter the grounds is a section of curtain wall to the right.

The castle's central keep, extensively remodelled in the 19th century, has been put to good use as the town museum. It's an intermittently enjoyable rummage and alongside the standard historical fare are several recreated interiors, including Basil Jones's grocery shop, the contents of which were transported here lock, stock and very large biscuit barrel following the death of his son, Jerry, in 1989. One of the more unusual exhibits is a Red Cross parcel sent to Rudolf Hess, Hitler's deputy. In June 1941, taking a flight between Germany and the UK, for reasons that never been entirely clear although some historians contend that Hess was on a quest to broker some kind of peace deal, Hess's plane crash-landed at Eaglesham in Scotland. He was originally detained in London, before being transferred to Maindiff Court Military Hospital in Abergavenny, where he remained for the best part of three years. Although his presence in the area was not a secret, his exact whereabouts was never revealed to the wider public at the time.

St Mary's Priory Church and Tithe Barn (Monk St; ✆01873 858787; w stmarys-priory.org; ⊕ 10.00–14.00 Mon–Fri; free) The earliest parts of St Mary's Priory Church, including the sanctuary, date from Norman times, when it was founded as a priory and home to a dozen or so monks, though the greater part of the church was completed in the 14th century under the patronage of John de Hastings, Lord of Abergavenny, a wooden effigy of whom lies in the north transept. This is one of many splendid medieval monuments, among them ten 15th- and 16th-century alabaster chest tombs holding members of the Hastings and Herbert clans; these are mostly grouped in the Herbert Chapel. Two tombs with particularly outstanding carvings are those of Sir Richard Herbert, encased with an elaborate window arch under an ornate heraldic canopy, and that of Sir William ap Thomas, carved with apostles and martyrs. Many of these were originally rich in colour, not that you'd know it now.

But the church's most spectacular piece of work is the Jesse Tree sculpture, a twice life-sized statue of King David's father that was hewn from a single piece of timber, although the author is unknown. This makes it singularly unique in that most 'Jesse Trees' (which represent the ancestors of Christ in the guise of a family tree) are more commonly found carved in stone or in stained-glass windows. Another of the church's timber treasures are the medieval choir stalls, the only one of Wales's one-time Benedictine churches to have retained their stalls. Take a look at the misericords, the carved shelves underneath the seats.

One of Wales's most important festivals, and one of the best of its kind in Europe, is September's two-day food festival, with talks, tutored tastings, demos and masterclasses by the best in the business. More than 200 artisan producers, stalls and street food vendors cram into the town's narrow streets and dozens of other venues, like the Market Hall, theatre and castle ruins.

The original purpose of the 16th-century Tithe Barn adjacent to the church was as a tax collection office, though stints as a coach house, theatre for travelling actors and a discotheque were among some of its more colourful incarnations. These days, it's home to an exhibition on the history of Abergavenny, though it doesn't usually take long for most people to gravitate towards the Abergavenny Tapestry, a beautifully assembled visual representation of the town's history, with characters, places and events – Blorenge, Sugar Loaf and Skirrid, the castle, Owain Gyndwr, the Jesse Tree sculpture, Foxhunter – woven into a 24ft (8m)-long piece of fabric. The work was undertaken by a small army of local volunteers and took them the best part of six years to complete, and was ready for display in 2005.

THE BLACK MOUNTAINS

Much like their near namesake in the western Beacons, the Black Mountains see relatively few visitors in comparison with the park's central tract, but for those that are tempted by this exhilarating corner of the national park, it's not somewhere easily forgotten. Geographically, the mountains lie roughly between Abergavenny, Crickhowell, Talgarth and Hay-on-Wye, at the same time forming a formidable natural frontier with England. And although far from being intimidatingly mountainous, like the mightiest peaks of Snowdonia, or even parts of the central Beacons, the Black Mountains retain a stark, elemental beauty that you won't find replicated anywhere else in Wales.

Walking in the Black Mountains is as rewarding, and in parts as challenging, as anywhere else in the Brecon Beacons. Moreover, you can go miles without seeing another soul here, almost as if human habitation has decided to forego this landscape altogether. If you're looking to bag a few peaks, the big ones here are **Waun Fach** (2,661ft) and **Pen y Gadair Fawr** (2,625ft).

It's not difficult to understand why these mountains and their 'hushed atmosphere' – as observed by the 12th-century cleric Giraldus Cambrensis – have exerted such a strong pull over the centuries: St Issui built a cell, and William de Lacy founded a hermitage here; later, Walter Savage Landor settled in Llanthony for a brief period, Turner painted here, while the diarist Kilvert found himself mildly apoplectic at the sight of 'two British tourists posturing among the ruins in an attitude of admiration.' There's also something in the raw physicality of this landscape that has managed to fire the imagination of many a great author, from Bruce Chatwin (*On the Black Hill*) and Raymond Williams (*People of the Black Mountains*) to more contemporaneous writers like Owen Sheers, whose World War II-based novel, *Resistance*, was set among these hills.

VALE OF EWYAS Described by Geraldus as 'a wilderness far removed the bustle of mankind', the Vale of Ewyas (also known as Llanthony Valley) is arguably the

Brecon Beacons   THE BLACK MOUNTAINS

7

Outlined here are four of the most popular and enjoyable short hikes in the Black Mountains, all taking around 2 hours and all of which are manageable for anyone with a reasonable degree of fitness. They are also all within striking distance of Abergavenny with each and every one offering gobsmacking views. But as always, go prepared, because even at these fairly modest heights, the weather can turn quickly.

HAY BLUFF (2,221ft) (3 miles) At the precipitous eastern end of the **Hatterall Ridge**, Hay Bluff is easily reached, starting at the car park at the top of the Gospel Pass, from where an obvious track runs up to the summit cairn for sensational views over the border into Herefordshire, and the Brecons to the west. Once at the top, an enjoyable continuation of the walk is along the ridge, walking southeast along the rim of the hill until you reach the Offa's Dyke Path, whereupon you drop down on to a switchback path back towards the car park. It'd be unusual not to see a hang-glider or two as well, even if there's just a slight hint of wind.

SUGAR LOAF (1,995ft) (10 miles) Probably the most popular outing of the lot. The typical ascent is from the south: from Abergavenny, head out on the A40 towards Crickhowell for about half a mile, turning right up Pentre Lane. Continue past the Sugar Loaf Vineyard (you can visit that afterwards) to reach Llanwenarth car park. From here, the initial part of the walk through open moorland is fairly sedate, but as the mountain face opens up, it becomes apparent that you've got a wee climb on your hands. As the gradient increases, the grassy track starts to give way to rockier terrain before you reach the summit. The 360-degree views are something else.

BLORENGE (1,834ft) (3 miles) A smooth, rounded cone, Blorenge (the only word in the English language that rhymes with orange) occupies the high ground between Abergavenny and Blaenavon to the south, so could be tackled from either town. The best route is from the car park at Keeper's Pond (Pen-Ffordd-Goch Pondon on the OS map) on the B4246 just north of Blaenavon. From here take the left-

loveliest vale in all of Wales. Running for some 12 miles north from Llanfihangel Crucorney up to the Gospel Pass, it's thoroughly enchanting, throughout history a siren call to artists, writers, monastics and recluses. Its ancient past is recalled in a triumvirate of memorable ecclesiastical buildings: **Partrishow Church**, the extraordinary lopsided enigma that is the **Parish Church of St Martin** in Cwmyoy, and the gaunt remains of **Llanthony Priory**.

Church of St Ishow

From Llanfihangel Crucorney, the road continues north into the Vale of Ewyas, and after a mile or so, a lane break off left towards Grwyne Fawr, location for the Church of St Ishow (or St Issui). The story goes that an early Christian called Issui (or Ishow) founded a hermitage near a well by St Mary's Stream some time in the 6th century. The hermit was later murdered by a passing traveller to whom he had given sanctuary, and thereafter the site became an important place of pilgrimage; one passing traveller, having been healed by the waters, left a crock of gold with which to build a church. The original stone church was rebuilt in the 14th and 15th centuries, and largely restored in the early 19th century, though it did hand path, which runs along the left-hand side of the pond and heads northeast. Where the path splits (at the stone way marker marked Llanfoist/Govilon), take the right-hand path, which continues around the contour of the hill. Shortly after, climb up into a grassy gully and, emerging from this, you'll soon see Blorenge's northern slopes. Beyond a small building, turn right and make for the summit and savour the view: the Brecon Beacons to the north and the Valleys to the south. From the summit take the gravel path south all the way down to the Foxhunter's car park (you can't miss it: it's flanked by two huge TV masts). Just before the car park is a plaque dedicated to Foxhunter, the 1952 Olympic gold-medal-winning horse whose hide is buried here (his skeleton was donated to the Royal Veterinary College); the ashes of his rider, Sir Harry Llewellyn, were also scattered here in 1999. At the car park, walk along the tarmac road for a couple of hundred metres then take the grassy path that breaks off to the right and back towards Keeper's Pond.

SKIRRID (1,595ft) (5 miles) Although by some distance the lowest of the four mountains, that doesn't mean that this hike is any less enjoyable. Quite the opposite: it's a surprisingly steep ascent so you'll have your work cut out, and the views from the summit of this charismatic mountain are every bit as rewarding as the others. Skirrid (Ysgyryd Fawr) has been known as a holy or sacred place ever since Christ's crucifixion, when a piece of the mountain is said to have broken off. The walk itself starts from a small roadside car park on the B4521, three miles northeast of Abergavenny and half a mile or so short of the Walnut Tree Inn. From the car park, walk up the gravel track towards the woodland and through a kissing gate at the top of the slope. Take the obvious path uphill and when you reach a wooden gate in the wall at the top of the woodland, turn left and follow the footpath as it contours around the hillside. At the top of the hill, take the waymarked footpath on the eastern side and round to the trig point. Having savoured the view, and taken a quick look at the scant remains of a medieval chapel, which was used as a clandestine meeting place during a period of Catholic persecution, head south along the ridge to the waymarked path and proceed back down the hill.

manage to escape the attention of the Victorians, as this place was evidently just too remote for them bother with. Inside, there is much fine detail to admire, not least a superb early-16th-century rood screen culled from Irish bog oak and beautifully carved with shallow reliefs of oak leaves and swirly-tailed dragons. There are some intriguing medieval wall texts too: one is a painting of a skeleton, hourglass in one hand and scythe and spade in the other – so called *Time and Death* – and it's been said that no matter how many times the image is painted over, it seeks to reappear... The well itself is located beyond the churchyard gate down a steep lane; it's easily identified thanks to the colourful ribbons tied to a tree, while a small tin cup allows visitors to draw water from the well.

The Parish Church of St Martin '...the cleft church at Cwmyoy, its gravity displaced', was how the poet Geoffrey Hill described the exquisite Parish Church of St Martin in *Comus*. And it's true. From whichever angle you approach it, Cymyoy's remarkable little church almost defies description: nothing at all matches up, from the lopsided tower and askew roof, to the buckled walls and the chancel slewing this way and that, looking for all the world as if it's been pieced together by a drunk draughtsman. Even the headstones in the cemetery are all of a wonk. The reason for this is subsidence: the church happened to be built directly below the site of an enormous landslide that occurred some 12,000 years ago (the Quaternary Ice Age??), and as this material slowly disintegrated, the church found itself subject to a series of minor disturbances.

The most appreciable changes to the original 13th-century structure were the 16th-century square-headed windows followed by the communal rails and six large bells in the 17th century, a superfluous addition, really, given the state of the tower – as it is, they stand idle. On one of the windowsills is a diminutive stone crucifix bearing a shallow relief of Christ with a mitred cap. It's had an eventful history: following Llanthony's dissolution, the cross was buried in the graveyard for safe-keeping (though in the event Henry's henchmen never bothered venturing this way as the church was evidently too remote), before it was retrieved by a local farmer in 1861. It was then stolen from the church in 1967, only for it to be traced to a London antique shop by the British Museum's Keeper of Sculpture (who better?) and returned to Cwmyoy. The church is usually open most of the time.

Llanthony Priory and Capel-y-Ffin

Few ruins anywhere in Wales can offer such a wildly romantic setting as those of **Llanthony Priory** (✆ 03000 252239; w cadw.gov.wales; ⊕ 10.00–16.00 daily; free), a construct of 11th-century warlord William de Lacy who founded the country's first Augustinian priory here; its name comes from Llandewi Nany Hodni – the Church of St David on the River Honddu. Travelling through the Vale in the late 19th century, Cambrensis observed that the priory – at that stage still under construction – was 'truly fitted for contemplation, a happy and delightful spot, established to supply all its own wants.' What remains today is largely 13th century: effectively the shell of the church, which includes the western façade, nave and southern transept (whose high, sharply pointed archways perfectly frame the sheep-speckled mountains) and several outbuildings. What remains is arguably one of the best examples of the Transitional style between Romanesque and Gothic in Wales.

As with many other places of worship, the priory was dissolved in 1539 but because of its remoteness, virtually nothing was plundered: instead its deterioration was down to neglect and decay. Part of it has been put to good effect though, with a hotel now occupying a track behind the ruins from where a track winds up to the Offa's Dyke Path.

Less than 4 miles up the narrow, tree-funnelled road is **Capel-y-Ffin**, meaning 'Chapel at the End'. Timeless in every sense, it has been a place of spiritual devotion for centuries, ever since de Lacy himself pitched up and became a hermit, before he emerged a few years later and decided to go and do something useful like construct a priory. For the record, the village has two chapels, a fenced-off monastery ruin built in 1870 by the Reverend Joseph Lyne (and confusingly called Llanthony Monastery) and not a lot else – certainly no houses, shops, or even a pub. Upon Lyne's death, the monastery was run by a group of Benedictine monks, but it eventually disintegrated and was purchased in 1924 by the controversial sculptor and typeface designer Eric Gill who established a small artists' colony here. As much as Gill and his motley entourage – among them the painter David Jones, to whom Gill was something of a father figure (Gill got engaged to one of his daughters too) – were able to draw inspiration from their surrounds, it was a hostile environment, particularly in winter, and four years later they decamped to the relative comfort of Piggotts Farm in High Wycombe. Gill left his mark, however, in an engraved headstone in the churchyard. Meanwhile, his great-granddaughter, Mary, now runs the Grange Trekking Centre (see below).

A short walk from the chapel is **Grange Trekking** (Capel-y-Ffin; ✆01873 890215; w grangetrekking-wales.co.uk), a long-established, well-run riding centre with a stable of 36 Welsh ponies and cobs. They offer half- and full-day treks (£44/75) through the mountains, neither of which require any riding experience. With an expert guide leading you, treks climb steeply up into the hills and into the belly of the Black Mountains: thrilling stuff. The full-day trek is particularly exhilarating as you get to ride towards Hay Bluff.

Where to stay, eat and drink

Llanthony Priory Hotel (7 rooms) Llanthony Priory; ✆01873 890487; w llanthonyprioryhotel.co.uk; restaurant & bar ⏱ summer 10.30–15.00 & 18.00–22.00 Tue–Fri, 10.30–22.00 Sat, 10.30–21.00 Sun, Nov–Mar 18.00–23.00 Fri, 11.00–23.00 Sat, noon–16.00 Sun. Fashioned from the remnants of the priory, this erstwhile hunting lodge offers 7 rooms, 4 of which are located in the quartet of towers. Owing to the building's age & configuration, none of the rooms have bathrooms, & so long as you're not bothered about other creature comforts (including mobile or Wi-Fi reception), & aren't restricted in terms of mobility (there are no lifts & the stairs are steep & narrow), then it's all to play for. It is overpriced for what it is, but given the location, it's worth it. There's a decent restaurant to boot, while the atmospheric bar occupies the vaulted medieval undercroft, a thirst-slaking beer here perfect after a hard day in the hills. **££**

Grange Trekking (3 rooms) Capel-y-Ffin; ✆01873 890215; w grangetrekking-wales.co.uk. Whether you're here to ride or not, this trekking centre has various accommodation available, from a comfy little B&B with 3 en-suite rooms & a riverside campsite with 20 pitches & an on-site compost loo to a shepherd's hut sleeping 3 & a pod sleeping 2; there are 'proper' loos & showers in the main house, which is also where you can have a filling cooked b/fast; guests of both the B&B & the campsite pay extra (£8) for this. **£**

The Gospel Pass and Hay Bluff
From Capel-y-Ffin, the road, still disconcertingly narrow, crawls up and over the **Gospel Pass**, one of the most thrilling short drives in all of Wales. As the road climbs and widens beside sheep-cropped verges, a vast tract of moorland layered with tight coils of russet bracken, heather and wildflowers opens up. To your right stands **Hay Bluff** (2,221ft), a favourite spot for hang-gliders, who propel themselves from the top when conditions are right. From the car park, the walk to the top of Hay Bluff is not a difficult one (page 186), but do be prepared if the weather looks like it might close in as it's very exposed along the ridge. Needless to say, the views from its windy summit – the Brecons to the west and Herefordshire to the east – are unbeatable. From Hay Bluff it's a gentle 5-mile descent to Hay-on-Wye, which of course could also be an alternative starting point.

HAY-ON-WYE

Books, books and more books. That's the essence of Hay-on-Wye (locals just call it Hay), a spruce little town slap on the border with England – it's surprising how many people think that Hay is *in* England – and it's been this way ever since the first secondhand bookshop opened here in 1961. Whereas many towns in South Wales have seen their shops and businesses ebb away in recent years, most here in Hay have just about managed to cling on and today there are in excess of 20 trading bookshops. It all comes to a climax each May with the **Hay Festival**, the world's largest and most prestigious literary jamboree (page 244).

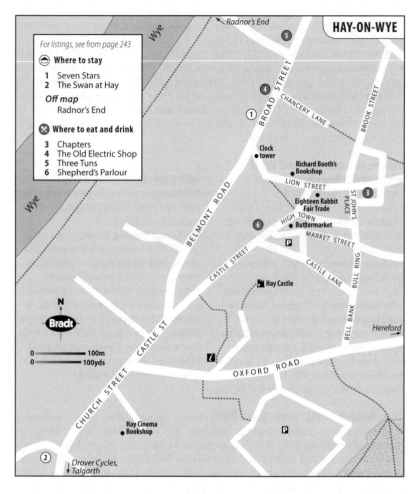

The phenomenon that is Hay has everything to do with Richard Booth (1938–2019), the flamboyant, Hay-born-and-bred bookseller. On 1 April 1977 (note the date), Booth declared Hay an independent sovereign state, at the same time proclaiming himself monarch, appointing his own ministers ('cabinet' meetings would be held in the pub) and issuing passports and rice-paper money; bonkers, maybe, but visionary too. It didn't take long for the strategy to work, for within a few years the town had become a mecca for bibliophiles. This spirit of contrariety has served the town well over the years, filtering down to other businesses and sectors within the community.

Apart from browsing and eating (and notwithstanding the newly renovated castle), there's not an awful lot else to see or do in Hay, but like Crickhowell, it's the ideal base for local outings, including the popular walk up to Hay Bluff.

GETTING THERE AND AWAY From Hay it's a 40-minute drive east to Hereford along the B4352 and A438. Heading west, it's a short run down to Talgarth, from where the A438/A470 continues to Brecon and the A479 scenically weaves its way south to Crickhowell and Abergavenny.

There is no train station in Hay, the nearest being Hereford 22 miles away. There are buses from Hereford (4 daily Mon–Sat, 3 Sun), which is actually the same bus (#T14) that serves Brecon and Talgarth; these stop on Oxford Road opposite the tourist office.

TOURIST INFORMATION AND ACTIVITIES

🛈 Tourist Information Bureau Oxford Rd; 📞01497 820144; **w** hay-on-wye.co.uk; ⏲ 10.00–16.00 Mon–Sat, 11.00–13.00 Sun. Small but helpful office opposite the main town car park with a raft of leaflets to hand & expert advice.
Drover Cycles Forest Rd; 📞01479 822419; **w** drovercycles.co.uk; ⏲ 09.00–17.30 Mon–Sat, 10.00–17.00 Sun. The area around Hay is fantastic for cycling so if you fancy a bit of 2-wheeling this excellent outfit has got an extensive fleet of bikes including road, mountain, e-bikes, tandems & trailers; prices start at £35 for a day's hire (£25 for kids). They also deliver within a 15-mile radius so long as you hire 2 bikes & for a min 2 days.

🏠 WHERE TO STAY *Map, opposite*

There's a reasonable stock of accommodation in Hay, though perhaps not as much as you might expect in a town that stages one of the world's great festivals. It goes without saying that if you do intend to stay here during the festival, you will need to book well in advance, and that means months ahead.

🏠 The Swan at Hay (19 rooms) Church St; 📞01497 821188; **w** swanathay.co.uk. the classiest hotel for miles around, the Swan occupies one of the oldest buildings in town, dating from 1812. Rooms (classic, superior & deluxe dbls & 1 sgl) are immaculate, decorated in gentle beige or blue tones, with floral lines & wall-bound botanical studies by local artist Lea Gregory; the 4 coach house rooms are all dog-friendly. Public areas extend to a gorgeous garden where you can breakfast on warmer mornings. The hotel does tend to lean heavily on weddings so check availability well in advance. **£££**

🏠 Seven Stars (9 rooms) 11 Broad St; 📞01497 820886; **w** theseven-stars.co.uk. A fabulous old stone building harbouring sunny rooms with thick-set walls & chunky oak beams, though the best surprise is the heated indoor swimming pool – not something you find in your everyday guesthouse. The very amenable owner, Di, does a mean breakfast – including haddock from the Black Mountain Smokery – to see you on your way. **££**
⚑ Radnor's End Radnor's End; 📞01497 820780. Clean back-to-basics campsite in a terrific location by the Wye & just a short walk into town; coin-operated showers & laundry/tumble dryer. **£**

✘ WHERE TO EAT AND DRINK *Map, opposite*

✻ ✘ Chapters Lion St; **m** 07855 783799; **w** chaptershayonwye.co.uk; ⏲ 17.00–21.00 Wed–Sat. Taking over where St John's left off a few years ago, Chapters is one of the finest restaurants in South Wales, & it seems only a matter of time before a Michelin star comes its way. It's an intimate space, occupying part of what used to be a part of St John's Church, & the owner, Charmaine, has been meticulous in ensuring that everything here was sustainability sourced, from the bar (old scaffolding boards) to the artwork (repurposed from old books). Care is also taken to ensure ingredients are in season & sourced from local producers, as well as their own kitchen garden, hence the 5-course set menu (£52) is likely to feature divine morsels like BBQ sprouting broccoli with goat's curd & wild garlic, & Herefordshire pork loin with confit carrots, cider jus & crackling. An absolute treat from beginning to end. Reservations required. **£££**
🍺 Three Tuns 4 Broad St; 📞01497 821855; **w** three-tuns.com; ⏲ noon–22.00 Mon–Thu, noon–23.00 Fri & Sat, noon–21.00 Sun. This rambling old pub has been serving satisfied punters since the 17th century (it's actually Hay's second-oldest building), & notwithstanding some slightly brutal modern extension work, the rippled flagstoned floors, stone walls & inglenook chimney make for a very welcoming prospect. After Chapters, this is some of the best-cooked food in town, essentially Italian, with the likes of white bean puree, rocket & chilli bruschetta, & rare-breed

pork ragu pasta. On Sun, attention turns to hearty, & very reasonably priced, roasts. ££

⌐ **The Old Electric Shop** 10 Broad St; ✎ 01497 821194; **w** oldelectric.co.uk; ⏲ 10.00–17.00 daily. Immediately likeable junk-shop-like space packed with vintage clothing, furnishings, gifts & books – it's one of the few bookshops in town that sells just new titles. But the café is even better, devoted exclusively to an all-veggie/vegan menu, plus tasty coffee & some belting homemade sticky treats. £

⌐ **Shepherd's Parlour** 9 High Town; ✎ 01497 821898; **w** shepherdsicecream.co.uk; ⏲ 09.30–17.00 daily. Jolly café/ice-cream parlour serving seasonally flavoured ices in myriad weird & wonderful flavours like gooseberry & elderflower crumble, & damson & sloe gin, all made with sheep's milk. Loads more too, including toasted sourdough sandwiches, soups & home-baked cakes. £

SHOPPING There isn't of course enough space to list even a fraction of the town's bookshops, so below are just two of the more popular and unusual, suffice to say that a stroll along Castle Street will yield a bookshop every few yards or so, with shops specialising in everything from murder mystery to ??

Eighteen Rabbit Fair Trade 2 Lion St; ✎ 01497 822882; **w** eighteenrabbit.co.uk; ⏲ 10.00–16.00 Mon–Fri, 10.00–17.00 Sat. There's not much that this fabulous little fair trade shop doesn't sell, which includes everything from wallets made from recycled tyres to chocolate, coffee & books.

Hay Cinema Bookshop Castle St; ✎ 01479 820017; ⏲ haycinemabookshop.co.uk; ⏲ 09.00–18.00 Mon–Sat, 10.00–17.30 Sun. One of the very first bookshops to open in Hay (1965), this venerable old place (in the town's former cinema, obviously) has piles & piles of

secondhand & remainder books on subjects you never even thought possible. With more books spilling out into the front courtyard, be prepared for a lengthy browse.

Richard Booth's Bookshop 44 Lion St; ✎ 01497 820322; ⏲ boothbooks.co.uk; ⏲ 09.30–17.30 Mon–Sat, 11.00–17.00 Sun. This place has come on a bit since Booth himself ran the gaff & today it's a beauty of a bookshop with shelves neatly stacked with every conceivable genre (both new & old titles); grab 1 or 2 that take your fancy & retreat to the sunlit café at the rear of the shop; they've even got their own cinema here.

HAY'S FESTIVALS

For ten days at the end of May, this small town of 2,000 becomes the centre of the literary universe. The first **Hay Festival** (**w** hayfestival.com) was held in 1987, playing host to no more than a few people, a far cry from the 100,000 or so that now pitch up each spring. From established authors to the biggest names in the world of politics and journalism, it's a stellar line-up. There's also a feast of live music, comedy and drama. In 2022, there were performances by Jimmy Page, Bryn Terfel, Marcus Brigstock, Benedict Cumberbatch and Catrin Finch with Seikou Keita. The festival is mostly self-contained in an enormous marquee-filled field at the entrance to town, which can be reached via shuttle buses from the town centre. Such is the festival's profile that it has spawned 'Hay Festivals' all across the globe, including as far away as Medellín in Colombia.

Running alongside the Hay Festival (for just four or five days) is **HowTheLightGetsIn** (**w** howthelightgetsin.org), a colourful, vibrant celebration of music and philosophy which typically features some of the world's greatest thinkers like Richard Dawkins and Slavoj Žizek – this, too, has spawned namesake events in other parts of the world.

WHAT TO SEE AND DO   Although most bookshops are located along Castle Street, Hay is essentially centred on a handful of creaky little streets leading to or from the colonnaded **buttermarket**, erected in 1830 on the site of the former marketplace; it's still home to a Thursday market (⊕ 09.00–14.30). Heading down Lion Street, and beyond Richard Booth's Bookshop – note the gorgeous glazed tiles painted with agricultural motifs on the façade – is the town **clock tower**, built in 1881.

The town's one conventional site is **Hay Castle** (☏01497 820079; w haycastletrust. org; ⊕ 10.00–17.00 daily; free), which, after years in a perpetual state of repair, has now seen the light of day again. Built in the 13th century by William de Braose, it was sacked the following century and promptly rebuilt by Henry III, before a Jacobean mansion was added to the existing structure in the 17th century. Fires in 1939 and 1977 further degraded the building and after a period of time spent as – surprise, surprise – another bookshop, it was eventually closed in 2015 pending the recent restoration. Booth himself bought the castle in the 1960s and remained its custodian until 2011 when he sold it to the Hay Castle Trust. Finally re-opened in 2022, there is a top-floor gallery for touring exhibitions, a platform at the top of the keep for views, and a café in the former coach house and kitchen. Below the castle walls, an open-air bookshop invites passers-by to browse – if there's anything you like the look of, pop your cash into the honesty tin.

8

Carmarthenshire

Carmarthenshire – Sir Gâr in Welsh – is one of Wales's original 13 historic counties, a sparsely populated, predominantly agricultural region patchworked with gently rolling fields and river valleys, and carved up by quiet back roads, in places almost appearing to be untouched by modern life. In many ways, the county's position, between Gower and Pembrokeshire, does it few favours, with most folk quick to chase the more obvious attractions further west. Conversely, it's almost inevitable that you'll be passing through at some point, so there's no good reason not to stop and explore some of its overlooked charms.

Save for a small pocket in the southeast, once heavily industrialised with coalmining, steel making and tinplate making, the county once had the largest agricultural labour force in Wales, but like most places these days it's the service industry that it now relies most heavily on. It's here, too, where you'll start to notice more Welsh being spoken, assuming you've come from the east, and although the most recent census indicated that the number of Welsh speakers here had declined in recent times, it's still a fairly healthy 44%.

On the surface, Carmarthenshire's two main towns, **Carmarthen** – the ancient county town – and **Llanelli**, have little going for them, but burrow a little deeper and there are gains to be had. Within Carmarthen's orbit there's the fun **Gwili Railway** – South Wales's only narrow gauge – and the **National Botanic Garden** – a world-class horticultural complex centred on the Sir Norman Foster-designed great glasshouse. Not for nothing is Carmarthenshire known as the Garden of Wales and there's another beauty a few miles northeast courtesy of the gloriously resurrected **Aberglasney** gardens.

Heading up the lush **Tywi Valley** – home to the River Twyi, the longest river entirely within Wales – the small, green-fringed market towns of **Llandeilo** and **Llandovery** lie close to some irresistibly charming countryside pockmarked by historical and industrial remnants: Newton House and Dinefwr Castle, and up towards the northern margins of the county within touching distance of the Cambrian Mountains, the Dolaucothi Goldmine, Britain's only known Roman goldmine. Close by, Carmarthenshire nudges into the western foothills of the Brecon Beacons, claiming the magnificent, muscular ruins of **Carreg Cennen** as its own.

Carmarthenshire's biggest draw by a country mile is the tiny township of **Laugharne**, by dint of its associations with Dylan Thomas (he is buried here), although both its castle and its setting at the mouth of the glistening Loughor Estuary offer other reasons to visit. Laugharne aside, few people gravitate towards the Carmarthenshire coast, but that is to miss out on some thrilling beaches, in particular the long silken stretches of sand at **Cefn Sidan** and **Pendine** and a brace of superlative fortresses at **Kidwelly** and **Llansteffan**. Here too is Wales's only **Wildfowl and Wetlands Centre** representative, just outside Llanelli.

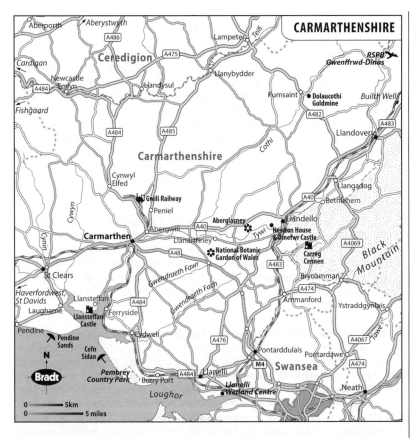

Getting around is easy. The A48 picks up where the M4 ends, while the A40 continues westwards into Pembrokeshire. Public transport is good. The main train line is the one that runs from Llanelli to Carmarthen via Burry Port and Kidwelly before it disappears into Pembrokeshire, while slower trains pootle along the lovely Heart of Wales line between Swansea and Llandovery before disappearing off into Powys and beyond. Apparently Dylan Thomas liked to travel by bus, and you can too, wherever you want, as even the most rural spots are well connected with the major towns. As much as anything else, this is wonderful cycling country, which is only set to get better with the recent announcement of a plan to construct a new cycle path in the Tywi Valley between Carmarthen and Llandeilo.

LLANELLI AND AROUND

Casting envious glances across the Loughor Estuary to the Gower Peninsula, Llanelli was once known as Tinopolis after the local industry that thrived here. Yet as elsewhere in South Wales, the post-industrial aftermath hasn't been kind to Llanelli. The town had been struggling for years before Covid-19 reared its head, but the pandemic has only compounded the sense of economic and social stagnation, something that's all too apparent in its downcast streets; there appear to be more empty units here than any other town in South Wales. As always, though, there is hope, and to this end various regeneration schemes have been proposed, so when (or if) any of these plans come to fruition, it won't be a moment too soon. For all its troubles, the wonderful Llanelly House is strongly recommended, while the nearby Wetlands Centre holds out the promise of fantastic wildlife.

Like so many towns in South Wales, Llanelli forged its identity in the industrial arena, in particular steel and tinplate manufacturing, and while output is a fraction of what it used to be, the Tata-owned Trostre plant still employs around 650 people, primarily producing tinplated steel for food cans. But as in other parts of the region, the ever-present threat of redundancies – or worse still, closure – casts a long shadow. Steelworks aside, the natives take great pride in their rugby team, the Scarlets, one of Wales's four regional professional clubs, and an afternoon spent watching the boys knocking seven bells out of one another at Parc y Scarlets is one not to be missed if you happen to be around on match day.

GETTING THERE AND AWAY

By car Coming by car from the east, you come off at Junction 48 of the M4 near Pontarddulais and transfer to the A138. Note that if travelling from Swansea, you can avoid going the long way round by using the Loughor Bridge on the A484 road, which also marks your entry into Carmarthenshire. The Thomas/Edgar car park just to the north of Llanelly House is the most convenient spot if you need somewhere to park in town. There is also a pay and display down by the water near St Elli's Bay restaurant.

By rail and bus The train station is just under a mile south of the town centre on Great Western Crescent. There are hourly services to Swansea, as well as Carmarthen, stopping at Kidwelly and Pembrey and Burry Port en route; around half of these continue to Haverfordwest and Milford Haven. There are also a couple of trains a day to Fishguard Harbour. Llanelli is also on the Heart of Wales line, which runs between Swansea and Shrewsbury in Shropshire, meaning that from Llanelli there are also services running along the western fringe of the Brecon Beacons to Pontarddulais and Llandeilo (4 daily Mon–Sat, 2 Sun) and then onwards to Builth Wells and Knighton in Powys.

The bus station is on Island Place on the eastern side of town. There are buses every 20–30 minutes to Carmarthen, Kidwelly, Burry Port, Pembrey and Swansea, as well as services to Ammanford (4 daily Mon–Sat).

WHERE TO STAY, EAT AND DRINK

Angharad Hotel (20 rooms) 88A Queen St; 01554 899734; w angharadhotel.com. Although it's unlikely that you'll need, or want, to stay the night in Llanelli, this is your best bet if you do. Located closer to the beach than the town centre, the hotel reopened in 2021 after a big refurbishment & now has 20 fashionably smart, if modestly sized rooms including small dbls, twin & family rooms; they've also got a very creditable restaurant & a neat little coffee shop. **££**

Llanelly House Bistro Plas Llanelly Hse, Bridge St; 01554 772857; w llanelly-house.org. uk/bistro; ⏱ summer 09.30–17.00 Mon–Sat, winter 10.00–16.00 Mon–Sat. After a tour of the house (see opposite), it'd be remiss not to partake in coffee, or perhaps lunch, in the house's civilised bistro, which occupies the old drawing room & parlour. If you fancy going posh, tuck into High Tea (£14), a selection of beautifully prepared sandwiches, cakes & scones, plus tea or coffee, served in Llanelly's fanciest china; you do need to book ahead for this. **££**

St Elli's Bay Discovery Centre North Dock; 01554 526006; w stellisbay.co.uk; ⏱ bistro 10.00–19.00 daily; brasserie noon–23.00 Wed–Sat, noon–18.00 Sun. A 10-minute walk south of the centre on the waterfront, the old Discovery Centre (& until recently home to the tourist office) is now a bright-&-breezy 2-floored bistro-brasserie. The downstairs bistro serves burgers, butties, fish & chips & the like, while the 1st-floor brasserie deals in more fancy fare (herb-crusted cod loin with crispy cockles, coconut panna cotta) along with providing superior estuary views. There's a very affordable 2-course fixed-price menu Wed to Fri lunchtimes. The gelateria serves luscious ice cream, all made on site. £–££

⌨ **Hywl** 20 Market St; ℘ 01554 775537; ⊕ 09.00–15.00 Tue–Thu, 09.00–23.00 Fri & Sat. Opened at the height of the pandemic, this foliage-drenched café-bar run by a Welsh-Hungarian couple is currently the best thing about Llanelli's dining scene. The products are a celebration of all things local: coffee from Coaltown in Ammanford, gin from the Gower & beer from the Tinworks Brewing Company here in Llanelli. Weekly pop-up nights could be anything from tacos & tostadas to chunky pies & chips. This should be the template for the future of food & drink in Llanelli. ££

WHAT TO SEE AND DO

Llanelly House (℘ 01554 772857; w llanelly-house.org.uk; ⊕ tours (90mins) at 11.00 Mon, Wed & Sat; £7) At the end of Bridge St, Grade I-listed Llanelly House is the town's one essential stop. It's a handsome three-stoeyed Georgian townhouse dating from 1714, and built by Thomas Stepney, fifth baronet and one-time Member of Parliament for Carmarthenshire, ostensibly in celebration of his marriage to Margaret Vaughan – you can detect the Stepney crest on the downpipes. It remained in the family until 1811, whereupon it was inherited by William Chambers, although his was a relatively short-lived ownership. Since this time it has been pretty much anything you can think of: a bank, bakery, sweet shop, saddler's, motorbike showroom – even a tax office.

Quite literally on the brink of collapse, an extensive restoration programme between 2011 and 2013 not only brought Llanelly House magnificently back to life, but the building also gave up some of its long-held secrets. This included a section of cobbled flooring that pre-dates the building by at least 100 years (it's now glassed off so you walk over it), along with a clay pipe, oyster shells and some Australian wine bottle labels (this was also once a wine merchant's house), leading experts to surmise that these probably belonged to the first ever importation of Aussie wine to British shores.

Although there's next to nothing by way of original fixtures and fittings, this doesn't diminish from what is a fabulously entertaining romp through the house. As much as the guides themselves, it's the cleverly conceived talking portraits that bring Llanelly's main protagonists to life (including a rather spiky Lady Stepney), in addition to a time capsule which transports visitors all the way back to medieval Llanelli, that make this so much fun. Among the half a dozen or so rooms you get to see are Lady Stepney's bedroom and ante-chamber, William Chambers' study and the chambermaid's attic room.

Like any self-respecting building of a certain age, Llanelly House has its ghosts. The story here goes that, having fallen pregnant, the chambermaid, Mira Turner, attempted suicide, though some suspected that she was pushed so as to keep her pregnancy out of the news. Whatever the manner of her death, Turner's presence in the house has loomed large ever since. A couple of other incidentals to keep an eye out for include a portrait of the eighth baronet John Stepney by Joshua Reynolds in the Great Hall, and a plaque dedicated to William Chambers distinguished sporting son, John Chambers, who not only rowed for Cambridge but also swam the English Channel and codified boxing's Queensbury Rules – they were only named as such as it was the Ninth Marquess of Queensbury who endorsed them. The house bistro is also one of the best places to eat in town (see opposite). There's nothing else to see in town, so once you're done with the house you could take a wander down to the beach for some sea air and gelato from St Elli's Bay (see opposite).

8

Parc Howard Museum and Gardens (Felinfoel Rd; ✆ 01554 742220; w discovercarmarthenshire.com) About half a mile north of the town centre stands this Italianate mansion, built in 1885 by the Buckleys, a successful local brewing family. It's now a shrine to all things Llanelli, with galleries pertaining to industry (principally tin-making), art and pottery, among other subjects. One of the museum's more curious specimens is the Stepney Spare Wheel, a spokeless rim fitted with an inflated tyre in case of a puncture – this in the days before motor cars carried a spare. The invention of local lad Thomas Davies (who was based in Stepney Street, hence the name), the 'Stepney' is still used as a colloquial term for a spare tyre in some countries, notably India. Take time too to stroll the early 20th-century gardens, all pristine lawns and colourful flowerbeds. Note that Parc Howard was closed at the time of writing but was scheduled to reopen in spring 2023, so do check the state of play before any potential visit.

Llanelli Wetlands Centre (Llwynhendy; ✆ 01554 741087; w wwt.org.uk/wetland-centres/llanelli; ⊕ 09.30–17.00 daily; £9.45) Opened by Sir David Attenborough in 1991, the Wildfowl and Wetlands Trust run Llanelli Wetlands Centre, some 450 acres of manmade lagoons, lakes and pools, scrapes and walkways adjoining the saltmarshes of the Burry Inlet Estuary. As well as being one of the most important sites for wildfowl and waders, it's a key flyway for migratory birds. Spring brings large numbers of migrant warblers to the site, such as blackcap, reed warblers and sedge warblers, though wild bird numbers peak in winter when you'll see healthy populations of gadwall, shelduck and tufted duck, as well as star waders like snipe and black-tailed godwit, another red-listed bird. Bittern is another overwintering bird, though you've a better chance of hearing its foghorn-like boom than actually catching sight of this notoriously hard-to-see bird.

One of the keys to the management of the site is its livestock: grazing by sheep, cattle and ponies helps to control the vegetation for ground-nesting birds like lapwing, a red-listed member of the plover family which is presently doing well here, with around ten breeding pairs at last count. There have been other success stories too: Llanelli is one of just two sites in Wales (the other is Magor Marsh on the Gwent Levels, page 106) where water voles have been reintroduced and are currently doing extremely well. Otters, too, are present in good numbers, though sightings are rare.

The **Millennium Wetland** is traversed by a well-laid-out nexus of paths that snake their way between the various bodies of water. Pick up a map at reception and you can select your walk according to how much time you have or how deep you want to go into the reserve, though there are usefully marked signposts indicating distances and times. One of three hides here is the Heron's Wing Hide overlooking Deep Water Lake, which usually yields a good variety of birdlife, for example little egrets and, to a lesser degree, great white egrets (both members of the heron family), as well as blackcap and reed and sedge warblers; otters like to fish here too. The website has a useful weekly update on recent sightings, which gives you some idea of what to expect, and roughly where, at any given time of the year.

The second part of the wetlands is the **Living Collection** area, a collection of ponds that's home to more than 60 species of captive-bred wildfowl – ducks, swans, geese and cranes, along with 60 cacophonous Caribbean flamingos corralled into their own watery paddock. The visitor centre harbours a tidy little café serving sandwiches, pasties, cakes, coffee and the like.

Burry Port and Pembrey Country Park Five miles west of Llanelli, along the ever-shifting sands of the Loughor Estuary, the small maritime town of **Burry Port**'s claim to fame is that this was where aviator Amelia Earhart completed her solo 21-hour transatlantic journey on 18 June 1928. A memorial commemorating the feat – the first woman to fly between the two continents – is located a 5-minute walk up from the harbour on Stepney Road. Another stone monument, on the eastern side of the harbour, was erected at the spot where she is alleged to have stepped ashore, though this rankles more than a little with the neighbouring village of Pwll, who assert that it was actually in *their* village that she disembarked – so naturally, they have their plaque too. Neighbours, eh?

Like so many harbours on the South Wales coastline, the small harbour here in Burry Port was built to ship coal that had come down from the Gwendraeth Valley. Alongside the harbour grew up tinplate, copper, silver and lead works, all long since vanished. There's nothing to do here except enjoy an ice cream while watching the boats come and go. If coming by train, the station is on Station Road, midway between the harbour and the memorial.

Burry Port merges imperceptibly into the village of Pembrey, unremarkable enough but the jumping-off point for **Pembrey Country Park** (✆ 01554 742435; w pembreycountrypark.wales; ⊕ 06.00–22.00 daily, parking £3.50/2hrs, £7/day, £4/day winter), a large tract of verdant woodland and pine forest. You could spend the best part of an entire day here invested in various activities, including golf, horseriding, dry tobogganing, cycling and walking; bikes are available to hire from the ski and activity centre, and there's more information about all these activities at the visitor centre (⊕ 10.00–16.00 daily except Thu).

Pembrey Park hasn't always been such a welcoming place. During both World Wars the surrounding 700 acres of woodland was the site of the country's largest **munitions factory**, employing more than 6,000 people, mostly women. It was dirty, dangerous

MUM'S ARMY

In 1969, the Ministry of Defence proposed transforming the old Pembrey airfield into a gunnery range, essentially as an extension of the missile-testing area in Pendine a few miles west. Such a plan would have meant annexing half of Cefn Sidan beach while effectively turning Pembrey into a garrison town – that's certainly how the locals saw it. But the consequences would have been more far-reaching, not least the impact on the local farming and fishing industries, as well as the very real possibility that both Milford Haven port and Swansea airport might have been forced to close.

As the scale of what was being proposed became clear, opposition groups began forming. One particularly well co-ordinated campaign, called Save Our Sands (SOS) and led exclusively by women – mothers, grandmothers, daughters, and subsequently dubbed 'Mum's Army' – became the standard bearers. Initial protests in November 1969 were peaceful – on one of the first occasions, a group of women forestalled a tank that was attempting to enter the airfield – but as protests gathered strength, the mood turned more sinister. Many women found themselves being followed and their phones tapped, the sort of activity you'd expect in Communist-era Romania, not South Wales. The women took their protests to Westminster, dropping leaflets at the Houses of Parliament, while beach bonfires were regularly lit all along the Carmarthenshire coastline, even as far as the Gower. In May 1970, exactly a year after the initial notice of the plans had been served, a public inquiry was launched, and in April 1971 the project was finally abandoned.

work which involved preparing high explosives, TNT and the propellant cordite. The park is scattered with remnants of the factory, including bunkers, magazines and many of the lead-lined tunnels in which explosive substances (including nitroglycerin) were stored – you're welcome to explore them, if you can find them.

The park lies adjacent to **Cefn Sidan** ('Silken Back'), an endless, 7-mile sweep of sand curving around the end of the Burrows. Wales's first blue flag beach, Cefn Sidan is popular with dog-walkers in winter, but even in summer (when dogs are restricted to certain sections of the beach) it hardly feels much busier, so vast is it. During the summer months, lifeguards patrol a small area close to the entrance of the park.

Up towards its western reaches, the algae-riddled hull of the SV *Paul*, a four-masted schooner, gradually reveals itself at low tide. There are others, too, buried deep beneath these sands, some of which resurfaced during the great storms of 2014; it's been said that more than 300 vessels have run aground here over the course of time. Both Burry Port and Pembrey are easily reached by train and bus from Llanelli.

KIDWELLY AND AROUND

Lorded over by its glorious castle, it's unlikely you'd visit Kidwelly for any other reason, although the old quays have been converted into a pleasant nature reserve, so you could comfortably make a good half a day of it. An unassuming small town, but with a big village feel, Kidwelly was established around 1115, although an earlier form of its name – Cetgueli – was recorded as early as the 9th century by the monk, Nennius. Industry in Kidwelly took the form of tinworks and brickworks, the history of which was, until recently, recorded in the excellent Industrial Museum. But this has now closed, with little indication that it will be resurrected any time soon.

From the castle it's a gentle walk down Castle Street, past the old Castle School on your right and through the gatehouse, which, along with the bridge, is one of the few extant remains from the medieval town. Once across the bridge, you are now on Bridge Street, Kidwelly's main thoroughfare, which then becomes Causeway Street. Assuming you have parked at the castle, you can return there by walking from the bridge back along the riverbank, which brings you to the base of its walls; it's all signposted.

With time on your side, it's worth considering venturing down to **Kidwelly Quay**, formerly, and still sometimes called, Kymer Quay after the quay and canal built here by Thomas Kymer in 1768, which was almost certainly the first of its kind in Wales. It's now a stable habitat for different kinds of wildlife but is especially popular with birders – little egrets, curlew, redshank and sandpipers can be seen skimming across the mudflats and old salt pans of the Gwendraeth Estuary. You can either walk the 2-mile loop of the canal and quay or once at the end, carry on back into town. The quay is a 5-minute walk south of the train station.

GETTING THERE AND AWAY Kidwelly is just off the A484, 10 miles south of Carmarthen. It's on the Llanelli to Carmarthen train line with more or less hourly trains to both towns, with those to Llanelli continuing to Swansea. The train station is a 10-minute walk southwest of the village along Station Road down towards the Quay. There are half-hourly buses (none on Sun) from both Carmarthen and Llanelli, which stop by the Fisherman's Arms on Causeway Street in the centre of the village, a 5-minute walk south of the castle.

✖ WHERE TO EAT AND DRINK

🍴 Kidwelly Deli 12 Causeway St; ☎01554 890313; ⊕ 09.30–15.00 Tue–Fri, 09.30–14.00 Sat. If you're feeling peckish after the castle, make a beeline for this homely little deli on the main street. They've a whole larder of scrumptiousness: focaccia sandwiches, quiches, pasties, salads, & loads more, all freshly made on the premises, or if you're after something a little lighter, try one of their hand-crafted Portuguese tarts washed down with a flat white. Sit down or take away. £

🍴 Parc y Bocs Carmarthen Rd; ☎01554 892724; w burnsfarmshop.co.uk; ⊕ 10.00–16.00 daily. A mile or so north of town, this capacious farm shop & café is as good as anywhere in the area to park up for a bite to eat, perhaps an eggy breakfast (benedict, florentine or avocado) made using the farm's free-range eggs, a sharing platter, or the super Sun roast (noon–15.00; booking required). £

WHAT TO SEE AND DO

Kidwelly Castle (Church Rd; ☎03000 252239; w cadw.gov.wales; ⊕ Mar–Jun, Sep & Oct 09.30–17.00 daily, Jul & Aug 09.30–18.00 daily, Nov–Feb 10.00–16.00 daily; £6.50) 'There is an air of solemn majesty in its appearance that bespeaks a noble origin', so recalled the Anglo-Irish writer and naturalist Edward Donovan. Spread across a large grassy knoll above the Gwendraeth Fach, Kidwelly Castle is indeed a magnificent fortress. It's also just as a castle should be: endless battlements, cannon ports, hidden staircases and other nooks and crannies that make it thoroughly explorable and inspiring.

As a satellite of Sherborne Abbey in Dorset, the castle's origins date back to around 1106 when a timber structure of some form went up here, before it may well have been captured by Rhys ap Gruffydd, prince of Deheubarth, some time later that century. The first stone defences then went up in the late 12th or early 13th century, and by the 1280s it was beginning to resemble a military stronghold that would rank alongside other great Welsh fortresses like Caerphilly and Carreg Cennen. The castle just about withstood Owain Glyndwr's early 15th-century onslaught, and neither did the castle appear to have played any part in the Civil War. Some later repairs were made to parts of the castle, and a few other bits tinkered with here and there.

Among the earliest structures were the four portentous corner towers, each of which would have been equipped to provide a variety of different accommodation. Each tower is also possessed of its own, uniquely distinguishing feature: the southwest tower, for example, is the only one with its floors intact and a stone-vaulted ceiling (hence you can climb to the top for views of the Loughor Estuary); the northwest tower retains an unusual kidney-shaped structure; while the northeast tower looks distinctly askew.

The great south gatehouse – five floors including battlements – was a relatively late addition, raised in the late 14th century. Not only was it designed to intimidate, but it also provided comfortable accommodation for the king's constable, which explains why there were originally 20 rooms here, many ornamented with a fireplace, chimney or some such feature. Within this tight warren of rooms was the main hall on the first floor, above which, on the second floor, was a larger solar room. Note the small stalactites bearing down from the ceiling arch on the first-floor room next to the great hall, and the thickly calcited entrance in the passageway between the kitchen and the east tower, also on the first floor.

In the unlikely event that the enemy did manage to breach the gatehouse, they would have entered the **outer ward**, an almost-perfect D-shaped enclosure with a curved battlemented wall punctuated by three mural towers along the west side. Ranged along the wall between the northwest and southwest towers, the two gable ends are all that remain of what would have been either a courthouse or stables, though it's not really clear which of these it was. Further round, pressed up into the curtain wall near the north gatehouse, is the late-medieval bakehouse with the clearly defined remains of the oven. If you've ever wondered where the phrase 'upper crust' (usually used to refer to the upper classes, or gentry) comes from: if the bottom half of a loaf of bread burnt, as it frequently did, only the top, or upper, half would be served to the lord of the manor.

Beyond the four impregnable-looking towers – yet another formidable layer of defence – is the **inner ward**. Towers aside, the courtyard held domestic quarters, including a kitchen, accommodation and a chapel. Last, but by no means least, is the **Chapel Tower**, reached via a spur buttress from the southeast tower. As well as being a place of worship it functioned as a flanking tower to protect the east curtain wall. Head through to the tiny sacristy on the south side with its fine stone cruciform ceiling. Incidentally, fans of Monty Python's *The Holy Grail* may recognise the castle from the opening shots of the film.

Llansteffan Castle (Church Rd; w llansteffancastle.com; ⊕ 10.00–16.00 daily; free) To the list of South Wales's formidable coastal fortresses you can add Llansteffan, marooned between two wide estuaries in the village, and on the peninsula, of the same name. As was the case with so many fortresses hereabouts, the original timber building (itself preceded by an Iron-Age promontory fort) was replaced by a much stronger Anglo-Norman fortress, designed by the incumbent de Camille family. A tug-of-war battle for power then ensued between the Welsh and English before the castle was conferred on Jasper Tudor by his uncle, Henry VII. In 2016, the castle entered private ownership for the first time, when businesswoman Marian Evans bought the property; one of the first things she did was to commission a pair of wrought-iron gates for the original medieval gatehouse, which had been blocked off for centuries. There's little to see otherwise, so just soak up the marvellous views.

Getting there and away Excitingly, the ferry service has been reinstated between Llansteffan and Ferryside on the opposite side of the estuary. The amphibious Carmarthen Bay ferry, the *Glansteffan* (✆ 01267 874010; w carmarthenbayferries. co.uk), shuttles back and forth between the two beaches between April and October, roughly every 15–30 minutes, though services are tide-dependent, ie: when there's enough water! It can also take up to four bikes and two wheelchairs.

✖ Where to eat and drink

🍴 **Inn at the Sticks** (5 rooms) High St; ✆ 01267 241177; w innatthesticks.co.uk; ⊕ noon–22.00 Wed–Sat, noon–17.00 Sun. If you've made the effort to come all the way to this relatively isolated spot, you may as well stick around for a bite to eat, or at least a drink. A short walk up from the beach, this early 19th-century inn run by a couple of West Wales boys has a warming, Welsh farmhouse feel about it, & the food is delicious. Ingredients are literally plucked off the doorstep: Llanelli Bay mussels, Llansteffan wild garlic, & pigeon from Pendine are all likely to find their way on to the menu at some stage; otherwise, they do a mean homemade organic garlic chicken kiev with parmesan & chips. In summer, there's often live music. If you just fancy a pint, & the ale is excellent, then join the locals at the bar for a natter. If overnighting appeals, they've got 5 en-suite rooms (mind the roof beams), 3 of which are hound-friendly. ££

LAUGHARNE

If Swansea was his 'ugly, lovely town', then Laugharne (simply pronounced 'laan'), it seems, fared little better when Dylan Thomas described it as 'the strangest town in Wales' – though to be fair, that was on the occasion of his first visit here in 1934. The poet was soon captivated by the place, as are most visitors, especially the many Thomas devotees who flock here from all over the world – much as they do to those other Thomas shrines, Swansea and Newquay, but Laugharne tends to be the first and most important stop on the pilgrimage, largely on account of the fact that this is where he lived during the last years of his life and where he is buried.

Inevitably the town exploits its Thomas connections to the full, but there's a refreshingly healthy irreverence about it, and it in no way detracts from what else Laugharne has to offer. Sitting on the sandy fringes of Carmarthen Bay, the town's tight cluster of Georgian townhouses and stone-built cottages wend their way down towards a stately castle ruin and the shifting sands of the Tâf Estuary. In summer, Laugharne feels more Mediterranean than British, or Welsh. A great time to be here is the end of March for the **Laugharne Weekend** (w thelaugharneweekend.com), a three-day mash up of music, film, comedy, food, book talks, town walks and much, much more in various venues around town; a weekend ticket entitles you to attend any of the events over the three days.

GETTING THERE AND AWAY Coming by car, the town lies 5 miles south of St Clears just off the fast A40. Laugharne's streets can get murderously busy in summer, so your best bet is to park up by St Martin's Church as you enter the village, from where it's a very pleasant walk into town. Laugharne is poorly served by public transport: the nearest train station is Carmarthen, 13 miles away, from where bus #222 (5 or 6 Mon–Sat) runs to Laugharne's main square (The Grist), before continuing to Pendine, with the same number going in the opposite direction.

🏠 **WHERE TO STAY, EAT AND DRINK**
Map, right

🏠 **Brown's Hotel** (14 rooms) King St; 📞01994 427688; w browns.wales. Thomas wouldn't recognise the place these days, which is probably just as well, though as you'd expect there's plenty of Dylan memorabilia knocking about, including

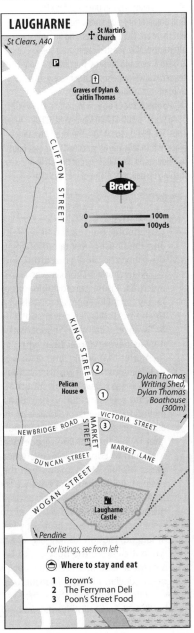

LAUGHARNE

St Clears, A40
✝ St Martin's Church
P
🏠 Graves of Dylan & Caitlin Thomas
CLIFTON STREET
N
Bradt
0   100m
0   100yds
KING STREET
② The Ferryman Deli
Pelican House ●
① Brown's
Dylan Thomas Writing Shed, Dylan Thomas Boathouse (300m)
VICTORIA STREET
NEWBRIDGE ROAD
MARKET STREET
③ Poon's Street Food
MARKET LANE
DUNCAN STREET
WOGAN STREET
🏰 Laugharne Castle
↙ Pendine

For listings, see from left

🏠 **Where to stay and eat**
1   Brown's
2   The Ferryman Deli
3   Poon's Street Food

volumes by the poet to pore over while supping a beer. Sympathetically made over a few years ago after lying redundant for far too long, the hotel interplays much of the old (wonky doors & creaky floors) with lots of the new (wall art, media bar & coffee pods), & no 2 rooms are the same. The independently run Dexter's Steak House & Grill prepares dry-aged meat from its own cattle, but there are plenty of appetising non-meaty alternatives, like roasted cauliflower steak & chips, & bean & avocado burritos. The flower-scented terrace is a welcome suntrap yet nicely shielded from the estuarine winds. **£££**

✗ **Poon's Street Food** 3 Market St; m 07967 334657; ⊕ 09.00–17.00 Mon–Wed, 09.00–20.00 Thu–Sat, 09.00–16.00 Sun. The locals love this place, which tells you all you need to know about just how good it is. When not in the kitchen rustling up delicious plates of mostly Asian-

inspired food (pad Thai, beef panang curry, papaya salad), the owner, Poon, is just as likely to pop out & say hello, as is her gregarious other half, Vince. If you've still got room, scour the chilled cabinet for one of her delectable desserts. It's cheap (you won't pay more than a tenner for anything), atmospheric, & on the whole really rather good. **£**

⌂ **The Ferryman Deli** King St; ☏ 01994 427398; ⊕ 10.00–18.00 Mon–Sat, 11.00–16.00 Sun. Neat & trim café-deli where they turn out a scrummy range of baguettes & ciabattas (Teifi Saval cheese; Manchego, serrano & quince) as well as proper coffee & a nice line in homemade cakes & tarts, like almond, & cherry bakewell muffins, with a few vegan options too. They've only got a couple of tables so you'll probably have to wait, though most things are available to take away. The deli beyond the seated area is a cornucopia of great produce. **£**

DYLAN THOMAS

'…a chubby, bulb-nosed little Welshman with green eyes, a generally untidy air and the finest lyrical talent of any poet under 40' was how *Time* magazine once described the prodigious drunk and literary titan that was Dylan Thomas.

Dylan Marlais Thomas was born on 27 October 1914 at 5 Cwmdonkin Drive, Swansea, into a comfortable, middle-class family. His parents, D J ('Jack' to the family) and Florence, were Welsh speakers, although it was not the language of the home and Dylan never spoke his native tongue. His father, an English master at Swansea Grammar School, was his greatest earliest influence, but as a child he was never happier than when at his aunt's farm in Fernhill, Carmarthenshire, memories that would later resurface in the eponymous poem.

Leaving school at 16, his first foray into the world of journalism was as a reporter for Swansea's *Evening Post*, but that was never really his *metier* and he continued to write zealously during his 18 months there – indeed much of his early work, including elements of *Portrait of the Artist as a Young Dog*, was informed by his experiences at the *Post*. His first publication, in 1930, was followed just two years later by his first volume of poetry at the age of just 18. Dylan's work frequently took him to London, which is where he was introduced to the Irish chorus-line dancer Caitlin Macnamara (then the mistress of the painter Augustus John), and the pair would marry in Penzance the following year, 1937.

Although Dylan had been a drinker since his days in Swansea, it was among his own kind – the *bon viveurs* of bohemian Fitzrovia – that he developed a real taste for hard liquor. His nightly bouts in Brown's, in Laugharne, remain the stuff of legend, though frankly, any old tavern would do; Caitlin was no slouch either when it came to the business of booze. Despite his hard-drinking ways, he was a meticulous and ferociously disciplined writer – he drafted *Fern Hill* 200 times before declaring himself satisfied with it.

As for Laugharne, Dylan first set eyes on the town in 1934, invited here by his friend and fellow writer Richard Hughes, and despite initial reservations –

WHAT TO SEE AND DO As good a place as any to begin your quest of the town is **St Martin's Church**, not only because this is a convenient and cheap place to park (£1 in the box), but also because this is where you'll find the **graves of Dylan and Caitlin Thomas**. Located in the overspill graveyard to the right of the little stone bridge, it's pretty obvious which ones theirs are, the bright white wooden cross marked with Dylan's name on one side and Caitlin's on the other. It is claimed that Caitlin once requested that Dylan's body be exhumed on account that the present location wasn't befitting 'Wales's foremost poet' – a request by the authorities for a £2 fee in order to accommodate her wishes to have him reinterred at the boathouse was never forthcoming, so in the event nothing happened and she now lies with him.

From the church, proceed down Clifton Street and King Street, where you'll eventually pass **Brown's Hotel** (page 255) on your left. Few buildings are as closely associated with Thomas as his erstwhile favourite watering hole, and there's enough memorabilia knocking about to satisfy even the most ardent fans, despite the hotel's boutiquey pretensions. In 1949 – the same year that he returned to Laugharne – Thomas moved his parents out of their Swansea home to the **Pelican House**, located, conveniently enough, opposite Brown's. A beautifully proportioned, three-storeyed Georgian townhouse, the green-painted Pelican was home to Dick (who died in 1952) and Florrie until Dylan's death in 1953, whereupon Florrie moved into the

and notwithstanding periods of time spent living in London and Newquay (in Cardigan), the latter for a year at the end of World War II – this was always home; the last of their three children, Colm, was born here in 1949. Strange as it is to consider, Dylan didn't really become a household name until 1945, until which point his work was only really known to a coterie of writers and artists. But he was nothing if not versatile, and as well as his poetry and short stories, he worked with Strand Films on productions for the Ministry of Information, in addition to working on radio scripts for the BBC, where he was a fixture between 1945 and 1948.

Thereafter, Thomas undertook lucrative lecture tours in the United States, and it was on one such tour that his life came to a premature end. Following a night of heavy drinking in the White Horse Tavern in New York, he is alleged to have said to the doctor 'I've had 18 straight whiskeys, I think it's a record', although the veracity of this utterance has never been proven. For years, the cause of his death remained the source of some contention, though it was widely assumed to have been as a result of *delirium tremens*, a drinker's condition – however, rather than having died from 'an insult to the brain' caused by alcohol, it was established that pneumonia was the most likely factor. Regardless, his death came just one month after he had completed his radio play *Under Milk Wood*, which to this day remains his most celebrated achievement. Loosely based on the lives of a Welsh seaside community over the course of 24 hours, the play brings Dylan's vivid verse brilliantly to the fore one last time.

Dylan and Caitlin's marriage was far from fulfilling. There were multiple adulterous affairs on both sides, and Caitlin was hugely resentful of Dylan's stateside success, yet for all that they remained together until his death in 1953. Caitlin then moved to Italy where she remarried, though she had always expressed a wish to be buried alongside Dylan, and when she died in 1994, she was interred next to him in the graveyard on the hill.

boathouse. It was here, too, that Thomas's body was laid out after his death and where the wake was held. The street bears right just before the castle ruins and continues down towards The Grist, the main square, and beyond to the car park by the estuary.

If you're hankering for more Thomas-inspired activity, then you might care to tackle the unimaginatively named **Birthday Walk** (w dylanthomasbirthdaywalk. co.uk), an easy 2-mile circular so-named after the little hike he undertook on his 30th birthday. His reflections of that walk subsequently made it into print in *Poem in October*, and it is lines from the poem that adorn the benches intermittently dispersed along the trail. Start from the car park below the castle and follow the signposts. The boathouse aside, Thomas lived in two other properties in Laugharne, one of which, Seaview (near the castle), is marked with a simple plaque; the other a small unmarked cottage in Gosport Street.

Dylan Thomas Boathouse and Writing Shed (Dylan's Walk; ☎01994 427420;

w www.dylanthomasboathouse.com; ⏲ Apr–Sep 11.00–17.00 Thu–Mon; for winter hours call ahead; £5.50) Reached via a narrow, tree-fringed lane, there's a palpable sense of anticipation as you approach the Dylan Thomas Boathouse, whose stilted setting high above the craggy, wave-bashed shoreline is much as you'd hoped it would be. Dating from 1830, this was Dylan and Caitlin's home for the last four years of his life, although it wasn't actually theirs: the boathouse had been bought for them by the Oxford don Margaret Taylor, whom Thomas had befriended some years earlier when visiting the city, although Thomas didn't endear himself to Taylor's husband, the distinguished historian and broadcaster A J P Taylor, who despised the poet.

The two upstairs rooms have Dylan's father's desk and chaise longue in situ, but most of the space is taken up with family photos and documents, most impressively a letter from former US president Jimmy Carter – one of the poet's biggest fans – presented to the house on the occasion of a visit here in 1979. Among the few personal effects is the only pair of cufflinks Thomas is said to have owned and a copy of the *Carmarthenshire Journal* announcing his death (though the disappearance of a local farmer appears to have taken precedence in the reporting). The two ground-floor rooms (kitchen and former living room) now constitute a sweet little tearoom, though it's more fun sitting outside on the terrace overlooking the water – unless the water's up, in which case it's not unusual for the terrace to flood.

More evocative than the boatshed is Thomas's green-painted writing shed, which you pass en route to the former. Actually a converted garage, it's much altered from its original state, in so much as the iconic sky-blue door is no longer there (it's on display in the Dylan Thomas Centre in Swansea, page 161) and there is little that's original inside. Instead, it's been mocked up as a working study, with books, pens, a simple wooden desk covered in scrunched-up balls of paper, and a cast-iron fire, which Thomas would sit in front of and write for 2 hours a day, when he wasn't admiring the ravishing views towards the Llansteffan Peninsula. It was here that he crafted some of his best-loved work, including *Under Milk Wood* and *Over Sir John's Hill*. Unfortunately, it's not possible to enter the shed, so you'll just have to content yourself with a peek through the narrow window of the door. Outside the writing shed, steps lead down to the rocky shore, from where you can walk (at low tide) back towards the village.

Laugharne Castle (☎03000 252239; w cadw.gov.wales; ⏲ Apr–Oct 10.00–17.00

Thu–Mon; £4.80) Teetering on a low cliff above Carmarthen Bay, the ivied ruins of Laugharne Castle make for an imposing sight, especially when viewed from the shoreline below. The oldest upstanding remains of the castle date back to the 13th century, though there was almost certainly an earthernwork structure here prior to this. Having been granted Laugharne by Elizabeth I in 1575, the castle – by that stage almost ruinous – was partly recast into a residence of some pretension by Sir John Perrot. Not that he had long to enjoy it, as he was imprisoned at the Tower of London in 1591 for high treason and condemned the following year. The Civil War did the castle few favours, though much of the damage occurred afterwards when it was purposely demolished so that it could no longer serve as a stronghold.

Having crossed the bridge through the inner gatehouse – remodelled at least three times – take a look about two-thirds of the way up on the right-hand side and you'll see an exquisitely dressed capital. The inner ward is a motley assemblage of half-bitten towers with hollowed-out windows, the most complete sections of which are the two north towers, just yards apart from one another: steps immediately to the left of the inner gatehouse allow access to the northwest tower, or keep, built in the middle of the 13th century, though the battlements – which afford superlative views of the Loughor Estuary – were part of the 1930s restoration. Halfway between the northwest tower and the half-eaten northeast tower stands the slender stair tower, distinguished by its square-headed Tudor windows on four unequal levels.

Opposite, the southern curtain wall is a jumble of different features: to the left a great oriel window, below and to the right of which is an obvious fireplace, and

DEMONS OF SPEED

For a few rip-roaring years in the 1920s, the long, flat sands of Pendine provided the backdrop to an extraordinary series of attempts on the world land speed record. Since the first documented land-speed record achieved by Gaston de Chasseloup-Laubat in Achères, France, in 1898, many drivers had attempted, and succeeded, in beating the original mark of 39.24 miles an hour. But the ante was upped quickly, and by the time Malcolm Campbell brought *Sunbeam* to Pendine Sands in 1925, that original record had been surpassed 29 times.

Campbell's latest effort landed him with a new record of 150.88 miles per hour, though he would go on to beat this on several more occasions. He pitched up again in 1927 with *Bluebird*, achieving a speed of 174.88 miles an hour, a mark that proved to be an irresistible challenge to another former record holder, the Wrexham-born racer J G Parry-Thomas. Just a month later, Parry-Thomas, with his 27-litre, chain-driven vehicle *Babs* (which had already broken the record twice, the year previously) had another go, but this time with fatal consequences. The car exploded, in the process decapitating Parry-Thomas, and ended up buried in the sand. It spent the next 42 years lying in respectful silence before being recovered in 1969.

Unlike Parry-Thomas and many of his peers, Campbell finished his racing career unscathed, instead dying of natural causes in 1948. Interestingly, his son, Donald, went on to achieve arguably even greater fame than his father, having also held both the land and water speed records at one stage, before his untimely, though sadly predictable, death on Coniston Water in the Lake District in 1967 when attempting a new record, also in a boat called *Bluebird*. There are various bits of footage of some of these, including Campbell's record attempt, on YouTube.

below that a couple of sub-basement windows. All these features would have been integral to the Great Hall, but there is next to nothing there now to indicate that this was once the grandest room in the castle. The far western end of the inner ward would have been consumed by the kitchen, and that much can be ascertained by the massive outline of the oven.

One of the castle's curiosities is the gazebo perched on the edge of the outer ward's trim gardens overlooking the water. Upon his arrival in Laugharne, Thomas became good friends with another eminent writer, Richard Hughes, author of *A High Wind in Jamaica*; in fact it was Hughes who had originally introduced Dylan and Caitlin to Laugharne. Both men used the gazebo, essentially an annex of the adjoining Castle House which Hughes had been renting, to write at various times. Thomas completed several pieces for *Portrait of the Artist as a Young Dog* here, while Hughes wrote another of his much-vaunted titles, *In Hazard*, in these small yet cosy confines. The small exhibition inside is deservingly dedicated to Hughes.

Pendine Sands   For all the massed ranks of caravan parks, souvenir shops and cheap eateries, Pendine Sands, 5 miles west of Laugharne, also boasts a glorious, 6-mile-long stretch of golden sand that's comparable to any other stretch of beach along the Carmarthenshire or Pembrokeshire coast. Another good reason to come is the **Pendine Museum of Speed**, although it's presently undergoing a major overhaul and there's no firm timescale with regards to its reopening. But when it does open its doors again, it should be a treat – as well as recalling those heady days of the 1920s, you can expect to see *Babs* in all her fully restored glory (page 259).

CARMARTHEN AND AROUND

Given its status as the county town and ancient capital of the region, and at one time the largest town in Wales, Carmarthen comes as quite a disappointment. One or two elegant buildings aside, there's not a lot to get worked up about, and however hard you try, the town warrants no more than an hour or two of your time. That said, the recent reopening of the county museum just outside of Carmarthen following a major revamp is cause for genuine excitement, as is the fact there are one or two really fine places to eat, although these are also out of town.

This relative poverty of cultural riches belies the town's long and proud history. Originally a Roman fort called Moridunum Demetarum (meaning 'fort by the sea'), Carmarthen was the civic centre for the Demetae, one of the five tribes that ruled over Wales, in this case the present-day territory of Carmarthenshire and Pembrokeshire. To this end, Carmarthen had all the attendant facilities: baths, a temple, and one of just seven amphitheatres in Britain, though there is next to no trace of any of these now. Carmarthen likes to claim one of the great legends as its own, too, in this case Merlin, of King Arthur's magical accomplice fame – in so much as the Welsh translation of Carmarthen is Caerfyrddin, meaning Merlin's Fort. What is true is that the old Roman fort was eventually replaced by a Norman castle, around which the town grew up, until it yielded to Owain Glyndwr during one of his customary attacks.

Carmarthen's position on the Tywi helped facilitate the town's recovery and it become an important industrial hub – initially for the wool trade then later heavy industry (iron, tinplate and rope works), and while nowhere near the scale of the huge coal-, iron- and steelmaking concerns further east in the Valleys, these trades were vital in securing the town's prosperity.

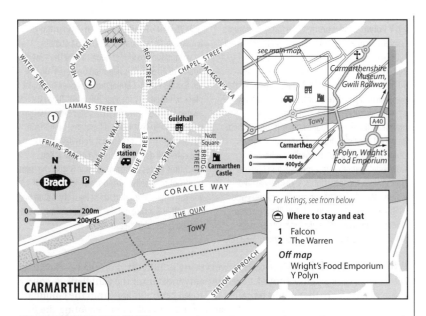

CARMARTHEN

For listings, see from below

⊝ **Where to stay and eat**

1 Falcon
2 The Warren

Off map

Wright's Food Emporium
Y Polyn

GETTING THERE AND AWAY Carmarthen is the easiest place in the county to reach by road, lying at the junction of the A48 (which joins the M4 near Swansea) and the A40, which runs east–west between Brecon and Haverfordwest.

The well-connected train station is on the south side of the Tywi, from where it's an easy walk back across Carmarthen Bridge to the town centre. There are hourly services to Swansea, with all trains stopping at Kidwelly, Pembrey & Burry Port, and Llanelli en route. Heading west into Pembrokeshire, there are trains to Fishguard Harbour (2 daily), Haverfordwest and Milford Haven (8 daily Mon–Sat, 3 Sun), and Tenby (9 Mon–Sat, 3 Sun), which is where you would need to change for Pembroke Dock.

The bus station is right in the centre on Blue Street, with plentiful buses serving most destinations in the county including half-hourly services to Kidwelly, Llanelli and Swansea, as well as Laugharne and Pendine (both 5 daily Mon–Sat), Llandeilo (10 daily Mon–Sat), Narberth and Haverfordwest (both 3 daily Mon–Sat).

🏠 **WHERE TO STAY, EAT AND DRINK** *Map, above*

🏠**Falcon Hotel** (16 rooms) 111 Lammas St; 📞01267 234959; **w** falconcarmarthen.co.uk. A family-run hotel for more than 50 years, the Falcon is more or less your one option for a sleepover, & it's not a bad one. While the rooms – a mix of sgls, twins & dbls – might not be brimming with personality, they are pleasing enough. The food, though, is very commendable, with an attractively priced 2-course lunchtime set menu your best bet. **£££**

✖**The Warren** 11 Mansel St; 📞01267 236079; **w** warrenmanselst.co.uk; ⊕ noon–15.00 & 18.00–21.00 Wed–Sat, noon–15.00 Sun. The one place worth eating at in Carmarthen itself, where the watchwords are sustainable, organic & local – & that's not just paying lip service. As much as possible, ingredients are foraged locally, resulting in dishes like organic farm beef with sautéed potatoes & seasonal greens, or seasonal quiche with lentils, red cabbage & aioli. The wine card is similarly well curated, with some choice organic wines in there. You'll find the place busiest on Sun when locals pile in for roast lunch, with a choice of meats (lamb, beef or pork) plus a veggie & vegan option available, though you should book ahead for this. The restaurant itself looks fab, with lots of intimate coves to dive into, corkboard walls & flooring, & twinkling fairy lights. **££**

Y Polyn 2 miles north of the National Botanic Garden & 8 miles east of Carmarthen in Capel Dewi; 01267 290000; w ypolyn.co.uk; ⏲ noon–14.00 & 18.30–21.30 Tue–Fri, noon–14.30 & 18.30–21.30 Sat, noon–14.30 Sun. Simon Wright's previous haunt before he set up the Emporium a few miles away, Y Polyn ('The Pole') has maintained the same high standards it had when he was at the helm. It's a refreshingly humble country inn with a determinedly unaffected way about it, for example mismatched tables & chairs minus the tablecloths, & casually attired waiting staff. Using the surrounding countryside as its natural larder, expect dishes like pan-fried woodpigeon breast with pickled beets or roast belly pork with hispi cabbage & cider jus. £££

Wright's Food Emporium Llanarthney, 8 miles east of Carmarthen; 01554 668929; w wrightsfood.co.uk; ⏲ noon–18.00 Thu–Sat, noon–16.00 Sun. This beautiful Georgian country inn 8 miles east of Carmarthen has been a popular place of hospitality for over 200 years. Today it's owned by food writer & broadcaster Simon Wright, who acquired what was a dilapidated building in 2010, in the process sparing it from developers. The café/deli delivers a short & concise menu of lunchtime plates (cream of organic British chestnut soup, hot pork belly cubano sandwiches), but if you can't make it for that, do at least try & stop by for a coffee & a slice of cake – perhaps some baked sultana & nutmeg cheesecake. ££

WHAT TO SEE AND DO More or less everything of interest is on the north side of the Tywi, where a dense knot of streets broadly meet up at the **Guildhall**, as good a place as anywhere that might be called the town centre. It was from the Guildhall, in 1966, that Gwynfor Evans gave his acceptance speech after becoming the first Plaid Cymru member to take a seat in parliament, a seat he took for a second time in 1974. Behind the Guildhall, **Nott Square** is named after the eponymous major-general, a statue of whom stands in the centre; here since 1851, it's cast from a cannon captured at the 1843 Battle of Maharajpur. Off to one corner of the square are the remains of Edward I's disconsolate **castle**, a pretty lightweight affair these days, with the shell keep, a few bits of tower and some curtain walls all that remain.

A walk back down past the Guildhall and beyond Darkgate brings you to **Lammas Street**, a fetching thoroughfare of high and handsome Georgian townhouses, many of them former coaching inns. Here too is the town's **indoor market** (⏲ 09.00–17.00 Mon–Sat), where you can find anything from fresh produce to crafty bits and bobs. On Wednesdays and Saturdays, the market spills over into the street, while on the first Friday of each month the farmers' market rolls into town. You'll also hear plenty of Welsh spoken here, Carmarthen being the first major town in West Wales in which the native tongue is more widely heard.

Carmarthenshire Museum (The Old Palace, Abergwili; 01267 234567; w discovercarmarthenshire.com; ⏲ 11.00–16.00 Tue–Sat; free) Following a protracted renovation programme, the Carmarthenshire Museum, 2 miles east of town in Abergwili, reopened to much relief all round in 2022. This mightily austere building was the unlikely home to the bishops of St David's from when they upped sticks from their appreciably grander lodgings in St David's in 1542 until 1974. This much is evident in the chapel, which remains in situ. The building was actually largely destroyed in 1903 but rebuilt just a few years later.

The museum offers a compelling trawl through the region's history, with rooms fashioned in chronological order. There are some intriguing items on show, among which are pistols and batons used in the Rebecca Riots, and some personal effects belonging to Thomas Picton, including his field boots and walking cane. There's also a mocked-up Victorian classroom and a reconstructed farmhouse, though all its contents are from the original, Penrhiwbeili farm near Talog, dating from 1920.

Gwili Railway (Bronwydd Arms; ☎ 01267 238213; w gwili-railway.co.uk; ⊕ check website for timetable; £15) South Wales's only standard-gauge tourist railway, Gwili Railway is named after the river alongside which it runs. Both steam- and diesel-hauled trains slowly puff along an 8-mile section of the old Carmarthen to Aberystwyth line (itself an extension of the old Great Western Railway), which was closed to passengers in 1965 owing to a combination of persistent washouts and more pertinently the infamous Beeching Axe, when many spur lines were cut. Finally closed to all traffic in 1973, it was taken over by the Gwili Preservation Society who eventually made good the track again, and it re-opened in 1988. Starting at the Bronwydd Arms station, the train chuffs through thick woodland alongside the Gwili up to Danycoed Halt, before returning from whence it came and continuing down to Abergwili Junction, this latest section of track inaugurated in 2017; the ride is about an hour in total. It is anticipated that, in time, Abergwili will have its own car park and visitor centre.

For now, all the facilities – including ticket office, shop and tea room – are at Bronwydd Arms, as is the beautifully restored 1875 signal box transferred here from Llandybie station on the Heart of Wales line, the original having been demolished in the 1960s. If you can, try and make it for one of the steam gala days, when there are shunting demonstrations, miniature steam traction engines and an opportunity to see the workings of the signal box.

THE TYWI VALLEY

From Carmarthen, the deeply incised **Tywi Valley** arcs northeast along the river of the same name. It's a captivating corner of the county, nestled in the foothills of the western Brecon Beacons and within touching distance of the Cambrian Mountains to the north. The valley's two main towns, **Llandeilo** and **Llandovery**, are imbued with a wonderful sense of timelessness, each worthy of a day's exploration, and with a trio of superb castles at **Dryslwyn**, **Dinefwr** and **Carreg Cennen**, plus two of the finest gardens in Britain (**National Botanic Garden** and **Aberglasney**), you'll hardly be scratching your head thinking of things to do. If you really are strapped for time in Carmarthenshire, then you could do a lot worse than spend that time here.

NATIONAL BOTANIC GARDEN OF WALES (Middleton Hall, Llanarthne; ☎ 01558 667149; w botanicgarden.wales; ⊕ Apr–Oct 10.00–18.00 daily, Nov–Mar 10.00–16.00 daily; £13.75 – tickets valid for 7 days; bus #279 departs Carmarthen each day at 11.05, returning to town at 16.25 – stopping at the train station en route) Eight miles east of Carmarthen, the National Botanic Garden of Wales opened to great fanfare in 2000 and has since shot up the ranks to become one of Wales's most popular attractions. The garden may feel a little too polished or too contemporaneous for some, but there's more than enough here to please horticulturists of all persuasions, and in any case it's easy to lose yourself among the vastness of its 550 acres.

The history of the site goes way back. Middleton Hall was here long before William Paxton, a financier for the East India Company, brought the estate in 1789, but it was Paxton's vision, and money, that brought one of the finest Regency-period landscapes of the time to actualisation. Upon Paxton's death in 1824, the estate passed over to the Adams family who accrued much of their wealth in much the same way – that is, through the business of slavery. The house burnt down in 1931 as a few stubby remains testify, but from this vantage point there are glorious views through the low mist that frequently lingers below the hill towards the parkland.

Formerly the brew house, laundry and kitchens, the adjacent building is all that remains of the Middleton Hall site.

Looking like an enormous spaceship that has just landed in the middle of a field, Norman Foster's **great glasshouse** looms very large indeed. It's a typically unrestrained Foster design, a huge curvaceous dome – the largest single-span great glasshouse in the world, longer than a football pitch – sheltering a dramatically landscaped interior by Kathryn Gustafson. The theme is endangered plant species from Mediterranean climatic zones: wild dagger and butterspoon trees from the South African Cape; red-eyed wattle and grass trees from Australia; curry trees from Chile; sagebrush and yucca from California – you could be forgiven for thinking you were taking a stroll through some of the world's great wine regions.

Far smaller is the drippingly humid **tropical glasshouse**, harbouring a steamy array of palms, ferns, orchids, cycads and aquatic plants, including some huge circular water lilies. For many, the glasshouses are eclipsed by Paxton's double **walled garden**, a fixture here for more than 200 years. The combination of an outer stone wall and an inner brick wall apparently has the effect of creating different microclimates for each of the garden's four quadrants, one of which is abundant with crops of fruit and vegetables that sustain the restaurant. The garden's latest triumph is the Regency Restoration Project, whereby some 300 acres of wooded parkland have been restored to something approaching their former pomp.

If you feel the need to justify every penny of your entrance fee, you could stray further and walk the 2 miles to **Paxton's Tower**, a castellated three-towered folly built in 1809. The story goes that, after being rejected by electors in his campaign to become MP for Carmarthenshire, Paxton built this tower – as opposed to a bridge over the Tywi which had been part of his original manifesto – as a measure of revenge, though he is just as likely to have built it in honour of Lord Nelson, whom he may have once met.

To the rear of Y Ty Melyn, the **Wallace Garden** has been laid out with ferns, pines, ginkgos and cycads in tribute to the eponymous explorer and naturalist, whose contributions to the study of evolution are frequently overlooked in the rush to acclaim Darwin's efforts (page 119). Close by, kids (and adults) can lark about in the ace little adventure playground and willow maze before heading for some refreshments in the stable yard café-restaurant, very pleasant outside on a warm summer's day. That said, there are so many lovely areas to picnic here that you're better off saving your money. For the elderly and those with mobility problems, buggies are available for use around the site – and if you are with pooch in tow, they are allowed in on Mondays and Fridays and the first weekend of each month. Another excellent initiative sees cyclists gain entry half price, but don't think you can get in just by turning up in lycra – you will need to hand in your helmet at reception as proof.

British Bird of Prey Centre
(National Botanic Garden; m 07444 177818; w britishbirdofpreycentre.co.uk; ⏲ Apr–Oct 10.00–18.00 daily, Nov–Mar 10.00–16.00 daily; £1, shows £3) Located within the grounds of the National Botanic Garden, the British Bird of Prey Centre was set up in 2018 as a centre dedicated to the welfare of native owls and raptors. The centre's large and well-kept enclosure house around two-dozen handsome, sharp-taloned beasts, all of which are hand-reared here, among them a gyrfalcon, goshawk, peregrine falcon, merlin (the smallest bird of prey), black and red kites, snowy owl, white-tailed (sea) eagle and golden eagle.

Led by experienced, well-informed falconers, the daily shows (3 Apr–Sep, 2 rest of the year) are not to be missed; most of those housed in the enclosure fly at least once a day, and six or seven of them make an appearance during any one display.

You'll have your own favourite, but perhaps the most charismatic birds are Hector the European eagle owl, Enzo the peregrine falcon, the kites, Salsa and Saffron, and Midas, the awesome golden eagle. For something a little extra special, the centre offers a range of flying experiences. Among the options available are 30-minute small-group experiences flying owls or kites (£20), and a 90-minute private owl (£60) or woodland (£50) walk, the last with an American Harris hawk called Maleki. These last two experiences must be booked in advance.

ABERGLASNEY (Llangathen; ☏ 01558 668998; w aberglasney.org; ⏰ Apr–Oct 10.00–18.00 daily, Nov–Feb 10.30–16.00 daily, Mar 10.30–17.00 daily; last entry 1hr below closing; £11) Beautiful and atmospheric at nearly every turn, Aberglasney is one of Britain's finest heritage gardens, packing more into its eight acres than most gardens two or three times its size. Yet less than 30 years ago both the house and the gardens were almost lost to posterity. With the 15th-century **house** a ruinous shell and the gardens unrecognisable as such, William Wilkins, founder of the Welsh Historic Gardens Trust, launched a stupendously ambitious plan to revive both, and sure enough, within five years both were ready for public viewing.

The house itself is of minor interest compared with the gardens, but is home to one particularly unusual botanical feature. Named after the garden of Ninfa near Rome, the **Ninfarium** (old kitchen) consists of two storeys of ruined walls topped by a modern glass roof, under which a panoply of sub-tropical species – aspidistras, begonias, mahonias, lilies and a whole variety of ferns – flourish in the cool semi-shaded environment. Look out too for the orchids growing high up on the walls in hessian sacks. The house also hosts temporary art exhibitions, which are worth checking out if that's your thing.

Fronting the house, the beautifully remodelled and neatly trimmed Elizabethan **Cloister Garden** – built on the orders of Bishop Rudd, a friend of Elizabeth I, and allegedly one of just two cloister gardens in the world (the other is in Italy) – presages Aberglasney's most picturesque spot, the Jacobean **Pool Garden** with its murky green stew pond and a **tearoom** built into the wall; a cuppa out on one of the terrace tables when the sun is shining is bliss. The neighbouring upper walled garden was the first to be coaxed back into life during the restoration, followed by the lower (or kitchen) garden, bursting with edible delights all year round: strawberries, blackberries, crab apples, asparagus, squash, leek, kale and an abundance of herbs.

The Jubilee **Woodland Garden** harbours huge stands of upright silver firs among its trickling streams and gentle waterfalls, alongside silver birch, magnolia and great laurel (rhododendron) from North America, and giant Chilean rhubarb plants, with leaves big enough to picnic under. Yet another intriguing feature of the garden is the 18th-century **Yew Tunnel**, whereby the trees were planted on just one side and the gnarly branches deliberately bent over, thereby rooting on the other side, a process known as 'layering'. Wander through the alpinum and up behind the house along Bishop Rudd's Walk to the top of the valley and the Asiatic garden, where you can park yourself on a bench and savour the view.

LLANDEILO AND AROUND Tucked away in the northeastern corner of Carmarthenshire, bright-and-breezy Llandeilo takes its name from the 6th-century saint Teilo, who chose to make this his base, although little else is known about him. It's the overall feel of the place rather than any specific sight that makes Llandeilo such an attractive proposition, and in that way it's not dissimilar to Crickhowell. And like Crickhowell, the town has a strong sense of its own identity, which is evident in the number of flourishing small independent businesses. Given that

Carmarthenshire THE TYWI VALLEY

8

there's little of substance to see or do in town itself, you'll need to cast your net a little wider for some meaningful action, but that's not difficult given Llandeilo's proximity to any number of outstanding attractions, in particular a fine pair of castles and a charismatic country house. Other than that, the town makes a useful base, with some excellent accommodation and dining options.

Getting there and away Llandeilo is just off the A40 road from Brecon to Carmarthen, while the A483 runs right through the centre of town on its way down to meet the M4. Llandeilo is on the Heart of Wales line, which means four trains a day heading south to Swansea via Ammanford and Llanelli, and the same number heading north into Powys, and ultimately Shrewsbury in Shropshire. Beyond that there are no other services. The train station is a 10-minute walk east of the centre on Heol yr Orsaf. Arriving and departing from New Road, there are bus services to Carmarthen (9 daily Mon–Sat), Llandovery (9 daily Mon–Sat) and Swansea (8 daily Mon–Sat).

Where to stay, eat and drink

Cawdor Hotel (24 rooms, 2 suites) Rhosmaen St; ☎ 01558 823500; w thecawdor.com. A bright-red-painted building with canted bay windows & a Doric-columned entry, this fine little hotel has been providing first-class hospitality, on & off, since 1765. Its rooms & indulgent top-floor suites come with gorgeous Melin Tregwynt fabrics & slate-lined bathrooms with deep soaking baths & enormous rainforest showers. The hotel also functions as the town's social hub, with both the restaurant & bar as popular with locals as they are guests – always a good sign that. In fact the restaurant is the best place in town for an evening meal: breads are baked daily here, meats are smoked in-house & the pasta is handmade. Some folk say the vegan burgers here are the best they've ever had. Good, safe car parking to the rear of the hotel. **££**

The Plough 1 mile north of Llandeilo in Rhosmaen; ☎ 01558 823431; w ploughrhosmaen.com; ⏰ 10.00–22.00 daily. A quick glance down the menu will have you scratching your head such are the many lip-smacking possibilities: perhaps pan-seared scallops with maple syrup, or chicken liver parfait with apple & pear chutney for starters, followed by roast Gressingham duck breast with beetroot & orange compote & Pinot Noir & rum sauce, or Moroccan spiced savoury crumble for a main. Whatever you settle on, The Plough serves the best food in town. For good measure they offer a tummy-filling Welsh afternoon tea (£22), or you could just pop in for coffee & cake. **££**

Ginhaus Deli 1 Market St; ☎ 01558 823030; w ginhaus.co.uk; ⏰ 09.00–16.30 Mon–Sat. True to its name, this cosy little bolthole just off the main street sells gin – hundreds of different varieties in fact – but it's the food that you're really here for: Welsh artisan cheeses, hand-crafted scotch eggs & Black Mountain salmon, alongside shelves groaning under the weight of olives & almonds from Spain. Before you walk away with an armful of goodies, treat yourself to a cup of coffee with beans roasted at Coaltown Coffee in nearby Ammanford (page 271). **£**

Shopping

Crafts Alive 133b Rhosmaen St; ☎ 01558 822010; w craftsalive.co.uk; ⏰ 10.00–17.00 Mon–Sat. A co-operative of local designers & makers, this brilliant little shop sells wares by practitioners of all things arty & crafty living within 30 miles of Llandeilo, from cards & textiles to pottery, ironwork & woodwork; there are galleries & workshops upstairs too.

Heavenly 60 Rhosmaen St; ☎ 01554 822800; w heavenlychoc.biz; ⏰ 11.00–16.00 Tue–Thu & Sun, 10.00–17.00 Fri & Sat. If the sight of fresh Welsh cakes being prepared in the window doesn't draw you in, then the irresistible waft of chocolate will. As well an eye-popping assortment of made-on-the-premises chocolates & cakes, there are shelves laden with confectionery & homemade organic ice cream for warmer days.

What to see and do The town's main thoroughfare, **Rhosmaen Street** (the A483), is flanked by gaily coloured buildings variously harbouring shops, cafés and tenements, but with traffic thundering through, it's quite a racket. However, there are enough side streets and little alleyways worth exploring, most of which are likely to yield something that piques your interest.

A short walk downhill from Rhosmaen Street's standout building, the rich red-painted Cawdor Hotel, is the well-kept and welcoming **St Teilo Church**, remodelled by George Gilbert Scott in 1848, although the existing medieval foundations and tower, mercifully spared the Victorian revamp, were incorporated into the new design. In fact the church stands on a site where there has been Christian worship for more than 15 centuries dating back to the mission of the eponymous saint – sometimes known by his Cornish name, Eliud – in the 6th century.

The church is actually more interesting for something that isn't there, namely the **Llandeilo Fawr Gospels**. A beautifully illuminated 8th-century manuscript, closely related to the more famous Lindisfarne Gospels, the manuscript had been in the church's possession for the first 200 years or so until it was purloined and taken to Lichfield Cathedral in Staffordshire, where it still resides. Although written in Latin, the manuscript is significant for having marginalia (marks or comments made in the side of a book) in Welsh, leading experts to conclude that these are the earliest surviving words written in the native language. Efforts to secure its return have so far proved unsuccessful, a situation that looks unlikely to change after so many years, much to the chagrin of the locals. The book may not be here, but you can view a digitised text in a specially curated exhibition.

Erected at the same time as the church, the immaculately proportioned single-span **bridge** – the largest single-span bridge in Wales – replaced a triple-arched structure that was swept away by falling trees during a great flood in 1750. The bridge has long had its admirers, including J M W Turner, whose *Llandilo Bridge and Dynevor Castle* is currently in the National Museum Cardiff.

Newton House and Dinefwr Castle (Dinefwr; ☎ 01558 825910; w nationaltrust.org.uk; ⊕ house: April–Oct 10.30–16.30 daily, park: 10.00–17.00 daily; £8) Casting a glance at the perkily turreted corner towers of **Newton House**, you could almost be forgiven for thinking that you were in the Loire Valley, though that might be overstating it a little. The towers were actually 18th-century additions to the main house, which was built in 1660 and for the next 300 years was home to the Rhys (Rice) family – descendants of the medieval warrior-prince The Lord Rhys (Rhys ap Gruffydd). The house's nicely lived-in feel possibly owes something to the fact that it was still squatted until the late 1980s, and it's still agreeably dishevelled in parts. That and the fact that because there's little by way of original fittings (some were pilfered by the squatters), most of what's here is from the National Trust's own stock, which includes a couple of ostentatious (and really quite uncomfortable) sofas from the set of Downton Abbey. Although visits are self-guided, cheery guides are on hand to offer all kinds of fascinating tit bits, though the guidebooks are well worth buying. There's a very agreeable café in the house too.

One room has been given over to an exhibition on the history of the estate, while another has a display of archaeological bits and bobs uncovered during the house's excavation in 1999, including nails, moulds, a wooden mortice lock, and scraps of the old hand-painted wallpaper. Another 120 or so random objects were found during this period, many of them buried under the floorboards; among this veritable cabinet of curiosities is a quill and paper fragment, a playing card,

8

a clay pipe, and even a Roman cremation urn, though none quite so strange as a mummified tortoiseshell cat, now displayed as it was found, frozen in time.

Outside, there's much to enjoy among the lush medley of gardens, lawns, ponds and parkland: the last is stalked by herds of fallow deer and rarely seen white cattle, a primitive breed that may well have been introduced here by the Romans. There are two loop trails, one of which – the 1½-mile-long Brown Trail – was conceived by the celebrated landscapist Capability Brown as part of his overall design for the park, although not all of his proposals met with the approval of the then owners George and Cecil Rice.

This walk can be extended to include **Dinefwr Castle** (⊕ open access), which is otherwise a gentle 20-minute walk from the house through Dinefwr Park. Perched atop a prominent crag above the Tywi River, this is where Rhys ap Gruffydd developed his seat of power in the late 12th century, though records suggest that there was a fortification here some 200 years prior to his arrival. It was a seat of some significance too, for the Rhys dynasty had established Deheuberth as the pre-eminent Welsh Kingdom at that time, taking in large parts of modern-day Carmarthenshire, Pembrokeshire and Cardiganshire, and a little bit of Breconshire for good measure. There's little of architectural merit here, but the views are scintillating.

Carreg Cennen (Trapp, Llandeilo; ✆01558 822291; w carregcennencastle.com & cadw.gov.wales; ⊕ Apr–Oct 09.30–18.00 daily, Nov–Mar 09.30–16.30 daily; £5.50) If you thought Dinefwr was impressive, wait until you get to Carreg Cennen, 4 miles southeast of Llandeilo. A mighty, heroic fortress grafted on to a vertiginous limestone outcrop on the Carmarthenshire/Brecon Beacons border, few superlatives do its location justice. Worth recalling is the story of how the castle ended up in private hands: essentially as a result of an administrative oversight. The current owners are Bernard and Margaret Llewellyn, but when Margaret's father bought the farm below the castle, having previously been the tenant, the deeds erroneously failed to omit the castle from the portion of land that he was purchasing, hence it became part of the overall property – and thereby the first Welsh castle to be privately owned. Although owned by the family, CADW are the guardians and maintain responsibility for the overall management of the site.

The present castle was raised by John Giffard, baron to Edward I, in 1248, but there was almost certainly an earlier fortress here, dating from around the same time as Dinefwr Castle a few miles away, when Lord Rhys ap Gruffydd was seeking to shore up his territory. In what proved to be a series of short but eventful campaigns, Carreg Cennen was taken by Edward I in 1277 during his first offensive, recaptured by the Welsh five years later, before the English pinched it back barely a year down the line. It last saw action in 1462 when it was partially destroyed by the Earl of Pembroke and has pretty much remained unaltered since. Its high, jagged, and occasionally gappy walls are still largely intact, though the structure is secondary to the constantly superlative panoramas.

Deep in the guts of the castle is a natural **cave**, which can be reached via a narrow, damp passage, though lots of head ducking is required. It's great fun – so long as you're not claustrophobic – and at its furthest extent (around 160ft) it's possible to detect some graffiti etched into the stone boulders bearing the date 1887. The cave isn't lit, so either make sure you have enough battery on your phone or bring some torches, which can also be rented from reception (£1.50). Note that it's a stiff 10-minute climb from the car park up to the castle entrance, and although perfectly

OK for pushchairs, those with certain mobility issues may struggle. Moreover, a few steps need to be negotiated to access the inner ward.

TOWARDS LLANDOVERY   Until 1800, the tiny farming village of **Bethlehem**, 6 miles north of Carreg Cennen below the glowering bluff of the Black Mountain, was known as Dyffryn Ceidric, but when the chapel changed its name to Bethlehem, so did the village – pandering to the wave of religious noncomformism sweeping the area. Bar a few years ever since, each Christmas the sub post office has done roaring business franking cards with the trademark Bethlehem postmark. (To be fair, it's done well to keep going at all, albeit these days it's just a mobile service, opening on Wednesdays, for just one hour between 15.30 and 16.30, but happily every day between 1 and 21 December.) Bethlehem is a good base from which to reach the massive Iron-Age hillfort of **Y Garn Goch**, as memorable for its bleak desolation as it is for the scope of its extant earthworks and stone ramparts. To give you some idea, it's only fractionally smaller than Maiden Castle in Dorset, which is Britain's largest hillfort. It actually comprises two forts: Y Gaer Fach and the far larger Y Gaer Fawr, with its half a dozen entrances and with views as exceptional as those at Carreg Cennen.

LLANDOVERY AND AROUND

Granted a royal charter in 1485 by Richard III, Llandovery was a key staging post for the West Wales drovers taking their cattle to market in London, which goes some way to explaining why there were once 70 pubs here. There are somewhat fewer these days, and it's presumably a lot quieter for it, but the town wears its sociability well. Physically, the town has changed little over the centuries, its houses painted in multiple eye-catching colours: burnt orange, rust red, maroon, navy blue, lime green and so on.

Llandovery was home to two of Wales's less-heralded characters whose respective contributions to Welsh culture often fly under the radar – and they've got blue plaques, so they must have been quite important. First is the vicar and poet Rhys Prichard, whose most famous composition was *Cannwyll y Cymry* (*The Welshman's Candle*), a collection of poetic teachings; one oft-told local story has it that he brought his beer-drinking goat along for a night out only for the goat to get blitheringly drunk and refuse to go out again the following evening, leading Richard to contemplate a more virtuous life. Then there is hymnologist William Williams Pantycelyn, who wrote *Arglwydd, arwain trwy'r anialwch* (*Lord, lead thou through the wilderness*), more familiarly known as *Guide Me, O Thou Great Redeemer* – whose gloriously anthemic refrain ('Bread of Heaven, Bread of Heaven, Feed me til I want no more') is often sung when the Welsh national rugby team plays. And while we're at it, there was also the outlaw Twm Sion Cati, aka the Welsh Robin Hood, who used to stake out a cave in Rhandirmwyn north of town.

GETTING THERE AND AWAY   Llandovery is at the crossroads of several important junctions, with the A40 running east–west from Brecon through the heart of the town, and continuing down to Llandeilo, and the A483 north to Builth Wells. The most convenient place to park is Castle car park (£1.20/2hrs).

On the Heart of Wales line, trains (4 Mon–Sat, 2 Sun) pass through here each day en route south to Swansea, and north to Shrewsbury, via Builth Wells and Knighton; the station is a 10-minute walk northwest of the museum just of Tywi Avenue (the A40). The main bus stop is in the Castle car park, from where there are services to Brecon, Carmarthen (9 daily Mon–Sat) and Llandeilo (8 daily Mon–Sat).

TOURIST INFORMATION

 Llandovery Tourist Information Kings Rd; ☎ 01550 720693; w llandoverymuseum.wales; ◷ 10.00–16.00 Tue–Sun). Inside the town museum, it's not an official tourist office but they stock plenty of literature & are more than helpful with any queries.

🏠 WHERE TO STAY, EAT AND DRINK

🏠 **Castle Hotel** (15 rooms) Kings Rd; ☎ 01550 720343 w castle-hotel-llandovery.co.uk; Llandovery's pre-eminent hotel (albeit in a town with few), the small, family-owned Castle has recently been refurbished to a good standard, with well-appointed – if hardly memorable – rooms. Just about shades it too as the best spot to eat in town; worth a go is the gut-busting Drover's Lunch, consisting of ham hock terrine, sausage meat & Scotch egg, with Welsh cheddar & chutneys. It won't quite get you to London, but it'll see you on your way. **££**

🍽 **La Patisserie** 2 High St; ☎ 01550 720375; ◷ 09.00–18.00 Tue–Sat. The irresistible waft of freshly baked bread is sure to lure you into this aromatic den of loveliness: cakes, pastries & tarts, & if you want something more filling, try one of their hot-out-of-the-oven pasties or rissoles. Decent take-away coffee too. **£**

🍽 **Penygawse** 12 High St; ☎ 01550 721727; w penygawse.co.uk; ◷ 09.00–16.00 Tue–Sun. Fabulous Victorian-styled tearoom just around the corner from La Patisserie that is far classier than the plastic bottles of ketchup on the tables might suggest. It's co-owned by a master barista so you can enjoy terrific coffee alongside a fortifying all-day b/fast or a slice of moist lemon drizzle cake. They've also got 7 perfectly acceptable guest rooms, one of which is a family room sleeping up to 6. **£**

SHOPPING

Myddfai 4 Market Sq; ☎ 01550 777155; w myddfai.com; ◷ 10.00–18.00 Wed–Sat, 11.00–16.00 Sun. Established in 2010 by the Myddfai village community but now based in nearby Llangadog (both villages just a few miles up the road), this excellent social enterprise has just opened its 1st shop. It's a small affair but packed with their ethically sourced products: hair & body items ranging from hand wash & shower gel to body lotions as well as items for the home including candles & reed diffusers. Myddfai are now one of the largest suppliers of guest toiletries to hotels in Wales, so the chances are that you'll have used their products before.

WHAT TO SEE AND DO Positioned atop a grassy knoll right under the nose of the main town car park and bus stop (there are much nicer views from the other side) are the sad, stumpy remains of the **town castle**. Originally a 12th-century fortification, ownership of the castle sallied back and forth between the Welsh and the English before it last saw action in the early 16th century. On 9 October 1401, local landowner Llywelyn ap Gruffydd Fychan was marched to the castle's gallows, whereupon he was disembowelled and dismembered on account of his support for Glwnydr's rebellion. The victim of this singularly gruesome incident is celebrated in the form of a bizarre statue on another mound just below the castle: an oversized stainless-steel carapace, completed by brothers Toby and Gideon Petersen in 2001, it looks a bit like Darth Vader in medieval garb.

From the castle, it's a short walk through the car park to the **Llandovery Museum** (☎ 01550 720693; w llandoverymuseum.wales; ◷ 10.00–16.00 Tue–Sun), which also doubles as the town tourist information office (see above). Housed in the town's old bakery, and run by an enthusiastic group of volunteers, its local history collection is crammed into just one room, the main focus of which is the town's drovers' heritage: Welsh Black cattle, along with a motley assortment of sheep, pigs, geese and whatever other livestock could be rounded up, would be assembled in Market Square before the long haul, on foot, up to London to be sold. It was the drovers, too, who founded the Black Ox bank, which will be more familiar to you

A former mining town on the southwestern tip of the Brecon Beacons, **Ammanford** doesn't have much going for it these days, but there are folk who travel here from all over for just one thing: coffee. Cleverly trading on the town's rich industrial heritage, **Coaltown Coffee** is a small-batch roastery established in 2014 by hometown boy Scott James, who, after initially starting out from his garage, identified a derelict coalshed next to the railway line on the outskirts of town to carry his vision forward. Coaltown now supplies dozens of cafés and restaurants across South Wales and beyond so you'll probably have tried it at some point or other. But the company's local roots remain strong, and you can try some of their coffee at the roastery (☎ 01269 400105; w coaltowncoffee.co.uk; ⏱ 09.00–16.00 daily) on Foundry Road. If the look of the building doesn't draw you in, then the aroma will. It's a fabulous space – dare we say it, straight out of Hoxton – with a cool front-facing bar and industrial-leaning décor.

The menu is concise, with the usual suspects, as well as pour-over filter coffee, but it is of course all about the beans, which are seasonally sourced from single-estate farms in some of the world's leading coffee-growing regions, such as Uganda's Kisinga coffee station. Sip with a rhubarb and custard blondie, or a single-origin brownie and watch the magic happen from behind the lead-framed windows that separate the drinking area from the factory floor. As well as the coffee shop here in Ammanford, they've just opened up another in Swansea – expect more to follow. While Coaltown Coffee won't transform the town's fortunes, it is an uplifting local story and one that might just inspire other potential businesses. Forget coal: coffee is the new Black Gold.

as the Black Horse bank, or Lloyds TSB. There are also displays on education – the high school has recently closed, though the private Llandovery College maintains a prestigious presence in town – and Welsh costume. Here is an example of the classic Welsh hat, a tall stovepipe with a stiff, flat brim and a high crown. Worn almost exclusively by rural women, typically when attending church, its popularity peaked in the mid 19th century before it quickly fell out of fashion, and the only time you're likely to see them adorned now is on St David's Day.

Cross the main road to the wide and handsome **Market Square**, bookended by the grey-painted **town hall**, now home to a modest craft market and one or two other low-key shops.

Dolaucothi Goldmine (Pumsaint; ☎ 01558 650177; w nationaltrust.org.uk; ⏱ 10.00–17.00 Wed, Thu & Sun (Wed–Sun during school holidays); £10) Heading northwest from Llandovery, the landscape becomes increasingly green and hilly as you approach the village of Pumsaint (Five Saints). It was here, to coin a quote from Mark Twain's 1892 novel *The American Claimant*, that the Romans discovered 'gold in them thar hills', and so it was that they remained at the Dolaucothi Goldmine for the best part of 200 years, long enough to take their share of the spoils. It is thus the only known Roman gold-mining centre in Britain.

The Romans established a vast operation here, employing various methods to mine the gold: one was open-cast mining – simply digging for gold in open pits – while another method entailed driving horizontal shafts, known as adits, into the hillside, the openings to which are now concealed by thick vegetation. Ever the engineers, the equipment used by the Romans was astonishingly advanced for the time, and included water-powered trip hammers and a 12ft waterwheel, parts of which would be recovered by miners in later years. The rewards were substantial (the Romans wouldn't have hung around otherwise), but they had to work hard for their return: a tonne of quartz yielded just one ounce of gold, which would then be transferred to Carmarthen before being destined for the Imperial Mint in Lyon.

There were effectively two further stages of mining here after the Romans: initially between 1888 and 1912, then in the 1930s. Encouraged by the success of gold-mining operations in South Africa and the famous Klondike gold rush, the Victorians picked up where the Romans left off, albeit some 1,800 years later. In his capacity as mine manager, Cornish mine engineer James Mitchell sank a shaft to a depth of around 100ft, but despite sporadic success the cost and effort to mine what ultimately gave very little by way of return was unsustainable and the mine closed in 1912. Mitchell returned to South Africa with his tail between his legs, but in the event he was far more successful there.

The third and final phase of mining here at Dolaucothi took place in the 1930s, continuing until the eve of World War II. At any one time during this period, there would have been up to 500 men and boys, some as young as 12, digging for gold. As far as health and safety was concerned, the goldmine was appreciably safer than, say, the coal mines, although many men did succumb to silicosis, an incurable and degenerative lung disease caused by breathing in quartz dust. Miners were well remunerated, though, earning a king's ransom in comparison to workers in other industries. The mine was eventually forced to close due to spiralling production costs, as well as the demand for alternative energy sources. It was then used to stockpile ammunition for World War II before the National Trust took over the site in 1942.

The yard is laid out with the remnants of these last two phases of operation – the towering pit-head frame, the tracks used for the drams (trucks) to shunt material back and forth, and half a dozen corrugated-iron sheds which variously housed machinery (winding shed, workshop, generator) or were used by miners in preparation for work, such as the kitting-up shed.

Despite the promise of lots of dark tunnels to root around in, the visit to the mine itself is fairly perfunctory, and the one slightly disappointing aspect of the tour. But the enthusiastic guide offers illuminating insight into the workings of the mine as you are led around the site, which bears many reminders of intense activity here, such as the spoil heaps, the closed-off entrance to the Lower Roman Adit, and the leats ranged across the hills in the distance which used to carry water into the mine for washing the ore. There are quite a few steps on the guided tour, so do bear that in mind when booking. You can even prospect for gold yourself using panning dishes.

✗ Where to eat and drink

Dolaucothi Arms Pumsaint; 01558 650237 w dolaucothiarms.co.uk; 17.00–23.00 Wed & Thu, noon–23.00 Fri & Sat, noon–20.00 Sun. It's not quite as old as the Roman mines, but this warming inn with rooms, just down the road in the village, has been knocking around since the 16th century. The menu is little more than well-cooked pub food, plus pizzas, but washed down with a pint of real ale from the nearby Evan Evans brewery, & you've got yourself a very pleasant lunch. The best thing about the place, though, is the beer garden, one of the finest in Carmarthenshire, which, with its views overlooking the valley, is gorgeous on a warm day. The 3 en-suite Arts-&-Crafts-style rooms are most pleasing on the eye, if a fraction small, & dogs are welcome to sleep over too. ££

RSPB Gwenffrwd-Dinas Nature Reserve and Llyn Brianne
If you've the time and inclination to venture, then you could do worse than head further north towards the Cambrian Mountains and the **RSPB Gwenffrwd-Dinas Nature Reserve** (car parking £2) – 11 miles northwest of Dolaucothi, or a more direct 11-mile route if you're coming from Llandovery. Birders should come armed with binoculars, as there are some top species here including pied flycatcher, redstart, common sandpipers and wood warbler, and you can expect to see plenty of red kites too as this is very much their territory. To get the most out of the reserve, tackle the 2½-mile-long marked trail which starts at the car park and which weaves through ancient woodland full of twisted trees alongside the fast-flowing River Twyi up to its confluence with the River Doethie – it's fairly rough and steep in places, but nothing too demanding.

If you thought the reservoirs in the Brecon Beacons were quiet, wait until you get to **Llyn Brianne**, a lovely spot just a few miles on from the nature reserve. Relatively modern by Welsh standards, Llyn Brianne was constructed in 1970 in order to supply Swansea and West Wales with drinking water. You can walk or cycle the perimeter, but you could just as usefully use the reservoir to strike out into the wilds of the Cambrians.

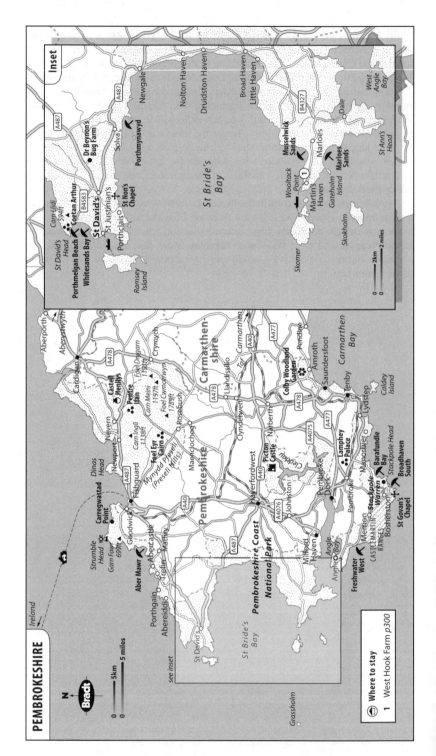

Inset

Ireland

N

Bract

0   5km
0   5 miles

see inset

Pembrokeshire Coast National Park

St Bride's Bay

Grassholm

PEMBROKESHIRE

Strumble Head
Carregwastad Point
Garn Fawr 699ft
Goodwick
Fishguard
Dinas Head
Newport
Cam Ingli 1138ft
Foel Eryr Cairn 1535ft
Mynydd Preseli (Presell Hils)
Maenclochog
Rosebush
Cam Meini 1197ft
Foel Cwmcerwyn 1759ft
Foel Drygarn 1199ft
Aberporth
Abenystwyth
Cardigan
Nevern
Castell Henllys
Pentre Ifan
Crymych
A478
A487
A40
A478

Aber Mawr
Abercastle
Trefin
Mathry
Porthgain
Abereiddio
St David's

Pembrokeshire

Haverfordwest
A40
A487
Johnston
A4076
Clynderwen
Llandissilio
Llawhaden
Narberth
A478

Carmarthen-shire

Teifi
Tâf
Carmarthen
A40
A477

Milford Haven
Angle
Angle Bay
Freshwater West
CASTLEMARTIN RANGES
Merrion
Bosherston
St Govan's Chapel
Stackpole Warren
Barafundle Bay
Stackpole Head
Broadhaven South
Manorbier
Lamphey Palace
Picton Castle
Cleddau
Pembroke Dock
Pembroke
A4075
A477

Colby Woodland Garden
Amroth
Saundersfoot
Tenby
Lydstep
Caldey Island

Carmarthen Bay

St Bride's Bay

St David's

Inset detail:

St David's Head
Carn-Llidi 594ft
Coetan Arthur
St David's
Porthmelgan Beach
Whitesands Bay
Ramsey Island
Porthclais
St Justinian's
St Non's Chapel
B4583
A487
Dr Beynon's Bug Farm
Solva
Porthmynawyd
Newgale
Nolton Haven
Druidston Haven
Broad Haven
Little Haven
Dale
B4327
West Angle Bay
St Ann's Head
Wooltack Point
Martin's Haven
Musselwick Sands
Marloes
Marloes Sands
Gateholm Island
Skokholm
Skomer

St Bride's Bay

0   2km
0   2 miles

Where to stay
1   West Hook Farm p300

274

9

Pembrokeshire

Pembrokeshire manifests the most illustrious stretch of coastline in all of Wales: beautifully sculpted cliffs scalloped by sheltered coves and white-sand beaches with pellucid waters, and headlands crowned by Iron-Age hillforts. Such uplifting beauty is best appreciated walking the **Pembrokeshire Coast Path**, but if that's not invigorating enough, try your hand at coasteering, sea kayaking or snorkelling. For many, the highlight of a visit to Pembrokeshire – indeed for some it's *the* reason for coming to Pembrokeshire – is the opportunity to see one of the largest seabird colonies in northwest Europe. From spring onwards, **Skomer**, **Skokholm** and **Grassholm** are seething with hundreds of thousands of nesting guillemots, gannets, razorbills, kittiwakes, fulmars, Manx shearwater and puffins: it's a heady sensation of sight, sound and smell.

The county can roughly be divided between south and north Pembrokeshire, as intimated by the so-called Landsker Line, an imaginary demarcation between the two halves of the county, which came about as a result of early Norman occupation – and anglicisation of – the southern portion, the country that Henry I turned into 'Little England Beyond Wales'. Nowhere in Pembrokeshire is more anglicised than **Tenby**, Pembrokeshire's star turn, which offers an undeniable shot of glamour allied to an old-fashioned charm that is shared in other seaside resorts like **Saundersfoot** and **Manorbier**. While the multiplicity of resorts strung out along **St Bride's Bay** lack much by way of charisma, the beaches are terrific and this is some of the coast's best surf.

Beyond St Bride's Bay, the road veers west to the pint-sized harbour of **Solva** and thence onwards to **St David's**, Britain's smallest city and the birthplace, in around AD550, of the eponymous saint. Its magnificent cathedral remains Wales's most important place of pilgrimage. The city sits squarely in the centre of the peninsula of the same name, the highlight of which is a walk out to **St David's Head**, from where you can make a satisfying circuit via a yomp to the top of Carn Lidl. Whitesands Bay is the beach of choice here, but clandestine coves lie in wait all around – you'll no doubt find yours. For the best of the wildlife, you'll need to head offshore to **Ramsey Island**, home to one of the largest seal colonies in southern Britain.

Less visited than its southern counterpart, the north Pembrokeshire coast has just as much appeal. It's here where the full elemental power of the ocean can truly be appreciated: cliffs resound to the thunder of waves and there are few settlements here of any appreciable size, just **Fishguard**, scene of one of the more bizarre events in Welsh history, and one of Pembrokeshire's two ferry terminals, and lovely **Newport**, though it's sometimes just as congested as some of the busier spots to the south. From here it's an easy escape from the crowds into the **Mynydd Preseli** (Preseli Hills), a beguiling landscape rich in antiquity, with awesome Pentre Ifan the most striking example in all of Wales of the building prowess of the New Stone Age peoples.

Often conveniently forgotten is just how industrial Pembrokeshire once was, and still is in some parts. **Milford Haven** is the UK's largest energy port and the mother of all bays, where monster-sized tankers ply the shipping channels. The town itself has managed to reinvent itself in recent times with serious investment in the waterfront giving it some leverage as a bona fide tourist destination, which certainly wasn't the case a few years ago. Sadly the same can't be said of **Pembroke Dock**, whose once-proud standing as one of Britain's foremost naval shipyards has long since been consigned to history, although its illustrious past is recalled in a fine museum. Moreover, as one of Pembrokeshire's two terminals from where ferries set sail for Ireland, there are reasons why you might end up here. Smaller **Pembroke** town has much more going for it, not least a formidable castle, much hyped as the birthplace of Henry II.

Inland Pembrokeshire is an almost uninterrupted collage of green pastures, just occasionally broken up by a small town or village. These include graceful Narberth and Haverfordwest, Pembrokeshire's county town and largest conurbation. The latter is more of a pit-stop of necessity rather than choice, acting as a busy hub for St David's to the west and the ferry ports to the south. Nearby Picton Castle offers one of the most enjoyable days out anywhere.

You'll get the most out of Pembrokeshire – and escape the worst of the crowds – if you visit outside of the tourist season, which enters full-throttle between mid-June and August. In any case, there's no guarantee that the weather will be any more favourable in high summer than in spring.

NARBERTH

One of the liveliest and most likeable small towns in South Wales, Narberth was a Norman stronghold on the Landsker Line (page 278) – the language border between the English- and Welsh-speaking parts of West Wales – hence the proportion of Welsh speakers is fairly high. You don't come to Narberth to see the sights, because there aren't any really. Rather, the attraction is the town itself, its narrow streets trimmed by a harmonious ensemble of styles, from pretty little cottages and tweedy shops to high-standing Georgian and Edwardian façades. And what it lacks in conventional sites, it more than makes up for in some great shops, a busy arts scene and some fabulous places to eat.

The best time to be here is September's two-day **food festival** (w narberthfoodfestival.com), when dozens of independent stallholders showcase their wares, chefs offer demonstrations, tastings and workshops, and there's plenty of live music to jolly things along. It's not as big as Abergavenny's equivalent of course, but it's just as much fun. The town's other big knees-up, and one that serves to underline the strong community spirit here, is **Narberth Civic Week** at the end of July, seven days of activities for all ages culminating in Saturday's colourful carnival, Pembrokeshire's biggest.

GETTING THERE AND AWAY Narberth is just a few miles south of the busy A40, which shoots east–west between Carmarthen and Haverfordwest. The busy High Street does have on-street parking (free for 1 hour) – if you can find a space – but otherwise there's Townmoor car park northwest of the High Street.

The train station is a good mile east of town, but if you don't fancy walking in, bus #381 picks up roughly hourly. Narberth is on the Pembroke to Carmarthen line (7 daily services to both, stopping at Tenby and Saundersfoot en route to Pembroke); with another line up to Whitland where you'd change for trains to Fishguard and

Milford Haven. Buses stop at the top of the High Street, with services to Carmarthen (3 daily Mon–Sat), Haverfordwest (hourly Mon–Sat) and Tenby (hourly Mon–Sat).

🏠 WHERE TO STAY, EAT AND DRINK

Aside from those places listed here, The Queen's Hall (see below) hosts a food and craft market every Thursday (🕐 10.00–16.00).

✳ 🏠 **The Grove** (13 rooms & suites in the main house) 2½ miles southwest of Narberth in Molleston; 📞 01834 860915; w grovenarberth. co.uk. For those of a sybaritic disposition, Pembrokeshire's smartest country house should do the trick. The site traces a history that goes back to the 15th century when it was a longhouse belonging to the Bailiff of Tenby before the house itself was raised in the 1680s. The rooms are simply gorgeous, fitted out with handmade furniture & soft furnishings like Welsh rugs & fine silks, in addition to items of locally produced pottery & artwork. The personal touches are everywhere: fresh flowers, turn-down service & a free minibar. Elsewhere the place is run through with decorative Welsh features, for example love spoons in the lounge & a slate-sided bar. The hotel's eco credentials are exemplary too: a biomass boiler, rainwater recycling system, & car-charging points; they also maintain their own veg garden, which sustains the 2 superb restaurants. The main Fernery restaurant (🕐 Wed–Sat eves) offers 5- & 8-course tasting menus, including pescatarian, vegetarian & vegan options, with the majority of ingredients harvested in their own kitchen gardens, while the more informal Artisan restaurant offers a more straightforward à la carte menu with dishes like chilli squid with pak choi & coriander, & lamb pudding with creamed potatoes & garden greens. B/fast, meanwhile, is a 2-course menu: expect the likes of smoked haddock omelette with laverbread, parmesan & Hollandaise sauce, possibly the best you'll ever have. **£££**

🍴 **The Angel** 43 High St; 📞 01834 860318; w theangelnarberth.co.uk; 🕐 noon–23.00 Mon–Fri & Sun, 10.00–23.00 Sat. Attractive & popular 18th-century inn with a choice of bar, lounge or suntrap terrace in which to eat, though the food offer is the same in all 3 settings: perhaps honey glazed goats' cheese to start followed by the Angel fish pie; alternatively, get your chops around one of their enormous burgers. **££**

🍴 **Plum Vanilla** 2 St James St; 📞 01834 862762; 🕐 09.00–17.00 Mon–Sat. Just around the corner from the old town hall, and unmissable with its mint green-coloured frontage & bright pink-painted doors & window frames, this subtly boho café is run by 2 sisters, Plum & Vanilla (yes, really), who are also at the forefront of the Plastic Free Narberth movement, so good on 'em. Part-café, part-deli, the food is mostly veggie-oriented, like spinach & feta pie & spicy vegetable fajitas, plus quiches, frittatas & baguettes to take away. Good coffee & cakes too. **££**

🍴 **Ultracomida** 7 High St; 📞 01834 861491; w ultracomida.co.uk; 🕐 10.00–17.00 Mon–Sat. Spain's finest comes to rural South Wales in this serious homage to all things Iberian. Beyond the front deli packed with lots of juicy goodies to take away is a buzzy tapas space where you can plough into generously portioned plates (of Iberian goodies), & it's the real thing: Picos de Europa (Spanish blue cheese), *cecina* (oak-smoked beef), & an assortment of *empanadas*. Or just stop by for a reviving *café con leche*. **£**

ENTERTAINMENT

The Queen's Hall 44 High St; 📞 01834 861212; w thequeenshall.org.uk. One of the county's most exciting & progressive venues, this great space hosts gigs, comedy, theatre, magic, & much more, while art lovers should have a peek at the Oriel Q Gallery. If you're staying in town, or even if you're just passing through, do check to see what might be occurring.

SHOPPING

Golden Sheaf Gallery 25 High St; 📞 01834 860407; w goldensheafgallery.co.uk; 🕐 09.30–17.30 Mon–Sat. Purveyors of all things good & gorgeous (as the website would have it) just about sums up this wonderful gallery, where a lengthy browse could yield just about anything. Its sister shop, Pembrokeshire Living (🕐 10.00–17.00 Mon–Sat), occupies the former town hall premises across the road.

Chapter One Bookshop Narberth Museum, Church St; ☎01834 860500; w narberthmuseum.co.uk; ⏱ 10.00–17.00 Tue–Sat. Surprisingly perhaps, for such a well-heeled town, this is the only bookshop in Narberth, & it's a little beauty: titles of all persuasions, including fiction, non-fiction, poetry & children's literature, & loads of Welsh-interest books too. What's more, they have an excellent roster of events. Grab a title & enjoy with a coffee next door.

WHAT TO SEE AND DO There's only one place to start really and that's the **High Street**, where there are plenty of opportunities for your wallet to take a serious bashing among the clothes and crafts emporia, delis, fruiterers and small, independent galleries. The one most obviously striking building here is the high and narrow **town hall**, nestled on its own little grassy wedge towards the bottom of the street. Originally of 18th-century origin, the third storey, embedded with a handsome little clocktower, was added just before World War I. Accessed via a double flight of steps, the building is now home to a gallery and gift shop.

Beyond the town hall, roads slope down left and right. Take the right and you come to the **town museum** (☎01834 860500; w narberthmuseum.co.uk; ⏱ 10.00–17.00 Tue–Sat; £4.50), occupying the old bonded stores on Church Street. More than 100 years old, the warehouse was built for storing and blending spirits – with whisky shipped from Scotland, and brandy, port and sherry from Europe – until its

THE LANDSKER LINE

Following their 12th-century invasion, the Normans drove the indigenous Welsh from the agriculturally rich lowlands of south Pembrokeshire and, just to make sure the natives were kept firmly in their place, a line of fortifications were hastily erected. And so the Landsker Line – '*landsker*' is Norse for 'frontier' – was created, the frontier in this case referring to an invisible but palpable line that wavers across the county dividing Cymric (Welsh) north Pembrokeshire from the anglicised, or English, southern part of the county – otherwise dubbed 'Little England Beyond Wales', a term first coined in the early 17th century.

Although it doesn't follow any obvious physical or topographical features, this ghost line runs from Newgale at the top of St Bride's Bay down to Amroth in Carmarthen Bay, and has since become recognised as a partition between the two areas on both linguistic and cultural grounds. Depending upon which side of the line they are, towns and villages are either demonstrably Welsh or English, for example Maenclochog and Clynderwen in the north, and Tenby and Milford in the south. While some view the term as an anachronism, particularly since devolution, others suggest that it is remains an important element of the county's history, and that it emphasises a distinct dichotomy in the region's language and culture. A partial concomitant of this divide are the differing political allegiances. Although these are by no means hard and fast, the north inclines to a combination of older Liberal traditions alongside the more nationalist tendencies espoused by Plaid Cymru, while the south, generally speaking, upholds more conservative-leaning views.

There is an official **Landsker Borderlands Trail**, a circular 58-mile-long route waymarked by a Celtic cross with a brown upright arrow – a relatively straightforward proposition best tackled over three or four days. The traditional starting point is Canaston Bridge, just west of Narberth. The best map for this walk is the OL36.

closure in 2003; the original barred windows and the dual-locking system on the entrance door (security was of the highest importance) remain in situ. The story of the store, and that of its owner, James Williams – who took his own life at the age of 63 – is vividly recalled in an otherwise thoroughly entertaining slice of Narberth life. Indeed, pubs have long been part of the fabric of life here in Narberth, with as many as 30 hostelries in town at one time, as the collection of old bottles and pumps testifies. Further industrial and social history themes covered include dairying, printing, textiles and milling (there were once a dozen mills around town), religion and carnival. The museum's star exhibit is an 1887 'geared facile' – a rare type of penny-farthing still with its hard rubber tyres, so rare in fact that there are believed to be no more than half a dozen in existence.

After the museum, have a poke around the **castle's** gappy ruins, which most visitors aren't even aware exist so you'll probably have the run of the place, although at present the site is closed so you may only be able to view it from the roadside. The castle's history pre-dates the current 13th-century remnants – no more than a few bits of two towers, a vaulted cellar and pantry – as there is thought to have been a Norman fortification here the previous century. It has its legends too: this was the supposed site of the court of Pwyll, Prince of Dyfed, whose adventures make up one of the four branches of *The Mabinogion*, the name given to the collection of 14th-century Welsh tales (page 27).

AMROTH AND SAUNDERSFOOT

The first coastal resort within the county boundary is **Amroth**, whose great, storm-washed beach provides ample excuse for rambling. At low tide these broad sands are sometimes studded with the petrified stumps of blackened trees, possibly up to 7,000 years old, and a sobering reminder that the coastline was once several miles further out to sea than it is today. Many people, though, come to Amroth to embark upon the first leg of the Pembrokeshire Coast Path (or finish it if starting at the other end in St Dogmaels). The first major stop after Amroth is **Saundersfoot**, some 3 miles distant.

A cheerful kind of place, Saundersfoot's salty harbour was originally built to service the needs of the coal and anthracite industries – anthracite in this area was said to be among the finest in the world – who would load up their wares here before it was shipped off to London and elsewhere along the southern Welsh coast. Tourism has long replaced coal and anthracite, and the only boats leaving the harbour these days are trawlers and charters.

From St Bride's Hotel's spectacular clifftop perch above the harbour at the southern end of the village, you could almost be forgiven for thinking you were on the Italian Riviera, as the eye follows the gentle curve of the beach towards the hazy headlands and coves beyond. Of course, it isn't anything like the Italian Riviera, and that much is evident when you reach its main street and harbour, inundated with cafés, chippies, pubs and ice-cream parlours all doing a roaring trade. Gluttony, alongside the usual beach-bound pleasures, is pretty much the sum total of things to do in Saundersfoot.

WHERE TO STAY, EAT AND DRINK

✳ 🏠 **St Bride's Hotel** (34 rooms) St Brides Hill, Saundersfoot; 📞 01834 812304; w stbridesspahotel.com. With its high-altitude panorama of the harbour, town & beach (all of which are just a 5min walk downhill), few hotels in Wales are blessed with such a superb outlook. Although the exterior is not the most promising, this is one of Pembrokeshire's most refined outfits, with a suite of supremely classy rooms, each of which either has a sea or hill view, although the sea-facing ones do come at a premium; regardless, all are beautifully appointed. All guests receive a complimentary 90min spa session. You might also want to get down to b/fast early to bag one of the window tables. £££

🗐 **Wiseman's Bridge Inn** Wiseman's Bridge; 📞01834 813246; **w** wisemansbridgeinn. co.uk; ⏲ 10.00–22.00 daily. Give the pubs in Saundersfoot a wide berth & head down here. Roughly midway between Amroth & Saundersfoot, in an attractive seaside hamlet with a small stone bridge, this traditional-as-they-come beachside pub commands one of the best beer terraces along the entire coast. Food is unsophisticated (burgers, fish pie, gammon) but tasty & generously proportioned while there's a decent selection of ales to choose from. The ideal spot to refuel if walking the Pembrokeshire Coast Path, which you

will have either just started or are about to finish, Amroth being less than 2 miles away. ££

🗐 **Harold O'Vinegar's Seafood Deli** Ocean Sq. The first in the cluster of wooden-built huts (the ones with the wavy roofs on) fronting the harbour, this little deli offers a cabinet full of morsels that have just wriggled their way straight off the boat: prawns, cockles, mussels & dressed crab, & if you're feeling decadent, oysters & champagne. £

🗐 **Hive** 35 Milford St, Saundersfoot; ⏲ 11.00–18.00 daily. You can't move for ice-cream stalls in Saundersfoot, but for the real deal head to Hive, set back from the seafront on the road up towards the community hall. This is an outlet of the original creamery in Aberaeron with the same offbeat flavours like honey Turkish delight, & salted peanut; fabulous sorbets too – try the blackcurrant. Take-away in tubs or cones, including gluten-free ones. £

COLBY WOODLAND GARDEN (📞 01834 811885; **w** nationaltrust.org.uk; ⏲ Mar–Oct 10.00–17.00 daily; £6 parking) A mile inland from Amroth, Colby Woodland Garden covers barely 8 acres yet it's one of the most atmospheric small gardens in South Wales – and that's quite something when you consider that this little corner of eastern Pembrokeshire was once heavily mined, the evidence for which is clear to see in the sealed-off mine entrance, the mine wheel and part of the old railway track. The estate, including the lodge (which is off-limits) is named after the former mine owner, Jim Colby, although it was the subsequent owner, the pharmacist Samuel Kay, who set about recultivating the landscape, work that continued right up until its last proprietors, Pamela and Peter Chance, bequeathed Colby to the National Trust in 1979. Nicely sheltered and consistently moist thanks to abundant streams and lots of Welsh rain, spring sees snowdrops, bluebells, daffodils, crocuses and golden trumpets have the run of the place before summer welcomes azaleas, rhododendrons and camellias. One legacy of the mine is the proliferation of oak trees, which were originally grown here to provide pit props. The Japanese redwood, meanwhile, confers a sense of grandeur.

TENBY

In the endless debates about Britain's most attractive seaside resort – pointless but good fun – Tenby is usually a frontrunner. One thing is for certain: its setting is peerless, and this much you'll appreciate when you reach The Norton and observe the curve of terraced buildings in all their pastel-coloured glory – mint green, salmon pink, lemon yellow, sky blue – above the tiny, stone-built harbour, itself surrounded by piles of lobster creels, with fishermen's cottages tucked into every nook and cranny in the cliff. Either side of the harbour lie Tenby's two great beaches, North Beach and South Beach, in between which is the smaller Castle Beach.

An attack on the town by Llywelyn ap Gruffydd in 1260 is likely to have been the spur to build the town walls you see today. Sustained port activity during the 14th and 15th centuries – trade was mostly high-end goods – was crucial in the town's

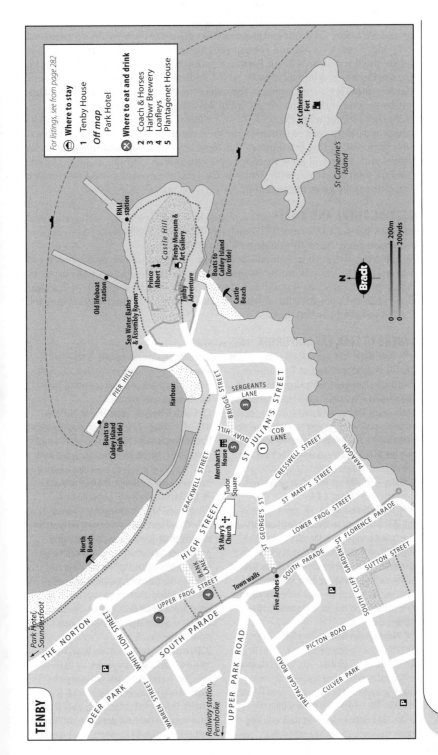

TENBY

For listings, see from page 282

Where to stay
1 Tenby House
Off map
Park Hotel

Where to eat and drink
2 Coach & Horses
3 Harbwr Brewery
4 Loafleys
5 Plantagenet House

0 ——— 200m
0 ——— 200yds

St Catherine's Fort
St Catherine's Island

RNLI station
Old lifeboat station
Castle Hill
Prince Albert
Tenby Museum & Art Gallery
Tenby Adventure
Castle Beach
Boats to Caldey Island (low tide)
Sea Water Baths & Assembly Rooms
PIER HILL
Boats to Caldey Island (high tide)
Harbour
North Beach
Park Hotel, Saundersfoot
THE NORTON
Merchant's House
Tudor Square
CRACKWELL STREET
HIGH STREET
BRIDGE STREET
QUAY HILL
SERGEANTS LANE
COB LANE
ST JULIAN'S STREET
CRESSWELL STREET
ST MARY'S STREET
St Mary's Church
BANK LANE
ST GEORGE'S ST
LOWER FROG STREET
UPPER FROG STREET
WHITE LION STREET
WARREN STREET
DEER PARK
Railway station, Pembroke
UPPER PARK ROAD
SOUTH PARADE
Town walls
Five Arches
SOUTH PARADE
PARAGON
SOUTH CLIFF GARDENS-ST
FLORENCE PARADE
SUTTON STREET
PICTON ROAD
TRAFALGAR ROAD
CULVER PARK

Bradt

Pembrokeshire TENBY

prosperity, before Civil War and plague followed, leaving the town depopulated and decaying. Tenby's revival and subsequent emergence as a bathing resort of some repute owed much to William Paxton, a Scottish-born businessman and MP for Carmarthenshire, who had already built Middleton Hall at the National Botanic Garden (page 263). The coming of the railway in 1863 further enhanced its status, and by the end of the 19th century Tenby was a grand tourist centre.

To that end, little has changed. Tenby's charms of course are no secret, and its streets and beaches can be tainted by the sheer numbers of tourists and day-trippers who flock here during the summer. But come any other time and this spectacular little seaside town will leave a lasting impression, for all the right reasons. The one genuine disappointment with Tenby is the lack of any really good restaurants, surprising really given its reputation.

GETTING THERE AND AWAY Between mid-July and September, cars are banned in Tenby between 11.00 and 17.00 each day. There are plenty of car parks, none of which are more than a 10-minute walk into the centre.

The train station is a 5-minute walk from the town centre at the bottom of Warren Street. Tenby is on the Swansea to Pembroke line, thus is well served by trains in each direction. Local buses stop on South Parade, at the top of Trafalgar Road and on Upper Park Road, while National Express coaches from London and Cardiff call at Upper Park Road.

🏠 WHERE TO STAY, EAT AND DRINK *Map, page 281*

🏠 **Park Hotel** (28 rooms) North Cliffe; 📞01834 842480; w parkhoteltenby.com. Three separate townhouses have been melded together to create this cracking little hotel in a quiet spot overlooking North Beach. They've got a suite of different rooms (though sea view are the only ones with a full view of the water), & although none are especially large, they are all beautifully appointed. The hotel's great selling point, however, is its heated outdoor pool (🕑 May–Sep), though the clifftop garden with sun loungers is fun too. **£££**

🏠 **Tenby House Hotel** (16 rooms) Tudor Sq; 📞01834 842000; w tenbyhousehotel.com. If you don't mind being right in the thick of the action, then William Paxton's former Regency home has a decent selection of white-on-white rooms, some of which overlook the square itself. For convenience's sake, you can take meals down in the lively bar any time of the day, or outside in the convivial beer garden. **££**

✗ **Plantagenet House** Quay Hill; 📞01834 842350; w plantagenettenby.co.uk; 🕑 10.30– 14.30 & 18.00–22.00 Wed–Sun. Tenby's standout restaurant is tucked away inside a 10th-century house, as evidenced by the fine medieval Flemish chimney. The food lives up to the setting too, with dishes like Pembrokeshire fillet steak with king oyster mushrooms & sea bass fillet with asparagus

informing mouthwatering land- & sea-based menus, but if you truly want to splash out, there's a gut-busting seafood platter or a whole Tenby lobster to get stuck into. **£££**

🍺 **Coach & Horses** Upper Frog St; 📞01834 842704; 🕑 noon–23.00 daily. This bright orange-fronted boozer claims to be the oldest in Tenby, & it probably is, but no-one's particularly bothered about that. What people do enjoy here is kicking back with a pint & taking in the local gossip. **£**

✳ 🍺 **Harbwr Brewery** Sergeants Lane; 📞01834 845797; w harbwr.wales; 🕑 noon–22.00 daily. One of South Wales's foremost independent brewers, these guys are doing great things at present. See for yourself in their quirky little bar with its tables & chairs spilling out along the alleyway, *à la* the continent, lovely on a sunny day, & away from the roving hoards too. Beers range from a lighter Celtic pale ale ('Sea Bass') to a powerful orange stout ('La Nossa Signora'), & much else besides. **£**

🍴 **Loafleys** Llandrindod Hse, Upper Frog St; 📞01834 843956; w loafley.wales; 🕑 09.00–17.00 Mon–Sat. Super bakery-deli, with everything prepared upstairs, including fresh breads & pastries. There's good coffee to take away or enjoy in the tiny gravelled courtyard to the rear, where it feels as if you could be anywhere, which is rather nice. They've also a cracking sandwich shop just a few paces up the street, with a chilled cabinet tempting you in with mouthwatering treats like Pembrokeshire smoked salmon with cream cheese, lemon & capers, perfect for lunch on the beach. £

TOURS AND ACTIVITIES Down in the harbour is **Tenby Adventure** (m 07880 746892; w tenbyadventure.co.uk), who run all kinds of coast-based activities including coasteering (£50/5hrs), kayaking (£50/5hrs) and snorkelling (£50/3hrs).

WHAT TO SEE AND DO Strengthened by Jasper Tudor (Earl of Pembroke and uncle of Henry VII), about half of the original 20ft-high **town walls** survive intact, including the **Five Arches**, about halfway along. Described by Augustus John as like 'a piece of cheese gnawed by rats', this semicircular barbican was used as an everyday entrance by town citizens, but unbeknownst to invaders had lots of hidden lookouts for surprise attack. So enamoured were the locals with their walls that in 1989 they founded the Walled Town's Friendship Circle, which some 150 other walled towns have since joined. Head through the arches and you'll find yourself on St George Street and now in the thick of it: cafés, restaurants, ice-cream parlours and sweet shops. Left and right are Upper Frog Street and Lower Frog Street respectively. At the end of St George Street bear left and you're in **Tudor Square** close to the main High Street, and the entrance to St Mary's Church.

St Mary's Church (High St; ☎ 01834 842068; w stmaryschurchtenby.co.uk) The
first thing you notice upon entering the mostly 15th-century St Mary's Church – a cool, quiet refuge from the hubbub outside – is the size of the place, looking much bigger inside than it does out. It's effectively a triple-naved church, so wide are its north and south aisles (as are the dividing arches), with all three taken up by rows of long, bleached pews covering almost every square inch of floorspace. By far the most compelling aspect of the church is the nave's wagon ceiling, which runs all the way from the west door to the high altar: a panel design, its warped-looking beams bear a total of 75 carved bosses that were gilded as recently as 1966. The building is rich in memorials, a clutch of them grouped together in St Thomas's Chapel to the right of the chancel as you face it. Prominent here are the two chest tombs with effigies of Thomas and Jon White, superbly carved and only marred for chunks having been chipped off here and there, including most of Thomas's face. Both erstwhile mayors of Tenby, it was Thomas White who helped secure the escape of Jasper Tudor and his nephew, the then 14-year-old Henry VII, from Tenby harbour in 1471, though only after the pair had apparently hidden in a cellar where the current Boots shop is. Similarly defaced is a relief of William Risam, a later mayor of Tenby, kneeling at a *prie-dieu* (prayer desk). It retains some of its original red and charcoal colouring, so one can only imagine how fantastic the whole must have once looked.

Merchant's House and the harbour From the church, the town's maze of
rough cobbled streets dive down to the superb **Merchant's House** (☎ 01834 842279; w nationaltrust.org.uk; ⊙ 11.00–16.00 Thu & Sat; £6.50) on Quay Hill. A high and narrow three-floored Tudor dwelling, the house is certainly 15th century, but is thought to have medieval origins. The top floor would have been the bedrooms, the middle floor the living quarters, and the ground floor an open shop selling wool, cloth, vinegar and spices; this is where, in 2017, late 18th- or early 19th-century floral wall paintings were discovered on the north wall of the entrance hall. The house is full of mostly replica 16th-century furnishings.

Pembrokeshire TENBY

9

From the Merchant's House, the street slopes steeply to the **harbour**, where people congregate around the wooden huts deciding which boat trip to take. Peer into the dockside arches with fishmongers selling the day's catch. During the late 18th century, the town developed into a fashionable bathing resort thanks to the patronage of William Paxton who, having settled in Tenby, financed the **Sea Water Baths and Assembly Rooms**, located just beyond the cluster of huts selling boat trips. Built in 1811, the baths would have incorporated two pools with dressing rooms, warm and cold baths, a cupping room and a bedroom for invalids; it's now under private ownership. Paxton also built, and lived in, the elegantly balconied **Tenby House** on Tudor Square back in the centre of town. Once the site of the Globe Inn, it's now the Tenby House Inn.

Spreading away from the harbour is the great golden expanse of **North Beach**, one of Wales's most-photographed stretches of sand, partly because of its spectacular backdrop. Smack bang in the middle of the beach is the pronounced mound of Goskar Rock.

Castle Hill From the harbour, a slipway leads down to **Castle Beach**, while a path veers left on to Castle Hill and **Tenby Museum and Art Gallery** (☏ 01834 842809; w tenbymuseum.org.uk; ⊕ 10.00–16.00 Wed–Sat; £4.95), one of the most attractive small museums in Wales. Packed to its rafters with biological, geological and nautical artefacts, it's the gallery that holds the real treasures, particularly a clutch of paintings by Augustus and Gwen John, both of whom spent their childhoods here in Tenby. Two of the pair's most striking pictures are a portrait of the writer Richard Hughes by Augustus, and *Portrait of Winifred John* (her sister) by Gwen. The earliest oil painting here (1799) is *Tenby from North Cliff* by William Golding (not of *Lord of the Flies* fame), a wonderfully evocative piece with bathing machines and nude bathers clustered around Goscar Rock on North Beach. Other artists represented include John Piper, Kyffin Williams and Nicky Wire, bassist in the Manic Street Preachers.

From the museum, follow the path down and around to the Victorian bandstand, where you can savour the wide-screen panorama. There's more Victoriana at the top of Castle Hill courtesy of the **statue of Prince Albert**. Hewn from Sicilian marble, the statue could certainly do with a clean.

The most compelling thing on Castle Hill – in Tenby in fact – is the enormous **RNLI station** (w rnli.org; ⊕ 11.00–15.00 Mon–Wed & Sat; free), which was built on top of the old town pier (opened in 1899 and all but demolished in 1953) to replace the old lifeboat station close by. Opened in 2005, it's a magnificent structure, and inside there's an equally magnificent vessel: the RNLB *Haydn Miller*, which you can view up close – better still time your visit to coincide with a launch (check website). The boat, which cost a cool £2.4 million and which entered service in 2006, is named after the Northamptonshire farmer who funded the majority of it through his will. Informative wall panels recall the lifeboat's history, and here too is the scorched lifebuoy from RFA *Sir Galahad*, destroyed during the 1982 Falklands War with the loss of 48 lives, including 32 Welsh Guards.

Fronting Castle Beach, and reached via a flight of 74 stone steps, is **St Catherine's Island**, so named after the eponymous saint of spinners and weavers and where a chapel once stood in her honour. The island is now topped by a **fort** of the same name, another of Lord Palmerston's follies (page 289), this one constructed in 1869. Closed for years, it can now be accessed at low tide (⊕ Apr–Dec; £5), and while there's not a huge amount to see, it makes for a pleasant short ramble and the views back across to Tenby are rather lovely.

Caldey Island (Tickets from the Caldey Island Kiosk in Tenby Harbour; ☏01834 844453; w caldeyislandwales.com; ⊕ Easter–Oct every 20mins; £15 return) Two miles offshore, Caldey Island – whose name was reputedly derived from the Viking Keld Eye, meaning 'Cold Island' – has been a place of God for more than 1,400 years, ever since Celtic monks pitched up here in the 6th century. Viking incursions briefly put a halt to religious proceedings, before order was restored in 1136 when Benedictine monks from St Dogmaels in northern Pembrokeshire founded a priory here. The dissolution resulted in much toing and froing of ownership before it was bought by a community of Anglican Benedictines in 1906 who were then forced to sell up and were succeeded by Reformed Cistercians (Trappists) from Scourmont Abbey in Belgium in 1929. Living a life of austere simplicity, the monks here take vows of poverty, chastity and obedience and observe a rule of silence between 19.00 and 07.00. In addition to study and prayer, the third tenet of their rule is work, and here the brothers cultivate chocolate, shortbread, cosmetics and perfume, samples of which you can buy in the village shop. You may spot some red squirrels, a small colony of which were reintroduced to the island in 2016, and they've been thriving ever since.

From the jetty, it's a short walk to the island's main settlement, consisting of no more than a post office (with a small museum), a perfume shop selling the monks' wares, and some sweet little tea gardens, from where you can see the imposing **abbey** itself. Beyond the abbey is the diminutive **St David's Church**, which is fairly plain save for a font with lettering by the controversial sculptor and typeface designer Eric Gill, founder of a craft community in Capel-y-Ffin in the Black Mountains in the 1920s (page 240).

Completing this triumvirate of ecclesiastical buildings is the 12th-century **St Illtud's Church** (in the grounds of the old priory), which is possibly the oldest church in England and Wales still used for Catholic worship. The first thing you'll notice is its steeple, stunted and with a slight lean, but it's inside the church – ancient pebble flooring worn to a slippery shine – where the treasures lie. Here is the 6th-century **Ogham Cross**, as rare and as important a find as the stones in the church of the same name in Llantwit Major in the Vale of Glamorgan (page 132). Ogham was a medieval alphabet and the stone here, retrieved from under the stained-glass window on the south side of the nave, bears an inscription that reads: 'And by the sign of the cross which I have fashioned upon this stone, I ask all who walk there that they pray for the soul of Catuocunus.' Seek out the medieval etchings graffitied on to another wall, one of which is a small skull and crossbones. Carry on down the lane to the island's lighthouse with hazy views straight ahead to the North Devon coast. Note that boats to Caldey Island depart from Tenby Harbour, but when the tide is out, they depart from Castle Beach.

THE COAST WEST OF TENBY

LYDSTEP From Tenby, the coast path continues south and west towards Manorbier, but it's worth pausing at Lydstep on the way. On the surface just one enormous caravan site, there is a very pleasant shingle beach here and the village itself passes for picturesque. The main draw here, though, is a chain of **caverns**, which can be reached via 100 steps from the top of the cliff, but only at low tide as there is little sand here. If you do make it (and you'll probably be alone), you can nose around several caves bearing names like The Droch, Bear Cave, and Smuggler's Cave, the last of which has three separate entrances and is about 300ft long. Of **Bear Cave**, the 19th-century naturalist P H Gosse wrote, 'it is a yawning chasm…in the centre of which there is a most excellent image of the face of a colossal bear, as if crouching in the cave, the pointed ears, the half-closed eyes, the nose and muzzle are all excellent, almost too good to be true; till on approaching, you discern that every feature is merely some natural crevice, or angle, or rounding of the wet and slimy rocks…' Just don't forget your torch. And now you've made it here, stay a while and do some rockpooling.

Although not part of the coast path, there is a designated National Trust walk (1 mile) around the headland, which starts at Lydstep Head car park and loops round via **Lydstep Point** – from where there are awesome views of Gower and the Carmarthenshire coast away to your left – and abandoned lime quarries that drop sheer into the Haven. From Lydstep, it's a mile or so further west to **Skrinkle Haven** and another sumptuous little cove reached via steep steps from the car park at the end of the little lane off the Manorbier road.

MANORBIER Gerald Cambrensis called it the most delectable spot in Wales, and there's no doubt Manorbier (pronounced 'manner-beer') oozes charm. So much so that quite the list of superstar names have deemed it worthy of a visit in years past: Augustus and Gwen John frequently spent time here, both George Bernard Shaw and Virginia Woolfe stayed at the resort, Woolf on at least two occasions, and the celebrated war poet Siegfried Sassoon penned *A Ruined Castle* here when visiting Walter de la Mare in 1924.

As for Cambrensis, one might reasonably suppose that the reason for his flattering comment about Manorbier was down to the fact that he was born in its **castle** (☎ 01834 870081; w manorbiercastle.co.uk; ⏱ 10.00–16.00 daily; £6) in or around 1146. Surrounding a beautiful, baize-like lawn, the castle was originally raised in the 12th century – its Norman walls remain extremely well preserved and come with some of the finest views along the coast – before the Cambrensis clan got their hands on it. Having exchanged hands several times thereafter, it became the property of the Philipps (of Picton Castle) in 1670, who subsequently leased it to J R Cobb, who was responsible for much of its 19th-century appearance. The waxwork figures are a bit daft, but other than that, this is great fun. Note that the castle is a popular wedding venue and does close fairly frequently, so check the website before visiting. Accessed via the road between the castle and the beach are the remains of a dovecote. On the opposite side of the car park stands the **church of St James the Great**, whose nave is of Norman origin while its ghostly white-painted tower – one of the coast's more distinctive landmarks – is probably late 13th century. Inside is an effigy of one of the de Barris (though which one has never been established) and some stained glass in the north aisle representing Cambrensis with St David.

As well as Manorbier's own very fine pebble and sand beach, there are other, less busy ones to target if you don't mind walking a little. One of these is **Presipe beach**, a 15-minute walk east of Manorbier beach. This deeply indented cove backed by huge crags of fossil-rich red rock is an absolutely gorgeous spot, but at high tide the beach can be completely cut off. From the path on the left-hand side of Manorbier beach, you gently ascend the headland known as the **Priest's Nose**, and en route to Presipe (beach) you'll pass the **King's Quoit**, a Neolithic burial chamber that dates from around 3000BC. From here, look back in the direction from whence you came for superb views of the castle and church. Heading west from Manorbier beach, just over 2 miles away, **Swanlake Bay** is another remote and quiet bay.

STACKPOLE ESTATE The coast path bumbles on from Swanlake Bay to Freshwater East, marred by a ring of chalets and in any case far inferior to Freshwater West on the other side of the Castlemartin ranges. The next major stop along the coast is the National Trust-run Stackpole Estate, an enchanting little enclave combining abundant wildlife, superb beaches and memorable clifftop walks. The visitor centre aside, the village itself consists of nothing more than a few houses and a very good pub. The estate is also just 5 miles down the road from Pembroke, a handy escape if it's raining.

Getting there and away Buses #387 and #388 (Coastal Cruiser) loop round from Pembroke Dock and Pembroke (3 daily), calling at Bosherston and Stackpole village, with two of these going to St Govan's; between October and May this service runs on Saturday only. There are National Trust car parks at Lodge Park (for the estate office) Stackpole village, Bosherston Lily Ponds and Broadhaven South (£5 per day).

Tourist information
National Trust Estate Office Lodge car park; ☏ 01646 623110; w nationaltrust.org. uk; ⏰ 10.00–17.00 Mon–Fri. The friendly folk here can dispense leaflets as well as advise on local walks.

✕ Where to eat and drink
🍴 **Stackpole Inn** Jason's Corner, Stackpole village; ☏ 01646 672324; w stackpoleinn.co.uk; ⏰ noon–15.30 & 17.30–23.00 daily. A low grey house with a tiled roof & large sloping lawn, the estate's one pub was originally the village post office, but has since gained a reputation as a bit of a foodie destination. The restaurant serves beautifully cooked dishes such as Pembrokeshire beef carpaccio with celeriac remoulade, & pan-fried pork loin with wild garlic & star anise (& if not foraged, most of the food is sourced as locally as possible), although your head is likely to be turned towards the daily specials board which typically features the best of the day's catch, such as lobster, crab claws, dover sole & so on. They've also got a handful of rooms styled with some panache (min 2-night stay in Jul & Aug). £££

What to see and do
Stackpole Quay and Barafundle Bay By anyone's reckoning, **Stackpole Quay** is a mere slip of a harbour, with barely enough room to squeeze more than two or three boats into. Built in 1878 by the Earl of Cawdor, one-time owner of the now-demolished Stackpole Court, the quay was used to export limestone from the earl's quarry, as well as to import luxury goods for him and his family to enjoy on the estate.

The delightful **Barafundle Bay** is one of those that regularly tops those 'best of' lists, if you're into that kind of thing. A broad stretch of golden sand with clean water and a lovely hinterland of gorse-flecked dunes and pinewoods, Barafundle is also just far enough away from Stackpole Quay (about a half a mile) to stop it from ever getting overwhelmed. Swimmers love it, especially when you can paddle round to the three natural arches on the south side of the beach. Behind the bay, the **Stackpole Warren** dune system is a fun place to go and explore for a bit.

Bosherston Lily Ponds Three spindly fingers of reed-fringed water formed in the 18th century when the Stackpole Estate sealed off a trio of limestone valleys to create a designated park, cactus-shaped Bosherston Lily Ponds now form part of a sylvan nature reserve. Of these three bodies of water, the Eastern Arm is the longest and largest, though the most rewarding is the Western Arm, which is also the one closest to Bosherston village. The time to see the purple lilies and tangles of fern in full bloom is late spring into summer, though June always seems to be a good time. Bosherston is one of the more reliable places in Wales to see otters gambolling, though there's plenty of other wildlife to pay attention to including herons, overwintering wildfowl, and bats – lots of bats. Tree-dwellers include jays, nuthatches and great spotted woodpeckers. It's also possible to fish here, though you will need a permit from either the Estate Office or the Ye Olde Worlde Café in Bosherston.

Stackpole Head and Broadhaven South Walking south from Barafundle Bay along the coast path brings you to **Stackpole Head**, a craggy limestone headland that's home to large colonies of seabirds including razorbills and guillemots, as well as choughs; there are thought to be around 20 pairs of these acrobatic birds here, easily distinguished from other members of the crow family owing to their bright-red beaks and feet. Those with wheels (and children) tend to make a beeline for **Broadhaven South** beach, owing to the proximity of the car park. But in any case, this is another terrific arc of sand, bright yellow sloping into calm waters. Rising from the sea ahead is the small jagged lump of Church Rock.

St Govan's Chapel Tucked away in a shadowy cleft just inside the western edge of the MoD's Castlemartin artillery range (check the website for range opening times – see below), St Govan's Chapel was named after the 6th-century Irish priest, Gobhan. Legend supposes that the priest was once attacked by pirates, probably from Lundy, whereupon the cliffs below swallowed him up thus saving him from inevitable death. The genesis of this extraordinary chapel is uncertain, but most commentators regard it as being of 11th- or 12th-century origin. One thing's for sure: it's austere, both inside and out, furnished with a simple slab altar and a few faint inscriptions, nothing more; if you're looking for some solitude, you'll probably find it here. Steps continue down to a small cell hewn from the rock – the spot where Govan supposedly sheltered – and thence down to the water itself.

THE CASTLEMARTIN RANGE The area between Bosherston and Freshwater West is known as the Castlemartin Range, which was first used by the army in 1939 before it was purchased by the MOD in 1948. Castlemartin is actually divided into two sections: **Range West**, which is not open to the public at any time owing to the danger of unexploded ordnance, though occasionally guided walks are offered by National Park rangers; and **Range East**, which is usually accessible at weekends and bank holidays – either way, you should always check (☏ 01646 662367; w gov.uk/ government/collections/firing-notice). Regardless, if red flags are flying or lights are hoisted, you should not enter. The same timings apply to the only road (lane) that runs through the range from the army camp at Merrion down to Stack Rocks.

If walking the coast path, there are two options: from St Govan's the path continues towards beaches at **Bullslaughter Bay** and **Flimston Bay** before reaching **Stack Rocks**, whereupon you turn right and walk up the lane to Merrion. When the range is closed there's an alternative inland route from Bosherston to Merrion, just beyond which you meet up with the other path.

FRESHWATER WEST AND ANGLE **Freshwater West** is superior to its counterpart on the other side of the Castlemartin Range on several counts, not least because it's largely devoid of the type of development that mars Freshwater East. Above all, though, this wonderfully unspoiled beach is one of the south coast's best for surfing – indeed, many rate it the best in Pembrokeshire. That said, it's generally the preserve of more experienced boarders, and isn't suitable for swimming owing to the strong currents. Freshwater West's relative seclusion has made it a popular location for film shoots: parts of *Robin Hood* and *Their Finest* have been shot here, while Harry Potter fans may recognise it as the location of Shell Cottage in *Harry Potter and the Deathly Hallows*.

Around 3 miles northwest of Freshwater West, on the eastern side of the peninsula of the same name, is the medieval village of **Angle**, although most of today's houses, or cottages, are of 19th-century origin. On this same side of the peninsula is **Angle Bay**, a Site of Special Scientific Interest on account of its tremendous birdlife, particularly waders. For a more traditional, albeit fairly low-key, slice of beach action, head a mile west of Angle to **West Angle Bay**, though again the currents here can be strong; there is parking above the beach. This stretch of coastline is replete with abandoned forts, dating from the Iron Age all the way through to World War II. Some, like the fort crowning **Thorn Island** just offshore from West Angle Bay, were built in the mid 19th century on the instruction of the then prime minister Lord Palmerston (along with many others along the southern coastal waters) in light of what were perceived to be deteriorating Anglo-French relations – although in the event none of these were ever used. After World War II, the fort was converted into a hotel, which closed in 1999, since which time it has been bought and sold on a couple of occasions, though at the time of writing it stood redundant.

✕ Where to eat and drink

✳ ✕ **Café Môr** The Old Point House, Angle; 📞07422 535345; **w** theoldpointhouse.wales/ about-cafe-mor; ⏱ noon–17.00 Wed & Thu, noon–20.00 Fri & Sat. Operating from a mobile, solar-powered seaweed boat (the *Josie June*), this fabulous seasonal street (or beach) food kitchen is the creation of chef Jonathan Williams, whose great passion is seaweed, which he forages in abundance along these shores. This is reflected in the menu – for example Welsh beef & laverbread burger, & egg butty with laverbread & Welsh sea black butter (there's even seaweed tea) – but there's much more besides including crab & lobster rolls, plus ice creams, cakes & coffee. **£**

PEMBROKE AND AROUND

The old county town of Pembroke nudges up against the southern bank of the River Pembroke, whose muddy brown waters flow in from the Cleddau Estuary. The first thing to say is that Pembroke town and Pembroke dock are two quite different entities, each with their own distinct character and history: the docks with its shipbuilding, and the town with its gargantuan castle. Like so many Welsh towns, Pembroke grew up around its castle, at the same time flourishing as a port from where it could ship goods to Ireland, France and Spain, as well as the rest of the British Isles. After being besieged by Cromwell, Pembroke came good again during the 18th century, thanks to several important industries, among them weaving, dyeing, tailoring and leather making.

GETTING THERE AND AWAY

By ferry Irish Ferries (**w** irishferries.com) operate two daily ferries from Pembroke Dock across to Rosslare in southeast Ireland, a crossing of around 4 hours.

By rail and bus A 10-minute walk east of the docks and heritage centre, Pembroke Dock train station – which opened in 1864 offering free rides to Tenby (no such luck these days) – is the last stop on the line from Carmarthen (7 daily);

all these stop at Pembroke, Manorbier, Tenby and Saundersfoot en route. Buses stop on Laws Street, just west of the train station, with hourly services to Pembroke, Milford Haven and Tenby. Easily accessible by car from the A477, which continues to Pembroke Dock, there are several car parks in the vicinity of the castle.

WHERE TO STAY, EAT AND DRINK

Lamphey Court Hotel & Spa (39 rooms) Lamphey; 01646 672273; w lampheycourt. co.uk. Early 19th-century Georgian mansion directly opposite the palace ruins, this is top-end accommodation with good-sized, fresh-faced rooms in both the main building & the Coach House. Leisure facilities, including a gorgeous indoor pool, sauna, gym & massage, a well-respected restaurant, & sweeping grounds, complete the package. £££

Food at Williams 18 Main St; 01646 689990; 10.00–15.00 Mon–Sat. Breakfasts & light lunches is what they do here, & they do it very well too; Welsh rarebit on sourdough, Glamorgan sausages & chicken noodle soup, plus sarnies & baguettes galore. Lush coffee & cakes too. £

WHAT TO SEE AND DO Before visiting the castle, it's worth a wander through the town itself, essentially one long thoroughfare – unimaginatively called **Main Street** – darting east from the train station all the way through to the castle walls. Bound by Georgian and Victorian houses concealing brightly painted frontages, you'll find all the amenities you need here, including one or two reasonable places to eat, as well as the **Pembroke Museum** (01646 683092; w pembrokemuseum.wales; 10.00–12.30 Mon–Fri; free), inside the town hall building towards the castle end of the street. On your way into the building take a moment to view the murals on the foyer and upper landing, a brazenly colourful pictorial history of the town through time. The museum itself is an enjoyably chaotic space with cabinets stuffed with maritime paraphernalia, Welsh costume, toys and games, and a lovingly recreated 1940s home.

Nicer still is a walk alongside the **Mill Pond**, which runs parallel to Main Street along the north side of the town walls. From the east end of Main Street, turn right down Mill Pond Walk to the waterside, following the promenade all the way down to the castle. Now a nature reserve, the pond is home to some waterfowl and even the occasional otter. At the end of this trail, **Mill Bridge** was actually a tidal barrage, though nothing, except for its old base, remains of the mill as it was demolished in 1959.

Pembroke Castle (01646 681510; w pembrokecastle.co.uk; Mar & Sep–Oct 10.00–17.00 daily, Apr–Aug 09.30–17.30 daily, Nov–Feb 10.00–16.00 daily; £8.50) Perched atop a limestone promontory above the Cleddau Estuary, and surrounded by water on three sides, Pembroke Castle quite reasonably sets much store on its associations with Henry VII (Tudor), who was born here in 1457. But the original castle pre-dates Henry's birth by around 250 years when Lord Roger Montgomery – taking advantage of the power vacuum that had been created in West Wales by the death of Rhys ap Thomas – pitched up in 1093 and built a wooden frontier fortress, one that effectively acted as a bridgehead between Wales, England and Ireland.

Notwithstanding later restoration, what you see today is the result of an almost complete rebuild in 1189 by William Marshal, Earl of Pembroke by dint of his marriage to Richard de Clare's (aka Strongbow) daughter, Isabel. In 1452, Jasper Tudor, with his brother's young widow, Margaret Beaufort, in tow, was granted the title and castle by his half-brother Henry VI, and it was here that Margaret gave birth to Henry, whose victory over Richard III at the Battle of Bosworth Field in 1485 would see him crowned King Henry VII of England. Until recently, it had been assumed (albeit without any real concrete evidence) that Henry had been born in what is now known as the **Henry VII Tower**, immediately to the left of the gatehouse. But archaeological digs in 2018 revealed some extant remains of a late-medieval house in the courtyard, pointing to the likelihood that this more modern residence was in fact his birthplace.

The castle last saw meaningful action during the Civil War, and despite managing to repel Cromwell for 48 days – testament to its enduring strength – it succumbed and most of the towers were demolished to some degree or other. Extensive decay followed. After a short period of restoration in the 1880s, there was a brief hiatus before the castle was acquired by local landowner Sir Ivor Phillips. Phillips set in train a thorough programme of restoration, the result of which is what we see today.

Entering through the towering **gatehouse**, the castle appears remarkably intact, though this is as much to do with extensive restoration as it is to do with the resilience of the original fortification. While it does look, and feel, like an exaggerated restoration in parts – which has inevitably quashed some of its historical charm – it's all good fun and eminently explorable, with lots of dark rooms and dank passages deep within the walls, themselves punctuated by hulking great towers. Walking around the walls, it's striking to see how thin they are, though for purposes of defence these were necessarily thicker on the one landward side.

To the rear of the courtyard, the inner ward is dominated by Marshal's colossal 13th-century **great keep**, quite possibly the mightiest in Wales. At 75ft high and with walls 18ft thick, it's an extraordinary symbol of authority, but to get a real sense of its scale, step inside its yawning innards – which at one time would have had five floors – and crane your neck upwards towards the domed roof. Tucked away under its immense shadow are a cluster of ruinous buildings, including the Norman Hall (the oldest masonry building in the castle) and the Northern Tower; from here, steps wind down to **Wogan's Cavern**, whose damp interior would have been used as a place of shelter for Stone-Age settlers centuries before the castle appeared. Open to the elements on one side, it's quite possibly the only castle in Britain to have been built over a natural cavern. It's worth partaking in one of the free guided tours which start from just inside the gatehouse four times a day in peak season.

Lamphey Palace ☎ 01646 672224; w cadw.gov.wales/visit/places-to-visit/lamphey-bishops-palace; ⊕ 10.00–16.00 daily; free)

From Pembroke, it's just 2 miles to the village of Lamphey and the fabulous ruins of the Bishop's Palace, the one-time country retreat of the bishops of St David's. Built in three separate stages between the early 13th and the middle of the 14th centuries, the palace was largely the work of Henry de Gower, chief architect of the far grander Bishop's Palace in St David's (and, indeed, bishop of St David's between 1328 and 1347); that much is obvious from the distinctive arcaded parapets ranged along the top of the Great Hall, which still looks in great nick. Don't miss the long, dark and atmospheric undercroft: alongside the Great Hall, there would have been some 20 or so well-appointed rooms.

Indeed, this was once quite the site, with a walled deer park to the south, and to the north a complex system of breeding and feeding ponds for fish, not to mention acres of orchards and pastures, fruit and herb gardens. The palace fell into the hands of Henry VIII in 1546 and thereafter the powerful Devereux family, who used it as a private residence and held it until the Civil War when it was garrisoned by Parliamentarians. Different owners followed, including Charles Mathias who restored many of the old buildings and redeveloped the old walled garden; he also acquired neighbouring Lamphey Court, now a smart hotel and spa (see opposite).

Pembroke Dock Just 2 miles northwest of Pembroke, and only separated from it by the River Pembroke and some housing, Pembroke Dock sprang up around the same time as Milford Haven across the estuary. It's a utilitarian place, though its wide, grid-like streets – in the same vein as those in Milford Haven – are flanked by some handsome Victorian buildings. Where Milford Haven had its whaling and fishing industries (then oil and gas), Pembroke Dock had its shipbuilding, the docks opening here in 1813, though they almost didn't come here at all. The first ships were built across the water in Milford Haven, before Nelson deemed the rent too expensive, so he transferred operations here. In the 113 years that followed, 283 Royal Navy vessels left these docks, including five royal yachts. At its peak in the 1890s, the Royal Dockyard was one of the largest in the world, employing more than 3,000 people, and at one stage it was the only place in Britain to have all three forces (Army, Navy and RAF) garrisoned here at the same time.

The docks' closure in 1926 devastated the community, with a quarter of the population moving away from the area, leaving most of those that remained unemployed. Decline was compounded by some of the heaviest bombing on Welsh territory during World War II, when the docks were blitzed on two occasions, firstly in May 1941 and then exactly a month later. Building of the refineries in the 1960s and 70s once again provided gainful employment, as did the construction of a power station for the Central Electricity Generating Board, and the construction of the **Cleddau Bridge**.

A 5-minute walk from the ferry terminal stands the dome-topped **Garrison Chapel**, the only Neoclassical Georgian chapel in Wales, whose restoration in 2014 was nothing short of a miracle given the condition it found itself in. It was originally built in 1831 to serve the soldiers based at the dockyard, but once they left it served as a cinema, dance hall and a motor museum, before being left to rot. Since 2016, it has been home to the **Pembroke Dock Heritage Centre** (Meyrick Owen Way; ☏01646 684200; w pdht.org; ⏲ 10.00–16.00 Mon–Fri; £6), whose largely volunteer-run team are running the place with gusto; by the time you leave, there won't be much you won't know about the dock's history. A good place to start is the timeline spread across the first wall.

One board lists each and every ship constructed at the docks, perhaps the best known of which was HMS *Erebus* (1826), whose doomed attempts to reach the fabled Northwest Passage alongside HMS *Terror* were brilliantly dramatised in the BBC series *The Terror*. Abandoned in 1848, the sunken wreck of *Erebus* was discovered by a Canadian expedition as recently as 2014. Another ship built here was the *Victoria and Albert*, though apparently Victoria never set food aboard; looking at the beautiful model, it's hard to believe that she was scrapped.

Entering service in 1938, the iconic **Sunderland Flying Boats** were in many ways one of the RAF's unsung aircraft, yet they provided a crucial role during World War II, their mission being to protect British convoys from attack by German U-boats; the RAF station here was the largest flying boat base in the world. The Sunderland remained in front-line service for 21 years before being retired in 1959, deemed obsolete with the coming of the jet. A Sunderland that had been on display at the chapel in the 1960s was subsequently transferred to the RAF Museum in Hendon over 50 years ago, and naturally the Trust are keen to reclaim it – they are working on it, so watch this space. In the meantime, a reconstructed cockpit illustrates just how roomy these aircraft were, but more impressive are some remains of a Sunderland that was blown off its moorings during a storm and ended up at the bottom of the Haven. After years resting on the seabed, parts of the plane were

On the evening of 15 February 1996, the 147,000-tonne Liberian-registered *Sea Empress* tanker, en route to the Texaco oil refinery at Pembroke Dock, became grounded on mid-Channel rocks at St Anne's Head. Initial attempts to salvage the vessel – which were hampered by atrocious weather – proved futile, and it wasn't until six days later, with the help of eight tugs, that she was finally floated clear of the rocks and brought into dock, all the while with oil still gushing into Pembrokeshire's waters (ten of the vessel's 18 tanks had ruptured). Within a week, more than 72,000 tonnes of crude oil had spewed into the sea, with slicks moving in every direction, as far as Fishguard on the north coast and Pendine Sands in Carmarthen Bay to the east, in what was the third-largest oil spillage on British shores.

As the weeks and months passed, the damage was all too clear: over 120 miles of the environmentally sensitive Pembrokeshire coastline (some 12% of the entire Welsh coastline), which included 26 Sites of Special Scientific Interest, had been oiled. Casualties to wildlife were immense: more than 20,000 seabirds perished – the common scoter duck was the main victim – and every kind of marine life was smeared with oil, including seaweed and shellfish, while in West Angle Bay, one of just seven British populations of the brooding cushion starfish was wiped out. There were major economic casualties too, with local fisheries closed for months and resorts the length and breadth of Pembrokeshire hard hit by the absence of tourists – and that's without taking into account the cost of the clear-up itself, which, in its final reckoning, amounted to some £60 million. The clean-up operation entailed environmental officers and armies of volunteers skimming oil from beaches and setting up bird-washing camps – even today locals still recall the pungent smell and the sea, black and thick like custard.

Investigations into the grounding determined that the cause was pilot error (it was subsequently revealed that he had never handled such a large vessel before), but ultimately that blame should lay with the Port of Milford Haven Authority. Lessons were learned, though: a national Port Marine Safety Code was enshrined, and at a local level, the Sea Trust was established, which continues its work today surveying and monitoring marine life. As for the *Sea Empress*, she was eventually repaired and rechristened MV *Sea Spirit*, going on to be renamed a further four times and spending the rest of her days in the Far East before finally being broken up in 2016.

retrieved in 2003, including one of the Bristol Pegasus engines and the front turret, as well as other sundry bits and pieces, some of which have been cleaned up. It now seems unlikely that any more is salvageable.

A little-known fact was that Pembroke played a key part in the Star Wars blockbuster, *The Empire Strikes Back*. It was here, working under a veil of secrecy in an old aircraft hangar, that engineers from the local docks constructed the iconic Millennium Falcon starship (mostly from wood and steel), before it was broken up and transferred to the film set in Hertfordshire. The story of how this all came about is now told in a new permanent exhibition, with initial displays entailing photographs, props, costumes and the like; future plans, funding permitting, are likely to include recreating some of the film sets.

MILFORD HAVEN

Long before it became Wales's most important fishing port, or even a town, Milford Haven had witnessed significant maritime activity, particularly as a base for a series of assaults on Ireland – Henry II in 1171, Richard II in 1387, and Oliver Cromwell in 1649 among them. But it wasn't until the arrival of Quaker whaling families from Nantucket in 1790 – invited here by Sir William Hamilton, whose wife Emma Hamilton later embarked upon a notorious affair with Admiral Nelson – that the town developed more or less as you see it today; among other things, they established Pembrokeshire's first bank. In the event, the whaling industry proved to be short-lived, largely on account of the emergent coal industry, but also because of the invention of the oil well.

Fast forward to 1888 and the arrival of *Sybil* – the very first vessel to enter Milford Docks – which ushered in a period of great prosperity for the town. Milford Haven emerged as one of the most prosperous fishing ports on these shores thanks to its proximity to good fishing grounds, a fine, natural sheltered harbour and excellent transport links. At the peak of the industry it rated some 130 vessels employing more than 4,000 people, with typically 40,000–50,000 tonnes of herring and mackerel caught per annum, which ranked it in the top five fishing ports in the UK.

Declining Atlantic fish stocks in the 1950s precipitated the demise of the industry, but the emerging petrochemical industry offered an alternative, and very lucrative, source of employment, and within a few years two massive refineries (the first being Esso in 1960) and an oil-storage plant secured Milford Haven's status as the most important oil port not just in Wales, but in Britain. By 1970 it had become one of the largest energy ports in Europe. In 2009, Milford Haven took its first delivery of liquid natural gas (LNG), on the site of the old Esso refinery, since renamed South Hook LNG Terminal, the largest LNG site in Europe; the only other two LNG terminals in the UK include another here in Milford Haven and one on the Isle of Grain in Kent. Arriving from the Arabian Gulf in tankers three-and-a-half times the length of a football field, the cargo is discharged into vast tanks, where it is stored at 160 degrees below freezing before being regasified and then pumped through huge pipelines to businesses and premises throughout the UK.

For visitors, the town's main draw is its waterfront marina, which emerged from the ashes of the old docks, whose demise was complete by the 1980s. In its place, over 300 berths were created and today are occupied by all kinds of leisure craft including some seriously swanky yachts.

GETTING THERE AND AWAY The two main roads leading into Milford Haven are the A4076 from Haverfordwest in the north, and the A477 from Pembroke Dock in the southeast, which crosses the River Cleddau. There's plenty of parking down by the waterfront as well as in the town centre (on Market Square and Robert Street).

The train station is below the Hakin road bridge, opposite Tesco and next to the docks; there are services to Haverfordwest and Carmarthen (8 daily Mon–Sat, 4 Sun), with most of these continuing to Swansea. Buses stop near Tesco as well as along Charles Street (going westbound) and Hamilton terrace (going eastbound), with destinations including Haverfordwest (every 30mins), Pembroke Dock and Pembroke (8 daily Mon–Sat), and Dale and Marloes (both 3 daily Mon–Fri, though two of these (09.25 & 13.25 from Tesco) are 'Dial-a-Ride' services for which you must call ☎01437 890230).

WHERE TO STAY

Floatel (4 cabins) Nelson Quay, Milford Waterfront; ☎ 01646 400810; w ty-hotels.com. Located at the far end of the pontoon, each of the 4 cabins here is named after something with a connection to the town – for example, Sybil, which was the 1st (fishing) ship to dock in Milford Haven in 1888. All 4 are more or less identically furnished, though Sybil is configured slightly differently in that the room itself is slightly smaller & the bathroom slightly larger in order to accommodate a wheelchair. Large, sliding windows give access to a decked terrace from where you can kick back with a beer or glass of wine & enjoy the comings & goings of the big posh boats. You may even wake up to the sight of a swan gliding past. Each cabin has a small fridge, & tea-making facilities; b/fast can be taken at Ty Milford for an extra cost. **££**

Ty Milford Waterfront (100 rooms) Nelson Quay, Milford Waterfront; ☎ 01646 400810; w ty-hotels.com. Another welcome addition to the waterfront (& the town's limited stock of accommodation), all but 16 rooms in this sparkling new hotel have views overlooking the marina (& those that don't are around £25 cheaper); room categories come as standard & deluxe, the latter slightly bigger & with balconies, though all have the same furnishings & AC. The in-house restaurant, Dulse (which is where b/fast is taken) has a fabulous waterside panorama & commendable food. A few useful little extras include an activi-ty suite (little play on words there), free car parking close by & charging points for electric cars. **££**

WHERE TO EAT AND DRINK

Madison's Unit 3, Nelson Quay; ☎ 01646 278274; w milfordwaterfront.co.uk; ⏰ 18.00–23.00 Wed–Fri, 11.30–midnight Sat, noon–16.30 Sun. Thoughtfully conceived 1930s-themed restaurant right above the water with film posters & photos splattered across the walls & music from that time playing – even the food is served on patterned china plates redolent of the era. The food is top drawer, & they also pay particular attention to the needs of vegetarians & vegans. **££**

Pembrokeshire Promise 95 Charles St; ☎ 01646 278519; ⏰ 09.00–17.00 Mon–Sat. Perky little coffee shop at the far end of Charles St. As well as top-drawer coffee & cakes, the chirpy girls here make freshly prepared bloomers, ciabattas & paninis packed with all kinds of yummy fillings in addition to some heartier plates. The entire space is decked out in wood using old pallets, including the floor, walls & bar, with tables culled from old beer barrels. **£**

WHAT TO SEE AND DO One of the most tangible legacies of the Quaker whalers is the distinctive grid pattern of streets they established high above what is today's marina. The first of these is **Hamilton Terrace**, graced by what were among the first buildings in Milford Haven, many now brightly painted including the Lord Nelson pub, so named after the admiral following his visit to the town in 1802. Running parallel to Hamilton Terrace, Charles Street essentially constitutes the town centre, though sadly this is as devoid of life as so many other high streets and therefore doesn't really merit a visit unless you fancy a coffee in the one excellent café here (see above) or require anything of a practical nature.

Any meaningful action in town is centred on the **marina**, whose trawlers have long since been replaced by fancy pleasure craft. The best way to get a handle on the marina is to walk the mile-long loop, which is also suitable for cyclists and wheelchair users – note, though, that for two 2-hour periods each day (before high tides), the locks are opened to allow vessels to come and go, periods known as 'free flow'; you can check the times online (w milfordmarina.com) or at the marina office on Nelson Quay. The red-brick buildings ranging along the south side of the marina – now packed cheek-by-jowl with cafés, restaurants and bars – were once the site of the old fish market, which would have run the entire length of the quay.

The town's maritime heritage is recalled in the wonderful **town museum** (Sybil Way; ☎ 01646 694496; w milfordhavenmuseum.co.uk; ⏰ Easter–mid-Oct 10.30–

16.00 Mon–Sat; £4), located behind the Ty Milford Waterfront hotel in the old Customs House. Reckoned to be the second-oldest building in Milford Haven (1797), this is where taxes would have been collected, for example, on barrels of whale oil. There are displays on all facets of life here, from the town's Quaker beginnings and the impact of the docks to the associated trades like net braiding, icing and the foundries. There's coverage, too, of World War II, when the town gave safe shelter to large convoys of ships; the war also saw many trawlers here commandeered as minesweepers.

Upstairs, attention turns to whaling, which was a hard and dangerous existence. Whalers would typically be out at sea for months, if not years, at a time, and even then there was no guarantee that they would return. On display here are some of the original harpoons, which were either wooden with an iron head, or all metal. Once killed, the animal would be hauled up and tied to the side of the ship before the skin and blubber was peeled off in long strips, from which the oil would be extracted – a grisly and very smelly business, but extremely lucrative. The oils were then sent to cities all over the UK, principally for use as street lighting, while the bones were used in a variety of products such as corsets.

The next-door display dwells on the town's energy industry and recent developments in the petrochemical industry, though oddly no reference is made to the *Sea Empress* oil spill in 1996 (page 293). Away from industry, there are displays covering the town's social history, with traditional costumes, old signs that once adorned telegraph poles, and cabinets containing various household items, among them some hand-embroidered tablecloths and wooden cotton reels – a real throwback those.

HAVERFORDWEST

A hilly town sliced in half by the River Cleddau and benignly overlooked by the shell of a 12th-century castle, Haverfordwest doesn't merit a special diversion, but if you are passing through – which is likely given its location on the A40, and as a key transport hub – then there are one or two points of interest.

GETTING THERE AND AWAY The train station, a 10-minute walk east of town, is served by trains from Carmarthen (8 daily), Milford Haven (8 daily) and Swansea (7 daily). For trains to Fishguard you have to change at Clarberston one stop away. The bus station, which is across the old bridge from the town centre, is served by hourly buses from Fishguard, Newport, Pembroke, St David's and every 30 minutes from Milford Haven and Tenby.

✘ WHERE TO EAT AND DRINK
✘ **Block and Barrel** 2 Castle Sq; ☎01437 768775; w blockandbarrel.co.uk ⏲ 10.30– 21.00 Mon–Sat, 11.00–20.00 Sun. Hidden away in one corner of the small main square, this intimate little space with just 4 or 5 tables is a welcome addition to Haverfordwest's limited dining scene. Monster steaks, gut-busting gourmet burgers & fiery chicken wings is what they do here, & they do it very well. Washed down with a local craft beer, you've got yourself a very satisfying meal. Best place in town for coffee too. ££

✘ **The George's** 24 Market St; ☎01437 766683; w thegeorges.uk.com; ⏲ 10.30–18.00 Thu–Sat. A handsome Georgian building in the older quarter, The George's has been a popular stop among local foodies since 1989 & remains a stalwart. Dishes – with many ingredients grown in their own kitchen garden – range from snacks like French-style filled butter crepes to mains such as beef casserole with cheesy mash or a Greek-style macaroni cheese; to their credit they've also got separate dairy-free, gluten-free & vegan menus.

Ethical, traders, they also sell natural remedies, toiletries & other gifts. Just a shame they keep such short hours. ££

WHAT TO SEE AND DO From **Castle Square**, the hub of town, pedestrianised Castle Street winds up towards the river and the old stone **bridge,** erected in 1726 by John Philipps of Picton Castle (see below). A monument in the centre of one side of the bridge acknowledges its founder's contribution, while also noting that King George IV passed over the bridge en route back from Ireland in 1821, having landed at nearby Milford Haven. The bridge was substantially widened in 1848. It's a pity more hasn't been made of the riverside, which is flanked by an ugly shopping precinct on one side and dull buildings on the other.

The High Street is infinitely more agreeable. From the criminally redundant Shire Hall at the bottom – built by William Owen in 1835 – variously coloured buildings climb steadily up the street to **St Mary's Church** on the corner of Market Street and opposite the preserved remains of a Georgian townhouse vault; the church itself is worth a peek for its Gothic-styled north arcade inlaid with some beautifully carved capitals. Halfway up the High Street, a passageway by the Castle Photography shop cuts through to the ivy-strewn **castle** (see below), whose towers loom large over the car park, but otherwise there is little that survives of the original medieval fortress. Fought over during the Civil Wars, but never completely destroyed, the castle then served as a mental hospital and a prison, before the Pembrokeshire police force took up residence, remaining here until 1968, since which time it has been left scandalously unheeded.

The former prison governor's house in front of the castle is home to the **town museum** (✆01437 763087; w haverfordwest-town-museum.org.uk; ⏰ 10.00–16.00 Mon–Sat; free), which has all kinds of curiosities, including what is claimed to be Wales's oldest letter box, an elegant seaweed-green-painted specimen dating from around 1850; one of the original cell doors alongside some menacing-looking equipment; and, at the top of the stairs, a couple of sketches by hometown boy Augustus John, though that still feels like a meagre return from one of Wales's most celebrated artists. Moreover, there's nothing on display by his equally talented sister, Gwen.

Picton Castle (✆01437 751326; w pictoncastle.co.uk; ⏰ Apr–Oct 10.00–17.00 daily, Nov–Mar 10.00–16.00 daily; £12) Retaining an air of baronial magnificence, Picton Castle was originally raised in 1280 by the one-time Justiciary of Ireland, John Wogan (though he never actually lived here), before it was acquired by the Philipps family in the 1490s, under whose ownership it remained for the next 500 years before it was handed over to the Picton Castle Trust in 1987. For several centuries, the Philipps were by some distance the most influential family in Pembrokeshire, among them Sir Richard Philipps, who became Lord Milford in 1776.

Visits to the castle are by guided tour only, which can't be pre-booked so you'll be given an allotted time when you purchase your ticket. The two most impressive rooms are the **circular library**, which conceals numerous clever contraptions including hidden bookcases and curtains that open outwards, and the Georgian-style **Great Hall**, at one end of which is a Minstrel's Gallery complete with organ. The room holds several portraits of Philipps family members painted by Graham Sutherland, who became a close acquaintance of the family in the 1940s. Here, too, is a fine stone and marble carved fireplace by Henry Cheer, one of several within the

9

castle, although the most infamous item here is a painting entitled *Boats on the Seine at Argenteuil*, which may or may not have been painted by Pierre August Renoir. Although it bears all the hallmarks of the celebrated Impressionist – including the pigments and canvas he would have used – the piece isn't signed. Alongside this small matter, the Wildenstein Institute, one of the world's leading art authorities, deemed the painting to be of a standard not befitting Renoir's work, and have so far refused to endorse it as genuine, despite the fact that another leading authority – the Bernheim-Jeune Gallery – have. The story of the painting was documented on the BBC programme *Fact or Fiction* in 2015, which can be viewed on YouTube and is well worth a watch. Upstairs, you'll get to see the octagon-shaped **bedroom**, complete with a lavish en suite, and next door, through a low, stone-vaulted arch, the private family **chapel** dating from 1754 with stained glass from 1894. Completed around 1790, the castle extension is a quite different structural beast, its ceilings much higher and its walls much thinner. In the dining room is another exquisite Cheer-designed fireplace alongside lead-lined mahogany urns, Meissen figurines and further portraits.

Every bit as satisfying as the castle are the **gardens**, all 40 acres of them. The estate is particularly renowned for its exceptional collection of azaleas and rhododendrons, whose glorious blooms peak in May. The Grade II-listed walled garden, meanwhile, has been spectacularly restored to its former glory following an expensive restoration project.

The third part of what makes Picton such a hugely enjoyable day out is the **Welsh Owl Garden and Zoo** (admission included in the castle and gardens ticket), which is home to some two-dozen species of owls and exotic birds. Depending upon the season, there are usually between one and three flying displays each day, as well as encounters with other animals including reptiles and otters.

During World War II the castle was requisitioned as a hospital, and there's a sobering reminder of this courtesy of the small **mortuary** – complete with cold stone slab – in one corner of the cobbled courtyard. Next to here is a fine assemblage of antique and vintage lawnmowers, collected by the Lumsden family, one of whose number, Nick Lumsden, married into the Philipps family – hence their presence here. All completely restored, there are some beautifully engineered models from all the established names: Shanks, Jefferies, Ransomes (including a superb New Automaton from 1890) and Greens. The most iconic piece of machinery here is a 1923-built Greens carrying a four-cylinder Dorman engine, the only working model of an early playing field petrol mower in existence today. Elsewhere in the courtyard is an art gallery and Maria's restaurant – a fully licensed bistro-style affair – shop and deli.

ST BRIDE'S BAY

A huge arc at the most westerly point of Wales, St Bride's Bay is for many the most memorable section of the Pembrokeshire coastline. Peppered with fantastic beaches, sunny coves and comely little resorts, you could spend weeks here and still only scratch the surface. At its southern extremity, the Dale Peninsula rates three wonderful beaches: the east-facing sands of **Dale** itself, the larger, south-facing beach at **Marloes**, and wilder west-facing **Musselwick**.

The Marloes Peninsula is the launchpad for trips out to **Skomer**, **Skokholm** and **Grassholm**, which, collectively, provide some of the most intense seabird-viewing experiences anywhere in northern Europe. The long and straight west-facing back of St Bride's Bay is pockmarked with a handful of resorts in between, eg: **Little**

Haven in the south and **Newgale** in the north, each with their own signature beach, but if it's surf you're after then Newgale is the one.

ST ANN'S HEAD AND THE DALE PENINSULA One of the most exhilaratingly desolate places in Pembrokeshire, **St Ann's Head** offers almost off-the-scale remoteness. A bold promontory (around 120ft high) located at the western point of the entrance to Milford Haven, the wind blows hard up here, so if you're walking this section of the Wales Coast Path, be prepared for a good buffeting. In 1485, Henry VII (then Duke of Richmond) ended his exile in France and landed at Mill Bay in the eastern lee of St Ann's Head, with 55 ships and 4,000 men, his sights firmly set on the British crown. He duly slew Richard III at Bosworth Field to become king. But St Ann's Head is probably better known for an incident that took place here in February 1996, when the tanker *Sea Empress* hit rocks, leaking more than 72,000 tonnes of crude oil into the surrounding waters, resulting in one of Britain's largest ever oil spills (page 293). The clean-up operation was phenomenal and you certainly wouldn't notice anything untoward today.

A mile or so north of St Ann's Head, the tiny village of **Dale** fronts a wide bay skirting the entrance to Milford Haven. What few houses there are here, which includes the village pub, are huddled together at the southern end of the beach. Out of season, it's one of the most restful spots along the coast but in summer, kayakers, windsurfers and yachties descend upon the place in big numbers. Down by the beach, **Celtic Sea Watersports** (℡ 01646 636642; w celticseawatersports. co.uk; ⏰ 09.00–17.00 daily) offer all kinds of rental including single and double sit-on kayaks, canoes and dinghies. They also do a range of sailing and powerboat courses as well as snorkelling tuition. Birdwatchers in the know, meanwhile, head out to the **Gann Estuary** just north of Dale, which is rich in waders: oystercatchers, curlew, redshank and grey plover among the most common avian foragers here.

✗ Where to eat and drink

🍴 **Griffin Inn** Dale; ℡ 01646 636227; w griffindale.co.uk; ⏰ Tue–Sun. After an afternoon's exertion on the water, head to Dale's sole pub, which we should be thankful still exists at all – records suggest that there were 15 here at one time. As appealing as the interior is – red quarry tiles, painted stone walls & wood panelling – eat outside if you can, & preferably up on the top terrace. Food, unsurprisingly, is of the fishy variety, fresh off the boat each day, with steamed cod loin, hake, dover sole, lobster & shellfish among the daily staples, but if you're not a fan of the wet stuff, there are alternatives like beef & stout pie. ££

MARLOES PENINSULA On the opposite side of the peninsula to Dale, the whacking mile-long **Marloes Sands** is frequently cited as one of the county's top beaches, and with its soft sand and shallow waters it's easy to see why. Yet it never comes close to feeling overcrowded, partly because it's a bit of a hike to get here (and there are no facilities), but also because it is so vast that it's not difficult to find your own space should the crowds start to build – the breakers here are great for bodyboards too. Geologically, too, this is one of the more interesting sections of the coastline, its cliffs layered with alternate bands of grey shale and red sandstone. Jutting into the sea at the beach's northern end is **Gateholm Island**, where dozens of Iron-Age hut circles have been found, together with pottery fragments: it is accessible at low to mid-tide so be mindful of the water levels here. The mile-long stretch of coast path from Gateholm up to the western tip of Marloes Peninsula is sublime, with opportunities to access a series of tiny coves en route.

At the very edge of the peninsula – though strangely the coast path doesn't follow the curve of the headland here – is **Deer Park**, a bit of a misnomer as there are no deer here and probably never were, and nor is it really a park. You are, though, likely to see seals in the two coves, while nearby **Wooltack Point** is a good spot for seeing porpoises. Lord Kensington is remembered in **Marloes village**, a mile or two back inland, by a sturdy roadside clocktower hewn from the locally quarried red stone in 1904 – his wife chose this as his memorial, owing to his 'remarkable punctuality', apparently. Often the odd one out here as people make a dash for the coast is **Marloes Mere**, a little area of wetland with some good birdlife, in particular lots of migrant wildfowl.

Just north of Marloes, and completing this triumvirate of beaches, is west-facing **Musselwick Sands** (pronounced locally as 'muss-lick'), another unspoilt gem hemmed in by high, black slate cliffs, though again it is prone to getting cut off at high tide – in fact Musselwick is only accessible for 4 hours each day, 2 hours either side of low tide.

Getting there and away The National Trust car park (£3/2hrs, £6/day) is half a mile or so beyond Marloes village. From the car park, paths lead south to Marloes Sands beach and north to Musselwick Sands, neither any more than a 15-minute walk. Beyond the car park, the road continues to Martin's Haven, where there's another car park (£6/day) above Lockley Lodge Visitor Centre, which is the departure point for boats to the islands. There are 3 buses (Mon–Fri) from Haverfordwest, via Milford Haven, to Dale, two of which are 'Dial-a-Ride' services.

Between the end of May and the beginning of October, the Puffin Shuttle bus operates 3 times daily (Mon–Sat) between St David's and Marloes village, stopping at all resorts in between (Solva, Newgale, Broad Haven, Little Haven). During the rest of the year these buses only run on Wednesdays.

 ## Where to stay, eat and drink

Ⅹ West Hook Farm [map, page 274] West Hook Farm; 01646 636424; w westhookfarm-camping.co.uk. High on the cliffs, with the golden Marloes Sands & Musselwick beaches both less than a mile away, this reassuringly simple site is all about location. Facilities are basic (coin-op showers, no hook-ups) but there is a barn for when it rains! They've also got a static caravan for hire. **£**

Runwayskiln Marloes Sands; 01646 636545; w runwayskiln.co.uk; ⏲ 09.00–18.00 Thu–Mon, 10.00–16.00 Tue & Wed. You'd do well to follow the sign from the National Trust car park, which points the way to this erstwhile youth hostel that has been converted into a daytime café. Fresh fish, veggie & vegan is what this place does best: the fish taco is sublime, as is the miso & sesame roast cauliflower, plus there's lots of coffee & cake. Just 7 tables so worth booking ahead to avoid disappointment, though the take-away kiosk pops up in Jun for the summer. **££**

SKOMER Home to one of northern Europe's great bird colonies, and Wales's largest population of ledge-nesting birds, Skomer, around a mile offshore, is a place apart. The numbers speak for themselves: 39,000 puffins, 120,000 pairs of Manx shearwater, 27,000 guillemots, 8,000 razorbills, 575 pairs of fulmars, and 1,400 pairs of kittiwakes, one of the few birds in the British Isles in decline. There are also currently three pairs of peregrines and roughly the same number of short-eared owls (thought to be around a quarter of the total Welsh population), which usually occupy the territory near the farmhouse and tend to feed by day. The endangered hen harrier might also put in an appearance. Most birds keep roughly the same season here on Skomer, typically arriving in March and staying through to mid–late July, though Manx shearwater stick around a bit longer, usually until early September.

The undoubted star of the show is (indeed) the puffin, 'that extraordinary clown-like bird with the aldermanic air', as described by Welsh naturalist Ronald Lockley. These charismatic birds, with their hinged, red-orange beaks and colourful eye ornamentation, begin their invasion of the island in late March or early April, typically congregating around the South Plateau and The Wick (where there is a rope cordon), as well as North Haven where the boat lands. They are remarkably unfazed by us and typically go about their business, whether that's excavating a burrow or having a bit of rough and tumble with a mate, completely oblivious.

By way of contrast, Manx shearwater – nifty flyers and useful underwater but hopeless on dry land – steer clear of the island during the day, returning only under the cover of darkness when there is less threat of predation, in theory at least. But there are so many of them that they still make for relatively easy pickings, particularly for the great black-backed gull, a bird of tremendous power and appetite it would appear, judging by the number of picked-over corpses around the island. These gulls aren't averse to a nice plump rabbit either, lots of which you'll see tearing about. If you're intent on targeting specific birds, places to concentrate on might be Bull Hole which is great for fulmars, and Pigstone Bay, a little further on, for choughs. Razorbills gather in big numbers at North Haven too.

Cetaceans (dolphins and porpoises) tend to frequent the waters off the north and west coasts, as do Atlantic grey seals, who also inhabit the sea caves around The Neck; their numbers are greatly increased during pupping season in September. Wildflowers, too, especially bluebells and red and sea campion, make a fleeting appearance between late April and June. Endemic to the island is the Skomer vole, though it has to be wary with its main predator, the owl, constantly on the hunt.

For all the astonishing wildlife here on Skomer, it's never been an island devoid of human existence. There's evidence of very early human settlement in the form of the 5,000-year-old Harold Standing stone, not far from the landing stage. Elsewhere there are Iron-Age hut circles – which points to there being a small farming community here around that time – while the most obvious recent evidence is the Old Farm near the centre of the island. This is where the only loos are, as well as a visitor centre, and is where you lodge if overnighting.

Getting there and away
Excluding the 15-minute ferry ride across to the island, you get just over 4½ hours to explore Skomer, which is ample time to complete a full circuit (3 miles) including regular stop-offs to take it all in and have some lunch. Upon disembarking, one of the wardens will offer a brief introduction, including what you are likely to see and where. There are very few designated paths on the island, which you must keep to. This does mean that you can't avoid other people, unfortunately, whichever way you go round. Binoculars are available for hire (£5) by the landing stage, and accommodation is available on the island with the Wildlife Trust of South Wales (page 303). There is, of course, no shop on Skomer so bring your own grub.

The following operators run tours to Skomer, although only the first of these is authorised to land:

Pembrokeshire Islands Boat Trip/Dale Sailing Martin's Haven; \01646 603123; w pembrokeshire-islands.co.uk. ⏰ Apr–Sep; sailings at 10.00, 10.30, 11.00, 11.30 & noon Tue– Sun; £40 (cruises £20; sea safaris £30; Grassholm gannetry experience £50). The venerable *Dale Princess* has been ferrying excited passengers across to Skomer for years. Departures are from the jetty on the beach at Martin's Haven, but you need to check in at the Lockley Lodge Visitor Centre 1hr before sailing. It's worth buying the excellent little booklet (£3) at reception, as it outlines the island's walking routes as well as all the wildlife you can see; otherwise, they have the obligatory souvenirs (mostly puffins) & a machine dispensing hot drinks. Parking is available at the National Trust car park at Martin's Haven (£6/day) just above the lodge. If you don't have 5hrs to spare, they also have a few trips of 60 or 90mins' duration including a Skomer cruise, a sea safari & an evening shearwater safari. Between Apr & Jul they also run a 90min Grassholm gannetry experience (£50).

Thousand Islands Expeditions Cross Sq, St David's; 01437 721721; w thousandislands. co.uk. Operate a daily 2hr trip to Skomer (£54; no landing) to see the puffins between Apr & late Jul, departing from St Justinian's.

Voyages of Discovery 1 High St, St David's; 01437 721911; w ramseyisland.co.uk. Offer a daily 2hr trip to Skomer (£54; no landing) to see the puffins between May & late Jul, departing from St Justinian's.

SKOKHOLM AND GRASSHOLM Two miles offshore, **Skokholm** was home to Britain's first bird observatory, established here in 1933, and while it doesn't attract nearly the same volume of birds to its clifftops as Skomer, the numbers of puffins, razorbills and guillemots – and by night Manx shearwater and storm petrels are still fantastic. Skokholm is one of the few places in Britain where you can see storm petrels, though like the Manx shearwater, this tough little seabird (smaller than a house sparrow) is vulnerable to predation and so spends the majority of its time offshore.

Managed by the Welsh Wildlife Trust, the island measures a mile long and around half that in width, allowing for easy exploration in a relatively short time. It was here on Skokholm that the concept of small-island wardening began, when the naturalist and writer Ronald Lockley took out a lease on the island in 1927, before setting up the aforementioned observatory. Lockley wrote prolifically on all aspects of island life, and by the time of his death at the age of 97 in 2000, he had written some 50 books: quite the life. Lockley left the island in 1940 when it was taken over by the military during World War II, but he was soon to embark on an even bigger project, namely the Pembrokeshire Coast Path (page 317).

Long before Lockley pitched up, 10th-century Vikings used the island as a springboard for raids on the Pembrokeshire coastline. Records recall that the island was heavily wooded during those days, though it's not quite as green now (albeit more verdant than Skomer) and is mostly red sandstone. Skokholm is also the only one of the three islands with a lighthouse, located on the southwestern tip looking out over Wildgoose Bay. Raised in 1916, it has been automated since 1983.

Eleven miles from the coast, which makes it the most distant of the three islands, **Grassholm** is also the only one of the three that has a strict 'no-landing' policy. A small, lumpy mass that appears to be covered in what looks like a light dusting of snow, Grassholm sees around 40,000 pairs of breeding gannets return here each spring, the only gannet colony in Wales and the third largest in the British Isles – the only two with greater numbers are Bass Rock and St Kilda, on the east and west coasts of Scotland respectively.

Currently amber-listed, which seems surprising given the vast numbers here, gannets, white with pollen-yellow heads and black-tipped wings, are known for their lightning-fast fishing techniques, which sees them attack the water at speeds of up to 60mph – wings folded back and with air sacs in their face and chest that inflate to cushion the impact – before emerging with a gobful of mackerel. The island is by no means an exclusive one-bird club, though, with guillemots and others here too, while Atlantic grey seals bask on the rocky shores. Pembrokeshire Islands Boat Trip/Dale Sailing (page 301) operate cruises and sea safaris around both islands, sometimes in tandem with Skomer.

Where to stay

Wildlife Trust of South and West
Wales ☏ 01656 724100; w welshwildlife.org.
Between Apr & Sep you can stay on both Skomer
& Skokholm in self-catering farmhouse-style
accommodation. As you'd expect it's fairly basic
but all the requisite amenities are there, including
well-equipped kitchens, electricity & compost
loos. Best of all, this is your only opportunity to
experience the island minus the crowds, as well
as see & hear the extraordinary Manx shearwater.
For Skomer, changeover days are Sat, Tue & Thu,
dictating stays of either 2 or 3 nights (Apr £60,
May–Jul £85, Aug & Sep £50; children 12 & under
half price). For Skokholm, you can stay for either
3 nights (from Fri) or 4 nights (from Mon) for
£150 (£110 in Aug & Sep); 7-night stays are also
possible (£270 & £170). The return boat fare is
£27.50. Whichever island you might be staying
on, be prepared for a last-minute change of plan
if the weather's not playing ball. Conversely,
you may well end up being stranded on either
island! **££–£££**

FROM LITTLE HAVEN TO NEWGALE The first resort on St Bride's Bay is **Little Haven**, contender for the county's prettiest seaside village. From the snuggle of stone houses in the centre of the village, steps lead down to a stony, well-sheltered beach popular with divers and rockpoolers, though it is considered a safe swimming spot for children. Not that you'd have any idea today, but Little Haven used to be a busy little coal port, lying at the westernmost edge of the Pembrokeshire coalfield, itself an extension of the South Wales coalfield.

At low tide, it's possible to walk to the next resort along, dipping in and out of the coves as you go, though **Broad Haven** does feel a bit like stepping into a cold shower after the sedate charms of its near neighbour. It's certainly brasher (but this is Pembrokeshire so it's all relative) and if you've an aversion to noise, or just people generally, then head somewhere else (or stay in Little Haven). The fine, golden-sand beach is much bigger here than at Little Haven, but by the same token it does get busier. Three miles on is **Druidston Haven**, where another gorgeous, secluded beach awaits. The hub of activity is its hotel (see below) which, at the end of June hosts the Druidstone Jazz Festival.

The last of the 'Havens' is **Nolton Haven**, though there's very little to it beyond a few houses and a shingled cove. The last resort before the left turn towards St David's Peninsula is **Newgale**, whose village is dull, but whose beach – **Newgale Sands** – is, in terms of its scale, immense and the one to head for along here if you're after some surf. Newgale also marks the westernmost extent of the Landsker Line (page 278).

The 4-mile walk from Newgale to Solva is one of the best short stretches of the entire coastal path. En route you'll pass **Porthmynawyd**, a secluded little bay with one of those 'secret' beaches that, well, isn't quite so secret anymore. Protected from the currents that run between the mainland and Ramsey Island, it's ideal for swimming, and there's plenty of sand to muck around in.

 ## Where to stay, eat and drink

Druidstone Hotel (10 rooms) Druidston;
☏ 01437 781221; w druidstone.co.uk. Unlike
anything else along this stretch of coastline, the
clifftop Druidstone has 10 rooms, half of which are
en suite, the other half with shared bathrooms. The
sea-facing rooms (including the 2 in the loft) have
peerless views (the others have garden views),
though all are simply furnished. 5 self-catering
cottages are also available, one of which is the
'cwtchy' solar-&-wind-powered Roundhouse.
Better still are the restaurant & bar that see the
occasional concert; the hotel also hosts the village's
annual folk festival. **££**

Swan Inn Point Rd, Little Haven; ☏ 01437
781880; ⊕ noon–midnight daily. One of the
bay's more worthwhile pubs, the Swan has been
going strong for more than 200 years. On warmer
days, most folk just kick back with a beer outside
or congregate on the wall & watch surfers &
rockpoolers do their thing. **£**

St David's Peninsula is Wales at its windiest, wildest best – a corrugated coastline gashed with coves and beaches. While St David's may be the cultural showstopper, there are rewards of a different hue to be had elsewhere. The peninsula's greatest offshore treasure is Ramsey Island, one of Britain's great seal-watching destinations and a gathering site for thousands of visiting birds each spring and summer. A trip to the island, be it a landing or a wildlife cruise, is not to be missed. There is of course wonderful walking to be had here: for many, the peninsula is one of the standout sections of the coast path, but there are plenty of shorter hikes (albeit likely to incorporate elements of the coast path), for example a circular walk to Carn Lidl via Whitesands Bay and St David's Head, or, in the opposite direction, a circular from St David's via St Non's Chapel and Porthclais. If that's too sedate, there are more invigorating ways to spend your time here, such as coasteering – an activity that originated right here.

Despite its relative isolation, and the time it can take to get here, St David's Peninsula still absorbs a hefty proportion of Pembrokeshire's visitors, but there's enough space here not to have to concern yourself with others. Although you can pretty much cover everything over a long weekend or a leisurely few days, this is a landscape that rewards slow travel, so stay longer if you can. Better still, come out of season when the crowds have thinned, even if the weather is likely to be more inclement.

SOLVA Sitting at the end of a long, deep ria (drowned glacial valley) framed by totem-like cliffs, this is actually a village of two parts – Upper and Lower Solva – though everything of interest is in Lower Solva and its long main street, liberally sprinkled with shops, galleries, restaurants and pubs. The chief pleasure here, though, is strolling around its salty stone harbour, filled with boats imperceptibly bobbing up and down on the water or resting on the tidal mud.

Getting there and away As it's on the main road to St David's, Solva becomes a bit of bottleneck during high season. The main car park is down by the harbour, though does gets filled up very quickly. Alternatively you can drive to Upper Solva where there are a couple of smaller car parks (big lay-bys really), from where it's a 5-minute walk back down into the village. Regular buses from St David's stop at various points along Main Street in Lower Solva.

Where to stay, eat and drink

The Cambrian Inn (5 rooms) 6 Main St; \01437 721210; w thecambrianinn.co.uk; ⏱ 11.00–23.00 daily. At the far end of the main street, this popular watering hole has immaculately prepared rooms (including a trpl), each named after a Pembrokeshire island. The food is also very definitely up to scratch, with above-average pub grub (duck bon-bons, baked mussels with anchovies). A very convivial stop off all round. **££**

35 Main St 35 Main St; \01437 729236; w 35mainstreet.co.uk; ⏱ 10.00–11.30 & noon–15.00 daily, also 17.00–21.00 Fri & Sat. The very

last in the row of buildings facing the harbour, this is Solva's one outstanding restaurant. Although the menu is full of mostly fishy things, there are some great options for vegetarians & vegans, such as spiced cauliflower pakoras & a selection of Lebanese wraps. If it's warm, scoop up a crab sandwich or a plate of calamari & chips & head out to one of the picnic tables overlooking the harbour walls. **££**

MamGu Welshcakes 20 Main St; \01437 454369; w mamguwelshcakes.com; ⏱ 09.00–17.00 Mon–Fri & Sun, 09.30–16.30 Sat. While the baked-on-the-premises Welsh cakes are obviously a very good reason to come here (gluten-free & vegan ones too), the freshly ground coffee is the perfect complement (take-outs too). Loads more besides, including a nice line in teas, hot chocolate & ice cream, plus more filling loveliness like crempogs (Welsh pancakes), cawl & rarebit. £

What to see and do The perfect complement to time spent down in the harbour or browsing the shops and galleries is a walk up to the **Gribin**, the eastern headland guarding the entrance to the harbour, which you'll walk along anyway if you're on the coast path. As well as the remains of an Iron-Age earthwork, you'll be rewarded with spanking views of St Bride's Bay.

Prior to World War I, the River Solva (Solfach) was powering up to seven mills along its valley floor, one of which, the **Solva Woollen Mill** (℡ 01437 721112; w solvawoollenmill.co.uk; ⊕ 10.00–17.30 Mon–Fri; free), located one mile inland from the village, is still going strong after more than a century in action – in fact it's one of just two working mills left in Pembrokeshire. Specialising in flat woven flooring (the only mill in Wales to do so) and floor rugs, Solva uses 100% British wool – mainly Herdwick and Welsh Mountain sheep – which is spun and dried in Yorkshire. After being woven on the loom – time your visit right and you can watch Tom, the owner, working his magic on the clattering Dobcross loom in the weaving shed – the runners and rugs are then cut and hand-fringed. The shop sells products made both here and elsewhere in the UK, but be prepared to spend a pretty penny whatever it is you are in pursuit of. If coming by bus, alight by the Cambrian Pub in Lower Solva, from where it's a 15-minute walk north along Prendergast Lane.

ST DAVID'S In 1995, the Queen conferred city status on St David's – the country's spiritual and ecclesiastical centre – thereby relegating Wells to second position in the list of the UK's smallest cities, by rank of population at least. In all but status, St David's is a large village, and were it not for the crowds (which makes coming out of season a very appealing proposition), there would be no reason for thinking otherwise. It was St David himself who effectively founded the city around AD550 when he established a monastery on, or near, the site of today's cathedral, and it quickly emerged as an important place of pilgrimage, counting William the Conqueror, Henry II and Edward I among its illustrious visitors. This didn't stop the Vikings from laying waste to the city, on more than one occasion, before it settled into a life of relative solitude, commensurate with its mellow, village-like surrounds.

In terms of sights, St David's Cathedral and the Bishop's Palace complete one of the most exceptional ecclesiastical enclaves in the British Isles, but once you've exhausted those two, there's little else to see here and you can turn your attention to exploring the rest of the peninsula.

Getting there and away If you've come by car, it'll be some relief to finally get here, such is the long and winding A487 road. Forget about parking anywhere near the High Street and instead aim for one of the two car parks located at the top (by the roundabout near the Oriel y Parc Gallery) and bottom (near the cathedral) of town respectively. Buses head to Fishguard (7 Mon–Sat) and Haverfordwest (hourly), departing from next to the City Hall on New Street.

Tourist information Situated inside the Oreil y Parc Gallery, the visitor centre (℡ 01437 720392; w pembrokeshirecoast.wales; ⊕ 09.30–17.00 daily) has a voluminous amount of material on both the city and the wider area, including maps if you're planning on doing any walking.

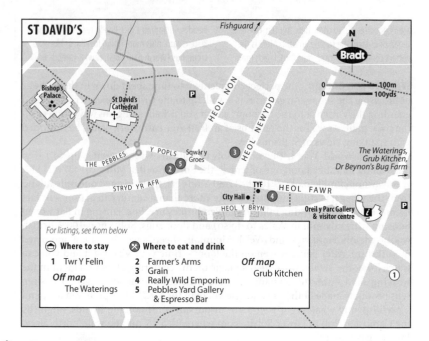

For listings, see from below

Where to stay

1   Twr Y Felin

Off map
    The Waterings

Where to eat and drink

2   Farmer's Arms
3   Grain
4   Really Wild Emporium
5   Pebbles Yard Gallery
    & Espresso Bar

Off map
    Grub Kitchen

Where to stay *Map, above*

✳ 🏠 **Twr Y Felin** (41 rooms) 📞 01437 725555; **w** twryfelinhotel.com. Less than half a mile southeast of the Oriel y Parc Gallery, this contemporary art hotel's name means 'mill tower', & it's had quite the history: part of the property was a windmill for the best part of century, the top floor was used as a GCHQ U-boat lookout during World War II, & thereafter the building operated as a temperance hotel. Throughout, more than 100 specially commissioned pieces, many reflecting the Pembrokeshire coast & countryside, decorate both the rooms & public areas, including the vaulted main lounge & restaurant; local heroes – Burton, Hopkins & Zeta-Jones – also feature. The gorgeously designed rooms typically sport polished boarded floors, grey fabric walls &

suede armchairs, as well as bespoke artwork, & depending upon which wing you are in (& what floor you are on), come with a private terrace or a balcony, though all have fabulous views. The hotel's eco credentials more than stand up to scrutiny too, with LED bulbs & water-saving taps throughout, plus solar panels & electric car charging points. **£££**

🏠 **The Waterings** (7 rooms) Anchor Dr; 📞 01437 720876; **w** waterings.co.uk. A short walk east of the Oriel y Parc Gallery, this restful guesthouse has a selection of nautically themed rooms (5 on the ground floor & 2 in the loft) in a nod to the building's former incarnation as a marine life centre; 4 of these have their own private sitting area. **££**

Where to eat and drink *Map, above*

✗ **Grub Kitchen** At Dr Beynon's Bug Farm (page 310); **m** 07966 956357; **w** thebugfarm.co.uk; 🕐 Apr–Oct 10.30–16.30 Thu–Sun (also Tue & Wed during school hols), Nov–Feb Sat & Sun. It's not quite *I'm a Celebrity*, but how does the thought of munching mealworms appeal? Here at the UK's only restaurant devoted wholly to entomography, you can sample the edible delights of insects: many of the meals, like burgers & lasagne, are

made using VEXo (plant & insect mince), but there are other interesting morsels like mixed insect pakoras & chillied crickets. Who knows, this concept may have legs. **££**

✳ ✗ **Really Wild Emporium** 24 High St; 📞 01437 721755; **w** reallywildemporium.co.uk. This sensitively restored 1924 Art Deco building (the original tiled frontage & stained glass remain) is now the coolest café/restaurant in town. Not only does it look brilliant – a corrugated-iron counter & salvaged pews among the quirks – but as much as possible on the menu is foraged, or at least sourced locally, so you'd be looking at dishes like sugar kelp & parsnip soup, seaweed cauliflower pakoras, & local wild plaice escabeche with pickled garlic stems & smoked paprika mayonnaise. There's a dedicated vegan menu too. This place will charm the socks off you. ££

🍴 **Farmer's Arms** 14–16 Goat St; 📞 01437 721666; w farmersstdavids.co.uk; ⏱ 11.30–23.00/midnight Mon–Thu & Sun, 11.30–midnight Fri & Sat. St David's has surprisingly few pubs, though that may be a hangover (excuse the pun) from the community's fervently religious past. Still, this is a cracking boozer, with good beer & food, a lively crowd, & a monthly quiz on the last Thu & live music most weekends. ££

🍴 **Grain** 1 High St; 📞 01437 454321; w grain. wales; ⏱ noon–22.00 daily. There's a very Welsh orientation to Grain's superb pizzas, for example 'Land of my Fathers' with roast leek, or 'Ndu-Ja Like it Spicy' with Pant y Sgawn goats' cheese & chilli flakes. With a cheeky craft beer from the Bluestone Brewery on the go, you're all set. They've only got 4 tables inside (which you can book ahead), but otherwise there are plenty more on the covered, & heated, outdoor terrace. Take-aways too. £

🍴 **Pebbles Yard Gallery & Espresso Bar** The Pebbles; 📞 01437 720122; ⏱ 10.00–17.00 daily. Given that this is prime tourist territory, it's more than a little surprising that St David's should be so bereft of anywhere to get a decent cup of coffee, so we should be thankful for this super little gallery-cum-bar just off Cross Sq (it's the 1st building on the left heading down towards the cathedral). Strong, well-prepared cups of caffeine & scrummy cakes best enjoyed outside in the tiny courtyard. £

Shopping

Really Wild Emporium 24 High St; 📞 01437 721755; w reallywildemporium.co.uk; ⏱ 10.00–15.00 Wed–Sun. On the 1st floor above the café (the entrance is to the side), this great shop has been designed with fixtures & fittings culled from bits of wood from the previous building. In keeping with John & Julia's ethos, every product here, from jam to gin, has been made as sustainability as possible, manufactured from one or more wild ingredient (often seaweed) & packaged in an eco-friendly fashion; there's also a vegan section. All the soaps & cosmetics are made on site by Julia. You can even buy your own foraging basket for those trips out to the coast. They also lead foraging trips to different destinations, for example Whitesands Bay or the Cleddau Estuary to root around for types of seaweed (it's much more exciting than it sounds), or hedgerow foraging for a variety of plants.

Activities

Falcon Boats 10 New St; 📱 07494 141764; e info@falconboats.co.uk; w falconboats.co.uk
TYF 20 High St; 📞 01437 721611; w tyf.com. Outdoor pursuits specialists who pioneered the sport of coasteering back in the 1980s, years before it became fashionable; other carbon-neutral coastal activities offered include kayaking, surfing, stand-up paddleboarding & rockpool safaris.

What to see and do St David's is not a big place and you could easily walk from one end of the city to the other in 10 minutes, and in all fairness there's nothing of tangible interest to see en route. All the main streets converge at **Cross Square**, which is not a square at all but a triangle. From here, The Pebbles slopes downhill to the cathedral and the Bishop's Palace, while Goat Street wends its way down and out of the city towards St Non's Chapel. Heading in the other direction, the **High Street** is a persistent thrum of activity, with cafés, ice-cream parlours, outdoor clothing stores and craft shops all doing brisk trade.

At the top of the High Street, on your right, is the **Oriel y Parc Gallery and Visitor Centre** (📞 01437 720392; w pembrokeshirecoast.wales/oriel-y-parc; ⏱ shop & visitor centre 09.30–17.00 daily, gallery 10.00–16.00 daily; free), a functional but well-designed building that's home to a long-standing collaboration between the Pembrokeshire Coast National Park and the National Museum Cardiff. It's a fabulous space for the rotating exhibitions, with themes usually pertaining to the ecology of the Pembrokeshire coast.

St David's Cathedral (✆ 01437 720202; **w** stdavidscathedral.org.uk; ⏱ 10.00–17.00 Mon–Sat, 13.00–17.00 Sun; free, but suggested donation £5) The most dramatic approach to St David's Cathedral, Wales's largest and most important ecclesiastical building, is via the thirty-nine steps – named after the Thirty-Nine Articles, the key tenets of Anglicanism – from the 14th-century Tower Gate at the bottom of the Pebbles. Like Llandaff Cathedral in Cardiff, the pretty hollow in which the cathedral resides was chosen ostensibly to ward off potential raiders, but whereas Llandaff was the unfortunate victim of the German Luftwaffe, St David's was ransacked at least half a dozen times, including by Cromwell in 1648. It was Bernard, the first Norman bishop of St David's, who not only initiated the campaign to elevate the diocese to an archbishopric, but who also commissioned the first cathedral here in 1131, though that was demolished and this one raised on or around the previous one in 1182. Most of what you see now is 12th to 14th century, although, inevitably, Sir Gilbert Scott – who first clapped eyes on the cathedral in 1854 – played a large part in proceedings, among his efforts including redesigning the four purple-flecked towers on the West Front with stone quarried from nearby Caerfai.

The first thing that strikes the visitor upon entering the cathedral is the wonderful wooden pendant-hung ceiling, an early 16th-century masterpiece culled from Welsh bog oak – that's if the gently sloping floor and outward lean of the massive arcades hasn't caught your eye first. This was the result of subsidence – there's a reason why this is called Vallis Rosina ('Valley of the Little Swamp'). And these aren't St David's only idiosyncrasies. One of the most unusual features of the cathedral is its *pulpitum*, a stone screen dividing the nave from the **quire** (choir) – unusual in that this is something more familiar to churches on the continent, whereas in the British Isles a typical church offers an unencumbered view from the West Door all the way through to the altar. Here in the *pulpitum* is Bishop Henry Gower's tomb. The quire is replete with fascinating detail, from the medieval floor tiles bearing the coats of arms of nobility to the choir stalls and their misericords ('misery seats', or more prosaically, flip-up seats), the undersides of which reveal differently carved images or scenes, a wild boar hunt and a group of seasick pilgrims among them.

Between the choir and the high altar is **St David's Shrine**, built in 1275 to replace an earlier one damaged during a Viking raid. The niches had lain empty for years until local artist Sara Crisp painted and gilded the motifs you see now, in 2012. A reliquary in one of the niches is said to contain St David's remains, but this is highly unlikely. In 1920, a cache of bones *was* discovered behind the High ltar, leading some to contend that these were those of the venerated saint, but later radiocarbon dating dispelled this theory. There are some notable tombs here, though, including those of Edmund Tudor, father of Henry VII and the first Tudor monarch, and erstwhile Prince of Wales, Lord Rhys ap Gruffyd.

More impressive than anything here is Bishop Vaughan's fan-vaulted ceiling in the **Chapel of the Holy Trinity**, itself walled off between the High Altar and the Lady Chapel. Here too in the Holy Trinity Chapel is an intriguing altar slab pieced together with different bits of medieval stone fragments that looks like a badly designed jigsaw puzzle – the Latin reads 'Behold the Lamb of God who takes away the sins of the world'. The chapel also holds a statue of the medieval scholar Gerald Cambrensis (aka Gerald of Wales), who himself had designs on becoming Bishop of St David's – elected three times, he was never enthroned.

Before leaving, take a look at the **Treasury** on the west side of the north transept, which houses a glittering array of bejewelled chalices, and other church artefacts, as well as objects retrieved from the graves of 13th-century bishops Thomas Bek and Richard de Carew. Here too is the cope (cape) worn by the Bishop of St David's at the coronation of Queen Victoria in 1838. The incumbent Bishop of St David's is Joanna Penberthy, who became the first female bishop in the Church of Wales when she was consecrated in 2017.

Bishop's Palace (✆ 03000 252239; w cadw.gov.wales; ⊕ Mar–Jun, Sep & Oct 09.30–17.30 daily, Jul & Aug 09.30–18.00 daily, Nov–Feb 10.00–16.00 daily; £4.80) Not to be outdone by its near neighbour just across the River Alun, the Bishop's Palace is every bit as impressive. Now roofless, the palace was built in two stages by two bishops, initially under the patronage of Bishop Thomas Bek (1280–93), and then under the sponsorship of Bishop Henry de Gower (1328–47). It's widely assumed that there was no further building work following de Gower's death. By the early 16th century, the palace had fallen out of favour, largely as a result of financial

A SHORT WALK TO ST NON'S BAY AND PORTHCLAIS

This short, easy walk starts and finishes in St David's, and takes in the alleged birthplace of St David and a fine little section of the Wales Coast Path which features one of the coast's prettiest harbours. From the main square in the city centre head down Goat Street, past the cottages on your left and continue walking along the road. On your right is the entrance to the now-derelict St Non's Hotel. Beyond here, around 450 yards further on, a small car park on your right leads to a field, whereupon you'll come to the scant remains of **St Non's Chapel**, named after St David's mother who, it is said, gave birth to the future saint here amid a wretched storm, some time around AD500. Now little more than a few crumbling stone walls, with an early Christian stone cross propped up in the corner, it looks and feels a little underwhelming, as if one somehow expected something more befitting for the birthplace of Wales's patron saint. Nearby is the healing **well** of St Non (particularly efficacious for eye diseases apparently), and a little further away, St Non's Retreat and a modern (1934) replica of the chapel with stained-glass representations of St David and St Non.

Carry on diagonally through the field until you meet the coast path. Turn right on to the path – narrow, twisting and affording glorious coastal views all the while; peek down occasionally and you may see basking seals. After half a mile or so, a deeply indented creek forces the path to veer sharply right. **Porthclais** once served as the city's Roman harbour, but these days ships have long since been replaced by pleasure craft. With the harbour on your left carry on walking until you come to a junction: the coast path continues up towards the road, but you need to go through the gate on the right and into the field. Walk through the field towards the caravan site, passing this and into the next field. At the end of that field and the entrance to the next, one sign points left and another continues straight on – take the left-hand path (although if you carried straight on you'd still end up in St David's, almost where you started) and follow the track to its conclusion. Beyond the gate (at the end of the field), you are now on the southwestern edge of the city. Turn right here on to Catherine Street and walk back into the centre.

constraints, and the bishop's main residence had moved nearly 50 miles away to Abergwili in Carmarthenshire (the current home of the Carmarthenshire County Museum). When Bishop William Barlow (St David's first Protestant bishop) had the roofs stripped, the palace's fate was sealed.

Beyond the gatehouse a spacious quadrangle lays wide before you, surrounded on all four sides by buildings in various states of disrepair. To the left of the gatehouse is Bek's Bishop's Hall, which is flanked by the kitchen and the Bishop's Solar (the private chapel). But it's de Gower's hand that reigns supreme, his Decorated Gothic style dominating what remains of the palace. His crowning glory was the **Great Hall**, which is reached via two flights of stone steps and through a monumental porch. In the east gable of the great hall – at nearly 120ft (36m), the second-longest medieval hall in Wales, trumped only by the one at Conwy Castle – is an elaborate Bath-stone wheel window, also known as the **Rose Window**. Separated from the Great Hall by the shin-high remnants of a wall is the Great Chamber, which would have served as a private space and bedroom for distinguished guests and royal pilgrims, while close by is the **Great Chapel**, in one corner of which is a piscina, a storage area for chalices and the like. Below the Great Hall, the undercroft was used for storage, accommodation, a buttery and so on.

Both the east and west ranges are adorned with arcaded parapets constructed from purple and yellow stone blocks in a chequerboard pattern – de Gower's signature motif – and dressed with more than 130 corbels (at one time there were as many as 200 around the palace) variously sculpted into human heads, animals and other mythical creatures. There's a much better view of the east range parapet from the outside garden.

Dr Beynon's Bug Farm (Lower Harglodd Farm; m 07966 956357; w thebugfarm. co.uk; ⊕ Apr–Oct 10.30–16.30 Thu–Sun (also Tue & Wed during school hols), Nov–Feb Sat & Sun; £7) One of Pembrokeshire's most unusual visitor attractions is Dr Beynon's Bug Farm, the brainchild of ecologist and entomologist Dr Sarah Beynon. Located 2 miles east of St David's, the farm has been in the family since the 1830s, but when Sarah purchased it in 2013 she came up with the idea of transforming it into a working insect farm and research centre, which was followed by the museum and bug zoo. This has since spawned other elements, like bug trails and the bug house, a rustic playbarn for little ones.

The one-room museum is packed with all kinds of (dead) exotic mini beasts, all collected by Sarah herself, along with lots of weird and wonderful facts, such as bugs don't have noses, spiders often have eight eyes, and ants can taste with their feet. There is also a grisly collection of exoskeletons, the name given to the hard protective exterior that spiders shed, a process called molting. The tropical bug zoo holds all kinds of fascinating (live) specimens: stick insects, scorpions, tarantulas, rainbow stag beetles, Madagascan hissing cockroaches, a Martinique pinktoe tarantula, and so on. The leafcutter ants are a particularly compelling watch: their mission begins by sawing off small bits of leaf 20 times their own bodyweight before returning to the other members of the colony who grind them into a mulch for growing fungus, which in turn acts as a food source for their larvae. Clever little things.

Complementing their work on the farm and in the field of insect research, Sarah and her partner Andy have become pioneers in entomography – in layman's terms, eating insects – a movement that is part of a drive to reduce the global environmental impact caused by the overconsumption of meat, and to this end they've established the Grub Kitchen, their on-site restaurant (page 306). It must be tried, at least once!

WHITESANDS BAY TO ST DAVID'S HEAD As far as Pembrokeshire's beaches go, **Whitesands Bay** (where the sand isn't very white) garners plenty of accolades, and there's no doubt it's a beauty: long, wide and big enough to lose yourself on should you start to feel crowded out. Moreover, the surf's terrific, though bodyboarders will appreciate the waves here just as much. There's also good parking and a café here, while lifeguards patrol a section of the beach in front of the café during high season. From Whitesands, there's a fabulous section of coast path out towards St David's Head, which should inveigle even the most reluctant walker. Starting at the car park, the path heads upwards, edging the precipitous cliffs before dropping down into the valley and skirting the soft blonde sands of **Porthmelgan Beach**, another of the coast's now not-so-secret beaches. So long as you've picked the right day, it is as gorgeous as everyone makes it out to be, though there are strong currents here so be careful. At mid and low tide, though, there are rock pools and a great little cave to root around in.

Back on the path, the long thin spit of **St David's Head** lies less than a mile ahead. On your approach, you'll see the remains of prehistoric hut circles, while St David's Head itself is the location for an Iron-Age coastal fortress. Clamber up on to the rocks to any number of fine viewing points. From here, you can either return whence you came or continue along the path which swings right, soon passing an impressive 20ft-long capstone called **Coetan Arthur** precariously supported by an orthostat (upright stone). Dating from around 3000BC, this would have been part of a passage grave linked to a long barrow. Beyond Coetan Arthur, a path breaks off right in the direction of **Carn Llidi** (594ft), or you can carry on along the coast path.

RAMSEY ISLAND The departure point for boats to Ramsey Island is St Justinian's, 2 miles west of St David's and named after the hermit who sought sanctuary on the island back in the 6th century – a roofless chapel in his honour stands alone in a private field near the ticket office. Boats to the island depart from the nearby RNLI lifeboat station, which has been responding to emergencies and saving lives since 1869, and on average gets called out around 45 times a year.

Just half a mile offshore, across treacherous Ramsey Sound, Ramsey Island (in Welsh 'Ynys Dewi' meaning 'St David') is an indeterminately shaped island that manifests two distinct geological entities: a northern half that is largely sedimentary, and a southern half that is volcanic. If you are on a landing trip, there's an easy but very satisfying 3½-mile circuit of the island, which traverses its three moderately sized peaks including the highest, Carn Llundain, at 446ft (136m). The most interesting offshore geological feature is the notorious 'Bitches' on the eastern side, a linear reef of needle-sharp rocks that are covered at high tide, hence why many a vessel has come a cropper attempting to negotiate safe passage – one of the worst incidents here occurred in 1910 when three crew from the lifeboat *Gem* lost their lives when tending to another stricken vessel.

Covering some 640 acres and owned and managed by the RSPB since 1992, the island was originally the property of the Church, until it was passed into private hands and run as farmland, which included a deer park. Red deer have proved to be a resilient presence on the island, and there's a good chance of seeing some. But it's really all about the birds. Come at the right time of year (spring through to summer) and you'll see large numbers of guillemots and razorbills plus fulmar petrels which tend to hang around longer, staying as late as September. Kittiwakes and Manx shearwater are also present in good numbers. Most of these birds are cliff-nesters, so are best observed from a vessel, though you won't see Manx shearwater as these birds only return to the safety of their burrows at night. Don't come expecting to

9

see puffins, though, as these are the preserve of Skomer (page 300) further south. Resident birds include shags, cormorants, oystercatchers and choughs, as well as peregrines – currently three pairs.

You'll also get to see grey seals, hundreds of 'em, dozing on the pebbly beaches and in the sea caves pressed into the cliffs all around the island. Although there is a small resident population here year-round, their numbers are swollen in autumn (September/October) when hundreds of pups, up to as many as 700, are born here, making Ramsey one of the largest breeding colonies in Britain. In what might seem like a harsh life lesson, pups are weaned off their mothers at just three to four weeks old, although by that stage they will have doubled, if not tripled, their birthweight. These waters are also frequented by common, or harbour, porpoises. Animals aside (there are lots of sheep here too which get transferred off the island for the winter), the island's only other residents are its two wardens, Greg and Nia – Greg has been tending the place for 17 years, but the unpredictable weather means it's not been unknown for him to be stranded here for weeks at a time.

Getting there and away   A couple of operators offer trips out to the island (only one of these is permitted to land), but if it's wildlife you want to see, you'll probably get more out of doing just a water-bound trip. In any case, all vessels tend to stick to the more sheltered eastern side, which includes a weave through the Bitches (great fun in the RIB), as the west side is too wet and wild for the types of craft used here.

Thousand Islands Expeditions   Cross Square, St David's; ☏ 01437 721721; w thousandislands. co.uk. The only operator permitted to land on Ramsey Island; 4-hour trips are at 10.00 & noon, & they also offer 90min wildlife adventure trips around the island in either a boat or a RIB.

Voyages of Discovery   1 High St, St David's; ☏ 01437 721911; w ramseyisland.co.uk. Operate 1-hour guided wildlife trips around the island on a RIB, which depart from the lifeboat station at St Justinian's. There are daily sailings from the end of Mar to mid-Nov with limited sailings in winter (check the website).

THE NORTH PEMBROKESHIRE COAST

The northern Pembrokeshire coastline presents a wilder side, with vertiginous cliffs and heart-stopping inclines. Much of this coastline's identity has been shaped by industry, in particular quarrying, with several visible remnants in many of its small harbour villages like **Abereiddi**, which has since been transformed into a mesmerising lagoon, and **Porthgain**. Beyond Abercastle, **Strumble Head**, which thrusts out into Irish Sea, offers wonderful walks and opportunities for seabird spotting. It also lies close to the scene of one of Wales's more bizarre contributions to folklore, an event that is relayed in **Fishguard**, the coast's main town and departure point for ferries across the water.

ABEREIDDI TO ABERCASTLE   It's 5 miles along the coast from St David's to **Abereiddi**. It's hard to reconcile this wild and wonderful landscape with the fact that this was once an area of heavy industry. From around 1850, good-quality slate was extracted from more than 100 quarries in the county, including the main quarry of the St Bride's Slate Company based in Abereiddi, which closed in 1910. The stark, yet hauntingly picturesque reminders are there in the guise of a few quarry buildings and workmen's cottages surmounting the clifftop. Following closure, the quarry was dynamited, which allowed the sea in to create a natural harbour, and thus the **Blue Lagoon** was formed, the colour derived by minerals leaching from the rocks.

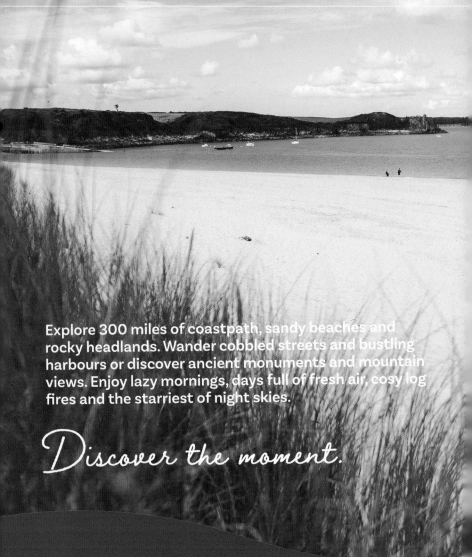

Explore 300 miles of coastpath, sandy beaches and rocky headlands. Wander cobbled streets and bustling harbours or discover ancient monuments and mountain views. Enjoy lazy mornings, days full of fresh air, cosy log fires and the starriest of night skies.

Discover the moment.

West Wales Holiday Cottages

For the unforgettable memories. Discover the *moment* in Wales

01239 810033   www.westwalesholidaycottages.co.uk

It's a fantastic colourscape: aquamarine, ultramarine, lapis lazuli and cerulean, and pretty though it may be, it is also very cold and deceptively deep at just over 80ft, which is why this is one of the best spots in Wales for coasteering (page 52). Come another time and you might see divers leaping forth from 100ft-high boards!

Trains loaded with cargo would trundle up the coast to **Porthgain**, from where it would be despatched to all parts of the United Kingdom. Following the closure of the slate quarries here, attention switched to extracting brick and granite, which continued until 1930. A small coastal hamlet with a sheltered harbour used for fishing boats and pleasure craft, Porthgain is reliant on tourism these days, but there are reminders of its past here too, both in the slate works (the pilot house and cottages with their lime-mortared roofs) and in the brickworks: the hoppers, a lime kiln and brick-drying shed, and the old brick-making shed which has been put to good use as a restaurant/café (see below).

The coastal path continues east via Trefin to **Abercastle**. Translating as 'Samson's Stone' after the eponymous saint and one-time resident of Caldey Island who allegedly lifted the 16ft-high capstone on top of the seven upright stones with just his little finger, **Carreg Samson** is another of the region's many impressive burial chambers. Slightly younger than Pentre Ifan (it just dates from 4,500 years ago), and although not as imposing as its near neighbour in the Preselis, it is nonetheless an awesome sight upon close inspection. The chamber is a short walk (1 mile) west of the village at Longhouse Farm, and is accessible via a trail that leads off the coast path. From Abercastle, the coast path carries serenely on to the headland of **Trywn Llwynog**.

Getting there and away The Strumble Shuttle (#404) connects St David's with Fishguard via all the coastal villages (Abereiddi, Porthgain, Trefin, Abercastle and Strumble Head). Between late May and September there are three buses Monday to Saturday in each direction, and during the rest of the year there are two buses on Thursdays only. The #T11 Haverfordwest to Fishguard bus (6 daily Mon–Sat) via St David's also stops in Trefin but none of the other villages.

Where to stay, eat and drink

✳ 🏠 **The Old School Hostel** (6 rooms) Ffordd Yr Afon, Trefin; m 07845 625005; w oldschoolhostel.com. In the tiny hamlet of Trefin, roughly halfway between Porthgain & Abercastle, this fine, ecologically oriented hostel is more akin to a good-quality budget B&B. Its 6 comfortable, colourful rooms sleep between 2 & 7 people, & all come with solid bunks, memory-foam mattresses & solar-powered showers. B/fast & packed lunches available upon request. **£**

🅰 **Trellyn Woodland Camping** (10 pitches) Abercastle; m 01348 837762; w trellyn.co.uk. A 5min walk south of the village centre, each of the 7 beautifully sited pitches here has its own picnic table, grill & covered campfire area. If you fancy an upgrade in the comfort stakes, there are 3 yurts, each with its own kitchen & campfire area too. Additional facilities include power showers, communal area, wood-fired pizza oven – which

roars into life in on Sun & Mon – & wood-fired sauna. Note, however, that because the site has so few pitches, bookings are for a week minimum for camping. *Camping* **£**, *yurts* **£££**

✘ **The Shed** 56 Llanrhian Rd, Porthgain; ☏ 01348 831518; w theshedporthgain.co.uk; ⏰ 10.00–12.45 & 17.00–22.00 daily. Restaurant, fish-&-chip take away & ice-cream shop, there's not much they don't do here inside the cleverly converted old brickworks shed. The fish & chips are decent but not world beating, but you won't mind that so much with a setting like this, especially when the sunsets can be so spectacular here. **£**

🍺 **The Sloop Inn** Porthgain; ☏ 01348 831449; w sloop.co.uk; ⏰ 11.30–23.00/midnight Mon–Thu & Sun, 11.30–midnight Fri & Sat. Packed to its oak-beamed rafters with nauticalia, this whitewashed 18th-century building is one of the most satisfying pubs in Pembrokeshire. It's won a ledgeful of awards for its menu, which uses best local produce & is skewed heavily towards seafood (salt & pepper squid, *moules marinière*, fish pie),

but there's more besides including a decent slew of burgers & steaks, plus veggie/vegan options like halloumi salad & purple gnocchi. £££

Activities

Celtic Quest Coasteering Abereiddi Bay; \01348 837337; w celticquestcoasteering.com. Rockhopping, cliff jumping & belly flopping are all part of the fun overseen by this excellent & very

experienced coasteering outfit; all sessions – which last 3hrs, 2 of which are in the water – finish with a leap (optional!) into Abereiddi's Blue Lagoon. £55 pp, though note that the minimum age is 8.

STRUMBLE HEAD The 10-mile stretch of the coast path from Abercastle to Strumble Head is fantastic. A succession of small sandy beaches, at **Abermawr, Aber Bach** and **Pwllcochran** are all plausible diversions, before the triple volcanic crags of **Garn Fawr** (699ft) loom into view. Most easily reached via the car park at its eastern ridge, on the lane up to Strumble Head, this not insubstantial Iron-Age fort is an easy enough climb, taking no more than 30 minutes to circuit the ditches, ramparts and hut circles. The views, on a clear day, are sensational: the Wicklow Mountains in Ireland, and even the Llyn Peninsula and Snowdon in North Wales.

From Garn Fawr it's just a couple of miles to **Strumble Head**, the closest that Wales gets to the Irish mainland. Located at the very tip of the peninsula known as Pen Caer, erected in 1908 on Ynys Meicel (St Michael's Island), the lighthouse is linked to the mainland by a metal footbridge, though this is closed to the public. This is another superb spot for seabird spotting: gannets, kittiwakes, fulmars and guillemots all make their presence loudly known here during late spring and summer. One beach you won't hear much about is **Porthsychan**, a 20-minute walk east from Strumble Head. A small, very quiet cove backed by low headlands and a trio of waterfalls, you can swim here safely, and you might even see seals close by. Beyond here is **Carregwastad Point**, the site of the last invasion of Britain (see opposite), an event marked by a headstone.

FISHGUARD

South Wales's main ferry terminal, Fishguard is a little more than just a place from which to catch a ferry to Ireland. The port, which is actually in the northwestern suburb of Goodwick, was built here by the Great Western Railway in 1906 as Fishguard was deemed to be the shortest route both to southern Ireland and the United States. While the terminal has always been the town's focal point – the effects of Brexit, with Fishguard closer to Rosslare than it is to Cardiff, are still yet to fully play out – the town is packed with history. One event in particular stands out: the Last Invasion (see opposite), which is celebrated in a glorious tapestry in the town library. Although the town – divided into two distinct parts, Lower and Upper Fishguard – now has some pretty decent places to stay and eat, you're unlikely to stick around long.

GETTING THERE AND AWAY

By ferry Stenaline Ferries (w stenaline.co.uk) operate two daily ferries from the harbour in Goodwick to Rosslare in southwest Ireland. These currently depart Goodwick at 13.00 and 23.45.

By car Fishguard is a straightforward 25-minute drive north from St David's along the A487, while Haverfordwest is a similar-length drive heading south along the

A40. There's a huge car park down on the Parrog in Goodwick, if you don't mind the walk up into town, but otherwise, you could use the Co-op car park just off the High Street if you're only stopping for a short while.

By rail and bus Trains from Carmarthen (3 daily Mon–Sat) call in at Fishguard & Goodwick station before terminating at Fishguard Harbour. For Milford Haven you need to change at Clarberston Road. Buses stop by the town hall in the Market Square, as well as on Station Hill and the Parrog in Goodwick. The excellent T5 Trans Cymru service departs nine–ten times daily for Aberystwyth, Cardigan, Newport and Haverfordwest.

WHERE TO STAY, EAT AND DRINK

The Manor House (6 rooms) 11 Main St; 01348 873260; w manortownhouse.com. Superior to anything else in Fishguard, guests couldn't be made to feel more welcome at this lovingly run, family-owned guesthouse in the centre of town. 4 of its rooms (superior sea view & junior sea view) have the outlook while the other 2 have town views, though all are furnished to the same high exacting standards. Public spaces include a lounge with honesty bar & a flower-bedecked garden terrace. There's also a handsome b/fast to see you on your way, whether that's to Ireland or elsewhere. **££**

Kitewood Camping (12 pitches) e camping@kitewoodcamping.co.uk; w kitewoodcamping.co.uk; ⏱ May–Sep. Superb, family-run woodland site about 1½ miles southwest of Fishguard with well-spaced-out pitches, each with its own sheltered campfire area & firepit (with free firewood), hot shower & compost toilet, which is about as good as it gets. Additional communal facilities include a games

9

room & wash house. Note, though, that if you can't live without your mobile (there are no charging points) or Wi-Fi, then this place is not for you: it's totally off-grid. Minimum 2-night stay in summer hols. ££

🛏 **Royal Oak Inn** Market Sq; 📞 01348 218632; w royaloakfishguard.co.uk; 🕐 11.30–23.00/ midnight Mon–Thu & Sun, 11.30–midnight Fri & Sat. It was here in the Royal Oak that Colonel Tate was coerced into negotiating surrender following the botched invasion of 1797, & rumour has it that the very table on which the surrender was negotiated is still here. History aside, this is a very convivial pub, with a terrific selection of ales, a very respectable menu & a cracking folk music night each Tue. ££

🛏 **Nourish** 12 High St; m 07546 086511; w nourishbakery.co.uk; 🕐 09.00–16.00 Wed–Sat. Superb little bakery just up from the main square where all the products are made exclusively with sourdough: brown & white loaves, sandwich loaves, as well as cinnamon swirls, *pains au chocolat* & jumbo-sized croissants; an early visit is recommended, however, as most things get snapped up pretty quickly. £

SHOPPING

The Gourmet Pig 32 West St; 📞 01348 874404; w gourmetpig.co.uk; 🕐 09.30–17.30 Mon–Fri, 09.30–16.30 Sat. Fabulous deli stocked with sumptuous goodies including cheeses & pâtés from France, salami & olives from the Mediterranean, & posh wines & proseccos from around the world; there's plenty of local produce too. You could quite easily end up spending a small fortune in here.

Seaways Bookshop 12 West St; 📞 01348 873433; w seawaysbookshop.co.uk; 🕐 10.00–17.00 Mon–Sat. Occupying a handsome Georgian building, this terrific indie bookshop is packed to the gills with all manner of genres: fiction, children's, biography, lifestyle & so on, plus there's artwork & CDs to purchase. Look out too for special events held here, including quite a few author signings & talks.

WHAT TO SEE AND DO Walking from the ferry terminal, on the Goodwick foreshore itself, the large curved glass-fronted building houses a café and the **Ocean Lab Aquarium** (📞 01348 874737; w seatrust.org.uk; 🕐 Apr–Sep 10.00–16.45, Nov– Mar 10.00–15.45; £6.50), a modest, child-oriented affair harbouring the usual suspects: moon jellyfish, conger eels and other exotic fish. In front of the building, an extended seawall offers an invigorating short walk out into the middle of the bay, from where you can get a closer view of the ferries coming and going, albeit just two a day. From here it's a short walk to the **Lower Town**, defined by its rows of coloured pebbledash cottages sheltered below wooded slopes. From here the road climbs steeply up West Street to the junctions of High Street and Main Street which brings you to the **Upper Town**.

Located inside the library on the first floor of the Town Hall is the town's one conventional site. Commissioned as part of Fishguard's bicentenary celebration in 1997, the **Last Invasion tapestry** (📞 01437 776638; w lastinvasiontapestry.co.uk; 🕐 Apr–Sep 10.00–17.00 Mon–Wed & Fri, 10.00–18.00 Thu, 10.00–16.00 Sat (Oct– Mar until 13.00 Sat); free) is a wonderful pictorial interpretation of those peculiar two days in 1797 (page 315). A legacy of artists Elizabeth Cramp, who designed it, and textile artist Audrey Walker, who co-ordinated its creation, the tapestry was stitched by some 77 local women over a period of four years: the embroiderers worked on different panels in small groups from their homes, pulling all 37 panels together at the end. With text in both English and Welsh, the 100ft-long piece (exactly the same length as the Bayeux Tapestry) recalls the story alongside illustrations of the main events, including the first sighting of the invaders, pitchfork-wielding women and weeping prisoners. Afterwards, pop across the road to the Royal Oak to view what is supposed to be the very table upon which the surrender was negotiated, and while you're at it, hang around for a drink and a bite

For many, the sole reason to come to Pembrokeshire is to walk all, or part of, the 186-mile (300km) Pembrokeshire Coast Path, often rated one of the world's top long-distance walking routes – it's certainly the highlight of the entire Wales Coast Path. If you were to do it all in one go at a reasonable lick, reckon on about two weeks, a couple of days less if you are super fit, a few days more if not! (The other thing to factor into planning is whether you want the occasional day off to go and explore, for example, Skomer.) While not technically difficult, nor requiring any specialist map skills – it's very well marked – it's nevertheless not to be taken lightly. To put it into perspective, the total ascent is around 33,000ft (10,000m), higher than Mount Everest.

The path was first mapped out by the naturalist R M Lockley in 1950, but it would be another 20 years before it finally opened: the intervening years were spent negotiating with more than 150 landowners in order to secure various rights of way, culminating in its inauguration in 1970. You can of course walk the path from either end (St Dogmaels in the north or Amroth in the south) and while many guidebooks now outline the route north–south (as per the direction of the Wales Coast Path), most aficionados prefer walking south to north. Generally speaking, the cliffs in the south are not as high as they are along the northern coast, and the terrain is also less rugged, so it might just be a case of saving the hardest, and most spectacular, legs until last.

Starting in Amroth on the south coast, the majority of the route is along unspoiled open coast, but there are enough small towns, villages and resorts along the way to break things up a little. En route there are an incredible 50 beaches, 40 Iron-Age promontory forts and dozens of other archaeological sites; you won't want for things to see. There are a few sections of the path where a greater degree of planning might be required, assuming you don't want to stray too far inland: specifically, around Milford Haven there are a couple of inlets that can only be crossed when the tide is out, while along the MOD's Castlemartin Range, access is forbidden through a 4-mile stretch when firing takes place.

Planning is all-important: while summer would seem like the best time, you are of course competing for path space with thousands of other people, while accommodation will be at a premium (both in terms of availability and price). Late spring (or September) is optimum, as the crowds are thinner and you should still get some of the best of the weather, while April and May will see the cliffs begin to teem with birdlife as huge colonies of guillemots, fulmars, kittiwakes and Manx shearwater start to settle. Summer does, though, bring with it the advantage of more local transport, should you require it, with buses shuttling back and forth along various sections of the coast. The best guide to the Pembrokeshire Coast Path is Cicerone's *Walking the Pembrokeshire Coast Path* (£16.95), which includes an excellent route map booklet. Or there's the website w pembrokeshirecoast.wales/coast-path.

to eat. You can also pick up fruit and veg, plus a few other goodies, from the small **indoor market** on the ground floor of the town hall.

Overlooking the harbour away to the east on the knobbly peninsula of Castle Point stands the somnolent remains of **Fishguard Fort**. It was here, during the

Pembrokeshire FISHGUARD

9

Last Invasion (page 315) that the garrison fired rounds of blanks to warn of the impending French attack; this was enough to send the invaders scurrying away in the direction of Strumble Head where they eventually landed. The fort doesn't merit a special detour, but if you're walking the Coast Path you'll pass right through it.

MYNYDD PRESELI

If you're seeking somewhere to decompress, a place to slow down for a few days of self-imposed exile from modernity, then Mynydd Preseli (Preseli Hills) should do the trick. Indeed, a walk through its treeless vales, spartan hills, and time-trapped villages with their secretive churches leaves you with little option but to dial out for a bit.

They may be of (relatively) unassuming height – the highest, **Foel Cwmcerwyn**, tops out at 1,759ft – but these stone- and sheep-spattered hills offer some of the most exhilarating, off-the-beaten-track walking outside the Brecon Beacons. The Preselis are also celebrated for being the source of the bluestone that was used at Stonehenge, though they don't shout out about it too much around these parts. It's little surprise then that these hills are rich in prehistoric pickings, manifest in a remarkable proliferation of standing stones, cromlechs and hillforts, such as those at **Carn Ingli**, **Foel Drygarn** and **Pentre Ifan**, as well as a reconstructed Iron-Age settlement at **Castell Henllys**. Charming, coast-bound **Newport** is the only town in the Preselis and therefore makes the most obvious base, which is just as well because it also rates a disproportionately good number of places to stay and eat. From here you can strike out towards Carn Ingli, the Preselis' most high-profile peak, and the gorgeous little church at **Nevern**, before venturing into the hills proper.

NEWPORT An altogether very different proposition from its namesake in Gwent (page 107), Newport was founded by the Normans in the 12th century, later developing into a port (the Parrog) of some importance thanks to expansion of the local wool trade, although as the recent discovery of a pottery kiln suggested, this too was a significant industry. You can view this, and take in one of the country's most adorable little museums, in a leisurely couple of hours (the town castle is in private hands) before checking out the beaches and indulging in some good food.

Newport is also unique for being the only town in Wales to still appoint an annual mayor, a tradition that dates back to the time when it was the seat of the Norman Marcher Lordship of Cemaes. Another joyful local custom is the so-called 'Beating of the Bounds', whereby the town's boundaries are laid out. The custom, whereby young boys would be beaten at certain markers along the way so they would not forget where the boundaries lay, is believed to date from the 5th century, but ceased to be in 1888. Revived here in Newport in 1964, this silly bit of fun takes place on the third Friday of August and anyone is welcome to join in this perambulation: walkers, riders, dogs – anyone that can get around basically. The 'Beat' used to be 26 miles long but is around 9 miles these days – and you do get a certificate if you complete it!

Getting there and away Newport is well served by buses, all of which stop on Bridge Street in the town centre. Newport is easily accessible by car, as it lies right on the busy A487 linking Fishguard and Cardigan.

Tourist information The **Community Library and Information Centre/Newport Information Centre** (☎ 01437 776651; ☼ 09.30–12.30 Mon & Sat, 12.30–18.00 Wed) opposite the car park on Long Street is a useful resource.

Where to stay, eat and drink

✳ **Llys Meddyg** (8 rooms) East St; ☎ 01239 820008; w llysmeddyg.com. If you fancy a bit of indulgence after a day out in the hills, look no further than this Grade II-listed Georgian townhouse, whose rooms are run through with classy touches like Egyptian cotton linen, woollen blankets from the nearby Melyn Tregwynt mill, & walls hung with original coastscapes; each room has its own idiosyncrasy, for example, a low-slung bed or a double vanity. In the guest lounge you can chill out with a newspaper or a book, or, on warmer days, escape to the sanctuary of the kitchen garden. **£££**

Pwnc East St; ☎ 01239 820100; ☼ 09.00–14.30 Mon & Thu–Sat. As the 'Fuel for Brave Living' sign outside would have it, this is food for the health-conscious, as avocado sandwiches with crispy halloumi, & spicy coconut dhal would seem to advocate. Beyond the colourful blue-&-orange frontage, bikes hang from the walls & ceiling, & a climbing wall invites kids to unleash some pent-up energy while you go and hide in the cute little courtyard garden. **££**

Blas at Fronlas Market St; ☎ 01239 820065; w blasatfronlas.com; ☼ 09.30–16.30 daily. Sweet little licensed café serving breakfast & lunch with the likes of quiche, cawl & toasted paninis. You can also pick up bits here to take away for a packed lunch; the home-baked bread is a good place to start. They also have 2 dbl rooms (**££**) offering all the requisite comforts, though there is a 2-night minimum stay Sat & Sun. **£**

Shopping

Carningli Centre East St; ☎ 01239 820274; w carninglicentre.com; ☼ 10.00–17.30 Mon–Sat. Marvellous little emporium packed with thousands of secondhand books (enough to give any shop in Hay a run for their money), maps, antique furnishings & railway signs (something for the mantelpiece?) in addition to a gallery selling mostly work by local artists. They also have a selection of bikes for hire (£15/22 half/full day, which includes all equipment), & can normally let out bikes when the shop is closed. Moreover, the owner, Graham, is a qualified trail rider & is more than happy to advise on routes as well as lead guided tours upon request.

What to see and do Newport's main thoroughfare is actually two contiguous streets, East Street and Bridge Street (basically the A487), from where Long Street dips down to the **Nyfer Estuary**. At the bottom, take a left turn along the path hugging the shoreline towards the **Parrog**, Newport's nearest beach – it's mostly a shingle affair but with a bit of sand at low tide. Better is the dune-backed **Traeth Mawr** (Big Beach) on the north side of the estuary, which is reached via an iron bridge beyond Feidr Pen-y-Bont. En route, keep your eyes peeled for a burial chamber, **Carreg Coetan Arthur**, dating from around 3000BC and somewhat incongruously located behind some holiday bungalows just before reaching the bridge on the left-hand side.

Back in the centre are a couple of minor delights. On Market Street, Ty Twt (the Little House), is home to the **Dolls' House and Toy Museum** (☎ 01239 820590; w dollshouseandtoymuseum.org.uk; ☼ all school hols 10.30–17.00 Mon, Wed & Fri; £3). Not only is this wonderful collection of dolls' houses – from 1840 to the present day – the private collection of the owner Val Ripley (now in her late nineties!), but this was the very house that she grew up in, along with her late sister Pam. The detail in each and every one is beyond exquisite, from the earliest house (1840) – a recreation of Tregear Manor – to some of the very personal items including a miniature dog that belonged to ballerina Margot Fontaine, and dolls' dresses given to Val from her childhood friend's father, *Gone with the Wind* star

Leslie Howard. The family toys, too, are a delight. Although opening is nominally restricted to school holidays, visits are welcome by appointment.

Beyond Bridge Street, on West Street, the **Newport Memorial Hall** (m 07966 370827; w newportmemorialhall.co.uk; ⊕ 09.00–17.00 daily; free) is the location of a remarkable recent find. In 2017, an almost-intact pottery kiln was unearthed on the site of the hall, along with thousands of pottery shards, leading experts to proclaim this the finest medieval pottery kiln of its kind ever discovered in Britain – it may even be the only one. Subsequent analysis revealed the kiln to date from the 14th or 15th century, suggesting that the town and surrounding area had been a pottery works of some importance. The kiln can be viewed through a window in one side of the hall with wall panels offering lucid interpretation.

CARN INGLI The Preselis' most high-profile peak, Carn Ingli ('The Mount of Angels' – 1,138ft) – exerts a powerful presence over the surrounding landscape. Its scree-strewn summit is crowned by the remnants of an ancient hillfort, one of the largest in West Wales, and although little is known about its earliest history, some experts have surmised that it may even have Neolithic or Bronze-Age provenance. For the most part, the fort interior is boulder-strewn but a number of hut circles can be discerned on the lower slopes close to the main entrance. The ramparts, which once provided a formidable barrier around the fort, are fairly well preserved to the north, from where there are wonderful views back across Newport and out to Cardigan Bay.

NEVERN In the village of Nevern, a mile or so east of Newport (roughly double the distance by foot along a pleasant riverside path), and nestled in a delightful spot by a rushing stream, is the **Church of St Brynach**, founded by the eponymous saint – known in Welsh as Brynach Wyddel, or Brynach the Irishman – around AD540, although the oldest extant part of the building is its 14th-century tower. The church is packed with interesting features, both inside and out: set into the sill of one of the south windows, the gravestone of the Romano-British worthy Maglocunus bears Ogham inscriptions from the 5th century, Ogham an early Celtic alphabet that arrived in Wales courtesy of Irish settlers at the end of the Roman Empire. Heading outside, in the south transept stands the 13ft-high Great Cross of St Brynach, a superb 10th-century specimen inscribed with characteristic Celtic inscriptions.

Typically garnering more attention than its monuments is the church's collection of ancient **yews**, and one in particular. Take a look at the second one on the right, which is said to mysteriously 'bleed' brown-red sap from its bark, hence its moniker 'the weeping yew'. A common feature in many church graveyards (planted by Normans and, before them, Christians), the yew's religious and cultural heft stems (excuse the pun) from its ability to regenerate and the supposed healing powers of its needles. Local legend supposes that the tree will continue to weep until a lord of the manor is reinstated in the castle, but that's not going to happen any time soon.

The **castle** (open access) can be reached via a circular walk beginning at a gate by the stream. A settlement of sorts since the Iron Age, it's said that the aforementioned lord of the manor who allowed Brynach to build the church lived here. What little is left of it now – a circular base of the keep – dates to around the 1170s when the castle was raised by Lord Rhys (Rhys ap Gruffydd). In a somewhat ignominious turn of affairs, Rhys was later, briefly, incarcerated here by his own sons, who then burnt the place down (after they had released their father) to avoid it falling into Anglo-Norman hands.

PENTRE IFAN Two miles south of Nevern is the Preselis' single most captivating monument. Pentre Ifan is a 5,000-year-old prehistoric tomb (or megalith, cromlech or dolmen – call it what you will) and the largest in Wales, a 16-tonne arrowhead top stone balanced atop three tapering stone legs. Two more upright stones watch on. It's every bit as impressive as anything Stonehenge has to offer, and once seen, is not easily forgotten – and nor are the views. According to experts, it would have taken (at least) a dozen men several months, using creepers as ropes and tree trunks as rollers, to raise this beast. Hard as it is to believe now, Pentre Ifan was originally buried under a pile of stones and soil more than 100ft deep. Less surprising is its location, as most *cromlechi* were typically erected near the sea, whether in Scotland or Wales. Since these were assumed to be the work of people who sailed the western sea routes, it is therefore not surprising that southwest Wales (and in particular Pembrokeshire) should have so many.

CASTELL HENLLYS (✎ 01239 891319; w pembrokeshirecoast.wales; ⊕ Mar–Jun 10.00–13.00 & 14.00–17.00 daily; £6.50) Five miles east of Newport, or a 4-mile walk south from Pentre Ifan, is Castell Henllys, a surprisingly evocative reconstruction of an Iron-Age village. In 1982, archaeological work uncovered the foundations of a complex of roundhouses, thought to date back some 2,000 years. Since its discovery, four roundhouses have been sensitively reconstructed on the original foundations, which gives this site some genuine gravitas. There's much more to enjoy beyond exploring the village itself, including an exhibition in the visitor centre, wool dyeing and wildlife watching opportunities plus other activities for kids, though usually just during the school holidays. Much fun is the Barefoot Trail, a cleverly conceived meander along the River Nant Duad where you get to experience what it's like to walk on different surfaces, like flint and clay, just as the Celtic warriors would have done – unlike them, though, you do have the option of keeping your shoes on.

GOLDEN ROAD A 4,000-year-old ridgeway, the Golden Road extends for 7 miles between Crymych in the east to the Gwaun Valley in the west. It takes its name from the time when gold from Ireland's Wicklow Hills was transported along this road en route to southern England. The only thing that lines the route these days is (a few) walkers, but as any of them will tell you, this is one of the most rewarding short trails in Pembrokeshire.

A mile or so west of Crymych, at a modest altitude of 1,191ft is **Foel Drygarn** ('Hill of the Three Cairns'). Aside from the 'Gop' in Flintshire, these three 10ft-high burial cairns are the highest in Wales. Within the two main enclosures are the remains of more than 100 platforms, areas that have been flattened so that other structures can be built on top. From Foel Drygarn you can see the length of the Golden Road all the way to **Foel Cwmcerwyn**, the highest point in Pembrokeshire no less, at 1,759ft. But before then, it's another mile or so from Foel Drygarn to **Carn Menyn** (1,197ft), which is where, it has been suggested, the bluestone subsequently transported to Stonehenge was cut. Various theories have been ascribed as to the reason why they were taken from here to Stonehenge; among them that it was believed that the stones had therapeutic properties. Either way, and if the stones did come from Preseli, it still hasn't been determined how they were transported such a long distance, and it probably never will be. A short walk from the western trailhead of the Golden Road is **Foel Eyr Cairn**, a large, conical Bronze-Age burial site. Like both it has a commanding presence and superb views.

✕ Where to eat and drink

🏠 **Tafarn Sinc** Bryn Ter, Rosebush; 📞01437 532214; w tafarnsinc.cymru; 🕐 noon–22.00 daily. An ox-blood-red, corrugated-iron shack marks the 'Zinc Tavern' out as something just a little bit different, & it doesn't disappoint. Originally built in 1870 as a hotel to promote health tourism in the area (it failed), the building ran as a staunchly Welsh-speaking pub for years before falling into disrepair; it was bought out by the local community in 2017 & is now going great guns. With a toasty woodburning fire, simple but well-cooked pub grub (chilli, Glamorgan sausages, that kind of thing), & best of all, their own brewery – try the Cwrw Tafarn Sinc – there's much to like about the place. **££**

Outstanding Wildlife Boat trips

On our fully guided marine voyages, explore echoing sea caves, towering rock gorges, marvel at seabird cities & enjoy close encounters with seals, porpoise, dolphins & more. Learn all about our unique wildlife, spectacular geology & local history & experience some of the fastest tidal races in the country.

We offer a variety of trips ranging from our **1.5 hour Ramsey Island Special** suitable for all the family to **a 2.5 hour Grassholm – Seabird, whale & dolphin trip** for the more intrepid wildlife enthusiast. Trips depart from St Justinians.

We also specialize in **bespoke trips**, be it photography, storytelling or a special event, we can create the perfect trip for you.

51°40.21' N   4°41.39' W

Feel like doing something a little different?

Tenby Adventure are adventure and activity specialists based in the picturesque seaside town of Tenby, Pembrokeshire.

Coasteering, kayaking, climbing & snorkelling

...around spectacular, fascinating and out-of-the-way parts of the famous Pembrokeshire coast.

We're experienced, qualified to the highest levels and ridiculously enthusiastic.

Explore awesome cliffs, weird caves, hidden beaches and picturesque rivers. You'll learn all about our rich wildlife, amazing geology and local history.

It's also possible we'll persuade you to jump off a cliff or two…

Appendix 1

LANGUAGE

According to the most recent census (2021), around 880,000 (more than a quarter of the population) are Welsh speakers, but that number is now thought to be much higher, and it is certainly growing, though usage inevitably varies a great deal by region. In 2010, the Welsh Assembly unanimously passed the **Welsh Language Measure**, which effectively puts Welsh on an equal footing with English, and since 2016, it has been mandatory for all new signs to be displayed in Welsh first. All children now learn Welsh in school. For more on the history of the Welsh language, see page 21.

THE WELSH ALPHABET AND PRONUNCIATION The Welsh alphabet – which has 29 letters – is similar to English, but there are no letters k, q, v, x and z, although these are sometimes found in borrowed words. Moreover, and this is where the Welsh trump the English, there are five vowels: a, e, i, o, u (the same as English), plus w and y.

Welsh consonants are pronounced in a similar way to English, with a few exceptions, such as c and g, which are always hard, as in 'call' and 'gate', while f is pronounced as v in 'vat'. Additional consonants are ch, as in a Scottish 'loch'; dd, as in 'this'; ff, as in 'four'; ng, as in 'thing'; ph, as in 'phone'; rh, as in 'pray' (trilled or rolled); and th, as in 'maths'. The most common, and problematic, Welsh consonant is ll, which features in place names all over the country, from Llanelli to Llangollen. The way to pronounce it is to lift the tongue behind the top row of teeth and breathe through it.

USEFUL WORDS
Basics

shwmae	hello	*croeso*	welcome
Hwyl fawr	goodbye	*heddiw*	today
bore da	good morning	*yfory*	tomorrow
nos da	good night	Cymraeg	Welsh
noswaith dda	good evening	Cymru	Wales
os gwelwch yn dda	please	Cymry	Welsh people
diolch	thank you	Lloegr	England
oes	yes	*fach*	small, lesser
nac oes	no	*fawr*	big, greater

The outdoors

afon	river	*bwlch*	mountain pass
bryn	hill	*carreg*	stone

clun	meadow	*glyn*	valley
coed	forest, woodland	*llwybr*	path
craig	rock	*maen*	stone
crannog	artificial island on a lake	*maes*	field
		môr	sea
cromlech	literally 'curved stone'; generally used to refer to megalithic burial chambers	*morfa*	coastal marsh
		mynydd	mountain
		nant	valley, stream
		pant	vale
		parc	park
cwm	valley	*sir*	county, shire
dŵr	water	*rhiw*	hill
dyffryn	vale	*traeth*	beach
fforest	forest	*ynys*	island
gardd	garden		

Sightseeing

ar Agor	open	*eglwys*	church
ar Gau	closed	*eisteddfod*	festival
amgeuddfa	museum	*fferm*	farm
caer	fort	*llan*	sacred enclosure, early church
canol	centre		
capel	chapel	*marchnad*	market
castell	castle	*melin*	mill
clwyd	gate	*neuadd*	hall
din or *dinas*	fort	*twr*	tower

Getting around

araf	slow	*porth*	port, gateway
bws	bus	*stryd*	street
ffordd/ heol	road	*tren*	train
pentre (f)	village	*tref*	town
pont	bridge		

Food and drink

bara	bread	*llaeth*	milk
cwrw	beer	*psygod*	fish
gwin	wine	*wyau*	eggs

Services

gwesty	hotel	*tafarn*	pub
heddlu	police	*ysbyty*	hospital
siop	shop	*ysgol*	school
swyddfa	office		

A1

Appendix 2

FURTHER READING

Welsh literature is flourishing like never before. For an overview of Welsh titles, the excellent *New Welsh Review* (**w** newwelshreview.com) is well worth consulting. A trio of terrific independent Welsh publishers driving things forward are Seren Books (**w** serenbooks.com), Y Lolfa (**w** ylolfa.com) and Parthian Books (**w** parthianbooks.com). For more on the history of Welsh literature, see page 27.

FICTION

Browning Wroe, Jo *A Terrible Kindness* Faber & Faber, 2022. The tale of a young man who volunteers to help in the rescue of the victims at Aberfan in 1966, but it's just as affecting when recalling his own trials and tribulations, which are laid bare throughout this engaging read.

Chatwin, Bruce *On the Black Hill* Vintage Classics, 1998. One of the great 20th-century Welsh novels, this is an affecting tale of identical twins who live for all their 80 years in almost near rural isolation on a farm in the Black Mountains, written in Chatwin's own inimitable style.

Cordell, Alexander *Rape of the Fair Country* Blorenge Books, 1998. First published in 1959, this is the first in a brilliant trilogy of books charting the lives of a family caught up in the hardships of life in the ironworks of Blaenavon in the throes of the Welsh Industrial Revolution and at the onset of Chartism. *Hosts of Rebecca* and *Song of the Earth* complete the set.

Davies, Lewis *Love and Other Possibilities* Parthian, 2009. A series of short stories set in different parts of the world, with personalities as diverse as a Muslim taxi driver in Cardiff to a gay playwright in Morocco. Quite different is *Work, Sex and Rugby* (1993), a fairly self-explanatory yet still hugely entertaining slice of Valleys life.

Griffiths, Niall *Broken Ghost* Vintage, 2020. Another fine contemporary writer, Liverpool-born Griffiths has won a legion of fans with his dystopia-driven novels touching upon themes like austerity, disconnection and social breakdown – and *Broken Ghost* does this to thrilling effect. Other titles worth seeking out include *Grits*, *Sheepshagger* and *Runt*.

Jones, Cynan. Currently Wales's pre-eminent writer, Jones is known for the economy of his texts, which come to the fore in novels like *The Long Dry* (Granta, 2014), which depicts, in warmly melancholic fashion, the daily grind of working the land, with a missing cow to boot. There's also *The Dig* (2014), a vivid depiction of badger baiting. The similarly sparse *Cove* (2017) is a tale of one kayaker's sea-bound travails, while the author's most recent book, *Stillicide* (2019), is a searing meditation on the climate emergency.

Jones, Tia *On Open Ground* (2008); *The Moss Gatherers* (2013); & *Curlew's Cry* (2016) Gomer Press. Engrossing trilogy that follows the fortunes of one hill farming family on the mid-Wales coast over the course of three generations.

Keane, Catrin *Salt* Gomer Press, 2020. Superb debut novel based on the lives of the author's great-grandparents, in which a young girl from Tiger Bay marries a Barbadian sailor. At a time when cultural identity and race are to the fore, this book strongly resonates.

Sheers, Owen *Resistance* Faber & Faber, 2008. This riveting novel, set in the Black Mountains during World War II, recalls the unlikely co-existence between a group of women villagers and their German occupiers as they gradually become accustomed to one another.

Thomas, Dylan *Under Milk Wood* Weidenfeld & Nicolson, 2014. First published in 1954, Thomas's lyrical masterpiece tells the story of a day in the life of the inhabitants of a Welsh seaside village.

Thomas, Dylan *Collected Stories* Weidenfeld & Nicolson, 2014. All of the author's prose pieces, including *Quite Early One Morning*, *A Child's Christmas in Wales* and the much-loved *Portrait of the Artist as a Young Dog*.

Trezise, Rachel *Easy Meat* Parthian, 2021. At the forefront of modern female Welsh writers, Trezise rarely pulls any punches, and so it is in her latest outing which recalls a day (EU referendum day as it happens) in the life of a Valleys boy, bound up in themes of grief, poverty and societal dysfunction. Other titles by Trezise include *Fresh Apples* (2005) and *Cosmic Latte* (2015).

Williams, Raymond *Border Country* Parthian, 2006. Originally published in 1960, this engaging semi-autobiographical novel recalls the experiences of one Welsh family's life in a small village (based on Williams's real-life home of Pandy) on the Wales/England border.

BIOGRAPHY, CULTURE AND SOCIETY

John, Angela *The Actor's Crucible* Parthian, 2015. An illuminating read in which the author looks back at the lives of the country's three greatest actors, Richard Burton, Anthony Hopkins and Michael Sheen, all of whom, remarkably, hailed from Port Talbot.

Jones, Ron and Lovejoy, Joe *The Auschwitz Goalkeeper: A Prisoner of War's True Story* Gomer Press, 2013. In conjunction with *The Guardian*'s former football correspondent, this is the compelling story of Jones's time incarcerated as a POW in Italy and then at Auschwitz; the title, incidentally, refers to the position Jones played for the camp football team (for Wales, natch). Jones died in 2019 aged 102.

Madgwick, Gaynor *Aberfan* Y Lolfa, 2018. An inevitably powerful account about the appalling disaster of 1966, and the aftermath, as recalled by one of its survivors, who lost her brother and sister to the tragedy.

Price, Angharad *The Life of Rebecca Jones* MacLehose Press, 2014. A fictionalised memoir that paints an affecting picture of farming life in a rural mid-Wales community over the course of the 20th century, the main protagonist being a member of Price's real-life family.

Sheers, Owen *Calon* Faber & Faber, 2014. As the Welsh Rugby Union's poet in residence, this is a compelling account of a year spent in the company of the national team but which at the same time examines the sport's role within wider Welsh society.

Thomas-Symonds, Nicklaus *Nye: The Political Life of Aneurin Bevan* Bloomsbury, 2016. The most thoroughgoing account of arguably Wales's most influential politician, warts and all, which at the same time offers a genuine understanding of Bevan's political philosophy.

HISTORY

Davies, John *A History of Wales* Penguin, 2007. If you're looking to delve into every nook and cranny of Welsh history, then this monster 700-page tome should just about do it.

Gower, Jon *The Story of Wales* BBC Books, 2013. Accompanying the excellent BBC One series, this is an insightful and hugely readable account of the country's history, from prehistory through to the formation of the Welsh Assembly.

Milne, Seumas *The Enemy Within* Verso, 2014. This lively, thoroughgoing account explains the lengths to which the British government went to destroy the power of the miners' union during the 1984 strike.

Paxman, Jeremy *Black Gold: The History of How Coal Made Britain* Harper Collins, 2022. Compelling and evidently well-researched book in which the former BBC presenter relays the history of the black stuff from Roman times through to the Industrial Revolution and beyond, with plenty of references to the South Wales coalfield.

Ross, David *Wales: History of a Nation* Waverley, 2019. Comprehensive coverage of the nation's history with chapters on all the key periods, beginning with Pre-Celtic Wales. This latest (third) edition has been updated to include Brexit developments.

TRAVEL AND TRAVELOGUE

Ansell, Neil *Deep Country: Five Years in the Welsh Hills* Penguin, 2012. This absorbing account of the author's hermit-like existence in a small cottage in the heart of rural Wales is the perfect antidote to modern living. In his follow-up, *The Last Wilderness: A Journey into Silence* (Tinder Press, 2018), Ansell retreats to the even more remote area of the Rough Bounds in the Scottish Highlands. This is slow living and some.

Borrow, George *Wild Wales: Its People, Language and Scenery* John Murray, 1862. Timeless, and eminently readable account of the English-born linguist's walking tour through Wales in 1854.

Cray, Martin & Nicholas, Alvin *Wild Woods* Bradt Guides, 2021. A collection of some of Britain's best woods, forests and woodland experiences, with a dedicated chapter on South Wales. Covers everything from campsites, bothies and quirky accommodation through to wild swimming and walking and cycling trails.

Finch, Peter *Real Cardiff: The Flourishing City* Seren, 2018. This builds upon the author's previous three books on the city (*Real Cardiff, Real Cardiff Two* and *Real Cardiff Three*). Others in this illuminating series, which delve into parts of cities and areas you'd never find in your average travel guidebook (or anywhere else for that matter), include *Real Swansea, Real South Pembrokeshire, Real Newport* (among many others), each of which is written by a different author.

Francis-Baker, Tiffany *The Dark Skies of Britain and Ireland: A Stargazer's Guide* Bradt Guides, 2021. Useful guidebook covering the International Dark-Sky Association's Certified Sites and Discovery Sites, including the Brecon Beacons and other places in South Wales.

Gower, Jon and Moore, Jeremy *Wales at Water's Edge* Gomer Press, 2012. Published to coincide with the opening of the Wales Coast Path, this big glossy hardback charts a course around the Welsh coast offering delightful nuggets along the way. If this doesn't inspire you to get out and have a crack at the coast path (or even just a small bit of it), then nothing will.

Lloyd Owen, David *A Wilder Wales: Traveller's Tales 1610–1831* Parthian, 2021. In distilling the writings of 36 authors over more than two centuries, Lloyd Owen has produced a memorable collection of short stories.

Morris, Jan *Wales: Epic Views of a Small Country* Penguin, 2000. Despite the unremitting pro-Welshness present throughout, the late, legendary travel writer espouses enthusiastically on the land, the language, the people and the very soul of the nation that she lived in for more than 50 years. In her last book, *Thinking Again* (Faber & Faber, 2021), Morris muses upon her life and travels in a somewhat more melancholic fashion.

Parker, Mike *Neighbours From Hell?* Y Lolfa, 2014. A trenchant account of English attitudes to the Welsh by English émigré Mike Parker, whose erudite, witty prose is also to the fore in *The Greasy Poll* (2016), in which he stood as a candidate for Plaid Cymru in the 2015 general election. His most recent offering, *On the Red Hill* (Heinemann, 2019), is a personal take on events following a surprise inheritance.

Perrin, Jim *Snowdon: The Story of a Welsh Mountain* Gomer Press, 2013. Written by *The Guardian*'s country diarist, this is the best read about Wales's most iconic mountain you'll come across. Perrin further expounds upon Wales's glorious landscape in the *Hills of Wales* (Gomer Press, 2016) and *Rivers of Wales* (Gwasg Carreg Gwalch, 2022).

Wheeler, Rupert & Bruning, Ted *Britain in a Bottle: A Visitor's Guide* Bradt Guides, 2020. A visitor's guide to Britain's finest gin distilleries, whisky distilleries, breweries, vineyards and cider mills, including many in South Wales.

POETRY

Minhinnick, Robert *Selected Poems* Carcanet Press, 1999. Drawing on nearly two decades' worth of his earlier poems, this fine collection draws upon themes such as industry and wildlife to dazzling effect.

Sheers, Owen *The Green Hollow* Faber & Faber, 2018. Originally created as a BAFTA-winning BBC drama about the 1966 Aberfan disaster, Sheers's book is a moving poetic portrait of that devastating day.

Thomas, R S *Selected Poems* Penguin, 2004. As well as being one of the greatest religious poets of the 20th century, the reverend also touches upon themes of family and Wales in what is probably the best overview of his work.

WALKING AND GUIDES The essential companion for walks in South Wales is Cicerone, who offer easy-to-use guides that are clear, concise and have good maps. Among those pertinent to South Wales are *The Wales Coast Path*, *The Pembrokeshire Coast Path*, *The Wye Valley Walk*, *Offa's Dyke Path*, *Walking on Gower* and *Brecon Beacons Walks*.

Index

Page numbers in **bold** indicate main entries; those in *italics* indicate maps

Thomas, Dylan 161, 163, **256–7**, 258
Three Cliffs Bay 167
ticks 37
Tinkinswood Long Cairn 131
Tintern 94–7
Tonypandy 206
tour operators and guides 34–5
tourist information 34 *see also* individual
   locations
travelling positively 53–4
Tredegar 184–5
Trefil 186–7
Trellech 97–8
Treorchy 206
Tretower Castle and Court 231–2
Tywi Valley 263–9

Usk 118–20
Usk Reservoir 213

Vale of Ewyas 237–41
Vale of Glamorgan, Swansea and Gower
   123–72, *122*
Vale of Neath 147–51

Valleys, The 173–209, *174*
visas 35

Wales Coast Path 50, 317
walking **50–1,** 92–3, 129, 134–5, 150, 170,
   183, 186–7, 218, 219, 232, 238, 309,
   317
watersports 52
weather 4, 31, 38, 39
Weobley Castle 171
Western Beacons 212–17
what to take 39
when to visit 31–2
Whitesands Bay 311
Wings of Wales 215–16
Worm's Head 169, 170
Wye Valley 92–8
Wye Valley Path 50, 92–3

Y Garn Goch 269
Ystradfellte 214

Zip World Tower 207–8

INDEX OF ADVERTISERS